THE PAGEANT
OF AMERICA

R.K.

Independence Edition

VOLUME XIV

THE PAGEANT OF AMERICA

A PICTORIAL HISTORY OF THE UNITED STATES

RALPH HENRY GABRIEL

EDITOR

JOHN CHESTER ADAMS   ARTHUR HOBSON QUINN

ASSOCIATE EDITORS

<table>
<tr><td>CHARLES M. ANDREWS</td><td>ALLEN JOHNSON</td></tr>
<tr><td>HERBERT E. BOLTON</td><td>WILLIAM BENNETT MUNRO</td></tr>
<tr><td>IRVING N. COUNTRYMAN</td><td>VICTOR H. PALTSITS</td></tr>
<tr><td>WILLIAM E. DODD</td><td>ARTHUR M. SCHLESINGER</td></tr>
<tr><td>DIXON RYAN FOX</td><td>NATHANIEL WRIGHT STEPHENSON</td></tr>
</table>

ADVISORY EDITORS

DAVID M. MATTESON

INDEXER

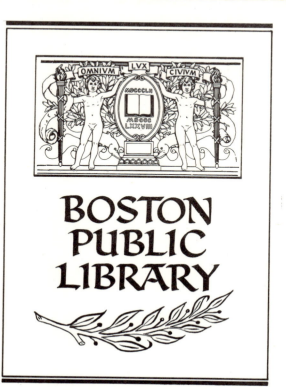

From an aquatint, published 1838, by J. Childe, Covent Garden, London

GEORGE H. HILL AS "HIRAM DODGE" IN *THE YANKEE PEDLAR*

THE YALE PAGEANT OF AMERICA

THE AMERICAN STAGE

BY

ORAL SUMNER COAD

EDWIN MIMS, JR.

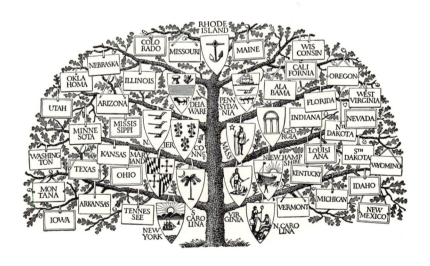

NEW YORK

UNITED STATES PUBLISHERS ASSOCIATION

TORONTO · GLASGOW, BROOK & CO.

TABLE OF CONTENTS

THE AMERICAN STAGE

OUT of the Mexico of the brilliant days of the Aztecs comes one of the most poignant dramas the world has known. Immediately following the month Toxcalt, Indian priests, clad in elaborate costumes and impressive headdresses sought among the young men of the empire a youth to play a divine rôle. They chose him for the perfection of his mind and the beauty of his body. They instructed him in order that for a year he might impersonate the god of the month Toxcalt. His stage was Tenochtitlan, the rich and aristocratic metropolis of Aztec Mexico, above the roofs of which towered lofty mountains and an occasional smoking volcano. Merchants and warriors, passing through the streets of Tenochtitlan, caught an occasional glimpse of the gaily attired young man followed by a retinue of pages, and perhaps paused to comment on whether or not he was playing well the part of the god of Toxcalt. The freedom of the city was his. Men honored him as they would the deity whom he impersonated. When the month Toxcalt entered, he was given brides who represented goddesses. In his honor was held a succession of brilliant festivals. On the last day of the month an eager and expectant populace awaited the climax of the piece. The waters of Lake Texcoco, which surrounded the old Aztec capital, were ruffled by a great fleet of canoes. Passengers, hushed by the solemnity of the occasion, watched the slowly dipping paddles as the boats paraded from the city to a point on the distant shore where a temple graced the top of a pyramid. At a certain piece of desert land near the holy place the young man paused, put off his gay garments, and bade a ceremonious farewell to the goddesses. With but a necklace of flutes about his neck he turned his face toward the temple. As he slowly climbed the pyramid he broke on each succeeding step a flute. Reaching the top a naked man he stood before the priests from whose girdles dangled decorated knives of the sharpest obsidian. A moment later his heart, still beating, was presented to the image of the very god he had impersonated.

This religious drama of the Aztec is not unique. In all parts of the world primitive peoples have given expression to their thoughts in dramatic dances and ceremonies that have served important functions in their lives. If their crops wilted in the heat of summer, they danced to the Sun God or the Thunder Bird. When a boy grew to manhood, he was initiated into the circle of hunters and warriors with symbolic ceremony and pageantry. When a tribe went forth to war upon its enemies, it first conquered them in the war dance. The drama is a human institution whose origins are lost in antiquity. Acting to express ideas is, perhaps, as old as speech. Behind both the red man and the white man who first met on the eastern edge of the American forest lay a long dramatic heritage.

The first settlers in the New World came from Elizabethan England. They knew of the poets and playwrights who had produced Elizabethan drama; perhaps some, even, had seen the acting of Shakespeare himself. The gossip of early Jamestown doubtless turned at times to wistful reminiscences of theater-going in the days of the Virgin Queen. But, in England, the drama had its enemies as well as its friends. The Puritans had arisen to scourge sin out of the land and symbolism out of the Anglican Church. Symbolism smacked of "Popery" and symbolism was the very foundation of the art of the theater. The Puritan, moreover, pointed a finger at the morals of the stage. In his eyes it was the dearest instrument of the devil to encompass the downfall of the righteous. The Puritan fathers planted the seeds of this prejudice deep in the soil of New England.

But this is not the sole reason why the drama did not at once spring up and flourish in the New World. In the cabin hamlets along the lonely western shore of the Atlantic, life was reduced to simple terms. The drama is peculiarly a social art which grows out of the group life of the people. It withers in isolation. Seldom in seventeenth-century America did group life achieve a cohesion that would make dramatic expression possible. The struggle for existence in an untamed environment demanded the full energies of the men and women who had risked their lives in the New World. Though they borrowed from the Indian his agriculture and his methods of adjustment to the forest, they had come too far along the road of cultural progress to revert to his dances and ceremonies. The complicated art of Shakespeare was out of adjustment with the primitive conditions of life in the American forest. Until the pioneers could free themselves from the hand to hand struggle with nature, the ancient dramatic method of expressing thought and feeling must, of necessity, remain in disuse.

The eighteenth century saw the beginnings of economic emancipation. In New England, coast villages became prosperous commercial towns in which moderate wealth appeared. In Maryland, Virginia, and the Carolinas an aristocracy of planters grew up. New York and Philadelphia waxed in economic and intellectual importance. The middle years of the eighteenth century saw life in America become rich in social, intellectual, and spiritual values. Colleges, some of them already old, were enriching the intellectual life. In the towns orchestras were playing the best music of Europe. In all the colonies the well-to-do lived in dwellings the artistic perfection of whose construction has remained a source of never-ending admiration to succeeding generations. The aristocratic tradition was still strong throughout America, and the aristocracy of the New World, provincial though it was, was cultivated and urbane. To communities dominated by such traditions and ideals the professional dramatic art of England was brought by the Murray-Kean Company and, in 1752, by Mr. and Mrs. Lewis Hallam. Not only the players but the plays and the traditions of acting were English — another illustration of that never-ceasing transfer westward across the Atlantic of the unfolding civilization of Europe.

The year 1767, which saw the appearance of *The Prince of Parthia*, the first American play produced by professionals on the American stage, was the same in which Charles Townshend secured the passage in Parliament of sundry new taxes, cordially disliked and vigorously opposed by the Americans. Eight years later bloody skirmishes at Lexington and Concord marked the opening of the Revolution. America was shaken from seaboard to farthest frontier cabin. Surging emotions swept through the New World communities. New thoughts were in the minds and on the tongues of everyone. Every known literary vehicle was rushed into service laden with argument, exhortation, satire, or abuse. Although in consideration of the gravity of the crisis the Continental Congress requested that the theaters be closed, the drama continued to express the thoughts and emotions of the people. The battles of the war, the mistakes of the Continental Congress, the hatred between the Whigs and Tories furnished plenty of themes to the writers of plays. Naturally, almost unconsciously, Americans, scarcely more than a quarter of a century after the professional theater had appeared among them, turned to the age-old institution of the drama to help them to express the emotions that grew out of their struggle for independence.

The Revolution was followed by swift national growth. The passing decades saw the frontier pushed west to the Mississippi and across it. Within half a century after the surrender of Yorktown America had acquired Florida and the vast territory of Louisiana; a second war with England had been fought and a new national consciousness gained. Growth and expansion were everywhere. The need of the times was for men to do things; to captain the ships of the merchant marine, to direct the new factories of the North, to lay out and manage the new cotton plantations of the South, to take up land in the swiftly moving life of the West. Though here and there appeared small centers of culture, the quiet thinker was not encouraged in the vigorous life of the young republic. As a people Americans, engrossed with doing, had little conception of the larger significance of their prodigious activity. In such times the drama was of small use as a vehicle of American thought. The theaters, reopened after the Revolution ended, continued to offer English drama presented by English actors. Side by side with the plays from London were adaptations of Paris successes. Neither native plays nor native actors were of importance. The theater in America remained exotic.

The theater of ancient Greece and that of Elizabethan England had developed in settled communities where families lived for generations and where change was slow. The life of both Athenians and Londoners was set against a background of history and tradition. These cities had individuality and were conscious of it. Change in America seemed to be everywhere and nowhere more marked than in the swiftly developing seaports of the East. The old communities of the Atlantic seaboard were giving up their people. Long trains of canvas-covered wagons filed through the passes of the Appalachians. New Englanders pushed into New York and on to Ohio. Planters from Virginia and the Carolinas sought the rich bottoms of Alabama and Mississippi. All America seemed on the move, drifting westward, westward, westward. The nation had no quiet towns where life was settled and stable and where the individuality of the community could emerge. America was in flux; individualism, rather than consciousness of the group, characterized its people. The folk of the quiet towns and cities of pre-Shakespearean England had developed the drama as a means of expressing their ideals and their emotions. They had begun with the miracle or mystery play. In course of time guilds had arisen which undertook the presentation of religious pageants and dramas. Then had come the secular plays and finally the Elizabethan era. Though the English heritage was the strongest single cultural element in American life, the dramatic development of the mother country could find no counterpart in the shifting communities of the young republic. Life itself was a drama for these people whose task it was to transform a wilderness into a nation. They labored, eagerly, hopefully, ceaselessly. Yet few there were who sensed the romance of the age whose destiny was theirs.

Because of adverse conditions native American drama developed slowly. In the growing cities of the coast and on the western circuit American plays were produced. Some depicted characters and reflected episodes in the national history. The heroes of the Revolution and the traitor, Arnold, appeared before the footlights. Politics, international complications, and war inspired dramatic pieces whose chief virtue was the patriotism of a youthful nation. Efforts were made to present American types: the Indians, Pocahontas and Metamora; Nimrod Wildfire of the frontier; Mose of the New York East Side; and perhaps greatest of all, Solon Shingle, the Yankee teamster. There were plays built on the foibles of contemporary society, and plays which sought the freedom of distant lands and ages to grapple with the problems and emotions of human life. Perhaps in the drama of society and romance Americans achieved their greatest successes. Twentieth-century Americans have seen revivals of Mrs. Mowatt's *Fashion* and Boker's *Francesca da Rimini*. Yet before the Civil War no dramatist arose to stand beside the makers of a great epoch in American literature. The audience to whom the playwright spoke was too limited to challenge the best efforts of the man who sought to fix his impress on the thought life of the nation. The plays of the day are largely forgotten. Nimrod Wildfire and Metamora, the Last of the Wampanoags, have vanished, but Leatherstocking and Uncas, the Last of the Mohicans, still live. Mose disappeared with the peculiar urban conditions of which he was a part. Solon Shingle has been forgotten by a generation that still laughs at and loves Sam Slick. America in the first half of the nineteenth century was not yet ready to express itself effectively through an art which from antiquity has portrayed the deepest emotions of men. America rather expressed itself in the westward march of the frontier, in the anti-slavery crusade, in the compromises which held a threatened Union together, and, above all, in that ceaseless activity which meant material growth. Yet for more than a generation before the first Confederate guns opened up against Fort Sumter great actors had stirred their audiences from the American stage.

The rise of Edwin Forrest in the 'thirties and the passing of Edwin Booth in the early 'nineties mark the limits of a brilliant period in American acting. Citizens of the United States who were still talking with wonder about the tremendous speed of thirty miles an hour attained by the new railroad trains, or who were watching with apprehension that growing rift between North and South, were going to theaters in New York, Boston, and Philadelphia to see many of the best artists that America has known. A majority, like the Kembles and Adelaide Neilson, were foreigners who had scored triumphs abroad. Some were sprung from the soil of the New World, like Forrest, Charlotte Cushman, the Jeffersons, and Booth. The memory of many of these artists still lives to enrich the national heritage. This brilliant galaxy on the stage at a time when the American drama was still of inferior quality presents a perplexing paradox.

The actors were, of course, not dependent upon American plays. English and French productions were freely used. Many artists rose to their greatest heights in the rôles of Shakespeare. Perhaps of even greater importance is the fact that conditions in the United States in the middle years of the nineteenth century stimulated acting if not the writing of plays. The almost universal medium for carrying ideas to the masses of the people was the public platform. The newspapers and the thoughtful magazines were but little developed in the 'forties and 'fifties. Edwin Booth and Charlotte Cushman must be set against the background of an age that listened to and was moved by the brilliant Clay, the impressive Webster, the fire-eating Yancy, the impassioned Wendell Phillips. Sumner was a master of invective; Douglas could face a hostile audience and dominate it; Lincoln could pronounce the Gettysburg address. An age accustomed to such public speaking was ready to hail the power of Forrest, when, as Metamora, he defied the white invader, or to sit breathless while the poetic Booth spoke the matchless soliloquies of Hamlet. The actor faced comparison with the greatest Americans of the day and the result was an art which has never been surpassed west of the Atlantic.

But other factors helped to make the stage prominent during the middle years of the nineteenth century. In the decades immediately preceding and following the Civil War, cities were growing rapidly and wealth was mounting. Urban Americans in increasing numbers were beginning to have leisure to play and could afford more expensive pleasures. Americans, as a people, however, knew very little about playing. Drinking, dancing, card-playing were the pastimes that had come down from the earlier time of struggle with a rough environment. Before the Civil War, the only sport that could pretend to national vogue was horse racing. By the middle of the century, Americans were ready to take a step forward in the national play life. The theater as an institution of entertainment quickly responded to the demands of the new day. The minstrels and the circus, two peculiarly American products, were given to the public. Down to the passing of Booth the theater was the chief source of entertainment for the people of the growing cities. That the great days of the stage should end at almost the precise time that the sports and out-of-door pastimes of the present age entered upon the period of their swift development is not without significance. Yet other factors were primarily responsible for the decline of the theater.

Industrialism developed swiftly in America after the war between the states. Gigantic combinations of capital took the place of individual enterprises. Within a generation the industrial revolution had turned the chief American cities into monster centers of population. In this new environment the theater offered unprecedented possibilities for profit. The opportunity attracted the attention of certain capitalists and the "Theatrical Trust" appeared. Compared with many of the enterprises of the time it was a small affair. Perhaps for this reason, perhaps for lack of general American appreciation of the possibilities for usefulness of the drama, the "Trust" did not attract the quality of leadership that, by the end of the nineteenth century, was common in American business. The theater was commercialized. Broadway became the theatrical Wall Street of the nation. The network of railroads which stretched from the Atlantic to the Pacific distributed to the American people the output of the New York manufactures. Theaters, the country over, became dependent upon the metropolis of the Atlantic seaboard for their supply of shows. As for player and playwright, they either bowed to the commercial will or no longer bowed to the public. The pursuit of art merged rapidly into the pursuit of the dollar. For a time the public accepted the situation without protest.

But the growth of industrialism in America brought with it the motion picture. In the first quarter of the twentieth century the "movie," out-distancing the older theater, became one of the half dozen largest business enterprises in the United States. The growth was the result of the fact that the "movie" met a national need. It carried entertainment to isolated farms and mountain villages whose play life had, hitherto, seldom felt the touch of outside influence. Even in the great days of acting the influence of the artists of the stage had rarely gone beyond the larger cities. They had failed to touch the mass of Americans. In the cities crowded with unassimilated immigrants, the "movie palace" furnished diversion to millions of people who could neither understand English nor afford the price which the "Theatrical Trust" asked for its product. The "movie" helped to blunt the edge of the discontent that was growing as a result of the congestion of the urban centers and of contact with an economic system built upon the automatic machine. However crude its art, the picture play was a step forward.

Undoubtedly the cinema mirrors the taste of the mass of the American people. Much good as well as evil flickers on the screen and the beautiful jostles the cheap. In one generation the motion picture has become a social force whose powers no man can estimate. Celluloid plays have become an important item in American export. They are distributed, not only in Europe, but in South America, among the yellow people of China and Japan and the brown people of southern Asia. The product which represents the average mind and the average taste of America is being spread over the world. Plays which reflect the peculiar prejudices and points of view of the white race are shown to all the races. What the end will be no one can tell. Already there are many who have recognized that the "movie" can be used for beneficent ends as well as for the making of money. It has artistic and educational possibilities which are outside the field of the older theater. Time only can make known the full significance of this new force for America and for the world. Meanwhile, it has become clear that the motion picture will not, as some hasty persons prophesied, supplant the spoken drama.

Curiously enough during the last two decades, when the "movies" have been so definitely in the ascendant, America has produced more able playwrights than at any other period in its history. Unlike the cinema, with its exaggerated and highly romanticized picture of life, these dramatists have tended toward a more or less veracious presentment of the American scene and American history. As early as Bronson Howard's Civil War play, *Shenandoah*, first acted in 1888, there began a succession of plays distinguished alike by the native material with which they dealt and the high competence of their writers. Some of the later dramas in this succession are *Shore Acres* by James A. Herne, *Secret Service* by William Gillette, *In Mizzoura* and *Arizona* by Augustus Thomas, *Barbara Frietchie* by Clyde Fitch, *The Girl of the Golden West* by David Belasco,

The Great Divide by William Vaughn Moody, *The Easiest Way* by Eugene Walter, *The Nigger* and *The Boss* by Edward Sheldon, *Beyond the Horizon* and *Desire Under the Elms* by Eugene O'Neill, and *In Abraham's Bosom* by Paul Green. These playwrights and others of comparable powers, most of whom have arisen during the twentieth century, have given to American drama an importance it never possessed before, but which there is reason to believe it will continue to possess in the work of their successors.

Other evidence is at hand which seems to point to a fuller and more normal use of the drama in American national life. The World War brought to America a new unity of thought and feeling. It gave to the vast republic a vivid national consciousness and a new world perspective. Powerful forces are making toward uniformity. News agencies and syndicates scatter the same material from one end of the country to another. Magazines whose circulations run into the millions distribute the same intellectual fare from the Atlantic to the Pacific. The radio has brought the jazz of the urban dance hall to the lonely mountain cabin and flung the words of the orator to the four corners of the land. The drift toward uniformity is strong but setting against it is a steady movement toward sectionalism. Like the unexpected turn in the plot, the theater is emphasizing the sectionalism rather than the unity of the nation.

The wheat belt differs from the cotton country. The mining valleys of Pennsylvania are unlike the orchard-covered slopes of California. Loyalty to the province is a factor of growing importance in American life, most conspicuous, perhaps, in California. But Virginia has a quiet pride, the Buckeye State is aware of its political importance and even the metropolis at the mouth of the Hudson is not without self-consciousness. Local pride and loyalty seem more and more to be leading to community self-expression. Cities and country villages have turned to the masque and the pageant to portray the ideas and the historical background of the community. The people have abandoned the rôle of the passive audience and have become active participants in dramatic exhibitions. The soundness of the new growth may be gauged by the fact that it has started with the less complicated forms of the dramatic art. But the movement has gone beyond the pageant.

In the heyday of the "Theatrical Trust," plays that succeeded in New York were put "on the road." But developing sectional taste which differs from that of New York, the amazing expansion of motion-picture houses, and an increased cost of transportation have made more and more hazardous the venture of sending a play about the country. As a result there are large and populous areas in America which see good plays rarely or never. For some of these the "movie" has not sufficed. The North Carolina Playmakers, centering in the university at Chapel Hill, have undertaken to write and produce plays, the inspiration for which is drawn from the life with which North Carolinians are familiar. Scattered over the nation are community organizations, different in detail, but manifesting the same desire on the part of the people of the locality to secure and, frequently, to share in the writing and production of the dramatic pieces they want. The amateur is becoming a person of importance. In American sport he has in some cases eclipsed the professional. In the theatrical world his significance is growing.

But the destiny of the theater lies in the hands of the professional artist and not the amateur, however good the latter's training or high his ideals. Perhaps the amateur's greatest importance in the large city where the theater flourishes is in the diffusion among the people of a more accurate knowledge of things theatrical and the raising of the standards of public taste. In this work a small group of skilled dramatic critics are also playing an important part in appraising the work of the dramatist and actor.

After all, the standards of the audience will be what determines the standards of the stage. And the audience which watches the art of a modern actor has quite a different background from those which were stirred by Forrest or Booth. The college man and woman has become a commonplace. Even the graduate of the high school has some knowledge of the European drama out of which American dramatic life has come. Practical training in the writing and production of plays is taking its place in the university curriculum. But more important than these elements of educational training is the fact that the years of the nation's youth have passed. National maturity is at hand. The urban population now exceeds that of the country districts and the old isolation of the farmer is disappearing. The growth of the new sectionalism in America with all its provincial loyalties is the result of the passing of the frontier and the stopping of the westward flood of population. Communities have become more settled, each more conscious of its peculiar heritage and opportunity. The flux in American life has become less important. Loyalty to the province is not antagonistic, but rather complementary, to the larger loyalty to the nation. In its turn the nation, as it takes its place in world affairs, is becoming conscious of its peculiar background and ideals. The voice of the thinker is more frequently heard above the industrial tumult. The ideas of the new day are finding expression in the universities, the churches, the newspapers, the magazines, and the books of men of letters. Through the acted and printed play the playwright also can carry his message to a vast audience. He can aspire to make an impress on his times and to produce work that will carry on into the future. In such an environment the ancient institution of the drama seems destined to achieve a place of importance and for the first time adequately to express in its unique way the life of the American people.

RALPH H. GABRIEL

CHAPTER I

OUR INFANT STAGE

WHEN the first rigors of pioneering in America came to an end about the beginning of the eighteenth century, the art of the theater began to make tentative bids for recognition. It met a various reception. In Puritan New England the stage was regarded as one of Satan's deadliest traps for ensnaring the soul of man; the drama was a "shameful vanitie" that would make of Christian Boston a rival of heathen Rome. Such an attitude is scarcely surprising in view of the antecedents of the New England colonists. The English Puritans, with whom they were allied in spirit, had seen the theater, during the reigns of James and Charles, grow increasingly licentious as the actors became more and more the entertainers and defenders of the loose-living, luxury-loving court circle. These same English Puritans had promptly padlocked the theaters in 1642 when they gained the supremacy in the civil struggle, only to see a vastly more immoral type of drama ushered in with the restoration of the Stuarts. Naturally the New England Puritans were resolved to avoid a duplication of this experience in the New World. But their hostility was not based solely on moral grounds. The New England colonists, by and large, were a struggling people whose circumstances compelled belief in the gospel of hard work. Why should they support by their scantily rewarded toil so expensive a luxury as the theater with its large staff of indolent parasites? What man wanted to see his son lured from the plow or the counter to a life of idleness by the pernicious example of the player-folk? The opposition that the stage encountered in New England was inevitable.

New York, during the first half of the century, though a smaller town than Boston, was becoming the most cosmopolitan city in America. Dutch, English, French, Germans, Jews, and other peoples met on its busy streets. In the valley of the Hudson to the north a landed aristocracy presided over their vast estates like American Sir Roger de Coverleys. Their gorgeous costumes and brilliant social affairs contrasted strangely with the plain habit and simple manners of the Quakers of Pennsylvania. Philadelphia, together with the surrounding country, however, was thriving commercially through the medium of agriculture, and like New York contained small groups of citizens enjoying wealth and culture. In each town the theater found friends when its struggle for existence began. But in the thrifty Dutch burghers of New York, as in the pious Quakers and Presbyterians of Philadelphia, it also found enemies.

The tobacco planters of Maryland and Virginia, and the rice and indigo planters of the Carolinas were a self-conscious aristocracy, who aped the fads and fashions in vogue among the English gentry. With their Cavalier and Church of England background, they hailed a play as a long-lost friend.

But even if the North had been as cordially disposed as the South, the establishment of the theater in the New World would not have been greatly hastened. The scattered nature of the population, the absence of large towns, and the wretched state of road travel, which made the trip from Philadelphia to New York a three-day journey beset with many perils, were circumstances scarcely calculated to attract professional actors from England. In the course of the years, however, some players who sought adventure or who found the competition in London too keen, resolved to try their fortune in the new province across the Atlantic. Anthony Aston, the first actor in this country of whom we have any definite information, was a soldier of fortune. Something of the quality of Murray and Kean's Company, which flourished briefly about 1750, is indicated by the announcement of a benefit for a member who "is just out of prison," and another for an actress "to enable her to buy off her time" — an indentured servant, who had sold her services for a limited period to meet the expenses of the voyage. Even the Hallam Company, whose coming in 1752 marks the beginning of more dignified drama in America, had suffered bankruptcy in London. But however far below the best English standards these pioneer actors fell, they found, south of New England, a considerable body of liberal minded colonists who gladly gave them a hearing. As a reporter in Charleston phrased it in 1754, "Last Monday evening the New Theatre in this Town was opened when a Company of Comedians perform'd . . . much to the satisfaction of the Audience."

This satisfaction is easy to understand. Colonial evenings were long, and diversions were few; books were expensive and hard to obtain. Into the daily routine the theater introduced entertainment, romance, escape. What though the costumes were dingy? What though the same sets of battered scenery were compelled to do duty from play to play? What though the house was mean, and the smoky oil lamps and tallow candles were inadequate to dispel the gloom, and the actors doubled their rôles? The players had come to town, and the irresistible magic that is peculiar to the theater was once more working its spell.

The audience that filed into the playhouse about six o'clock on the nights of the acting was a representative one. In the boxes sat the members — especially the ladies — of the "first families," who provided their own system of reservation by sending the negro servants early in the afternoon to hold good seats for them. The young gentlemen of the town exercised the ancient prerogative of sitting on the stage, and no doubt took occasion to ogle the actresses shamelessly and perhaps even to chat with them during the play. The pit was occupied only by men, who, before the performance began, stood on the uncomfortable benches that were their seats in order to inspect the audience. In the gallery sat the vociferous rabble, who did not hesitate to express their disapproval either by words or by missiles. At times actors, orchestra, and audience alike suffered from their attentions.

But with all its crudity our early theater performed an invaluable service for the colonists. It brought a new form of diversion, a new element of satisfaction, into their circumscribed lives, and in the process it gave them an acquaintance with the great masters of English drama — Congreve and Farquhar, Fielding and Otway, Ben Jonson and Shakespeare.

YE BARE AND YE CUBB

MANY of the first colonists who sailed in 1607 to Jamestown may well have carried with them memories of the Globe and the Blackfriars Theaters in London, where they had seen Richard Burbage and Shakespeare himself interpreting the great rôles of the living Elizabethan dramatists. But in the privations and dangers of those first experimental years on the distant Virginia frontier, there was neither time nor inclination to

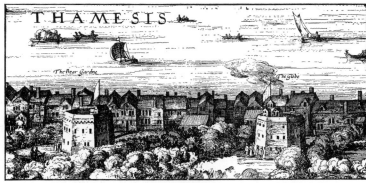

1   View of the Globe Theater, London, detail from a reproduction of the C. J. Visscher map of London, 1616, in the New York Public Library

transplant to the new world this lighter phase of English civilization. The odium attached to the name of professional actor, which Shakespeare bemoaned in his sonnets, influenced the capitalists promoting the Virginia venture. It cannot be determined how long this original barrier against actors was maintained. Greater leisure and security among the Virginia aristocrats undoubtedly widened the range of interests and amusements. With increasing economic prosperity, the colonists began to return occasionally to London. Country gentlemen with current London tastes began to appear on the tidewaters of the James. By the time that we pass in 1665 to the first actual fact in our theatrical history, the romantic plays of the Elizabethan period had been brought to an end by Puritan opposition, and a new school had already begun to usher in the classical French formulas of Restoration comedy and tragedy. Five years after the restoration of Charles II, there is given the first historical glimpse of actors in Virginia. In Accomac County on the eastern shore of the James, a play was given called *Ye Bare and Ye Cubb*. We know nothing further of the play, or of the actors, Cornelius Watkinson, Philip Howard, and William Darby, although it has been conjectured that they were local amateurs. The records do show, however, that hostility to the acting profession still motivated one Edward Martin, who informed the authorities of the existence of the play. The three men were haled to court and ordered to "give a draught of such verses or other speeches and passages, which were then acted by them." The passages proving innocent, the actors were acquitted and the informant was assessed with the payment of court expenses.

2   Governor William Berkeley, ca. 1610–77, detail from the portrait by Sir Peter Lely (1617–80), in the possession of M. du P. Lee, Wilmington, Del.

A PASTORAL COLLOQUY

AT the time that Edward Martin brought complaint against the three Virginia actors, William Berkeley was royal Governor of the colony at the capital in Jamestown. Before coming to Virginia, he had been to Canada, where he had written a play called *The Lost Lady*, and in London he had been a student and patron of the current theater. His career as Governor of Virginia was a long and colorful one, culminating in the famous Nathaniel Bacon Rebellion of 1675. Though there are no existing facts which connect him with theatrical development in Virginia, it is a warrantable assumption that his original interest in the theater persisted, and that he gave official sanction and encouragement to whatever embryonic attempts may have been made. L. G. Tyler, in his *Williamsburg, The Old Colonial Capital*, wrote of a slightly later period, when Alexander Spotswood, a successor of Governor Berkeley, attended the theater at Williamsburg. "The fact that in 1702 'a pastoral colloquy' was recited by the scholars of William and Mary College is indicative of an active interest felt by the Virginia people in such things, which doubtless was manifested in frequent but unreported exhibitions on the theatrical boards."

3   Scene from *The Fool's Opera* with medallion portrait of Anthony Aston, from a print in the Robert Fridenberg Collection, New York

THE FOOL'S OPERA; OR, THE TASTE OF THE AGE

A MORE definite indication of theatrical interest in the South was the appearance of the first known professional actor in America, Anthony, or Tony, Aston. Tony was an English strolling player and soldier of fortune, who in 1701 found his way to Jamaica. From there he migrated to "Charles-Town," South Carolina, where he acted for a short time, apparently in 1703, before pushing on to New York in 1703–04. In 1704 he returned to England and continued his barnstorming career for many years.

Aston, a writer of sorts, about 1730 published *The Fool's Opera*, a negligible play with occasional songs. Interest in this piece arises from the fact that to it Tony appended a sketch of his life, from which we gather that our first player was a low comedian, mountebank, and wag rather than a dignified artist. But we also gather that he was a vivid, engaging, and versatile person. At the outset of his autobiographic sketch he addresses the reader thus:

> "*My merry Hearts,*
> You are to know me as a Gentleman, Lawyer, Poet, Actor, Soldier, Sailor, Exciseman, Publican; in *England, Scotland, Ireland, New-York, East* and *West Jersey, Maryland,* (*Virginia* on both sides *Cheesapeek,*) *North* and *South Carolina, South Florida, Bahama's, Jamaica, Hispaniola,* and often a Coaster by all the same."

Fate was not always kind to him in his wanderings, for, as he tells us, he landed at "Charles-Town" "full of Shame, Poverty, Nakedness, and Hunger: — I turned *Player* and *Poet*, and wrote one Play on the Subject of the Country." Unfortunately all trace of that play has been lost, but it could scarcely have been livelier than his brief autobiography.

THE WILLIAMSBURG THEATER

THE years immediately following the "pastoral colloquy" of 1702 and the brief appearance of Tony Aston again must be filled in by the imagination. No further facts come to light until 1716 when it is definitely recorded that William Levingston, a dancing master in the adjoining New Kent county, bought a plot of land in Williamsburg, and almost immediately thereafter began the construction of a theater. Charles Stagg and his wife, Mary, became the leading actor and actress of this pioneer American theater, the first of which there is a clear record. Alexander Spotswood, Governor of Virginia at the time, mentions that, on the King's Birthday in 1718, a play was presented before him by Charles and Mary Stagg and their company. No specific mention is made of the theater, but Tyler assumes logically enough that it was the one built by Levingston. On the death of Charles Stagg in Williamsburg in 1735, his widow turned from the theater to the giving of dancing lessons. In the years immediately following there are only occasional references to theatrical activities. In 1736 Addison's tragedy of *Cato* — a perennial favorite with the American colonial — was given by the students of William and Mary College, while the "young Gentlemen and Ladies of this Country" gave *The Busy Body*, *The Recruiting Officer*, and *The Beaux' Stratagem*. The deed books of Yorktown state that in 1745 the theater "had not been put to any use for several years." In 1748 it was sold to the civic authorities as a city hall.

4   Early View of William and Mary College, Williamsburg, Va., from William Meade, *Old Churches in Virginia*, Philadelphia, 1857

"RUDE ESSAYS"

THE aristocracy of Charleston, South Carolina, was more concentrated than the tidewater planters of Virginia and even more closely in touch with the social amenities of London. The plantations of the rice growers and merchants surrounded the town, and on most of them were found the tastes and pastimes of the English squire. There were horse racing and hunting, dancing and music. *The Gentleman's Magazine* and *The Imperial Magazine* brought the news and fashions of London. During the winter the Planter's Hotel, known as "The Jolly Corner," was the rendezvous for those who had come to enjoy the busy social season. On January 18, 1735, the year that Charles Stagg died at Williamsburg, the *South Carolina Gazette* carried the arresting announcement that there would be presented in "Charles-Town" a tragedy of Otway, *The Orphan or The Unhappy Marriage*, and that the price of the tickets would be forty shillings. Though it has been conjectured that the troupe which played in New York in 1732 may have toured on to Charleston, nothing authoritative is known of the identity of the cast. *The Orphan* and the plays which followed it during this first season must have been given in the Court-room and Council Chamber above the Exchange. The first American

Prologue spoken to the ORPHAN, *upon it's being play'd at* Charleſtown, *on Tueſday the 24th of* Jan. 1734-5.

WHen firſt Columbus touch'd this diſtant Shore,
And vainly hop'd his Fears and Dangers o'er,
One boundleſs Wilderneſs in View appear'd!
No Champain Plains or riſing Cities chear'd
His wearied Eye. ——
Monſters unknown travers'd the hideous Waſte,
And Men more Savage than the Beaſts they chac'd.
But mark! how ſoon theſe gloomy Proſpects clear,
And the new World's late horrors diſappear.
The ſoil obedient to the induſtrious Swains,
With happy Harveſts crowns their honeſt Pains,
And Peace and Plenty triumph o'er the Plains.
What various Products float on every Tide?
What numerous Navys in our Harbours ride?
Tillage and Trade conjoin their Friendly Aid,
T'enrich the thriving Boy and lovely Maid.
Hiſpania, it's true, her precious Mines engroſs'd,
And bare her ſhining Entrails to its Coaſt.
Britannia more humane ſupplys her wants,
The Britiſh Senſe and Britiſh Beauty plants.
The Aged Sire beholds with ſweet Surprize
In foreign Climes a numerous Offspring rize.
Senſe, Virtue, worth and Honour ſtand confeſt,
In each brave Male, his proſp'rous hands have bleſt,
While the admiring Eye improv'd may trace
The Mother's Charms in each chaſt Virgins Face.
Hence we preſume to uſher in thoſe Arts
Which oft have warm'd the beſt and braveſt Hearts
Faints our endeavours, rude are our Eſſays;
We ſtrive to pleaſe, but can't pretend at praiſe;
Forgiving Smiles o'erpay the grateful Task;
They're all we hope and all we humbly ask.

5 First American Prologue, from the *South Carolina Gazette*, Feb. 1–8, 1734–35

prologue — written anonymously for *The Orphan* — appeared in the *South Carolina Gazette* of February 1–8, 1734–35, a modest apology for the "rude essays" with which the audience must at first be content. In this

ON Tueſday the 28th Inſt. in the Court-room will be acted the ſecond time a TRAGEDY called, *The Orphan*, or *the unhappy Mariage*. Tickets to be had at Mr. *Shepherd's*, at 40 s. each.

6 From the *South Carolina Gazette*, Jan. 18–25, 1734–35

same season was given the first opera in America, *Flora or Hob in the Well*, which was followed later by Dryden's *Spanish Friar*. So great was the success of the season that the planters and merchants of Charleston decided to erect a building devoted exclusively to the stage. The building, which was located in an outlying section of the town, near the Old Burying Ground, was not opened, however, until the season of 1736–37. The identity of the company during the second season is also obscure. Only one name emerges, that of Thomas Dale, M.D., associate justice of the Province of South Carolina, who wrote the epilogue for Farquhar's *Recruiting Officer*, an epilogue typically "Restoration" in the frankness of its details. *The London Merchant or History of George Barnwell* and Addison's *Cato* with a prologue by Alexander Pope were included in the second season's program. Thereafter with the exception of a season in 1754, the theater in Charleston was inactive until new life was infused into it by the arrival of a highly trained troupe of professional actors from New York in 1763. During the interval the prosperity of the South Carolinians increased, and the culture of their community mellowed with increasing age.

7 Map of Charles-Town, 1739, showing the site of the first Theater (T), from a reprint in *The Charleston Year Book*, 1884

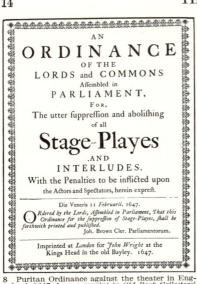

8 Puritan Ordinance against the theater in England, 1647, from a reprint in *Old Book Collectors' Miscellany*, London, 1873

9 Samuel Sewall, 1652–1730, from an engraved portrait in *The Diary of Samuel Sewall*, Massachusetts Historical Society, 1878–80

"PAINTED VANITIES"

The religious pioneers of Massachusetts and Connecticut were but the adventurous representatives of the great section of English society which, during the seventeenth century, demanded, and for a time obtained, a radical simplification of the artificialities of religious and social customs. To them ritual and symbol and decoration stood in the way of direct communion with their deity. Drama in any form, whether in church or theater, was the ally of the arch-tempter. From 1642 to the restoration of Charles II in 1660 the theaters of England were closed. Even for many years after that the Puritans of New England lived free from theatrical performances. In 1685 Judge Samuel Sewall of Boston recorded in his diary that the Puritan conscience was being tortured by the prevalence of wickedness, especially by the presence of dancing masters who contended that more morality could be drawn from a single play than from hours of homiletics and pages of Scripture. Increase Mather lamented in the preface to a diatribe against sin, published in 1687, that "there is much discourse of beginning Stage-Plays in New England," which he placed in the circle of iniquity with "promiscuous dancing." Both Sewall and Mather were disheartened in 1687 by the ceremonies of the May Pole, and by a stage pantomime in which there was a colorful clashing of swords. An evil was becoming prevalent whose deep roots must be eradicated by restraining legislation. And Samuel Sewall in 1714 took definite steps of suppression. The colonial records of Massachusetts, Rhode Island, Pennsylvania, South Carolina, and New York, are full of protests against the theater. Not only the Puritans, but also the Quakers, the Lutherans, and other religious groups were watching anxiously to stamp out any evidences of this increasing evil. When professional troupes began more systematic attempts to establish the theater in America, the opposition of religious sects became in proportion more violent. The antagonism to the Hallams and to Douglass in New York and especially in the Quaker City was most bitter. In 1750, when two English actors attempted to give a performance in Boston, there was a small riot, whereupon the Commonwealth of Massachusetts passed a drastic law, forbidding play-acting, and rendering liable to a heavy fine anyone who by his presence or otherwise gave countenance to such "painted vanities."

ANDROBOROS

If the southern colonies were more active in presenting plays in the early years, to their northern neighbors goes the honor of having created the first play written and printed in America. It was the work of that able colonial Governor of New York, Robert Hunter. *Androboros* (man-eater), printed in 1714, was composed as a satire on certain of Hunter's enemies, including the officials of Trinity Church, who were hostile to him because he had refused grants of land to the parish. Hunter, who had associated with Addison, Steele, and other wits before coming to America, had a caustic pen that made up in vigor what it lacked in delicacy. It is interesting to see American drama at its inception using local incident and political motives.

ANDROBOROS
A
Bographical Farce
In Three Acts, VIZ.
The SENATE,
The CONSISTORY,
AND
The APOTHEOSIS

By Governour Hunter

Printed at Monoropolis since August, 1714

10 Title-page of *Androboros*, 1714, from The Huntington Library and Art Gallery, San Marino, Cal.

BEGINNINGS IN NEW YORK

In spite of the attempts in the northern colonies to suppress theaters and public amusements, there had been, from the time of Richard and Francis Hunter at the beginning of the eighteenth century, various manifestations in New York of the desire to cater to the increasing public demand for group entertainment. Scattered references in New York newspapers of the time to pageantry, concert, variety, and circus, supply adequate substance for such a generalization. The beginnings of the legitimate drama in New York are still, however, not entirely clear. For many years scholars were content with the assumption that New York stage history began in 1750. The discovery of an isolated reference to a

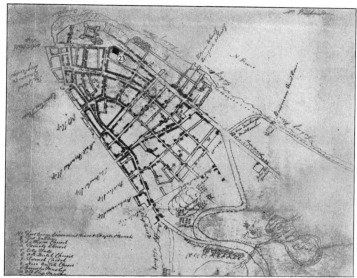

11   Plan of New York City, 1735, showing site of the Theater (23), from a print in the New York Public Library

production in 1732 of Farquhar's *Recruiting Officer* suggested an earlier date, which is apparently authenticated by a notice in the *New England & Boston Gazette* of January 1, 1733, that includes an item from New York of the preceding December 11. "On the 6th instant the *New Theatre* in the building of the Hon. Rip Van Dam, Esq., was opened with the comedy of *The Recruiting Officer*, the part of Worthy acted by the ingenious Mr. Thos. Heady, Barber and Peruque Maker to his Honor." The addition of details to this meager account must be left to speculation. The location of the theater, the status of the players, whether professional or amateur, the connection of this troupe with the Charleston troupe of 1734, have not yet been determined. The next ascertainable fact is that on a map of Manhattan of 1735, republished in I. N. Phelps Stokes' *Iconography*, there is marked a playhouse, situated on the east side of Broadway just above Beaver Street. It is not known whether this contained the stage on which in 1739 Henry Holt, who had danced for a number of years at the Theater Royal in Drury Lane, London, exhibited a *New Pantomime Entertainment in Grotesque Characters, called the Adventures of Scaramouch and Harlequin, or the Spaniard Trick'd.* We can only assume from a prologue to its second opening that plays were given with some regularity and received with some favor:

"This gen'rous Town which nurs'd our infant Stage
And cast a Shelter o'er its tender Age. —"

In February of the same year there is a reference to a production at the new theater on Broadway of *The Beaux' Stratagem* by actors all but one of whom had had previous stage experience. On the whole subject of the early New York theater Dr. George C. D. Odell's monumental *Annals of the New York Stage* is the outstanding authority.

View of New York City, 1717–46, from a print in the New York Historical Society

13 First known Playbill in America, New York, March 20, 1750, from the original in the Harvard Theater Collection, Cambridge, Mass.

MURRAY AND KEAN

In the *New York Gazette or Weekly Post Boy* of February 26, 1750, appeared an announcement that a troupe of actors had arrived from Philadelphia. They would open shortly in Colley Cibber's adaptation of the famous historical tragedy of *Richard III*. This and subsequent plays were to be presented in the building owned by Rip Van Dam on Nassau Street, "where they intend to perform as long as the season lasts provided they meet with suitable encouragement." The theory is generally accepted that with this company were the actors Thomas Kean and Walter Murray, the former probably playing the rôle of the hunchback king on the opening night. During the first season six different plays and three farces were given, including *The Spanish Friar*, Otway's *The Orphan*, Farquhar's *The Beaux' Stratagem*, Lillo's *The History of George Barnwell*, and Congreve's *Love for Love*, all popular plays of the contemporary London stage. The second season was surprisingly long, running from September 1750 to the following July. The presentations often took the form of benefit performances for a particular actor, who on the announced date would be given the entire receipts. From the record of such benefit performances we learn the names of Thomas Kean and Walter Murray, Charles Somerset Woodham, and

several other associates. But in spite of regularly recurring benefits, and earnest pleas to the readers of the *Post Boy*, the receipts gradually fell off. Kean became discouraged and announced that he would retire from the stage, but, instead, left with Murray and Woodham for Williamsburg, Virginia, where they erected a theater and gave a season of plays. In the second New York season they had added to their repertory *The Recruiting Officer*, the moral *Cato*, the immoral *Amphitryon* of Dryden, Gay's *Beggar's Opera*, Rowe's *The Fair Penitent*, and other pieces.

Last week arrived here a company of comedians from Philadelphia, who, we hear, have taken a convenient room for their purpose, in one of the buildings lately belonging to the hon. Rip Van Dam, Esq; deceased, in Nassau street; where they intend to perform as long as the season lasts, provided they meet with suitable encouragement.

14 Arrival of Murray and Kean in New York, communication in *The Pennsylvania Gazette*, March 6, 1750

Thursday Evening last, the Tragedy of CATO, was play'd at the Theatre in this City, before a very numerous Audience, the greater part of whom were of Opinion, that it was pretty well perform'd: As it was the fullest Assembly that has appear'd in that House, it may serve to prove, that the Taste of this Place is not so much vitiated, or lost to a Sense of Liberty, but that they can prefer a Representation of Virtue, to those of a loose Character. The *Recruiting Officer*, will be presented this Evening.

15 Murray and Kean's second New York season, from the *New York Gazette or Weekly Post Boy*, September 24, 1750

By his EXCELLENCY's Permission:
At the Theatre in *Nassau-Street*,
On Monday the 5th Day of *March* next, will be presented,
The Historical Tragedy of King RICHARD III.
Wrote originally by *Shakespeare*, and alter'd by *Colly* Cibber, Esq;
In this Play is contain'd, The Death of K. Henry VI. the artful Acquisition of the Crown by K. Richard; the Murder of the Princes in the Tower; the Landing of the Earl of Richmond, and the Battle of Bosworth-Field.
Tickets will be ready to be deliver'd, by Thursday next, and to be had of the Printer hereof; PITT, 5 s. Gallery, 3 s.
To begin precisely at Half an Hour after 6 o'Clock, and no Person to be admitted behind the Scenes.

16 Performance of *Richard III*, from the *New York Gazette or Weekly Post Boy*, February 26, 1750

Mr. KEAN, by the Advice of several Gentlemen in Town, who are his Friends, having resolv'd to quit the Stage, and follow his Employment of Writing (wherein he hopes for Encouragement;) and Mr. Murray having agreed to give him a Night, clear of all Expences, for his Half of the Cloaths, Scenes, &c. belonging to the Play House; it is resolved, that for the Benefit of said Kean, by his Excellency's Permission, on Monday the 29th of this Month will be perform'd KING RICHARD the III: The Part of RICHARD to be perform'd by Mr. Kean; being the last Time of his appearing on the Stage. To the above Tragedy will be added a Farce called, THE BEAU in the SUDDS.

17 Kean's "Resignation" from the Stage, from the *New York Gazette or Weekly Post Boy*, April 22, 1751

ROBERT UPTON

On December 30, 1751, a new company of comedians appeared at the Nassau Street Theater, giving for the first time in America Shakespeare's *Othello*. Robert Upton, the leading actor and manager of this new company, had been sent out to America by a London producer named William Hallam "in order to obtain permission to perform, erect a building, and settle everything against our arrival." The

By his Excellency's Permission.
ON Thursday Evening next, at the Theatre in Nassau-Street, will be presented by a new Company of Comedians, a Tragedy, call'd OTHELLO, Moor of Venice; to which will be added, a Dramatick Entertainment, wrote by the celebrated Mr. Garrick, called LETHE :----- To begin precisely at Six o'Clock.
Boxes, 5*s.* Pitt, 3*s.* Gallery, 2*s.*

18 Upton's Company of Comedians at the Nassau Street Theater, from the *New York Gazette or Weekly Post Boy*, December 23, 1751

advance agent, arriving in New York, found his problem complicated by the presence of a theater already in existence and of a professional company with an appreciable repertory. Upton simplified the problem — unjustifiably, from the irate Hallam's point of view — by joining the Murray-Kean organization, by cutting all ties with the Hallams, and, after the departure to Virginia of his new associates, by attempting himself to carry on the New York theater which they had begun. The response to his efforts was disappointing. Two weeks after opening he inserted in the *Post Boy* a notice to the effect that "Mr. Upton (to his great disappointment) not meeting with encouragement enough to support the company for the season, intends to shorten it, by performing five or six plays only, for Benefits." The potential audience of New York in 1752 was very small. Upton's repertory was meager and inadequate, and frequent repetitions of the same play were unpopular. In less than two months the season was ended. *Othello* was Upton's most significant contribution. The final performance, on March 4, was of Otway's *Venice Preserved*, in which Mr. and Mrs. Upton took the leading rôles. It is interesting to note that prior to the arrival of the Hallams, so often considered as marking the real beginning of the American stage, colonial audiences were already familiar with plays by Shakespeare, Dryden, Otway, Congreve, Farquhar, Rowe, Ambrose Philips, and Addison — authors at the height of their popularity among London audiences.

19 Mrs. Upton's Benefit, from the Fridenberg Collection, New York

THE ARRIVAL OF THE HALLAMS

The year 1752 marks a turning point in the history of the American stage. In that year William Hallam, 1712–58, bankrupt manager of a minor London theater, sent a company of players to America under his brother, Lewis. The leading lady was Lewis' wife, who had had a considerable amount of experience on the London stage, and first created for America many Shakespearean rôles. Another member was Lewis, Jr., then about twelve years old, who later became a favorite with the public and held a prominent place on the boards of numerous of our early theaters until his retirement in New York in 1806. The wanderers, wisely preferring the Cavalier South to the Puritan North, landed on the coast of Virginia, and opened at Williamsburg, September 15, 1752, in *The Merchant of Venice*, with the farce of *The Anatomist* as afterpiece. There can be little doubt that on this historic night America saw acting superior to any it had previously witnessed. Our stage as a dignified as well as continuous institution may be said to have sprung into being with the Hallams. The company soon developed an extensive repertory consisting of some twenty-four plays and eleven afterpieces, including the most popular of Shakespeare's dramas as well as the outstanding works of more recent playwrights who were filling the English theaters.

20 Announcement of The First American Performance of the Hallams, from the *Virginia Gazette*, August 28, 1752

21 Lewis Hallam, Jr., 1740(?)–1808, from a miniature, artist unknown, in the Harvard Theater Collection, Cambridge, Mass.

New-York, November 12, 1753.

By a Company of COMEDIANS,
At the New-Theatre, in *Naſſau-Street*,
This Evening, being the 12th of *November*, will be presented,
(By particular Deſire)
An *Hiſtorical Play*, call'd,

King RICHARD III.
CONTAINING
The Diſtreſſes and Death of King *Henry* the VIth; the artful
Acquiſition of the Crown by *Crook-back'd Richard*; the Murder
of the two young Princes in the Tower; and the memorable
Battle of *Boſworth-Field*, being the laſt that was fought between
the Houſes of *York* and *Lancaſter*.

Richard,	by	Mr. *Rigby*.
King Henry,	by	Mr. *Hallam*.
Prince Edward,	by	Maſter L. *Hallam*.
Duke of York,	by	Maſter A. *Hallam*.
Earl of Richmond,	by	Mr. *Clarkſon*.
Duke of Buckingham,	by	Mr. *Malone*.
Duke of Norfolk,	by	Mr. *Miller*.
Lord Stanley,	by	Mr. *Singleton*.
Lieutenant,	by	Mr. *Bell*.
Catesby,	by	Mr. *Adcock*.
Queen Elizabeth,	by	Mrs. *Hallam*.
Lady Anne,	by	Mrs. *Adcock*.
Ducheſs of York,	by	Mrs. *Rigby*.

To which will be added,
A Ballad FARCE, call'd,

The DEVIL TO PAY.

Sir John Loverule,	by	Mr. *Adcock*.
Jobſon,	by	Mr. *Malone*.
Butler,	by	Mr. *Miller*.
Footman,	by	Mr. *Singleton*.
Cook,	by	Mr. *Bell*.
Coachman,	by	Mr. *Rigby*.
Conjurer,	by	Mr. *Clarkſon*.
Lady Loverule,	by	Mrs. *Adcock*.
Nell,	by	Mrs. *Beccelor*.
Lettice,	by	Mrs. *Clarkſon*.
Lucy,	by	Miſs *Love*.

PRICES: BOX, 6ſ. PIT, 4ſ GALLERY, 2ſ.
No Perſons whatever to be admitted behind the Scenes.

N. B. Gentlemen and Ladies that chuſe Tickets, may have them
at Mr. *Parker's* and Mr. *Gaine's Printing-Offices*.
Money will be taken at the DOOR.
To begin at 6 o'Clock.

22 The Hallam Company in New York, 1753, from a playbill in the Fridenberg Collection, New York

ON TOUR

AFTER nearly a year in Virginia the London company moved on to New York in 1753, where serious obstacles were encountered. Their predecessors, Murray, Kean, and Upton, it seems, had conducted themselves in such a fashion as to prejudice many influential people against play-actors, and an unsuccessful effort was made to prevent the newcomers from performing. Furthermore, the New York playhouse was found to be so inadequate that they were compelled to tear it down and build a new one on the same site. What must have been a fairly successful season, however, closed in March, 1754. The company then invaded Philadelphia in spite of

PHILADELPHIA, June 20.

LAſt Evening, at the *New Theatre* in *Water-ſtreet*, the *Careleſs
Huſband*, and *Harlequin Collector*, were acted before a very crowded
and polite Audience, for the Benefit of the *Charity Children* belonging to the Academy of this City; on which Occaſion the following Prologue was ſpoken by Mr. *Rigby*.

OUR humble *Prologue* means not to engage
    Candor for Scenes that long have grac'd the Stage;
Nor vainly ſtrives to pay with Words, at laſt,
    For cheering Smiles, and kind *Protection* paſt.
Weak is the Power of Language to explain
    The ſacred Feelings, or th' ingenuous Pain
And ſilent Strugglings of the virtuous Breaſt,
    Beneath the Load of *Gratitude* oppreſt.
    But tho' no Words can picture what we feel,
Our *Aims* may ſpeak it, and our *Actions* tell.
To Night we glory in the double View
Of pleaſing ſoft-ey'd *Charity*——and You.
For this our cheerful Service we beſtow,——
'Tis all our ſlender Fortunes will allow;
    " And thoſe who give the little in their Power,"
The *Skies* acquit.——and *Earth* can aſk no more!
    Thrice happy you, whom kinder Fates have given,
With liberal Hand, to eaſe the Care of Heaven!
To raiſe the drooping Head of modeſt Worth;
From Fortune's Blaſt to ſhield the *Orphan-B*irth,
To pierce the dark Retreats where Miſ'ry ſighs,
And wipe the trickling Tear that dews her Eyes;——
If Deeds like theſe picture what we feel,
With Joys ſincere——what Boſom glows not now?
For ſure, if aught be gen'rous, great or fair,
It muſt be ——TRUTH and *public* WORTH to rear!
    Where *Virtue* blooms in yonder hallow'd * Ground,
With each ennobling Science op'ning round;
How many † *Maids* and *Youths*, with kindling Fires,
Now grow in all that living Worth inſpires,
Whom Fortune, in their Dawn, neglected laid,
To pine untutor'd in the barren Shade,
Where *Wiſdom* never did her Page unrol,
And Want ſtill froze the Current of their Soul;
Till, by your bounteous Hand, redeem'd from Fate,
You bade them riſe to grace a riſing State.
    Thus pinch'd beneath ſtern Winter's rigid Reign,
The Flowers lie mourning thro' the frozen Plain,
Till *Spring*, ſoft iſſuing from her ſouthern Hall,
Sweeps o'er the Dew-bright Lawn, with breezy Call,
And wakes them into Life:——They ſtraight unfold
To th' orient Sun their vegetable Gold;
And in Return embia'm the foſt'ring Air,
Or grace the lovely Boſoms of the Fair.

* *The Academy*.   † *The Charity Children.*

23 Charity Performance by the Hallams at the Water Street Theater, Philadelphia, from the *Pennsylvania Gazette*, June 20, 1754

much opposition on the part of moralists, and carried on a season of two months in what had once been a warehouse in which Murray and Kean had played. During this campaign they attempted to placate their enemies by offering a performance for the benefit of the charity school belonging to the College of Philadelphia.

DAVID DOUGLASS

BEGINNING in October, the Hallam Company conducted a campaign of about four months in Charleston; then, packing up the modest wardrobes and scenery which they had brought from London, and to which they had perhaps added but little since coming to America, they repaired to Kingston, Jamaica. In this city, which had seen considerable theatrical activity for a number of years, Hallam found a company of players in operation, with whom he united his own forces. His death followed shortly upon this event, and his widow in due time married David Douglass, an actor who had come out from England to Jamaica in 1751. When the reorganized troupe returned to America in 1758, Douglass was in control. Lewis Hallam, the younger, was the leading man, and his mother, Mrs. Douglass, a woman of much beauty and charm, was the leading lady. Perhaps the colonists derived less amusement than would a modern audience from seeing this mother and son playing together as Juliet and Romeo. Douglass, excellent man though he apparently was, found his career in this country beset by many opponents and hindrances.

24   The Kingston Theater, from a lithograph by A. Duperly in the Institute of Jamaica, Kingston, Jamaica

Then the Houſe adjourned to Three o'Clock, *P. M.* Adjournment

An Addreſs from the Society called *Quakers*, was preſented to the Houſe and read, *Poſt Meridiem* ſetting forth, that they have, with real Concern, heard that a Company of Stage Players are preparing to erect a Theatre, and exhibit Plays to the Inhabitants of this City, which they conceive, if permitted, will be ſubverſive of the good Order and Morals, which they deſire may be preſerved in this Government, and therefore pray the Houſe to frame and preſent to the Governor, for his Aſſent, a Bill to prohibit ſuch enſnaring and irreligious Entertainments. *Ordered to lie on the Table.*

25   Protest of the Philadelphia Quakers against Douglass, May 22, 1759, from the original *Journal of the General Assembly*, in the Pennsylvania Historical Society, Philadelphia

A "WANDERING THEATER"

IN New York, where Douglass landed with his players, the magistrates looked with a jaundiced eye on the actor's art, and consequently, after having gone to the expense of erecting a new theater on Cruger's Wharf, he was denied the privilege of using it. His subsequent announcement that it was his intention to open a "Histrionic Academy" in which he proposed "to deliver Dissertations on Subjects, *Moral, Instructive* and *Entertaining,* and to endeavor to qualify such as would favour me with their Attendance, *To speak in Publick with Propriety,*" deceived no one; but finally he was permitted to conduct a brief season. At Philadelphia also he found it necessary to erect a new theater and was compelled to wage another campaign against the opposition of the moralists. For years he transported his "wandering theater" about the colonies, visiting Annapolis, Williamsburg, Charleston, and smaller towns in Virginia and Maryland, and usually being compelled to erect a playhouse in each new town he entered. He even ventured intrepidly into the virgin territory of New England and played at Newport and Providence. He found it expedient to advertise *Othello* as a "Moral Dialogue, in Five

26   View of Philadelphia, 1761, detail from a sketch in the *London Magazine,* October 1761

Parts, Depicting the Evil Effects of Jealousy and other Bad Passions," and in other ways to disguise his offerings. An act to prevent stage plays was the immediate result of this incursion. In the face of such obstacles and of increasing hostility against British players, which led even to the demolition in 1766 of a theater he had built in Chapel Street, New York, Douglass nevertheless pursued his profession zealously until the Revolution, when he returned to Jamaica and retired from theatrical life.

AUNT AND NIECE

ALTHOUGH Mrs. Douglass' supremacy as the leading actress of the company was never disputed, there were a number of her first husband's nieces and cousins who achieved considerable popularity in certain rôles. The identity of these various Miss Hallams has become somewhat confused. But one Miss Hallam, the niece of Mrs. Douglass, became the first idol of the American theater. From various critics, especially in Maryland, she evoked superlative adulation.

27   Mrs. Douglass (d. 1774, ca.) as Daraxa, from a print in the Ohio Historical Society, Cincinnati

POETS CORNER.

To Miss H A L L A M,
On ſeeing her laſt Monday Night in the Character of
I M O G E N.

SAY, HALLAM! to thy wond'rous Art
    What Tribute ſhall I pay?
Say, wilt thou, from a feeling Heart,
    Accept this votive Lay?

A votive Lay to Thee belongs,
    For many a pleaſing Tear,
That fell, for IMOGEN's foul Wrongs,
    On fair FIDELE's Bier.

Fair, fair FIDELE! how thy Charms
    The Huntſmens Pity mov'd!
Artleſs as theirs, ſuch ſoft Alarms
    My melting Boſom prov'd.

In Nature's Breaſt, ſuperior Joy
    The Pow'r of Beauty wakes;
And the wild Motion of her Eye
    An eaſier Priſoner takes.

From earlieſt Youth, with Rapture, oft
    I've turn'd great SHAKESPEARE's Page;
Pleas'd, when he's gay, and footh'd, when ſoft,
    Or kindled at his Rage.

Yet not till now, till taught by Thee,
    Conceiv'd I Half his Pow'r!
I read, admiring now I ſee,
    I only not adore.

Ev'n now, amid the laurel'd Choir
    Of bliſsful Bards on high,
Whom liſt'ning Deities admire,
    The Audience of the Sky!

Methinks I ſee his ſmiling Shade,
    And hear him thus Proclaim,
" In Weſtern Worlds, to this fair Maid,
" I truſt my ſpreading Fame.

" Long have my Scenes each *Britiſh* Heart
" With warmeſt Tranſports fill'd;
" Now equal Praiſe, by HALLAM's Art,
" AMERICA ſhall yield."
                              PALADOUR.

28   Poem in praise of Miss Hallam, from *The Maryland Gazette,* 1771

29 John Henry (d. 1795), as Ephraim Smooth in *Wild Oats*, from an engraving by C. T. after a drawing by C. B., in the Harvard Theater Collection, Cambridge

JOHN HENRY

A PROMINENT figure in "the American Company," as Douglass' players came to be called, was John Henry, an actor from London, who went to the West Indies and thence to America, where his first appearance was made October 6, 1767, at Philadelphia. He was a tall and handsome Irishman and became popular as a comedian, especially in Irish characters. Henry was a picturesque and unconventional figure, whose morals might perhaps have been improved. Being a sufferer from gout, he kept a carriage ornamented with his coat of arms, which consisted of a pair of crossed crutches with the motto: "This or these." In this carriage he always drove his wife to the theater, already costumed for her night's part. Because of her immense hoop skirt, he found it necessary to slide her out sidewise and carry her to the stage door. According to William Dunlap in his *History of the American Theatre*, Henry was "one of the best performers in the colonies," but unscrupulous rivals kept him from achieving the distinction he deserved.

JUVENILE POEMS
ON
VARIOUS SUBJECTS.
WITH THE
PRINCE of PARTHIA,
A
TRAGEDY.
BY THE LATE
Mr. THOMAS GODFREY, Jun.
of PHILADELPHIA.

To which is prefixed,
Some ACCOUNT of the AUTHOR and his WRITINGS.

Poeta nascitur non fit.   HOR.

PHILADELPHIA,
Printed by HENRY MILLER, in Second-Street.
M DCC LXV.

30 Title-page of *The Prince of Parthia*, 1765, from the collection of Montrose J. Moses, New York

THE PRINCE OF PARTHIA

WHILE the actors were struggling to put the American theater solidly on its feet, our writers were making tentative efforts toward an American drama. In 1759 Thomas Godfrey, Jr., 1736–63, of Philadelphia wrote *The Prince of Parthia*, the first American tragedy, and the first American play to be acted professionally. It was printed in 1765 and produced at the Southwark Theater, Philadelphia, April 24, 1767. The play, written in flexible blank verse, has a considerable amount of dignity of the kind adhering to the formal English school of tragedy of the eighteenth century. It is, on the whole, a creditable beginning for American dramatic poetry. Being the work of a young student of books, it deals as do its British models with a remote time and scene, in interesting contrast with the very local *Androboros*, which was written by an active man of affairs.

Robert Rogers
Commandeur der Americaner.

31 Robert Rogers, 1727–95, from an engraved portrait in the collection of Montrose J. Moses, New York

THE FIRST INDIAN PLAY

EARLY American plays were chiefly outgrowths of contemporary situations and, however neglible otherwise, they often have a certain historical value. Major Robert Rogers, a pioneer backwoodsman, demonstrates this fact in his one drama. *Ponteach* (Pontiac), published in 1766, soon after the uprising of that great Ottawa chieftain, is our first Indian play. Dramatically, to be sure, there is little to be said for Major Rogers. His tragedy is crude and formless, but his contact with the Indians in his capacity of soldier and his quick observation enabled him to present the problem of the Indian with sincerity and feeling. To our surprise it is the white man's cunning greed in his dealings with the redskin that is indignantly exposed. *Ponteach* may be styled our earliest problem play.

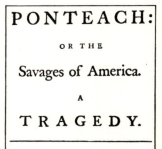

PONTEACH:
OR THE
Savages of America.
A
TRAGEDY.

LONDON:
Printed for the Author; and Sold by J. MILLAN,
opposite the *Admiralty*, *Whitehall*.
M.DCC.LXVI.

32 Title-page of *Ponteach*, 1766, in the New York Public Library

33 Chorus of Yankee Doodle from *The Disappointment*, in Oscar G. Sonneck, *Early Opera in America*, New York, 1914, courtesy of Schirmer & Co.

34 Title-page of *The Disappointment: or, The Force of Credulity*, in the Library of Congress, Washington

OUR FIRST OPERA LIBRETTO

A DEFINITE start having been made in the matter of native playwriting, the work went forward with considerable briskness, and some effort was made to try out forms hitherto unattempted in America. A popular type of dramatic entertainment of the time was the so-called comic opera, a comedy with songs interspersed. What was apparently the first representative of this species to be written by an American was *The Disappointment: or, The Force of Credulity*, by Andrew Barton, perhaps a pen name for Colonel Thomas Forrest. Arrangements were being made for its stage presentation on April 20, 1767, at Philadelphia, but on the 16th the *Pennsylvania Gazette* carried the announcement that it had been withdrawn because of personal reflec-

35 Charlotte Lennox, from a mezzotint by Bartolozzi, 1794, after the portrait by Sir Joshua Reynolds (1723-92), in possession of the publishers

tions that made it unfit for the stage. It was a satire on the current mania of searching for the hidden treasures of Blackbeard the Pirate; and the folly of certain well known Philadelphians was held up to such lively ridicule that the manager decided, probably under pressure, to drop the whole matter. *The Disappointment*, though one of the coarsest of early American plays, is distinctly vigorous, and, in its crude way, not unamusing. Nor does the author wholly fail at his self-announced task — "to point out vice" and "to make virtue fair," which, despite the puritanical language, is after all the office that comedy has aimed to perform since the days of Aristophanes.

CHARLOTTE LENNOX, 1720–1804

THE first woman born in America to write a play was Charlotte Lennox, who left this country for London at the age of fifteen. *The Sisters*, said to be a dramatization of her own novel, was not written until 1769; consequently America's share in her small achievement is but slender. Though *The Sisters* was equipped with an epilogue by Oliver Goldsmith, it failed on the stage. It was, however, printed and even translated.

36   Nassau Hall, Princeton, N. J., from an engraving by H. Dawkins, after a drawing by W. Tennant, in *An Account of the College of New Jersey*, 1764

COLLEGES AND THE EARLY DRAMA

In spite of religious prejudice the eighteenth-century American college encouraged drama. We have already observed the "pastoral colloquy" at William and Mary in 1702. The College of Philadelphia, later the University of Pennsylvania, from about the middle of the century gave considerable attention to "dialogues,"

37   President John Witherspoon, 1723–94, from an engraved portrait in the Madigan Collection, New York

38   Rev. William Smith, 1727–1803, from a portrait by Benjamin West (1738–1820), in the Historical Society of Pennsylvania, Philadelphia

sometimes written by the students. Francis Hopkinson and Nathaniel Evans, among others at the Philadelphia institution, turned their hands to these exercises. This type of entertainment was also familiar at Princeton, then known as the College of New Jersey, where it enjoyed the approval of President John Witherspoon. *The Military Glory of Great Britain*, of unknown authorship, "an Entertainment given by the Late Candidates for the Bachelor's Degree at Nassau Hall, September 29, 1762," presented to Princetonians a very different point of view from *The Rising Glory of America*, written by Hugh Henry Brackenridge and Philip Freneau for the commencement program of 1771. It is one of the interesting contradictions of dramatic history that, while pulpits were anathematizing the iniquity of the playhouse, and legislators were bandying back and forth laws for the suppression of the vagabond actor, such severe representatives of education as Provost William Smith of Philadelphia, and President Witherspoon of Princeton, had under their wings the early exponents of American playwriting.

39   College of Philadelphia before the Revolution, from an engraving, courtesy of the University of Pennsylvania, Philadelphia

40   The Death of Warren, frontispiece to *The Battle of Bunker's Hill*, Philadelphia, 1776, from an engraving by Norman after a drawing by "N. G."

41   Hugh Henry Brackenridge, 1748–1816, from an engraving after a contemporary drawing, in the collection of Montrose J. Moses

42   The Death of General Montgomery, frontispiece to Brackenridge's poem of that name, from an engraving by Norman after a drawing by "N. G."

THE TEMPER OF THE TIME

DURING the stirring years of the Revolution Brackenridge, remembering his efforts at Princeton, wrote a dialogue of a much more ambitious sort than any so far mentioned, to be used as an exercise in oratory by the "young gentlemen" of Sommerset Academy in Maryland, where he was teaching. *The Battle of Bunker's Hill* (1776), though devoid of action, is divided into five acts and approximates drama more closely than any of its predecessors. It is written in blank verse of a rather vigorous sort. In 1777 it was followed by a similar exercise, *The Death of General Montgomery in Storming the City of Quebec*. Both these pieces are charged with the most intense hatred of all things British and the most ecstatic admiration of all things American. One is not surprised to learn that Brackenridge deserted the classroom to deliver vigorous political sermons to the soldiers. Taken as a whole the school and college dialogues described above can scarcely be called dramatic, but at least they indicate the presence of the dramatic impulse. Polemical they undoubtedly are, and consequently they are a measure of the temper of the time.

43   Mrs. Mercy Warren, 1728–1814, from an engraving in the collection of Montrose J. Moses

A FRIEND OF ADAMS AND JEFFERSON

JUST preceding the Revolution patriotic ardor was by no means an exclusively masculine prerogative. Mrs. Mercy Warren, sister of James Otis and wife of James Warren, both prominent American statesmen, was actively in touch with political events and carried on a correspondence with John Adams, Thomas Jefferson, and other leading men. To express her hostility to the British oppressors, she resorted to dramatic satire. Her first play, *The Adulateur* (1773), was directed especially against Thomas Hutchinson, Governor of Massachusetts, who, because he was a native of the colony, was intensely hated for attempting to enforce British measures. This was followed in 1775 by *The Group*, in which Mrs. Warren pilloried those Americans who sanctioned the king's recent abrogation of the Massachusetts charter — a group including prominent citizens of the type of Foster Hutchinson, the Governor's brother, from whom patriotic leadership might have been expected. These sketches, which were never acted, give expression to the sense of intolerable wrongs common at this period, and *The Adulateur* ends with a glowing prophecy of the future glories of America, a note frequently heard in our early drama.

44 St. John de Crèvecœur, 1735–1813, from an engraving
by L. Massart in Robert de Crèvecœur, *St. Jean de
Crèvecœur*, Paris, 1883

A TORY VIEW

IF the dramatic form was useful for patriotic propaganda, it could also serve pro-British purposes. Among those who thus employed it was the author of *Letters from an American Farmer*, St. John de Crèvecœur, a Frenchman who emigrated to America in 1754 and subsequently took up agriculture in New York. Because he was an aristocrat and saw the rebellion of the Colonies as an uprising of the misguided and over-ambitious common man against the aristocracy, Crèvecœur championed the Tory cause. During the Revolution he wrote six dialogues, which he called *American Landscapes*. The leading figure in these sketches is the commissioner for selling Tory estates, a deacon, who, with his fellow commissioners, imprisons and tortures Loyalists and sells or appropriates their property. The Deacon and his wife are represented as conscienceless hypocrites, whose mouths are full of Puritanical cant and whose hearts overflow with malice and greed. Says the Deacon, "God is good; God is great; His mercy is immense. If we serve Him faithfully, I am sure He will reward us with the spoil of our enemies." The *Landscapes* are written with sprightly vigor and obvious feeling. The remark of one of Crèvecœur's Tories that the Deacon is a "perfect epitome of the times" is as sincere and mistaken as corresponding comments upon the British made by patriot playwrights.

THE SOUTHWARK THEATER, PHILADELPHIA

THE American playhouses that arose in the early years of the eighteenth century are to-day disquietingly shadowy and elusive. What they looked like we can only conjecture. Their history, except for a few bald facts, we shall probably never know. A few years before the Revolution, however, two theaters were erected that still occupy a definite and important place in the story of our stage. The first in point of time was the Southwark Theater at Philadelphia, constructed by David Douglass in 1766. A lower part of brick, an upper part of wood, and a coat of glaring red paint over the whole combined to produce a most unsightly and primitive looking edifice. The interior was scarcely less ill-contrived and ugly. Plain oil lamps without glasses lighted the stage and the view of this dim and probably smoky platform was interrupted by large wooden pillars supporting the balcony and the roof. Unprepossessing as this sounds, it was an advance over the temporary structures that had preceded it. It was situated on South Street above Fourth in what was apparently a desolate and uninviting spot. Consequently Douglass' patrons must have read with pleasure his announcement in February, 1770, that "a footpath is made across the common to the corner of Pine Street, in Fourth Street, on which those ladies who are not provided with carriages may come to the house without dirtying their feet." It is to be hoped this footpath aided in leading large audiences to the theater, for in it were to be seen the best actors the colonies could boast. Some interesting first performances in America were offered here, among them that of *King John*. When competent acting failed to induce the public to risk dirtying its feet, the enterprising Douglass resorted to displays of fireworks upon the stage. The Southwark continued to serve as a playhouse until the early years of the nineteenth century, when, after partial destruction by fire, it was converted into a brewery, and was not finally demolished until 1912.

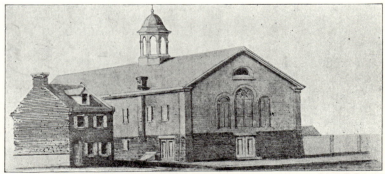

45 The Old South Street Theater, Philadelphia, from a reconstructive drawing by Edwin F. Durang
in Durang's Extra-Illustrated Edition of his *History of the Philadelphia Stage*, in the Library of
the University of Pennsylvania, Philadelphia

THE JOHN STREET THEATER, NEW YORK

A YEAR after the erection of the Southwark Theater, a companion playhouse was put up in New York on John Street, near Broadway. It was situated about sixty feet back from the street and was provided with a covered passageway leading from the pavement to the doors. It was built principally of wood, and like its Philadelphia twin was painted red. Dunlap might have applied to it the same phrase he employed in describing the Southwark — "in its appearance no ornament to the city." That historian further wrote: "Two rows of boxes, with a pit and gallery, could accommodate all the playgoing

46 Interior view of the John Street Theater, from an engraving by S. Hollyer, in possession of the publishers

people of the time." The pit benches were occupied entirely by gentlemen, while the side spaces, which no doubt represent boxes, were filled with ladies. One makes out two proscenium doors opening upon the stage, and it is possible to identify the openings above them as balconies for spectators. From the row of reflectors across the front of the stage it is evident that footlights were a part of the equipment, but we cannot be sure when this drawing was made, and consequently it does not provide a clue to the date when footlights were first used in America. If other overhead lights than those shown in the picture were employed for the stage, they may have been hoops of candles so suspended that they might be raised into the flies when a dark scene was desired. This simple but famous house was opened by Douglass, December 7, 1767, with *The Beaux' Stratagem,* and during the thirty years of its career it housed many of the greatest dramas of the English language, while its narrow stage was trodden by more than a few actors whose names are still cherished by students of the American theater. In off seasons rudimentary circuses, assembly dances, itinerant horse riders, rope walkers, and the like were called on to regale the public within these classic walls.

THE GENERAL MANAGER

TEN years later, during the winter and spring of 1777, after Washington's retirement to the Jerseys had brought relief from immediate danger to the British and Hessian garrison in New York, the John Street Theater was taken over by a company of British military actors, and, as a taunt to the patriot sympathizers, renamed The Theater Royal. The first play presented was Henry Fielding's *Tom Thumb,* with prologue and scenery by British officers. Six plays and nine afterpieces were presented during the season, including Farquhar's *The Inconstant,* Addison's *The Drummer,* and Beaumont and Fletcher's *Rule a Wife and Have a Wife.* In January, 1778, General Clinton took over the managership of the Theater Royal, and the direction of "Clinton's Thespians." For a number of months the manager was away, having been ordered to Philadelphia to replace Howe. But by July he was back, and with him had come additional dramatic candidates, "the strolling company" of Howe's army, who had performed in the Old Southwark Theater in Philadelphia.

Clinton maintained his headquarters in New York until the British army embarked for home after the treaty of peace in 1783. A list of the excellent plays given by them has been preserved. Their most significant contributions were productions of Sheridan's contemporary London successes, *The Rivals,* and *The School for Scandal.* "Crouded" and "brilliant" audiences were the rule, and the theater was financially successful, though a very small fraction of the receipts found its way into the hands of the war victims, who were supposed to be the beneficiaries and the justification of the entire scheme. It was run with a definite policy, and General Clinton may well be considered one of the first successful commercial managers in the early American theater.

On Monday,
The Sixteenth Inſtant, *February 1778,*
At the Theatre in Southwark,
For the Benefit of a PUBLIC CHARITY,
Will be repreſented a Comedy
CALLED THE
Conſtant Couple.
To which will be added,
DUKE AND NO DUKE.
The CHARACTERS by the OFFICERS of the ARMY and NAVY

47 Playbill announcing theatrical performance by British Troops in Philadelphia, February 1778, from Smith and Watson, *American Historical and Literary Curiosities,* Philadelphia, 1847.

48 Sir Henry Clinton, 1738–95, from the *Oxford Book of Historical Portraits,* Vol. III, Oxford University Press, Oxford, England, 1919

49   Receipts in the Theater Royal Account Book for Current Expenditures, from
        the original in the New York Historical Society

DRESSES AND WIGS

THE Theater Royal account books for 1779–80 show that Clinton's Redcoat actors went to great expense to secure first-class costumes. Nine pounds were paid for "Cupid's dress," and thirty-seven pounds, six shillings, for wigs. Under their management the orchestra was also developed to a higher point than it had reached before in America. There was an orchestra of fourteen instruments, all well played and well rehearsed. The scenery on the other hand was wretched. The parts were usually taken by men, but it quite often happened at this time in New York that the leading female part was played by one of the garrison mistresses who had accompanied the British officers to America. During the season of 1778 twenty-one performances were given. The following year there were approximately thirty, with a repertory of sixteen plays and eighteen accompanying afterpieces. During the fourth season there were thirty-five performances. One great difficulty that the actors had to face was that of getting sufficient copies of a play from which to learn their parts. In the *Royal Gazette* for December 22, 1779, appeared the following advertisement: "The managers of the theater, understanding that a gentleman purchased a set of Garrick's works from Mr. Robertson the printer, will be much obliged to that gentleman if he will resign the purchase over to the theater for the benefit of charity, or lend them the particular volume that contains the comedy of *Catherine and Petruchio*."

A FRIEND OF GARRICK'S

ANOTHER Redcoat manager, General John Burgoyne, was in charge of the theatricals given by the British in Faneuil Hall. He wrote for his players a farce entitled *The Blockade of Boston*. It was ready for production on the night of January 8, 1776, when the audience was thrown into a panic by an announced attack on Charlestown by the Americans. It was a local skit — unfortunately lost. That Burgoyne was a dramatist of some power is shown by the fact that one of his plays was produced in London by David Garrick, who may have been prompted by a certain snobbish desire to be closely affiliated with titled people. Burgoyne was also an actor of ability, but there is no evidence that he acted with his soldiers. He did give orders, however, that the handbills of the theater should be sent to the American commanders, probably in order to show them how gay the British were, and also as a taunt to the Puritanical. Seilhamer, in his *History of the American Theatre*, wrote, "So thoroughly had Burgoyne infused the theatrical spirit into his soldiery that when his captured army was in captivity at Charlottesville, in 1779–80, they erected a theater for their own amusement."

50   British Theater run by General John Burgoyne's soldiers at Charlottesville, Va., detail from a sketch in Thomas Anburey, *Travels through the Interior Parts of North America*, London, 1789

51   General John Burgoyne, 1722–92, from the portrait by Allan Ramsay (1713–84), in the collection of Mrs. Morton Philips, England. Photo by Rischgitz, London

52 Major John André, 1751–80, from an engraving by J. K. Sherwin after a self-portrait by André, in possession of the publishers

53 Ticket for the Meschianza, in the Library Company, Philadelphia. Photo by P. B. Wallace

54 Headdress for the Meschianza, from a drawing by André, reproduced in Scharf, *History of Philadelphia*, Philadelphia, 1884

THE FIRST PAGEANT

On the enemy side there is also the figure of the romantic André working among the canvases of the theater, painting scenery and curtains, and designing costumes. He might be regarded as America's first pageant creator, for it is to him that much of the glory belongs for the success of "The Meschianza," which was given, May 18, 1778, in honor of Lord Howe, on the occasion of his recall to England. Burgoyne had written *The Maid of the Oaks* for a similar *fête champêtre*, and "The Meschianza" leaned heavily on former celebrations of the kind. The affair was given at the country seat of Mrs. Wharton, which included a section of the Delaware River. "The Meschianza" was a variety of entertainments combined; there were a grand regatta, and galleys of beautiful Tory women of Philadelphia, music, ballrooms paneled with eighty-five mirrors, and a supper room where three hundred tapers lit the table and four hundred and thirty covers were laid. André's costume designs were elaborate, those for the Burning Mountain and the Blended Roses being particularly resplendent. André possessed taste; his brush and pen were ever ready to aid the Redcoat theater.

55 Congressional Resolution of 1778 denouncing theatrical performances, from the original in the Library of Congress, Washington

DRAMA AT VALLEY FORGE

It is less generally known that dramas were also given before American audiences. A soldier at Valley Forge on May 14, 1778, wrote the following description: "The theater is opened. Last Monday Cato was performed before a very numerous & splendid audience. His Excellency [Washington] & Lady, Lord Stirling [an American officer], the Countess . . . & Mr. Green [General Nathanael Greene?] were part of the Assembly. The scenery was in Taste, & the performance admirable."

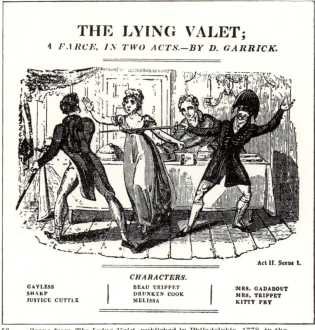

THE LYING VALET;

A FARCE, IN TWO ACTS.—BY D. GARRICK.

Act II. Scene 1.

CHARACTERS.

GAYLESS	BEAU TRIPPET	MRS. GADABOUT
SHARP	DRUNKEN COOK	MRS. TRIPPET
JUSTICE CUTTLE	MELISSA	KITTY PRY

56   Scene from *The Lying Valet*, published in Philadelphia, 1778, in the
Library of Congress, Washington

REPUBLICAN AMATEURS

WHEN the Continental Army returned to Philadelphia in 1778, a number of plays were produced in September and October at the Southwark Theater by a group of players whose names are not known. The copy of Garrick's farce, *The Lying Valet*, a scene from which is here reproduced, was "printed at the desire of some of the officers of the American Army who have suffered in the War for American Liberty." It is recorded that Washington, remembering Congress' recommendation against plays, was forced at this time to refuse Lafayette's invitation to attend the theater in Philadelphia. In the same year *Cato*, ever popular because of the intensity of its republican sentiments, was produced in Portsmouth, New Hampshire. In the final year of the Revolution, *The Revenge* and *The Lying Valet* were produced by American troops at Reading, Pennsylvania. Following the surrender of Cornwallis, the first French play in America, Beaumarchais' *Eugénie*, was presented by the pupils of a French professor in Philadelphia before Washington, the French Minister, the French officers, and others assembled at the Southwark Theater. It was a period of rejoicing, in which Luzerne, the distinguished French Minister, seems to have taken the lead in fêting Washington at concerts and oratorios, with fireworks and balls and suppers.

57   View of Annapolis, 1797, showing the State House (large building in background), from an engraving in possession of the publishers

58   The Reëntry of the Americans into New York, from an engraving after a drawing by Chapin, in possession of the publishers

THE RETURN OF THE PROFESSIONAL

IN the majority of the colonies, acting during the Revolution was carried on by soldiers or not at all, but things were ordered differently in Maryland. No local prohibition having been enacted there, the recommendation of Congress was not binding. Consequently Mr. Wall, formerly of the American Company, and Adam Lindsay, a tavern keeper, taking advantage of the situation, organized a company of professional players and conducted a season in Baltimore from January 15 to about June 14, 1782. They were housed in the city's first theater, built the year before. During the second season the company was strengthened by the addition of Mr. and Mrs. Dennis Ryan from Dublin. Early in 1783 Ryan took over the control of the organization, which, after two short visits to Annapolis, closed its season in June. The company then proceeded to New York and held forth at the John Street Theater for over two months, after which they returned to Maryland. The next spring the company disbanded and Ryan died two years later.

CHAPTER II

IN THE DAYS OF THE JOHN STREET THEATER

IF certain over-zealous citizens of the new nation congratulated themselves that their hard-won freedom from British dominance would involve freedom from the profane vanity of that British institution, the theater, they were doomed to early disillusionment. Within a few months after the treaty of peace, tentative efforts were made by the pre-Revolutionary dramatic leaders to reinstate themselves in their former territory. The opposition was vigorous at first, but through the strategy of the players, the tolerance of the more liberal members of the community, and the potent appeal of the dramatic art, the forces of the theater in a few years had won more ground than they had ever yet occupied. New York capitulated quickly. Philadelphia, with its various rigid sects, offered more resistance, but six years after the peace the managers were relieved of the necessity of presenting plays disguised as "serious moral lectures." The most signal triumph of the theater, however, was the successful invasion of New England, where hitherto intolerance toward the stage had most vigorously flourished. The conquest was complete when, in the early 1790's, the prohibitory acts of many years standing were repealed in Rhode Island and Massachusetts. This surrender should cause little surprise, however, for the impulse toward art was already strong in New England, as is evidenced by the rise and popularity of John Singleton Copley and Gilbert Stuart, portrait painters of the first order, and of the distinguished architect Charles Bulfinch. Puritan severity notwithstanding, New England loved art, and the art of the actor could not be indefinitely denied.

This territorial expansion was accompanied by a natural multiplication in the number of theatrical companies. The Hallam organization, from its first appearance in this country, enjoyed a virtual monopoly of the field until after the Revolution, but it was both desirable and inevitable that this position, sooner or later, should be successfully disputed. When Thomas Wignell seceded from the Old American Company and assembled a rival troupe in 1794, a new era in the American theater began. The old organization now centered its activities at New York, while Wignell's forces gained control of Philadelphia and the adjacent territory. Philadelphia quickly became the dramatic capital of America, and for three decades its position was not seriously challenged. Superior equipment and greater initiative in obtaining new and promising actors kept that city steadily in advance of her less aggressive rival to the north.

Progress, however, was not confined to Philadelphia. During the post-Revolutionary period drama invested itself with much more dignified and impressive equipment than America had yet known. In several towns new theaters were built on a scale of size

and beauty yet unattempted. Taste and money were employed to make them as attractive as possible. Competent musicians and scene-painters were secured. The
managers of these new houses were wise enough always to bear in mind the democratic
spirit of the new republic. When Wignell built his splendid theater in Philadelphia,
a lady who led the first society of the town proposed to purchase a box "at any price
to be fixed by the manager." Wignell was tempted, but he realized that he was an
American manager, and that within the walls of his playhouse all men — and women
— must be free and equal. Consequently he declined the offer.

In respect to the playwrights of the time the public was less insistent on applying the
doctrine of republicanism. The theatergoers, prejudiced in favor of the foreign writer,
doubted whether anything good in the shape of a play could come out of America;
hence the home-bred dramatist sometimes found it to his advantage to suppress the
fact that his work was a native product. But in spite of this deterrent, the final years
of the eighteenth century saw a noticeable increase, both in quantity and quality, in
the output of our playwrights. Several interesting innovations in types of play or
of character were made, which distinctly widened the range of American drama. Furthermore, this period was marked by the activity of the first professional playwright
in the United States. Clearly, then, dramatic literature was pushing forward along
with the other aspects of the theater.

Yet the main distinction between the colonial theater and that of the years after
the Revolution lies in the quality of the acting. During the later period, thanks especially to the Philadelphia directors, a procession of gifted British players moved to these
shores, many of them to remain here permanently. Most of these newcomers had had
sound training in the provincial theaters of England or even in the leading London
houses, and had sometimes played with the great actors of the time. Indeed, among
these visitors a substantial number had risen to eminence before leaving for the New
World. In consequence the tone of American acting was raised to such a level that
it deserved serious consideration even when compared with the London stage. These
representative British artists set a pattern that must have been a source of stimu-
lation to the older actors in America long out of touch with the English theater. That
they also exerted an influence on the dress and manners of the playgoing public may be
discovered from various records. In an age when foreign travel was difficult and infre-
quent, they brought something of European culture to the raw country of their adoption
and undoubtedly were distinctly, though intangibly, beneficial in diluting, particularly
in the theater towns, the provincialism which they found there. Among other things
it is interesting to speculate upon the effect which these imported actors must have had
on American speech. How much did they aid in keeping urban speech along the Atlantic
seaboard approximately parallel with that of London? Obviously the answer is not
forthcoming, but it is not fantastic to suppose that their influence was far from negligible.

In general during the last decade of the eighteenth century the American theater
felt an impetus toward improvement and expansion that was a natural sequel to the
successful conclusion of the war and the establishment of the new nation. Among
the various manifestations of the progressive spirit of the time, the theater was not
the least vigorous and not the least creditable.

"VIVAT RESPUBLICA"

As soon as the Revolution was safely over, the actors who had withdrawn to Jamaica returned. Lewis Hallam was in Philadelphia as early as January, 1784, in an effort to gain legal permission to resume his activities. Although many citizens and some of the newspapers supported him in his attempt, he met with no success. The opponents of the stage now had an additional grievance against the actors — the fact that they were British sympathizers who had deserted their foster-country during her struggle for independence. Naturally this intensified the prejudice against them. On April 1, however, Hallam began offering public entertainments, consisting of lectures, especially the popular "Lectures upon Heads," and "poetical addresses." In December we find him joint manager with a Mr. Allen of a feeble company that reopened the Southwark Theater at Philadelphia on April 7, with a bill involving "A *serious* investigation of Shakespeare's morality illustrated by his most striking characters faithfully applied to the task of *mingling profit with amusement*." This was obviously a disguise for a play or perhaps scenes from several plays, but the authorities apparently offered no serious objection, for it was repeated twice during the month, and was followed by other entertainments of a similar nature. In August, 1785, Hallam and Allen opened the John Street Theater in New York with lectures and kindred amusements. But by September 20, they were frankly announcing plays. The season was brief but it was not interrupted by magisterial intervention.

The last Night of Performance.
THEATRE.
On WEDNESDAY EVENING next, being the 9th Instant, June—Will be delivered,
A NEW Course of

Lectures upon Heads,

Serious, Comic and Satiric; with Alterations and Additions.

The first part will chiefly consist of a Poetical Address to the Audience, and a Dissertation upon the Passions, with Examples selected from the most eminent dramatic writers.

The second part will exhibit a Groupe of Female Portraits, faithfully drawn and characteristically represented ; and

The third part will consist of various Male Caracatures, with a concluding Address to the audience.

The whole will be properly diversified with Music, Scenery, and other Decorations.
Previous to the first part of the Lecture will be recited, a

MONODY,

In honor of the CHIEFS who have fallen in the Cause of America, accompanied with suitable Decorations.

Tickets to be purchased at Mr. Bradford's Book-Store, in Front-street, near the Coffee-house, and places for the Boxes to be taken at the Theatre from 9 till one o'clock each day. The doors will be open at 6, and the Lecture begin at seven o'clock.

Boxes 7/6—Pit 5/—Gallery 3/.
No Money to be received at the door.
Vivat Respublica.

59 Announcement of Hallam's Lectures upon Heads, from *The Pennsylvania Packet*, June 5, 1784

OPERA-HOUSE, Southwark.

Positively the last Week.

THIS EVENING, the 23d of July, will be presented,
A CONCERT;
Between the Parts of which will be delivered, (*gratis*)
A SERIOUS

Historical Lecture,
In Five Parts—On the

Fate of Tyranny;
Exemplified in the Life and Character of

King *Richard* the IIId.

Containing the Distresses and Death of King *Henry* the VIth and his Son *Edward* ; the artful Acquisition of the Crown by *Richard* ; the Murder of the two Princes in the Tower; the Fall of the Duke of *Buckingham* ; the Landing of the Earl of *Richmond*, and the famous Battle of Bosworth Field. Which put an End to the Contention of the Houses of *York* and *Lancaster* ; with many other historical Passages.

"Thrice is he arm'd, that hath his quarrel just,
"And he but naked, tho' lock'd up in steel,
"Whose Conscience with Injustice is corrupted :
"The very Weight of *Richard's* Guilt shall crush him."
Shakespear's RICHARD the IIId.
The Whole to Conclude with a
COMIC LECTURE,
In Two Parts—Called, The

Credulous Steward :
OR,
A new Way to get Money.
The doors will be opened at seven, and the curtain drawn up precisely one quarter before eight o'clock.

60 *Richard III*, disguised as "a serious Historical Lecture," "Opera-House," Philadelphia, from *The Pennsylvania Packet*, July 23, 1788

HALLAM AND HENRY

WHILE Hallam was holding forth in New York, John Henry arrived in Philadelphia with a few members of the pre-Revolutionary troupe as well as several recent recruits from the West Indies — a company considerably superior to that of Hallam and Allen. After performing for a time in Philadelphia, Henry entered into a partnership with Hallam some time late in 1785, and the new organization applied to itself the name of The Old American Company. For several years it held a monopoly of the field and visited the principal towns from New York to Charleston. In certain communities opposition was still active. This was especially true of Philadelphia, where for a time the managers found it expedient to call the theater an opera house, to advertise the performances "gratis," and to disguise

OPERA-HOUSE, SOUTHWARK,

THIS EVENING, the 16th of July, will be performed
A CONCERT;
Between the Parts of which will be delivered, (*gratis*)
A Serious, Moral and Instructive TALE, called,

The Penitent Wife:
OR,
Fatal Indiscretion.
Exemplified in the History of JANE SHORE.

" If poor weak woman swerve from virtue's rule,
If, strongly charm'd, she leave the thorny way,
And in the softer paths of pleasure stray,
Ruin ensues, reproach and endless shame,
And one false step entirely blasts her fame.
In vain with tears the loss she may deplore,
In vain look back on what she was before ;
She sets, like stars that fall to rise no more "
Rowe's Jane Shore.
To which will be added a COMIC OPERA,
In Two Acts, called,

Love in a Camp :
Or, Patrick in Prussia:
Being the second part of the POOR SOLDIER. With the Original Overture and Accompaniment, New Scenery, a View of the Camp at Grosnitz, &c. N. B. The public are respectfully acquainted, that to avoid the inconvenience of late hours, the Lecture will begin precisely at the time advertised.

The doors will be opened at seven, and the curtain drawn up precisely one quarter before eight o'clock. Places in the Boxes may be had of Mr. Ryan, at Mr. North's, next door to the Opera-House ; where also Tickets may be had, and at Mr. Bradford's Book-store.

The Proprietors respectfully request, that their friends and patrons will supply themselves with Tickets, as the door-keepers are in the most particular manner prohibited from receiving any money.
BOX 7/6, PIT 5/ GALLERY 3/9

61 *Jane Shore*, disguised as "a Serious, Moral, and Instructive Tale," from *The Pennsylvania Packet*, July 16, 1788

the plays with moral captions. Thus *Hamlet* became "Filial Piety"; *She Stoops to Conquer*, "Improper Education"; *Richard III*, "The Fate of Tyranny"; and *The School for Scandal*, "The Pernicious Vice of Scandal." But at last in 1789, thanks to the efforts of the more cultured and influential people in Philadelphia, the prohibition against the theater enacted in 1778 was repealed.

62   Mrs. Owen Morris (d. 1825, ca.), from an engraving by D. C. Johnston, in the Harvard Theater Collection, Cambridge, Mass.

SOME PLAYERS

THE leading actress of The Old American Company was Mrs. Owen Morris, who made her first American appearance about 1770, and after the Revolution assumed a commanding position on the stage. She was a tall and imposing lady, who captured her audiences in elegant comedy and more stately forms of drama. As Katherine in *The Taming of the Shrew*, Mrs. Hardcastle in *She Stoops to Conquer*, and other characters, she was for years the greatest attraction in the theater. The leading actor was still Lewis Hallam. Though his tragedy was at times formal and declamatory, he was competent in all branches of his profession. He was, however, particularly qualified for genteel comedy, in which he was notable for ease and vigor, performing with credit almost every prominent rôle in the plays of his time. John Henry, although primarily a comedian, was a good general actor. According to Dunlap he played Othello better than any actor before him in America, but he was most thoroughly at home in Irish parts.

"LUXURIANT IN HUMOUR"

THE best low comedian of the company was Thomas Wignell, a cousin of Lewis Hallam. He came from an English theater to America in 1774 but transferred his activities to Jamaica along with his fellow actors. He first appeared on the American stage in 1785, and, being the best natural comedian this country had yet seen, was soon in high favor. Dunlap described him as "below the ordinary height, with a slight stoop of the shoulders; he was athletic, with handsomely formed lower extremities, the knees a little curved outwards, and feet remarkably small. His large blue eyes were rich in expression, and his comedy was luxuriant in humour, but always faithful to his author. He was a comic actor, not a buffoon." The truth of the last sentence is indicated by the fact that one of his best liked characters was Joseph Surface in *The School for*

63   Thomas Wignell, in the character of Darby, from an engraving after a drawing by William Dunlap, in O. G. Sonneck, *Early Opera in America*, New York, 1914, courtesy of Schirmer & Co.

Scandal. But the part that came to be inextricably associated with his name was that of the Irish Darby in O'Keeffe's *The Poor Soldier*. Whenever President Washington visited the theater, as he often did, it was Wignell who, in a full dress of black, with his hair powdered, and holding two candles in silver candlesticks, received him at the box door and escorted him to his seat.

64   Thomas Wignell, 1753(?)–1803, from a portrait, artist unknown, in the Houdini Collection, New York

WASHINGTON GOES TO THE THEATER

GEORGE WASHINGTON was always intensely interested in the theater. Paul Leicester Ford, in a brochure, *Washington and the Theatre*, has conclusively traced his constant and lively delight in the current playhouse. At an early age he went to the theater in the Barbadoes, November 15, 1751, to see George Lillo's *George Barnwell*. He was a gallery god, April 30, 1752, at Fredericksburg, Virginia. His thoughts were sometimes on the theater during the French and Indian War, 1759, and during the session of the House of Burgesses in Virginia in

65 Facsimile of Washington's Diary, 1773, recording three consecutive visits to Annapolis Theater, from Paul L. Ford, *Washington and the Theatre*, Dunlap Society Publications, New York, 1899

66 George Washington, 1732–99, from an engraving by H. B. Hall after the crayon portrait by C. B. J. St. Memin (1770–1852), in possession of the publishers

1771. He enjoyed wax works and sleight-of-hand performances. After he became President theater parties were often given by Washington, at which such men as Chief Justice Jay were present. His favorite plays were *The School for Scandal* and the comic opera, *The Poor Soldier*. A newspaper in 1792 observed that the President paid a certain play "the tribute of a tear." After Washington's death many monodies in his memory were delivered in the theaters, and for weeks afterward the playhouses throughout the country were draped in mourning.

THE FIRST SUCCESSFUL AMERICAN PLAY

THE excellence of The Old American Company was bound in time to inspire some native writer to create a play that would not be wholly unworthy of their talent. Such a play emerged in 1787, the year of the framing of the Constitution. The piece was the work of Royall Tyler, who had never been inside a theater until, in that year, on a visit to New York, he went to see *The School for Scandal*. Three weeks thereafter Tyler's manuscript of *The Contrast* was ready, and it was produced April 16, 1787, by the best members of the company. It was given six times during the next two months in New York, with several performances elsewhere, and it thus became the first native play that could boast of anything resembling a "run." Its theme, a

reflection of the prevailing exuberant patriotism, is the contrast between the folly and affectation of the Europeanized American and the sterling worth of the home-bred citizen. The plot is somewhat devoid of action, but the dialogue is lively and the humor is noticeably original, centering as it does about the New England servant, Jonathan, Tyler's distinctive contribution to drama. In this quaint figure the long-popular stage Yankee, a mixture of ignorance, awkwardness, and shrewdness, makes his bow to the world.

67 Royall Tyler, 1757–1826, from an engraved portrait in the collection of Montrose J. Moses

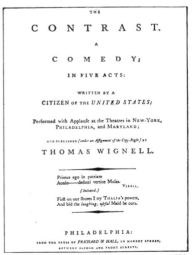

68 Title-page of *The Contrast*, Philadelphia, 1790, in the New York Public Library

NEW THEATRE.

FOR THE BENEFIT OF THE AUTHOR.

THIS EVENING WILL BE PRESENTED

A Tragedy, founded on the Death of

MAJOR JOHN ANDRE,

Adjutant General of the British Army in North America,
Who was executed as a Spy, in Nov. 1780. With
new dreſſes, and appropriate Scenery, never before exhibited.   The Prologue to be ſpoken by Mr Martin.

General	Mr Hallam,
Bland,	Mr Cooper,
McDonald,	Mr Tyler,
Seward,	Mr Martin,
Nelville,	Mr Williamſon,
American Officer,	Mr Miller,
British Officer,	Mr Hogg,
Children,	Miſs Hogg, and Maſter Stockwell,
And, Andre,	Mr Hodgkinſon,
Mrs Bland,	Mrs Melmoth,
And, Honora,	Mrs Johnſon.

End of act 2d, the popular Song of "Return enraptured
Hours," ſaid to be written by Major Andre, during his
confinement, by Mr WILLIAMSON.

Between the Play and Farce, the Hiſtorical Pantomime of

THE OLD SOLDIER.

To which will be added, a Farce called, The

PRISONER AT LARGE.

69   Performance of *Andre* at the John Street
Theater, from an announcement in the New
York *Weekly Museum*, April 17, 1798

70   William Dunlap, 1766–1839, from a reproduction of a contemporary lithograph, in the
possession of the publishers

YANKEE CHRONOLOGY;

OR,

HUZZA FOR THE CONSTITUTION!

A MUSICAL INTERLUDE,

IN ONE ACT.

To which are added,

THE PATRIOTIC SONGS OF

THE FREEDOM OF THE SEAS,

AND

YANKEE TARS.

BY W. DUNLAP, ESQ.

NEW-YORK.

PUBLISHED BY D. LONGWORTH,
At the Dramatic Repository,
Shakspeare-Gallery

Dec—1812

71   Title-page of *Yankee Chronology*, New
York, 1812, in the New York Public
Library

DRAMATIST AND PAINTER

THE unprecedented "run" of *The Contrast* was one of the determining influences in the life of the man who became the leading playwright of this period.

72   Dunlap the Painter, detail from the painting by Dunlap,
Artist Showing his First Picture to his Parents, in the New
York Historical Society

A young painter just home from three years of study under Benjamin West in London, William Dunlap heard much talk of Tyler's successful comedy, and he resolved to try his hand in the same field. His first play, written in 1787, failed to reach the stage; but with his second, *The Father; or, American Shandyism* (revised as *The Father of an Only Child*), he entered the then slender ranks of the practical playwrights of America. This piece, which was produced at the John Street Theater on September 7, 1789, with Hallam, Henry, Mrs. Henry, and Wignell in the principal parts, is a sentimental comedy of the same general sort as *The Contrast*, though involving more action than the latter. Its reception during seven performances was sufficiently favorable to induce Dunlap to cast in his lot with the theater. Other plays followed in steady succession — comedies, tragedies, and operas. An important play of his, which marked an innovation for America, was *Fontainville Abbey* (1795), a drama of mystery and terror of the sort just coming into favor in England. Dunlap's source was *The Romance of the Forest* by the English novelist, Mrs. Ann Radcliffe, one of the leaders of the so-called Gothic school of romance. Other similar plays followed from his pen, and the new type was soon caught up by his contemporaries. Dunlap's best known play is *André* (1798), a tragedy presenting with considerable sympathy and force the story of the famous British spy. It is written in smooth and dignified blank verse. Of our early dramatists Dunlap was by far the most versatile, prolific, and important. He was our first professional playwright, and as a pioneer in the field he exerted a pronounced influence on the work of his fellow practitioners. His career was cast in the Federalist period of Washington and Adams and of those inveterate rivals, Hamilton and Jefferson. (See No. 123.)

THE NATIVE ACTOR APPEARS

PIONEERS of another sort were Miss Tuke, afterward Mrs. Hallam, and John Martin. Although a Mr. Greville, who had joined Douglass' company in 1767, probably merits the distinction of being the first native American to venture upon the professional stage, his known career was so brief and his rôles so unimportant that we need not dwell upon him. Miss Tuke, whom Hallam introduced about 1785, was a young woman of more beauty than natural aptitude for the stage. She was criticized at the beginning for her lifeless and uninteresting manner of acting, but within a few years she had developed sufficiently to become one of the leading ladies of the company. Martin made his début at Philadelphia on March 13, 1790, as Young Norval in Home's *Douglas*. Dunlap wrote of him: "He was of fair complexion, middle height, light figure, and played the youthful characters of many tragedies and comedies in a style called respectable . . . a useful, though not a brilliant actor. He laboured hard, lived poor, and died young." A critic in *The Evening Post*, February 10, 1802, wrote: "Mr. Martin is an assiduous and useful performer. The public hold him in much estimation both in his professional and private capacities."

73　John Martin, 1770–1807, as Charley in *The Highland Reel*, from an engraving by Scoles, after a drawing by Martin, in the Fridenberg Collection

"THE PROVINCIAL GARRICK"

THE last decade of the eighteenth century saw the arrival of many actors who had already made a reputation in England and who greatly enriched the American stage. The first and perhaps the most remarkable of these was John Hodgkinson. This player had acquired in the principal English theaters outside of London a reputation that earned for him the designation of "the Provincial Garrick." Henry engaged him and his wife for The Old American Company. He made his first appearance at Philadelphia, September 26, 1792, and a few months later was seen at New York. It was at once recognized that he was the most gifted performer this country had yet seen. He was equally at home in comedy, tragedy, and opera. His figure, his voice, his energy, and his imitative faculty all fitted him so peculiarly for his profession that his contemporaries insisted on regarding him as one of the greatest natural histrionic geniuses the world had ever known. Hodgkinson's art was in harmony with the gentility and the artistic tradition that characterized the Federalist society of the period.

74　John Hodgkinson, 1767(?)–1805, as Robin in *No Song no Supper*, from an engraving by C. Tiebout, after a drawing by W. Barr, in the Harvard Theater Collection

MRS. HODGKINSON

THOUGH by no means so distinguished a person as her husband, Mrs. Hodgkinson was a valuable addition to The Old American Company. She had been a competent singing actress at Bath and Bristol, and her coming meant the strengthening of the vocal department of the company. Although her specialty was opera, she was charming, by reason of her youthful figure and manner, in the rôle of a lively young girl. In some tragic parts, notably Ophelia, she was also very appealing. In her private life she was, according to Dunlap, "an amiable woman and a good wife."

75　Mrs. Hodgkinson (d. 1803), from an engraving by S. Hollyer after a drawing by William Dunlap, in the Harvard Theater Collection

76 Mrs. Charlotte Melmoth, in the rôle of Queen Elizabeth, from an engraving by Collyer after the drawing from life by Dodd, in the possession of the publishers

MRS. MELMOTH, 1749–1823

MRS. CHARLOTTE MELMOTH, another player with an honorable reputation in Great Britain, made her American début at New York, November 20, 1793. Although past her prime, she was, Dunlap thought, "the best tragic actress the inhabitants of New York, then living, had seen." Unfortunately, with the passage of the years her figure had grown more matronly until she was now of most impressive proportions. This fact almost made shipwreck of her opening performance, when, as Euphrasia in *The Grecian Daughter*, she implored the tyrant to kill her instead of her emaciated father, crying "Strike here, here's blood enough!" By her merit, however, she was able to live down the roar of laughter that greeted this too appropriate speech. Her versatility was in proportion to her size, for in the opinion of many her Mrs. Malaprop ranked alongside her Lady Macbeth.

WIGNELL AND REINAGLE

THE monopoly of The Old American Company came to an end in 1794, when a rival organization began its career at Philadelphia. In 1791 Wignell, because of differences with Hallam and Henry, had resigned and entered into partnership with Alexander Reinagle, a prominent Philadelphia musician. Wignell spent the next two years in England securing actors for the new venture, and in 1793 returned to the United States with the best group of players that had ever performed in this country. Their first season at Philadelphia, which began in February, 1794, was the most brilliant that city had ever enjoyed, and their subsequent seasons were not less successful. Wignell and Reinagle quickly gained control of the field from Philadelphia southward; so that The Old American Company was compelled to confine its activities to New York and the northern region. To extend their sway the Philadelphia partners built a theater in Baltimore in 1794 and another in Washington — the first in that city — in 1800, in which their company performed between seasons, but in spite of constant activity the proprietors were sometimes unable to make ends meet, largely because one of their special hobbies was operatic production, which they found to be a distressingly expensive luxury.

77 Alexander Reinagle, from an engraving after a miniature in possession of the family, in O. G. Sonneck, *Early Opera in America*, New York, 1914, courtesy of Schirmer & Co.

78 Alexander Placide, prominent Wignell recruit, 1793, and founder of a distinguished American actor family, from an engraved portrait in the Harvard Theater Collection

THE CHESTNUT STREET THEATER — PHILADELPHIA

WHEN Wignell departed in 1791 to recruit his actors, plans were already on foot among the citizens of Philadelphia for erecting a new theater to house the enterprise. On his return he found awaiting him a practically completed building on Chestnut Street near Sixth. With a luxurious interior modeled on the Theater Royal at Bath, and a tasteful exterior, it completely surpassed in

79 Interior of Wignell and Reinagle's Chestnut Street Theater, from an engraving by Ralph after a drawing by S. Lewis, in the *New York Magazine*, 1794

beauty and impressiveness any playhouse this country had yet known. The auditorium was spacious, its seating capacity being about two thousand. Its shape, as well as the arrangement of boxes and balconies, is suggestive of an Elizabethan theater or a modern opera house, though the backless benches of the pit could scarcely have been as comfortable as are the Metropolitan orchestra seats. The stage was of good size for the time, having a front of thirty-seven feet between the boxes. An apron, projecting as much as twelve or fifteen feet, it would seem, in front of the proscenium arch, gave added depth to the stage, and provided ample space for the proscenium doors and stage boxes. The department of scenery was in charge of Charles Milbourne, a capable and experienced scene painter from London, and the excellence of the stage decorations was one of the many attractions of the theater. During the next quarter of a century the Chestnut Street boasted a stock company which was generally reputed the finest in the country.

80 Exterior of the Chestnut Street Theater, from an engraving by M. Marigot in the New York Public Library

MRS. OLDMIXON

PERHAPS the most distinguished member of this notable band was Mrs. Oldmixon, formerly Miss George, who had served with high distinction as a singing actress at the Haymarket and Drury Lane Theaters in London. Her voice, unusual in range and sweetness, her vivacious manner, and her expressive and pleasing features fitted her admirably for the stage. Probably the best vocalist yet heard in America, she soon became a ruling favorite in Philadelphia, and her success was duplicated in New York, with whose stage she was intermittently connected from about 1797 until her retirement about 1814.

81 Mrs. Oldmixon (d. 1836), from an engraving by Orme, after the portrait by Miss Howell, in the Harvard Theater Collection

82 Eliza Kemble Whitlock, 1762–1836, from an engraving, 1792, by Audinet after a painting by DeWilde, in the Fridenberg Collection

"THE SIDDONS OF AMERICA"

ANOTHER actress of outstanding merit was Mrs. Whitlock, sister of the famous Mrs. Siddons, whom she is said to have resembled and imitated. She had been a favorite at the Haymarket, and as a tragic actress in America she repeated her success. Her work was said to be notable for the absence of "theatrical imposture," and for the presence of an educated mind and discriminating taste.

FENNELL AND OTHER ACTORS

THE outstanding man among Wignell's recruits was James Fennell. Educated at Eton and Cambridge, he had tried his fortunes on the stage, and was soon playing at the Covent Garden Theater, London. At Philadelphia his impressive appearance and noble bearing made him, especially in tragic characters, an idol of the theatergoers. His Othello was a favorite rôle. Though sometimes criticized for indistinctness of utterance, he was described by Dunlap as "a remarkably handsome figure, although above the just height, being considerably over six feet. His complexion and hair light, with a blush ready for every occasion on which a blush could be graceful. His features were not handsome, his nose being round, thick, and too fleshy, and his eyes a very light gray, with yellowish lashes and brows. His appearance in the Moors, Othello and Zanga, was noble; his face appeared better and more expressive, and his towering figure superb." A player who, after a modest beginning, steadily developed ability that placed him among the most popular and gifted comedians of his time was John E. Harwood, who, after transferring to New York, died in 1809. According to Dunlap, he was "from talents and education, one of the brightest ornaments of the Philadelphia company. A young man at the time of forming his engagement with Wignell, he was engaging in manners, and remarkably handsome in the form and expression of his countenance." Indulgence and indolence lessened his powers, but he seems never to have lost the ability to delight an audience. As Falstaff he achieved a special success. He married Miss Bache, the granddaughter of Benjamin Franklin.

83 James Fennell, 1766–1816, from an engraving by Snyder in the *Polyanthos Magazine*, Boston, March 1807

84 William Francis as Sir George Thunder, from the portrait by John Neagle (1796–1865), in the possession of the Players Club, New York

MINOR ACTORS

A LESSER performer whom Wignell obtained in England was William Francis, of whose career before his coming to America little is known. At Philadelphia and later at New York he played old men creditably, but his specialty was dancing and pantomimes, the latter a very frequent feature of the evening's bill. An actor who prided himself on excelling in small characters was Francis Blissett (1773–1850), son of a Bath comedian. In a part of twenty or thirty lines he would frequently set a standard that the more important players could scarcely equal. An artist said of him: "He reminds one of an exquisite miniature."

A CORRESPONDENT

Cannot help remarking the continued Impudence of thofe Vagabonds in Society, the Company of ftrolling Players, who have come to this Town to fleece the giddy Youth of their Money—One of thefe Mendicants, in an Addrefs to the Inhabitants in the Centinel, modeftly fays, that "*at the requeft of the Selectmen*" the Company forebore to act on the Evening of Friday laft! When they knew, as well as others, that it was the *abfolute determination* of the Governor and Council to put a final ftop to the further Progrefs of the Theatre in this Town.

85   Protest against "Vagabond" Players, from the *Boston Gazette*, December 10, 1792

For the Benefit of Mr. HARPER.

New Exhibition-Room, Board-Alley.

THIS EVENING, 15th October, Will be exhibited, A Moral Lecture,—In Five Parts : In which the Difadvantages of a neglected Education, will be ftrikingly defcribed in

She Stoops to Conquer :

Or,

The Miftakes of a Night,

Delivered by Meffirs. MORRIS, HARPER, ROBINSON, MURRY, SOLOMON,—Mrs. ROBERTS, Mifs SMITH, Mrs. GRAY, Mrs. SOLOMON, and Mrs. MORRIS, After the Moral Lecture a Favourite MUSICAL ENTERTAINMENT ——— Called,

ROSINA :

Or,

The Reapers.

Delivered by Meffirs. HARPER, MURRY, SOLOMON, ROBINSON, ROBERTS,——Mrs. GRAY, Mrs. SOLOMON, and Mrs. MORRIS.

The whole will conclude with.

A HORNPIPE.

By Mifs SMITH.

☞ Mr. HARPER moft refpectfully informs the Ladies and Gentlemen, of this town and its environs, that every poffible care and attention will be paid to render the Evening's Entertainment, worthy the patronage of fo liberal and generous a community.

86   Advertisement of Harper's "Exhibition Room," from the *Boston Gazette*, October 15, 1792

THE INVASION OF NEW ENGLAND

YEARS after the theater had come to be taken more or less for granted in Philadelphia and New York, New England was still holding out stanchly against this ally of Satan. When in 1790 Hallam and Henry appealed for permission to open a theater in Boston, the prohibitory act of 1750 was successfully invoked against them. But in 1792 a group of theater lovers erected a building which they called the "New Exhibition Room." Though the wicked word was not used, this was the first theater in Boston. It was opened, August 16, 1792, under the management of Joseph Harper, formerly of The Old American Company, who offered programs of dancing, tumbling, and the like. After some weeks Harper took counsel of his courage and attempted plays — *Hamlet*, *Richard III*, Home's *Douglas*, and others. On December 5, during a performance of *The School for Scandal*, the sheriff, uninvited, made an appearance on the stage and brought to a close Boston's first theatrical season. Harper forthwith moved his company to Providence and obtained the use of a courthouse for plays disguised as moral lectures. The house was full at every performance. In February, 1793, the prohibitory law of the state was repealed, and in the spring a large brick building, once a market, at Newport was converted into a theater. Here with his modest company Harper conducted a season of about three months, offering, among other plays, *Othello*, *The Tempest* (Dryden's version), and *She Stoops to Conquer*. Further brief seasons under his management followed during the next year or two, and the transformed market continued to do duty as a theater for half a century.

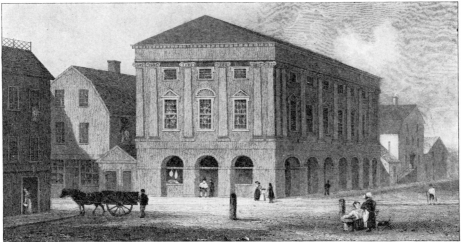

87   Harper's Theater, at Newport, R. I., from an engraving, 1831, by Fenner Sears & Co., after a drawing by W. Goodacre, Jr., in the Goodspeed Collection, Boston

88   The Federal Street Theater, Boston, opened to the public February 3, 1794, from an engraving in the Boston Public Library

89   Medal showing the Federal Street Theater, from Justin Winsor, *Memorial History of Boston*, Boston, 1880–81

THE FEDERAL STREET THEATER, BOSTON

MEANWHILE the friends of the theater in Boston were not idle. Early in 1793 they brought about the repeal of the prohibition of 1750, and at once set about building a new theater on the corner of Federal and Franklin Streets. Designed by the distinguished American architect, Charles Bulfinch, the playhouse was a handsome though simple structure, one hundred and forty feet long, sixty-one feet wide, and forty feet high. Before its completion the trustees appointed Charles Stuart Powell, an actor from Covent Garden, who had played in Harper's company, sole manager, and he shortly sailed for England to assemble a group of actors. The theater was opened February 3, 1794, with much ceremony. An innovation was the appointment of a master of ceremonies, whose office it was to prevent indecorum of any kind, such as the hurling of apples, stones, etc., at the orchestra. To gain the good will of the pious citizens, the manager announced that performances would not be held on nights that might be devoted to religious services. After two seasons Powell found himself, partly because of the inferiority of his company, in a state of bankruptcy, and was asked to retire from the management. For the season of 1795–96, Colonel John S. Tyler, "master of ceremonies," was made director of the house, and he was succeeded by John Brown Williamson, an actor from the London Haymarket who had recently come to Boston.

"LITTLE PICKLE"

WILLIAMSON made his first American appearance as Othello, January 25, 1796, and was moderately praised for the propriety of his elocution. But the critics were extravagant in their admiration of his wife as Little Pickle in the afterpiece of the evening, Bickerstaffe's *Spoiled Child*. This was one of the very popular pieces of the time because of the character of Little Pickle, a romp and tomboy, who gave the singing ingénues a splendid opportunity to display their sprightly charms. Mrs. Williamson, formerly Miss Fontenelle, had already delighted London audiences at Covent Garden and the Haymarket by her amazingly nimble and high-spirited impersonations of similar characters; and the American critics did not hesitate to pronounce her Little Pickle the most astonishing and brilliant display of theatrical genius ever witnessed in this country. John Bernard in his *Retrospections of America* styled her "that most buoyant and charming of all reckless romps." She was the delight of Boston in the heyday of its commercial and shipping success. After a year or two she and her husband joined the company at Charleston, and there she died in 1799.

90   Miss Fontenelle in the rôle of Maggy McGilpin, from an engraving by August Toedteberg, in the Fridenberg Collection

MRS. SUSANNA ROWSON, 1762–1824

ONE of the most interesting figures whom Williamson added to the Boston company was Mrs. Susanna Rowson. Though born in England, she had been brought to America by her father, a British officer, and had lived here between 1767 and 1778. In 1792 she and Mr. Rowson, whom she had married in 1786, had, because of the failure of his business, gone on the stage at Edinburgh. Wignell brought them to America as members of his first Philadelphia company, assigning minor rôles to her and employing him as a prompter. At Boston, where Mrs. Rowson acted during the season of 1796–97, she was given rather more important characters but she was never a distinguished performer. She was, however, a prominent writer, her novel *Charlotte Temple*, one of the famous books of its time, having been written before her return to America. In this country she wrote several plays, all of them performed. Among them are *Slaves in Algiers, or a Struggle for Freedom* (1794) and *The Volunteers* (1795), both of which

91   Susanna Rowson, from an engraving by H. W. Smith, in the Fridenberg Collection

deal with contemporary events. The former was called out by trouble with the Barbary States — Algiers, Morocco, Tripoli, and Tunis — which at this time were engaging in high-handed piracy in the Mediterranean, seizing Christian vessels and selling their occupants into slavery. The first offense against the United States was committed in 1784. But, instead of taking measures to drive the pirates from the seas, the United States followed the shameful example of the European nations by purchasing protection with tribute. In 1794, the year of *Slaves in Algiers*, Congress took steps for the building of warships to be used against the Algerians, the boldest of the Barbary corsairs. Little enough came of this gesture, however, and it was not until Stephen Decatur's vigorous naval attack in 1815 that the United States was freed from this menace. Mrs. Rowson's play tells a highly romantic story based in part on *Don Quixote* but involving a group of American captives, who are eventually released. *The Volunteers*, which was not published, concerned itself with the Whiskey Rebellion of 1794. This dangerous insurrection, the result of an excise placed on hard liquor by the Federal Government to replenish the treasury, was confined to the western counties of Pennsylvania, where stills were probably more numerous than in any other section of the Union. When the Government agents undertook to collect the tax, they were set upon by the mob, and some were tarred and feathered. Scenes of riotous violence were enacted, in which several persons were killed or wounded, until in September, 1794, President Washington sent a force of militia against the "Whiskey Boys," who submitted without bloodshed. It would be of considerable interest to know how Mrs. Rowson treated this event, which had its importance in demonstrating the power of the infant Federal Government. At any rate these two plays are significant as showing the readiness with which our early playwrights seized upon contemporary affairs as material for drama.

SLAVES IN ALGIERS;

OR, A

STRUGGLE FOR FREEDOM:

A PLAY,

INTERSPERSED WITH SONGS,

IN THREE ACTS.

BY MRS. ROWSON.

AS PERFORMED

AT THE

NEW THEATRES,

IN

PHILADELPHIA AND BALTIMORE.

———

PHILADELPHIA:

PRINTED FOR THE AUTHOR, BY WRIGLEY AND BERRIMAN, Nº 149, CHESNUT-STREET.

M,DCC,XCIV.

92   Title-page of Mrs. Rowson's *Slaves in Algiers*, 1794, in the New York Public Library

93   The Haymarket Theater (back-center), Boston, from a water-color, 1798, by Robertson, in the Public Library,
Boston.   Photograph © George Brayton, Boston

POLITICAL PROPAGANDA

CHARLES S. POWELL was not pleased with the way in which his management of the Federal Street Theater had terminated, and in 1796 he resolved to make a fresh start in a new theater. For this project he obtained a group of backers, who were more influenced by political than artistic considerations. The Federalist party was strongly suspected by its rivals, the Democratic-Republicans, of using the stage of the Federal Street Theater for political propaganda. The French, whom the followers of Jefferson championed, were made the butt of many an interpolated jest on the Federal Street boards. This may account for the fact that shares in the proposed building were sold with surprising rapidity, and that before the end of the year the new play-house, christened the Haymarket, was finished. This enormous wooden structure stood near the corner of Tremont and Boylston Streets. During its construction Powell had gone to England to engage his actors. Among those he secured were Mr. and Mrs. Giles L. Barrett and the three Westray sisters, all of whom were later prominent on the American stage. (See No. 147.) The theater opened December 26, 1796, with what proved to be a very fair company. Powell brought out many new English and a few American plays. But Boston was incapable of supporting two theaters, and at the end of the season Powell again gave up and disbanded his company. The Haymarket was later used as a summer theater, but was finally abandoned altogether.

HALLAM AND HODGKINSON

WHILE Wignell and Reinagle were establishing themselves in Philadelphia and Powell was active in Boston, important developments were taking place at New York. Hodgkinson, though a remarkable actor, was an ambitious and unscrupulous man. By 1794 he had driven Henry from the management and installed himself in his place. He then began depriving Mr. and Mrs. Hallam of as many rôles as he could appropriate for himself and his wife. Bitter enmity was the inevitable result. Under the new management some notable additions were made to the staff.

94 John Hodgkinson, from an engraving by Leney after a drawing
by Groombridge, in the Harvard Theater Collection

95   Thomas Jefferson, the earliest actor of the famous theatrical family, from an engraving in the Harvard Theater Collection

96   Joseph Jefferson, I, 1774–1832, from an engraving by D. Edwin after the portrait by John Neagle, in the New York Public Library

NEW NAMES IN THE OLD COMPANY

PROMINENT among the newcomers was Mrs. John Johnson, who was said to be the most perfect fine lady of comedy America had yet seen and the model in dress and deportment for all the belles of the town. Mrs. Johnson, together with her husband, was introduced to this country at Boston during a brief season in 1795–96 under the auspices of The Old American Company. From her first appearance in New York, February 10, 1796, she maintained, except for considerable absences in England, a commanding position on the stage of that city for over twenty years. The most famous name that Hallam and Hodgkinson brought into our theater was that of Joseph Jefferson. This first bearer of the name, the grandfather of the beloved "Rip," was the son of Thomas Jefferson, an actor long associated with David Garrick at the Drury Lane Theater, London, and afterwards manager of the theater at Plymouth. In his father's company Joseph received the rudiments of his theatrical education. Coming early to the United States, he made his American début on December 16, 1795, at the Federal Street Theater in Boston during the New York company's short season there already referred to. He soon won for himself a place among the best comedians ever seen in this country. Dunlap described him at the time of his arrival as "then a youth, but even then an artist. Of a small and light figure, well formed, with a singular physiognomy, a nose perfectly Grecian, and blue eyes full of laughter, he had the faculty of exciting mirth to as great a degree by power of feature, although handsome, as any ugly featured low comedian ever seen." Jefferson continued with the New York theater until 1803, when he left for Philadelphia, there to remain until 1830, two years before his death at Harrisburg, Pennsylvania.

97   Joseph Jefferson, I (left), and Francis Blissett in *A Budget of Blunders*, from an engraving by D. Edwin after a drawing by C. R. Leslie, in the Fridenberg Collection

98 Mrs. Lewis Hallam, Jr., in the rôle of Marianne, from an engraving by Tiebout after the drawing by William Dunlap, in the Harvard Theater Collection

HALLAM, HODGKINSON, AND DUNLAP

IN the spring of 1796 Dunlap was persuaded to buy a quarter interest in The Old American Company, and thus to become a partner of Hallam and Hodgkinson. One of the strong inducements was the prospect of producing his own plays. He quickly discovered that his two associates, being rival actors, were bitter enemies of each other, and that it was his unpleasant task to be mediator between them. "Hallam laid open his grievances," wrote Dunlap in his *History of the American Theatre*, "complaining of Hodgkinson's encroachments, and usurpations of power and of parts; having deprived him of all those characters which gave him consequence with the public, either playing them, or contriving to keep the plays from being played. His wife, he said, was likewise aggrieved, misrepresented, and deprived of her consequence by the introduction of others." The quarrel over parts and lines of business was unceasing, but its most picturesque manifestation occurred in March, 1797. Mrs. Hallam, née Tuke, had contracted a habit of frequent intoxication, and in that state she sometimes appeared on the stage. Hodgkinson seized the opportunity to make an agreement with Hallam that she be kept out of the theater. But on the night in question just as Hodgkinson came on to begin his performance, Mrs. Hallam, dressed in black and looking "beauty in distress,"

appeared at the other side of the stage. Hallam, likewise clad in black, also entered and requested that she be heard. Thereupon Mrs. Hallam read a statement complaining that she had been deprived of the means of

earning her living. Something very like a riot ensued, which of course did nothing to allay the feud. At the end of this season Hallam saw fit to withdraw from the management, although he and his wife continued as salaried actors. Hodgkinson now took it upon himself to conduct a summer campaign in New England. After a few lean nights at Hartford he moved the company to Boston, where the losses steadily mounted. But before the summer was over Hodgkinson had sent another troupe into New York to compete with the excellent Philadelphia company, which had descended upon the town. The result was that Dunlap was compelled to borrow heavily to back two losing companies.

99 Hodgkinson in title rôle of a native play, *Tammany*, 1794, from a program in the Harvard Theater Collection

100 Lewis Hallam's Benefit, from an announcement in the *New York Post Boy*, June 10, 1797

MRS. MERRY, 1769–1808

WHILE the theatrical directors at Boston and New York were experiencing a variety of vicissitudes, the Philadelphia managers were likewise confronted by a serious problem. Some of their important actors had left, and others were losing their hold on the public; consequently the patronage during the season of 1795–96 fell off sharply. To remedy this situation Wignell made a second visit to England to reinforce his company. Some of the performers with whom he returned in the fall of 1796 were of such marked excellence that the Philadelphia stage now became by far the most brilliant in America. Foremost among them, from the British point of view, was Mrs. Merry. When she first ventured on the stage, at the age of fifteen, she swept the town of Bath off its feet, and an engagement for Covent Garden was at once forthcoming. After several years of marked success at that house she retired, having married Robert Merry, a fashionable poet. But the diminution of her husband's fortune induced her to accept Wignell's offer, and she made her first Philadelphia appearance as Juliet, December 5, 1796. From that day until her death her hold on the American public was complete. Though lacking the commanding stature and beauty that a *tragédienne* might seem to require, she made an indelible impression by virtue of a truly

101 Anne Merry as Horatia in *The Roman Father*, from an engraving, 1792, by Leney, in possession of the publishers

rare personality. Gentle, simple, sincere, she was said to appeal to the emotions as profoundly as the majestic Mrs. Siddons. The American stage has known few actresses more worthy of admiration than Mrs. Merry.

SUPERB PASSION AND POWER

DURING his stay in England, Wignell heard of the fame of one Cooper, who, after an unimportant career in the provinces, had appeared as Hamlet at Covent Garden in October, 1795, and had won high praise from the critics, but had failed to secure an advantageous engagement from the manager of that theater. When Wignell made him a substantial offer, therefore, he readily accepted it, and made his first Philadelphia appearance, December 9, 1796, in the rôle of Macbeth. He was soon recognized as the greatest of American tragedians, and for thirty years his preëminence was not seriously disputed. Though he relied less on art than on impulse, and though his memory was sometimes treacherous and his study careless, his remarkably handsome face and figure and his marvelous voice carried him triumphantly through. And at his best, as in Macbeth and various Roman characters, he conveyed a sense of superb passion and power. During much of his career

102 Thomas Abthorpe Cooper, 1776–1849, from an engraved portrait by Harris in the *Polyanthos Magazine*, Boston, Jan. 1806

Cooper was a more or less itinerant star, and at one time or another visited every state then in the Union, sometimes traveling in a covered wagon which he drove himself. He made a fortune by his acting, and for a time after his marriage in 1812 to Mary Fairlie, the leading belle of New York, he was prominent in the first social circle of the city. But owing to his reckless and extravagant mode of living, his last years were spent in greatly reduced circumstances.

103 Cooper as Pierre in *Venice Preserved*, from an engraving by J. O. Lewis after a drawing by C. R. Leslie, in the Fridenberg Collection

A CLASSIC COMEDIAN

104   William Warren, 1767–1832, from an engraving, 1811, by D. Edwin after a drawing by Sully, in the Fridenberg Collection

105   Warren as Sir Peter Teazle, from an engraving by J. B. Longacre after a painting by John Neagle, in the Fridenberg Collection

THE ship that brought Mrs. Merry and Cooper to these shores carried another of Wignell's recruits, who was destined to make for himself an important place in the theatrical world of the time. William Warren had been initiated into the actor's calling at the age of seventeen through membership in a very inferior strolling company. But he was industrious and attentive to work, and four years later he was playing opposite Mrs. Siddons during her engagement at York. Wignell found him a favored provincial actor in 1796 and engaged him for Philadelphia. In this country he achieved a high reputation in the rôles of irascible old men, such as Sir Anthony Absolute, Sir Peter Teazle, and Brabantio, and he was an admirable Falstaff. Warren was peculiarly at home in classic comedy, that is, in the works of Shakespeare and of Sheridan. In such plays he displayed an authority that set him somewhat apart from the other comedians of his time. Not only was he an admirable actor, he was also a man of the highest integrity.

"IN THE REARWARD OF FASHION"

A YEAR after this trio of famous actors were added to the Philadelphia company, that troupe was further strengthened by the engagement of a most finished comedian. John Bernard had been on the British stage from the age of sixteen, and had played important comedy parts at Covent Garden. But an attempt to operate a provincial circuit, coupled with extravagant living, so reduced his circumstances that he gladly accepted an offer from Wignell, and made his American début August 25, 1797. For six years he remained at Philadelphia, "enjoying," according to William B. Wood's *Personal Recollections of the Stage*, "an enviable degree of favoritism." The same chronicler, describing a certain performance of *Everyone Has his Fault*, says, "Bernard (the worst dresser on the stage) was as usual in the rearward of fashion at least half a century, but acted Sir Robert so well that his dress was wholly overlooked, or pardoned." One of his most popular parts was Charles Surface in *The School for Scandal*, in which play he was mated by Wignell as Joseph Surface. "These characters," wrote Wood, "were so completely identified with Wignell and Bernard that their successors felt themselves somewhat in the state of men going to execution." After leaving Philadelphia Bernard was for some years connected with the Boston Theater, and in 1813 opened, as manager, the first theater in Albany. In 1819 he returned to England where he died in poverty.

106   John Bernard, 1756–1828, from an engraving by S. Harris, in the *Polyanthos Magazine*, Vol. II, 1806

107 Mrs. Wrighten (Mrs. Pownall), from an engraving, 1777, by Thornthwaite after a drawing by I. Roberts in the Fridenberg Collection, New York

AT CHARLESTON

ALTHOUGH the major theatrical developments were in the northern cities, Charleston continued to be an interested patron of dramatic art. In 1792 Bignall and West, who were in control of a not incompetent Virginia company, had erected a theater in the city, where they conducted occasional brief seasons. At this time there was another playhouse in the town apparently erected as Harmony Hall in 1786, and now known as the

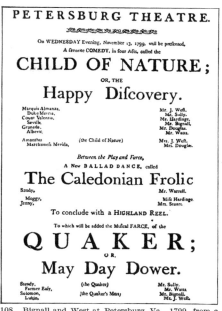

108 Bignall and West at Petersburg, Va., 1799, from a playbill, in the New York Historical Society

City or Church Street Theater. The proprietor of this building, John Joseph Leger Sollee (or Solee), in the summer of 1794 let it to a traveling company of French pantomimists, dancers, and tumblers headed by Alexander Placide (see No. 78). During their occupancy it was known as the French Theater. The next season it was taken by a Mr. Edgar and his company of actors, most of whom had recently been associated with Bignall and West. But Edgar's season failed in February, 1795, and Sollee now assumed control of the affairs of his theater. When the Boston Company disbanded for the summer, he secured a number of the players for Charleston. Chief among these were Mrs. Pownall and her twin daughters by a former marriage, Mary and Charlotte Wrighten. Mrs. Pownall had been a member of Garrick's company at Drury Lane, and had played opposite John Philip Kemble. Both as actress and singer, she quickly became highly popular in Charleston, and her two daughters were soon playing leading rôles. Altogether the season of 1795–96 was considered a brilliant one, thanks partly to a visit by Chalmers of the Philadelphia theater. The following season the company was deprived of Mrs. Pownall's services by her untimely death, August 11, 1796, apparently caused by the shock resulting from her daughter Charlotte's elopement with Alexander Placide.

FAREWELL TO THE JOHN STREET THEATER

IF New York could not pride itself on a company capable of holding its own with its Philadelphia rival, at least there was the consolation that, early in 1798, it would be able to boast a new theater, the equal of any in the land. As far back as 1794 the idea of a more adequate playhouse was seriously taken up by interested citizens, but construction was not begun until 1797, and then it proceeded with exasperating slowness. The situation was further complicated by the proprietors of the new building, who greatly curtailed the term of the manager's lease and demanded free tickets for all the stockholders. By the beginning of 1798, however, the managers resolved to take possession of the building even in its unfinished condition. Accordingly, after the performance of January 13, the curtain was lowered for the last time at the John Street Theater, and that outgrown house, which had nevertheless made important stage history for thirty years, passed quietly out of existence.

109 Announcement of the closing of the 'John Street Theater, from the *Weekly Museum*, New York, January 13, 1798

110   View of New York from Long Island, 1796, from an engraving in the New York Historical Society

LITTLE OLD NEW YORK

It is small cause for wonder that the citizens were demanding a more elegant playhouse than the humble edifice on John Street. New York, toward the close of the century, was a city of fashion, alive to all the developments then comprised within the term "modern." The stern memories of the war had been quickly softened by time, and, according to an English visitor writing in 1797, "New York is the gayest place in America; the ladies, in the richness and brilliancy of their dress, are not equalled in any city of the United States." The source of inspiration for feminine styles was the "light, various, and dashing drapery of the Parisian belles." The gentlemen affected a plain but "elegant and fashionable" dress, in close conformity with the English costume. The members of the first social group, consisting of "government officers, divines, lawyers, and physicians of eminence, with the principal merchants and people of independent property," are said to have lived in a style little inferior in splendor to that of the Europeans. The city was growing rich, and modern luxury had taken firm root. The winter was given to a round of entertainments — theater parties, dinner parties, tea and card parties, concerts, balls, and sleigh rides. Broadway and the Bowery, where the "best people" lived, were the scene of a steady program of activities. Withal it was not an undemocratic society. Actors of personal charm, though without family pretention, were sometimes admitted to the inner circle. Thomas A. Cooper, shortly after the turn of the century, married the reigning belle of the town and took a conspicuous position among the social leaders.

But gayety was by no means the exclusive preoccupation of the New Yorker; the things of the intellect were given most earnest attention. It was a time of many literary clubs, whose members met together with great solemnity for the improvement of their minds. Most famous of these organizations was the Friendly Club, which flourished during the last two decades of the century, and which counted among its adherents William Dunlap, dramatist, Charles Brockden Brown, our first professional man of letters, Anthony Bleecker, lawyer and leader in public affairs, Samuel Latham Mitchill, physician and scientist, and James Kent, celebrated jurist. It is said that Washington was fond of attending the weekly sessions of the Friendlies. Throughout the better class of citizens it had become fashionable to attend lectures on moral philosophy, chemistry, botany, mineralogy, mechanics, and similar subjects, the ladies in particular applying themselves to such abstruse branches of learning. The English visitor already referred to remarked that dress was not the sole absorption of New York women, for "there are many who are studious to add to brilliant external accomplishments the more brilliant and lasting accomplishments of the mind. Nor have they been unsuccessful, for New York can boast of great numbers of refined taste, whose minds are highly improved, and whose conversation is as inviting as their personal charms; tinctured with a Dutch education, they manage their families with good economy and singular neatness." As we see it to-day, eighteenth-century New York was a quaint little town, but it was progressive and ambitious, and, unknowing, it carried a mighty promise.

CHAPTER III

THE FIRST PARK THEATER

THE years between the opening of the Park Theater and the War of 1812 were a period of continued struggle for the American stage. The moral conflict had almost come to an end, but the absence of hostility was not enough. For its successful operation our theater needed a large playgoing public, whose attendance could be counted on with fair regularity. Such support came slowly, and consequently the expansion in the form of better buildings and more adequate actors, which we have noted in the preceding chapter, resulted not so much in added returns as in added perplexities for the managers. Not the least of the forces that militated against the success of the theater was the scourge of yellow fever, which, with tragic frequency, descended upon the larger towns and, as Charles Brockden Brown has so graphically represented it in his Philadelphia novel, *Arthur Mervyn*, swept off appalling numbers of the inhabitants. As a result of these visitations the opening of the season, which, for sound financial reasons, should occur early in September, was sometimes deferred as much as three months. Even when the doors of the playhouse could be opened without fear of contamination, the populace was often inclined to apathy. This indifference is attributable in part to the dearth of effective plays. Although our dramatists were increasing in numbers and talent, the public showed little inclination to flock to an American play. As for the English drama, upon which our producers had always mainly relied, it was entering on a period that had not been matched in barrenness for over two centuries. Moreover the state of affairs within the nation tended to unsettle men's minds and turn their thoughts away from the peaceful arts. This was the time of the strife between the Federalists and the anti-Federalists, one of the bitterest conflicts in our early political annals. For a time shortly after 1798 informal war with France was waged, and the country resounded with preparations for the struggle. From across the Atlantic came news of the progress of the Napoleonic wars, which, after 1806, worked severe hardships on American commerce. Moreover the British impressment of American seamen continued to outrage the honor of the nation, and in 1812 the United States threw down the gage of battle to England. That conditions worked against the prosperity of the early nineteenth-century theater is obvious. The bankruptcy of Dunlap at New York in 1805, although hastened by his lack of business acumen, was largely a result of the theatrical depression that was familiar also at Boston and Philadelphia — in the latter city partly offset, to be sure, by an all-year program that involved Baltimore, Annapolis, and Washington.

If Philadelphia suffered less than her rivals, her good fortune must be attributed in no small measure to the superiority of the Chestnut Street company, which still contained an impressive number of the most gifted actors in America. When the new century began, the remarkable group that had been assembled in the seventeen-nineties was still almost intact: Thomas Wignell, artist in humor; William Warren with his broad, human comedy; Mrs. Merry, whose beautiful sincerity was irresistible on the stage, and whose gracious personality won her a prominent position in the society of the town; the brilliant Cooper, dividing his time between Philadelphia and other cities; the mercurial Fennell, whose occasional appearances between sojourns in jail were enthusiastically received; and John Bernard, the poorest dresser and the most finished player of them all. In addition to these, new and important names were frequently added to the roster. What Dunlap wrote in his *History of the American Theatre* concerning the Chestnut Street company in its inception was still entirely applicable: "Wignell's talents and influence laid the foundation of that theatrical establishment in Philadelphia which flourished for many years more uniformly, and with actors of more general estimation as citizens and artists, than the rival institution in New-York."

On the whole this was not a period of material prosperity for the American theater, and in an effort to improve their financial situation the managers introduced a procedure which eventually wrought far-reaching changes. As an added attraction, a leading player from another city, such as Cooper or Mrs. Merry, would be engaged to appear for a limited time with the resident company at New York, let us say; and thus came into being the starring system which later proved fatal to the stock companies that it was calculated to fortify.

During these unstable years, however, the theater continued its evolution toward the fully developed institution it ultimately became. Perhaps the most evident progress achieved in the period now under review was in the matter of scenic effects. In this particular our stage had been content with simple beginnings. From the stage directions of a play printed in 1766 and acted in 1773, *The Conquest of Canada* by George Cockings, we learn how impoverished the colonial theater was on the physical side. To represent a night attack of the French fire-ships upon the British fleet, the stage is darkened and a ship is pushed out from the wings, while men behind the scenes roar and bawl incoherently, and others on the boat make a great clatter of oars. Twice a light appears, to indicate the approach of the fire-ships, but, as we gather from the shouting, these are successfully staved off. In the same play a land battle is suggested by the simple method of discharging artillery behind a lowered curtain and then raising the curtain to reveal the dead and wounded. With the passage of time our stage mechanicians gained an ingenuity that would have filled a colonial audience with wonder and amazement. In the last years of the eighteenth century and the first of the nineteenth, thanks to expert scenic artists imported from England, complicated displays that attained a surprising degree of realism were frequent attractions in several theaters. For instance one might witness the wrecking of a ship against the rocks in a violent storm, or the destruction of a fleet by the cannon of a fortress; or one could behold the transformation of Cinderella's pumpkin into a splendid carriage, and of the six white mice into horses richly caparisoned. All this, while no doubt more crudely executed, was no less ambitious than the effects achieved in the most elaborate revues and operas to-day.

The corner ſtone of
this Theatre was laid
on the 5ᵗʰ day of May
AD 1795

Jacob Morton } Com-
Wᵐ Henderson } miſſion
Carlile Pollock } ers
Lewis Hallem } mana
John Hodgkinſon } gers.

PARK THEATRE

CORNER-STONE OF PARK THEATRE, PRESERVED AT
"WINDUST'S."

111 Cornerstone of the First Park, from a print
in the New York Historical Society

ALL IN A BUSTLE

THE John Street Theater being closed, the attention of Dunlap and Hodgkinson was now concentrated on completing as quickly as possible the more spacious and elegant theater which was to replace it, and which, they hoped, would bring to an end the financial difficulties which had so sorely beset them as joint managers. Neither threats nor bribes, however, could hasten the slow plodding of the workmen. Likewise the negotiations over the exact details of management and policy were protracted during weeks of wrangling. At last the Park Theater opened

THE NEW THEATRE
Will open on MONDAY EVENING next,
With an Occaſional ADDRESS,
To be delivered by Mr. HODGKINSON.
And a PRELUDE, written by Mr. Milns called,
ALL IN A BUSTLE,
Or, The NEW HOUSE.
The Charaſters by the Company.

After which, will be preſented, Shakeſpeare's Comedy of
AS YOU LIKE IT.
To which will be added, the Muſical After-Piece, of
The PURSE:
Or, American Tar.

Places for the Boxes, will be let every Day, at the Old Office, in John-Street, from Ten to One, and on the Play Day, from Three to Four in the Afternoon.

Tickets can alſo be had at the above Office, any Time previous to Monday, 4 o'clock after which Hour, they muſt be applied for at the Ticket Office in the New Theatre.

Subſcribers will be made acquainted with the Mode a-dopted for their Admiſſion, by Application at the Box Office.

The Offenſive Praſtice to Ladies, and dangerous one to the Houſe, of Smoking Segars during the Performance, it is hoped every Gentleman will conſent to an abſolute Pro-hibition of.

Ladies and Gentlemen, will pleaſe to direſt their ſer-vants to Set Down, with their Horſes Heads towards the New Brick Meeting, and Take Up with their Heads to-wards Broad-Way.

The future Regulations, reſpeſting the taking of Seats, will be placed in the Box Office, for general Information.
VIVAT RESPUBLICA.

112 Announcement of the opening of the Park
Theater, from the New York *Weekly Museum,*
January 27, 1798

its doors on January 29, 1798, with *As You Like It* and a farce *All in a Bustle, or, The New House.* The farce visualized for the audience the commotion and excitement back stage and the enthusiasm over the spacious new theater, beautiful in spite of its present uncompleted form. Costing one hundred and thirty thousand dollars and seating two thousand persons, it was, wrote Joseph Norton Ireland in his monumental *Records of the New York Stage,* New York, 1866, "one of the most substantial buildings ever erected in New York." A contemporary account of the opening described the pit as "remarkably commodious," and praised the three semi-circular rows of boxes, unsupported by the customary pillars which heretofore had proved such a "common and great obstacle to the view." The gallery was "thrown back of the upper front boxes." The stage was also described as "remarkably commodious," and the scenery, for which Dunlap apologized as still crude, was, according to this eulogist, superior to "everything of the kind heretofore seen in America." The perfection of the architect's plan here shown was not attained for a number of years, if at all.

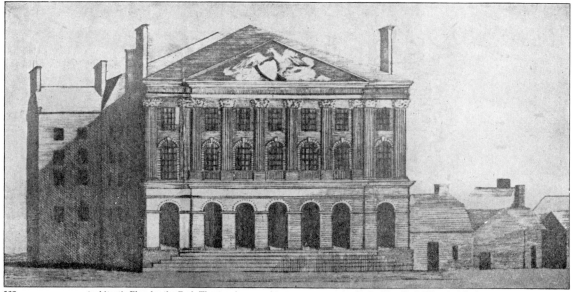

113 Architect's Plan for the Park Theater, from a contemporary engraving in the New York Historical Society

114   Interior of the Park Theater, copy from an old woodcut used as a frontispiece to the Rejected Address
of the Opening, in the New York Historical Society

OLD JEALOUSIES IN THE NEW HOUSE

ACCORDING to the agreement reached with the one hundred and thirteen stockholders promoting the Park Theater enterprise, Dunlap was to be treasurer and Hodgkinson stage manager. Patrons of the John Street in their new unsupported boxes or in the "commodious" pit and gallery of the Park saw familiar faces on the "commodious" new stage. There were few changes in casting. Lewis Hallam, the patriarch, the symbol of the earlier, cruder days of the American theater, appeared year after year, growing older and more garrulously quarrelsome until he became a burden too heavy to carry. Other notable members of the company were Hallam's wife, who still drank on occasion before performances, Hodgkinson's wife and her family retinue of the Bretts, Joseph Jefferson for comedy, and James Hogg for old men's parts. With them appeared George Tyler, John Martin, Mrs. Whitlock, Mrs. Oldmixon, Mrs. Melmoth, and for a too brief period Mrs. Johnson. Stage manager Hodgkinson must have realized this first year that his cast, with the exception of Mrs. Johnson, was, in comparison to such a company as Wignell's at Philadelphia, a somewhat inferior one at best. Yet the company of the early Park, owing to internal dissension, seldom realized its maximum efficiency. The treasurer and the stage manager were often at odds. Dunlap, in spite of his recognition of Hodgkinson as the greatest American actor, distrusted him away from the footlights. The feud between the Hallams and the Hodgkinsons continued. The Hallams sulked, appeared at rehearsals, but refused at times to speak to Dunlap. Hodgkinson and Jefferson quarreled over salaries. Dunlap wrote in his Diary: "Hodgkinson talked in a very cavalier manner, and Jefferson told him not to put his name on the bills for Friday." Hodgkinson, losing his temper, "said that he wanted not his services." Dunlap, the peacemaker, alone prevented an open breach. The tribulations of the treasurer increased. The new theater had not proved a solution to the financial difficulties. Receipts fell off — often below the four hundred and fifty dollar minimum necessary for profits. The stockholders complained. The stage manager, disappointed at results, began to talk of going to Boston.

115   Scene from a performance of *The School for Scandal* (Jefferson, Hodgkinson, Mrs. Whitlock and Tyler), from the painting by William Dunlap in the Harvard Theater Collection

A BROKEN CONTRACT

THOMAS A. COOPER had been one of the audience at the new theater on its opening night. He had helped in the handling of the crowd. A line in the farce had referred to his presence in the wings. After his summer season with Wignell and Reinagle at the Greenwich Street Theater, New York, 1797, he had, in spite of a contract that bound him, refused to return to Philadelphia, where the enormous popularity of Fennell's tragic rôles dimmed the rising star of the younger tragedian. In the Park cast there would be no rival

116 Cooper in the rôle of Hamlet, from an engraving by D. Edwin in the Robert Fridenberg Collection, New York

NEW THEATRE.

THIS EVENING WILL BE PRESENTED

(BY DESIRE)

Shakespeare's grand Historical Play of

KING JOHN.

John,	(King of England)	Mr Cooper,
Philip,	(King of France)	Mr Tyler,
Lewis,	(Dauphin of France)	Mr Martin.
Prince Henry,		Mrs Collins,
Prince Arthur,		Miss Harding,
Hubert,		Mr Hallam,
Earl of Salisbury,		Mr Williamson,
Earl of Pembroke,		Mr Hallam, jun.
Earl of Essex,		Mr Seymour,
Cardinal Pandulph,		Mr Prigmore,
Duke of Austria,		Mr Fawcett,
Chatillon,		Mr Hogg,
Citizen,		Mr Johnson,
English Herald,		Mr Jefferson,
French Herald,		Mr Simpson,
Robert Faulconbridge,		Mr Miller,

Messengers and Soldiers,

Messrs Woolls, Lee, Roberts, Leonard, M'Knight, Shapter, Stowell, &c. &c.

Philip,	(the Bastard)	Mr Hodgkinson,
Queen Elinor,		Mrs Simpson,
Lady Blanch,		Miss E. Westray,
Lady Faulconbridge,		Mrs Brett,
And, Constance,		Mrs Melmoth,

117 Announcement of Cooper as King John, from the New York *Weekly Museum*, March 24, 1798

in his favorite rôles. Dunlap and Hodgkinson were eager to bolster their rickety finances by the addition of an actor with such prospects for a long, brilliant career. Yet for a month it was impossible to come to any definite agreement, because all parties were frightened by the prospect of the legal entanglements and difficulties that Wignell might raise over the broken contract. Theatrical enthusiasts in New York, anxious to conciliate the Philadelphia manager, raised five hundred pounds as damage money. Cooper went to Philadelphia to offer it to Wignell. The money was refused; Wignell's threat persisted; and yet by some legal manipulation, the exact details of which are not now clear, Cooper's legal position was strengthened, and on February 28 he dared make his début at the Park as Hamlet. He was received with acclaim. The treasurer lapsed into superlatives: "never, probably, was the Danish prince so well played in America." "His performance was transcendently excellent," wrote a newspaper critic on March 2. "It may be proper to say," he

The Retrospect,

OR AMERICAN REVOLUTION,

In the course of the piece will be represented the principal events of the American Revolution, with views of places where the occurrences happened.

The most striking scenes in act III, are —A view of SANDY HOOK, the LIGHT HOUSE illuminated, and the Ocean. The BRITISH FLEET is discovered at anchor within the Hook. At break of day, boats with soldiers are seen putting off from the ships and approaching LONG ISLAND. Firing. Troops land, to military music.

THE TEMPLE OF AMERICAN INDEPENDENCE.

End of the act, the Declaration of Independence will be read by Mr Cooper.

The principal scenes of act 2d are.—A view of the RIVER DELAWARE and TRENTON in possession of the British. Americans cross the river, under command of Gen'l WASHINGTON, attack and defeat the enemy.

THE LAST SCENE

Will exhibit an elegant perspective view of the lower part of BROADWAY, with the BOWLING-GREEN, FORT, BARRACKS, &c as they stood at the time commemorated, when just evacuated by the British. The English flag still flying. The BAY is seen, and the ENGLISH FLEET departing.— GEN. WASHINGTON enters, attended by the patriotic citizens of New York, who had been in voluntary exile from their home, while it was in possession of the enemy—the AMERICAN ARMY follows. During the procession is seen the well-known action of the Sailor, who, when it was found that the lines of the flag-staff on the Fort were destroyed, climbed to the top, and striking the English colors, displayed the AMERICAN FLAG TRIUMPHANT.

The whole to conclude with a GRAND CHORUS.

The curtain will draw precisely at half past 7.

118 Announcement of a Public Reading by Cooper of the Declaration of Independence, from the New York *Weekly Museum*, July 3, 1802

continued "that never did this country witness a more magnificent exhibition. . . . They who were incapable of feeling the excellencies . . . must relinquish their pretensions to judgment and sensibility." In the rôle of Romeo, to Mrs. Johnson's Juliet, Cooper was extremely popular. The youthful enthusiasm and matured craftsmanship of his Shakespearean interpretations brought in crowds which raised the receipts well above the four hundred and fifty dollar mark. In this exploitation of Cooper, there are inherent, if not actually present, the beginnings of "starring."

119 Cooper in the rôle of Leon, from an engraving by Edwin after a drawing by C. B. L. in the Fridenberg Collection, New York

120 Hodgkinson (left) in *The Children in the Wood*, from an engraving in G. C. D. Odell, *Annals of the New York Stage*, Vol. II, Columbia University Press, New York, 1927. Courtesy of Prof. Odell.

121   Giles L. Barrett, 1744–1809, from an engraving after a drawing, in the Harvard Theater Collection

DEPARTURE OF THE STAGE MANAGER

But in spite of the "transcendent excellence" of the new "star," the spring and early summer months of 1798 witnessed a steady decline in the fortunes of the Park. Stage manager Hodgkinson, increasingly ambitious, and growing more irascible from the trying responsibilities of joint managership, announced that he intended to end his rôle as an executive. He refused to hamper his genius with the burden of helping to raise the five thousand dollars for next season's rent. He would remain as an actor with a salary of fifty dollars a week. Otherwise he would go to Boston, reëstablish the Federal Street Theater, which had recently burned, and at the same time control the Haymarket. Dunlap refused to pay the fifty dollars. Hodgkinson went — and with him Mrs. Hodgkinson and her relatives, the Bretts. The loss of Mrs. Johnson, the most popular actress of the first season, who returned with her husband to Covent Garden, was another blow to Dunlap, who now was alone responsible for the success of the new theater. Apparently the only available actors to fill these losses were Giles L. Barrett of Boston and Mrs. Barrett. Dunlap's negotiations with the Barretts reveal the difficulties that must often have plagued the early managers in their dealings with the members of the cast. Barrett, in a Hodgkinsonian manner, had tried to stipulate what parts he should play, and with such insistence that the manager was at last forced to tell him firmly: "I would wish it to be clearly understood that while I direct the stage, my opinion must be paramount to any other." And yet Barrett's opinion on the matter of salary was paramount. Balking at the original contract price, the Boston actor demanded an additional ten dollars a week, which Dunlap was forced to grant on condition that nothing be said of it to the other members of the cast. It would seem that the additional ten dollars was a bad investment, for the Barretts, in spite of their Federal Street reputation, were "past the meridian" and never popular in New York. At the end of a year they returned to Boston.

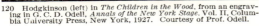

122 Announcement of the Benefit of Mrs. Giles L. Barrett, from the New York *Commercial Advertiser*, June 3, 1799

"DUTCH STUFF"

THE Barretts did not make their New York appearance until December, 1798. The fall season, which Dunlap estimated as potentially the most lucrative of the entire year, owing to the presence of many visitors in New York, had been completely lost. The fortunes of our early theater seem intimately connected with the epidemics of yellow fever, which with autumnal regularity, visited the theatrical centers of America. Many patrons were carried off by its ravages, and the theater was forced to wait with empty benches and closed doors until the survivors dared congregate again. By December Dunlap was in despair. He had waited impatiently for the pestilence to spend itself. Yet he was incessantly working. There appeared one solution, one road to financial security. During the preceding season "having got possession of a wretched publication in which the plot and part of the dialogue of Kotzebue's play were given, in language neither German nor English, he wrote a play founded on these materials." Thus Dunlap recorded the beginnings of a commercial practice which constituted one of the salient characteristics of his seven years managership. August Friedrich Ferdinand von Kotzebue, called by his adulatory European contemporaries "The German

123 William Dunlap, from the portrait by Charles Ingram, in the National Academy of Design, New York

Shakespeare," wrote countless dramas, saturated with bizarre theatrical sentimentality; and because he was, in addition, the first to project on the stage the new spirit engendered by the French Revolution, he had become a favorite medium with European producers, who sensed the eager response of their audiences. He

THE

VIRGIN OF THE SUN:

A PLAY,

IN FIVE ACTS.

———

FROM THE GERMAN OF

AUGUSTUS VON KOTZEBUE.

WITH NOTES MARKING THE VARIATIONS FROM THE
ORIGINAL.

124   Title-page of Dunlap's Adaptation of *The Virgin of the Sun*, in the New York Public Library

was for a short time official court dramatist at Vienna and later was made director of the German theater in St. Petersburg by Czar Paul I. The Kotzebue play, mentioned by Dunlap as "written in language neither German nor English," was *The Stranger*, and the success of Dunlap's adaptation had alone enabled the adapter-manager to keep open the theater during the first season. Safe from yellow fever in his home at Perth Amboy, he had perfected the study of German, that he might adapt other Kotzebue successes more rapidly. The second season was kept going by the success of *False Shame*. Others followed in quick succession, the most popular of all being *Pizarro*, of which Sheridan had made an earlier adaptation for Drury Lane. Dunlap realized as well as any critic of the present day the inferior quality of most of Kotzebue's work, and yet it was his primary duty to keep open the Park. And the profits from Kotzebue nights were great. His actors likewise held the German dramatist in contempt, referring always to that "Dutch stuff." But they too realized whence came their salaries.

HODGKINSON IN "DUTCH STUFF"

125   Hodgkinson as Baron Wellinghorst, from an engraving after the drawing by William Dunlap, in Dunlap, *The Wild Goose Chace*, New York, 1800

UNFORTUNATELY for Hodgkinson there had been no Kotzebue adaptations in Boston to stave off failure. It is not surprising to hear that the gruff new manager of the Federal Street and the Haymarket quarreled with the proprietors. In the spring of 1799 Dunlap in New York received a letter containing Hodgkinson's offer to return to the Park stage on condition that he and his wife receive a hundred dollars a week between them. Dunlap dared not refuse again. Barrett had proved a miserable substitute for the great actor, who now offered to play any one of one hundred and forty-six rôles. Cooper was paid only thirty-two dollars a week, but his list of rôles was limited, and he was not an ideal Kotzebue hero. Dunlap, watching Hodgkinson's first Kotzebue rôle, that of Erlach in *False Shame*, must have felt that any salary and any degree of toleration of Hodgkinson's meanness and deception off stage were more than justified by the perfection of his acting. "Never was part better suited to Mr. Hodgkinson than that of Erlach" wrote the manager, "and never was part better played." Of Ellen Westray, the ingénue of the company, who in *False Shame* played opposite Hodgkinson, Dunlap remarked, "Her youth and beauty contrasted finely with Hodgkinson's figure and manner . . . and the exquisitely natural playing of both made an impression never to be forgotten, and rendered the comedy useless to the theater of New York when they ceased to perform the parts." The English Shakespeare yielded precedence to the German. Erlach was more popular than Hamlet, Hodgkinson than Cooper. The young "star," deprived of his favorite rôles, performed indifferently those that were allotted to him. His weakness of misspeaking lines was exaggerated under the circumstances into a glaring fault that the critics attacked energetically. New complications arose from the old feud with Wignell over the broken contract. His negotiations in Philadelphia with Wignell extended over a longer period of time than he had anticipated. As a result two performances at the Park had to be canceled because he did not return on the specified date. Smarting under his position of inferiority to Hodgkinson, he resented Dunlap's attitude on the two broken engagements. He refused to return to the Park, and for the next season was in Philadelphia. The one check on Hodgkinson's domination was removed. There was no buffer between the tyrannical actor and the compromising manager.

126   August von Kotzebue, 1761–1819, from an engraving after the drawing by William Dunlap, in Dunlap, *The Wild-Goose Chace*, New York, 1800

127   William Coleman, 1766–1829, from an engraving by H. B. Hall after an original portrait, artist unknown, in the possession of the publishers

128   Washington Irving, 1783–1859, from an engraved portrait in the collection of Albert Davis, Brooklyn, N. Y.

"THE SHAKESPEARE"

As far as can be determined, Hodgkinson, during the season of 1800–01, performed many rôles of Kotzebue, and of other authors now forgotten, to the great delight of himself, of the audience, and of the critics, who sat in a large box occupying the front of the second tier and directly in front of the stage. This box, called "The Shakespeare," was capable of accommodating between two and three hundred persons, and it was there that the critics of New York, William Coleman of the *Post*, Washington Irving and others, assembled in the days before the Park was remodeled in 1807. And it was to the influence exerted from this box that the beginning of Hodgkinson's decline can be traced. Cooper was called back to the Park for a season during the summer of 1801, and with him came a much greater attraction in the person of Mrs. Anne Merry, who was by far the most popular actress in America at the time. At the end of the engagement there were the usual benefits. Pleading the necessity of an immediate return to Philadelphia, Mrs. Merry refused to play in Hodgkinson's benefit. To the anger of Hodgkinson she remained, however, long enough to play in Cooper's benefit. Hodgkinson's recriminations and attempts at bribery angered Mrs. Merry, and to her defense rushed William Coleman. From this unpleasant scene dated the antagonism of the critics. Shortly afterward the critics found another convenient occasion for attack in Hodgkinson's increasing corpulence. Smarting under the lash of the critics, Hodgkinson introduced into Fennell's farce, *The Wheel of Truth*, a scene portraying a critic as a goose. The critics retaliated, ridiculing his fatness, and deriding his acting. "His tragedy we pronounce rant," wrote Coleman, "his comedy frequently degenerates into vulgar farce." Irving, under the nom de plume of Jonathan Oldstyle, was even more caustic, " . . . I was so disgusted with the Merry Andrew [his favorite name for Hodgkinson], that in spite of all his skipping and jumping and turning on his heel, I could not yield him a smile." "The Merry Andrew's" extravagant salary demands for 1802–03 were flatly refused by Dunlap. Cooper became more excellent in his own rôles, the attacks of the critics more bitter against Hodgkinson's. In September of 1803, after Mrs. Hodgkinson's death, her somewhat chastened widower left New York for Charleston, where he played two seasons under the Placides. In the spring of 1805 he was appointed manager of the Park, and in the same summer, while recruiting his new company, was stricken in Maryland, where he died.

FOR THE COMMERCIAL ADVERTISER.

While there was room to ascribe Mr. Hodgkinson's rudeness to Mrs. Merry either to precipitancy or to a deficiency in manners, I was willing to allow him the full benefit of such an apology. It is with much regret therefore, for I am not personally his enemy, that I read in yesterday's paper a renewal of his ill grounded complaint against that lady, expressed with such deliberate formality, as will I fear expose him in the opinion of many to the imputation of motives the most disingenuous and unjustifiable. His address to the public on the subject is framed with art ; a suppression of some circumstances, a discolouring of others and some little misrepresentations give the whole an appearance very different from the truth. With any misunderstandings between Mr. H. and the Manager I shall not meddle further than may be necessary to the defence which Mrs. Merry has done me the honor to commit to my discretion.

The most material part of this address is, the assertion that Mr. Hodgkinson " knew nothing of any settled number of nights for Mrs. Merry's *first* engagement, nor was ever made acquainted that there had been an alteration, nor *that the alteration would or might affect his security of her services for his Benefit.*"

129   Coleman's Attack on Hodgkinson, in the New York *Commercial Advertiser*, July 17, 1801

THEATRE.
Mr. & Mrs. Hodgkinson

Respectfully acquaint their friends and the public in general, that their Benefit is fixed for To-Morrow Evening, July 15.

They feel it a duty they owe themselves and their friends, to state that the nature of their engagement with the manager rests their principal emolument for the present, in the patronage of this evening ; and by express agreement with him, they were assured the services of Mrs. Merry, in case it had been in her power to fulfil her first engagement ; but it is with painful regret they add, that after repeated solicitations, that lady absolutely declines performing in New-York one evening more.

The novelty they have gained for the evening will be Mrs. and Mons. PLACIDE, the latter of whom will, previous to the play,

Dance a Hornpipe on the Tight Rope.

Afterwards play the Violin, and display the American Flag in several attitudes.

After which will be presented the celebrated comedy of

THE SUSPICIOUS HUSBAND.

Mr. Strickland, Mr. Cooper ; Frankley, Tyler ; Bellamy, Martin ; Ranger, Hodgkinson ; Jack Meggot, Jefferson ; Buckle, Robinson ; Tester, Wilmot ; Servant to Ranger, Macdonald ; Simon, Lee ; Chairmen, messrs. Lee, &c ; Mrs. Strickland, Mrs. Placide ; Clarinda, Hallam ; Jacintha, Hodgkinson ; Lucetta, Hogg ; Landlady, King ; Milliner, Brett ; Maid, Miss Hogg.

After the Play, the ANTIPODEAN WHIRLIGIG by Mr Robertson. In the course of which he will stand upon his head, and whirl round at the rate of 60 or 100 times a minute, without the assistance of his hands.

130   Protest of the Hodgkinsons at Mrs. Merry's Departure, from an announcement in the New York *Commercial Advertiser*, July 14, 1801

THE UNDEPENDABLE FENNELL

NEITHER in his Diary nor in his *History of the Theatre* does Dunlap expatiate on his feelings as he read Hodgkinson's final refusal to accept the terms offered to him for the season of 1803–04. The letter came from Philadelphia, where the great actor had temporarily stopped, and quite laconically wished the manager success in his negotiations with other people. Hodgkinson was gone, and the preceding spring, Cooper had left the Park for Covent Garden to fill a vacancy caused by the absence of the famous English actor, John Philip Kemble. For the coming season the heavy burden of tragedy would have to be borne on the now feeble shoulders of James Fennell. Fennell has already been seen (No. 83), the idol of the Philadelphia audiences when Cooper was an overshadowed tyro. In 1799 he had come to the Park and been received with unqualified praise. "Few things can excel the performance of the excellent Fennell," wrote the critic in the *Commercial Advertiser* of May 2, "The power of expression by countenance and gesture he possesses in an eminent degree. . . . We have only to lament that our stage is so seldom honored with the performance of this admirable actor. . . ." The cause of the infrequency of this admirable actor's appearance lay in a strange quarter. His primary interest,

131   James Fennell, from an engraving by Boyd after a portrait by Wood, in the Fridenberg Collection

after leaving the scene of his triumphs at the Chestnut, was in a great project for making salt on a cheaper and more extensive scale, and incidentally a fortune that would gratify his extravagant desires. The stage was for him never again more than a stop-gap, when, as in the autumn of 1800, after a year's quixotic enterprise in his salt works on the Battery, he returned, "oppressed by poverty and debt, and in the possession of those who would not receive promises as current coin." The *Commercial Advertiser* was now forced to say, qualifying the praise that it had earlier given him, "But there was such a languid finish that he did not appear to be the same man." His "mellow commanding tones" and "accurate discrimination" were never

quite blunted, but Dunlap, regretfully looking over Hodgkinson's words of refusal, or following in the London papers Cooper's brilliant success at Covent Garden, realized that Fennell was now but a secondrate tragedian at best, and that at worst he might appear any night at the debtor's prison instead of on the "commodious" stage of the Park. Yet there was no other tragedian for the coming season and Dunlap was forced to accept with as good grace as possible.

SALT WORKS, *NEW YORK.*
THE share-holders are respectfully informed that the sale of the shares advertised for distribution, being completed, the erection of the works will commence without delay, and the proprietors flatter themselves with the hope, that without issuing an additional number of shares they shall be enabled to have the works in full operation by the first of June next.
The shares for which obligations have been given for delivering them to the original purchasers, will be ready for distribution before the month of January next.
In the mean time such persons as may have purchased with an intention of selling again are informed, that the receipts will be received at their pleasure, and the obligations made payable to their assigns at the expense of one shilling per share, and as frequent applications have been made since the completion of the sales, for more shares than the proprietors feel inclined at present to distribute, the holders of many shares are informed that advantageous transfers may be made by leaving them for sale at the Office, where punctual attendance is given every day, (Sundays and Holidays excepted) from 9 till 5 o'clock.
nov. 49.   FENNEL & Co.

132   Advertisement of Fennell's Salt Works, from the *Commercial Advertiser*, New York. November 28. 1799

THEATRE.
The Public are respectfully informed, that the Managers have engaged,
MR. FENNELL,
FOR SEVEN NIGHTS ONLY.
His first appearance will be
ON FRIDAY EVENING, JAN. 3.
When will be presented,
Shakespeare's Celebrated Tragedy of
HAMLET,
PRINCE OF DENMARK.

Hamlet,	MR. FENNELL.
Claudine, King of Denmark,	SHAPTER.
Polonius,	JOHNSON.
Horatio,	TYLER.
Laertes,	YOUNG.
Rosencrants,	BAILEY.
Guildenstern,	ROBINSON.
Francisco,	RINGWOOD.
Marcellus,	CHARNOCK.
Bernardo,	BURD.
Ghost of Hamlets Father.	HALLAM.
Grave Digger,	HOGG.
Ostrick,	MARTIN.
Player King,	HOGG.
Gertrudy, Queen of Denmark,	MRS. BARRETT.

133   Fennell as Hamlet, from the New York *Evening Post*, January 3, 1806

A NEW COMEDIAN

THE prospect for the comic rôles during the coming year must have seemed in comparison less discouraging. Jo Jefferson, it is true, had gone at the end of the season of 1803 to the Chestnut Street company in Philadelphia. But as compensation Dunlap had secured from that same company the services of John E. Harwood, whom Wignell had brought from London to Philadelphia ten years before (see p. 38). In the intervening decade at the Chestnut Harwood had established a reputation as one of the finest comedians ever seen in America. According to Dunlap he became very soon a favorite with the audiences at the Park, "although the remembrance of Mr. Hodgkinson in many parts made it impossible for any performer to follow him with perfect success." Dunlap has listed a great number of Harwood's characters, which the manager considered "superior . . . to those of any man yet seen in this country." One of the chief difficulties encountered by the present day student of the early phases of our theatrical history arises from his lack of familiarity with the great mass of forgotten plays that were produced at the time.

134 John E. Harwood, 1771–1809, from an engraving by David Edwin after the portrait by Robert Field, in the Harvard Theater Collection

Unless he knows, for example, the play in which Dennis Brulgruddery is the great comic character it does not greatly stimulate his imagination to be informed by Dunlap that "Dennis was in Harwood's hands one of the richest pieces of comic acting that we have ever witnessed; nothing overcharged, nothing vulgar, but ripe and having all the flavor of perfect ripeness in the mellow fruit of an author's genius." He can only realize from such a statement that Harwood's excellence lay in the rôles of polished and refined comedy, as contrasted with the low comedy of the buffoon. Upon the addition of Twaits to the cast (see No. 146), Harwood gladly relinquished to him the low comedy rôles. Until the arrival of George Frederick Cooke in 1810 Harwood was recognized as the greatest Falstaff the country had yet seen.

"THE INTERIOR OF AN ESTABLISHMENT, BADLY ORGANIZED"

135 John Hogg, 1770–1813, from a portrait by Thomas Sully (1783–1872), in the possession of Mrs. Jonathan Bulkley, New York

BUT the essential flavor of the old stock companies would be lost were attention confined to such outstanding leaders as Cooper, Hodgkinson, and Harwood, whose reputations extended well beyond the borders of one theatrical center, and who could move at will to Philadelphia or to Boston, or on occasion to London. Year in and year out at the Park, or the Federal Street, or the Chestnut, the great body of the company, playing a variety of secondary rôles, remained the same. For example, when the doors of the Park opened in 1798 John Hogg, who had performed at the John Street, was still found playing the rôles of old men. Such actors improved slowly, almost imperceptibly. Hogg continued at the Park until his death in 1813. And Mrs. Hogg was in all her old women "a most able actress." During the twelve crowded nights of 1804, when Cooper, fresh from his triumphs in London, was starring at the Park, Dunlap must have felt that the stock company, in the sense in which it had been understood, as it was typified by actors like the Hoggs, was doomed. For when Cooper left to continue his starring at Philadelphia and Boston, the discouraged New York manager realized that his years of effort had been in vain. "After the departure of Mr. Cooper," he wrote, "the theater sunk irretrievably. . . . After a struggle of years against the effects of the yellow fever, and all those curses belonging to the interior of an establishment, badly organized when he found it, the manager's health yielded to disappointment and incessant exertion, and his struggles became proportionably fainter."

136   William B. Wood, 1779–1861, as Stephen Foster, from
the portrait by John Neagle (1796–1865), in the possession
of The Players' Club, New York

137   Wood as Charles de Moor, 1810, from the painting
by Thomas Sully (1783–1872), in the possession of the
Misses Hutchinson, Philadelphia

"OLD DRURY"

WHEN Cooper left New York in December of 1804, after his twelve brilliant Shakespearean performances, he went to Philadelphia, and opened at the Chestnut Street Theater.   Thomas Wignell, who had been primarily instrumental in building up the fine company there, was no longer in control. Shortly before his death in 1803, he had married Mrs. Anne Merry and it was that excellent actress who, in partnership with Reinagle, nominally carried on the managerial duties in the years immediately following. But William Warren (see No. 104), an excellent high comedian whom Wignell had brought from England in 1796, became more and more the trusted adviser and actual executant. The responsibilities of manager began to be assumed by him. In 1806 he married Mrs. Wignell, and the theatrical policy was now entirely in his hands. Warren's most able assistant was William Wood, a Canadian, who had come with a letter of introduction to Wignell. His early attempts at tragedy having proved a failure, he had gone for a time to the West Indies, and then returned, deciding on the second attempt to play comedy. His success was great. Wignell had recognized not only his talents as a comic actor but also his unusual executive ability, and had made Wood the treasurer of the Chestnut Street Theater. When Wignell died, it was Wood who was sent to London in search of new recruits.   He made many influential connections, and his rise in the managerial field was rapid, culminating in 1809 in a joint managership of the Chestnut with William Warren. No other theater in America enjoyed the prestige of the Chestnut.   "Wignell's friendly relations with London managers and authors," wrote Wood in his *Recollections,* "gave him the advantage of an early manuscript of each new piece, on condition of its use being confined to his theater."   The theater prided itself on its nickname of "Old Drury," which suggested its affinity with the great London prototype.   Not only in Philadelphia, but also in Baltimore, Annapolis, and in Washington, the cast of "Old Drury" was welcome. No company could boast a quartet of comedians approximating Jefferson, Blissett, Warren, and Twaits. Yet for an accurate perspective, it is necessary to have Wood's qualifying record that "in spite of the Old Drury reputation inferior parts in tragedies were almost uniformly butchered."

New=Theatre.

THIS Evening, February 15, 1806,
Will be presented,
An Opera, (for the first-time) called
THIRTY THOUSAND,
Or, Who's the Richest.
Written by T. Dibden, author of the Jew and Doctor, &c.
And performed at the Theatre Royal, Covent Garden, with the most unbounded applause.
With the original music by Messrs. Braham, Reeve and Davy. The Orchestra parts by Mr. R. Taylor.

Lawyer Plainly,	Mr. M'Kenzie.
Mr. Dubious,	Mr. Francis.
Arable,	Mr. Robbins.
Fbressil,	Mr. Woodham.
Windmill,	Mr. Harwood.
Clump,	Mr. Blissett.
Gangway,	Mr Jefferson.
Teddy,	Mr. Cross.
Jenkins,	Mr. Bray.
Clodpole,	Mr. Mestayer.
Harry,	Mr. Durang.
Sailors,	Messrs. Seymour, Taylor, &c.
Rosanna,	Mrs. Woodham.
Mrs Arable,	Mrs. Jefferson.
Henrica,	Mrs. Seymour.
Mrs. Notable,	Mrs. Francis.
Margery,	Mrs. Durang.

After which (for the Ninth time in America) a new grand allegorical pantomimic spectacle, called
CINDERELLA;
Or, the Little Glass Slipper.
Invented by Mr. Bryne, and performed at the Theatre Royal, Drury-lane, upwards of 100 nights the two last seasons, to overflowing houses.— The Scenery, Machinery, Dresses and Decorations, entirely new.   The Scenery and Machinery designed by Mr. Holland, and executed by him, assisted by Mr. Robbins and H. Reinagle. The Pantomime got under the direction of Messrs. Francis and Cross. The Dresses by Mr. Mascubin. The Dances composed by Mr. Francis. With the original Music by Mr. Kelly.
IMMORTALS.

Hymen,	Mr. Woodham.
Cupid,	Master Jefferson.
Venus,	Mrs. Seymour.
Nymph,	Miss Hunt.

138   The cast of the Chestnut Street
Theater, Philadelphia, from a playbill
in the New York Historical Society

139 The Walnut Street Theater, Philadelphia, from an engraving after a drawing by C. Burton in the New York Public Library

140 The Second Holliday Street Theater, Baltimore, from an engraving in the City Library, Baltimore, Md.

THEATRICAL SUBURBS

THE Park, the Chestnut Street, and the Federal Street were the principal, but not the only, theaters in America. Wignell and Reinagle, having decided to make Baltimore a theatrical adjunct to Philadelphia, had built a new playhouse in 1794 on Holliday Street. It was replaced by the second Holliday Street Theater, a much more commodious structure, which was finished in 1814 despite various hindrances occasioned by the War of 1812. When the Capital was established at Washington in 1800, Wignell and Reinagle opened the town's first playhouse in a large building, erected as a hotel, which became known as the National Theater. Although the project was almost a failure, other promoters built a second theater on Pennsylvania Avenue a few years later. It was destroyed by fire in 1820. At Philadelphia the Chestnut Street house had a competitor in a new theater on Walnut Street. Built in 1809 for a circus, it was improved in 1811 and the name changed from the Olympic to the Walnut Street Theater. It became a legitimate theater during the season of 1811–12, opening January 1, 1812, with *The Rivals*. After many vicissitudes it still stands to-day — the oldest extant playhouse in America.

THE FEDERAL STREET

HAVING completed his Philadelphia performances, Cooper, at the invitation of Snelling Powell, went on to Boston. When Hodgkinson left Boston in the summer of 1799 the theatrical promoters with whom he had quarreled proposed to Giles L. Barrett, finishing an unsuccessful year at the Park, that he should return to Boston, to take over the management of the Federal Street. Barrett accepted, but seems to have made as little a success of managing as of acting. The following season he was succeeded by Mr. Whitlock, husband of the actress who had made such a reputation in London and Philadelphia. But things went no better.

141 Snelling Powell, 1774–1843, as Sir George Airy in *The Busybody*, from an engraving by S. Hill after a drawing by W. Lovett, in the Harvard Theater Collection

The old prejudice against the theater had not entirely died. There is no real continuity to Boston theatrical history until the opening of the Federal Street Theater on October 27, 1802, with Snelling Powell as manager. The new manager, a brother of Charles Powell (see p. 40), had acted at the Park during the season 1801–02 without attracting attention. But his ability as a manager was greater, for he introduced a period of financial prosperity hitherto unknown in the Boston theater. From 1802 to 1805 he was in sole control of the Federal Street. In 1803 the Haymarket, the only rival, was sold at auction, leaving Powell with a monopoly of the Boston market. "Mr. Powell" wrote William W. Clapp in his *Record of the Boston Stage*, "was thus the first successful manager of a theater in Boston. He adopted a straightforward course, and honorably kept his engagements, and by offering to the public entertainments worthy of patronage, 'conjured back into the boxes,' to borrow an expression of a critic of those days, 'the long absent taste and beauty of Boston.'" One of the most significant incidents arising out of Cooper's visit to Powell's theater, was the quarrel between the visiting star and the native stock actors, who, at the time of Cooper's interruption, were anticipating a series of benefits for themselves. For the first time the antagonism between the stock and the star became audible in disturbances that were difficult for the straightforward manager to quiet.

142 Thomas A. Cooper, from the portrait by Gilbert Stuart (1755-1828), in the possession of The Players' Club, New York

THE NEW MANAGER OF THE PARK

DUNLAP's struggles to continue, growing "proportionably fainter," finally, on February 18, 1805, ceased altogether. A new administration was necessary, and yet there was no outstanding figure at the Park to whom the proprietors could turn. In the interim a makeshift organization was attempted. John Tyler, a steady player of secondary rôles, who had been at the Park since its opening, and John Johnson, who, after his return to Covent Garden with his wife in 1798, was again at the Park, were chosen by the Commonwealth of Players to represent them as nominal heads of the company. The actors comprising the Commonwealth soon made it evident to Tyler and Johnson that neither of them had been given any real power. Tyler and Johnson attempted to specify the salaries which the Commonwealth should pay to them; but they were quickly voted down and powerless. There was no possibility of success in such an arrangement. To be sure there were two excellent actresses in the cast, Johnson's wife, and a Mrs. Jones, who unfortunately died the following spring; Harwood could be relied on for a brilliant performance of high comedy, and the two managers were wise enough to concentrate on comedy. But a great deal more was required. In desperation they resorted to starring. Fennell, after his years of appearing and disappearing, was now starred in a series of engagements, which did little to improve the financial depression of the theater. Jo Jefferson was brought from the Chestnut for four nights. Cooper was announced for early March; and days before his appearance all the boxes were taken for the entire five nights. On the opening night "a fashionable house assembled . . . to give him welcome." But at the end of the five nights, the proprietors were as far from a solution of their problem as ever. Receipts immediately fell to an impossible figure. Exactly what occurred during the next month is not known. The first definite news is in the *Post* of April 22, which announced that for the low price of fifty thousand dollars the Park Theater had been sold by the one hundred and thirteen proprietors to John Jacob Astor and John K. Beekman, who, continued the announcement, "have already written to Mr. Cooper and committed to him the sole management of it; who on his part has engaged that . . . he will introduce to us . . . a better company than we have ever had in this city." Fifteen thousand dollars was appropriated for the alteration of the building, and Dunlap was engaged to take general superintendence of the business. But the responsibility was to rest on the now matured shoulders of Thomas Abthorpe Cooper.

THEATRE.

The public are respectfully informed, that on account of the want of patronage, the manager is under the necessity of closing the Theatre, and this evening is positively the last night of the present season.

MONDAY EVENING, FEB. 18,
WILL BE PRESENTED,
Beaumont and Fletcher's celebrated Comedy of
RULE A WIFE AND HAVE A WIFE.

Duke of Medina,	Mr. DARLEY,
Don Juan de Castro,	TYLER,
Perez, (the Copper Captain)	HARWOOD,
Alonzo,	HALLAM, jun.
Sancho,	ROBINSON,
Leon,	COOPER,
Cacafogo,	HOGG,
Lorenzo,	MACDONALD,
Perez's Servant,	KINOWOOD,
Margaretta,	Mrs. DARLEY,
Estifania,	JOHNSON,
Altea,	DARBY,
Clara,	Miss PATTON,
1st Lady,	WHITE,
2d Lady,	Mrs. PETIT,
Old Woman,	Mr. JOHNSON,
Maid,	SHAPTER,

TO WHICH WILL BE ADDED,
(Under the direction of M. Labottierre)
A Grand Pantomime, in 2 acts, called,
MIRZA & LINDOR.

MIXED WITH VOCAL AND INSTRUMENTAL MUSIC
AND COMBATS.

The Governor,	Mr. SHAPTER,
Lindor,	DARLEY,
Adulph,	LABOTTIERRE
Commandant,	CLAUDE,
Pontiff,	HALLAM, jun.
Officers, Sailors, &c.	
The Countess,	Mrs. CLAUDE,
Mirza,	DARBY,
Betsy, (negro confidant of Mirza)	WHITE.

IN ACT II,
A CONCERT.
IN ACT II,
A COMBAT WITH THE SWORD,
BETWEEN LINDOR AND ADULPH.
☞ *The Doors will open at half past five, and the Curtain rise at half past six*

143 Dunlap's Retirement, from an announcement in the New York *Evening Post*, February 18, 1805

THEATRE.

The attention of the Patrons of the Drama, is respectfully solicited to the present state of the New-York Theatre.

The Performers, having suffered inconvenience from the interruption of the business of the Theatre, destroying not only the reasonable expectations from their respective contracts, but also the customary remuneration from the public at the close of the Season, will open the Theatre under the management of Messrs. Johnson and Tyler; and hope, by unabating diligence and assiduity, to merit the public patronage.

MONDAY EVENING, MARCH 4,
WILL BE PRESENTED,
The celebrated Comedy of
THE SOLDIER'S DAUGHTER.

Gov. Heartall,	Mr. JOHNSON,
Frank Heartall,	HARWOOD,
Malfort, Sen.	ROBINSON,
Malfort, Jun.	TYLER,
Capt. Woodley,	DARLEY,
Mr. Ferret,	HARPER,
Timothy Quaint,	HOGG,
Simon,	HALLAM,
Tom,	KINGWOOD,
William,	MACDONALD,
Footman,	Master STOCKWELL,
Widow Cheerly,	Mrs. JOHNSON,
Mrs. Malfort,	DARLEY,
Mrs. Townley,	DARBY,
Mrs. Fidget,	HOGG,
Susan,	HARPER,
Julia, (Malfort's Child)	Miss MARTIN,

TO WHICH WILL BE ADDED,
A favorite Farce, in two acts, called,
RAISING THE WIND.

Plainway,	Mr. JOHNSON,
Diddler,	HARWOOD,
Fainwould,	CLAUDE,
Richard,	ROBINSON,
Sam,	HOGG,
Waiter,	SHAPTER,
Messenger,	MACDONALD,
Miss Laurelia Durable,	Mrs. HOGG,
Peggy,	CLAUDE.

☞ *The Doors will open at half past five, and the Curtain rise at half past six*

144 The New Management of Tyler and Johnson, from an announcement in the New York *Evening Post*, March 4 1805

FOR THE CONVENIENCE OF THE SPECTATORS

THE fifteen thousand dollars appropriated by the new proprietors, Beekman and Astor, for alterations was spent under the direction of John Joseph Holland, a New York architect whose secondary interest happened to be theatrical art. By the autumn of 1807 the alterations had been completed. Dunlap in his history has left a full description of the novelties that the audience witnessed on the opening night: "This Theater has lately undergone considerable alterations, which have materially added to the comfort and convenience of the spectators. The audience part, which is entirely rebuilt, now consists of four rows of boxes; in the lower lobby there is a handsome colonnade, with mirrors, and fireplaces at each end, the whole lighted by glass lamps between the columns. . . . There are several coffee rooms, one of which is fitted in an elegant style for the accommodation of the ladies. . . . The boxes will accommodate upwards of sixteen hundred persons, and the pit and gallery about eleven hundred. The ceiling painted as a dome, with panels of a light purple, and gold mouldings; the centre a balustrade and sky. The box fronts (except the fourth row) are divided into panels, blue ground with white and gold ornaments;

145 John Joseph Holland, from a miniature by J. Evers, in the New York Historical Society

a crimson festoon drapery over each box. The lower boxes are lighted by ten glass chandeliers, projecting from the front, and suspended from gilt iron brackets, and the whole house is extremely well lighted. . . . A beautiful effect is produced by a large oval mirror at the end of the stage boxes, which reflects the whole of the audience on the first row."

A LOW COMEDIAN

IMPROVEMENTS in the cast were equally imperative. The greatest need was a low comedian, who could relieve Harwood of the rôles for which he was not particularly fitted and allow him to concentrate on those polished characters which he relished. At the Chestnut Cooper had watched the work of William Twaits, a young actor whom William Wood had brought to this country in 1803. Cooper, impressed by his acting, had persuaded young Twaits to accompany him to Boston, where they had become close friends; and nothing delighted Twaits more than to tell anecdotes at the expense of the great tragedian "Tom." Now that "Tom"

146 William Twaits, 1781–1814, as Sir Adam Contest in *The Wedding Day*, from an engraving by J. R. Smith, in the Fridenberg Collection, New York

was manager of the Park he persuaded the singing comedian to remain permanently in New York. The choice was a happy one. He was an admirable foil to Harwood, and according to Dunlap's estimate it was the work of these two comedians that tided over the theater during the uncertain days of Cooper's early managership. Dunlap has left a most graphic description of the new comedian: "Neither his style of playing, nor his face or person, was like any other individual on or off the stage." Twaits was "short and thin, yet appearing broad; muscular yet meagre." He had a "large head with stiff, stubborn, carroty hair; long colourless face, prominent hooked nose, projecting large hazel eyes, thin lips, and a large mouth which could be twisted into a variety of expression, and which, combining with his other features, eminently served the purposes of the comic muse. . . . He had played everything, but he was only fitted for comedy — and for that he was eminently fitted." And yet, with a certain perverseness, Twaits nourished, until his death in 1814, the desire to play tragic rôles. At times his insistence could not be ignored, and we find him appearing, to the great amusement of the critics, as Prince Hal, as Richard III, and even as King Lear. General ridicule followed, until he would appear again in one of those inimitable low comic rôles which rendered him the most striking theatrical figure of this period of our history.

147 Mrs. John Darley (Ellen Westray), 1779–1848, from
an engraving by Leney after the portrait by William
Dunlap, in the Fridenberg Collection, New York

148 Mrs. William Wood (Juliana Westray), 1778–1836,
from an engraving by Edwin after a portrait by Rembrandt
Peale, courtesy of the Columbia University Press, New York

THREE SISTERS

DURING the first years of the Park when Dunlap had been manager, Mrs. Simpson had divided old women's parts with Mrs. Hogg. Mrs. Simpson had had by a former marriage three daughters, the Westray sisters, all of whom had acted at one time or another for Dunlap. Juliana Westray, after a few seasons at the Park, had married William Wood of Philadelphia, the enterprising co-manager with William Warren of the Chest-

nut Street Theater (see p. 60). Elizabeth Westray had substituted in some of Mrs. Hodgkinson's parts the year that actress was in Boston with her husband (see p. 54). Ellen Westray, the third of the sisters, whose "exquisitely natural acting" opposite Hodgkinson in *False Shame* has already been noted (see p. 56), married a Philadelphia sea captain named John Darley, who had a well cultivated voice and aspirations toward the stage. In 1804–05 the Darleys appeared at the Park. The next year they were at the Federal Street, but in 1806–07, the second year of Cooper's management, they were permanently attached to the Park, remaining with an occasional off year until 1818. Mr. Darley, Dunlap remarked, "gave great pleasure as a singer, and in many characters in comedy. His Frenchmen were approved, and his fine manly figure and face gave him a superiority to most who represented the second gentlemen of the drama." But it was Mrs. Darley on whom Manager Cooper relied for more important rôles. With her sister, Elizabeth Westray, who in the meantime had married Mr. Villiers, she now divided the leading rôles. Mrs. Darley also had a beautiful voice, and was almost as popular for her singing as for her acting, and both had greatly improved, Dunlap tells us, since the early days when she played seconds to the great Mrs. Melmoth and Mrs. Hodgkinson and Mrs. Johnson. On the death of her husband, Mrs. Villiers married "the muscular yet meagre" Twaits, trying, no doubt, until her death in 1813 to discourage her husband's weakness for tragic rôles.

149 Benefit of Mrs. Villiers (Elizabeth Westray), 1787–1813,
from the New York *Evening Post*, May 9, 1806

150 Mrs. William Warren, from a miniature by William Dunlap, in the possession of T. S. Woolsey, New Haven, Conn.

151 John Bernard as Jack Meggot in *The Suspicious Husband*, from an engraving by Maguire after a drawing by De Wilde, in the Houdini Collection, New York

"SUPERIOR EXCELLENCE"

YET neither Twaits, nor Harwood, nor the Westray sisters, nor even Cooper on his acting nights was sufficiently attractive to the patrons of the Park to guarantee financial prosperity. Importations for limited engagements were necessary. As Cooper cast his eye about for possible attractions, the figure of John Bernard in Boston seemed promising. Bernard we have already seen as the veteran comedian since 1797 at the Chestnut (see No. 106). In 1806 he had gone to Boston, to take over the joint managership of the Federal Street with Snelling Powell and Dickson. He had not appeared in New York since the summer of Wignell and Reinagle's season at the Greenwich Street in 1797. On January 19, almost ten years later, he arrived at the Park and gave a series of nine performances. There is no evidence, however, that Cooper chose wisely. Bernard's engagement came to an end on January 30. The *Post* of that date announced: "this evening, we understand, is the last of Mr. Bernard's performance for the manager. For his benefit on Monday night . . . we hope he will receive some *solid proof* of the high respect [in] which his theatrical talents are held by the citizens of the metropolis." The "solid proof" of money, however, seemed lacking. Cooper had persuaded Bernard to come only by agreeing to go himself to Boston. This fillip to starring was increased still more the following year, when Cooper, Harwood, and Twaits all starred together in Boston, in return for Bernard's engagement at the Park. But between Bernard's first and second visits, the greatest of all the early stars had made her last appearance at the Park — Mrs. Anne Warren, who had been Mrs. Anne Wignell, and before that Mrs. Anne Merry. No other actor or actress of the period before Cooke aroused such enthusiasm. Of her rôle of Calista the critic of the *Post* of February 20 wrote: "Those well remembered tones — those eloquent pauses — that graceful motion — that expressive countenance — all spoke to us in language that is never conveyed to us by any other human being. The unbroken silence — the fast falling tear . . . were involuntary tributes to her superior excellence. . . ." The "well remembered tones" were soon to be silenced, for the next year, against the advice of her physician, Mrs. Warren accompanied her husband on a trip to Richmond where she died.

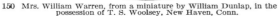

THEATRE.
FOR THE BENEFIT OF
MR. BERNARD.
The last night of his performance here.
ON MONDAY EVENING, FEB. 2d,
Will be presented,
THE FAVORITE COMEDY OF,
JOHN BULL,
OR,
AN ENGLISHMAN'S FIRE SIDE.

Peregrine,   Mr. TYLER.
Honorable Tom Shuffleton,   TWAITS.
Job Thornbury,   HOGG.
Dennis Brulguddery,   BERNARD.
Lady Caroline Braymore, Mrs OLDMIXON.
Mrs. Brulguddery,   SIMPSON
Mary Thornbury,   OLDMIXON.
End of the play, the
ORIGINAL MUSICAL EPILOGUE,
BY MR. BERNARD.
The much admired Song, of
"THE TUNEFUL BIRD."
BY MR. BERNARD.
The celebrated comic Song of "The Town Cryer,"
BY MR. TWAITS.
The which will be added,
A CELEBRATED FARCE, CALLED THE
LYING VALET.

Sharp.   Mr. BERNARD.
Gayless,   MARTIN.
Justice Guttle;   HOGG.
Melissa,   Mrs VILLIERS.
Kitty Pry,   OLDMIXON.
.*. *Doors open at one quarter past five and curtain rise at one quarter past six.*

152 Bernard's Benefit, from an announcement in the New York *Evening Post*, February 2, 1808

153 Stephen Price, d. 1840, from an engraved portrait in the Madigan Collection, New York

THE FIRST PROFESSIONAL MANAGER

At the beginning of the season of 1808–09, Stephen Price bought from Cooper an interest in the management of the theater. With a shrewd mind devoted entirely to the commercial phases of theatrical management, with no distractions caused either by acting or playwriting, Price established the finances of the theater on a much sounder basis. Our first theatrical speculator, at one time manager of Drury Lane, London, he brought to this country many distinguished European stars with whom he had made connections during a long residence abroad; our first monopolist, he controlled their bookings and contracts not only in New York but throughout the whole country. He freed Cooper's mind from many of the troublesome worries of managership, and gave the tragedian more time for starring. It was Cooper's practice at this period to divide his week between the Chestnut, the Park, and the road. Cooper and Price became great friends, living in adjoining houses, which soon came to be the center of a group of young wits, who loved wine and spirited dialogue and an occasional bet. From their increasing extravagance they suffered in the end; but during Price's early days as co-manager with Cooper he was, as Ireland wrote, "a man of great perseverance and energy of character, strict and severe though honorable in his dealings, and for a long period displayed good taste, judgment, and liberality in all his dramatic arrangements."

THE POES

The mother of Edgar Allan Poe often played in rôles opposite the youthful Payne. Born Elizabeth Arnold, she first married a light comedian, C. D. Hopkins. She played chiefly in the South, though it is recorded that she filled engagements in Maine, at the old John Street Theater in New York, at the Baltimore Theater, and from 1798 to 1802 at the Chestnut Street, Philadelphia. While in Baltimore she met David Poe, an actor of inconsiderable merit, to whom she was married in 1805, shortly after the death of Hopkins. Mrs. Poe rose above mediocrity as an actress, playing with Cooper and Fennell as well as with John Howard Payne. In 1809 the Poes were regular members of the cast of the Federal Street Theater in Boston, where on January 19, 1809, a son Edgar was born. Mrs. Poe continued acting until 1811, closing her career in Richmond, Virginia. On November 29, of that year *The Virginia Enquirer* published, in behalf of her destitute family, one of the most pathetic pleas in all theatrical history. On December 8 Mrs. Poe died.

154   Elizabeth Arnold Poe, from an engraving after an original miniature, in John H. Ingram, *Edgar Allan Poe*, London, 1880

Edgar's connection with the stage lay in his attempted playwriting and his notices of contemporary plays and acting. On May 4, 1885, at the New York Metropolitan Museum of Art, a tablet was unveiled to the memory of Poe's parents. Edwin Booth presided at the ceremonies.

THE RICHMOND FIRE

155   The Burning of the Richmond Theater, from an engraving in the Fridenberg Collection, New York

In 1811, the year of Mrs. Poe's death, there occurred in Richmond the most disastrous theater fire this country had seen. During the performance on December 26, the scenery caught fire, and the flames quickly spread through the whole building. Trapped in the narrow stairways or crushed by leaping from the windows, seventy-one people lost their lives. The enemies of the stage looked upon the catastrophe as Heaven's judgment, and the more liberal-minded hesitated to expose themselves to the hazard of fire. Consequently for months the theaters suffered a falling off in attendance.

156 Payne as Young Norval, from an engraving in the Fridenberg Collection, New York

HOME, SWEET HOME

BORN in New York, June 9, 1791, John Howard Payne developed early a love of journalism and of drama. At the age of fifteen he went to Union College, Schenectady, having already attracted the notice of older New York critics by his dramatic reviews in his own magazine, which he called *The Thespian Mirror*. In the same year that he went to Union his play, *Julia*, was presented at the Park, and though it was not a success the youthful author must have been sufficiently satisfied. On February 24, 1809, he began his acting career as Young Norval, at the Park,

157 John Howard Payne, 1791–1852, from an engraving by H. B. Hall in the collection of Montrose J. Moses, New York

where his beauty and grace were warmly applauded. He was heralded everywhere as the "American Roscius," worthy rival to young "Master Betty," the infant prodigy who had thrilled England a few years before. George Frederick Cooke, with whom Payne played, suggested his going to London; he sailed January 17, 1813. On June 4 of that year he made a successful appearance at Drury Lane, receiving the congratulations of the veteran painter, Benjamin West. There followed a period of association with Samuel Taylor Coleridge, Robert Southey, Charles Lamb, and Washington Irving. To meet the demand for translations from the French for the English stage, Payne began a series of adaptations of the luxuriant melodramas which were then the rage at the Comédie Française, where he came under the sway of the great French actor, Talma. He served as agent for Stephen Price of the New York Park Theater, who was on the lookout for foreign materials and also for Douglass Kennaird, the manager of Drury Lane. His own original play, *Brutus, or the Fall of Tarquin*, was produced, December 3, 1818, at Drury Lane, and at the Park the following year; and it continued throughout the century to be one of the dramas most popular with managers and audiences. His *Home, Sweet Home*, with music by Sir Henry Bishop, appeared in *Clari; or The Maid of Milan*, given at Covent Garden, London, May 8, 1823; the lyric was first sung by Miss Maria Tree. In America the piece was given at the Park, November 12, 1823. With Washington Irving, Payne collaborated in the preparation of *Charles II*, and to Irving he dedicated his *Richelieu*.

Home. Sweet Home

Mid pleasures and palaces though we may roam
Be it ever so humble, there's no place like home
A charm from the sky seems to hallow us there
Which, seek through the world, is ne'er met with elsewhere!

Home, home, — sweet, sweet home!
There's no place like home! there's no place like home!

II.

An exile from home, splendor dazzles in vain!
Oh, give me my lowly thatchèd cottage again!
The birds singing gaily that came at my call! —
Give me them, with the peace of mind dearer than all

Home, home, — sweet, sweet home!
There's no place like home! there's no place like home!

For the honorable
General G. McKim }

John Howard Payne /
Washington City, August 18. 1841.

158 Facsimile of *Home, Sweet Home* from Payne's *Clari*, in the Historical Society of Pennsylvania

159 Performance of Payne's *Clari* at Nashville, Tenn., from an announcement in *The National Banner and Nashville Whig*, October 30, 1829

THE
INDIAN PRINCESS;
OR,
LA BELLE SAUVAGE
AN OPERATIC MELO-DRAME.
IN THREE ACTS.
PERFORMED AT THE THEATRES PHILADELPHIA AND
BALTIMORE.

BY J. N BARKER

FIRST ACTED APRIL 6, 1808

PHILADELPHIA,
PRINTED BY T & G PALMER,
FOR G E BLAKE, NO 1, SOUTH THIRD-STREET
1808.

160 Samuel Woodworth, 1785–1842, from an engraving by J. H. Morrell, in the Fridenberg Collection, New York

161 Title-page of James Nelson Barker, 1784–1858, *The Indian Princess*, in the New York Public Library

162 Mordecai M. Noah, 1785–1851, from an engraving after the drawing by J. R. Smith, in the Harvard Theater Collection

NATIVE CHRONICLE PLAYS

In May of 1809 the young American Roscius had made his second appearance at the Park. The next month there was presented at the same house a play by another American, James Nelson Barker, who was older than Payne, and whose plays were the antithesis of all of Payne's later dramatic work. Barker was an active citizen of Philadelphia, absorbed in the development and welfare of his native country. Instead of turning for his themes to historic characters of antiquity or of seventeenth-century Europe, he saw — and was one of the first to see — the rich dramatic possibilities of the historic background of his own country. Free from the perverting influence of French melodrama and English Gothic romance, he turned to the almost untouched field of American history. It was the third of his plays, *The Indian Princess; or, La Belle Sauvage*, that was presented at the Park in June, 1809. He took the now famous story of John Rolfe and Pocahontas from John Smith's *Generall Historie*, adapting the historic facts to the demands of a well-built drama. It had already been given at the Chestnut the preceding year, the first Indian play by an American author actually to be produced, and twelve years later it was given in London, the first original American play to be presented in England after an initial performance in America. Previous to *The Indian Princess*, Barker had written *Tears and Smiles*, in which the hero returns to his native city of Philadelphia after brilliant triumphs over the Barbary pirates (see Vol. VI, Chap. XI). *Embargo, or What's News*, a play suggested by Blissett and attacking the embargo restrictions of President Jefferson's government (see Vol. VIII), was performed with great success in 1808 at Philadelphia. Barker's best historic play, *Superstition*, not presented until many years later, combined in its intensely dramatic treatment two episodes of our history, the flight of one of the regicides to New Haven (Vol. I) and the whole social and religious phenomenon of the witchcraft craze (Vol. X). Mordecai M. Noah, likewise a practical citizen intrigued by the background of his country's history, gave in *She Would Be a Soldier* (1819) a stirring description of the Battle of Chippewa (Vol. VI), which follows quite closely the historical facts, and which depicts most vividly the scorn felt by the regular army for the cowardice of the frightened militia. In *Marion*, Noah presented the background of the Battle of Saratoga, and the surrender of Burgoyne (Vol. VI). His *Siege of Tripoli* again dealt with the disturbing question of the ravages of the Barbary pirates. All of these proved successful for many years. There were other such plays, dealing with the Battle of New Orleans, in which Jackson was a prominent figure; the Battle of Eutaw Springs with General Greene as the hero; the Battle of Lexington; and the death of General Montgomery at the Falls of Montmorency. One of the best done of all the historical plays was *The Widow's Son*, by Samuel Woodworth, which portrays the bitter struggle of the preceding generation between the Whigs and Tories.

THEATRE.
IN HONOR OF THE DAY.
This Evening, July 4.
WILL be presented, an Historical Drama, in 3 acts, written by M. M. Noah, Esq. of New-York, called
She would be a Soldier,
OR
THE PLAINS OF CHIPPEWA.
Between the Play and Farce, an OMNIUM GATHERUM, consisting of Songs, Recitations, &c. The whole to conclude with an admired Farce, called
'TIS ALL A FARCE.
(For particulars see bills.)

163 Announcement of a performance of Noah's *She Would be a Soldier*, at Nashville, Tenn., from *The Nashville Whig*, July 4, 1821

GEORGE FREDERICK COOKE, 1775–1812

"THE Theater was in a decline"; wrote Dunlap, "when, lo! George Frederick Cooke arrived, and all was well again." Early in 1810 Cooper had sailed for Europe. Returning the following autumn, he brought back — to his own surprise and to the amazement of American theatergoers — the famous English actor whom London critics had eulogized as greater even than John Philip Kemble. Fortunately for Cooper's designs, Cooke had, at the moment, lost considerable popularity with his English audience because of periods of drunkenness when he would appear on the stage, hopelessly incapable of reaching the tragic heights which he attempted. Rumors persisted for many years that the American manager had kidnapped the depressed actor, helpless in a drunken stupor. From the Atlantic voyage Cooke arrived in better physical condition and in better spirit than he had enjoyed in months. His performance of Richard III, whom he portrayed without the conventions of hump or crooked legs, was brilliant. The doors of the Park were besieged by thousands of spectators, eager to see the distinguished English star, and so great was the rush that many were pushed in without paying. "He returned the salutes of the audience," wrote Dunlap, "not as a player to the public on whom he depended, but as a victorious prince, acknowledg-

164 George Frederick Cooke as Richard III, from a portrait by Thomas Sully, in the Pennsylvania Academy of Fine Arts, Philadelphia

ing the acclamation of the populace on his return from a successful campaign — as Richard, Duke of Gloster, the most valiant branch of the triumphant house of York." And at the end of the performance "reiterated plaudits expressed the fulness with which expectation had been realized, and taste and feeling gratified."

A BEWILDERED CATO

THE receipts were one thousand eight hundred and twenty dollars, and when, on November 23, he appeared as the popular Sir Pertinax MacSycophant, "notwithstanding a violent snow storm, which would have made a 'heartless void' of the theater on a common night, the receipts were fourteen hundred and twenty-four dollars." And so the heavy receipts continued to December 19, when Cooke attempted the rôle of Cato. But Cooke had drunk so heavily that he was incapable of reading a line to freshen his faulty memory. "The

165 Cooke as Sir Pertinax MacSycophant, from an engraving by D. Edwin after the drawing by C. R. Leslie, in the Fridenberg Collection, New York

house filled. An audience so numerous or more genteel, had never graced the walls of the New York theater. The money received was eighteen hundred and seventy-eight dollars. Soon, very soon, it was perceived that the Roman patriot; the god-like Cato — was not to be seen in Mr. Cooke. The mind of the actor was utterly bewildered — he hesitated, repeated, substituted speeches from other plays, or endeavoured to substitute incoherencies of his own . . . the audience which had assembled to admire, turned away in disgust." The receipts for the next performance dropped to four hundred and sixty-seven dollars — making a total, however, of twenty-one thousand, five hundred and seventy-eight dollars for the seventeen New York performances.

166 Cooke as Lear in Shakespeare's *King Lear*, from an engraving by D. Edwin after a portrait by C. R. Leslie, in the Fridenberg Collection, New York

167   Tombstone erected over the grave of Cooke, New York, 1821, (by Edmund Kean), from the water-color by Smith in the New York Historical Society

ON TOUR

On January 3, Cooke opened in Boston for a series of fourteen engagements which filled to overflowing the Federal Street Theater. It is interesting to recall that Stephen Price, the shrewd New York monopolist, was the one to receive the profits of the Boston engagement, for Cooke had been hired on a fixed salary of one hundred and twenty-five dollars a week, with a benefit in each city, and traveling expenses of twenty-five cents a mile. The receipts of

168   Cooke as Iago, from an engraving by G. Ward after the portrait by James Green, in the possession of the publishers

the sixteen nights in Philadelphia at the Chestnut were seventeen thousand three hundred and sixty dollars. Washington Irving's letter to Henry Brevoort on Cooke's interpretation of Macbeth in Philadelphia is one of our finest early critiques. "The old boy absolutely outdid himself . . . I place the performance of that evening among the highest pieces of acting I have ever witnessed . . . there is a truth and of course a simplicity in his performances that throws all rant, stage-trick, & stage-effect completely in the background. Were he to remain here a sufficient time for the public to perceive and dwell upon his merits, he would produce a new taste in acting. One of his best performances may be compared to a masterpiece of ancient statuary where you have the human figure destitute of idle ornament. . . . Such a production requires the eye of taste & knowledge to perceive its eminent excellences; . . ." Price arranged later for Cooke to go to Baltimore, where he played opposite Cooper.

EDMUND SIMPSON, 1784–1840

On May 29, 1812, the public was "respectfully informed" that Mr. Cooke had agreed to appear at the Park in the benefit performance of Edmund Simpson, the "acting-manager." Simpson had made his début at the Park in October of the year preceding Cooke's arrival from England. "Unless we are very much mistaken," wrote Thespis of the *Evening Post*, October 26, 1809, in praise of Simpson's performance, "this gentleman is to prove the greatest acquisition the American Theater has received for a long period." However pleasing Simpson may have proved in his rôles of dashing good fellow, the praise of Thespis must have smacked of hyperbole during the months of Cooke's triumphs. Yet with the perspective of the years, Simpson looms as a much more permanently influential figure than Cooke. Cooke's acting was cut short by his death in September, 1812, before it had the chance, hoped for by Irving, of influencing to any degree American histrionic tradition. Simpson, on the other hand, was intimately connected with the history of the Park for over thirty years, as actor, as joint-manager with Edmund Price, and, during the long periods when the latter was in Europe, as sole director. Dunlap had nothing but praise for Simpson: "And, although he has doubtless experienced the miseries of management, no man has borne the weight with better grace. . . . He has invariably yielded his rank to give an opportunity for the display of new talent; and played second fiddle ofttimes when he was entitled to play first. He cannot be charged with the besetting sin of actor-managers, the seeking to thrust himself into every character that gave a chance of gaining applause or enhancing consequence . . . he has had good sense to direct him as a manager, an actor, and a man."

169   Edmund Simpson, from an engraving by Henry Inman (1801–46), after the portrait by J. W. Jarvis (1780–1834), in the Fridenberg Collection, New York

WAR YEARS

BEFORE Cooke's death, war had again been declared between England and America, and during the three years that followed the fortunes of the Park sank to a low ebb. It is not known exactly when Cooper withdrew from his share in the managership, but, after Dunlap's final retirement, Price and Simpson were, to all intents and purposes, responsible for keeping alive interest in the peaceful drama of the stage. The cast on which they were forced to rely was mediocre in comparison with that of the days of Hodgkinson and Jefferson. Harwood had been dead for a number of years. Twaits and Mrs. Twaits were away. The one compensation was Thomas Hilson, a London actor, who had made his American début on April 8, 1811. He remained with Price and Simpson steadily until 1818, playing one of his successful rôles more than two hundred nights, and becoming a great favorite with the audiences. Approximating Twaits' effectiveness in low comedy, he was at the same time, what Twaits so longed to be, a first-rate tragedian. Cooper considered his Iago the best on our stage. His unusual versatility has been commented on again and again — his parts ranging from Falstaff, to Richard III, to Sir Peter Teazle,

170   Thomas Hilson, 1784–1834, as Tyke, from the engraving by A. B. Durand (1796–1886), after the portrait by John Neagle (1796–1865), in the Fridenberg Collection, New York

to Touchstone. His fine baritone voice enabled him to assume an unrivaled leadership in buffo characters in opera. During his years, 1812–15, the Park often reflected phases of the great military and naval drama that was being staged along the Canadian border and on the Atlantic. The brilliant naval victories over British frigates were reënacted in miniature on the stages of the Park, the Chestnut, and the Federal Street. The theaters were brilliantly illuminated to receive visits from General Harrison or Commodore Chauncey or Perry. But the normal contacts and channels of communication with London theaters were closed.

THEATRE.

" Let the Rallying Word be Liberty or Death."
BUNKER HILL.
FIFTH OF JULY

In commemoration of the Declaration of the Independence of the United States of America, the inside of the Theatre will be ILLUMINATED, and a grand transparent painting exhibited in allusion to the day. Description, on the right hand is Liberty, represented by an Allegorical Female Figure, clad in robes of Yellow, beneath her feet a Globe—in one hand she holds the Standard of the United States, and is supposed to be in the act of planting it upon that part designated America. In the other hand an Olive Branch. The Standard forms the outer drapery. Beneath is likewise seen a White Lilly, the most approved symbol of purity and sincerity. On the left are three boys ; one of whom is holding and pointing to a book, in the open leaf of which is seen written, DECLARATION OF INDEPENDENCE, JULY 4, 1776. Hovering over and covering a Globe.

The entertainments of the evening will commence with,
THE GLORY OF COLUMBIA,
'HER YEOMANRY :
Or, WHAT WE HAVE DONE, WE CAN DO

Gen. Washington,   Mr. Green.
Andre,   Simpson
Williams,   Hilson
Paulding,   Darley
Van Wert,   Jones

The three glorious columbian Yeomen, whose incorruptible honesty preserved West-Point and the American Army.
Honora,   Darley

171   Patriotic celebration at the Park, from the New York *Evening Post*, July 3, 1813

THEATRE.

The public is respectfully informed that the Theatre will be ILLUMINATED THIS EVENING in commemoration of the late
GLORIOUS AND BRILLIANT VICTORY
OBTAINED BY THE
U. STATES FRIGATE CONSTITUTION.

On WEDNESDAY EVENING, February 24th, Will be performed (for the first time in America) the Historical Drama of,
THE RENEGADE,
By J. Reynolds, Esq author of Exiles, Free Nights, &c. as now performing in London with great applause.

Between the Play and Farce a Patriotic Sketch in one act, called America, Commerce and Freedom. View of the sea, the Genius of America descends in a Car, the Temple of Naval Glory rises out of the ocean. A Letter Dance by the Infant Vestris, Miss Jones and Mast. Whale ; in which the names of Hull, Jones, Decatur, and Bainbridge will be displayed. A naval column will rise from the Stage in honor of Hull, Jones, Decatur and Bainbridge, surmounted by a full length portrait of COMMODORE BAINBRIDGE. The whole exhibition to conclude with a painting in transparency, descriptive of the
BLOWING UP OF THE BRITISH FRIGATE JAVA,
On the 31st December, 1812.

In course of the sketch the following songs will be sung, America, Commerce & Freedom, by Mr. Darley—Yankee Chronology, by Mr. Yates : Yankee Frolicks by Mr. M'Parland.
To which will be added,
HOW TO DIE FOR LOVE.
The Box office will be opened on Friday morn-

172   Celebration at the Park of a Naval Victory, from the New York *Evening Post*, Feb. 23, 1813

173   Joseph George Holman, 1764–1817, as Cyrus, from an engraving by Audinet after a painting by De Wilde, in the Fridenberg Collection, New York

BEGINNINGS OF COMPETITION IN NEW YORK

In spite of the war New York city continued to expand in area and population. The market seemed to give evidence of being able to support another theater. Even before the days of Price and Simpson there had been occasional rivals disputing the Park's monopoly. But they had produced no first-rate actors and had quickly died. In the first year of the war a more serious competitor entered the field. John Dwyer, a versatile comedian, and a partner named M'Kenzie, who had had a turbulent career in Philadelphia, took over the Broadway Circus, the chief attraction of which seems to have been a bar at the end of the foyer, where drinks were sold during intermissions. The New Olympic, as it was now called, closed at the end of the season, but reopened the following year under new managers, Twaits, Charles Gilfert, ex-leader of the Park orchestra, and John J. Holland, who in 1807 had remodeled the Park. The name of the company was the Commonwealth, or, as they were sometimes called, The Anthony Street Company. The most prominent actors of this new rival company were the Holmans, father and daughter, who in spite of the war had come to America in the fall of 1812. They had both played the preceding season at the Park and at the Chestnut, where their performances had been highly praised. The father, an Oxford man, was one of the best known figures on the London stage, "maintaining a powerful rivalship with Kemble." "Mr. Holman's Lord Townley," wrote Dunlap, "and the Lady Townley of Miss Holman have been considered among the perfections of the art histrionic." Mrs. Burke, later Mrs. Jefferson, and mother of Joseph Jefferson, III, divided with Miss Holman the leading feminine rôles, and was immensely popular. Thomas Burke was also with the Commonwealth this first season, as was Mrs. Twaits, who, however, died shortly after the opening. On January 10, 1814, the Commonwealth closed but reopened in April with Holland and Twaits as managers. In August the latter died, and after September there is no further mention of the Anthony Street players. Price and Simpson hired the best of the rival actors, and the monopoly of the Park was again established for a number of years.

174   Joseph George Holman, from an engraving in the Fridenberg Collection, New York

175   Mrs. Charles Gilfert (Miss Holman), from an engraving by S. Hollyer, courtesy of the Columbia University Press, New York

ON THE ROAD TO PROSPERITY

As soon as the war was over in 1815, Stephen Price sailed
for London to recruit new strength for the decrepit Park.
The number and quality of the players whom he secured
are eloquent testimonial to his ability and to his taste.
The arrival in New York of Mr. and Mrs. John Barnes on
the 17th of April, 1816, may be considered as marking the
opening of the final period of the first Park. During the
next five seasons it improved steadily in acting and in gate
receipts, a foreshadowing, in a sense, of the great brilliance
of the Second Park. Mrs. Barnes was from the Theater
Royal, Drury Lane, and with her came her sister, Mrs.
Baldwin, from the Theater Royal, Newcastle. Both opened
in *Romeo and Juliet*, the former as the heroine, the later
as the nurse. "On the whole," wrote the enthusiastic critic
of the *Post* after enumerating her excellencies in the various scenes, "we consider Mrs. Barnes decidedly the best
Juliet on the American stage, and offer our congratulations
to her with perfect sincerity." And of Mr. and Mrs.
Baldwin the same critic wrote, "we do not doubt their
soon becoming established favorites with the New York

176 Mrs. John Barnes, from an engraving by A. B. Durand
after the portrait by John Neagle, in the Fridenberg Collection

audience. . . ." "With the coming of Mr. and Mrs. Barnes," estimates Professor Odell, "the New York
company was at last, and perhaps for the first time since 1793, the best on the continent. . . ." Professor
Quinn, on the other hand, after analyzing the evidence of various conflicting contemporary critics, is
convinced that this supremacy did not pass from Philadelphia to New York until about 1825.

FOUNDER OF A DYNASTY

THE year 1818 was made memorable by the American début of the first bearer of the name of Wallack to
appear in this country. James William Wallack came of theatrical stock, both his father and his mother
being London actors, and as a youth he saw Mrs. Siddons, Edmund Kean, John Philip Kemble, George
Frederick Cooke, and other great players. Small wonder that he chose the theater in preference to the
navy, for which his parents had intended him. At about the age of twelve he was taking juvenile parts at
the Drury Lane Theater in London. When Wallack first appeared at the Park Theater he was a remarkably
handsome young
man, highly gifted
in both comedy
and tragedy, and
he aroused the
greatest expecta-
tions in the pub-
lic. Nor was
the public dis-
appointed during
his subsequent
career of forty-
one years. For a
time he alter-
nated between
England and the
United States,
but about 1851
New York be-
came his perma-
nent home.

177   James W. Wallack, 1795–1864, as Jacques in *As You
Like It*, from an engraving in the Albert Davis Collection, Brooklyn

178 Wallack as Rolla in Kotzebue's *Pizarro*, from an
announcement in the New York *Evening Post*, February 20, 1820

CHAPTER IV

FROM KEAN TO KEMBLE

WHEN the War of 1812 was over, a new period of national development began. The so-called "Era of Good Feeling," under the presidency of James Monroe, and the years immediately following saw, among other changes, a marked growth in the cities along the Atlantic seaboard. Boston, New York, and Philadelphia were rapidly expanding in size and prosperity. Especially were New York and Philadelphia pushing steadily ahead, and a keen rivalry had risen between them; but it was not long before New York took the lead over its southern competitor and gained the distinction of being the metropolis of the United States. By 1825 it contained one hundred and sixty-two thousand inhabitants, an increase of forty thousand in five years. To house this unprecedented addition to the citizenry over three thousand new buildings were in process of construction, and in the upper wards whole blocks of fine brick residences now stood where a few years before there had been nothing but marshes or a few straggling huts. In 1823 the city took the forward step of installing gas as a means of street lighting, in this matter following by one year Boston's adoption of the system and anticipating conservative Philadelphia by almost a decade and a half. At about this time New York contained twelve banks, while applications were being made to the Legislature for charters for twenty-seven others, and in the early months of 1825 five hundred new business firms were said to have been established in the city. Such prosperity was made possible first of all by New York's unmatched harbor, into which thirteen hundred vessels sailed annually, bringing cargoes from every corner of the world. In one year ten million dollars in duties was collected at the custom house, a sum exceeding by eighty thousand dollars the combined receipts at the ports of Boston, Philadelphia, Baltimore, Norfolk, and Savannah. The commercial activity of the city was further increased by the inpouring of agricultural produce from the rich country districts to the west and north, and when in 1825 a line of cannon extending from Buffalo to Manhattan Island boomed across the state the news of the opening of the Erie Canal even the Great Lakes and the Ohio valley became a part of New York City's hinterland. In an effort to recover its lost leadership the business men of the Quaker City urged the swift completion of the Pennsylvania system of canals reaching from Philadelphia to Pittsburgh, but these were finished much later than the Erie and never successfully competed with that great waterway.

The commercial status had its inevitable effect on the relative positions of the theaters of the two rival towns. By 1825 Philadelphia was compelled to surrender the theatrical leadership which it had held since the close of the Revolution, and the supremacy passed to New York where it has remained to this day. Not only did the northern city possess a rapidly increasing and prosperous population from whom a large body of playgoers would naturally be drawn, but it was also visited by merchants from every foreign country as well as from every part of the United States, and such visitors, as the Broadway managers of to-day well know, were among the most reliable patrons of the theater. Tangible evidence of the solid position that the stage had now attained in New York is seen in the erection of the Bowery Theater in 1826, the first playhouse to offer a serious and continued challenge to the monopoly long enjoyed by the Park. The placing of this immense theater in a neighborhood so far removed from the traditional center of the town is merely a measure of the rapid expansion the city was undergoing. As though to confirm the assumption of leadership by New York, at the same time that the Bowery was successfully launched, competition between two theaters in Philadelphia resulted in disaster for both. At Boston, likewise, when a second theater was opened in 1827, it was found after a short period of intense rivalry that a double failure could be avoided only by closing one of the houses.

During the years now under review the New York managers, and after them the other important managers of the country, brought to their theaters a succession of distinguished visitors from the English stage. This experiment had first been tried with George Frederick Cooke in 1810 and had proved so successful financially that after the War of 1812 it was undertaken on a much more extensive scale. Edmund Kean, Charles Mathews, William Charles Macready, and Charles Kean were brought over within a brief term of years for engagements of varying lengths. The starring system, which, as we have seen, came into being about 1800, had by this time taken so firm a hold on the fancy of the playgoers that the announcement of a foreign celebrity in one of his favorite rôles supported by the local company was certain to bring flourishing business to the box office. Some of the more thoughtful friends of the theater deplored the system, inasmuch as it inevitably reduced the esteem in which the hard working resident actors were held and sometimes served as an excuse for curtailing their salaries, while it bred in them discontent and indifference, and in the audience a taste for mere novelty and sensational histrionism. In passing, it is interesting to observe that the guest players from England seem to have been undeterred by the stream of comment that at this time was flowing from the British press in condemnation of our artistic achievements, our social conduct, our institutions, our ethics — in a word, of what our English cousins called our unmitigated barbarism. Perhaps they considered that American money was acceptable whatever was to be said of American manners, or perhaps they recognized that the American stage was worthy of their best efforts. Of more significance for the future of the American theater than the appearance of such visitors was the rise, during these years, of a group of native actors who later achieved high distinction. The emergence of James H. Hackett, John Gibbs Gilbert, James E. Murdoch, and above all of Edwin Forrest, our first great native star, was a happy omen. As yet our stage had depended overwhelmingly on England for new recruits, but before the art of the drama could be considered in any genuine sense an American institution it was essential that we begin to find our resources within ourselves. By the end of the first quarter of the nineteenth century the theater in the United States was giving evidence that it was rapidly coming of age.

179   Edmund Kean, 1787–1833, in the rôle of Richard III, from
      an engraving in the New York Public Library

180   Kean in the rôle of Gloster, from an engraving by R. Cooper after a
      painting by G. Clint, in the New York Public Library

"BEYOND MATERIAL BARRIERS"

THE appearance of Edmund Kean at Drury Lane in 1814 brought to an end the long period of supremacy which John Philip Kemble had for so many years enjoyed in the tragic rôles of the English theater. Years before, when, on his return from a sea-roving escapade, Kean had begun to be coached for Shakespearean rôles under a professional actress, he had asserted his own individuality of interpretation, his "unstudied impulses of nature," which had contrasted so sharply with the heavy declamation and the formal attitudes of Kemble. His Drury Lane début as Shylock roused the audience to a high pitch of emotional enthusiasm. On a later appearance, as Sir Giles Overreach, so great was the intensity and sincerity of his acting that the entire pit rose to its feet to acclaim him, while the other actors and actresses remained spellbound watching him. "His countenance was strikingly interesting and unusually mobile," wrote a contemporary critic. "His fine eyes scintillated even the slightest shades of emotion and thought. His voice, though weak and harsh in the upper register, possessed in its lower range tones of penetrating and resistless power, and a thrilling sweetness like the witchery of the finest music. Above all, in the grander moments of his passion, his intellect and soul seemed to rise beyond material barriers and to glorify physical defects [his small stature] with their own greatness." On November 19, 1820, this great English star made his début at the Anthony Street Theater, which, since the burning of the Park, was the only available New York theater worthy of him. His first rôle of Richard III was followed by Othello, Shylock, Hamlet and Lear. It is estimated that the receipts during his engagement averaged above one thousand dollars a night.

181   Kean in the rôle of Shylock, from an engraving by C. Goodman after the drawing by John Neagle, in the Davis Collection

KEAN AT BOSTON

GREAT as was the enthusiasm in New York, that in Boston was even greater. Long before Kean arrived, the tickets had been sold at auction and the unprecedented profits given by the managers, Snelling Powell and Dickson, to the charitable institutions of the city. "The Kean fever," wrote William W. Clapp, in his *Record of the Boston Stage*, "broke out and raged without cessation. His acting was the all engrossing subject of fashionable discussion, and Kean himself became the lion of the day." Over three thousand, three hundred dollars was taken in during his nine nights. He was immediately reëngaged for six nights. Kean's self-confidence knew no bounds. It was fed still further by his triumphs during his tour of southern theatrical centers. Although it was nearly summer, Kean desired to return for an engagement at Boston. Powell and Dickson remonstrated, warning of the dangers of the dull season. Kean's confidence recognized no seasons. Whatever Boston customs might have been in the past, they could be changed. For two nights the audience was fair. On the third night Kean, gazing at the sprinkling of people in the pit and boxes, refused to appear and left the theater in high dudgeon. A substitute was found for the star, and the play given, but the disappointment of the audience found voice in scathing denunciations in the Boston papers of the recalcitrant actor. The phobia against Kean spread rapidly to New York. In reply to protests the actor issued a patronizing, sarcastic note, which only angered still further the New York theatergoers. Since further appearances were judged unwise, Kean sailed for England. He did not return for four years. Contrite now from disappointments and misfortunes at home, he approached with the more timid step of an apologist. "I visit this country now," he wrote in a communication to a New York newspaper, "under different feelings and auspices . . . the spark of ambition is extinct, and I merely ask a shelter in which to close my professional and mortal career. I give the weapon into the hands of my enemies; if they are brave they will not turn it against the defenceless." But the unpleasant memories in the minds of the audiences of Boston and New York still persisted. In each place there was a riot, and the voice of the actor was drowned. The discouraged actor returned to England where his reputation and popularity were equally tarnished.

BOSTON THEATRE.

☞The Managers have the pleasure of announcing the engagement of

MR. KEAN,

From the Theatre Royal, Drury Lane, London,

FOR EIGHT NIGHTS.

☞Aware of the public anxiety to witness the performances of this celebrated Tragedian, and wishing, as far as possible, to accomodate ALL, the Managers respectfully announce, that not more than ONE Box can be taken by any One Person. As the Boxes will contain from eight to twenty each, they presume that this arrangment will meet general approbation, and at the same time prevent that unfair monopoly, which has heretofore been practised by certain individuals, who purchase tickets only for the purpose of selling them again at an advanced price. It rests with the frequenters of the Theatre to remedy this evil, by positively refusing to purchase a Ticket of any one except at the regular price.

••••••••••••••

ON MONDAY EVENING, FEBRUARY 13,

WILL BE PERFORMED,

Shakspere's admired Tragedy, in five acts, called

RICHARD THE THIRD.

RICHARD, • • • • • • • • • • MR. KEAN

To conclude with other Entertainments.
(Particulars in small bills.)

On Tuesday evening, Mr. KEAN will appear in the character of Othello.

☞The Nights of Performance, during Mr. KEAN's engagement, will be Monday, Tuesday, Thursday and Friday.

☞Places for Monday, Tuesday, (or both) may be taken on Saturday, and for Thursday, Friday, (or both) on Wednesday of each week.

182 Engagement of Kean for Eight Nights in Boston, from an announcement in *The Columbian Centinel*, Boston, Feb. 10, 1821

BOSTON THEATRE.

MR. KEAN'S BENEFIT

☞The Managers are highly gratified to find that the plan proposed by them, and approbated by the Selectmen, of offering the choice of Boxes by Auction and giving the proceeds to Charitable Institutions, meets the approbation of the public generally. They therefore propose to continue it during MR. KEAN's engagement.

THIS DAY, (Saturday)

Mr HAYWARD will offer for sale by Auction, on the floor of Merchants' Hall, the whole of the Lower Boxes and seventeen Boxes in the Second Row. The Tickets will be sold at $1 each; and whatever premium may be given for the choice of Boxes will be appropriated to various Charitable Institutions. The proceeds of *this* day's sale will be given to the Boston Dispensary.

••••••••••••••

ON MONDAY EVENING, FEBRUARY 26,

WILL BE PERFORMED,

Shakspere's admired Tragedy, in five acts, called

KING LEAR

AND HIS THREE DAUGHTERS.

KING LEAR, • • • • MR. KEAN

To which will be added, the favorite Farce, called

THE WEATHERCOCK.

TAKE NOTICE.

The Box Office will be open this day at 12 o'clock, for the sale of Green Box, Pit, and Gallery Tickets. Gentlemen who may purchase Box Tickets at auction, can receive the same at the Box Office at 5 o'clock, P. M

183 Boxes sold at Auction for Kean's Benefit, from *The Columbian Centinel*, Boston, Feb. 24, 1821

184   Henry Wallack, from a photograph
        in the Davis Collection

HENRY WALLACK, 1791–1870

WHILE Kean was on his first Southern tour, Henry Wallack, an older brother of James W. (see No. 177), made his New York début at the Anthony Street Theater, on May 9, 1821. In England he had appeared at the York and the Hull theaters without having approximated, however, the reputation of his younger brother. In America he was never a "star," but his acting was so uniformly good that Ireland felt justified in classing him as one of the very best stock actors of the time. Possessing unusual versatility, he was equally at home in tragedy, comedy, melodrama, opera, farce, and pantomime. He ranged without effort from Hamlet and Richard to Mercutio and Benedick, from Hotspur to Malvolio, from Henry VIII to Falconbridge, and "frequently," added Ireland, "with an ability entirely eclipsing the more pretending efforts of self-exalted stars." He was even more influential as a manager. On the death of Barriere (see p. 85), Wallack took over the lease of the Chatham Garden, which he opened on March 26, 1826, and ran with moderate success until it was overshadowed by the Lafayette. At the Chatham, at the Lafayette, and later at the Bowery, Wallack was a great favorite with the audiences. From 1837 to 1839 he was stage manager of the National Theater. (See No. 261.) In 1843 he was lessee of Covent Garden, London, but failed to make a success. After 1847 his activities were confined to the Old Broadway (see No. 500), where he played the first line of old men, in which, however, he never attained his former popularity. His last appearance was at the National Theater on October 18, 1858.

185   Interior of the Park, showing a performance
by Charles Mathews, from a water-color by
John Searle in the New York Historical Society

186   Exterior of the New Park Theater, from an engraving in the New York Historical Society

THE NEW PARK

IN the autumn following Henry Wallack's début, the new Park Theater, standing on the site where its predecessor had burned the year before, opened its seven doors to the public on September 1, 1821. The entrances faced Park Row, along which the façade extended for eighty feet. The building, calculated to hold twenty-five hundred people, had a depth of one hundred and sixty-five feet to Theater Alley. Five of the seven arched doorways, reached by a low flight of steps, opened into a long vestibule communicating with the first row of boxes. The other doors, one on each side of the steps, gave access to the pit and to the gallery, which was used primarily for the accommodation of negroes. Over all of the doorways except the central one were great arched windows, preserving the classic design of the house. The unoccupied space over the central door was later converted into a niche, in which was placed a statue of Shakespeare. At the opening, however, the patron bard was slighted, for the play offered was Mrs. Inchbald's comedy, *Wives as They Were, and Maids as They Are*. Perhaps the main event of the evening, to the mind of the audience, was the reading of the prize poem, or poetical address, for which the management had offered as reward the freedom of the theater to a resident or a gold medal to a non-resident. The program took place in an interior "neatly and conveniently" fitted up, and lighted by patent oil lamps hung in three chandeliers of thirty-five lights each.

187   Junius Brutus Booth, 1796–1852, from a daguerreotype
in the Madigan Collection, New York

188   Booth in the rôle of Sir Giles Overreach, from a print
in the Madigan Collection, New York

"THE VERY MAN"

On October 5, 1821, there appeared on the stage of the new building one of the greatest tragedians of the century, and the founder of a family that for many decades was prominent on the American stage. Having made his début at Covent Garden in 1815, Junius Brutus Booth in 1817 had played Iago to Edmund Kean's Othello at Drury Lane, and had come to be recognized as Kean's greatest rival. In 1821 on a trip to the Island of Madeira he had suddenly decided to sail to Norfolk, Virginia, and had opened at the Richmond Theater in the July preceding his appearance at the Park. His New York début as Richard was followed by Othello, Brutus, Hamlet, and Lear. He had been accused of being merely an imitator of Kean; but the individuality of his performances became more marked. "Charles Kemble and Macready," wrote Ireland, "with their studied attitudes and enunciation, were, in comparison but as plodding, wire-drawing critics. Booth was the very individual he represented; he imagined himself the very man, and the exquisite modulations of his voice, the wonderful mobility of his countenance, and the inspiration of his transcendent genius, thoroughly identified him with the most diverse characters. . . . In Richard, Shylock, Iago, Lear . . . he was allowed, by universal suffrage, to have been unrivaled here for near a quarter of a century." And on the other hand he delighted on occasion to play low comedy, in which he could invariably convulse the house with laughter. Or again, as when he was manager of the Adelphi Theater in Baltimore, and Kean appeared, he played the insignificant rôle of the "Second Actor" in *Hamlet*, and was able to produce a telling effect from his six lines. He was associated with many theaters as actor and stage manager: at the Chatham Garden under Henry Wallack, at the New Orleans theater under Caldwell, and at the Tremont when Pelby left Boston. He was an invariable favorite, drawing huge crowds at the Bowery, despite his occasional outbursts of violent temper and his frequent failures to appear. After his final New York appearance in 1843, he made an extensive tour of the country, going as far as California and then returning to New Orleans. He died in 1852 on a Mississippi steamboat which was headed for Cincinnati.

CHATHAM THEATRE

SOLE PROPRIETOR AND LESSEE........MR. F. S. CHANFRAU
Acting Manager.................... Mr. Hield

Boxes...........25 Cents. | Pit.... ...12½ Cents.
Private Boxes....................$3

Alteration of Time—In future
The Doors will open at 7—Performance commence at 7½ precisely
☞ Checks not Transferable. ☜
☞ All Free Admissions suspended, with the exception of the Press.

Third Week of the New Management.

Talent   Combined !

THE

Two Great Tragedians On the same night.

The Manager is pleased to announce to the Public that he has secured the services
for this night only of the DISTINGUISHED TRAGEDIAN

MR. BOOTH,

Who being en route for Boston, to fulfil an Engagement, has been prevailed upon to
remain in the City for this night, and appear in conjunction with MR.

A. A. ADDAMS

Mr. ADDAMS....as....William Tell
Mr. BOOTH..as..Sir Giles Overreach

189   Booth at the Chatham Theater, New York, from a
playbill in the Davis Collection

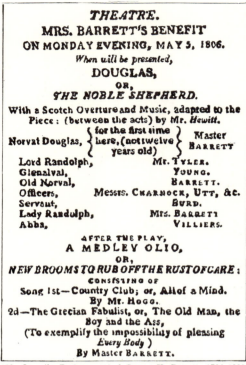

190 Juvenile Performance of George H. Barrett, 1794–1860,
     from an announcement in the New York *Evening Post*, May 3,
     1806

191   George H. Barrett, from a sketch by August Toedteberg, in the
       Harvard Theater Collection

"GENTLEMAN GEORGE"

GEORGE H. BARRETT, the son of Giles Barrett (see No. 121), was on the stage from his earliest childhood.
Born on June 9, 1794, at Exeter, England, he appeared four years later at the Park as one of the children in
Dunlap's adaptation of Kotzebue's *The Stranger*. On the return of his parents to Boston the following year,

he made his début on the stage of the Federal Street. His first
appearance after reaching manhood was at the Park on March 5,
1822, in *The West Indian*. His great skill in the lighter rôles of
genteel comedy soon elevated him to a position of importance
in that field of acting. Mrs. Ann Henry, who in 1825 became
Mrs. Barrett, was one of the most beautiful actresses of the period,
praised by Fanny Kemble as "a faultless piece of mortality in
outward loveliness." She was in addition an excellent actress in
graceful and refined comedy and the less heavy tragic rôles.
Before their unhappy divorce the Barretts were for many years
extremely popular both socially and professionally. Under
Gilfert's managership Barrett was stage manager at the Bowery
in 1828. In 1847 he was first acting-manager of the Broadway,
and at other times manager of the Boston and New Orleans
theaters. After fifty-seven years of active connection with the
stage, Barrett made his formal farewell in 1855. "As years increased," wrote Ireland, "health declined, and fortune frowned;
and, in impoverished circumstances, Mr. G. Barrett, once the
center of all admiration, the 'Gentleman George' of the Union,
and 'the best fellow in the world,' was forced to eke out a scanty
subsistence by preparing aspirants for a profession, from which,
with prudence, and under favorable circumstances, he should
have acquired a fortune."

THEATRE.

MANAGERS—LUDLOW & SMITH
Leader of the Orchestra—Mr. Mueller.
☞Public attention is invited to the cast of the
pieces this evening, including the names of
Mr BARRETT, (his last night,)
Mr CONNER,
Mrs MAYNARD,
Mr LUDLOW,
Mr SOL SMITH,
Mr FARREN,
Mr MAYNARD,
Mr SANKEY,
Mrs RUSSELL, &c. &c.
SATURDAY, September 5
Holcroft's admirable comedy of the
ROAD TO RUIN.

Goldfinch,	Mr Barrett
Harry Dornton,	Mr Conner
Old Dornton,	Mr Farren
Mr Silkey,	Mr Sankey
Sophia,	Mrs Farren
Widow Warren,	Mrs Russell
A Dissertation on Faults, by	Mr Ludlow
Comic Medley, by	Mr Sol Smith

To conclude with the
MARRIED RAKE.

Mr Flighty,	Mr Maynard
Mrs Trictrac,	Mrs Maynard
Susan Twist,	Mrs Farren

In rehearsal the YOUTHFUL DAYS OF HAR-
RISON, & PAUL JONES.

192   Barrett in St. Louis, from an announcement in the
      Daily Missouri Republican, September 5, 1840

193 Charles Mathews, 1776–1835, from an engraving by Woolnoth after a painting by Wageman, in the Goodspeed Collection, Boston

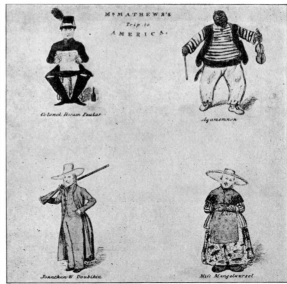

194 Mathews in various character skits, from *Mathews at Home; or Travels in Air, on Earth, and on Water*, New York, 1822

"CHAMPAGNEY AIRINESS"

ON November 7, 1822, Charles Mathews, who nineteen years before had made his début at the Haymarket, London, and who had remained ever since one of the most popular of English mimics and comedians, appeared for the first time on the stage of the Park. Previous to his New York appearance he had been for a short time at Baltimore, where he had opened on September 23. His stage method and entertainment, with his imitations of Kean and Kemble and other contemporary stars, were unfamiliar to American theatergoers, but he gradually won their unqualified enthusiasm; for his sense of language, dialect, and idiosyncrasy was inimitable. One of his most popular entertainments, which was repeated many times with unfailing success, was entitled *Mathews at Home*, a combination of songs, stories, anecdotes, mimicry, and ventriloquism. Another favorite monologue was called *La Diligence*, in which he impersonated seven French and English characters thrown together in a stage coach. His first stay in America, though regrettably short, was lucrative to him and a source of great amusement to the theatergoers at the Park. He was received everywhere, and socially lionized. Shortly before Mathews' second visit in 1833, there were rumors that he had ridiculed America in a playlet. To counteract the damaging effect of this gossip, which had come to his ears, Mathews read extracts from what he had written, and by the obvious sincerity of his denial, rewon for a time the enormous popularity

195 Mathews in other character sketches, from a lithograph by A. Ducote after a drawing by Auguste Hervieu, in the Fridenberg Collection, New York

which he had formerly enjoyed. But it gradually became apparent that he was suffering from nervous excitability, which dimmed the brilliance of his comedy. His last appearance at the Park was on February 11, 1835. Shortly afterward he returned to England. Thomas Babington Macaulay said of him: "Mathews was certainly the greatest actor that I ever saw. . . . I laughed my sides sore when I saw him." "He was," wrote E. A. Sothern, an old friend of Mathews, "undoubtedly, the founder of the present school of light comedy. His force consisted in his excessive — well, I may call it his champagney airiness." He was the father of Charles Mathews, Jr. (See No. 276.)

196   The New Chestnut Street Theater 1822–56, from an engraving
in the New York Public Library

THE NEW CHESTNUT STREET THEATER

In December a new theater, with an old name, was opened in Philadelphia. After the burning of the Chestnut Theater, April 2, 1820, Warren and Wood leased the theater in Walnut Street which had been built in 1809 (see No. 139). Though the managers incurred great expense in redecorating and insuring the house, it failed of success. After two unprofitable seasons, yielding to a growing popular demand, they began plans for the rebuilding of the Chestnut Street. The new theater opened on December 2, 1822, with the old Sheridan favorite, *The School for Scandal*, in the cast of which appeared Warren, Wood, Henry Wallack, and Jo Jefferson, I. To expedite entrance and exit the doors leading to the boxes had been placed on a different side from those leading to the pit, while there was still a third entrance to the gallery. This unfamiliar differentiation so aroused the indignation of certain patriotic frequenters of the pit that they issued inflammatory handbills, one of which concluded with the ringing exhortation, "The national spirit of America has triumphed over the pride of European armies; shall that spirit slumber under the degradation of European distinctions?" The management had no alternative. At the cost of alterations it was forced to provide a common entrance for the one and indivisible public. After much discussion the motto chosen for the new house was, "To raise the genius and to mend the heart." A feature of the opening, already noted at the first night of the new Park, and one which was fast becoming a national institution, was the reading of the "favored" poem. For the next three years the theater enjoyed great success and the visits of many notable stars.

ACTOR AND MANAGER

Francis Courtney Wemyss (see p. 162), for many years one of the outstanding personalities in the American theater, was first brought to America in 1822 to open at the new Chestnut Street Theater. Born in London in 1797, Wemyss had begun as an amateur, made some reputation as an agreeable drawing-room comedian, and had finally appeared at the London Adelphi in 1820. Though he always considered himself — as is evident from his pleasing autobiographical sketch, *Twenty-six Years of the Life of an Actor and Manager* — a first rate artist, his chief contribution was as manager. Following the withdrawal of Wood from the Chestnut (see p. 88), Wemyss had been sent by Warren to recruit new strength in London. But Warren, in spite of the new actors, failed to keep the enterprise going; and the historic old theater was turned over on December 25, 1828, to Wemyss and Lewis Pratt. But, as Wood remarked in his *Personal Recollections*, bankruptcy and failure were the only permanent elements left in the theater. On the 27th of the following May Pratt and Wemyss closed the Chestnut, and ended their management. Pratt made application for a new lease, and entered the managerial field alone. Wemyss tried to leave Philadelphia, but there were openings neither in Boston nor New York. Pratt's management went from bad to worse. Wemyss, to the great annoyance of the managers, published the following notice: "Starved Out! The unprecedented depression of Theatricals in the city of Philadelphia, having deprived the managers of the different theaters of the means of paying their actors, or fulfilling their contracts, the profession no longer affords the means of procuring the humble fare of bread and cheese for the support of a family." — with which preface he begged his old friends to support a ticket lottery which he was opening.

197   Francis C. Wemyss, 1797–1859, as Rolando, from an engraving, 1826, by J. B. Longacre after a portrait by John Neagle, in the Fridenberg Collection

198 Henry Placide, 1799–1870, as Polonius, from an engraving in the Davis Collection

"A GENUINE COMEDIAN"

HENRY, the son of Alexander Placide, the leader of the troupe of gymnasts and rope-walkers which Thomas Wignell had brought to Philadelphia in 1803 and which had later moved to Charleston (see page 47), had made his first appearance in New York at the Anthony Street Theater in 1814 at the age of fourteen. He attracted little attention, however, until his mature début at the Park in 1823 as Zekiel Homespun. He became an im-

199 Thomas Placide, 1808–77, from a photograph in the Davis Collection

mediate favorite with the audience, a position which he held during more than twenty years of service at the Park. At first he was called on to play minor comic rôles, while the more conspicuous parts were given to Thomas Hilson (see No. 170) and to John Barnes (see p. 73). It soon became obvious, however, that he was not inferior even to these veteran stars, and he became an equal in the comic trio, which, according to Ireland, "has never been equaled in a stock company at any other period in the history of the New York Stage." "Critically analyzing the smallest part intrusted to his care, and throwing around it a finish, an elegance, and a completeness rarely attempted by a less careful and discriminating actor," he soon began to outshine his elders. In a short time he was accorded undisputed choice of whatever rôles he preferred. "From clowns of the broadest Yorkshire dialect," continued Ireland, "to the most mincing Cockney cit, in the garrulous Frenchman and the high-bred English gentleman, the simplest rustic, or the keenest London footman, in the clumsy hobblede-hoy, or the pathetic childishness of extreme old age, he was equally at home and equally superior. . . . In fact, no other actor has ever so completely exemplified our idea of what a genuine comedian ought to be." Thomas Placide, a brother, having been brought from the New Orleans Theater, made his New York début in 1826 at the Chatham. He gradually gained a reputation as an excellent low comedian, and played throughout the country without ever approximating, however, the genius of Henry.

200 Tom and Henry Placide as the Twin Dromios in *A Comedy of Errors*, from an engraving in the Harvard Theater Collection

201 Mary Ann Duff, 1794–1857, in the rôle of Ophelia, from the portrait by John Neagle, in the possession of The Players' Club, New York

"UNIFORMITY OF EXCELLENCE"

MARY ANN DUFF, who with her husband had made her American début in Boston in 1810, appeared on September 5, 1823, at the Park. During the thirteen intervening years her progress as an artist had been extraordinary. Until 1817 her "tame and feeble" style had attracted little attention, and she had been generally considered subordinate to her husband. In that year, however, there had been a remarkable change. She had risen rapidly in the favor of the Boston public, and when she had gone to the Chestnut Street, Philadelphia audiences had been similarly enthusiastic over the sudden brilliance of her performances. By the time of her arrival at the Park she had come to be regarded as the undisputed American queen of tragedy. Her successes in New York at the Park, at the Chatham, and at the Bowery were overwhelming. "Mrs. Duff has *one* great characteristic . . ." wrote a critic in the *New York Mirror* of May 5, 1827, "*uniformity of excellence.* . . . The unity of her conception, the *oneness* is remarkable. No temptation can induce her to break it. . . . She seems to have a separate existence during the continuance of the play, and to have lost all knowledge, and even all power of seeing the realities around her. . . . Mrs. Duff pours out one unceasing blaze during the whole time that she occupies the stage. . . ." Ireland, in a long enumeration of excellencies, praised especially her voice, "which, for plaintive tenderness and thrilling expression, we have never known equaled." The arrival of the illustrious Fanny Kemble in 1832 diverted public attention from Mrs. Duff, who for a number of years was forced to play minor rôles and even suffered financial difficulties. She went on tour and played for a number of years in the leading theatrical centers of the country. Her daughter, Mary Duff, was for years a popular star in the southern and western theaters.

THEATRE--A CARD.

MISS MARY DUFF respectfully informs her friends and the public that her Benefit will take place on Tuesday evening, November 11, on which occasion will be performed, by particular request, R. Shiel's admired Tragedy of

EVADNE--OR THE STATUE.

EVADNE,	Miss MARY DUFF.
Olivia,	Mrs. J. Sefton,
Ludovico,	Mr. Oxley.
Colonna,	W. Sefton.

After which, the Melo Drama of the

SOMNAMBULIST,
OR THE VILLAGE PHANTOM.

Ernestine Dormieul, (Somnambulist)	Miss Duff.
Madam Gertrude,	Mrs. Kent.
Edmund Beauchamp,	Mr. Oxley.
De Rosambert,	J. G Porter.

With other entertainments, as will be expressed in bills of the day.

202 Mary Duff in Pittsburgh, from the *Daily Pittsburgh Gazette*, November 10, 1834

AN INSPIRER OF FORREST

WILLIAM AUGUSTUS CONWAY, an English actor with all the finish and elegance of the Kemble and Macready schools of histrionics, had in youth been educated for the law, but, prodded by an undeniable urge to go on the stage, had in 1812 secured an engagement at the Dublin Theater. After starring in the provinces, he went to the Haymarket, acclaimed by practically all the critics. But morbid and sensitive, in spite of his general popularity, he became incensed at a personal attack by an unprincipled critic, threw up his engagement, and remained a lowly prompter, until he was persuaded by his friends to try a complete change of scene by going to America. He opened at the Park on January 12, 1824, and proved a great success, especially in his appearances with Mary Ann Duff and Thomas Cooper. He is popularly supposed to have been one of the chief inspirers of Edwin Forrest, who in his early years played Mark Antony to Conway's Brutus. His American success did not, however, dispel the cloud of melancholia, which seemed on the contrary to thicken. He became more sensitive about his unusual height, which set him off from the other actors.

203 William Augustus Conway, 1798–1828, from a mezzotint, 1815, by W. Say after a portrait by G. H. Harlow, in the Harvard Theater Collection

His persecution complex became more developed, until he finally decided to leave the stage, and began the study of religion. But in 1828, on a passage to Charleston, his depression overcame him, and he threw himself overboard.

NEW THEATERS

THE summer entertainments at Barriere's Pavilion Theater, Chatham Garden, having achieved great success for two seasons, the proprietor determined in 1824 to erect a permanent theater. The result was the Chatham Garden, located between Duane and Pearl Streets, with an entrance between the private residences on the west side of Chatham Street. The new house "fitted up with great neatness, taste, and convenience," was opened on May 17, 1824, with *The Soldier's Daughter.* The company

204   Interior of the Chatham Garden Theater, 1825, from a lithograph by H. A. Thomas, in the New York Historical Society

engaged at the Chatham, which, according to Ireland, had never been surpassed in a New York theater, included such names as Henry Wallack, George Barrett, Thomas Burke, and Jo Jefferson II. The first year was eventful and successful, one of the outstanding features being the visit of General Lafayette on his final trip to America. On the death of Barriere in 1826, Henry Wallack leased the theater. But although such well known players as Conway and the Duffs made frequent appearances, and though for three months Booth was stage manager, Wallack ended in bankruptcy. Perhaps one reason for the deficit was that extensive renovations were made in the house during the summer of 1826. Jo Jefferson, II (see No. 437), was one of the decorative artists who succeeded in rendering the house "one of the most beautiful in the Union." In April 1827, Wallack closed the establishment, and though it was later reopened under various managements, it never again enjoyed its first success and reputation. Its patronage was diverted by the Park, the new Bowery, the Lafayette, and the summer concerts at Castle Garden. The Lafayette, situated on the west side of Laurens Street, was opened on July 4, 1825, by C. W. Sandford, as the Lafayette Amphitheater, and was devoted to circuses with occasional equestrian dramas, farces, and ballets. Two years later it was reopened as the Lafayette Theater, Sandford now confining his efforts solely to standard comedies, operas, and melodramas. It gained little popularity during its short career, which ended in April, 1829, when the theater was destroyed by fire. Sandford also built Mount Pitt Circus and opened it November 8, 1826, with a combined dramatic and equestrian company. Of its subsequent history nothing is known.

205   Signor Garcia as Othello in Verdi's Opera, from a French engraving in the Harvard Theater Collection

MANUEL GARCIA, 1782–1836

THE autumn season of 1825 introduced to the American stage a welcome novelty. On November 29, Signor Manuel Garcia, a Spanish tenor, celebrated throughout Europe as singer, teacher, and composer, opened at the Park with a well-trained company of Italian opera singers. The performance of Rossini's *Barber of Seville* was attended and applauded by one of the largest and most elegant audiences ever assembled at the Park. The receipts amounted to almost three thousand dollars. Encouraged by the success of the first night, Signor Garcia thereafter engaged the theater two nights in each week, and though the price of seats was double that of ordinary nights, he enjoyed large houses the remainder of the season. The voices of the entire Garcia troupe as well as the playing of the twenty-five piece orchestra were uniformly praised.

206   Maria Felicita Garcia Malibran, 1808–36, from a lithograph by
C. Basene after a drawing by Grevedon, in the Harvard Theater
Collection

THE QUEEN OF SONG

BUT praise changed to ecstasy in the case of Signorina Maria Felicita Garcia, who, though but seventeen, had already made a brilliant début in London. An extract from a contemporary newspaper gives an indication of the intense enthusiasm which she aroused. "The Signorina seems to us a being of a new creation; a cunning pattern of excellent nature, equally surprising by the melody of her voice and by the propriety and grace of her acting. . . . Her person is about the middle height, slightly *embonpoint* — her eyes dark, arch and expressive, and a playful smile is almost constantly the companion of her lips. She was the magnet who attracted all eyes and won all hearts." In 1827, tempted by Charles Gilfert's offer of five hundred dollars a night, Maria Felicita — now, by her marriage with a wealthy French merchant of New York, Madame Malibran — appeared in English opera at the Bowery Theater. Her final appearance on the American stage was on October 28, 1827. In November she sailed for Europe, where, until her death in 1836, she reigned as the greatest queen of song.

A MASTER OF DIALECT

JAMES HENRY HACKETT, born in New York city of a Dutch father and an American mother, had for a number of years been engaged in mercantile pursuits. Confronted with the crisis of a business failure, he decided to remedy his fortunes by adopting a career on the stage. On his first appearance at the Park, March 1, 1826, he suffered so from stage fright that he gave what must have been a blundering performance. His second venture was much more successful. Like Charles Mathews, Hackett was a master at mimicry and imitation of the mannerisms of other actors. On one occasion when he and John Barnes were playing the twin Dromios he imitated Barnes' voice and intonation so perfectly that the audience was unable to tell the two apart. His mastery of dialect was equally great, and brought amusement to two generations of theater goers.

207   James Henry Hackett, 1800–71, from
a photograph in the Madigan Collection,
New York

208   Hackett as Falstaff, from a playbill
in the Davis Collection

209   Hackett as Falstaff, from an engraving in the
collection of James K. Hackett, New York

210 Hackett as Rip Van Winkle, from the painting by Henry Inman (1801–64) in The Players' Club, New York

211 Hackett as Solomon Swap, from a drawing by Clay, in the Fridenberg Collection

YANKEE RÔLES

In his Yankee rôles, especially those of Uncle Ben and Solomon Swap, Hackett was the delight of New York and London audiences. In 1832, on his second visit to London, he attempted for the first time the exacting rôle of Falstaff. It was received enthusiastically, and soon became his favorite, and that on which his reputation most securely rests. He was at different times associated in the management of various of the New York theaters, but his prestige was primarily from his comic rôles. He was a keen student of Shakespearean drama, a subject which he discussed at length in an animated correspondence with ex-President John Quincy Adams, who likewise prided himself on his Shakespearean scholarship. Hackett's *Notes and Comments on Shakespeare*, which occasionally contains illuminating observations, was sent to Lincoln and drew from him a note of acknowledgment. The tragic rôles of Hackett were less enthusiastically received. George Vandenhoff, a later tragedian, expressed this feeling: "When I say that his Kentuckian never ceases to amuse me by its hearty, audacious oddities; that I consider his Solomon Swap the most natural and unexaggerated Yankee I ever saw upon the stage; that I have alternately smiled and wept at his Rip Van Winkle, one of the most artistic and finished performances that the American Theater ever produced, — he will, I know, not take it ill, that I could not discover the merit or the design, if it had any, of his Richard III."

A BOSTON THEATER WAR

Since the bitter riot caused by Edmund Kean's second Boston appearance in 1825, the fortunes of the Federal Street Theater had been on a steady decline. Instead of searching for the deeper causes the proprietors assumed that Finn and Kilner, the managers, were at fault. An open case against the management presented itself in the unfair treatment alleged to have been accorded William Pelby, whose demands for an increase in salary Finn had declared himself unable to meet. Pelby collected around himself a group of friends determined to repay the Federal Street managers by erecting a rival house. After much excitement and zealous wrangling between the sentimentalists who clung to the theater of Hodgkinson and Cooke and Cooper, and the rivals who were promoting the sale of shares in the new enterprise, the building on Tremont Street opened on September 24, 1827. For two years the competition between the Federal Street and the Tremont continued with unrelaxing intensity. Finn had immediately rushed to England for new recruits. Pelby had offered high salaries to actors in America. Star followed star in a rapid succession of short engagements. Junius Brutus Booth succeeded Pelby as manager of the Tremont. Joe Cowell (see No. 383) succeeded Booth. Prize poems, free tickets, balloon ascensions, extravagant orchestras, humorous ads — all devices were tried to draw crowds away from the rival house. The advantage which the Federal enjoyed of a superior stock cast was offset by the elegance of the Tremont's new establishment. Both theaters suffered, and it became increasingly apparent that Boston was metropolis enough to support only one. Double extinction or a compromise was the alternative. Negotiations were opened between the groups of proprietors. The Federal Street retired in favor of the younger rival, which leased the old historic building — and kept it closed.

212 William Pelby, 1793–1850, from an engraving after the portrait by J. G. Cole, in the Fridenberg Collection

213 The Tremont Theater, from a print in the New York Public Library

214 William B. Wood, from an engraving by A. W. Graham after a daguerreotype, in the Harvard Theater Collection

"A COMPLETE DEBACLE"

In Philadelphia there was similar dissension. The long years of joint-managership, during which William Wood and William Warren had gradually and patiently built up the Chestnut Street Theater and established it finally on a sound financial basis, were brought to an unhappy end in the autumn of 1826. It has been stated that the breach between the two men was but an inevitable climax to long years of bad feeling and mutual distrust. William Wood in his *Personal Recollections* asserts most forcibly the contrary. He was warm in his praise of Warren as an actor, as a manager, and as a co-worker. Wood's qualities were those which Warren needed, and vice versa. They proved, according to Wood, an ideal co-partnership, until Warren began to consult outside amateur advisers, who persuaded him to be more secretive in his discussions with Wood. Suggestions of policy were made by Warren which could not have emanated from an experienced manager. Wood, with

deepest anxiety, saw the work of twenty years endangered. He remonstrated. Warren accused him of personal spite against the outsiders. When Wood saw that the former open, frank intercourse with Warren was ended, he resigned as manager, but agreed to remain as an actor. With Warren in single control, innovations were made, which Wood sensed to be fatal. Others were dissatisfied with Warren's new policy. A group of proprietors opened a new theater on Arch Street and asked Wood to serve as manager. He finally consented, although with great reluctance at leaving this theater toward which he felt almost as toward a child. The venture at the Arch Street failed. There was no discipline on the part of the actors — nor support from the proprietors. Wood tendered his resignation. The Arch Street passed into younger hands, and in 1831 Warren retired permanently from the Chestnut. "There had been a complete debacle," wrote Wood. "I never became lessee again, nor very permanently connected with any theater as a stock actor." More and more rapidly New York usurped Philadelphia's position as America's theatrical center.

215 Warren at the Chestnut, Wood at the Arch Street, from announcements in the *National Literary Gazette*, Dec. 4, 1828

216 Warren's Last Night at the Chestnut, from an announcement in the *National Literary Gazette*, Jan. 4, 1831

217 William Charles Macready in the rôle of William Tell, from *The Autobiography of Joseph Jefferson.* © The Century Company, New York, 1889

WILLIAM MACREADY, 1793–1873

In his youth William Charles Macready had received the classical education of an English gentleman. His father, who had acquired some means as a theater manager in the English provinces, intended that the son should become a great barrister. Before the law courses began, however, the elder Macready faced financial ruin, and to meet the emergency William was forced to change his career to the theater. But the early legal training left an indelible mark on the scholarly, meticulously planned histrionics of the actor. After a début at Covent Garden in 1816, he rapidly became one of the outstanding tragedians of England. William Hazlitt declared him to be "by far the best tragic actor that has come out in our remembrance with the exception of Mr. Kean."

PARK THEATRE.

MR

Macready

AS THE

Cardinal Richelieu

Being the Last Night but ONE of his Engagement.

☞The Manager most respectfully announces that

MR. MACREADY

will This Evening appear for the LAST TIME, during his present Engagement, in his original Character of the

Cardinal Richelieu!!

Boxes 1 dollar.　Pit 50 cts.　Gallery 25 cts.

☞ **TIME ALTERED** ☜

Doors open at quarter to 7　The Curtain will rise precisely at quarter past 7 o'clock.

TUESDAY EVENING OCTOBER 17. 1843.

Will be performed, the Play of

Richelieu !

OR

THE CONSPIRACY !

Cardinal Richelieu......**Mr. MACREADY**
Louis XIII .... Mr. Barry
Gaston, Duke of Orleans, brother of Louis XIII .... Lyne
Count de Baradas, Favorite to the King, first Gentleman of the Chamber, Premier Ecuyer, &c ... . Ryder
The Chevalier de Mauprat, ...Wheatley
The Sieur de Berringhen, in attendance on the King, one of the Conspirators .... Andrews
Count de Clermont, ...Crocker
Father Joseph, a Capuchin, Richelieu's confident, ... Chippendale
Huguet, an officer of Richelieu's householdguard, a Spy ...Fisher
Francois, first Page to Richelieu................ ....Lovell
First Secretary of State ....Bridges
Second Secretary of State ....Freeland
Third Secretary of State ....Toomer
Page............ ....Miss Bedford
Governor of the Bastile.......... ....Vache
Gaoler ....Povey
Gamester ....Gallot
Captain of the Archers..,........................ King
Courtiers, Conspirators, Officers, Soldiers, Gamesters, &c.
Julie de Mortemar, an Orphan, Ward to Richelieu...Mrs. H. Hunt
Marion de Lorme, Mistress to Orleans, in Richelieu's pay ...Lovell

218　Macready as Cardinal Richelieu, at the Park Theater, 1843, from a playbill in the Davis Collection

When ten years later Macready sailed for America and made his début at the Park on October 2, 1826, he was universally acclaimed as the greatest living tragedian on the English-speaking stage. After his opening night, patriotic American critics still contended that Cooper was a greater actor, but at the end of Macready's engagement, the preëminence of the new arrival was universally recognized. His manner was a direct contrast to the impulsive spontaneity of Booth. Long before a performance Macready had planned out each move and each shade of intonation that was required to project the particular character, as he had come to analyze it after a most scholarly reading of the text of the play. Jo Jefferson has left an account of this predominant characteristic of Macready's acting. "He would remain in his dressing room absorbed with the play; no one was permitted to enter. . . . If the mechanism of the play remained intact, he became lost in his character and produced grand effects, but if by some carelessness he was recalled to himself, the chain was broken and he could not reunite it." His second visit to America was in 1843, when he received an even greater welcome on his tour of the country. Six years later he came again and would probably have remained, had he not been subjected to the humiliation and actual danger of the Astor Place Riot (see No. 309).

219   Drop Curtain of the first Bowery, from an engraving in the Fridenberg Collection

THE OPENING OF THE BOWERY

On the night following Macready's début at the Park, a formidable rival to the old theater opened its doors. Each year the increasing population of New York city pushed northward, up Manhattan Island, and to the east, where in the Bowery section many new improvements were being made to attract the fashionable classes of society. As more and more prosperous families moved into the neighborhood, complaints began to be raised at the great distance which separated them from the nearest theater. The time had come to build a new theatrical center, which by its superior elegance and more convenient location would eclipse the Park. There were numerous promoters, the best known of whom, from a theatrical standpoint, was Charles Gilfert, for many years musical director of the Park, who, ten years before, had failed in an attempt to set up an organization to destroy the Park's monopoly (see p. 72). But this second venture of Gilfert's was projected on a much surer foundation. In the course of the following year a handsome structure with imitation white marble and stately columns gradually rose on the site of the old Tavern and Cattle Market. The new theater, which was finally opened to the public on October 23, 1826, was the largest and most imposing in the country. The auditorium seated about three thousand five hundred people, the stage was enormous, and the decoration of the entire interior much superior to that of any rival. The first nighters were thrilled likewise by the gas-lighting arrangement, which here made its first appearance in New York — ten years later than in Philadelphia. After a preliminary adjustment the scale of prices was seventy-five cents for boxes; thirty-seven and one-half cents for the pit; and twenty-five cents for the gallery. With an assurance, perhaps not quite warranted, Manager Charles Gilfert and stage manager George Barrett called the new playhouse, The New York Theater, Bowery, feeling sure that the Park and the Chatham Garden would soon be driven out of the competition. When Hamblin and Hackett became managers in 1830, it was known simply as the Bowery — a name famous in our theatrical annals. On successive stages on this site appeared practically all the leading actors and actresses of the century.

220   The First Bowery Theater, from an engraving after a drawing by A. J. Davis, in the New York Historical Society

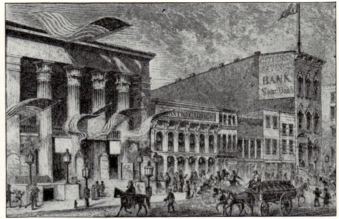

221   The Second Bowery Theater, from an engraving by Richardson after a drawing by A. C. W. (Waud?), in the New York Historical Society

222 Thomas S. Hamblin, 1798–1853, as Coriolanus, from an engraving in the Davis Collection

THE "BOWERY SLAUGHTER HOUSE"

Thomas S. Hamblin, whose name is closely linked to the Bowery, had been trained for a mercantile life in England, but the attraction of the theater had interfered. He had first appeared at the Adelphi Theater in London as a ballet dancer. In 1817 he had been at Drury Lane and then for a number of years in the provinces. He had made his début at the Park as Hamlet on November 1, 1825. For a number of years he was a popular touring actor in the Ohio and Mississippi Valley

THEATRE.—MELO-DRAMATIC.
Corner of Third Cross and Jefferson Streets.

Mr. Hamblin and Mrs. M'Clure's
Last appearance in this City.

THIS EVENING, (SATURDAY,) DECEMBER 5,
Will be performed, SHAKSPEARE's universally admired
Tragedy of

HAMLET—Prince of Denmark.
HAMLET, ... MR. HAMBLIN.
OPHELIA, ... MRS. M'CLURE.

The Evening's entertainment to conclude with the laughable Farce of
LOVER'S QUARRELS,
OR....LIKE MASTER, LIKE MAN.
SANCHO, - - - - - - Mr. M'CAFFERTY.
LEONORA, - - - - Mrs. JACKSON.
☞For further particulars, see Bills of the day.

☞On MONDAY, the Grand Eastern Spectacle of
EL HYDER,
With New Scenery, Dresses and Decorations.

☞Price of admission, 75 Cents, for all parts of the House—Colored people, 50 Cents. Performance to commence precisely at 7 o'clock.
Box Book open at Mr. STEELMAN's Steam boat Hotel, where seats can be taken for the evening, and retained until the end of the first act. No money taken at the doors. ☞Entrance to the Boxes, on Jefferson Street—to the Gallery, on the sides of the House. Smoking not allowed in the Theatre.
Tickets for sale at the Washington Hall, City Hotel,

223 Hamblin on a Western Tour, from the Louisville *Public Advertiser*, December 5, 1829

theatrical centers. Though at the beginning he gained considerable reputation as an actor, "with all the mechanism of tragic art in the Kemble School," his main contribution to the American theater was as manager of the Bowery Theater, of which he became joint lessee with James H. Hackett in 1830. Except for occasional absences in England he was connected with the Bowery until his death in 1853. In contrast to the earlier work of Gilfert as a producer, he made no pretensions to literary ambitions or elevated sentiment, which his company was incompetent to portray and his audience incapable of appreciating. He concentrated instead on melodramas of blood and thunder, which became such a marked characteristic of the Bowery, under Hamblin's

224   The Burning of the Second Bowery, from an engraving in *The Illustrated London News*, May 24, 1845

managership, that the theater became known as the "Bowery Slaughter House." In spite of the notoriety of his private domestic entanglements, Hamblin's reputation in his business relationships was always excellent. He was strictly honest and fair, and, as a friend, was in addition generous and benevolent. He suffered many reverses, but managed to retire at the end with a fortune of one hundred thousand dollars. James H. Hackett, his business associate for many years, has left the following description of Hamblin. "His head was remarkable for its covering by a shock of thick and curly dark-brown hair; his nose was high and thick, and long like his visage; . . . his eyes were of a dark hazel, small, sunken, and set very close to each other and not either penetrating or effective, and his other facial features were more rigid than plastic." When in 1848 Simpson withdrew from the management of the Park, Hamblin succeeded him for a short time until the destruction of the entire property by fire (see p. 122).

EDWIN FORREST, 1806–1872

DURING these early years of the Chestnut, the second Park, the Walnut and the Bowery, when each year witnessed the arrival of some famous English star from Covent Garden or Drury Lane, a young Philadelphian, a native American, was patiently learning on the boards of the western theaters the technique of the profession which from childhood he had loved. When in 1820 the fourteen-year-old Edwin Forrest was allowed by Manager Wood to make his début at the Walnut Street Theater, in the favorite début rôle of young actors,

225 Edwin Forrest, from a photograph in the Davis Collection

Young Norval, the intensity and spontaneity of his acting were praised by the critics of his native city. He went to the veteran Thomas Cooper for advice. He was told that his task was just beginning, that years of practical apprenticeship were essential, and that openings in the West were much more numerous. It was a stimulating field for an apprentice.

NEW THEATRE.

MR FORREST *for one night more!* And positively the LAST NIGHT of *the season.*

In compliance with the many requests made to see *Mr Forres* in KING LEAR, the manager has the pleasure to announce to his patrons, that he will appear in that character.

ON SATURDAY JULY 25,

Will be presented Shakspeare's popular tragedy of

KING LEAR.

KING LEAR . . . . MR FORREST.

After which the Operatical Farce entitled

OF AGE TO MORROW.

In which *Mr Caldwell* will sustain five characters.

226 Forrest as King Lear, from an announcement in the *National Banner and Nashville Whig,* July 24, 1829

Forrest's wanderings and quarrels with western managers (see Chapter VI) form an interesting prelude to his years of starring. Reports of the young actor began to get back to New York. Charles Gilfert engaged Forrest for his theater in Albany, where the young actor enjoyed the invaluable experience of playing subordinate Shakespearean rôles to Edmund Kean. A larger opportunity was at hand. He was invited to play at the benefit of an old friend, one of the cast of the Park. This initial New York appearance aroused such enthusiasm that he was immediately offered an opening by Simpson of the Park, and one by Gilfert, which latter he accepted. For the next three years he was at the Bowery, starting at forty dollars a week. His best rôles at the Bowery were Damon, Jaffier, William Tell, and Marc Antony. Shortly he began appearing in all the leading cities of the country and his fame and fortune grew rapidly.

227   Forrest as Spartacus, from a photograph in the Davis Collection

228 Forrest as Oralloossa, from a photograph in the Davis Collection

229   Forrest as Richard III, from a photograph
in the Davis Collection

"TURBULENT CHARACTERS"

When Gilfert died in 1829, Forrest left the Bowery to join the Park, which was the center of his activities for the next seven years. William Winter in his *Wallet of Time* has left a vivid portrait of Forrest at this period of his development. "Forrest was then in the prime of manhood and the first flush of popularity, a person remarkable for muscular force, a voice

230   Forrest as Metamora, from a photograph in
the Davis Collection

of prodigious volume and melody, and a cogent style of depicting the emotional experience of turbulent characters. He had, within a brief time, acquired an extraordinary vogue and distinction. The local stage, not then able to exult in much tragic talent distinctively American, proudly claimed for the American actor a rank equal with that of the best foreign representatives of tragedy." It would require chapters to sketch with any detail Forrest's long period of ascendency: from the Park in 1836 to Covent Garden and a tour of the English provinces; to the Chestnut and back to the Park; and in 1845, after a period at the Arch Street, and long tours and huge receipts through the states of the Union, back for a second visit to London in 1845. His career extending over five decades is a powerful link connecting the early days of Cooper and Warren with the modern theater of Augustin Daly and John Drew, the crudities of the Park and the Chestnut with the elaborate finish of the Fourteenth Street Theater, where he made his last appearance in 1871. As a personality he aroused violent reactions — wildly enthusiastic or bitterly hostile. He was never free from an imperious braggadocio and selfish vanity, intensified by his self-conscious Americanism. Many resented his acting for its untutored, savage spontaneity, which, though accidentally effective and thrilling at times, inevitably descended often to cheap bathos and mouthing. Yet no number of critics, however convincing, can undermine his position as the first great native American star, who, by his unfailing sincerity and honesty and individuality of interpretation, thrilled three generations of theatergoers in every part of our country. The age of impassioned oratory, typified by Webster and Calhoun, was reflected in his stirring periods.

231   Forrest as Macbeth, from a photograph in the Davis
Collection

232   Caricature of Forrest as Spartacus, in the Houdini
Collection

LAST NIGHT BUT THREE
Of the engagement of
EDWIN
FORREST
Who will appear this
Monday Ev'ng, Oct. 17th, 1864,
For the
First time this Season
In his powerful impersonation of
SPARTACUS
GLADIATOR
In Dr. Bird's Grand American Tragedy, the

Gellius, a Roman Consul	Mr. E. Barry
Crassus, a Praetor	Mr. J. W. Collier
Scropha, a Quaestor	Mr. Neil
Jovius, a Centurion	Mr. J. F. Hagan
Centurion	Mr. Rendle
Phasarius, brother to Spartacus	Mr. J. McCullough
Lentulus	Mr. J. Nunan
Bracchius	Mr. J. G. Burnett
Florus, son to Lentulus	Mr. Geo. Becks
Enomaus	Mr. H. Danvers
Crixus	Mr. J. W. Blaisdell
Fighting Gaul	Mr. E. B. Holmes
Artificer	Mr. Dennison
Slave	Mr. Burke
Child, son to Spartacus	Miss Le Brun
Julia, niece to Crassus	Miss Isabel Freeman
Senona, wife to Spartacus	Mrs. Farren
Female Slaves, Roman Ladies, Guards, &c.	

233 Forrest as Spartacus, from a playbill
in the Davis Collection

234 Edwin Forrest, from a photograph
in the Davis Collection

THE GENIUS OF FORREST

ONE of the most illuminating criticisms of Forrest's acting was given by Francis Courtney Wemyss (see No. 197) in his *Twenty-six Years of the Life of an Actor and Manager*. Wemyss, as manager of the American Theater at Philadelphia, had gone to enormous expense to secure costumes, chairs, tables, and scenery which would reproduce the exact spirit of the age of Richelieu, and give a setting worthy of Forrest's genius. "Of Mr. Forrest's performance of this part I can scarcely find words to speak in terms of sufficient praise; it was one of those masterly efforts of genius that sets criticism at defiance, full of beauty, full of faults; but an endeavor to analyze the latter would lead your pen into a strain of panegyric before you had completed half a dozen sentences, by the discovery of a flash of genius so brilliant, as to make you doubt the correctness of your judgment, and pronounce the fault you had determined to expose, a necessary foil to the excellent effect which followed. He evidently devoted no time to the study of character, but committed the words of the part to memory in a hurry; appeared in it before the public in a hurry; before them, to polish his crude ideas of the author as chance might direct . . . an effort no one but a great actor would have dared attempt." He succeeded in "taking his audience by surprise, and charging onward, until their admiration broke forth into an involuntary acknowledgment of his excellence, continuing several seconds after the fall of the curtain hid the actor from their view. . . . Richelieu will never find a better representative."

235 Forrest as Richelieu, from a photograph
in the Davis Collection

236 Forrest as Lear, from a photograph
in the Davis Collection

METAMORA AND THE GLADIATOR

IN order to secure a new medium for his vigorous style of acting, Forrest in November, 1828, offered a prize of five hundred dollars and half the third night's receipts for the "best tragedy, in five acts, of which the hero, or principal character, shall be an original of this country." The winning play was *Metamora, or the Last of the Wampanoags,* written by an actor, John Augustus Stone. Here for the first time the Indian appeared as the theme of a successful play. Since Robert Rogers' crude *Ponteach* (see p. 20) in 1766, the Indian had been employed with surprising infrequency by our playwrights until about the time of *Metamora,* when the theme began to enjoy a certain favor, partly inspired, it may be, by James Fenimore Cooper's contemporary "Leather-stocking" series. *Metamora* exists only in a manuscript containing the speeches of the title character, but from these one discovers that it was filled with the violent and exaggerated heroics in which Forrest specialized. The part was so

237   John Augustus Stone, 1801–34, from an engraving in the Fridenberg Collection, New York

well adapted to this actor that, after the première at the Park Theater on December 15, 1829, he played it constantly to the end of his career. Another successful writer of plays for Forrest was Robert Montgomery Bird, a young Philadelphian who, when his first manuscript was accepted in 1831, had recently renounced medicine for literature. *The Gladiator* possesses unmistakable dramatic and literary excellence, and in it the muscular Forrest, as Spartacus, leader of an uprising among the Roman gladiators, was able to sweep his audiences off their feet in hundreds of performances. The next year Forrest produced another drama by Bird — *Oralloossa,* the scene of which is laid in Peru. Lacking the dramatic power of *The Gladiator, Oralloossa* was dropped from Forrest's repertory after two seasons. Bird's final play was a more restrained domestic tragedy, *The Broker of Bogota* (1834), which provided Forrest with a vehicle for the display of his subtler gifts, and which was long a favorite with him. After *The Broker* Bird wrote no more plays, apparently discouraged by Forrest's unscrupulous treatment of him. That actor, taking advantage of a verbal understanding between them, refused to pay certain royalties which Bird understood that he was to receive. After a stormy quarrel the sometime friends parted forever, and Bird turned to novel writing and journalism. In 1837 was published his *Nick of the Woods,* one of the most thrilling of all Indian novels. It was dramatized the following year by Louisa Medina and enjoyed a stage success. In all Bird's plays the tendency toward frank romanticism, which was at that time widespread in both American and English drama, is very evident. The theater was then a place of escape and release for the imagination. Modern realism was yet to be invented.

238   Robert Montgomery Bird, 1806–54, from an engraving in the Gottschalk Collection, New York

239 Richard Penn Smith, 1799–1854, from an engraving by John Sartain after a portrait by I. Williams, in the Fridenberg Collection

240 Robert Taylor Conrad, 1810–58, from an engraving by John Sartain, in the possession of the publishers

241 George H. Miles, 1824–71, from an engraving, courtesy of Mount St. Mary's College, Emmetsville, Md.

OTHER FORREST DRAMATISTS

EDWIN FORREST made a frequent practice of adding American plays to his repertory. Among the writers whom he thus distinguished was the Philadelphian, Richard Penn Smith, whose *Caius Marius* he brought out in 1831. Since the tragedy was not published, we cannot estimate its worth, but in other plays of Smith's, such as *The Eighth of January* (1829), dramatizing Jackson's victory at New Orleans, and *The Triumph at Plattsburg* (1830), based on another "1812" theme, we see a lively sense of theatrical effectiveness. In *William Penn* (1829) Smith brings the Indian into our drama again. Robert T. Conrad was another able Philadelphia playwright. His chief play is *Jack Cade*, produced in 1835 and later revised for Forrest as *Aylmere*. Presenting as it does a defiant rebel, it became a favorite with that actor. George H. Miles received the prize in one of Forrest's competitions, but, although his *Mohammed* has some merit, Forrest did not use it. Most important of Miles' plays is *De Soto* (1852), in which the Indian theme prominently recurs. Between *Metamora* and *De Soto*, according to A. H. Quinn's *History of the American Drama*, some thirty-five Indian dramas were produced. Miles' play is among the best of the lot.

JAMES E. MURDOCH, 1811–1893

STIMULATED by the success of Forrest and Hackett, other native actors made preparations for serious theatrical careers. Born in Philadelphia of a good American family, but with no theatrical connections, James E. Murdoch (see No. 416) owed his success to close study and to self confidence rather than to inherited talent. At an early age he became absorbed in dramatic studies and elocution, and, in spite of the objections of friends, made an appearance on October 13, 1829, at the Arch Street Theater as Frederic in *The Lovers' Vows*. His next Philadelphia appearances as Young Norval, Octavian, and Selim in *Barbarossa*, were received with enthusiastic approval. After a tour in various theatrical centers of the South he occupied for several years an honored position at the Arch Street and Chestnut Street theaters. On June 4, 1838, he was engaged for the first time at the Park Theater to support Ellen Tree (see No. 251). He withdrew temporarily from the stage in 1842 for study, and at the same time gave elocution lessons to students and practitioners of law and divinity, as well as Shakespearean lectures in the larger eastern cities. Returning to the theater in 1845 he played Hamlet at the Park for the first time, and afterward traveled throughout the country, and made a successful trip to England. He was adapted to the performance of both comedy and tragedy. Wemyss called him the best light comedian of the day. Cornelius Mathews described his style of acting as hitting "the middle line, below the severe and terrible requirements of tragedy, and above the broad effects of comedy."

242 Murdoch as Count Waldbourg in *The Stranger*, from a photogravure by Gebbie & Husson Co., in the possession of the publishers

243 John Gibbs Gilbert as Sir Peter Teazle in *The School for Scandal*, from the portrait by John W. Alexander in the Rhode Island School of Design, Providence, R. I.

244 Gilbert as Sir Anthony Absolute in Richard Brinsley Sheridan's *The Rivals*, from a photogravure by Gebbie & Co., in the possession of the publishers

JOHN GILBERT, 1810–1889

ONE of our finest native comedians was John Gibbs Gilbert, who, born in Boston in 1810, spent his boyhood as next door neighbor and playmate of Charlotte Cushman. At nineteen he made his stage début at the Tremont Theater in the rôle of Jaffier in *Venice Preserved*, opposite the Belvidera of Mary Ann Duff (No. 201). His performance was unusually successful, and, although marked by some awkwardness of bearing and some crudity of expression, showed such discrimination and originality as to foreshadow his later career of sixty years. After his début he went to New Orleans where, with the exception of short engagements in such western towns as St. Louis and Nashville (see No. 392), he remained until 1834. During the period from 1834 to 1846 he was on the stage constantly in Boston, New York, and Philadelphia. In 1846 he appeared in London at the Princess Theater. His next appearance in America was at the Arch Street Theater, where he acted from 1858 to 1862, at which time he joined Wallack's New York Stock Company at Broadway and Thirteenth Street in the capacity of actor and, at one time, as stage manager. With this company he remained until it disbanded in 1888 — the year preceding his death. Gilbert was essentially a creator of old men's parts, and in this field had no rivals, whether he appeared as Old Norval, Sir Peter Teazle, the Abbé Constantin, or Sir Anthony Absolute. "He was sometimes a great actor; he was always a correct one," wrote William Winter. "In such characters as Sir Sampson Legend and Sir Anthony Absolute no man of his time approached him, and it is doubtful whether in that line of individuality he was ever equalled."

245 Louisa Lane at the age of eight, in the five characters in *Twelve Precisely*, from a lithograph by Pendleton after a drawing, 1828, in *Scribner's Magazine*, October 1899. Original in the John Drew Collection

LOUISA LANE, 1820–1897

LOUISA LANE, who, as Mrs. John Drew (see Nos. 528, 603), was to become the most famous actress manager of the United States, and whose dramatic career spans as great a period of theatrical history as that of Edwin Forrest, entered upon her profession at the age of twelve months, interpreting, with éclat no doubt, the rôle of a crying baby. Born in England, of player parents, at the age of five she was sustaining regular rôles in melodrama. In 1827 her mother brought her to Philadelphia where she appeared at the Walnut Street Theater, taking the part of the Duke of York to Junius Brutus Booth's Richard III. Immediately successful, she was sent to Joe Cowell's Theater in Baltimore to appear as Albert to Edwin Forrest's William Tell. She then made her New York début at the Bowery in 1828 as Little Pickle. Afterward she acted with all the famous players of her day — Macready, Forrest, Jefferson, Tyrone Power, Murdoch, George Holland, and Charlotte Cushman. Her versatility was extraordinary, allowing her to play in one season more than forty parts. In 1850 she married John Drew, an Irish comedian, with whom she played many rôles. In 1861 she assumed control of the Arch Street Theater, inaugurating a brilliant period in Philadelphia's theatrical history. She not only secured the best actors of the day as visiting stars, but developed a stock company, many members of which later became famous. Changing theatrical conditions forced her to abandon her stock company in 1869. From 1880 to 1892 she traveled with Joseph Jefferson, acting her most famous rôle of Mrs. Malaprop in *The Rivals*. Her powers were fast failing, and in 1897 she died.

246 Clara Fisher, from an engraving, 1818, by J. Alais after a portrait by Rose Emma Drummond, in the Gottschalk Collection, New York

CLARA FISHER, 1811–1882

BORN in 1811, the daughter of a Brighton librarian, who later became a London auctioneer, Clara Fisher at the age of six made her début on the "Lilliputian" stage at Drury Lane in an impersonation of Richard III. So tremendous was her success that she soon became famous throughout England. She first appeared in America at the Park in 1827, as Albina Mandeville in *The Will* and as the four Mowbrays in *Old and Young*. Some slight disappointment was felt in the first play, until she introduced for the first time in America "Hurrah for the Bonnets of Blue" — a song which produced

247 Clara Fisher Maeder, from a photograph in the Davis Collection

an electrifying effect on the house. From then on for many years her popularity in America was immense. In 1834 she married James C. Maeder, a musician of Boston, and the vocal instructor of Joseph Wood (No. 259), Charlotte Cushman, and others. As Mrs. Maeder, she formally bade farewell to the stage in the rôle of Lydia Languish, but after 1850 appeared again at Brougham's Lyceum and at Niblo's. The range of her acting was remarkable, though the characters in which she obtained the most success were the mischievous boys and rollicking girls of the stage, the saucy chambermaids and coquettish belles of the salon. She played also Ophelia in a touching and winning manner, and by her rendition of Clari's song of *Home, Sweet Home* she invariably moved her audience to tears. In opera she showed a thorough knowledge of music, but a limited vocal range. It was in her singing of ballads, however, that she attained the greatest popularity. Equally popular were the curls, the delicate lisp of Clara Maeder, which all the ladies of fashion at that time imitated.

CELINE CELESTE, 1818–1882

IN the same year that Louisa Lane and Clara Fisher first came to America, Celine Celeste made her American début at the Bowery in a "pas seul" from the ballet *The Twelve Pages*. Born in Paris in 1814, she had been placed at an early age as a pupil in the Conservatoire of the Academie Royale de Musique, and on one occasion had appeared with Talma, the great French actor. At the time of her New York appearance she could not speak a word of English, but danced with success in many American cities, admired everywhere for her grace and beauty. Later, having mastered English, she became a melodramatic actress of the first rank. In 1830 she performed in all the leading theatrical centers of England, and afterward made a tour of Italy, France, and Germany. In 1834 she again appeared at the Bowery in *The French Spy* — generally considered her most successful rôle. From 1834 to 1837 her receipts rose to the fabulous total of forty thousand pounds. In 1844 she became co-manager of the Adelphi Theater in London, continuing there for fifteen years both as directress and actress. Her farewell tour of the United States was made in 1865.

248 Celine Celeste, from a photograph in the Davis Collection

249 Celeste at the Camp Street, New Orleans, 1829, from a playbill in the Louisiana Historical Society, New Orleans

250 Charles Kean, 1811–68, in the rôle of King John, from an engraving by E. Clement in *The Autobiography of Joseph Jefferson*, New York, 1889. © The Century Company

251 Ellen Tree Kean, 1806–80, as Hermione in *The Winter's Tale*, from an engraving by Whitney, in *The Autobiography of Joseph Jefferson*, New York, 1889. © The Century Company

MR. AND MRS. CHARLES KEAN

CHARLES, the son of Edmund Kean, in order to support himself and his neglected mother had in 1827 accepted the offer of Stephen Price, then manager of the Drury Lane in London, and made his début as Young Norval. After three years on the English stage, he made his first American appearance at the New York Park, September 1, 1830, in *Richard III*. He remained in this country for over two years, enjoying to the full that popularity which British and European audiences still continued to withhold from him, despite his years of patient effort. On March 25, 1833, he returned to London and played at Covent Garden with his father, Edmund being Othello, Charles Iago, and Ellen Tree Desdemona. In 1839 he returned to the United States under the Wallack management. In 1842 he married Ellen Tree. He brought her to America when he came in 1845 to make a triumphal tour of the country until his return to Europe in 1847. On April 26, 1865, he appeared in New York in *Henry VIII* and received unstinted praise for his characters of Louis XI and King Lear. Mrs. Kean had previously been here, in 1836–37, when she had played Rosalind at the Park Theater, December 12, 1836, and Julia in *The Hunchback* in Philadelphia; and, according to Ireland, the great success of the tour of 1845 to 1847 was due more to the excellence of Ellen Tree than to that of her husband. Charles Kean, when he assumed the management of the Princess Theater, London, entered upon a career of Shakespearean productions that set the pace for such archæologists in the theater as Henry Irving. His career as an actor was never brilliant. Handicapped by an unprepossessing face and carriage, never able to free his voice from a rasping harshness, he was forced to secure his effects by the intelligence and cultivated perfection of his art. That he was able to produce increasing effects as he grew older is a tribute to his perseverance and character. He was not only admired but deeply liked by his fellow players. "He was a man charitable by nature," wrote Noah Miller Ludlow, the great western manager, "and liberal with his purse."

252 Josephine Clifton, from a lithograph by Pendleton after a drawing by T. Campbell, in the Harvard Theater Collection

JOSEPHINE CLIFTON, 1813–1847

THE short but brilliant stage career of Josephine Clifton began September 21, 1831, in her eighteenth year, under the management of Thomas Hamblin, when she appeared at the Bowery Theater as Belvidera in *Venice Preserved*. Endowed with exceptional beauty, a fine voice, and sound dramatic ability, she enjoyed an almost unprecedented success. Thanks to the indulgence of a wealthy mother she had been so well-trained that she soon occupied a commanding position in the theatrical world. After traveling throughout the United States, she appeared at Drury Lane in her original rôle of Belvidera, the first starring appearance of an American actress in England. In 1837 at the Park she produced the tragedy of *Bianca Visconti*, written by Nathaniel P. Willis, the successful competitor for the prize which she had offered to American dramatists. In 1846 she married Robert Place, manager of a New Orleans theater, and died there in 1847. Ireland says that at the time of Miss Clifton's death no other native actress had ever created such a wide sensation.

CHAPTER V

THE LAST DAYS OF THE PARK THEATER

DURING the 'thirties and 'forties the American stage continued to draw many of its leading players from England. As was proved by the rise of a group of gifted native performers, this country was now capable of producing actors of the first rank, but the managers continued to seek foreign stars, and for the very good reason that they could be relied on to exercise a greater drawing power than the American-born players. At this time the United States was suffering from an inferiority complex in respect to the arts — a complex which, as a matter of fact, it has not yet wholly outgrown. Sydney Smith's famous questions: "In the four quarters of the globe, who reads an American book? or goes to an American play? or looks at an American picture or statue?" received a disparaging answer even from a large section of the American public. Something of this prejudice manifested itself in connection with the art of acting. But there were those who resented any assumption of superiority on the part of the visiting stars and who took vigorous means to express their resentment. This animosity culminated in the bloody Astor Place Riot of 1849, in which William Macready represented, in the popular mind, the overbearing British actor, and Edwin Forrest the slighted native son. Although Forrest's jealousy seems to have been the immediate cause of the disturbance, the rhetorical question of the rioters' proclamation, "Shall Americans or English rule in this city?" and their cry of "Washington forever!" suggest that back of it all lay a sense of wounded national pride, which was easily fanned into a flame in an age when rioting was almost a common practice. The American stage, however, vindicated its existence and asserted its independence not by insulting British guests but by developing such remarkable players as Charlotte Cushman, Mrs. Mowatt, "Yankee" Hill, E. L. Davenport, and William Warren, Jr., all of whom were born on American soil, and all of whom appeared with great success before British audiences.

The achievements of these distinguished actors were not the sole evidence of expansion and increasing maturity in our theatrical life. In New York particularly, new theaters were being built with a frequency hitherto unparalleled. The monopoly of the Park and the Bowery was ended by the opening of the Franklin, the National, the New Chatham, the Olympic, and Palmo's. Every company contained the names of competent actors, and in each house there was a growing tendency toward specializing in one particular type of entertainment calculated to appeal to the tastes of its own clientele. In other words, New York, having left far behind the simple days when the John Street or the Park enjoyed the patronage of the entire theater-going public, was assuming the semblance of a theatrical metropolis and was already setting out on that course of development which has to-day made it a city of a bewildering and almost unbelievable multitude of playhouses. While Philadelphia manifested no unusual activity during this period, Boston displayed an enterprise not far behind that of New York. New theaters made their appearance in such numbers in the former stronghold of Puritan opposition as to indicate that the stage was steadily becoming a normal and even indispensable element in American life. It must be said, however, that the increase in the number and quality of our actors and theaters was not matched by a commensurate improvement in the dramatic fare offered by these agencies. Apart from the Shakespearean favorites, the stage was largely given over to inconsequential contemporary British pieces — and it cannot be denied that contemporary British pieces have seldom been more mediocre than during the middle decades of the nineteenth century. *The French Spy, Rory O'More, His Last Legs*, and their ilk are plays that the world has willingly let die. Yet these were the popular offerings that took the place occupied, when our theater was still in its infancy, by *The Beaux' Stratagem, Venice Preserved, Love for Love*, and *Jane Shore*. During this period the most encouraging hope for the future was to be found in the greatly increased number of plays written by American authors.

Granted that many of the current plays left something to be desired, it is nevertheless true that our theater was at this time in a healthy state, and that it was meeting more adequately than ever before the conscious need of the urban public for stimulating entertainment. Confirmation of this point may be seen in the fact that the devastating panic of 1837–41, which wrecked many banking and business establishments, did not spell disaster for the theater. While some managers inevitably suffered, others, such as Mitchell and Wallack, by lowered prices or other special bids for favor, were able to lay during these lean years the foundations of an enduring prosperity.

In the 'thirties and 'forties not only did the spoken drama gain a more assured place in the general esteem, but the lyric drama again asserted its claim to recognition. That a house was erected expressly for Italian grand opera in 1833 is evidence that there existed in America a sincere desire to enrich our civilization with the best products of European culture. That the enterprise failed after two seasons merely indicates that this desire was not yet generally felt. Eleven years later, when Palmo made another attempt to domicile Italian opera in America, his undertaking met a like fate. These failures clearly demonstrated that grand opera was a highly expensive form of entertainment, and that only by the generous support of people of wealth could it hope to survive — witness the later success of the Academy of Music and the Metropolitan Opera House.

In general during the final years of the Park Theater the American stage enjoyed a period of material growth. Not only did it expand in the cities where it had long been entrenched, but it was steadily invading regions remote from the Atlantic seaboard (see Chapter VII). The country as a whole also entered upon an era of expansion. Texas was annexed in 1845, Oregon followed in 1846, and in 1848 the Stars and Stripes floated above California. America's dream of becoming a nation that would stretch from the Atlantic to the Pacific was coming true, and the theater in pursuing its program of development was only endeavoring to keep pace with the national progress.

253 Charles Kemble, 1775–1854, as Charles Surface in *The School for Scandal*, from an etching by Richard Dighton, in possession of the publishers

254 Kemble as Hamlet, from an engraving in the Houdini Collection

THE COMING OF THE KEMBLES

IN 1832 the American playgoer experienced a thrill of expectancy he had not known since the days of Cooke and Kean, when it became known that Charles Kemble and his daughter, Frances Ann, were about to visit this country. Charles Kemble, a brother of Mrs. Siddons and of John Philip Kemble, was a member of the most distinguished actor-family England has ever produced. Though less gifted than his brother and sister, Charles was noted for his grace and refinement. In parts requiring the manner of a gentleman he was the first player of his time. His Mercutio and Benedick were unsurpassed, and in spite of a weak voice his Hamlet was greatly admired. Kemble made his American début at the Park Theater, September 17, 1832, as Hamlet. His success was immediate and continued throughout his visit. Joseph Norton Ireland in his *Records of the New York Stage* wrote of him: "His great, unvarying merits were his elegance of action, his taste and propriety in costume, his intimate knowledge of his author, and his refinement of manner, which always impressed

upon an audience the fact that Mr. Kemble, the high-bred gentleman, stood before them — a fact that he himself never for a moment forgot. There was generally a languor and want of energy about his performances, and his representations of the more violent passions always came tamely off; so that, while he uniformly pleased the scholar and the man of taste, he rarely reached the hearts of the multitude." During this first season the Kembles also played two long engagements at Philadelphia, and the enthusiasm there was as great as at New York. Not only to the audiences but to the actors of America they endeared themselves by their generous practice of performing at the benefits of their fellow players without remuneration. When on February 28, 1833, an elaborate performance was arranged at the Park Theater for William Dunlap, former manager of that house, who in his old age was suffering from illness and poverty, the Kembles were engaged to take part. After the performance they insisted on presenting to Dunlap their entire honorarium of four hundred dollars. In June, 1834, the Kembles retired from the American stage, to the great regret of the public.

255 Charles Kemble, from a lithograph by Lane, in the Houdini Collection

A FRANK CRITIC

KEMBLE's daughter, Frances or Fanny, a more gifted artist than her father, had come out on the London stage in 1829 as Juliet and had won the highest favor. In America, where she first appeared on the next night after her father, she repeated her London success. "To the state and dignity of the Kemble school, she added," according to Ireland, "all the fire and impetuosity of her own original genius. . . . No actress that preceded her in America ever held so powerful and deep a sway over the hearts and feelings of her auditors." The theatrical profession, however, was distasteful to her, and she did not make an effort sufficient to achieve true greatness. In 1834 she married Pierce Butler, a southern planter, but the marriage was not happy, and in 1847 she returned for a time to the English stage. In her later years she won a high reputation as a dramatic reader. She was also an author of some slight pretension, having written several acted plays and a *Journal of a Residence in America* (1835). In the latter Mrs. Butler expressed opinions of the United States which were by no means wholly complimentary. In contrast with England America seemed raw and only partially civilized.

256 Frances Ann Kemble, 1809–93, from the painting by Thomas Sully (1783–1872), in the Pennsylvania Academy of Fine Arts, Philadelphia

"The women dress very much," she noted, "and very much like French women gone mad." Society, she felt, lacked grace and dignity because, instead of being led by married women, it was dominated by "chits" and in consequence was noisy and flirtatious. Everybody talked at once — through the nose and in the highest possible voice. The language thus uttered was generally "unrefined, inelegant, and often ungrammatically vulgar." Clerks and shop keepers were too friendly, washer-women sat while she stood talking to them, and delivery boys kept their hats on in her drawing-room. At the same time Mrs. Butler found us not without our virtues. Unescorted women could walk the streets in perfect safety. The absence of poverty and the happiness of the lower classes deeply impressed her. She saw here no brutality to animals such as one witnessed hourly in any English town. Honesty and truthfulness were common qualities. New England she found to be superior in taste, intellect, and dignity to the rest of the United States. In Boston society lacked the vulgarity that offended her in New York and Philadelphia. Finally she discovered that the regions remote from the Atlantic cities contained many of the most admirable people in America — people who made no pretence to high social rank, who possessed originality of mind, intellectual cultivation, purity of morals, hospitality and simplicity.

257 Fanny Kemble and her aunt, Mrs. Siddons, from a painting by Briggs in the Boston Athenæum

NIBLO'S GARDEN

Doors open at Seven.   Commence at half-past Seven.

LAST WEEK BUT ONE of the Renowned

RAVELS

GABRIEL & FRANCOIS

And their Numerous Company.

MLLE. MARIA HENNECART

WILL APPEAR.

Tuesday Eve'ng, Dec. 27th, 1859

Second night of the Grand Fairy Comic Pantomime, called

RAOUL

OR THE MAGIC STAR.

258   The Ravels in the Pantomime, *Raoul*, from a playbill in the Davis Collection

GROUND AND LOFTY TUMBLING

MUCH as the American playgoer admired the acting of artists like the Kembles, he found it to his taste to intersperse courses of a lighter nature. Of such interspersion one type was represented by the Ravel family, a company of gymnasts, ropedancers, and pantomimists, who came to America from Paris in 1832 and opened at the Park on July 16. This group of ten performers soon won such unqualified approval for their grace and dexterity that on many nights it was found profitable to give the theater over entirely to them. For years they performed in the leading playhouses of New York, Philadelphia, and Boston, as well as touring the South and West. In 1847 the principal members returned to Europe. Two years later three of them, reinforced by the Lehman family, were again in this country; and in 1851 Gabriel, the most talented of the Ravels, returned to the American theaters. With various alterations in the formation of the troupe, and with the frequent assistance of the most noted gymnasts and ropedancers of the day, the Ravels continued their hold at least as late as 1860. Richard G. White praised the Ravels for having "given . . . side-shaking, brain-clearing pleasure to more Americans than ever relaxed their sad, silent faces for any other performers!"

MR. AND MRS. JOSEPH WOOD

A DIFFERENT form of variation from conventional dramatic fare was provided by Mr. and Mrs. Wood, operatic singers from England, who were first heard here September 9, 1833, at the Park Theater. It was said that Wood had been taken from the plow to make his first appearance on the London stage in 1828. A year later he was singing leading tenor rôles at Covent Garden. Mrs. Wood, formerly Mary Ann Paton, had been an infant prodigy who, at the age of eight, had given public recitals under the patronage of ladies of high rank. In 1822 she made her stage début at the Haymarket, and was immediately engaged for three years at Covent Garden. Here she more than held her own with the best vocalists of the day. In America the Woods were received with the highest delight; Mrs. Wood in particular created a furore, being regarded as the best English singer ever heard in the United States. During their three visits to this country they made a large sum of money, but unlike the Kembles they often displayed an attitude of illiberality toward their professional associates, which at one time created considerable ill will against them. They finally left these shores in 1841.

259   Joseph Wood in *Fra Diavolo*, from a lithograph by Endicott in the Fridenberg Collection

260   Wood as Ivanhoe in *The Maid of Judah*, from an engraving in the Fridenberg Collection

AMERICA'S FIRST OPERA HOUSE, 1833

THE coming of such singers as the Woods and the recent success of Garcia and Malibran indicated that the American public was hospitable to the vocal art. Accordingly Lorenzo da Ponte, an aged maestro, persuaded some wealthy New Yorkers to erect a theater expressly for opera on the corner of Leonard and Church Streets at a cost of one hundred and fifty thousand dollars. On November 18, 1833, the Italian Opera House, the first building in America erected exclusively for opera, was opened with Rossini's *La Gazza Ladra*. By an arrangement hitherto unknown in this country, the first tier communicated directly with the pit, where for the first time ladies sat.

261 The Italian Opera House, afterward the National Theater, from an engraving by Richardson in the New York Historical Society

The second tier was composed wholly of private boxes. In its furnishings and decorations the building was most luxurious. The seats were of mahogany, upholstered in blue damask; the floors were carpeted; and a splendid chandelier lighted a dome adorned with pictures of the Muses by special scenic artists brought from Europe. During the first season, which was devoted entirely to Italian opera, there was a deficit of almost thirty thousand dollars. The next season was entrusted to a different manager, but he was equally unsuccessful in making the venture pay, partly because of the unfortunate location of the house in a neighborhood difficult of access and bearing a bad reputation. After this failure the building was taken over by Henry Willard and Thomas Flynn, who opened it as the National Theater, August 24, 1836, with the *Merchant of Venice*. It was destroyed by fire in 1839 while in the hands of James Wallack. (See No. 274.)

262 Performance at the National Theater, from a playbill in the New York Historical Society

FRANKLIN THEATER

DURING these years new theaters were springing up in New York with a frequency that testified to a rapidly growing interest in the drama. In 1835, largely because of the prosperity of the Bowery Theater, a small house called the Franklin Theater was erected in the same neighborhood on Chatham Square. It would, according to Ireland, "probably seat (uncomfortably) about six hundred persons." The stock company assembled by William Dinneford, the manager, included several excellent players. Among them were the Sefton brothers, William and John, already popular in other American theaters, and Mrs. Duff, who was received with great enthusiasm after a two years' absence from the New York stage. Another member who deserves mention was the second Joseph Jefferson (see No. 437), who served as a scene painter and an actor in minor rôles. An able company, new plays, and half prices enabled this small theater to enjoy public favor for some years.

263 Benefit Performance at the Franklin Theater, from a playbill in the Davis Collection

264 George Handel Hill, 1809–49, from an engraving by T. Kelly after a portrait by George W. Twibill, in the possession of the publishers

AMERICAN THEATRE
CAMP STREET.

Mr HILL'S First night.

ON MONDAY EVENING, DEC: 22th,
Will be enacted the celebrated comedy of
JONATHAN IN ENGLAND.
SOLOMON SWAP,   :   :   :   Mr HILL,
Torrent,   :   :   :   " Farren,
Sir Larry McMurrough, :   :   :   " Thorne,
Barford,   :   :   :   " H G Pearson
Fanny,   :   :   :   Miss Petrie.
After which the laughable farce, entitled
HOW TO DIE FOR LOVE.
Capt Blumenfeldt,   :   :   :   Mr Williamson,
Trick,   :   :   :   :   " Thorne.

TO-MORROW EVENING
SHE WOULD BE A SOLDIER.
FREEDOM'S JUBILEE,
HURRAH FOR COLOMBIA,
THE STAR SPANGLED BANNER;
And a new piece, called
MY DAUGHTER, SIR !
In which Mrs KNIGHT will appear.

265 Hill in the West, from an announcement in *The Bee*, New Orleans, December 22, 1834

"YANKEE" HILL

THE most interesting figure associated with the Franklin Theater was George Handel Hill, the famous Yankee impersonator. Born in Boston, he was destined for trade, but the stage proved irresistible. When in 1825 he saw Alexander Simpson as Jonathan Ploughboy in Woodworth's *Forest Rose* his career was determined. He soon secured a position on the stage as a low comedian, but it was not until 1831 at the Arch Street Theater, Philadelphia, that he had an opportunity to distinguish himself in a Yankee rôle, that of Jonathan Ploughboy. The next year he was starring at the Park and thereafter toured the Union. In 1836 and again in 1838 he appeared in the leading British theaters to the increase of his fame and fortune. In the latter year he even gave two Yankee entertainments in Paris. In 1840 Hill took over the Franklin and renamed it Hill's Theater. It remained under his management, however, for only one short season. At about this time, apparently, Hill withdrew from the stage except for occasional appearances in various parts of the country in his favorite line of characters. Of all the impersonators of "Down East" eccentrics, a type extremely popular in

266 Hill as Sy Saco in *The Knight of the Golden Fleece*, from a playbill, 1848, in the Davis Collection

this period of our dramatic history, Hill was probably the most successful. Furthermore it may not be too much to say that he was one of the most completely American actors the country has ever produced. Born and trained in America, he devoted his best talents to plays by American writers in which native American characters were featured. Besides Jonathan Ploughboy, he included in his repertory of amusing New Englanders such distinguished representatives as Sy Saco in J. A. Stone's *The Knight of the Golden Fleece*, and Solon Shingle in J. S. Jones' *The People's Lawyer*. In this type of play the Yankee usually had but little connection with the main plot, yet he was the chief reason for the popularity of the piece because he had about him a touch of reality and because he was brought to life by the rich and truthful acting of Hill. Beginning with the *Letters of Jack Downing*, the flood of Yankee literature reached a climax in the *Biglow Papers*. One of the greatest of the characters created during this period was Judge Haliburton's "Sam Slick," the itinerant clockmaker from "Onionville, Connecticut." With a wealth of material upon which he could draw, the gifted Hill was irresistible, and the play shrank into insignificance beside the character which he portrayed.

267 Charlotte Cushman, 1816–76, from a photograph in the Davis Collection

268 Miss Cushman as Romeo, from a photograph in the Davis Collection

"OUR CHARLOTTE"

THE greatest actress America had yet produced — perhaps the greatest America has ever produced — made her début in 1835. Boston-born like Hill, Charlotte Cushman was descended from Robert Cushman, one of the original Massachusetts Puritans. When, at the age of fifteen, she was compelled by her father's death to begin supporting herself, she undertook a career as a contralto singer. She soon attracted the attention of a liberal patron, who made possible three years of training under the best teacher in Boston. On April 8, 1835, Miss Cushman made her first stage appearance at the Tremont Theater, Boston, as the Countess in *The Marriage of Figaro*, and was at once engaged as prima donna for the New Orleans theater. Here by indiscreet use of her voice she soon destroyed her possibilities as a vocalist. She was now persuaded to attempt tragedy, and in spite of her youth her first appearance as Lady Macbeth was triumphant. Returning to the North, she secured a position at the Bowery Theater at twenty-five dollars a week and made her New York début as Lady Macbeth, September 12, 1836. After three nights the Bowery Theater was destroyed by fire, and with it Miss Cushman's wardrobe. A winter engagement at Albany preceded her appearance the next April at the National Theater, where she played, among other parts, that of Romeo, and Meg Merrilies in the operatic play of *Guy Mannering*. Her success in New York was followed by a similar one in Boston, where at the Tremont Theater she appeared under the management of Thomas S. Barry, one of the most capable and enterprising managers of the middle decades of the nineteenth century. In the fall of 1837 she was secured as the leading stock actress at the Park Theater, New York. Her rise to fame was slow, but when she appeared as Nancy Sykes in *Oliver Twist* in February, 1839, she was recognized as a great actress. During the season of 1842–43 she was leading actress and stage manager of the Walnut Street Theater, Philadelphia. In 1844 at Macready's suggestion she went to England, and her début at the Princess Theater, London, was declared by one critic to surpass anything seen in an English theater since the first appearance of Edmund Kean in 1814. After enjoying several years of brilliant success, she returned to the United States in 1849 and made a triumphal tour of the country. Miss Cushman's later years were occupied with further American tours, New York engagements, and foreign visits. Among the new rôles she assumed was that of Cardinal Wolsey in *Henry VIII*. During the greater part of the Civil War she lived in Europe, but her love of country was strong, and in 1865 she returned to America to help the cause of the Union. By a series of performances in the principal cities of the East, she brought in over eight thousand dollars for the use of the United States Sanitary Commission. Miss Cushman's final appearance took place in her native city of Boston, May 15, 1875, at which time she was accorded a great public demonstration.

269 Charlotte Cushman, from a photograph by Conly, Boston, in possession of the publishers

270 Charlotte and Susan Cushman as Romeo and Juliet, from an engraving in the Harvard Theater Collection

"A STREAM OF FIRE"

IN the height of her power Miss Cushman made an indelible impression on all who saw her. Even those who spoke unfavorably of her acting could not escape her impressive power. On both sides of the Atlantic critics were forced into superlatives to express their emotion. An English writer said: "In kindling and uniting the heart of a whole audience, in transmitting a stream of fire through a thousand brains at once, Miss Cushman has no superior. In the last two acts of Julia, and in the whole portrait of Bianca, she displays a quality, a variety and an amount of emotion that we believe were never exceeded in any one performance. Here she quits all English rivalry, and challenges even Rachel." Ireland wrote of her in 1867: "Miss Cushman is tall and commanding in person, but somewhat ungraceful and awkward in her movements; . . . her expressive eyes of bluish gray are her finest features, and give an air of refinement to an otherwise plain and unattractive face. . . . Her true *forte* is the character of a woman where most of the softer traits of womanhood are wanting . . . ; or in characters where, roused by passion or incited by some earnest and long cherished determination, the woman, for the time being, assumes all the power and energy of manhood." According to Mary Anderson in *A Few Memories*, "During her prophecy [in the rôle of Meg Merrilies] . . . she stood like some great withered tree, her arms stretched out, her white locks flying, her eyes blazing under her shaggy brows. She was not like a creature of this world, but like some mad majestic wanderer from the spirit land." Of her Lady Macbeth John Ranken Towse has said in his *Sixty Years of the Theatre*: "I do not believe her conception was the right one, but the power with which she realized it compelled admiration and wonder. It was melodrama 'in excelsis.' . . . She was the source and mainspring of the whole tragedy. She was inhuman, terrible, incredible, and horribly fascinating." In the words of William Winter: "The greatness of Charlotte Cushman was that of an exceptional, because grand and striking personality, combined with extraordinary power to embody the highest ideals of majesty, pathos, and appalling anguish. She was not a great actress merely, but she was a great woman . . . she poured forth . . . such resources of character, intellect, moral strength, soul, and personal magnetism as marked her as a genius of the first order. When she came upon the stage she filled it with the . . . brilliant vitality of her presence."

271 Charlotte Cushman as Lady Macbeth, from an engraving in the Davis Collection

272 Charlotte Cushman as Meg Merrilies in *Guy Mannering*, from an engraving in the Harvard Theater Collection

"FROM THE HEART ITSELF"

IN sharp contrast to Miss Cushman was another native player, whose first appearance on the stage almost coincided with hers. When, at the age of fourteen, Charles Burke made his début as the Prince of Wales in *Richard III* at the National Theater, New York, he probably gave little enough evidence of the comic talent that was latent within him. But in later years his half brother, Joseph Jefferson III, said of him, "We get as near Burke as we can and he who gets nearest succeeds best." Jefferson has further remarked that his comedy was "subtle, incisive, and refined. . . . He had an eye and face that told their meaning before he spoke, a voice that seemed to come from the heart itself, penetrating, but melodious." Burke's rise to great popularity followed his apprenticeship of a year or two at the National in various boy's parts and his period of training in the West in the troupe of his stepfather, Joseph Jefferson II. (See No. 437.) From his reappearance in New York at the Bowery in 1847 to his early death from tuberculosis he held a prominent place among the leading comedians of America. Among his successful characters were Touchstone, Sir Andrew Aguecheek, Launcelot Gobbo, and Bob Acres. He was

273 Charles St. Thomas Burke, 1822–54, from an engraved portrait by August Toetdeberg, in the collection of Montrose J. Moses

also admirable in Yankee and other rustic rôles, and, dramatizing Irving's *Rip Van Winkle*, stage versions of which tale were already in existence, he added to his fame by acting that eccentric, lovable ne'er-do-well.

RIVALRY FOR THE PARK

THE theater in which Burke made his début was shortly purchased by a Mr. Mauran, a New York merchant, and James H. Hackett, and was leased to James W. Wallack. Under his management it was opened September 4, 1837, with a most effective and evenly balanced stock company. The courage required for this enterprise becomes evident when it is remembered that in the spring of 1837 one of the most disastrous panics in the history of the nation broke out. Prosperity did not fully return until 1842. James and Henry Wallack were outstanding members of the company, which included also several recent arrivals from England, among them James W. Browne, who had passed his prime but was still a versatile and accomplished artist in light and eccentric comedy; W. H. Williams, one of the best low comedians of his time, who specialized in Yorkshire and Cockney dialect; and John Vandenhoff, a tragedian of the first rank. The National under Wallack's

274   Burning of the National Theater, 1839, from a print in the New York Historical Society

management offered, according to Ireland, "the first opposition to the Park that had not been quickly overcome, and though it may not have proved a profitable speculation to its projectors, it resulted in so dividing the patronage of the public and in showing what improvements could be made in the general mounting and getting up of even old standard plays, that the hitherto proudly styled Old Drury of America lost its supremacy as the leading theater, and never again fully recovered that position." With programs selected from the plays of Shakespeare, standard English comedy, current London successes, and Italian opera, Wallack continued to draw large audiences to the National until its destruction by fire September 23, 1839.

"JIM" WALLACK

AN interesting member of Wallack's stock company was his nephew, James W. Wallack the younger, son of Henry Wallack. Born in London, he made his stage début in Philadelphia at the age of four as the child in *Pizarro*. He later played youthful parts at the Bowery, but his first significant appearance occurred January 20, 1837, at the National, where he soon assumed a leading position. Handsome of face and figure like all the Wallacks, he shone in rôles that gave play to the picturesqueness of his attitudes and the spirit of his declamation. Perhaps his most famous part was that of Fagin in *Oliver Twist*. In 1851 Wallack played for a time at the Haymarket, London, as Macready's successor, and thereafter became manager of the Marylebone Theater, London. Later he starred throughout Great Britain, Australia, and the United States from New York to California. While less highly endowed than some of his kin, he was extremely popular in tragedy and melodrama, and in a minor class of theaters was recognized, wrote Ireland, "as a star of the first brilliancy."

275 James W. Wallack, Jr. (right) and J. Lester Wallack, from an engraving by H. Davidson after a daguerreotype. © The Century Co., used by permission

CHARLES MATHEWS, JR.

ANOTHER actor to carry a distinguished stage name into the second generation was Charles Mathews, Jr., who visited America in 1838. Though distinctly inferior to his father, Mathews, by his quiet, unobtrusive comedy, appealed to the most intelligent part of his audiences. He was accompanied by his wife, formerly Madame Vestris, whose reputed beauty and whose fame as a singing actress aroused high expectation in this country. But forty-one years had taken their toll of her beauty, and her finished style of acting was inadequate compensation in American eyes for her diminished charm and her dubious moral reputation. Moreover, the public was much disappointed by the inferior grade of pieces in which the pair appeared. Consequently this visit of Mr. and Mrs. Mathews was brief and unsuccessful. In 1857 and again in 1871 Mathews revisited this country with more fortunate results. At the time of his third visit he was said to be "an unequaled incarnation of the spirit of youth and jollity."

276 Charles Mathews, Jr., 1803–78, from an engraving in *The Autobiography of Joseph Jefferson*, New York, 1887. © The Century Co.

277 Madame Vestris, 1797–1856, from an engraving by Woolnoth after a drawing by Wageman, in the Gottschalk Collection

278 Charles Mathews, Jr., from a sketch *Our Only Comedian* by "Spy," in *Vanity Fair*, London, 1875

THE NEW CHATHAM THEATER

LESS than three weeks after the destruction of the National Theater, another playhouse, the New Chatham, opened its doors to the public, September 11, 1839. It was situated on Chatham Street between Roosevelt and James. The original manager was Thomas Flynn, who, with Henry E. Willard, had projected the enterprise. Among the performers in the early days of the establishment were James W. Wallack the younger, Mr. and Mrs. Henry Wallack, and their two daughters, Julia and Fanny. During its career the house passed through the hands of various managers, and many famous actors appeared on its stage. Among the latter were

279   The New Chatham Theater, from a print in the New York Historical Society

Junius Brutus Booth, "Yankee" Hill, Mlle. Celeste, Edwin Forrest, Mary Duff, George Barrett, Edwin Booth, and Ada Isaacs Menken. By means of elaborate spectacles and other popular novelties, including *Uncle Tom's Cabin*, which were sure to appeal to East Side audiences, the New Chatham (rechristened the New National in 1848) maintained a continuous existence for twenty years and enjoyed a number of highly prosperous seasons before it was abandoned about 1860. The life of the New Chatham lay in two of the most eventful decades of American history. While the series of famous actors just noted were appearing on its boards, restless and eager Americans were carrying the national frontier west to the Pacific. Seven years after the founding of the theater the Mexican War broke out. Three years later occurred the great gold rush to California. Finally in the decade of the 'fifties the nation was drifting rapidly toward civil war.

"THE ELSSLER"

A MORE than nine days' wonder was the far-famed danseuse, Fanny Elssler, who, fresh from European triumphs, made her first American appearance, May 14, 1840. Ireland thus lyrically described her: "The perfection of grace attended every attitude; the airiness of gossamer every step. All that can be imagined of lightness indefinable and of movements seemingly effortless were displayed in her various performances, and in these important requisites she has eclipsed every dancer known to the American Stage. In person she was tall, but of exquisite womanly proportions, and her German cast of features was set off by a complexion of delicate whiteness, contrasting charmingly with the rich glossiness of her classically-braided chestnut hair. Fascinating beyond description was Fanny Elssler. . . ." Small wonder, then, that the theater-going public was intoxicated by her charm and did unaccountable things. At New York the whole house rose and gave such a shout as might greet a conqueror; in Baltimore the people loosed the horses from her carriage and drew her triumphantly to her hotel; the Senate at Washington rose as she entered, and the House insisted that she sit in the Speaker's chair; at Richmond she was met by a delegation of leading citizens, who had pressed a brass band into service; and in New Orleans the pillows of her carriage were sold to the highest bidder. To be sure the over-conscientious frowned and protested, but little good it did them with the public packing every theater in which she appeared. But the full houses, strange to say, did not mean enrichment for the local managers; on the contrary, the result was sometimes financial loss. "The Elssler" was adamant in her demands — never less than five hundred dollars a night or else half the gross receipts, and always a clear benefit. When Fanny Elssler returned to her native Germany, after two years in the United States, she was the richer by some eighty-five thousand dollars, a very great figure for those days, but of her American managers there was quite a different story to tell.

280   Popular Song Cover, showing a dance by Fanny Elssler, lithograph by N. Currier, after a drawing by W. K. Hewitt, in the New York Public Library

281   Fanny Elssler, 1810–84, from *The Illustrated London News*, 1843

282   Performance at Mitchell's Olympic, from a playbill in the Davis Collection

MITCHELL'S OLYMPIC

THE burning of the National Theater in 1839 threw various actors out of employment, among them an inconspicuous comedian named William Mitchell. In this dilemma Mitchell hit upon the idea of taking over the Olympic Theater, built two years before by Henry E. Willard and William R. Blake on Broadway near Grand Street. It was a small theater of unusual intimacy and charm; indeed it was said to display a more tasteful and beautiful interior than any other theater in America. But New York was oversupplied with playhouses, and the Olympic's refined programs of light comedies, witty farces, and burlettas failed to draw profitable audiences. When Mitchell leased the Olympic in 1839, he reopened it as a half-price theater and presented musical

283   William Mitchell, 1798–1856, from an engraving in the Davis Collection

travesties and other types of entertainment of a lighter sort than were to be found at the statelier houses of the city. It was still a time of serious financial depression, and the low price and the merry atmosphere of the Olympic served to draw the public in most gratifying numbers. The theater became cosmopolitan; it was a fashionable place of resort for the gentlemen of the city, while on Saturday nights the pit was reserved for newsboys and butcher boys at an admission of twelve and one-half cents each. Mitchell's mode of announcement was individual and calculated to catch the popular fancy. On one occasion, for instance, he advertised a "Grand Complimentary Benefit Given by Mr. Mitchell to Himself," and advised his patrons that "the prices will be, for this night only (being the last night of the season), the same as usual." Parodying the announcements of his rivals, he instructed drivers of conveyances, "to prevent confusion, [to] set their company down with the horses' heads in front and their tails behind." When Mitchell took over the Olympic, Dickens was the great literary sensation of the English-speaking world. With the appearance of *The Pickwick Papers* in book form in 1837 his place was assured. During his first visit to the United States in 1842 a "grand Boz ball" was held in his honor at the Park Theater, and between dances elaborate tableaux representing scenes from the Dickens novels were presented. According to Ireland, "the Dickens mania . . . excited the town almost to frenzy." Taking advantage of this situation, Mitchell, like other managers, presented numerous adaptations of the famous novelist's tales, and gained tremendous applause for his impersonation of various Dickens characters, among them Squeers, Crummles, and Sam Weller. Mitchell's company contained at one time or another a number of prominent players, including George Holland (see No. 405) and Mary Gannon (see No. 541). But none was more popular than Mitchell himself, and by virtue of this popularity he maintained the Olympic through eleven prosperous seasons before his retirement from the management in 1850.

284   Mitchell's Olympic, 1848, from a print in the New York Historical Society

THE VANDENHOFFS

JOHN and George Vandenhoff, father and son, were British actors of distinguished ability, both of whom created a notable impression in America. John Vandenhoff first appeared in this country at the National Theater, New York, September 11, 1837, as Coriolanus. This was followed by his impersonations of Macbeth, Shylock, Brutus, and Hamlet. The American critics agreed with their British brethren that in "grandeur of presence and heroic dignity" he was not surpassed by any actor of the age. After his first season Vandenhoff returned to England, but revisited America in 1839 and played at various New York theaters until his final leave-taking in 1841. His son, George, who, after some success on the British stage, came to this country in the year of Fanny Elssler's departure, spent most of the rest of his life here. His début occurred at the Park Theater as Hamlet, September 21, 1842. Though deficient in passion, his interpretation of the rôle was considered near perfection as a studied work of art. In such other parts as Richard III, Hotspur, Mercutio, Benedick, and Claude Melnotte in *The Lady of Lyons*, he delighted the judicious by his fine personal appearance, his gallant bearing, and his familiarity with the con-

285 John Vandenhoff, 1790–1861, as Shylock, from a lithograph, 1839, by Lane, in the Gottschalk Collection, New York

ventions of polished society. In his autobiography, *Leaves from an Actor's Note-book* (1860), the younger Vandenhoff recounted some of his experiences and observations in the United States. At the time of his arrival he found the country to be suffering from a financial depression, as a consequence of which the theatrical business was in a decline. He noted that Boston was not much given to supporting good drama, though panto-

286 John Vandenhoff as Sir Giles Overreach in *A New Way to Pay Old Debts*, from an engraving by Woodman after a drawing by R. W. Buts, in the possession of the publishers

mime, equestrian shows, and other spectacles prospered in that city of culture. The year after his American début Vandenhoff undertook a southern tour. He first appeared at the St. Charles Theater in New Orleans under the management of Ludlow and Smith. The critics praised him warmly, but the hard times were widespread, and, as in the North, audiences were discouragingly slender. One of his New Orleans experiences is perhaps worth relating. On a certain night while playing *The Lady of Lyons*, he was carrying the fainting Pauline upstage, when one of the spectators, carried away by his enthusiasm, shouted out: "Kiss her! by ——, kiss her!" The actor advanced to the footlights in an effort to espy the offender. What was his surprise to see a man suddenly lifted bodily from his seat and passed through the air from hand to hand until he was safely outside the door. The performance was then resumed with great applause. From New Orleans Vandenhoff went on to Mobile, where he found a shockingly bad company and almost no audience at all. After six "tolerable" nights at the Holliday Street Theater in Baltimore, he returned to New York and here he continued his career for several years. About 1856 he quit the stage, feeling that it was steadily sinking as a source of intellectual amusement, and devoted himself to public readings from his beloved Shakespeare.

287 John Brougham, 1814–80, from a photograph in the Davis Collection

ECCENTRIC CHARACTERS

THE year of George Vandenhoff's coming saw also the arrival of an Irish comedian who was destined to occupy a distinctive place on the American stage. Before coming to this country John Brougham had attained some prominence both as actor and manager in London. His first appearance at the Park Theater, October 4, 1842, made it evident that an important addition had been made to the ranks of the New York actors, and his subsequent career continued to disclose new phases of his

288 Brougham as Sir Lucius O'Trigger in *The Rivals*, from a photogravure by Gebbie and Husson, in the possession of the publishers

comic versatility. His too great familiarity with his audiences, and his habit of introducing constant interpolations into the text were sometimes criticised, but his popularity, both personal and professional, was unsurpassed by any contemporary. Brougham was at his best in the comedy of eccentric characters, being possessed of a great supply of animal spirit and vigor. He was ill equipped, however, for the delineation of pathos and sentiment. He was especially notable in Irish rôles, such as Dennis Brulgruddery in *John Bull*, Sir Lucius O'Trigger in *The Rivals*, and O'Callaghan in *His Last Legs*. As Captain Cuttle in *Dombey and Son* he also gained great favor. Desiring to attempt theatrical management in this country, in 1850 he had a playhouse built on Broadway, which he called Brougham's Lyceum. Although a high level of production was maintained, the venture failed, and he then became a member of Wallack's company until 1856, when he took over the management of the Bowery for a short season. During the remainder of his life he was a member of various stock companies, except for a brief period in 1869, when he unsuccessfully undertook the control of a second Brougham's Theater. He made his last appearance in 1879 at Booth's Theater.

289   Exterior and Interior of Brougham's Lyceum, New York, from an engraving by J. C. Taylor in *Frank Leslie's Illustrated Newspaper*, February 1863

290 John Brougham, from a photograph in the Davis Collection

WINTER GARDEN.

Lessee and Manager...W. STUART
Stage Manager...J. G. HANLEY
Treasurer...H. J. JACKSON

GREATEST SUCCESS OF THE SEASON.

This evening, Brougham's world famous Extravaganza, **Pocahontas!** The Great Comedian **John Brougham** as **Pow-ha-tan.** The young and beautiful Comedienne, **Miss Emilie Melville** as **Pocahontas.** **J. C. Dunn** as Capt. **John Smith.**

This Evening, will be presented, with **New Scenery, Costumes,** and **Appointments,** John Brougham's Original—Ab-original—Erratic—Operatic—Semi-Civilized, and Demi-Savage Extravaganza, in 2 acts, Being a Per Version of Ye Trewe and Wonderfulle History of Ye Renowned Princess,

PO-CA-HON-TAS!

Or, Ye Gentle Savage.

Dramatis Personæ—of Ye Englishe.

Capt John Smith, the undoubted original, vocal and instrumental, in the settlement of Virginia, in love with Po-ca-hon tas, according to this story, though somewhat at variance with his story..J. C. DUNN
Lieut. Thomas Brown, second in command a hitherto neglected genius, whose claims on posterity are now, for the first time, acknowledged as his right..............J. MILOT
William Brown, sometimes called Bill, another of the same sort............DUN BROWN
Mynheer Rolff, the real husband of Pocahontas, but dramatically divorced, contrary to all law and fact...C. M. WALCOT, Jr
Benjamin Brace...........(Splicers of main braces, shiverers of timbers)......MR. GO-AHEAD
John Junk...............(general dealers in single combats, double)........MR. COME-UP
Henry Halyard...........(hornpipes, and altogether amazingly naughty.)......MR. SPARK
William Buntline........(cal people.................................)......MR. MAST HEAD

Of Ye Savages.

H. R. H. POW-HA-TAN I, King of the Tuscaroras—a crotchety Monarch—in fact a Semi-Brave...MR. JOHN BROUGHAM
Right Hon. Quash-al Jaw, Speaker of the Savage House of Lords—straightener of unpleasant kinks, an oiler of troubled waters, unraveller of knotty points, adjuster of pugnacious diffi-culties, and Grand Eye Parliamentary Factotum and Fogleman...............T. J. LEIGH
O po dil-doc, one of the Aboriginal F. F. V's, an indignant dignitary..............J. DUELL
Col-o-gog, another warm headed and hearted son of Old Virginia, the untiring...W. S. ANDREWS
Bi-jin-ksk............Sergeant-at-Arms, a friend to swear by...............MR. WADDLETON
Ip-pah-kak...L. CARLAND
Sae-sa-prll..............(Medical Men of the Saultz)......................J. BULL
Kod-liv-royl............(and Senna-ca Tribes)............................A. FISH
Katomel.................(   )......................A. GEW
H. R. H. PRINCESS PO-CA-HON-TAS, the Beautiful and very properly undutiful Daughter of King Powhattan, married according to the ridiculous dictum of actual circum-stance to Mastaf Rolff, but the author flatters himself much more advantageously disposed of in the acting edition..................................MISS EMILIE MELVILLE
Poo-tee pet...........(Interesting offshoots from the a istocratic stock,)...MISS FANNY STOCQUELER
Di-mun-di............(superior be the first families of Virginia, embody-)..MISS DUNN
Wee- he-ven-da......(ing the rigid principles of the Tuscorora Fashion-).MISS MARY CARR
Kros-as-kan be......(able Finishing School.........................)......MISS MOORE

Music Incidental to the Piece.

Solo and Chorus—"O, how abet'd"?"...........................Pow-ha-tan and Chorus
Air—"Wid a Dundeen,"..Pow-ha-tan
Solo and Chorus—"Come Forward"..............................John Smith and Indians
Grand Scena—"As you are, oh "................................Po-ca-hon tas
Various—"Where the Idlers"...................................John Smith and Indian
Quintet and Chorus—"Fill now the Flowing Glass".....Powha tan, Po-ca-hon-tas and Smith
Grand Finale—"Effectuoso—Furioso—ε Conglomeroso".........Po-ca-hon-tas and Indians
Come, let us now like Watch,Dogs Bark......................John Smith and Po-ca-hon-tas
Operatic Duet..John Smith and Po-ca-hon tas
Characteristic Concerted Piece—" Now for a jolly encounter"...Po-ca-hon-ta , John Smith , Pow-ha tan
Grand Finale—"And now we have done our duty......John Smith, Pow-ha-tan, Po-ca-hon-tas and Chorus

THE SCOTIA POLKA,

Composed by **JOHN BROUGHAM**, and dedicated to Captain JUDKINS.
The orchestral arrangement by ROBERT STOEPEL.

Part 1.—The Departure—"Warning Bell"—Steam up—Paddle Wheel Accompaniment—Dinner—"Life on the Ocean Wave.
Part 2.—A Dark Day—Trouble Ahead—The Chief Engineer puts on his "foul weather shirt"—The "Deck" in a Storm—The Winds Whistle, so does the "Bos'n"—The Thunder Speaks, so does the Commodore.
Part 3.—"All's Well"—Glass rises—Sea falls—Passengers jolly—An eight day trip—The "Arrival" and the "Welcome Home."

291 "Brougham's World Famous Extravaganza, *Po-Ca-Hon-Tas!*" from a playbill in the possession of the publishers

JOHN BROUGHAM AS PLAYWRIGHT

BEFORE coming to America Brougham had tried his hand at dramatic composition, and in this country he added a large amount of playwriting to his activities as an actor and manager. Among his productions were several adaptations of Dickens' novels, including *Dombey and Son, Bleak House*, and *David Copperfield* (Brougham playing Micawber in the last named). Another of his adaptations was *Dred*, based on Mrs. Stowe's novel of that name. Sensational melodramas, Irish comedies, opera librettos, and at least one historical drama likewise came from his pen. His native bent toward lively satire displayed itself in a revamping of the then famous English burletta *Life in London, or The Day and Night Adventures of Tom and Jerry*, a play presenting with considerable vividness glimpses of the underworld of a great city. Under the title of *Life in New York, or Tom and Jerry on a Visit* (1856), Brougham continued the adventures of this lively pair. But it was not so much in this hasty sketch that the author displayed his dramatic talent as in a few burlesques, one of which bears the title *Much Ado about a Merchant of Venice* (1852), "from the original text — a long way." Best known of this species is *Po-Ca-Hon-Tas, or the Gentle Savage* (1855), in which Brougham created the part of H. R. H. Pow-Ha-Tan. The piece is a satire on the excessive use of monotonous and unreal Indian themes. This type of drama very nearly vanished after the appearance of *Po-Ca-Hon-Tas*. Laurence Hutton has said in his *Curiosities of the American Stage:* "If America has ever had an Aristophanes, John Brougham was his name. His *Pocahontas* and *Columbus* are almost classics. They rank among the best, if they are not the very best, burlesques in any living language."

292   Exterior of Palmo's Opera House (afterward Burton's Theater), from a print
in the New York Historical Society

PALMO'S OPERA HOUSE

SINCE the failure of the Italian Opera House in 1835, opera had been without a home in New York. To remedy this situation Signor Ferdinand Palmo, successful proprietor of the Café des Milles Colonnes on Broadway, erected an opera house on Chambers Street in which the music of his native Italy might be presented to the best advantage. Palmo's Opera House was a small and tasteful structure—"parlor-like" according to Ireland. A competent company of Italian singers was assembled. As a further inducement to the public Palmo affixed this notice to his announcements, "Arrangements have been made by the management with the Rail Road Company [the Harlem line], for the accommodation of ladies and gentlemen living up town, so that a large car, well lighted and warmed, will start after the Theater closes, and Police officers will be in attendance to prevent disorder." The opening occurred February 3, 1844, with Bellini's *I Puritani* — its first performance in New York. This was followed by such operas as *Il Barbiere di Siviglia*, *La Sonnambula*, *Lucia di Lammermoor*, and *L'Elisir d'Amore*. But the public found other ways of entertaining itself, and after two short seasons Signor Palmo, his modest fortune eaten up by expenses, was compelled to accept a position as barkeeper in a hotel. Under other management a few more seasons of opera were offered here until the house was converted into Burton's Theater in 1848. Among the able singers who appeared at the Palmo at one time or another were Signora Borghese, Signor San Quirico, Madame Damoreau, Signora Pico, Signor Tomasi, Signorina Barili (half-sister of Adelina Patti) and Signor Benedetti. One of the most interesting events that occurred at Palmo's Opera House was the presentation there, following recent successes in London and Berlin, of Sophocles' *Antigone*, April 7, 1845, probably its first professional performance in America. The production, superin-

tended by George Vandenhoff, was provided with a new Grecian proscenium, a double stage in accordance with the then prevailing conception of a Greek theater, and new costumes and properties consonant with classic drama. An orchestra and a chorus of forty voices performed the music of Mendelssohn. The part of Creon was taken by Vandenhoff, that of Haemon by F. S. Chanfrau (see No. 497) and that of Antigone by a Miss Clarendon. Scholars and artists cordially approved the production, but the public stayed away. In Vandenhoff's words, "We repeated this *classic disentombment* twelve successive nights, and then 'quietly inurned' the mighty Greek, to sleep in undisturbed and unprofaned repose."

293   Interior of Palmo's Opera House, from a print in the New York Historical Society

294 Mrs. Mowatt as Rosalind, from an engraving
in the Goodspeed Collection, Boston

295 Anna Cora Mowatt, 1819–70, from an engraving by I. C. Buttre,
in the collection of Montrose J. Moses

"BEAUTY, GRACE AND REFINEMENT"

THE year of this performance saw the emergence of one of the most interesting native actresses America had yet produced. Anna Cora Ogden was born in Bordeaux, France, but was descended from an old American family. At the age of fifteen she married James Mowatt, a wealthy New York lawyer, and for some years she led a pampered, carefree existence. About 1840, however, Mr. Mowatt lost his fortune through speculation, and, because of his failing sight, Mrs. Mowatt courageously undertook the support of herself and her husband. From childhood she had shown what her friends considered talent in home theatricals, and in her dilemma, stimulated by hearing the elder Vandenhoff in a course of readings, she determined to become a public reader. In this endeavor she achieved great success at Boston, New York, and elsewhere. Later, under the stress of necessity, she set about becoming an actress. Friends and relatives protested. For a woman of high social station to adopt the dubious profession of the stage was little short of a scandal; "but," in her own words, "entreaties, threats, supplicating letters could only occasion me much suffering — they could not shake my resolution." Her stage début was made, June 13, 1845, at the Park as Pauline in *The Lady of Lyons*. After her initial appearance Edgar Allan Poe wrote in the *Broadway Journal:* "We have to speak of her acting only in terms of enthusiastic admiration — let her trust proudly to her own grace of manner — her own sense of art — her own rich and natural eloquence." Mrs. Mowatt soon rose to the rank of a star and toured the country. In 1847 she visited England, playing first in the provinces and later at London to the great satisfaction of the British audiences. After her husband's death Mrs. Mowatt returned to America in 1851 and continued her starring tours with undiminished prosperity. Ireland explained her success thus: "Delicacy was her most marked characteristic. A subdued earnestness of manner, a soft musical voice, a winning witchery of enunciation, and indeed an almost perfect combination of beauty, grace and refinement fitted her for the very class of characters in which Miss Cushman was incapable of excelling, and in which *she* commanded the approbation of the British public." On June 3, 1854, she took her farewell of the stage at Niblo's Garden in the character of Pauline and a few days later married William F. Ritchie of Richmond. In the words of one of her contemporaries, she "has since dedicated her brilliant talents solely to the social circle of which she is the admired center."

296 Mrs. Mowatt, from an engraving in *Fashion*,
        London, 1850

FASHION

MRS. MOWATT's dramatic activities were not confined to the acting of others' plays; she gained much contemporary fame and a modest niche in American literature by writing plays of her own. Indeed before her stage début she had written her most noted play, *Fashion; or, Life in New York*, which was produced at the Park, March 24, 1845. Though the work of an American and a woman, it had a continuous run of three weeks before it was withdrawn, still at the height of its popularity, to make way for stars previously engaged. It also had a run at the Walnut Street Theater, Philadelphia, during the New

FASHION;

or,

LIFE IN NEW YORK

A Comedy

IN FIVE ACTS

BY

ANNA CORA MOWATT.

AUTHOR OF "ARMAND," "EVELYN," "THE FORTUNE HUNTER
ETC., ETC

How'er it be—it seems to me
'Tis only noble to be good,
Kind hearts are more than coronets
And simple faith than Norman blood."
                                    TENNYSON

LONDON

W NEWBERY 6 KING STREET HOLBORN
—
1850

297   Title-page of *Fashion*, in the
        New York Public Library

York engagement. *Fashion* is a descendant of our first important social comedy, *The Contrast* (see No. 68), and like it is a lively satire on the affectations of those Americans who make themselves ridiculous by stupidly aping foreign manners. Mrs. Tiffany, aspiring to the leadership of the New York "*ee-light,*" provides herself with a French *femme de chambre*, a few atrociously pronounced French phrases, a set of furniture with a "*jenny-says-quoi*" look about it, and the attentions of a spurious French count. The solid principles of republican America are exemplified by the speech and actions of the sterling Colonel Howard and hearty old Adam Trueman from Cattaraugus, New York. Though the plot is trite, the dialogue is lively, and the characters are vivid and not unveracious. Allowing for the necessary exaggeration, it mirrors one phase of contemporary society with considerable accuracy. *Fashion* had a run of two weeks during Mrs. Mowatt's London engagement, and by at least one critic it was compared favorably with the plays of Garrick and Sheridan. That the comedy is well adapted to the theater was proved when it was revived in something of a burlesque spirit by the Provincetown Players in New York during the season of 1923–24. When Mrs. Mowatt wrote her second play, *Armand*, she incorporated a part well suited to herself, a feature not present in *Fashion*. This romantic drama was produced at the Park, September 27, 1847. Later it was given at Boston and in 1849 at London — always, it seems, with the approval of the public. But for the modern reader this conventional play, lacking the contemporaneousness of its forerunner, has less interest. Another of Mrs. Mowatt's writings is her *Autobiography of an Actress* (1854), an entertaining record that gives valuable information concerning the American theater.

298 Scene from a revival of Mrs. Mowatt's *Fashion* at the Provincetown Theater,
        New York, from a photograph in the collection of Montrose J. Moses

299 Edward Loomis Davenport, 1816–77, from a
photograph in the Davis Collection

A REMARKABLE RANGE

DURING several of her years of stardom Mrs. Mowatt was supported by Edward Loomis Davenport, whom she had engaged to act as her professional companion. He had made his début at Providence, Rhode Island, in 1836, and had created so favorable an impression as to be invited to join the company of the Tremont Theater, Boston. He first appeared at the Park in 1846 as Romeo to Mrs. Mowatt's Juliet. The next year he accompanied her to England and played, among other parts,

300 Davenport as Adam Trueman in *Fashion*,
from an engraving in *Edward Loomis Davenport*,
edited by E. F. Edgett, New York, 1901, Dunlap
Society Publications, No. 14

that of Adam Trueman in *Fashion*. The next seven years were spent in England, where he gained the favor of the critics, and on his return to America he was recognized as one of the outstanding artists. In later years he managed in succession theaters in New York, Boston, Washington, and Philadelphia. Ireland regarded him, "with one exception, as the most chaste, refined and intellectual of American tragedians, and the most graceful and polished of native performers in genteel comedy, with a versatility of general excellence rarely approached." John Ranken Towse, in *Sixty Years of the Theater*, indicated something of his remarkable range in these sentences: "Second only to Booth's, his Hamlet was an exceedingly able performance, princely, thoughtful, tender, gravely humorous, sympathetic, and, in the crises, finely passionate. His Bill Sykes was one of the most terrific exhibitions of savage blackguardism ever witnessed on the stage, while only Booth could excel him in the craft and finesse of Richelieu." James G. Huneker has left this estimate in *Steeplejack:* "E. L. Davenport is one of my choicest memories. Next to Salvini's and Booth's, I never enjoyed such acting. . . . Davenport, it has always seemed to me, never received his critical due."

301 Davenport as Brutus in *Julius Caesar*, from a photograph in the Davis Collection

302 Davenport as Sir Giles Overreach, from a photograph
in the collection of H. A. Ogden, New York

303   View of Tremont Street, Boston, showing Boston Museum, from *Gleason's Pictorial*, Boston, 1853

NEW THEATERS FOR BOSTON

ALTHOUGH New York had become, years before the period with which we are now concerned, the dramatic capital of America, it must not be assumed that only in that city was the theater an active institution. During the 'forties Boston, once the citadel of the play actor's foes, experienced considerable expansion in its theatrical affairs. There was still a sizable and influential element in Boston who looked with an inherited disapproval upon the stage. In order to capture the patronage of this group it occurred to the canny mind of Moses Kimball, proprietor of the Boston Museum and Gallery of Fine Arts, located at the corner of Tremont and Bromfield Streets, to offer dramatic performances in connection with his exhibition of stuffed beasts and wax figures without employing that disquieting word — theater. A large music room over the Museum was admirably adapted to this purpose and in 1843 John Sefton and Mrs. Maeder (see No. 247) were secured to produce operettas. Later in the same year a stock company was formed with W. H. Smith as director, and the Bostonians found the offerings so much to their liking that the large music room soon proved inadequate to house them. Accordingly in 1846 a new museum was erected on Tremont near Court Street, which continued to do duty for decades, and for nearly half a century ranked as one of the important theaters of the country. As the old Federal Street Theater had made a pious gesture by discontinuing performances on meeting nights, the Boston Museum for years closed its doors on Saturday nights, the eve of the Sabbath. The sacrifice of an acting night proved to be good business. Other changes in the theatrical situation in Boston were the passing of the old Tremont Theater in 1843; the conversion of a tabernacle of the Millerites into the Howard Athenæum in 1845; the reopening of the old Federal Street Theater in 1846 with J. W. Wallack, Mr. and Mrs. Charles Kean, Edwin Forrest, and Charlotte Cushman as visiting stars; and the opening of the Adelphi Theater in 1847 with John Brougham as one of the managers. By 1846 Boston, once the leading seaport of the Atlantic Coast, had dropped in importance to third place — behind New York and Philadelphia. Still strongly influenced by Puritan tradition, its cosmopolitan population was yet to come.

304   The Boston Museum's Famous Stock Company, from an engraving in the possession of the publishers

WILLIAM WARREN, JR.

305 William Warren, Jr., 1812–88, from a photograph by Mottman and Campbell, in the possession of the publishers

306 Warren as Herr Weigel in *My Son*, from an albertype in the Goodspeed Collection, Boston

THE most popular of Boston's actors during this period and for many years after was William Warren, Jr., distinguished son of a distinguished father. Born in Philadelphia he made his début in 1832 at the Arch Street Theater, as Young Norval in *Douglas*. In 1843 he appeared briefly at the Park Theater, New York, and two years later was acting in London. He joined the company of the Boston Museum in 1847, and for many years was the outstanding member of that organization. Like his father he was preëminently a comedian. In that field an artist of remarkable versatility, he ranged easily from the best of Shakespeare's comedies through delicate French comediettas to the broadest and noisiest of farces. Pathos he could achieve as well as laughter. In *Reminiscences of a Dramatic Critic* Henry Austin Clapp has said of Warren: "In him Boston had a Théâtre Français, situated on Tremont Street, as long as he lived and played." His career as an actor covered exactly fifty years, from 1832 to 1882, and during that period he gave thirteen thousand three hundred and forty-five performances and appeared in five hundred and seventy-seven characters. Among the characters which, in the minds of Bostonians, were inseparably associated with Warren were Touchstone, Dogberry, Polonius, Launcelot Gobbo, Bob Acres, Sir Peter Teazle, Dominie Sampson (in a dramatization of Scott's *Guy Mannering*), and Micawber. And he continued to master new parts until the end of his career. Of Warren, the citizen, Clapp has given this description: "For many years Mr. Warren was a most interesting figure in Boston, not only upon the stage, but upon the streets over which he took his deliberate and slightly varied walks. His tall, large, well-formed figure, and his easy, rather peculiar gait, which seemed always about to become, but never quite became, a roll or swagger; his noble head, with the bright penetrating eyes and the extraordinarily sensitive mouth, made equally to utter mirth or pathos or wisdom, produced the effect of a unique personality. His manners were the finest I ever saw in a man."

307 Warren as Batkins in *The Silver Spoon*, from an albertype in the possession of the publishers

308 Warren as Launce in *Two Gentlemen of Verona*, from an engraving in the Davis Collection

309   Astor Place Riot, 1849, from an engraving in *The Illustrated London News*, June 2, 1849

THE ASTOR PLACE RIOT, MAY 10, 1849

ONE of the least creditable episodes connected with the American theater occurred just two months before the opening of Burton's Theater. The Astor Place Opera House was built in 1847 and managed for a season by San Quirico and Salvatore Patti. Then Niblo and Hackett leased the house and announced Macready for a Shakespearean series in May. The adherents of Edwin Forrest, who had intensified the recent unpleasantness between the American and English stars by giving wide publicity to Macready's alleged hissing of Forrest at the Edinburgh theater during the latter's tour of Great Britain, joined hands with chronic Anglophobes easily persuaded to participate in any anti-British agitation. Their activities commenced sometime before May 10, the day set for the performance of Macready's Macbeth. They were determined that the Englishman should not act, and hung posters blazing with such sentiments as: "Workingmen, shall Americans or English rule this city? . . . Washington forever! Stand by your rights. American Committee." Allston Brown, in his *History of the New York Stage*, gives a stirring account of the occurrences on the night of May 10, when partisans inside and outside the theater made riot. Police quieted the storm that arose in the auditorium when Macready appeared in the third scene, but none of the first act was audible because of the uproar in the streets. "In front and rear the fierce assaults of the mob, as they thundered at the door, resounded over the theater, while the shouts and yells of the assailants were terrific." The crowd pelted with paving stones the soldiers sent to dispel them, but finally after a bitter struggle, in which the military fired several volleys, the assailants were driven back. The square was then patrolled, and at one o'clock, when the play ended, quiet prevailed. In this riot, many people were severely wounded and seventeen were killed. Macready barely escaped with his life, and left immediately for Boston, whence he sailed for England. Forrest, though he strenuously denied all connection with the disgraceful fracas, never regained the support of the theatrical aristocracy, although his popularity with the common people increased.

THE END OF THE PARK

THE second Park Theater was for nearly three decades so dominant an institution in the dramatic activities of America that its destruction by fire may well serve to mark the end of an era. When, on December 15, 1848, a file of handbills hanging at the stage entrance swung against a burning gas jet, a conflagration began which, in hardly more than an hour, wiped from the roster of New York theaters the name which for a full half century had held a preëminent position among the playhouses of the city. The contemporary playgoer probably spent little time lamenting its end; for him its pristine splendor had departed and it had become a dreary and antiquated relic. To one of these contemporary playgoers, Richard Grant White, we are indebted for this description of the old house: "Across them [its boxes] were stretched benches consisting of a mere board covered with faded red moreen, a narrower board, shoulder high, being stretched behind to serve for a back. . . . The floor was dirty and broken into holes; the seats were bare, backless benches. Women were never seen in the pit, and although the excellence of the position and the cheapness of admission (50 cents) took gentlemen there, few went there who could afford to study comfort and luxury in their amusements. The place was pervaded with evil smells; and, not uncommonly, in the midst

310   Unromantic Glimpse of an Early American Audience, from a lithograph by A. Ducote, after a drawing by A. Hervieu, in Frances Trollope, *Domestic Manners of the Americans*, London, 1832

of a performance rats ran out of holes in the floor and across into the orchestra. This delectable place was approached by a long underground passage, with bare whitewashed walls, dimly lighted except at a sort of booth at which vile fluids and viler solids were sold. As to the house itself, it was the dingy abode of dreariness. The gallery was occupied by howling roughs who might have taken lessons in behaviour from the negroes who occupied a part of this tier, which was railed off for their particular use."

CHAPTER VI

THE FRONTIER THEATER

"FOR the greater part of my life I have entertained the opinion that the pioneers on the various roads of the world's broad highways were among the most interesting objects for the study of the coming generations of men." These words, written in 1880 by Noah Miller Ludlow, an American actor and theatrical manager, were an afterglow of the spirit which at the opening of the nineteenth century stirred thousands of restless Americans along the Atlantic seaboard to penetrate the barrier of the Alleghenies, and cross to the broad cheap lands of the Ohio and the Mississippi valleys. Following the trails blazed by Daniel Boone and other frontiersmen, families from Virginia, Maryland, and North Carolina poured each year in increasing numbers into the unsettled plains of the West. Before the opening of the century Tennessee and Kentucky had taken their places in the Union alongside the older states to the east.

In spite of the crudities and hardships of life along the new frontier, the settlers of Tennessee, and especially of Kentucky, were able gradually to transplant a number of the more cultural phases of their former homes. Lexington, Kentucky, which was permanently settled in 1779, two years before the end of the Revolutionary War, came to be known as the "Athens of the West." In 1787 the first western newspaper was begun there, and shortly afterward Transylvania University opened its doors, with a group of well-trained scholars and students drawn from a wide radius. It is not surprising that these Kentucky settlers, coming almost entirely from the southern states and inheriting that Cavalier spirit which had fostered the first beginnings of the theater in America, should at a very early date have turned to the production of plays in their new home. It was not by accident that in 1797, only five years after Kentucky was admitted to the Union, the inhabitants of the hamlet of Washington, Kentucky, gave a dramatic performance, which, as far as is known, was the first west of the Alleghenies. In the next twenty years the number of amateur theatricals increased, not only in Kentucky, but in the territory of Missouri, which was being filled by the same southern strains, and also in the state of Ohio, which had been settled by emigrants from New England and New York.

Lexington took the lead in amateur theatricals as it had in other cultural activities. In 1810 the Lexington promoters brought to Kentucky a group of professionals from Montreal, who, for a number of years, gave performances on a circuit which included Lexington, Frankfort, and Louisville. But owing to internal dissensions and disagreements with local promoters, the Montreal players proved unsatisfactory, and the lovers of the drama in the West were forced in 1815 to open negotiations with members of an American company, located in Albany, New York. In December of 1815, the honorable members of the Twenty-Third Kentucky Legislature and the inhabitants of the capital of Frankfort, witnessed the arrival of a group of "showmen," who during the next twenty years were to provide theatrical amusement for the increasing thousands in the leading centers of the Ohio and upper Mississippi valleys.

The newly arrived actors were not famous stars. They were minor members of a second-rate eastern theater, who had come to the West, like so many of their first night's audience, because competition in the East had made the prospect discouraging. It was soon known throughout Frankfort, and in Lexington, which was only twenty miles away, that these actors had made the long overland journey from Albany in the meanest style — the younger men afoot or on the narrow decks of a "broad-horn" ark, the women in common road wagons over narrow rough roads or in improvised cabins, afloat. But to the drama-starved audiences of Frankfort, Lexington, and Louisville, their performance of such favorite plays as *Richard III* and *Pizarro*, and even more of the lighter afterpieces which completed each program, were a welcome diversion from the seriousness of life on the frontier. In addition, the members of the troupe, in spite of the warnings of the preachers, soon proved themselves respectable citizens, pleasant off-stage, and patient both with the limitations of the crude theater accommodations and with the rowdy disturbances sometimes caused by the less desirable sections of the audience in the gallery. As the months went by, the friendship between the actors and the various classes in the audience increased. The political and social aristocracy of the towns received the actors in their homes and invited them to their "functions."

This warmth of contact between actor and audience was illustrated most completely in the career of Noah Miller Ludlow, who, beginning as a minor member of the Drake troupe, broke in 1817 from the parent organization and for the next two decades promoted theatrical production in all the leading towns and in countless backwoods hamlets between the Alleghenies and the Mississippi. Always responding to the restless, pioneering spirit that was directing the currents of "western" life, Ludlow in his wanderings felt the same enthusiasm for those whom he called the "dear, good unsophisticated mortals" of the small village, as he did for the fine ladies of the town, who, to satisfy their craving for the drama, would sit through five long acts of tragedy and an afterpiece, on a backless bench ten inches wide.

The Albany Theater was the nursery for another "stage-mad" boy, who, like Ludlow, carried his enthusiasm for the drama to thousands of primitive playgoers from the Gulf of Mexico to the Ohio. Sol Smith was even more of the wandering backwoods barnstormer than his predecessor, and his love of humorous anecdote and strange types brought him even more closely into contact with the variegated population which flocked into the improvised theaters of Tennessee and Alabama and Georgia to witness the crude performances of his troupe. The rambling account of his life which Smith has left in *Theatrical Management in the South and West*, and the more orderly and historical record found in Ludlow's *Dramatic Life as I Found It*, furnish an invaluable picture of the pioneer actor and of pioneer civilization. When in 1835 Ludlow and Smith terminated their years of rivalry in a co-management at Mobile, the frontier, which they had amused, had passed to the West, leaving a broad stretch of cultivated land and thriving communities.

"UNBRIBED BY GAIN"

"No practis'd actor here your passions charms,
Nor magic brush the vary'd scen'ry warms;
Our house, our equipage, our all but rude,
And little, 'faith, but our intentions good.

When wealthy cities shall extensive rise,
And lofty spires salute our western skies;
When costly theaters shall loud resound
With music, mirth, & ev'ry joyous sound;
Twill be remember'd that in days of yore,
Between a ragged roof and sorry floor,
The laughing muse here for the first time sate,
And kindly deign'd to cheer our infant state."

THE "infant state" was Ohio — the city Cincinnati, and the year 1801. A theater was being opened; O'Keeffe's comic opera, *The Poor Soldier*, was about to be presented, and to honor the occasion a pompously impressive prologue was spoken, which included the lines quoted above. Although this is the earliest prologue which has been preserved, other companies of amateurs and at least one theater were in existence prior to the Cincinnati opening. Early in 1799 amateur performances were announced in the town of Lexington, Kentucky, which by that date had come to be the cultural center of the new country west of the Alleghenies. *The Busy Body* and a farce, *Love à la Mode*, were presented by the students of Transylvania University; and shortly afterward *He Would be a Soldier*, and *All the World's a Stage* were performed by a different band of amateurs in the Lexington Court House. By the opening of the nineteenth century there was a definite center in Lexington referred to as "The Theater," and in 1808 there is mention of a "New Theater" in which the Lexington Thespian Society performed, and of which Noble Usher, one of the most active leaders of early amateur and professional theatricals in the West, was probably manager. Cincinnati and Lexington were not the only centers for amateur theatricals. In 1808 a Dramatic Institute was formed by certain citizens of Louisville, Kentucky, and amateur performances were given for a number of years, even after the arrival of the professionals. In 1815 we find amateur theatricals in St. Louis. In 1816 we have the first authenticated mention of a theater in Detroit, organized and conducted by the officers of the military garrison under the command of General Alexander Macomb, a distinguished American soldier, in which both male and female parts were taken by the men. In many of the smaller towns there were Thespian and Roscian Societies, sponsored by enthusiastic amateurs of the vicinity. As early as 1814 there was a Thespian Society in Vincennes, Indiana, and by 1840 there were similar organizations in Lafayette, Indianapolis, Logansport, New Harmony, Dayton, and Springfield. Scant newspaper notices and announcements give us our only clues. With the exception of the Cincinnati prologue, there are no descriptions of theaters, no critiques of the acting, no memoirs to give life to this unusual phase of our theatrical history.

ON THURSDAY EVENING, OCTOBER 12th,
Will be performed at the Court House,
BY THE
THEATRICAL SOCIETY
IN THIS TOWN,
The Celebrated Tragedy of
DOUGLAS;
To which will be added,
The Celebrated Comedy of
LOVE-A-LA-MODE,
And the Musical entertainment of the
PADLOCK.
☞ No Admittance behind the Scenes.
Washington Sept. 29, 1796.

311 First known theatrical performance west of the Alleghenies, from an announcement in *The Mirror*, Washington, Kentucky, September 30, 1797

THEATRICAL.

On the evening of the 21st instant,

Will be presented to the public, at the Court-House in Lexington,

THE WEST-INDIAN,

A COMEDY, in Five Acts.

To which will be added,

THE CITIZEN,

A FARCE, in Two Acts.

. The doors to be opened at five, and the curtain to rise at six o'clock.
††† Tickets to be had at the stores of Mr. James M'Coan, and Mr. John Mancarrow, price 75 cents
¶¶¶ A considerable addition of scenery.
§§§ No money received at the door.
‖‖‖ No admittance behind the scenes.

313 Amateur performance in Lexington, Kentucky, from an announcement in *The Kentucky Gazette*, November 14, 1799

A number of the young gentlemen of St. Louis, having raised a dramatic corps, made their debut in the performance of the comedy of the School for Authors, with the farce Budget of Blunders. Much curiosity was excited and a great many attended to witness the *blunders*; — but all were pleased — all were surprised to see tacticians in a parcel of recruits.

On thursday, the admired Comedy of

312 Amateur Theatricals in St. Louis, from an announcement in *The Missouri Gazette and Illinois Advertiser*, February 4, 1815

THEATRE.

To bring relief to meagre want and pain,
Unawed by bigotry—unbribed by gain ;—
To touch the heart, with sentiments refin'd,
Amuse, instruct and dignify the mind.

THE THESPIAN CORPS
WILL EXHIBIT, ON
WEDNESDAY EVENING,
16th inst.
At their new Play-house,
THE WELL-KNOWN COMEDY OF
JOHN BULL;
Which will be preceded by an original Prologue, and followed by an amusing Farce, in two acts, called
FORTUNE'S FROLIC.

☞ The *HARMONICAL SOCIETY* have politely offered to assist in entertainining the

314 Amateur Performance by "The Thespian Corps" in Cincinnati, Ohio, from an announcement in *Liberty Hall*, March 14, 1815

315 First Theater in St. Louis, from a painting in the Missouri Historical Society, St. Louis

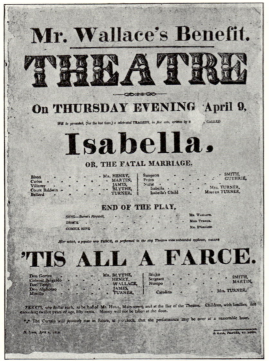

316 Performance of *Isabella, or, The Fatal Marriage*, by the Turners, St. Louis, 1818, from a playbill in the Missouri Historical Society, St. Louis

"DISPELLING THE GLOOM OF THE SEASON"

ELEVEN years after the first amateur performance in Lexington, a troupe of professional actors, recruited in Montreal and Quebec by a Mr. Douglas, were persuaded to venture forth on the long overland journey from Quebec to Lexington. By the middle of December, 1810, the main body of the company had arrived and been enthusiastically welcomed. "It is with sincere pleasure," wrote a contributor to the *Kentucky Gazette*, of December 18, 1810, "we are at length enabled to congratulate the lovers of the Drama, and the fashionables of the town, upon the arrival of Mr. *Douglas*, with a company of *Theatrical Performers* from *Montreal* and *Quebec*. . . . The citizens of Lexington and Frankfort will be gratified during the present winter with their performances, which in addition to the usual amusements of assemblies &c. will contribute much to dispel the gloom of the season." After a two weeks' run the company moved on for a month's stand at Frankfort, the capital of Kentucky, where the legislature was in session at the time. Performances were given on Wednesday and Saturday nights. Dissension soon arose in the company. William Turner, an actor, along with his wife and the Ciprianis, also actors, left Douglas and went to Cincinnati to give professional performances there. For a number of years Douglas continued to alternate between Lexington and Frankfort, arranging his schedule so that he should never miss a session of the state legislature. In the spring of 1814, he gave a three months' season in Louisville, where he had probably appeared at occasional intervals since his arrival in Kentucky. William Turner confined his activities to Cincinnati. In 1815 he went East for recruits, and when he reappeared in the West he styled his troupe the "Pittsburg company of comedians on their way to Kentucky." With Turner was a Joshua Collins, who for a number of years was an important figure in western theatricals. From Cincinnati Turner and Collins proceeded about the first of June, 1815, to Lexington, where Turner anticipated a long lease on the theater now owned by Luke Usher, an uncle of Noble L. Usher.

317 The "Pittsburg Company" in Cincinnati, from an announcement in *Liberty Hall*, April 22, 1815

218 Mr. Collins and Mrs. Turner in Cincinnati, from an announcement in *Liberty Hall*, May 2, 1815

THEATRE.

On Thursday Evening, April 15,
Will be presented the celebrated Tragedy of
THE GAMESTER.
After which, for the first time, the Grand Melo
Drama called
TEKELI,
OR THE SIEGE OF MONTGATZ.
HUNGARIANS

Count Tekeli,	Mr Fisher,
Wolf, (his friend)	Lewis,
Alexine, (the heroine of Montgatz)	Mrs. Groshon.
Counsellors, citizens, &c by Supernumeraries.	

AUSTRIANS.

Count Caraffa,	Mr Douglas,
Edmond,	Heran,
Bras de Fer,	Alexander,
Maurice,	S Drake,
Conrad, (a Miller,)	Drake,
Isadore,	Groshon,
Christina, (Miller's Daughter)	Miss Julia Drake,
Villagers,	By the company

Light Infantry and Peasants, by Supernumeraries.

ACT I

Scene I — A Wood, dark night and stormy — Tekeli being cut off from his army, and pursued by
the enemy is discovered lying on the branch of a
large tree, and Wolf, asleep at the foot of it—
after waking Wolf, and complaining of his distres-
sed situation, almost famished with hunger a party
of the enemy in search of Tekeli enter, having
heard their voices — Tekeli and Wolf throw themselves on the ground, shielded only by a little shrub-
bery The officer challenges who's there? and then
gives the word for the soldiers to fire among the
bushes, and afterwards charge and follow Tekeli
and Wolf rise unhurt, and return thanks to Providence directly another soldier is heard in the wood
calling for his comrade—he enters with a basket
of provision, which he is carrying to the out-post of
his general, Count Caraffa but his comrade Maurice, persuading him to recruit their stomachs, they
spread a cloth just under the tree where Tekeli and
Wolf have concealed themselves—some of the provision not suiting their taste they put it aside, and
Wolf with great caution and dexterity, feeds his
fainting friend Tekeli. After refreshment, the two
soldiers begin to talk of Tekeli, and the reward that
is offered to secure him, and the coward makes use
of such severe language as forces Tekeli and Wolf
from their retreat—Maurice is disarmed by Tekeli,
who gives him his life Wolf likewise spares the life
of the braggart, & they are left to contemplate their
own happy situation Music and a chorus of Villagers are heard at a distance—day-light appears, and
the villagers enter who are gathering to celebrate a
marriage at the Mill of Keben Wolf persuades
Tekeli to feign himself sick and lame and then en-
treats the peasants to assist him in taking his friend
to the Mill They cut down boughs and form a lit-
ter, on which Tekeli is placed, and they all go forward to the mill with the same chorus they had
chaunted before.

ACT II.

The Mill of Keben — A partial view of the internal part of the Mill, with a wide and wild ex-
panse of Scenery about it—On the left quite a wa-
ter-mill, on the right a wind-mill and between both,
in an oblique view a bridge that crosses the Torza
—At a great distance is seen the Castle of Montgatz, Tekeli's Citadel The villagers arrive and
introduce Tekeli as a sick traveller, who wants protection and assistance and Conrad the miller gives
him hearty welcome and reception, orders refreshment, talks of the wedding, and the peasants perform a Rural Dance After the dance Te-
keli discovers himself to the honest miller, and ob-
tains his promise of protection—Drums at a distance—peasants bring word that a guard is coming
to search the mill, and they have just time enough
to conceal Tekeli in a hogshead Wolf mixes with
the Peasants—orders are given for a general search,
and one of the Peasants, hearing the description
and reward offered by the officer, supposes it is
Tekeli in the hogshead, and wants to betray, but
honest Conrad gives him the portion intended for
his daughter to keep him quiet Maurice the soldier that Tekeli subdued in the forest, is of the
party, and recognizes, Wolf, but promises fidelity
—The soldiers make a search, make a bet that
one of them, at a proper distance, shall fire three
bullets right through the bung-hole of the hogshead,
which occasions an altercation that baffles the intent—The barrel is moved off, and the soldiers return to the wood to decide the wager Conrad then
tells Wolf that he has some corn going across the
bridge that evening to his store-house, and that no
other way can be found to save Tekeli, but by his
condescending to be covered over in one of the
sacks, which, with some pursuasion, he con-

319 The Drakes in Louisville,
Kentucky, from an announce-
ment in the *Louisville Public
Advertiser,* April 14, 1819

THE DRAKE CIRCUIT

In the fall of 1814 the younger Usher had made a special trip to Albany, with the hope of recruiting strength for his western circuit. He had found the prominent actors of the eastern company little disposed to risk the dangers or endure the hardships of a season on the Kentucky frontier. Samuel Drake, John Bernard's stage manager at the Greene Street Theater, Albany, New York, an Englishman with many years' experience of management in the provinces, ambitious, and seeing no opening of consequence in Albany, promised the Kentucky manager to organize a company and bring it across the mountains. On his nephew's death shortly afterward, Luke Usher continued negotiations with Drake, offering to lease him the Lexington, Frankfort, and Louisville theaters, if Drake would agree to manage them on his own account. In May 1815, Drake, with his three sons, his two daughters, and five assistants began the difficult journey to the West. The Drakes in early December reached Frankfort, where the Kentucky legislature was in session. From Frankfort Drake extended his influence to Louisville and Lexington — a circuit which, after eliminating Douglas and driving Turner to Cincinnati, he controlled for many years. He was never stationary. He appeared again and again in Cincinnati and Lexington. We find him going for short seasons to Vincennes and to St. Louis. In 1822 he went on a southern trip to Nashville, Tennessee, Huntsville, Alabama, and to Fayetteville, Tennessee, and returned again in 1826 for a short southern tour.

Theatre.
By the Company from Kentucky.

THE Public are respectfully informed that the Company under the management of Mr. Drake, will perform for a few nights in a temporary Theatre, erected in Mr. Bennet's Ball Room.

On Wednesday evening March 22.
Will be presented, the celebrated and genuine Comedy as written by G. Colman the Elder, in 5 acts, called
THE
JEALOUS WIFE.

Mr. Oakly,	Mr. Fisher;	Tom	Mr. Smith,
Major Oakly	Mr. Lewis,	Harman	H. Lewis,
Charles Oakly	Mr. Drake,	Lady Freelove	Mrs John Vos,
Russet	S. Drake,	Mrs. Oakly	Mrs Lewis,
Mr Harry Beagle	Alexander,	Harriet	Mrs. Harman,
Captain O'Cutter	Douglas,	Toilette	Miss M Drake.

END OF THE PLAY,
A Comic Song—"The Bag of Nails," By Mr. Alexander.
"Jessy, the Flower of Dumblane," — Mr. O. Lewis.

TO WHICH WILL BE ADDED, THE ADMIRED AFTERPIECE, CALLED

The Adopted Child,
OR, SECRETS OF MILFORD CASTLE.

Sir Bertrand	Mr. G. Lewis,	Michael the	With the song of
Record	Mr. Drake,	Foundling	"Will Watch,"
Spruce	Drake,	Le Sueur	Mr. Fisher,
Flint	Mr. Harman,	Nelly	Mrs. Morgan,
Record	Alexander,	Miss Nest Roch	Fisher,
Le Sueur	Douglas,		Miss Julia Drake.

☞ Doors to be opened at 6 and the performance to begin at a quarter before 7 o'clock.—Price of admission One Dollar.
Tickets to be had at the Bar of Mr. Bennet's Tavern, and at the Enquirer printing office.—No money to be taken at the doors.
The number of tickets for sale will be limited to the magnitude of the building.
Smoking Segars prohibited.
March 21, 1820.

Printed at the Office of the St. Louis Enquirer.

320 The Drakes in St. Louis, from a playbill, 1820, in the Missouri Historical Society, St. Louis

THEATRE
AND GREENVILLE SPRINGS.

THE Theatrical Company under the direction of A. Drake, will perform all the present month, (July) and perhaps longer, at the Greenville Springs. The subscriber has the pleasure to inform the public, that in addition to the former springs he has discovered a Chalybeate spring, which is now prepared for use. THOS. Q. ROBERTS.

321 The Drakes in Greenville Springs, Tenn., from an announcement in the *Nashville Whig,* July 9, 1825

THEATRE

For several weeks past the lovers of the Drama have been feasting their mental appetites on the chaste productions of Mr. Drake, the Manager of the company now performing here.

Perhaps there never was a man who deserved the public favor and support in a higher degree than this gentleman. He has grown old in his endeavors to please the public, and we believe his attempts generally meet with success. His company is composed of the most respectable class of performers, and what is perhaps singular, the private character of each member of his corps stands unimpeached! —This is as it should be; yet, it is so seldom we see so large a company of players, all standing on such fair ground, we deem it worthy of notice. With the exception of one or two, they are sterling performers in their respective lines; in short, we recommend to such of the public as are fond of rational amusements to pay a visit

322 Typical waterfront of Frontier Town, from the painting *Pittsburgh in 1825,* by Leander McAndless, in the Historical Society of Western Pennsylvania, Pittsburgh

323 Tribute to the Drake Company, from a communication to the *Independent Press,* Cincinnati, June 24, 1826

324   Mary Frances Denny (Mrs. Alexander Drake), from
        an engraving in the Fridenberg Collection

THE STAR OF THE WEST

WITH the Drakes was a young unknown Albany actress, Mary Frances Denny, who was destined in the following years to outshine all her emigrant companions. Born in Schenectady, New York, in 1797, she had at an early age moved with her family to Albany, the home of an older sister. Her "education," recorded Ludlow, "was confined to the simple rudiments of an old-fashioned school; but she was an industrious student and soon made rapid advancement in her profession." Before leaving the East she had played only minor rôles in Albany, Cherry Valley, and Cooperstown. During the earlier stages of the westward journey the Drakes played more or less the same pieces in every town at which they stopped, and, in consequence, her roles were limited to eight or ten — all "of a light and not exacting grade." When the troupe stopped at Pittsburgh, however, "she was called upon for greater exertions, and in meeting them she showed considerable capacity and development of talent, giving satisfaction generally to the manager and her audiences. On reaching Kentucky her progress in her profession became marked and highly encouraging, and it was not long before she became a great favourite." After four years with the Drake company in Lexington, Frankfort, Louisville, and Cincinnati, she went East, appearing in Montreal, Quebec, Boston, and on April 17, 1820, making her début at the new Park, New York. "Her abilities were well adapted to every walk of the drama," wrote Ireland, "but she excelled in the heavier characters of tragedy, in which line she has rarely been equalled on the American stage." In 1823 she married Alexander Drake, second son of Samuel Drake, an excellent low comedian, who was entrusted by his father with more and more responsibility in the management of the Drake Circuit. In Cincinnati and in Louisville Mrs. Alexander Drake was the reigning favorite on the boards of Drake's small theaters and in the social life of the towns. Mrs. Trollope, usually so bitter against all things American, had nothing but praise for Mrs. Drake as an actress and as a woman. Joe Cowell, another supercilious Britisher, passing through Cincinnati in 1829 on his way south to New Orleans, gave an interesting account of the financial instability of Drake's Cincinnati Theater, and a charming picture of young Mrs. Drake. "I perched myself on a throne-chair, by the side of Mrs. Drake, who was seated next the fire on a bass-drum. I found her a most joyous, affable creature, full of conundrums and good nature; she made capital jokes about her peculiar position; martial music — sounds by distance made more sweet; and an excellent rhyme to drum, which I am very sorry I have forgotten."

THEATRE.

MRS. DRAKE.

The managers have the pleasure of announcing an engagement with this lady for five nights.
TUESDAY EVENING, August 15th.
The Tragedy of
ADELGITHA, or The Fruits of a Single Error.

Guiscard,	Mr. M. Field.
Michael Ducas,	Mr. Anderson.
Lothair,	Mr. J. M. Field.
Adelgitha,	Mrs. Drake.

326   Mrs. Drake in St. Louis, from an announcement in the *Missouri Republican*, August 15, 1837

Theatre.
═══
MISS DENNEY'S NIGHT.
═══
THIS EVENING April 10,
Will be presented the celebrated
Comedy, called
THE HONEY MOON.

To which will be added an admiried
comedy, called
THE LIAR.

☞ *For particulars see bills.*

325   Miss Denney's Benefit, Louisville, Ky., from an announcement in *The Western Courier*, April 10, 1817

AMERICAN THEATRE.

The public are respectfully informed that the celebrated
Tragedy actress,
MRS. A. DRAKE,
Is engaged for seven nights, and will have the honor of
making her first appearance this evening.

ON TUESDAY EVENING, NOV. 25th.
Will be enacted *Milman's* tragedy of
FAZIO;
OR, THE ITALIAN WIFE.

Geraldi Fazio,	:	Mr. H. G. Pearson.
BIANCA,	: :	MRS. A. DRAKE.

Previous to which the laughable farce of
LOVERS QUARREL.
Sancho,   Mr. Bristow, *his first appearance here.*
The eveng's amusement to conclude with the petite comedy of
THE SECRET.

On Wednesday,
Mrs. KNIGHT'S second appearance.
───
Doors open at 6 o'clock, and curtain to rise at 7 o'clock
precisely.   Box office open every day from 10 o'clock A. M.

327   Mrs. Drake in New Orleans, from an announcement in *The Bee*, November 25, 1834

A VOYAGE OF ADVENTURE

BUT, in spite of the superior brilliance of Mrs. Drake's acting, by far the most important member of the little Drake troupe that left Albany in 1815 was Noah Miller Ludlow, at that time an altogether insignificant member of the Green Street cast. Eighteen years before, on July 5, 1797, Ludlow had been born in New York City, "in an old Dutch-fashioned house, built of bricks imported from Holland, the front of which was the gable-end, with an old iron weathercock crowning the peak of the gable." In childhood he had often gone to see the favorites of the old Park, Cooper, John Darley, Ellen Westray, Mrs. Old-mixon, the Hoggs, Thomas Hilson, and the others. In 1813, on the death of his father, he had moved to Albany where he had formed connections with the theater which John Bernard had taken over in 1813. Gradually he was allowed to play small parts. Then in the spring of 1815 came his opportunity. "Mr. Drake was somewhat puzzled to find the persons required to make up his company. . . . He told me very candidly that he was going on a voyage of adventure, which possibly might result disastrously. . . . I was too glad of an opportunity to embark in what had

328 Noah Miller Ludlow, 1797–1886, from an engraving in the Fridenberg Collection

become now my entire ambition, to hesitate an hour in giving him an answer." Arrangements were completed, and Ludlow was sent ahead as advance agent to make arrangements for the first performance at Cherry Valley, where two years earlier Mary Frances Denny had made her début. On the way to Kentucky and during the first two seasons of the Frankfort, Lexington, and Louisville circuit, Ludlow played in the main low comedy rôles, and assisted in a minor capacity with the trying problems of management. In the spring of 1817 there was talk among certain members of the Drake troupe of forming a "commonwealth of players" to carry the drama to the benighted regions of Tennessee where there should be a good market free from competition. Ludlow turned a deaf ear to their entreaties, until he became enamoured of a young widow, whose home was in Nashville. Thereupon he eagerly joined

For the National Banner.

MR. LUDLOW'S BENEFIT.

On Wednesday evening next, Mr Ludlow, the enterprising and judicious manager of our theatre, takes his benefit. In calling the attention of the lovers of the drama to this fact, it is but an act of justice to Mr Ludlow to say, that he has long been known to the citizens of this place, as a worthy and honorable man. His abilities as an actor are universally acknowledged, and he has ever been indefatigable in his efforts to please. It is, therefore, confidently expected that his merits as an actor and a man, will receive a substantial reward on his benefit night.   **H.**

329 Tribute to Ludlow from a Nashville admirer, from a communication to the *National Banner and Nashville Whig*, November 14, 1831

in with Aaron J. Phillips and Henry Vaughan. After several performances en route and a short season of three weeks in a primitive theater in Nashville, Phillips and Ludlow returned to Cincinnati for recruits. They found William Turner disbanding his Cincinnati troupe, signed them up, and returned for a fall season of about six weeks — during which time Mrs. Noah Miller Ludlow became a regular addition to the cast.

330 The Home Town of Mrs. Ludlow, from an engraving by W. E. Tucker after a drawing *View of Nashville*, 1832, by T. V. Peticolas, in the Department of Education, Nashville, Tenn,

SPECTACLE.

Mardi Gras, 2 Mars 1813,
A MIDI.
Une représentation du
BOURGEOIS GENTILHOMME.
Comédie en cinq actes, de Molière, orné de
tout son spectacle, danse, cérémonie Turc,
et costumes analogues ; Mde. Douvillier dan-
sera deux pas différedds.
Suivie d'une représentation du
MILICIEN,
Opéra en un acte, musique de Duni.
Mr. Champigny fils, fera ses débuts par le
rôle de Cléonte dans la première pièce, et
celui de Dorville dans la seconde.

Incessament,
AU BENEFICE DE MR ROCHEFORT,
FRANCOISE DE FOIX,
OU
*Les Amours de François 1er. Roi de
France*

331 Molière's *Bourgeois Gentilhomme,* at
the St. Philippe, from an announcement
in the *Courrier de la Louisiane,* March 1,
1813

332 Le Théâtre St. Pierre, from a sketch in
Joseph G. Baroncelli, *Le Théâtre-français, à la
Nlle. Orleans,* New Orleans, 1906, G. Muller

SPECTACLE.

Jeudi prochain, 10 Octobre,
(Au Bénéfice de Mde. Brunet,)
Une représentation du .
MISANTHROPE,
Comédie en cinq actes et en vers de Molière,
dans laquelle Mr. Fontaine jouera, en
qualité d'amateur, le rôle d'Alceste, (*Misan-
thrope*)
Cette pièce sera suivie d'une représentation de
BION
OU LES
Philophes de la Grece,
Opéra en un acte et en vers d'Hoffman, musique
de Mehui, orné de tout son spectacle.

333 Molière's *Le Misanthrope,* at the St.
Philippe, from an announcement in the *Courrier
de la Louisiane,* October 11, 1813

THE FRENCH THEATER

In 1791, six years before the earliest recorded English drama west of the Alleghenies, a group of professional comedians, for the most part first-rate artists from Paris under the direction of Louis Tabary, made their appearance in the city of New Orleans. No preparations had been made for them, and their early performances had to be given wherever opportunity dictated — in inns, under tents, and often entirely in the open air. The second floor of a house on the rue St. Pierre was finally selected as a permanent location for the stage. Unfortunately the first floor became in 1793 a dance hall, which year by year so degenerated that in 1799 it had to be closed by the police. The bitter partisanship of the French Revolution was reflected in this small second-story room on the rue St. Pierre. Jacobin songs resounded; feeling ran high until the police were forced to interfere. With the ascendancy of Napoleon order was restored, and for a number of years many French classics were well presented. In 1806 Tabary, in order to accommodate the increasing crowds, enlarged the seating capacity by adding a parquet. In 1808, complaints having been made that the St. Pierre structure was unsafe, an official investigation was ordered, which resulted in the building's being condemned. A syndicate had already been formed to build a more worthy theater and on September 14, 1808, the new St. Pierre opened its doors. In spite of the fact that much new talent had been imported from Paris the theater ran only two years, being sold at auction in December of 1810. A more elaborate one, the St. Philippe, had been built at the close of 1807, at a cost of one hundred thousand dollars and had opened on January 30, 1808, with Tabary as director. The new theater, consisting of a huge parquet and two rows of loges, could seat seven hundred persons. Still another theater, the Orleans, begun in the early days of 1809, had opened in November of that year. It was burned in 1813 and for a number of years was not rebuilt.

SPECTACLE.

Jeudi prochain, 16 Décembre
(Au Bénéfice de la Régie.)
Grande Fete Patriotique.
EN L'HONNEUR
*Des victoires remportées par es armées Améri-
caines en Canada, er des succès brillants de nos
braves marins depuis le commencement*
DE LA GUERRE,
Une Représentation de
WASHINGTON,
OU
L'Amérique et la France
REUNIES,

334 Celebration of the Franco-American Alliance, 1778-83, at the St. Philippe, from an
announcement in the *Courrier de la Louisiane,*
December 13, 1813

THEATRE D'ORLEANS.

Dimanche, 1er. Octobre,
(Pour l'ouverture du Théâtre
d'Orléans.)
La première représentation du
MARIAGE DE FIGARO,
Comédie en 5 actes, de Beaumarchais, ornée
de tout son spectacle.

335 Beaumarchais' *Le Mariage de Figaro,*
at the Orleans, from an announcement
in the *Courrier de la Louisiane,* September 25, 1820

THEATRE D'ORLEANS.

Dimanche, 16 Octobre,
La première représentation de
PHEDRE,
Tragédie en 5 actes et en vers de Racine.
Suivi de la première représentation de

336 Corneille's *Phèdre,* at the Orleans, from
an announcement in the *Courrier de la
Louisiane,* October 12, 1825

THEATRE D'ORLEANS.

Jeudi prochain, 13 Janvier 1825,
POUR L'OUVERTURE,
(ABONNEMENT COURANT)
Le Tartuffe ou l'Imposteur,
Comédie en 5 actes et en vers de Molière,
dans laquelle débuteront Messrs. Marchand, Clo-
zel, Ancelin, Varnet, Anglaise, Leblanc, Mdes.
Clozel, Souplar et Ancelin—Suivie de
MICHEL ET CHRISTINE,
Vaudeville en un acte de Scribe.
Messrs. Leb anc, Clozel ; Mde. Clozel.
☞Les personnes qui sont abonnées et celles
qui ont pris des loges, sont priées de faire pren-
dre leurs billets à l'administration, et d'en en-
voyer le montant selon les clauses du prospec-
tus.
Dimanche, 16 du courant,
LA BELLE ARSENE,

337 Molière's *Tartuffe,* at the Orleans, from an
announcement in the *Courrier de la Louisiane,*
January 13, 1825

338 Ludlow's First Performance in New Orleans from an announcement in *L'Ami des Lois et Journal du Soir,* January 10, 1818

339 Théâtre St. Philippe, from a painting in the Louisiana Historical Society, New Orleans

"NO CONTEMPTIBLE PROFIT"

DURING the course of his first season in Nashville it came to the ears of the young bridegroom, Ludlow, that with all the theatrical activity of New Orleans, it had never known a company speaking the English tongue. Seeing an opportunity to secure a foothold in new territory, Ludlow wrote seeking information from Richard Jones of New Orleans, whose acquaintance he had made at Pittsburgh on that first overland trip with the Drakes. From Jones he learned that there was a small theater to be rented, and that the prospects should be good. There were two deterring factors — the danger from yellow fever and the hostility of the French population to American intruders. Aaron Phillips and several others of the Nashville company balked at the danger. Only two of the men were willing to join Ludlow in his daring venture, John Vaughan and Thomas Morgan, the latter of whom had performed for two or three years in the West Indies. The three agreed to a joint management, sharing losses or gains. They purchased a keel boat and on October 17, they and their actress wives began, with no experience and without the least technical knowledge of navigation, the slow journey down the Cumberland and down the Ohio to the treacherous Mississippi. Stopping at Natchez, they were finally persuaded to give a performance at that small Mississippi town — the first ever to be given there. The captain of the steamboat which carried them from Natchez to New Orleans was a brother of the famous naval commander, James Lawrence (Vol. VI, No. 603), and there was much discussion of the naval engagements of the War of 1812, in which Ludlow, as a boy, had been so eager to participate. On their arrival at New Orleans they called on Coquet, the manager of the St. Philippe, who was surprisingly hospitable, and accommodating. Preliminary business arrangements completed, Ludlow called on the mayor of the city and obtained permission to give plays in English. Ludlow and his co-managers had come at an opportune time. There was no French competition, the Orleans not having yet been rebuilt. The French population was eager to see plays, whatever the language of the actors. On January 13, 1818, Ludlow opened with *The Honeymoon.* From then until the middle of the following April they gave performances four times a week, charging an admission of one dollar. At the end of the season they had cleared fifteen thousand dollars to be divided into thirds. "No contemptible profit," recorded the surprised Ludlow. His success was evidence of the importance of the rapidly growing American population in this seaport of the West.

340   Sam Houston, 1793–1863, in the costume of a Cherokee Chief, from a photograph of a miniature. © Boone Photo Co., Austin, Texas

THEATRICAL.—Will be presented, this Evening, by the *Nashville Thespian Society,* with the aid of a part of the company of Comedians that were here last season, the Tragedy of *Douglass,* together with other entertainments. The emoluments arising from the exertions of this Society, will be appropriated to charitable purposes.

341   Performance of *Douglas* by the Dramatic Club of Nashville, from an announcement in the *Nashville Whig and Tennessee Advertiser,* September 12, 1818

The Members of the Thespian Society are requested to meet at the Theatre on Monday next, at half past 4 o'clock, P. M. By order of the President.
SAM. HOUSTON, *Sec. pro tem.*

342   Sam Houston as Secretary of a Theatrical Club, from an announcement in the *Nashville Whig and Tennessee Advertiser,* September 19, 1818

THE DRAMATIC CLUB OF NASHVILLE

In the following July Ludlow, after the various amusing and unpleasant experiences of a horseback ride through the Choctaw and Chickasaw Indian nations, arrived back in Nashville, and was persuaded to settle down for a time to the less disturbing problems of housekeeping. Various Nashville citizens were eager, however, to organize a dramatic club, and persuaded Ludlow to act as stage manager, agreeing to his ultimatum that his acceptance was on the understanding that he have absolute authority. General John H. Eaton, husband of Peggy Eaton, and later Secretary of War in Jackson's Cabinet, was manager of all the outdoor business. General Andrew Jackson himself was an honorary member, and the most enthusiastic of all the members was a young lieutenant named Sam Houston, later to be president of the Republic of Texas. Their first play was the perennial favorite *Douglas,* and Ludlow timidly confessed that he could not say much for Houston's Glenalvon, because his excellent appearance was more than offset by his poor declamation. For the afterpiece to the second performance a month later, Ludlow selected a farce, *We Fly by Night,* in which Lieutenant Houston was assigned the low comedy rôle of a porter with two scenes. Walking in and examining the cast, "where it had been placed for the notice of the members of the club . . . he said to me: 'Ludlow, my boy, what is this you have got me up for in the afterpiece?' I replied 'Lieutenant, I am about to test the versatility of your genius; that character is a very fine bit of low comedy. . . .' He turned around, and looking me full in the face, said 'What! low comedy? Sam Houston in low comedy. Great God! my friend Ludlow, what are you thinking of. . . . "By the Eternal," sir, the people will hiss me.' His admiration of General Jackson was so great that he often indulged in the general's favorite oath." Houston's anger and dread continued. Seeing himself in his final make-up he "roared out, with stentorian voice '"By the Eternal" can this be Sam Houston.' . . . He paced the floor like a mad lion, swore by all the gods he would not go on the stage." Ludlow through General Eaton tipped off the audience that they should applaud Houston to the limit. Houston's performance was brilliant. "I have never seen it performed so well by anyone into whose hands it has fallen in the course of the regular profession," testified Ludlow. But Houston remained unconvinced and for a long time resentful toward both Ludlow and the audience which "ridiculed" him by what he felt to be exaggerated applause. Whether Houston's vanity and dignity were wounded by Ludlow's enthusiasm for his comic potentialities, or whether the fervor of the audience was dampened by enforced applause cannot be said. But it remains that this second performance was also the last by the Dramatic Club of Nashville. Ludlow's disappointment at the outcome was probably slight, for like Sol Smith he had considerable contempt for amateur organizations.

TAILORS AND CABINET–MAKERS

Such theatricals, though productive of amusing incidents and anecdotes, were scarcely sufficient to satisfy Ludlow's ambitions. He was restless; yet did not know where to turn. He had been especially urged to try another season in New Orleans, but the old company had scattered, and it was impossible to find substitutes worthy of the discriminating Louisiana audiences. At this time there arrived in Nashville an actor, Alexander Cummins, and his wife, the latter of whom had appeared on the

343 Typical cross-country Caravan, from a sketch in Seymour Dunbar, *History of Travel in America.* © 1915, courtesy of the publishers, the Bobbs-Merrill Company, Indianapolis

stage of the old Park. Cummins' proposal of a joint managership was accepted by Ludlow, and strenuous efforts were begun to secure eastern recruits for the company. But, wrote Ludlow, "the actors of the Eastern cities, with few exceptions, had no idea at that time what the West really was. The population of that region was supposed by many to be semi-barbarians; and to go to Kentucky or Tennessee was banishing yourself from civilization. When actors were asked to go to these new States or Territories, they would shake their heads and say, 'No, I've no desire to be devoured by savages.' When, then, the month of December arrived we found that all the company we were able to muster consisted of seven males and three females . . . Flanagan [Fawcett?] and Willis were cabinet-makers and had never performed at all on the stage. Frethy was a 'stage-struck' tailor, from Pittsburgh, who had performed a few times in an amateur company of private theatricals. Finlay, also a tailor, had been a *sailor*, and lost one leg; and young Clark, an orphan, had neither trade nor friends to help him along in the world. . . . While Cummins and myself were hunting around for actors, our wives and their assistants were busy getting up a few stage-dresses, that we might be enabled to produce decently a few comedies and farces." Ludlow, not daring to inflict this make-shift organization on his Nashville friends, decided to experiment in Huntsville, Alabama. Cummins was sent ahead, and in a few days Ludlow "succeeded in making arrangements for the hire of horses and wagons; and taking with me six small scenes — those we had used on our way from Louisville to Nashville in the summer of 1817 — and our recently acquired luggage, started for Huntsville." Their stay of ten weeks, the first professional season in the territory of Alabama, was surprisingly good, considering the cast and the theater, which was a room over a confectionery store. The price of admission was one dollar. Alabama at the time was rapidly filling up with planters or the sons of planters from the older southern states along the Atlantic.

THEATRE.

MR. JONES' BENEFIT

THIS EVENING, DEC. 15.
Will be presented *Shakspeare's* celebrated historical play of

KING HENRY 4th,

OR

THE HUMORS OF SIR JOHN FALSTAFF.

King Henry,	-	Mr. Cargill.
Prince of Wales,	-	Hanna.
Prince John,	-	Mrs. Ludlow.
Westmoreland,	-	Mr. Young.
Worcester,	-	Lucas.
Northumberland,	-	Addison.
Hotspur,	-	Vos.
Poins,	-	Ludlow.
Bardolph,	-	Cummins
Francis,	-	Frethy.
Carrier,	-	Finlay.
Sir John Falstaff,	-	Jones.
Lady Percy,	-	Mrs. Cummins.
Hostess,	-	Jones.

In act 5th, a Combat between the Prince of Wales and Hotspur—death of Hotspur.

BETWEEN THE PLAY AND FARCE,
Song—*Bay of Biscay.*
Recitation—*The Doctor and his Apprentice, or Infallible Signs.* - Hanna.
Song—*The Rivals, or a new mode of Duelling,* - - Cargill
To conclude with the laughable musical Farce, called

Sprigs of Laurel,

OR

THE RIVAL SOLDIERS.

Captain Cruizer,	-	Mr. Cummins.
Major Tactic,	-	Lucas.
Lenox,	-	Ludlow.
Sinclair,	-	Cargill.
Corporal Squib,	-	Young.
Nipperkin,	-	Jones.
Soldiers,		
Mary Tactic,	-	Mrs. Cummins.

344 The Ludlow Company, after its return from Huntsville, from an announcement in the *Nashville Whig and Tennessee Advertiser*, December 5, 1818

THEATRE.

On Tuesday Evening, March 16.
Will be presented a celebrated Comedy in 3 Acts, written by *James Kenney, Esq.* called

TURN OUT !

OR

A Peep at Politics.

Restive,	-	Mr. Ludlow,
Capt. Somerville,	-	Cummins,
Forage,	-	Fawcett,
Gregory,	-	Frethy,
Dr. Truckle,	-	
Marian Ramsay,	-	Mrs. Cummins,
Peggy,	-	Ludlow,

BETWEEN THE PLAY AND FARCE,
Songs { Alderman Gobble } Mr. Findlay
       { Clowns Bazaar }

After which the favorite Farce in 2 Acts, translated from a French piece entitled *La Jeune Femme Coliere,* called the

Day after the Wedding

OR

A Wife's first lesson.

Col. Freelove,	-	Mr. Ludlow,
Lord Rivers,	-	Cummins
James,	-	Fawcett,
Groom,	-	Frethy,
Lady Elizabeth Freelove,	-	Mrs. Cummins,
Mrs. Davis	-	Ludlow.

345 Performance of Ludlow Troupe in Nashville, March 16, 1819, from an announcement in the *Nashville Whig and Tennessee Advertiser*, March 13, 1819

346   The Théâtre d'Orleans, from an engraving in *Gibson's Guide and Directory of the State of Louisiana*, New Orleans, 1838, courtesy of the Louisiana Historical Society

THE ARRIVAL OF CALDWELL

In the autumn following the departure of Ludlow, Vaughan, and Morgan from New Orleans, the second Théâtre d'Orleans was completed on the same site where the first had burned in 1813. Its manager, John Davis, whose English name is misleading, was a Frenchman both in language and in manners. He brought over from Paris a company of actors worthy of the beautiful new building. His first season of 1818–19 was a great success artistically and financially. By the beginning of the season of 1819 Aaron J. Phillips, who had been afraid to join forces with Ludlow in 1817, had in the meantime summoned courage to try the New Orleans experiment, and made with Davis an arrangement whereby the French company should perform on Tuesday, Thursday, and Sunday nights at the Orleans, leaving the remaining four to Phillips' American actors. Phillips' company was at best a make-shift organization recruited according to the exigencies of the moment from western material; so that, when in January, 1820, James H. Caldwell, an English light comedian, with several years' experience at Charleston, South Carolina, and Petersburg, Virginia, arrived from the coast with a full-strength, carefully recruited company, Phillips realized that his own short-lived monopoly was ended, and that the only alternative to bankruptcy was a quick capitulation to Caldwell. Caldwell began by leasing the St. Philippe, but shortly afterward completed negotiations with Davis to take over the Orleans for the former Phillips' nights — at the same time continuing to play at the St. Philippe on the nights when the French were performing at the Orleans. The competition with the native actors proved unsuccessful, and the new American manager closed the smaller theater, making a three-year contract with Davis for the four nights a week at the Orleans. At the end of the first season, Caldwell and his company returned by boat to the Petersburg, Virginia, theater which during the following years they used for their summer season.

American Theatre
St. Philip Street.

On Monday Evening, January 17th, 1820,
Will be presented Shakespeare's celebrated
Tragedy of

HAMLET,
Prince of Denmark.
To which will be added, Macklin's Farce of
Love a la Mode.

On Tuesday Evening, January 18,
Will be presented Goldsmith's Comedy of
She Stoops to Conquer,
Or The Mistakes of a Night.
To which will be added, by particular request,
the Opera of
ROSINA.

☞ Tickets can only be admitted on the evening for which they are purchased—this regulation is necessary to prevent counterfeits among the door keepers.

Doors to be opened at half past 5 o'clock and the curtain to rise at half past six o'clock precisely.—Places for the Boxes to be taken every day of Mr. Thos. Caldwell, from 11 o'clock till 3 at the Theatre, from whom may be purchased a few Season Tickets.
Admittance to the Boxes $1—Gallery 75cents.

The Theatre will be open every evening, Sun days excepted.

347   The opening of James H. Caldwell at the St. Philippe, from an announcement in the *Louisiana Gazette*, January 17, 1820

American Theatre
St. Philip Street.

THEATRICAL NOTICE.
MR. PHILLIPS,
Late of the Orleans Theatre

Has the satisfaction of announcing to the public, that in consequence of the arrangement effected between himself and Mr. Caldwell, Manager of the St. Philip street Theatre, by which he is released from his previous engagements, he will appear on the Boards of the latter Theatre in the character of

ROMEO,
In Shakespear's celebrated Play of ROMEO AND JULIET,
On Friday Evening, Jan. 21,
And that the Profits of the house on that night will be appropriated to
HIS BENEFIT.

He trusts that the deference he has shewn to public opinion, and the sacrifices which it has cost him, will be taken into favorable consideration.

Between the Play and the Farce Mrs. GRAY will sing
"The Soldier tir'd of war's alarms."
And Mr. BOYLE will sing the favorite ballad of
"Black ey'd Susan."

348   Union of Phillips and Caldwell, from an announcement in the *Louisiana Gazette*, January 21, 1820

American Theatre
ORLEANS-STREET.

The Manager of the American Theatre most respectfully announces to the citizens of New Orleans that, in obedience to the wishes of many respectable American families, and particularly with a desire, on his own part, of gratifying the expectations of the French population, he has concluded an arrangement, through the medium of his friends, for the ORLEANS THEATRE. The Manager will not comment on the increased expences which he will necessarily subject himself to in the present arrangement, but merely say that, as he considers himself the public's humble servant, he is happy in having met the wishes of those disposed to patronise the Native drama, and his best reward will be in the assurance that he has their approbation.

On MONDAY EVENING, Feb. 14,
Will be presented Tobin's celebrated comedy of the
HONEY MOON.
In Act 4,
A RUSTIC DANCE,
Incidental to the Piece.
After the Play will be acted, an eccentric comic Drama in three acts called the
THREE and DEUCE.

349   Caldwell opens at the Orleans, from an announcement in the *Louisiana Gazette*, February 14, 1820

350 James H. Caldwell, 1793–1863, from an engraving by Illman and Pilbroie after a painting by John Wesley Jarvis, in the possession of the publishers

MONOPOLIST AND COMEDIAN

FOR the next two decades James H. Caldwell dominated the theatrical life of the Mississippi Valley. Successful from his first season, he gradually expanded his activities to include not only the vicinity of New Orleans but the upper Mississippi and the Ohio valleys. In contrast to the restless pioneering spirits of Ludlow and Sol Smith, he directed his maneuvers from a central headquarters, entrusting the minor tactics to moving lieutenants. A great part of the history of the western drama of the 'twenties and the 'thirties could be told from his point of view. Again and again Ludlow and Smith crossed his path, and were forced, in moments of temporary failure, to fall back, however much they disliked it, on the superior strength and permanency of the New Orleans manager. The rivalry between the three western managers was most bitter. In the end it was Smith and Ludlow who emerged victorious. But that was not until after 1840. *The Cincinnati Daily Gazette* of November 16, 1836, gives an insight into the powerful influence of Caldwell at his height. "MR CALDWELL of New Orleans, not satisfied with owning all the theaters between the falls of St. Anthony and the Balize, and managing two or three of them, with being the proprietor of a bank, and the largest bathing establishment in the Union — and with holding contracts for lighting three or four cities with gas, has a new project on foot — the formation of an Ocean Steam Company for running a line of packets between New Orleans and Liverpool. While he is thinking about it, he is amusing himself with a scheme for paving the streets of New Orleans with octagonal blocks of stones." It is misleading, however, to picture Caldwell solely as promoter and public benefactor. Sol Smith, whose condemnation of Caldwell rose at times almost to anathema, was always unstinted — just as Ludlow and Cowell were — in his praise of Caldwell as an actor: "I can express my opinion of Mr. Caldwell as an actor in no better way than by saying I have never yet beheld his equal as a light comedian. . . . Mr. Caldwell played the whole range of tragedy and but for some mannerisms . . . no other actor gave greater satisfaction to southern audiences than he did. He was scrupulously guarded in giving the fine text of Shakespeare when performing his characters. In the later years of his life he only appeared in comedy — and in that he was unapproachable." The Mississippi Valley, whose theatrical life Caldwell dominated, stirred with a prosperity, partly specious, which ended only with the panic of 1837.

THEATRE.

THE ladies and gentlemen of Nashville and its vicinity are respectfully informed, that the Theatre will be open *for a short season*, which commenced on Thursday evening last.

The Manager begs leave to call the attention of the public to this establishment, the arrangements for which have been attended with considerable difficulty and heavy expenses, that nothing but their unequivocal approbation and support can enable him to sustain. In locating himself with his establishment in the western country for a moiety of this year, the Manager turned his thoughts to this place and Cincinnati, associating the Huntsville Theatre with the former, and that of Lexington with the latter, as circumstances or terms of occupation might lead to his election. During the present season every attempt will be made to secure sufficient patronage to continue a regular dramatic establishment in Nashville.

This evening, Saturday, July 2d, will be presented Reynolds's admired Comedy of

LAUGH WHEN YOU CAN;

OR THE

Laughing and Crying Philosophers

Gossamer, (the Laughing Philosopher.) Mr. Caldwell

351 Caldwell's Nashville-Huntsville and Cincinnati-Lexington Circuits, from an announcement in the *Nashville Whig*, July 2, 1825

FRIENDS OF IRELAND, IN ST. LOUIS.

—An adjourned meeting of the friends of civil and religious liberty, will be held on SATURDAY evening, the 23d inst. at the house of Mr. John Pigott, Church street, St. Louis. The public are respectfully invited to attend, as the object of the meeting is a benevolent one, to assist those in Ireland who are struggling for their liberty

June 20th.

TO THE CITIZENS OF ST. LOUIS.

THE Proprietor and Manager of the AMERICAN THEATRE, at New Orleans, begs leave, most respectfully, to announce to the Citizens of St. Louis and its environs, that he is anxious to establish the Drama in their city, upon a liberal and respectable footing. The Manager conceives that, in conjunction with New Orleans and Nashville, St. Louis will enable him to keep the whole of his establishment together, throughout the year, which advantage will afford the lovers of the Drama much better entertainment than they could expect, if a company were divided in the summer and fall, and then, again obliged to be collected together for the winter. The Manager intends to bring the whole of his establishment to St. Louis, and he has every confidence in the liberality of its citizens for an ample support.

Every novelty possible will be brought forward, and every exertion made to make the theatre a fashionable and general resort. JAMES H. CALDWELL.

AMERICAN THEATRE, ⎱
New Orleans, May 10th, 1827. ⎰

N. B. The Theatre will be opened about the 25th of June.

☞ Due notice of the pieces for the occasion will be given. *May 30th, 1827.*

352 Caldwell's arrival in St. Louis, from an announcement in the *Missouri Republican*, June 21, 1827

CITY THEATRE.

NEW-ORLEANS COMPANY

For a Few Nights.

☞ THIS EVENING, Oct. 24th—Will be presented, Shakspeare's fashionable Comedy, entitled

MUCH ADO ABOUT NOTHING.

Benedick,	· · · ·	Mr. Caldwell.
Prince,	·	Raymond.
Dogberry,	·	Cowell.
Beatrice,	· ·	Miss Placide.

At the end of the Comedy splendid FRENCH WALTZING, By MADAME EDOUARD, from the Grand Opera, Paris

353 Performance of Caldwell's company in Louisville, from an announcement in the *Louisville Public Advertiser*, October 24, 1831

NEW CINCINNATI THEATRE.

THE Proprietor and Manager of this establishment, which he now names the CINCINNATI THEATRE, has the honor to announce to the citizens of Cincinnati and its environs in particular, and of the state of Ohio in general, that he will dedicate it to the *Drama*, on

WEDNESDAY, THE FOURTH OF JULY, 1832.

In the face of much prejudice and against some opposition, this extensive edifice has been raised—a single, though a strong proof that I do not think the Drama conquerable by such arms as have been used against it, and determined by making it more worthy of the support of the enlightened and liberal part of the community, that it shall never sink itself by vices and abuses of its own.

It has been my peculiar aim to organize an efficient Stock Company, competent to represent a well selected number of our best Tragedies, Comedies and Melo-Dramas. I shall endeavour to shew in the course of my managerial career in Cincinnati, that if not the *first*, the Theatre is *amongst* the first and highest schools of Literature and the Arts; and that Poetry, Painting and Music are no where so perfectly combined as within its walls.

JAMES H. CALDWELL, Proprietor.
Richard Russell, late lessee of the Richmond Hill Theatre, New York, will undertake the Stage department.
James S. Rowe, Treasurer.
A. Mondelli, Principal Artist.

354 Opening of Caldwell's Theater in Cincinnati, from an announcement in the *Cincinnati Daily Gazette*, July 4, 1832

TO ST. LOUIS

355 General William Clark, 1770–1838, from an engraving after the painting by George Catlin, in the possession of the publishers

In the autumn of 1819, while Phillips was completing his arrangements with John Davis, the outlook for Ludlow was most discouraging. His wife and her family had strenuously urged him to give up the theater and study law. In the spring following his return from Huntsville, he had made a sincere effort to comply, but the craving for the theater was too strong to be denied. Again he tried to secure recruits from the East with the same lack of success. Hearing at this time of possibilities in St. Louis, a growing town on the upper Missouri, he wrote to Isaac N. Henry, the publisher of a St. Louis newspaper. Henry was enthusiastic, and Ludlow began searching for additional recruits, this time with better success. These actors were all printers by vocation, but with a year or two of experience in eastern theaters and with considerable natural endowments. Two of them were married to fairly creditable actresses. On the twentieth of November, 1819, the little company embarked from Nashville in a "keel-boat," which was to pick up a load of iron castings further up the Cumberland and carry it to St. Louis. The shores of the Cumberland and the Ohio were by now familiar to Ludlow and his wife, but the laborious ascent of the muddy waters of the Mississippi was depressingly slow. Finally, in desperation the Ludlows transferred themselves and their baggage to the steamer *Missouri Packet*, which proved, however, not much faster. Arriving at St. Louis about the middle of December, Ludlow offered his customary opener, *The Honeymoon*. "Prior to the opening night," wrote Ludlow, "I waited on the principal officer of the city and Territory, Governor William Clark (of the celebrated Lewis and Clark expedition). . . . I told Gen. Clark what my object was in coming to Missouri; and as I had known of one instance . . . in the West where a tax had been levied on the Drama, I wished to ascertain whether it would be required in St. Louis, and if it were, what the tax would be. He . . . said: 'Mr. Ludlow, we feel too much complimented by you and your company visiting us to think of committing such an uncourteous act as *taxing* you. . . .' He . . . entered into conversation with my friend and myself on the advantages he conceived there were to be derived in any community from well regulated dramatic performances . . . when the season commenced I waited on the Governor and presented him with a *carte blanche* for our theater." In spite of this official favor the season was a failure. The theater was capable of seating about six hundred persons; the scenery, painted in water-colors, was neat and tasteful; but it was impossible to keep the building warm. At the most critical time the Drakes, not knowing of the presence of Ludlow, arrived and temporary amalgamation of the two companies was effected for the remainder of the season. The streets of St. Louis during this winter of Ludlow's stay saw many a trapper and an occasional Indian, for it was the center of the rich fur trade of the plains.

---

356 Ludlow's Greeting to the citizens of St. Louis, in the *St. Louis Enquirer*, March 8, 1820

---

357 The Drakes' Arrival, from an announcement in the *St. Louis Enquirer*, May 3, 1820

THEATRE.

THIS EVENING, August 23, will be performed, a very elegant Comedy, written by the late R. B. Sheridan, Esq. M. P. called the

SCHOOL FOR SCANDAL.

Sir Peter Teazle, - Mr. Jones.
Charles Surface, - - Collins.
Joseph Surface, - - Green.
Lady Teazle, - - Mrs. Groshon.
End of the Play, Mr. R. Jones will sing a Comic Song, culled

"Corn Cobbs."

After which, Shakspeare's celebrated Comedy of

Catharine & Petruchio,

OR,

THE TAMING OF THE SHREW.

Petruchio, - - Mr. Collins.
Catharine, - - Mrs. Groshon.
(For further particulars see bills.)

358   The Collins-Jones Nashville Season, 1820, from an announcement in the *Nashville Whig*, August 23, 1820

"THE HUNTERS OF KENTUCKY"

AFTER the first St. Louis season, Ludlow and his wife returned to Nashville where they hoped to find employment with the company of Joshua Collins and William Jones, which was playing there, and afterward to continue their journey further south to Pensacola, where Ludlow planned to open a fine new theater. Instead, however, Ludlow was persuaded by Jones to return again to St. Louis and try a season with him, which, wrote

THEATRE.

The Managers respectfully inform their friends and the public, that having made a permanent engagement with Mr. LUDLOW, his re-appearance will take place on Wednesday evening.

MRS. GROSHON'S BENEFIT.

ON WEDNESDAY EVENING, NOV. 1, will be presented, a grand historical tragedy, founded on an interesting fact which took place during the reign of Richard III. written by N. Rowe, called

JANE SHORE.

To which will be added, a ballet pantomime, called

FLORA'S BIRTH DAY.

The whole to conclude with a very laughable Farce, called

LOVER'S QUARRELS,

Or, like Master like Man.

Don Carlos, - Mr. Ludlow.
Sancho, - - Jones.
Lopez, - - - Groshon.
Leonora, - Mrs. Groshon.
Jacintha, - - Jones.
(For particulars, see the bills of the day.)

359   Ludlow joins Collins-Jones Company, from an announcement in the *Nashville Whig*, October 31, 1820

Ludlow, was "short and unprofitable, a mere repetition of what I had previously experienced." Jones returned to Cincinnati, and Ludlow took a steamer down the Mississippi on his way, he still believed, to Pensacola. Stopping in New Orleans, however, he was introduced in April of 1821 to James H. Caldwell, who was impressed by Ludlow's acting and quickly made terms with him. After the summer season of 1821 in Petersburg, where he saw the American début of Junius Brutus Booth (see No. 187), Ludlow returned for the following season under Caldwell. For his benefit in May 1822, Ludlow decided to introduce a song which his brother had clipped out of the New York *Mirror* and sent along to him. It was called "The Hunters of Kentucky," and was written by Samuel Woodworth (see No. 160), author of the "Old Oaken Bucket." "When the night came," wrote Ludlow, "I found the pit, or parquette of the theater, *crowded full* of 'river men' — that is, keel-boat and flat-boat men. There were very few steamboat men. These men were easily known by their linsey-woolsey clothing and blanket coats. As soon as the comedy of the night was over, I dressed myself in a buck-skin hunting-shirt and leggins, which I had borrowed off a river man, and with moccasins on my feet, and a rifle on my shoulder, I presented myself before the audience . . . I came to the following lines:

'But Jackson he was wide awake, and wasn't scared with trifles,
For well he knew what aim we take with our Kentucky rifles;
So he marched us down to Cyprus Swamp; the ground was low and mucky;
There stood 'John Bull' in martial pomp, but here was old Kentucky.'

As I delivered the last five words I took my old hat off my head, threw it upon the ground, and brought my rifle to the position of taking aim. At that instant came a shout and an Indian yell from the inmates of the pit, and a tremendous applause from other portions of the house, the whole lasting for nearly a minute. . . . The whole pit was standing up and shouting. I had to sing the song three times that night before they would let me off." And all that summer on his trip with the Drakes to Fayetteville, Tennessee, and Huntsville, Alabama, he was called on to sing the new favorite.

American Theatre.

ORLEANS-STREET.

On Saturday Evening,

January 18, 1823.

Will be presented, (for the first time in New-Orleans) the new and interesting Melo Drama, entitled the

WANDERING BOYS, or the
The Castle of Olival,

(*Performed at the London, and New-York Theatres, with the most unbounded applause.*)

Count De Croissy - - - Ludlow.
Justin, } { Miss Seymour,
& } The Wandering { &
Paul, } Boys { Miss Placide,
The Baroness - - - Mrs. Baker.

In Act 1st. The Original Ballad, called the
Wandering Boys of Switzerland,
By Miss Seymour.
(*For other Characters see Bills.*)
To which will be added the laughable Farce of

THE LADY & THE DEVIL,

Wildlove - - - Mr. Ludlow.
Zephyrina - - - Miss Placide,

360   Ludlow at the Orleans Theater, 1823, from an announcement in the *Louisiana Gazette*, January 18, 1823

361   Edwin Forrest, from an engraving after a daguerreotype, in the
possession of the publishers

362   Forrest in Cincinnati, from an announcement in
the *Independent Press*, March 6, 1823

THE ARRIVAL OF FORREST

AT the conclusion of the unsuccessful Jones-Ludlow St. Louis season of 1820, Jones was forced to return with empty hands to his partner Collins, who had remained in Cincinnati. Their long cherished ambition of creating a Cincinnati-Nashville-St. Louis circuit had failed. Thereafter they confined themselves to competing with the Drakes in the Ohio Valley theatrical centers. The Columbia Street Theater, which in March, 1820, Collins and Jones had built in Cincinnati, was the most imposing in that section. Although they were very prominent in western theatrical history for the next two or three years, they are remembered to-day chiefly because of the fact that they were the ones who first brought to the West the young Philadelphia actor, Edwin Forrest. After his début as Young Norval at the Walnut Street in 1820 (see p. 92), Forrest had been advised by Thomas A. Cooper to serve his apprenticeship in the West, where the field was less crowded. Signing a contract with Collins and Jones, Forrest appeared for the first time in the West at Lex-

ington, Kentucky, during the season of 1822–23. From Lexington he went with the company to Cincinnati and from there to Louisville. It is believed that he was one of the seceding players who left Collins and Jones in Louisville, and returned for an unsuccessful summer season at the Globe Theater, Cincinnati, where he certainly performed. He was again with Collins and Jones during their final season of 1823–24. In the spring of 1824, Collins and Jones disbanded, and Forrest was uncertain as to his own best course. At the Globe Forrest played Othello and many other characters for the first time, "but with scarcely any knowledge of the text," wrote Sol Smith, "his taste generally leading him to prefer the low comedy characters!" His salary was eighteen dollars a week.

363   Forrest at the Globe Theater, Cincinnati, from an announcement in the *Independent Press*, June 5, 1823

364 First Stage Appearance of Solomon Franklin Smith, 1801–69, from a drawing by F. O. C. Darley, in Sol Smith, *Theatrical Management in the South and West*, New York, 1868

365 First Theater in Pittsburgh (right), from a sketch in Palmer's *Pictorial Pittsburgh and Prominent Pittsburghers*, 1758–1905, courtesy of the Historical Society of Western Pennsylvania

"STAGE MAD"

WITH the break-up of the Collins-Jones management in the spring of 1824, a new figure entered western theatrical history, who for the following thirty years was destined to influence that history most profoundly. Sol Smith, like Ludlow — and in striking contrast to most of our early actors and managers — was born in America of American parents, in a log cabin, in the backwoods of Oswego County, New York. After a childhood of rigorous apprenticeship on the farm, he set off on foot for Boston where his brothers kept a store. But in the autumn of 1814 they were all back in Albany, and young Sol was clerking for them, and reading Shakespeare during every spare minute, except when he slipped off and went to Bernard's Green Street Theater. "My head was full of acting from that time forward," he wrote, "my duties at the store became irksome to me. I became as thousands had become before me, and thousands will become after me — stage mad!" Unfortunately his brothers were a portion of that righteous minority opposing the theater. But Sol soon made friends with the young Drakes, who, after he had slid down a sheet rope from his bedroom window, would let him in free behind the scenes. When the Drakes and Ludlow left, however, there were no more chances for free admission. Ruses of various kinds were necessary. On one occasion to get a good view of *Richard III* he hid in the casket which was supposed to contain the body of Henry VI. Entranced in peeping at the performance, Sol forgot to make his exit at the proper time, and was carried onto the stage. As the supers were bearing him off, he made a slight noise, sat up in the casket, and so startled the four men that they fled in terror. Shortly afterward Sol ran away from home and tried unsuccessfully to join a dramatic company at Troy, New York. When he returned to Albany he found that his brothers were planning to go to the West. So Sol set out by himself, expecting to meet one of them at an appointed rendezvous. For some reason they did not connect, and Sol arrived finally at Pittsburgh, alone, and with a last dollar, which he spent for lodgings at a tavern and for a theater ticket. The next morning he tried to get a job with the Pittsburgh company. He was refused and worked his way on a flatboat to Marietta, Ohio, where he still searched for his missing brother.

XIV—10

THEATRICAL.—Mr. Forrest.—We witnessed the representation of Richard on Friday evening last, by this young gentleman, and we intended to have expressed the satisfaction we received—but our correspondent "Thespis" has anticipated us, and fully expressed our sentiments on the subject. We are told that when Mr. *Kean*, the celebrated English tragedian, saw Mr. F. play Richard in New York or Philadelphia, he was heard to say "that young man never ought to stay in this country— he ought to *go to England.*" But we do hope it will not be necessary for him to leave his native country to have his talents acknowledged—that the time will come, ere long, when *native talent* will be permitted to live *at home.*

366   Smith's Tribute to Forrest, from an editorial in the *Independent Press*, March 27, 1823

SMITH AS DRAMATIC CRITIC

BEFORE many weeks the brother arrived with others of the family, and they all made their way together down to Cincinnati. The next three years were restless ones for young Sol. From Cincinnati he went further down the river to Louisville, where he apprenticed himself to a printer and spent much time behind the scenes at the theater which was owned by his old friends, the Drakes. When they left, Sol pushed on to Vincennes, Indiana, where he played a season as low comedian for the local Thespian Society. Still restless and discontented, he went on foot overland to Nashville, and then the three hundred miles back to Cincinnati. His activities were most varied: law student, clerk in his brother's store, organist, psalm-leader; and in the spring of 1820 he became leading actor with the Cincinnati Thespians, whose amateurishness he despised. In the winter of 1821–22 after a year's attempt to settle down to the law, Smith gave up and secured a job as prompter in Collins and Jones' Cincinnati Theater. At the close of the season he married, and decided to run a newspaper. The first issue of the *Independent Press* appeared on July 4, 1822. A little more than a year afterward, Collins and Jones brought to Cincinnati a new actor named Forrest. "The opening play was *The Soldier's Daughter,* the part of young Malfort by Mr. Edwin Forrest. Being editor of a paper, I was, of course, and ex-officio, a judge of theatrical matters, but when I gave a very favorable opinion of Forrest's acting in the comparatively trifling character of Malfort my brother editors laughed at me — and afterward, when he played Richard for his benefit and I prophesied his future greatness, they set me down as little less than a mad man." Smith's interest in Forrest — one was twenty-two, the other seventeen — dates from this time. The following summer Forrest was again in Cincinnati at the Globe. Smith, feeling that the young Philadelphia actor was wasting his talents, advised him to proceed to New Orleans and join Caldwell. Forrest was persuaded and the Caldwell contract made. As already noted, Collins and Jones disbanded in the spring of 1824. Smith at last saw an opening to managership. He took over their company, and proceeded for a season to Cincinnati. Forrest was anxious to join him. Smith, out of respect for the Caldwell contract, refused his services. Forrest, losing his temper, joined a low-class traveling circus, until Smith heard of it, pointed out the folly of such a course, and finally persuaded him to go on to the Camp Street Theater in New Orleans.

THE
INDEPENDENT PRESS
IS PRINTED AND PUBLISHED EVERY
THURSDAY MORNING,
BY
Solomon Franklin Smith,
Main Street, nearly opposite the Globe Inn.

TERMS.

TWO DOLLARS per annum, if paid in advance

TWO DOLLARS & FIFTY CENTS. in six months.

THREE DOLLARS at the end of the year.

Advertisements not exceeding a square, will be inserted three times or less, for One Dollar—each continuance 25 cents—larger ones in the same proportion.

Letters addressed to the Editor by mail must be post paid or they will not be attended to.

A failure to notify a wish to discontinue, at the end of the time subscribed for, will be considered as a new engagement.

No paper will be discontinued, (unless at the option of the Editor,) until all arrearages are paid

367   Smith as Newspaper Publisher, from an advertisement in the *Independent Press,* July 25, 1822

Theatre.

☞ELECTION NIGHT!!☜
—
THIS EVENING, OCT. 8,

WILL be presented, the humorous piece in 2 acts, called the

PRIZE! OR 2, 5, 3, 8.

The evening's entertainments to conclude with the admired Petit Comedy called

Each for Himself,
OR
THE RIVAL CANDIDATES!!

Immediately on the closing of the Theatre, there will be a grand ascension of

TWO BALLOONS

from the Vauxhall Gardens, with the name of one of the Candidates for Congress inscribed on each,

368   Theatrical Activity in Cincinnati before Forrest's Arrival, from an announcement in the *Independent Press,* October 8, 1822

369 Smith's opening at the City Theater, Cincinnati, from an announcement in *Liberty Hall*, January 23, 1824

"AN UNFORTUNATE BEGINNING"

THE rest of the company went to Cincinnati, where Smith commenced his managerial duties at the City Theater. "The season failed as I might have expected it would," wrote Smith in *Theatrical Management in the South and West*, "and we removed to the Columbia Street Theater. My funds ran out, and most of my actors scattered, as actors generally do when they find no money is to be had — and they are right,

370 Smith's Transfer to the Columbia Street Theater, Cincinnati, from an announcement in *Liberty Hall*, February 6, 1824

for they cannot live on air — though I have almost done so on several occasions. At the close of the theater I found myself in debt eleven hundred and fifty dollars. Rather an unfortunate beginning." Enough of the company remained, however, to begin another experiment in new territory. They proceeded first to Wheeling, Virginia, and then to Steubenville, Ohio, where performances were given in improvised quarters with indifferent success. In each new town along the way there was constant danger from the sheriff whose duty it was to see that all entertainers had proper licenses. At Wellsburg, Virginia, Smith was served with a warrant, a complaint having been entered that his company was showing without license. Receipts for the evening performance were fifteen dollars — the penalty was forty dollars. There were no funds with which to pay. Prison would be most awkward. Fortunately it was Saturday night, and more fortunately the sheriff had a taste for the drama, and an appreciation of the additional songs which Smith tacked on at the end. For by the time that the representative of the law found his way to Smith's dressing room it was after twelve, and therefore the Sabbath, on which no man should transact business, "particularly law busi-

371 Smith's Benefit, Cincinnati, from an announcement in *Liberty Hall*, March 2, 1824

ness." A later difficulty with the sheriff in Pittsburgh was less easily solved. Smith's creditors were most pressing. The Pittsburgh sheriffs, "who, to do them justice are the most indefatigable set of personages I ever met with," had thrown a cordon around the theater. There seemed little hope of escape. However, Smith disappeared beneath stage through the trap door and threw the sheriffs off the track long enough for him to be secreted away to the home of a friend. It was two days before the excitement had died down sufficiently for him to proceed to Philadelphia.

OUTWITTING A SHERIFF.

372 Smith's Encounter with the Sheriff, Wellsburg, Virginia, from an engraving after a drawing by F. O. C. Darley, in Smith, *Theatrical Management*, New York, 1868

373   Supers in a Frontier Performance, from an engraving by M. H.,
      after a drawing by D. in Smith, *Theatrical Management*, New York,
      1868

374   Smith's Return to Cincinnati, from an announcement in the
      Independent Press, November 4, 1826

ON THE NEW YORK FRONTIER

THE first attempt at management had proved a complete failure. The prospect of acting under settled conditions must have seemed tempting to Smith and his wife, as they paid their way to Philadelphia by giving small concerts in the villages along the turnpike. Great disappointment was in store. There was no opening at the Chestnut. Twice Smith tried at the Park, only to be refused. He was forced to turn his talent to everything except acting. He and his wife gave a concert at Princeton; he kept a bookshop in New York; rented a telescope and on the Battery sold peeps at the moon; edited a paper in Trenton; gave vocal concerts in Perth Amboy; and, finally, unable to keep away longer from the theater, at a salary of eight dollars a week joined the traveling company of H. A. Williams, which was on its way to western New York. The company played three nights in Schenectady, and then proceeded to Little Falls, Utica, Saratoga Springs — where DeWitt Clinton attended Smith's benefit — to Syracuse, and to Auburn. At this point Smith left Williams and assumed joint-managership of a company which planned to tour what was then known as upper Canada, now the province of Ontario. The venture was a failure financially, though productive of numerous amusing experiences such as the fist fight with the Canadians at Niagara, and the interview at Toronto with the Governor, whom Smith alienated by calling him "Mister." The last stop was at Auburn, New York, where in the play of *Damon and Pythias*, Smith's partner had costumed the supers to appear as Syracusan senators. "Not having sandals prepared, he permitted them to wear their own coarse brogans, and as they stood ranged on the stage, stooping down to make the shirts reach below the knee, their appearance was irresistibly ludicrous." Through such glimpses one can visualize quite clearly the conditions of these primitive outlying theaters. That some of the people off-stage were equally primitive is illustrated by a curious encounter near Jamestown, New York, when Smith and his small company were playing their way back to Cincinnati. A native, believing he would live forever, had on one occasion when selling a farm inserted a clause in the deed to the effect that after nine hundred and ninety-nine years the land should revert to him, provided he himself appeared to claim it. In October 1826, Smith was again in Cincinnati, where he played for a short season with his old friends, the Drakes. Convinced now that his future must lie in the West, he joined their company in an overland barnstorming tour through Shelbyville, Maysville, and Paris, Kentucky, to Nashville From Nashville he managed for a while a branch of Drake's company, carrying it to Clarksville, Tennessee, and to Russellville and Hopkinsville, Kentucky.

THE CAMP STREET THEATER

On May 29, 1822, long before Smith had contemplated theatrical managership, James Caldwell had laid the cornerstone of an American Theater in New Orleans. From the profits of his three previous seasons at the Orleans he had capital enough to use as security for floating further loans. He borrowed in lumps of three hundred dollars. For each such loan the subscriber was entitled to a ticket for every season of Caldwell's management in that city until the principal was paid back. On the 16th of May, 1823, the building was sufficiently advanced to allow a performance of *The Dramatist*, but the real opening did not occur until January 1, 1824. Caldwell's selection of a site for his theater was at first very severely criticized, it being earnestly pointed out that none of the better classes would repair to such a deserted quarter of the city. Experience soon proved, however, that the very presence of the theater elevated enormously the character of the vicinity. It is interesting to note that gas was used for the illumination of this New Orleans theater two years before it was introduced into any New York theater. (See p. 90.) The building was referred to generally as the Camp Street Theater, and less frequently as the American Theater. For eleven years, until the completion of the St. Charles in 1835 it was by far the finest playhouse west of the Alleghenies. In the summer of 1823, Caldwell for the first time began to extend his influence northward, giving a summer season in Nashville. In 1827, going still further away from his base of operations, he opened a theater on Second Street in St. Louis, which, from the

American Theatre

☞ The manager feels it his duty to explain to the public. that he is under the necessity of opening this Theatre in an unfinished state, for a few nights, in order to avoid those defects, which have been found to exist in many Theatres, where the precaution has not been taken of ascertaining how far the construction of the building was sufficient for assuring a complete opportunity of *seeing and hearing*, in every part of the house devoted to the audience. This proof is necessary not only for the saving of time and trouble, but will avoid the immense expense and inconvenience which would arise in the event of any such defect being discovered in the *finished* state of the house.

The opening night will be for the Benefit of the Theatre.

[Prices unlimited.]

ON WEDNESDAY evening May 16.
Will be presented Reynold's admired comedy of the

DRAMATIST, or Stop Him who Can,

Vapid [the Dramatist].   Mr. Caldwell,
Lord Scratch   "   Gray,
Floriville   "   Drake,
Louisa Courtney   Miss Placide,
Marianne   Mrs. Rowe.

To which which will be added the favorite farce of

ROMP.

Priscilla Tomboy   Miss Placide,
(For other characters see Bills,)

375   Opening of Caldwell's American Theater, May 16, 1823, from an announcement in the *Louisiana Gazette*, May 12, 1823

fact that it was an altered and enlarged salt house, was always referred to as "the Salt House theater." After a successful season of three months, the New Orleans company proceeded to Nashville. There Sol Smith and his wife, leaving the Drakes, joined forces with the successful promoter and manager, with whom for two years they remained secure under the sheltering prestige of the Camp Street, and free from the torturing uncertainties and responsibilities of independent management.

The American Theater (center), from a sketch in *Gibson's Guide to the State of Louisiana*, New Orleans, 1838

377   View of Mobile, 1823, from a sketch in P. J. Hamilton, *Colonial Mobile*, Boston, 1910.   Houghton Mifflin Co.,
Boston, courtesy of the publishers

MANAGEMENT AT MOBILE

LUDLOW, on the other hand, had not enjoyed the protection of Caldwell since the end of the 1824 season. It was the custom at the Camp Street Theater for the actors intending to return the following season to check their names on a list posted in the green room of the theater. The manager, seeing that the names of the Ludlows and certain others were not checked, called Ludlow into his office, asked the reason, was told that the young actor intended to resume independent management, and replied quite coolly that he hoped he would succeed. Later Ludlow learned that the older manager nourished a grudge against him, suspecting him of inciting the other players to rebellion, a suspicion which Ludlow claimed to have been unfounded. Whatever the facts, before leaving with his company for Nashville Ludlow took a steamer to Mobile to complete arrangements for a theater of which for some time he had contemplated the management. According to an agreement reached with a Mobile promoter the brick theater was to be completed and ready for occupancy, with six scenes and their appurtenances, by the first of the following November, at which time Ludlow would end his tour, and take up permanent head-quarters in Mobile.

THEATRE.

THE Subscribers to the New Theatre are requested to meet at the Mobile Hotel, on Friday evening, Dec. 20th, 1822.
Dec. 19.

378   Plans for a New Theater in Mobile, from an announcement in the *Mobile Commercial Register*, December 19, 1822

Because of the excessive heat the summer seasons in Nashville and Huntsville were bad, and the troupe had pushed on to Cahaba, Alabama, when a letter was received saying that work on the Mobile theater was not progressing. Ludlow hastened to Mobile and, finding the leading men of the city unusually sympathetic, pushed to completion the theater and the scenery, and to the surprise of all managed to open on December 24, 1824. For the next four years Ludlow gave full seasons in Mobile, with side trips to Montgomery and Nashville. Twice during this period he went to New York, appeared at the Park, and made tentative arrangements for a co-partnership, which was never effected, with Thomas Cooper at the Chatham. The four years at Mobile were colorful ones, with visits from Lafayette and John Quincy Adams and from many of the leading stars on their way to and from New Orleans. In the spring of 1829 the Mobile theater burned, and while waiting for a new one to be finished, Ludlow decided to compete in the Drake territory, and on October 5 opened in Louisville, Kentucky, which had the reputation of being a good theatrical town.

MOBILE Commercial Register.

MONDAY EVENING, APRIL 7.

The first corner of the new brick Theatre was laid on Thursday evening last. The entire foundation is now completed, and if a reason able degree of public spirit is manifested in the way of subscribing and *paying*, not more than six weeks will elapse before a building will rise up, both ornamental and creditable to the city.

379   Laying of Cornerstone of First Mobile Theater, from an announce-ment in the *Mobile Commercial Register*, April 7, 1823

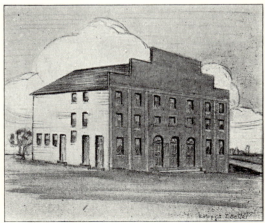

380   First Mobile Theater, 1824, redrawn from a contemporary view of Mobile, 1824, in P. J. Hamilton, *Colonial Mobile*, Boston, 1910.   Houghton Mifflin Co.

381 Ludlow's Louisville Season of 1829, from an announcement in the *Louisville Public Advertiser,* November 7, 1829

A "POVERTY-STRUCK" CONCERN

IT is interesting to learn from an outside source of Ludlow's traveling company at this time. One of the visiting stars who appeared with Ludlow during the Louisville season of 1829 was a young English actor, who had come to America and made his début at the Park in 1821. Later Joe Cowell, whose real name was Witchett, had managed an equestrian show in New York for Edmund Simpson and Stephen Price, who, in addition to managing the Park Theater, also promoted other theatrical enterprises. Cowell had afterward been acting-manager of the Chestnut Street Theater, Philadelphia, after the retirement of Wood; had managed equestrian shows in Philadelphia and Baltimore; had been manager of the Tremont Street Theater in Boston; and was now on his way to New Orleans to join Caldwell. Ludlow was enthusiastic about the acting of Cowell and of his little son, Sam. "In the character of

382 Joe Cowell and son in Louisville, from an announcement in the *Louisville Public Advertiser,* December 12, 1829

Crack in the operatic farce, *The Turnpike Gate,*" Ludlow wrote, the elder Cowell was "never in all probability equalled." The picture that Cowell gave of Ludlow was less flattering. "The regular theater at Louisville, an excellent brick building, belonging to old Drake, was closed; but a cattle shed or stable had been appropriated to that purpose, and fitted up as a temporary stage. The yard adjoining, with the board fence heightened and covered with some old canvass, supported by scaffold poles to form the roof, and rough seats on an ascent to the back, and capable of holding about two hundred persons, constituted the audience part of the establishment, the lower benches nearest the stage being dignified by the name of *boxes,* and the upper, nearest the ceiling, the *pit.* Here I found a strolling company on a *sharing scheme,* at the head of which was N. M. Ludlow. Nothing I had ever seen in the way of theatricals could be likened to this deplorable party . . . here there was not one redeeming point. Who they all were, or what has become of them, Heaven only knows. . . . The strict financial correctness, with the diligence and skill displayed by Ludlow in conducting this 'poverty-struck' concern, is above all praise." Things went from bad to worse with Ludlow. From Louisville he moved his little company to the Columbia Street Theater at Cincinnati, where he remained with only mediocre success until June 30, 1830. Without much hope of improvement he pushed on to Pittsburgh, where he managed to keep open the doors of the theater until James Caldwell passed through on his way back to New Orleans. Caldwell, looking for an agent to manage his increasingly numerous theatrical enterprises in the Ohio Valley, made moderately good offers to Ludlow, who was in no position to refuse. For he had heard in the meantime that the new Mobile Theater on St. Francis Street had also burned before it was even completed.

383 Joe Cowell, right (with Edwin Adams, left), J. W. Wallack, Jr., and Kate Bateman, from a photograph in the Davis Collection

384 Cowell's Farewell Benefit, St. Louis, from an announcement in the *Daily Missouri Republican,* June 27, 1840

385   Thomas A. Cooper, from a lithograph in the
            Fridenberg Collection

"THE WAYS OF GLORY"

DURING the season of 1830–31 at the Camp Street, Ludlow saw a performance by Thomas A. Cooper (see Nos. 102, 116) which greatly saddened him. "In the scene between Wolsey and Cromwell," he wrote, "at the close of the third act, Mr. Cooper was so affected by the words and the situation that tears flowed copiously from his eyes and coursed down his cheeks, so as to be visible to the performers at the side-scenes of the stage. . . . I felt very sad, for my mind went back to the days when Thomas A. Cooper 'trod the ways of glory'; but now his star had sunk to rise no more. He had just been in a manner crowded off the boards of the Park Theater, New York, by younger and more popular actors — Forrest, Booth, and Charles Kean, — and began to feel the full force of those lines of Dr. Samuel Johnson, 'Superfluous lags the veteran on the stage.' As my eyes gazed upon the old man, standing as he did before me, my memory travelled back to my boyhood, when Mr. Cooper was the god of my idolatry; when I used to look at him, as he passed my door, with feelings amounting almost to worship. On this occasion I could not restrain my tears of sympathy with the great actor that now stood before me in grandeur, like a magnificent old castle mouldering into ruins."

A RIVAL OF JACKSON'S

TOWARD the end of the season of 1829 at the Camp Street, Sol Smith, ever restive when working under the direction of a superior, decided to leave Caldwell, and with Lem Smith, his brother, organized "a small strolling concern to operate in the principal towns of Mississippi and West Tennessee." After two weeks at Port Gibson and four at Vicksburg, in both of which places Smith and his company were well known and popular, they proceeded to Memphis, where a small room next to an old warehouse was fitted up for them. After eight nights, with receipts of three hundred and nineteen dollars, the "journey work" commenced in reality. Common road wagons bore this small band through the "Western District, if not in very great style, certainly in great safety, and at an extremely moderate pace." Their first stop was Somerville, whence they

moved on to other frontier towns of Tennessee, whose names to-day are seldom heard. "The people seemed to come out of the woods," and, although the performances were given with inadequate lighting and without scenery, the receipts were surprisingly good. There was something primitive in these people to which the art of the actor appealed. Smith told an anecdote of an old landlord at Middleton, Tennessee, who was waiting up anxiously to see the actor Smith, whose reputation had preceded him. It was almost midnight when Smith and his fellow travelers arrived. The landlord rushed forward eagerly to find from the waybill which was the man he wanted to see. Smith, tired, and wishing at the moment to avoid publicity, disclaimed his identity. Great was the disappointment of the landlord, who proceeded to expound on the mysterious powers of that man Smith. "They tell me he can take any shape he pleases, and that he is one person today and another tomorrow, assuming as many characters as suits him; and he makes people *pay* for seeing him perform his tricks. Some people say he is as good as a caravan." And still grumbling at his misfortune in missing Smith, he went down the hall muttering, "Curse me if there is but one other man on earth I would have stayed up for, AND THAT'S GENERAL JACKSON HIMSELF."

386   The Arrival of Sol Smith at a Frontier Inn, from a
            drawing by F. O. C. Darley, in Sol Smith, *Theatrical
            Management*, New York, 1868

CELEBRITIES ON THE FRONTIER

AT Jackson, Tennessee, the company played in a log theater to good receipts; at Florence, Alabama, in the garret of the principal hotel. From Florence they proceeded in their common road wagons "at an extremely moderate pace" to Tuscumbia, Alabama, and then to Huntsville, where for a change they played in a "beautiful little theater which graced the city." From September 9 to January 4 they played at Tuscaloosa, an unusually long run but with practically no profit. Smith had leased Caldwell's theater at Natchez, Mississippi, for the spring season, and was preparing to go, when he received a pressing invitation from the citizens of Montgomery, Alabama, to visit their new theater which the Thespian Society had just erected. The Montgomery season, which was remarkably profitable, furnished, incidentally, an instance of the striking contrasts which a study of the frontier theater occasionally reveals. The most famous star who visited Montgomery at this time was Madame Feron, the famous European prima donna. According to Ireland, "no songstress of equal European repute had previously appeared here, Malibran not having achieved her transatlantic triumphs when she entranced our western world." Madame Feron, daughter of a French refugee, was born in London in 1797, and at the age of eight was already attracting great attention by the brilliance of her singing. In 1811 she made her début at Covent Garden and then toured for a number of years on the continent, appearing as an equal with the greatest voices of Europe, and becoming one of the favorite pupils of the great composer Rossini. In 1827 she returned to England, made her début at Drury Lane, and shortly afterward came to America. Two backgrounds could hardly be more different than those of Smith and Madame Feron; and equally different the crude little Montgomery theater from the great opera houses of France and Italy. And yet all went well. "The great singer performed with us two nights," Smith wrote, "and as we were without a regular orchestra various means were resorted to for an accompaniment to her songs. A piano-forte was introduced upon the stage, and she accompanied herself in some pieces, in others she pressed me into service." One song, to which Smith played the accompaniment, "was gloriously breathed forth by the great prima-donna of Europe, in a theater surrounded by uncut trees, and occupied by an audience whose appreciation was as warm as that of the dilettanti of Europe. Madame Feron seemed to enjoy herself very much, imparting her good humour to all around, both before and behind the curtain." The Montgomery planters were far from being rough frontiersmen.

387 Madame Feron, from an engraving after a drawing by Henri Hindeman, in the Harvard Theater Collection

388 Frontier Hotels, Tuscaloosa, and Milledgeville, Georgia, from advertisements in the *Mobile Commercial Register,* July 31, 1823

389 Sol Smith, from an engraving by W. G. Jackman after a drawing by J. Gunney, in the possession of the publishers

"BRAVING THE MUD"

From Montgomery Smith proceeded with great hopes to Natchez. But it soon became obvious that there would be no profits. So he tried the daring experiment of splitting his company, which was rather large, between Natchez and Port Gibson. Thus by giving performances on alternate nights and appearing himself in both places, he could double the receipts. The mathematics was good, but the strain on Smith himself is revealed in a page of his diary.

"*Wednesday:* Rose at break of day. Horse at the door. Swallowed a cup of coffee while the boy was tying on leggins. Reached Washington at eight. Changed horses at 9 — again at 10 — and at 11. At 12 arrived at Port Gibson. Attended rehearsal — settled business with stage-manager. Dined at 4. Laid down and endeavored to sleep at 5. Up again at 6. Rubbed down and washed by Jim (a negro boy). Dressed at 7. Acted the *Three Shingles* and *Splash*. To bed at 11½.

Thursday: Rose and breakfasted at 9. At 10 attended rehearsals for the pieces of next day. At 1, leggins tied on, and braved the mud for a fifty miles ride. Rain falling all the way. Arrived at Natchez at half past 6. Rubbed down and took supper. Acted *Ezekiel Homespun* and *Delph* to a poor house. To bed (stiff as steelyards) at 12.

Friday: Cast pieces — counted tickets — attended rehearsal until 1 P.M. To horse again for Port Gibson — arrived at 7. No time to eat dinner or supper! Acted in the *Magpie and Maid. . . .*"

MRS. SMITH IS SLIGHTED

At the end of this trying season Smith with a light heart and an unusually heavy purse left for Cincinnati to pay off the long-standing debts which had so sorely oppressed him. After a starring performance with the Drakes and a short summer season with Caldwell and George Holland in Nashville, he, with the rest of the Nashville troupe, steamed down to New Orleans on a "very slow boat, called *The Rapid.*" Caldwell soon afterward went East, as already noted, and, on his return trip, picked up Ludlow at Pittsburgh to serve as subordinate manager in outlying towns. For a

390 Early Travel between New Orleans and Natchez, from an advertisement in *The Bee*, New Orleans, December 30, 1831

short time the names of Smith, Ludlow, and Cowell were all posted in the green room of the Camp Street Theater. But in February 1831, Ludlow was sent to Natchez to manage a company which Caldwell had assembled for him. The theater, which had been built by a local Thespian association, was a brick building about a hundred feet by forty, located in an outlying section of the city near — much too near, according to Smith — an abandoned graveyard. "The company that had been put in charge by Mr. Caldwell," wrote Ludlow, "was an incongruous and ill-assorted one, with many conflicting pretensions as to lines of business, and the consequence was that I had great difficulties to encounter in the management of them." Soon afterward Sol Smith was conscripted to go to Natchez. "With great reluctance," he wrote, "we departed for the City of the Bluffs." Thus the scene was laid for the first direct encounter between Ludlow and Smith. Harry J. Finn, a prominent eastern actor in New York and Boston, who in addition was a good dramatist and clever painter, and for a time manager of the Federal Street Theater, Boston, was giving starring performances in Natchez, opening with *A Roland for an Oliver.* Ludlow was stage manager and in control of the casting. Sol Smith claimed the leading feminine rôle for his wife. Ludlow gave it to another, "because she was a better actress." Smith withdrew his wife from the cast, and, nursing his resentment against Ludlow, himself withdrew at the end of the St. Louis season, which followed the Natchez. It was several years before these roving spirits were again thrown together.

391 Harry J. Finn (left) as Paul Pry, from a lithograph in the Fridenberg Collection

392   John Gibbs Gilbert, as Dogberry, from an engraving in the Fridenberg Collection

THEATRE.

A CARD.——MR. GILBERT respectfully announces to the *ladies and gentlemen* of Nashville, that on WEDNESDAY EVENING next, he presents his name to them for a *BENEFIT* On which occasion he has selected a beautiful play by Dimond (never acted here) author of Foundling of the Forest, &c. called *The Conquest of Taranto, or the Algerine Corsair* To conclude with an entire new Melo-Drama, called *Charles the Terrible.* Between the pieces the storm scene of THE PILOT, will be exhibited—with other entertainments, as will be expressed in the bills of the day Mr GILBERT hopes in presenting his name to the Nashville public, to receive that patronage it has ever been his study and ambition to deserve.   nov21.

393   Gilbert's Benefit, from an announcement in the *National Banner and Nashville Whig*, November 21, 1831

THEATRICAL.
A CARD.

N. M. LUDLOW has the pleasure of announcing to the ladies and gentlemen of Nashville and its vicinity, that he intends opening the Theatre in that city on or about the 10th of October, for a short season—during which time many of the most successful and late productions of the drama will be produced, and he doubts not but his old friends and patrons will see him well recompensed for the expense and exertion required in producing the same. The following is a list of pieces he intends presenting for their patronage during the season:—MELO-DRA-MAS—PAUL JONES, or the *Pilot of the German Ocean*, a nautical Melo-Drama; ANTOINE THE SAVAGE, or the *Rocks of Le Charbonnier;* THE BOHEMIAN MOTHER, or *Presumptive Evidence;* CHARLES THE TERRIBLE; THE MONSTER, or the *Fate of Frankenstein;* JOAN OF ARC, or the *Maid of Orleans;* THE BRIGAND; THE INCH CAPE BELL; THE FATAL RAVINE; OVERY, or the *Miser's Daughter;* RIP VAN WINKLE, or the *Spirit of the Catskill Mountains;* DEVIL'S ELIXIR; FLYING DUTCHMAN, or the *Phantom Ship;* MURDERER, or *Devoted Son;* RUFFIAN BOY; MAY QUEEN; RED ROVER; WOMAN OF THE TREE, or the *Highland Widow;* MELMOTH THE WANDERER; THE EVIL EYE; THE SHEPHERD OF DERWENT VALE; THE TROUBADOURS—and the NEW FARCES of THE FIRST OF APRIL; 53, JOHN STREET; SNAKES IN THE GRASS; POPPING THE QUESTION; PERFECTION, or the *Maid of Munster;* YOUTHFUL QUEEN; HUSBAND AT SIGHT; DEAD SHOT; MARRIED BACHELOR; INVINCIBLES; WILLIAM THOMPSON; BILLY TAYLOR—with occasionally some of the most favorite Comedies and Tragedies.   sept23

394   Ludlow's Nashville Season of 1831, from an announcement in the *National Banner and Nashville Whig,* September 23, 1831

THE "EATON NIGHT"

THE last performance of the season of 1831 at St. Louis was on July 6, and three days later, on "a miserable apology for a steam-boat" Ludlow embarked with his company, minus the Smiths, for Nashville, where they opened in the theater which Caldwell had erected in 1826 on Summerville Street. "It was a very sufficient one for the population at that day, but the arrangements inside were of the roughest and plainest kind. The walls of the lobbies were not plastered, very little convenience in the auditorium, and only a few scenes, of the plainest character, were painted for the stage." The season began on July 23 with the comedy *A Cure for the Heartache* in which John Gibbs Gilbert took the part of Vortex. Gilbert had been a regular member of the company during the St. Louis season and became afterward one of the most famous native comedians, appearing with great success in the eastern theaters, and going on starring tours through the West and South. The profits at first were not good, but from September 1, with the return of many citizens from their summer vacations, until the end of the season, the houses were very remunerative, and Ludlow was able to send several hundred dollars to Caldwell, who had begun the construction of a new theater in Cincinnati. It is interesting to observe an instance, during this season, of how national excitement over the Peggy Eaton scandal (see Vol. VIII) reflected itself in Ludlow's theater. Eaton, an old friend and co-manager of Ludlow's (see p. 132), was in Nashville at the time with his wife. At his request *The Honeymoon* was performed, and was attended by a large and brilliant house, mostly Eaton partisans who resented the bitter attacks on Mrs. Eaton that had almost broken up Jackson's Cabinet. At a particular point of the dialogue — with the words "The man that lays his hand upon a woman, save in the way of kindness, is a wretch. . . ."— "there was a univeral burst of applause such as I have never heard in any theater since that time. . . . The applause was so great and general that even the chandeliers seemed to join in with it, for their glass drops rang out a joyous peal, in token of their pleasure." There were other gala nights, one sponsored by Governor Branch, Jackson's Secretary of the Navy, and an anti-Eatonite, and another when the Tennessee State Legislature attended *en masse*. But none was comparable to the enthusiasm of the "Eaton Night." Ludlow displayed considerable acumen in turning to his advantage the American zest for politics.

395   Thomas D. Rice, from an engraving by Henry Meyer after a drawing by J. W. Childe, in the Houdini Collection

"JUMP, JIM CROW"

CALDWELL had ordered Ludlow with his Nashville company to report at Louisville not later than November 10. The season which lasted from November 17, 1831, to February 3, 1832, was significant chiefly for one of the first dramatic performances of *Rip Van Winkle* west of the Alleghenies. The character of Rip, played by C. B. Parsons, who later became a well-known western preacher, was for a time enthusiastically received. At the end of the Louisville season Ludlow's company was greatly strengthened by the addition of Thomas D. Rice, who was to become one of the most famous comedians in America. Cowell is authority for the story that Rice, appearing as a super at the Park, unconsciously aroused such laughter in the audience that the veteran comedians, Hilson, Barnes, and Placide, forced Simpson to dispense with his services. In 1828 Rice was property man at the Mobile Theater, and then joined the Drakes. He had already begun to sing the negro song of "Jump, Jim Crow" which, according to Ludlow, he picked up in the following manner. "One spring season of the Louisville Theater, on a clear, bright morning, during the rehearsal of some play in which Mr. Rice had but little to do, as he was standing on the stage, at a back-door that looked out upon the rear of a stable-yard, where a very black, clumsy negro used to clean and rub down horses,

he was attracted by the clearness and mellowness of this negro's voice, and he caught the words, the subject of his song; it was the negro version of 'Jump, Jim Crow.' He listened with delight to the negro's singing for several days, and finally went to him and paid him to sing the song over to him until he had learned it. About this time the manager, Mr. Drake, was bringing out a small local drama, entitled *The Rifle*, in which Mr. Rice had been cast for a Kentucky Corn-Field negro, and when the piece was produced he requested Mr. Drake's permission to introduce and sing his newly acquired song of 'Jim Crow,' which Mr. Drake reluctantly consented to. The result was that 'Jim Crow' ran the piece to full houses for many nights. . . ." During the Cincinnati season, Rice was Ludlow's chief attraction, the audience invariably calling for him to step out of the character he was playing and sing the Jim Crow song. At the end of the season Rice went East, where he had a brilliant career. Ludlow returned to Louisville, and shortly afterward Caldwell with the New Orleans company arrived at Cincinnati to open his elegant new theater on July 4.

397   Rice as the original Jim Crow, from a sketch in the Houdini Collection

CITY THEATRE.

N. M. LUDLOW, (*Agent for* J. H. CALDWELL, *Manager of the New-Orleans Theatre,*) has the honor of informing the citizens of Louisville, that the Theatre will open here under his management, for a short season, some time next week—an arrangement having been made with Mr. Drake to that effect. ☞Due notice will be given of the first performance.   july 16

396   Ludlow as Caldwell's Agent in Louisville, Season of 1831, from an announcement in the *Louisville Public Advertiser,* July 19, 1831

For Tuscaloosa,
AND INTERMEDIATE PLACES,
THE Steam-boat TOMBECKBE, now lying at Hallett's wharf, having most of her cargo engaged, and will commence loading to-morrow, and positively start on Tuesday next. For freight or passage, apply on board to

Jas. H. Dearing.

may 1--42tf

The Steam Boat Columbus,
WILL leave for *MONTGOMERY and INTERMEDIATE PLACES,* in all, next week, for freight or passage, apply to Capt Ashbridge, on board,

J. Macnair,

398 Early Travel between Tuscaloosa, Mobile, and Montgomery, from an advertisement in the *Mobile Commercial* Register, May 1, 1823

FIFTY CENTS AND A GLASS OF WHISKY

WHILE Ludlow was devoting his energy to bringing in profits for Caldwell to apply toward building handsome new theaters in established centers, Sol Smith, having left St. Louis at the end of the unpleasant 1831 season with Ludlow, returned to Louisville and recruited a number of actors into a company to go on a long "gagging tour" over the southern circuit. Before he returned again to the Ohio in the spring of 1833 he had played forty-six weeks, had traveled five thousand miles, and had cleared four thousand dollars in profits. The early part of the trip was in familiar terri-

399 Sol Smith's Mobile Season, 1832, from the *Mobile Commercial* Register, February 13, 1832

tory. In Tennessee they passed again through Memphis, and were welcomed by old friends in Bolivar. They went on to Florence and Tuscumbia, Alabama; crossed the boundary twice again, to Columbia and Pulaski, Tennessee, and then back to Huntsville, Alabama. The first long stand was one of eight weeks at Tuscaloosa, where for the first time Smith performed before the Alabama Legislature, and where the receipts were unusually good. On January 15, 1832, Smith went to Mobile, "a city which he had long wished to visit professionally," but finding a strong competitor, J. Purdy Brown, already lodged there, he took his company on to Montgomery and then in the late spring made the surprising decision to penetrate into the Creek Country as far as Columbus, Georgia. "It was Sunday," wrote Smith of their arrival, "and the streets of Columbus were filled with gayly-dressed citizens and Creek Indians. The arrival of a theatrical company created quite a surprise." A bit later the Creek Indians in turn created "quite a surprise." Smith fancied that it might lend realism to the mob scenes of *Pizarro*, if some real Creek Indians could be secured. Arrangements were made. The Indians were paid their fifty cents and, alas! their glass of whisky. Instead of representing an Inca background, they took the center of the stage, putting on a real Creek war dance, which drowned out all other sounds and caused the actors to fly for shelter. There were no casualties, and the company appeared in numerous other Georgia towns — in Macon, and Milledgeville, the state capital, at Athens and Monticello, finally closing in Montgomery, Alabama, on the 29th of March, 1833. Not many years elapsed before Georgia and Alabama were practically cleared of Indians, and white planters occupied their rich cotton lands.

400 The War Dance of the Creek Indians, from a drawing by A. R. Waud, in Smith, *Theatrical Management*, New York, 1868

401   William Chapman's Floating Theater, from a sketch by Dr. Judd, in Arthur Hornblow, *History of the Theater in
America*, Philadelphia, 1919. © Lippincott, Philadelphia

AN EXTRAORDINARY FAMILY

When Sol Smith returned to Cincinnati in the spring of 1833, he made the acquaintance of the Chapman family, who were operating a "floating-theater," which plied up and down the Ohio and Mississippi, stopping at various towns along the shore and giving performances aboard for the inhabitants. Smith, however, told us little of the history of this family beyond their consuming passion for fishing, in which they all indulged even during the progress of the play, whenever they happened to be off stage. Our chief information comes from Ludlow, who had "never met with, in the profession of the stage, so many members of one family possessing such versatility and remarkable ability." There were the father and three brothers and two sisters, all born in England — the father at one time having held a "very respectable position" on the London stage. One of the brothers had made his American début at the Bowery in 1828 and had been a great favorite in Philadelphia; another was a "comic actor of more than ordinary ability"; another was a fair melodramatic actor. "But Caroline possessed more stage ability than any other member of this singularly gifted family. . . . My first knowledge of this family was, if my recollection be correct, about the year 1831 or 1832, when I beheld a large flat-boat, with a rude kind of house built upon it, having a ridge roof, above which projected

a staff with a flag attached, upon which was plainly visible the word 'Theater.'" Ludlow first saw them at Cincinnati where "they were on their 'winding way' south to New Orleans, and as I heard afterwards, stopped at every town or village on the banks of the river where they supposed they could get together a sufficient audience, and gave an entertainment at a small price of admission." On one occasion certain youths, resentful of the fifty cents admission demanded, quietly cast the boat from its moorings. When the performance was concluded the audience found themselves more than a mile down stream and were forced to trudge their way home in the best way they could. "In a few years after the commencement of their floating business, the Messrs. Chapman purchased a steam-boat, which they fitted up very comfortably, after the fashion of a theater, and placing on board a pilot, engineers, and deck hands, they navigated their way at pleasure, down and up the rivers of the West, playing at all the towns adjacent." The Chapmans were later in Mobile, New Orleans, and in **California.**

402 A Floating Circus, 1853, from a sketch in Archer B. Hulbert,
The Ohio River, New York, 1906. © Putnam Bros., New York

NEW TERRITORY

ON the 12th of August, 1833, following his meeting with the Chapmans, Smith, still in Cincinnati, hired Thomas A. Lyne as a member of the troupe he was organizing to follow up the theatrical connections made during the preceding year in Georgia. Instead of going the old familiar way by Memphis and West Tennessee and Alabama, the Smith troupe branched off to the southeast, planning to go through Cumberland Gap and making their first stop at Paris, Kentucky. The manager had started from Cincinnati with only three hundred dollars to cover the expenses of the entire trip to Georgia. He had anticipated no trouble in at least paying their way by performances in the towns through which they would pass. He soon learned, however, of the presence of cholera, and of the general dread of contamination. No one dreamed of congregating at a theater. From Paris they pushed on to Richmond, where they were forced to carry their trunks for a half-mile up a painfully steep hill. By the time that they had passed through London and reached Barboursville, the three hundred dollars had practically vanished. At the latter place they were persuaded to give a concert to an audience

403   Thomas A. Lyne, from an engraving in Horace G. Whitney, *The Drama in Utah*, Salt Lake City, 1915, Deseret News

of twenty-two, who stoutly refused to pay more than twenty-five cents "for any show." The total receipts were found insufficient to meet the hotel bill. Paying toll next day through a gate near the Cumberland Gap reduced the company's ready money to eight dollars and fifty cents. An impromptu performance in the dining room of the hotel at Tazewell did little to improve their finances. Later Smith tried to pawn his gold watch. He failed, and was in despair until a fellow voyager, who had passed them several times on the road and been struck by Smith's honest face, volunteered to tide him over the difficulty. At Bean's Station, East Tennessee, the company gave a concert in the dark, there being no light of any kind in the village. At Greenville, Tennessee, their receipts were three dollars. On September 11 Smith was at Warm Springs, North Carolina, where he finally succeeded in pawning his two hundred dollar watch for fifty dollars and in selling a wagon. With this money he started for Greenville, South Carolina, where Thomas A. Lyne, the leading tragedian of the company, had already gone ahead. The best performance to date was at Asheville, North Carolina, with receipts of six dollars and seventy-five cents. On September 17, the entire company was at Greenville and on the next night, having "completed the necessary alterations in the Masonic lodge room," they presented *The Honeymoon*. They remained only four nights with receipts totaling one hundred and fifty dollars, and then moved on to Pendleton, South Carolina, where they were taxed two-thirds of their receipts; to Washington, Georgia, where they played to nine people; and finally to Milledgeville, Smith's goal, where on November 4 the Georgia Legislature assembled, "when the tide turned in our favor, and we continued to perform to good houses to the end of the session and season."

404   Frontier Travel in Georgia and Alabama, from an advertisement in the *Mobile Commercial Register*, May 19, 1823

405   George Holland, 1791–1870, from a photo-
       graph in the Davis Collection

SMITH AND HOLLAND

By Christmas Smith was in Macon, Georgia, "where, in consequence of bad weather, we made but a poor season." When the company reopened in Montgomery, Alabama, on January 16, 1834, George Holland had been taken in by Smith as co-manager. "George Holland," wrote his new partner, "came to this country under an engagement for three years at the Bowery Theater. After performing in that establishment for a short time, he received so many offers of *starring* engagements that he *bought himself out*, and started on a tour through the states, making money at every step. In a year or two he accumulated sufficient means to purchase a cottage at Harlem, New York." His attempt to turn the cottage into an inn and commercialize the friends who lionized him proved a failure, and Holland was forced again to go on the stage. He first went on a tour with Thomas A. Cooper and William Barton, giving performances in all the principal towns from Baltimore to New Orleans. Shortly afterward he joined Smith at Montgomery, where the co-managers enjoyed a "moderately good" season, lasting until April 26. "My business connection with George Holland was a very pleasant one," wrote Smith. "We parted at the close of the season with mutual good feelings, and he proceeded to New Orleans, where he soon became the principal clerk of James H. Caldwell. . . . In prosperity and adversity he adhered to the fortunes and misfortunes of Mr. Caldwell

until 1843 . . . then attached himself to the Little Olympic, under Manager Mitchell, where he remained seven years, as great a favorite as New York ever knew. On the retirement of Mitchell from the management in 1849, Holland accepted an engagement offered him by Mr. Thomas Placide, manager of the 'Varieties,' New Orleans, where he enjoyed a popularity never perhaps achieved by any other actor in that city. Mr. Holland is now [1868] a fixture at 'Wallack's,' where he is deservedly esteemed both as an actor and a man." After the departure of Holland from Montgomery in April, 1834, Smith made a trip to New Orleans to secure new recruits. This brief interruption was followed by two additional weeks at Montgomery with a reorganized company; four at Columbus, Georgia; six at Macon, Georgia; and then, at the request of many of the most respectable citizens of Augusta, Smith agreed to lease their new theater for a year. But, losing very heavily during the first month, he was forced to abandon the enterprise. At Augusta we get an interesting picture of Smith in the "Directors' Room," attending personally to the payment of salaries for the final week, with pieces of silver and banknotes laid out on the table before him. For seven weeks Smith's company played at Milledgeville before the State Legislature, where many of the most legitimate tragedies and comedies were given, including an excellent Shakespearean repertoire. At the conclusion of this season they journeyed the three hundred miles back to Montgomery.

406   Holland as Bunbury Knobb, in Lester Wallack's *Rosedale*,
       from a photograph in the Davis Collection

407 Joseph M. Field, from an engraving in the Fridenberg Collection, New York

408 Joseph M. Field in Mobile, from an announcement in the *Mobile Mercantile Advertiser*, December 5, 1835

THE END OF THE SECOND ACT

DURING these final Georgia and Alabama seasons Joseph M. Field had been the leading actor, and was especially praised by Manager Smith for his interpretation of the Shakespearean rôles before the legislature in Milledgeville. He afterward became one of the outstanding actors of the St. Louis, New Orleans, and Mobile theaters. On January 3, 1835, at Montgomery, Alabama, Field was made Smith's assistant; and, wrote Smith, "urged by the citizens of Wetumpka, I sent my dramatic forces, under the temporary command of Brev. Gen. J. M. Field, to that remarkably primitive city, where a considerable business was done in a billiard room, hastily transformed into a theater, during a season of two weeks." One of the most amusing of all of Smith's engagements was at Haynesville, Alabama, where "for twelve successive nights we exerted ourselves for their edification, and to this day I am in utter ignorance whether our efforts were satisfactory or not, for not a hand of applause greeted us during the entire time; neither did a smile — a laugh was out of the question — shed its ray, to cheer us on in our task." On June 10, 1835, the Montgomery season ended — and "here," wrote Smith, "ends my Second Act and rather a long one it is; but I wanted to get through with my 'management' in the rural districts before taking the reader with me into my metropolitan experiences which I propose to hurry through with less regard to detail, than has characterized the recital of the incidents of the first 12 years of my theatrical life." Immediately afterward Smith left with Joseph M. Field for St. Louis, where they gave short starring engagements, and then on to Cincinnati where they did the same. Shortly they separated and Smith went to Philadelphia and New York, where he made successful appearances at the Walnut and the Park, whose doors ten years earlier had closed in his face. Field was the author of numerous dramas, the best known of which were *Oregon, or the Disputed Territory, Victoria,* and *Family Ties,* which won a prize offered by Dan Marble for the best Yankee play of the year.

409 Sol Smith Stops at St. Louis, from an announcement in the *Missouri Republican*, July 11, 1835

CHAPTER VII

THE WESTERN CIRCUIT

WHEN in 1835 James H. Caldwell opened the doors of his magnificent St. Charles Theater, with a gesture of self-confidence and pride typical of the city of New Orleans, he called it "the temple" of the drama. For fifteen years Caldwell, an Englishman by birth, an actor and theatrical manager by profession, had been a citizen of New Orleans, identified in an increasingly prominent way, not only with its theatrical life, but with the manifold activities of a city which fancied itself a center of trade, destined, by reason of its unique geographical position, to assume its place with New York as a commercial metropolis of a powerful nation. This unfaltering optimism, amounting at times almost to arrogance, which pervaded the minds of Caldwell and his fellow citizens of New Orleans, was a natural reflection of the spirit of the great mass of settlers in the West, who in the course of a few decades had transformed by their own indomitable energy an unproductive wilderness into a commercial empire which was fast outstripping the older states along the Atlantic. When Caldwell first came to New Orleans, in the winter of 1819, he found a sleepy village languidly clinging to its French and Spanish traditions, and attempting to ignore the alien population of boisterous jeans-clad bargemen from the hinterland, who in increasing numbers were docking at the wharves of the Faubourg Ste. Marie. Four years later Caldwell, sensing more astutely than his conservative advisors the great transformation that was taking place in the city, opened his new theater, the American, on Camp Street in the Faubourg Ste. Marie, on a site alarmingly distant from the old French quarters of Orleans Street. During the twelve years of Caldwell's régime at the American Theater, from 1823 to 1835, the Faubourg Ste. Marie developed with almost miraculous speed. On its wharves, within easy access of the theater, the raftsmen from the up-river towns and the crews of the powerful steamboats landed their valuable freight by day, and by night sought strenuous relaxation in the noisy gambling halls and ballrooms of the neighborhood, or in the gallery of Caldwell's theater, boisterously cheering songs commemorating Jackson's victory of New Orleans (see page 137). Near Caldwell's theater also rose the powerful new bank of New Orleans, which supplied the basis of credit for still further exploitation of the resources of the great valley which poured its riches into the hands of the Americans of the Faubourg Ste. Marie. By 1833 the value of the annual exports of New Orleans had reached almost thirty-seven million dollars. On the broad verandas of the St. Charles Hotel, Caldwell, seeking diversion from the routine of rehearsals on Camp Street, discussed his numerous commercial projects with the wealthy planters and promoters who were drawn to his city from Mobile and Natchez and even as far north as Cincinnati and St. Louis. During the early years of the St. Charles Hotel there seemed no restrictions to what the imagination of Caldwell and his friends might prescribe for New Orleans' future glory. In population she had far surpassed her western rivals and by the next census she would be the fourth city of the land. Mobile, where Ludlow and Smith were about to experiment with a permanent stock company, was, in spite of the millions of acres of rich cotton land for which it was the port, a village in comparison; Cincinnati, where in 1832 Caldwell had opened an elegant new home of the drama, though dominating the life of the upper valleys had fallen far short of realizing its vision of becoming the trade center of America. Natchez, with its brick theater on the bluff near the burying ground, was but the northern port of the cotton trade, insignificant in comparison to the southern terminus. And in 1833, Caldwell, reflecting the prevailing attitude of New Orleans, disposed of his minor up-river theaters to subordinates, and concentrated on erecting as near to the heart of the universe as possible a "temple" of the drama, which, surpassing all western rivals in magnificence, and housing a versatile and brilliant stock company, supplemented by the most famous stars from the East, should be a fitting adornment for the proudest city of the West.

In the same year that Caldwell opened the St. Charles Theater Noah Miller Ludlow and Sol Smith, the circuit riders of the frontier theater, abandoned their restless wanderings and their jealousies, and combined their experience and savings in the management of the Mobile Theater. And for the summer season of 1836, they were able, thanks to the perfection which the Mississippi steamboat service had reached, to transfer their company to the ambitious, growing town of St. Louis. By July 3 of the following summer they had, with the coöperation of the boosters of St. Louis, completed a beautiful theater, much more spacious than the actual population and resources of the city would seem to justify. But they had caught the spirit of the citizens of St. Louis, who in a grandiloquent style, that would have done justice to Edwin Forrest, their favorite actor, trumpeted the coming glories of their city. "When experience shall have fully tested the hazards of trade in lower latitudes," wrote the editor of the *Missouri Gazeteer* of 1837, with a veiled thrust at New Orleans, "true wisdom will point to St. Louis as the place where the purchase and sale of merchandise . . . shall be carried on . . . and all balances can be settled at the mammoth city of the West." With a prophetic sense, striking as well by its essential soundness as by the exaggerated language in which it is couched, the editor of the *Gazeteer* proceeded to enumerate the mineral resources and the growing manufactures of St. Louis, emphasizing the development of canals and railroads, which would bring the city into easy contact not only with the East, but with the vast far-western territory soon to be colonized. The analysis of the St. Louis editor is substantiated by the verdict of historians of the present, looking back on the events which followed. Though the full effect of these economic forces was not felt until long after the passing of Caldwell and Ludlow and Smith, the later development of the western theatrical circuit was profoundly affected by them.

In the decades following the Civil War, the famous stars and stock companies of New York, with a speed that would have shamed the fastest racing pilots of the Mississippi, traveled on luxurious private cars to such mammoth industrial cities as Chicago and St. Louis, and to the well-managed theaters of San Francisco, Salt Lake City, and the other theatrical centers in the regions beyond the Mississippi. While the railroad stimulated the growth of the theater in such cities, New Orleans, now isolated from the main arteries of American commerce, witnessed a steady decline of the theatrical prestige which she had enjoyed during the days of the St. Charles planters.

THEATRE.

MISS RIDDLES' SECOND NIGHT.

This Evening, November 10,

Shakspeares' Tragedy of
ROMEO & JULIET,

ROMEO,	- - -	MR. J. M. FIELD,
Mercutio,	- - -	Ludlow,
JULIET.	- - -	MISS RIDDLE,

SONG,   -   -   -   MRS. MINNICH

To conclude with the Farce of the
WEDDING DAY.

Sir Adam Contest, (his first appearance,) Mr Riddle,
LADY CONTEST,   -   MISS RIDDLE,

☞ For other particulars, see bills.

410   Second Night at the St. Emanuel Theater, Mobile, from an announcement in the *Mobile Mercantile Advertiser,* November 10, 1835

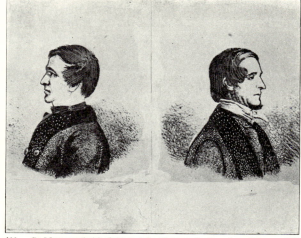

411   Co-Manager Smith (left) and Co-Manager Ludlow, from lithographs in the Louisiana Historical Society, New Orleans   412

CO–MANAGERS

In June, 1834, Smith heard of the death of J. Purdy Brown (see p. 151), who, since the departure of Ludlow in 1828, had had a monopoly of the Mobile theatrical market. The vagrant manager had had for a long time "a desire to visit Mobile professionally." Here was an excellent opening. Realizing, however, that Ludlow, owing to his four years of Mobile management, 1824–28, had a prior claim, Smith wrote to him suggesting a partnership. Ludlow received the letter in St. Louis, where in the preceding spring, after leaving Caldwell's employ, he had gone to open a theater for himself. He likewise had heard of the Mobile opening and had already taken steps to make the most of it. Smith's offer was, therefore, a surprise. Mrs. Ludlow, since the unpleasantness in Natchez in 1831, was prejudiced against the Smiths, and pointed out to her husband the various embarrassments that would arise from joint-managership. Ludlow was finally persuaded by Smith, however, that the difficulties of joint-managership were preferable on the whole to two competing theaters in one small town. So a meeting was arranged for October 1, 1834, in Mobile. Why Smith did not appear will, perhaps, never be determined. He, himself, claimed that he was unavoidably delayed by sickness in his family, and that he wrote Ludlow instructing him to lease the theater in both their names. Ludlow denied that he received any word from Smith, and finally, in despair at his non-appearance, leased the theater in his own name. This action was always a point of bitterness between the two managers. Whatever the true facts in the case, we know that in July, 1835, when Smith was playing at Ludlow's St. Louis theater, a final agreement was reached between them, and, as already noted, Smith left for New York to test his dramatic powers on the metropolitan stage and secure recruits for the new Mobile company. The first season of Ludlow and Smith's management opened at the St. Emanuel Theater at Mobile, November 9, 1835, with the performance of *The Hunchback.* Two of the most prominent resident actors during the first season were

THEATRE.

MISS RIDDLES' LAST NIGHT.

This Evening, November 14,
The excellent Comedy of
SCHOOL FOR SCANDAL.

CHAS SURFACE.	-	- - MR. LUDLOW,
Joseph Surface,	-	- - J M Field,
Sir Peter Teazle,	-	- - Riddle,
Lady Teazle,	-	- MISS RIDDLE,

COMIC SONG,   -   MR. SOL SMITH

To conclude with the after-piece of the
WEATHERCOCK.

Tristam Tinkle,   -   -   -   Mr. J. M. Field,
For other characters see Bills.

MISS RIDDLE'S BENEFIT ON MONDAY.

413   A Comic Song by Co-Manager Smith, from an announcement in the *Mobile Mercantile Advertiser,* November 14, 1835

Joseph M. and Matthew Field, the latter of whom soon afterward married Ludlow's daughter, Cornelia Burke. "Talented men were the brothers Field," wrote Smith, "and honorable in all their dealings." Elizabeth Riddle and Elizabeth Vos were the most striking actresses of the stock company, and were great favorites in the prosperous town of Mobile.

414   Eliza Riddle, from an engraving in the Fridenberg Collection

HERCULEAN SUPERS

ONE of the first stars to appear on the boards of Smith and Ludlow's Emanuel Street Theater in Mobile was James Barton, an English actor of some repute, who four years earlier had come from the Edinburgh theater to America. He was an excellent Shakespearean scholar and a gentleman of refined tastes. Ludlow praised him as a "sensible and classic actor, and very particular in his stage business. He was unfortunate in diseased nerves, that made him fidgety and irascible. He was grievously afflicted at times with asthma, which finally caused his death. For some time he was stage-manager for James H. Caldwell at New Orleans. . . . Mr. Barton was a gentleman in every respect and enthusiastically fond of his profession." According to Smith, one of Barton's favorite rôles was William Tell. Before his first performance at the Emanuel Street he recommended that the four guards who seize him in the second act should be selected from non-professional supers, who, far from the artificialities of second-rate theatricalism, would give a convincingly natural scene. In addition Barton specified that the four strongest be selected, and

415 William Barton at the St. Emanuel, Mobile, from a sketch *William Tell "Crushed,"* by A. Waud, in Sol Smith, *Theatrical Management*, New York, 1868

that they be instructed to crush him to the floor with all the strength they had. His instructions were closely followed. Smith impressed on the four giants that he had chosen the necessity of carrying out their original orders, however great the protest from the prisoner. The effectiveness of the actual scene exceeded Barton's fondest hopes. He was overwhelmed. His remonstrances fell on deaf ears. Harder and harder he was crushed to the floor until he lay helpless. Ludlow dismissed this along with the rest of Smith's stories as "funny, but lacking in point of fact, having but a slight foundation in reality." But the historical scholar demands less prejudiced evidence than that of Ludlow to dismiss thus lightly Smith's record.

A MODEST STAR

JAMES E. MURDOCH (see No. 242), who in 1835 was a member of the St. Charles company of New Orleans, requested permission of Smith to give a series of starring performances at the Mobile theater. It was agreed that he should give a round of comedy characters for six nights. "Even at that early period of his career Mr. Murdoch was a very pleasing actor. and had very few if any equals as a light comedian." Smith qualified this tribute elsewhere by placing Murdoch second to James H. Caldwell. Murdoch often appeared at the Ludlow-Smith theaters in Mobile, St. Louis, and New Orleans. Of his appearance at St. Louis in 1846 Ludlow wrote: "Mr. Murdoch pleased the people, and his engagement was a success. The theater-goers

416 James E. Murdoch as Petruchio, from an engraving in the Gottschalk Collection, New York

preferred his tragedy to his comedy; they considered his comedy rather sententious and heavy. I was particularly pleased with Mr. Murdoch's rendition of Hamlet. I thought it then, and do still think it, the best representation of the Danish prince that I have ever seen; his readings, his action, his appearance — in short his *tout-ensemble* was my *beau ideal* of the character. Much of Mr. Murdoch's career as an actor was passed in the South and West, where he was admired for his talents and highly respected as a gentleman in all associations of private life. . . . In comedy, such characters as Young Mirabel, in the *Inconstant;* Alfred Evelyn, in *Money;* and Rover, in *Wild Oats* — in short any character in comedy depending on the good delivery of fine sentiments, — Murdoch could give more effect to than any actor I have ever seen. Mr. Murdoch possessed a strong, full-toned, clear voice, sonorous, but mellowed by discretion; his stature of the medium height, manly and well-defined features, capable of varied and unlimited expression; but he possessed one quality that was a great hindrance in the way of his reaching the topmost niche in the temple of fame — he was too modest."

417   Architect's Plan for the St. Louis Theater, 1837, from J. C. Wild, *The Valley of the Mississippi*, St. Louis, 1841, in the Missouri Historical Society, St. Louis

A PERMANENT FOOTHOLD IN ST. LOUIS

THERE were numerous other stars at the St. Emanuel, and the first Mobile season was a great success, bringing in, according to Smith, a profit of twenty thousand dollars, which, compared to the former earnings of the two men, must have seemed colossal. Mobile, in the new arrangement, was to be the center for Ludlow and Smith's winter season, and in the summer the same company was to go to St. Louis. It was decided that in view of the extreme heat which often prevailed in St. Louis the season should be divided, with a short recess during the hottest weeks of July and August. Theater accommodations in St. Louis were most unsatisfactory. "The old 'salt-house' building, fitted up by James H. Caldwell in 1827 . . . was," wrote Ludlow, "a miserable apology for a theater, uncomfortable in every respect." In the summer of 1835, even before he had taken Smith into the man-

agement, Ludlow had succeeded in raising thirty thousand dollars by subscription. A site was selected at the southeast junction of Third and Olive Streets. Meriwether Lewis Clarke, "a gentleman of classical taste in literature and art, and possessed of exalted sentiments in regard to the Drama," proposed doubling the amount of existing subscriptions, thus making possible the erection of a magnificent building. The rent of course would be doubled, and Smith, returning at this point from the East, was asked for his approval. "Feeling a strong desire," wrote Ludlow, "to give the St. Louis public a building that they might feel proud of, we consented to the increased cost of the contemplated theater, against convictions in our own mind that we would be subjecting ourselves to a rental that the population of the city would hardly justify."

418   Theater (left) as it actually appeared, from a print in the Missouri Historical Society

The stone foundation was laid during the autumn of 1836. Work was slow, and it was only after exerting great pressure that Ludlow finally managed to open the doors on July 3, 1837. "The inside of the theater was very conveniently arranged, consisting of three tiers or galleries of seats and a parquet. The first tier or 'dress-circle,' would seat about three hundred persons; the second tier, or 'family-circle,' about three hundred and fifty; the third tier or 'gallery' about four hundred and fifty, and the parquet about four hundred. . . . The stage was about forty-five feet in depth, from the front of which to the front of the dress-circle was about fifty feet. The house, being designed for a summer theater, was constructed with a number of very large windows on each side, and the seats in the first and second tiers surrounded with handsome balustrades, turned of cherry wood, which being highly varnished looked like mahogany." On the first night, "the scaffolding, that had been used to put up some decorations for the front of the boxes, was being pitched out of side windows as the audience were coming in at the front doors. . . ."

419   Theatrical Billboard in front of the theater, from a print in the Missouri Historical Society

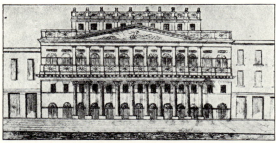

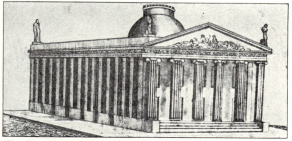

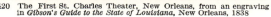

420 The First St. Charles Theater, New Orleans, from an engraving in *Gibson's Guide to the State of Louisiana*, New Orleans, 1838

421 The New American Theater, New Orleans, from an engraving inserted in *Gibson's Guide to the State of Louisiana*, New Orleans, 1838

"CLEAN, BRIGHT, AND BEAUTIFUL"

FOR five years Ludlow and Smith maintained their monopoly of the Mobile and St. Louis markets, at first alternating winter and summer between the two termini of their circuit, then in 1837 trying the unfortunate experiment of keeping both houses running at once, and then returning to the original arrangement. Caldwell ruled supreme in New Orleans. In 1833 he made the gesture of retiring from theatrical life by selling out his rights in his Ohio Valley theaters. But instead of retiring, in 1835 he opened a magnificent new theater, the St. Charles, which ranked for beauty and convenience with any in the country. During the years immediately following, his company was by far the most brilliant in the West, and it was he who drew the famous visiting stars. Not content, however, he began in 1840 to look with envy at the Ludlow-Smith monopoly in Mobile, and, learning that their theater had been visited with fire, decided it was a good time to strike. At the time, Ludlow was in St. Louis, with Smith in charge of the southern branch. The latter, hearing of Caldwell's new move, and, like Ludlow, always suspicious that Caldwell was trying to crush them, hurried to New Orleans and as a retaliatory threat began negotiations for a theater site on Poydras Street. He realized that there was no time to lose. In short time he had the New American Theater finished and ready for opening. Beginning weakly, their competition, which combined dramatic and equestrian shows, gradually during the next two years gained strength. In 1842 Caldwell's St. Charles burned to the ground, and shortly afterward the Ludlow-Smith Poydras Street American suffered the same fate. Then followed an involved transaction, the details of which cannot be condensed. As a result Caldwell, by means which Smith and Ludlow always denounced as dishonest, obtained control of the American Theater site and Ludlow and Smith were compelled to rebuild the St. Charles. And for the ten years that followed it was the St. Charles of Ludlow and Smith that dominated the Crescent City. Their revenge on Caldwell was speedy. In 1843 he announced his failure, closing the doors of his New American, and releasing to Ludlow his Mobile Theater, which had never prospered. In 1846 the St. Charles was "remodelled and re-decorated entirely in the interior arrangements; . . . large and commodious cushioned chairs had been introduced in the dress-circle and parquet and the second tier or family circle; and everything looked clean, bright, and beautiful."

422 Opening of Caldwell's Mobile Theater, January 11, 1841, from an announcement in the *Mobile Daily Advertiser and Chronicle*, January 11, 1841

423 Benefit Performance of A. A. Adams at the First St. Charles, February 12, 1837, from a playbill in the Louisiana Historical Society, New Orleans

424   South side of Fifth Avenue, Pittsburgh, 1840, showing Theater (second from right), from an engraving in *Palmer's Pictorial Pittsburgh and Prominent Pittsburghers*, 1758–1905, Pittsburgh

THE SMOKY PALACE

In the same year that Caldwell sold his theaters in the Ohio Valley to Russell and Rowe, Francis Courtney Wemyss (see No. 197), an English actor with several years of managerial experience in Philadelphia, opened a new theater on the Ohio at Pittsburgh, a town at which both Ludlow and Smith at various times had played. The opening night was September 2 and *The Busy Body* was presented by members of the company, which, according to the manager, "would bear comparison with the best in either of the Atlantic cities." The first season was not a financial success. Wemyss soon discovered that he had employed twice too many actors, and that his new audience of miners and boatmen was without the slightest gift of accurate discrimination. They enthusiastically applauded the worst actors, and hissed the most talented member of the cast because he "dressed like a gentleman and would persist in wearing white kid gloves in the street." The carpetings and furnishings of the dressing rooms, and the piano, ottomans, elegant chairs, and looking glasses of the green room were unusual luxuries for the Pittsburgh of the 'thirties. The receipts of the first season which lasted from September 2, 1833, to January 8, 1834, were seventeen thousand six hundred and twenty-seven dollars. For the next five years Wemyss kept the Pittsburgh Theater running at a moderate profit, though his main centers of activity after the fall of 1834 were Philadelphia and Baltimore. The Pittsburgh season of 1840 was disastrous to Wemyss. "The weather was so inclement," wrote Wemyss in his autobiography, "that the stars, both from the east and west, met half frozen at the top of the Allegheny mountains, which was the barrier beyond which none could proceed for three weeks. . . . The theater was open for seventy-two nights, the average receipts sixty-two dollars!! . . . The weather, and my own folly in yielding to the wishes of a few, in converting the pit into a parquette, (which the gallery were determined should not be so occupied in peace, jeering every one who took a seat in it, until it was replaced as a pit,) were the chief causes in bidding farewell to the theater. . . . My old Pittsburgh friends condescend to call upon me, when business brings them to Philadelphia, and we laugh at the happy times we have passed within the walls of the now smoky palace — the Pittsburgh Theater."

425   Early Travel between Pittsburgh and Philadelphia, from an advertisement in the *Daily Pittsburgh Gazette*, November 20, 1834

426   Opening of the New Theater, Pittsburgh, from an announcement in the *Daily Pittsburgh Gazette*, September 2, 1833

"A QUIET PORTRAIT OF NATURE UNDEBASED"

THE years of Wemyss' managership of the Pittsburgh Theater covered also the three American visits of Tyrone Power, the most famous comedian in Irish characters on the English stage. After a début in 1815, on the Isle of Wight, and a London apprenticeship at the Olympic, Arnold's Opera House, the Lyceum, and the Adelphi, "Paddy" Power made his appearance at Covent Garden, where in 1827 he performed his first original Irish character, O'Shaughnessy in Peake's farce, the *One Hundred Pound Note*, "with such *éclat*," recorded Ireland, "that his fame was established as the only legitimate representative of an Irishman on the Irish stage, though it was not until his absence in America revealed to the public how far superior he was to every Hibernian competitor, that he arose to the high pitch of popular esteem and favor with which he was overwhelmed on his return, and which ever after continued to attend him." On August 23, 1833, Power made his American début at the Park, as Sir Patrick O'Plenipo in the *Irish Ambassador*, followed by Dennis Brulgruddery, Major O'Flaherty, Pandeen O'Rafferty, McShane, and the Irish Tutor. In more or less the same rôles he delighted the audiences at the Walnut and the Chestnut in Philadelphia; at the Tremont in Boston; at the Front Street and the Holliday in Baltimore; for seven nights at the theater in Washington; at Pittsburgh,

427   Tyrone Power, 1799–1841, from a sketch, 1839, by A. D'Orsay, in the Harvard Theater Collection

where his friend Wemyss was manager; at Albany, New York; at Charleston, South Carolina; at Savannah, Mobile, New Orleans, and Natchez. It was feared at first that his unexaggerated acting, his ideal of a "quiet portrait of nature undebased" would fail

428   Power as Major O'Dougherty, from an engraving by Pense after a drawing by Clay, in the Fridenberg Collection

to satisfy the audiences, who had been accustomed to the highly spiced Irish caricature of other actors. But, with few exceptions, his audiences were enthusiastic. Unfortunately for the historian of the theater, Power in his *Impressions of America* deliberately emphasized the non-theatrical phases of his wanderings. Yet it was this modesty about his own work that captivated the audiences and the managers with whom he was thrown in contact. Cowell, Wemyss, Ludlow, Smith were in accord, for once, in their praise of the acting and of the personality of Power, and in their grief at his untimely death in 1841, when the steamship *President* was shipwrecked on its way to Liverpool. During Power's brief day upon the American stage many folk from his native Erin were migrating to the United States, though the flood of Irish immigrants did not begin until seven years after his death.

429   Power as Murtoch Delany, from an engraving by Woolnoth, after a drawing by Wageman, in the collection of Montrose J. Moses, New York

430   View of Natchez, Miss., detail from a lithograph in Henry Lewis, *Das Illustrirte Mississippi-Thal*, Düsseldorf, 1844–45

BORDER GALLANTS

OCCASIONAL theatrical descriptions are to be found in Power, the brilliance of which increases the reader's disappointment at their infrequency. In 1835, when the comedian was giving a series of performances in Natchez, Mississippi, the old haunt of Ludlow and Smith, he took a ramble in the early evening, while the lamplighter got ready his theater for the night's performance. Meeting his audience from nearby plantations coming to town on horseback, gaily caparisoned men and women, he returned with them to the theater yard. Picturesque was the scene, with the men "clad in a sort of tunic or frock, made of white or of grass green blanketing, the broad dark-blue selvage serving as a binding, the coat being furnished with collar, shoulder-pieces, and cuffs of the same colour, and having a broad belt, either of leather or of the like selvage; broad leafed Spanish hats of beaver were evidently the *mode*, together with high leggings, or cavalry boots and heavy spurs." Power had the fortune to see the folk of a western province of the Cotton Kingdom in holiday mood and attire. This audience went to the theater in full regalia; even their horses bore evidences of the festive occasion. "They bore *demi-pique* saddles, with small, massive brass or plated stirrups, generally shabracs of bear- or deer-skin, and in many instances had saddle-cloths of scarlet or light blue, bound with broad gold or silver lace." Such were the border gal-

431   Tyrone Power, in three rôles, from a print in the Fridenberg Collection

lants who for the moment forgot the gaming table and the race course for the gentler art of comedy or tragedy. "The whole party having come up, they walked leisurely into the theater, the men occupying the pit: whilst in the boxes were several groups of pretty and well-dressed women. The demeanor of these border gallants was as orderly as could be desired; and their enjoyment, if one might judge from the heartiness of their laughter, exceeding. . . . Indeed, to look on so many fine horses, with their antique caparisons, piquetted about the theater, recalled the palmy days of the Globe and Bear-garden."

432   View in front of the Natchez Theater, from a sketch in Tyrone Power, *Impressions of America*, London, 1836

BY LOCOMOTIVE AND HORSE

IN Power's descriptions are likewise found the most graphic pictures of the life of the itinerant fashionable actor, giving his "starring" performances in the widely separated theatrical centers of the West and South. When Power was in America, he divided his time of travel between horseback, steamboat, and locomotive; from a train that ran only twenty-five miles or little more he would have to be packed into a stagecoach or privately rented vehicle to go another twenty miles, and again, no matter what the time, back into another locomotive.

433 St. Louis as Power saw it in 1840, from a lithograph in the Missouri Historical Society, St. Louis

Sometimes the engine would not work and horses were requisitioned; at other times the "thoro'-brace" of the engine would snap, and a wooden rail would have to take its place; then it was that passengers would be forced to get out and climb mountains, to allow the crude engine to pant its way up an incline. Fortunate for him that he liked horseback riding. Power confessed that even inconvenience had its blessings since he saw more of America than he would have otherwise. The traveler could distinguish between the varying life of the East and West — for St. Louis was very far west those days. It was indeed a period of adventure, of weltering through mud, now driving forward through sheets of blinding rain, now stepping aside to allow an emigrant train to pass. Cities, Power found, grew before his very eyes, and from visit to visit great changes could be noted, and a sure, steady growth and improvement in the scattered theaters of the frontier.

434 Power as Connor O'Gorman, from an engraving after a painting by N. J. Crowley, in the Fridenberg Collection

NEW ORLEANS IN 1842

GEORGE VANDENHOFF (see No. 286), another recognized "star," has set down in his *Leaves from an Actor's Note-book* a colorful description of one phase of life in the leading theatrical center of the Southwest. Vandenhoff was connected for a number of years with Caldwell and Ludlow and Smith. At the second St. Charles he was the leading man in tragedy and comedy. In 1849 he played Cassius to Macready's Brutus, and Iago to Macready's Othello. "Sometimes," he wrote in his description of New Orleans, "the ordinary flow of life was ruffled by a squall or two, which troubled its surface, dashed a little spray around, and all was right again. Now and then, a *duel à l'outrance* would furnish a day's interest; sometimes the immense bar-room, in which thousands assembled at a time, was the scene of a little excitement: high words would be heard at one end; a scuffle, perhaps; a general clearing took place for a moment, a pistol-shot or two were fired, a body was carried out, the lookers-on closed up again, and the matter was forgotten. Or, the orderly current of a quadrille in a ballroom, or the mazy movements of the waltz, were broken by a quick and fatal stab, that left some much coveted damsel *unpartnered* for a moment; but the music scarcely stops. . . . eyes sparkle, feet twinkle, white shoulders shine beneath a thousand lamps, swelling bosoms heave, and pant and sigh, as triumph, love, or envy moves them." New Orleans was at the height of its mid-nineteenth century prosperity and the Mississippi was one of the greatest trade routes of the nation. Inevitably to this port were drawn, as temporary residents, many disorderly and undesirable people — adventurers and parasites.

LUDLOW & SMITH PROPRIETORS & MANAGERS

435 Exterior of the Second St. Charles Theater, New Orleans, 1842, from a lithograph in the Louisiana Historical Society, New Orleans

436

Interior of the St. Charles Theater, New Orleans, from an engraving in the Louisiana State Historical Society, New Orleans

"THE MOST ELEGANT-LOOKING AUDITORY OF THIS COUNTRY"

POWER described New Orleans life at its best as displayed in the theater. ". . . the parquette and dress-boxes were almost exclusively filled by ladies, coiffées with the taste which distinguishes Frenchwomen in every country. . . . All were more dressed than it is usual to be at theaters in America. This attention to costume on the part of the ladies, added to their occupying the pit, obliges the gentlemen to adopt a corresponding neatness; and hence it occurs that, when the New Orleans theater is attended by the belles of the city, it presents decidedly the most elegant-looking auditory of this country . . . a greater degree of repose and gentility of demeanour I never remember to have noticed in any mixed assembly of any place. So much for report, which informed me I should find the American house here filled by noisy planters from the up-country and boisterous Mississippi boatmen."

THEATRICAL BEGINNINGS IN THE NORTHWEST

IN the sparsely settled regions of the Great Lakes there were no theatrical centers like New Orleans to draw such stars as Vandenhoff and Power. During the 'thirties the Ohio Valley was the northern boundary of theatrical activity; St. Louis the only town further north that attracted eastern actors. In the year 1838, however, Joseph Jefferson, II, son of the famous comedian for so many years one of the mainstays of the old Chestnut Street Theater in Philadelphia, decided to bolster his tottering managerial fortunes in the "El Dorado" of the Northwest. In 1834 Tyrone Power had acted under Jefferson's management at the theater in Washington, which, according to the visiting actor, was in no way worthy of the National Capital. Jefferson, ever sanguine, held out hopes of a new theater, which, however, like most of his dreams failed to materialize. From 1835 to 1837 Jefferson had been connected as scenic artist with the Franklin Theater and Niblo's Garden in New York. In the autumn of 1837 it was decided to proceed to Chicago, where an uncle, Alexander MacKenzie, had invited Jefferson to join him in the management of a new theater. It was hoped that performances

437 Joseph Jefferson, II, 1804–42, from an engraving in the Harvard Theater Collection

along the way might defray the expenses of transportation. Rain interfered, however, and young Joseph, III, then a boy of eight, was called upon to give a private performance as part payment to the captain of the boat.

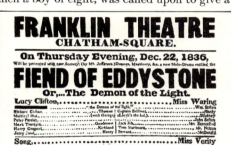

438 Jefferson as Scenic Artist at the Franklin Theater, New York, from a playbill, 1836, in the New York Historical Society

It is from the autobiography of Joseph Jefferson, III, written many years afterward, that we get a surprisingly modernistic description of the voyage along the Erie Canal and the Great Lakes, and of their arrival at Chicago: "At sunrise we are all on deck looking at the haven of our destination, and there in the morning light, on the shores of Lake Michigan, stands the little town of Chicago, containing two thousand inhabitants . . . busy little town . . . people hurrying to and fro, frame buildings going up, board sidewalks going down, new hotels, new churches, new theaters, everything new. Saw and hammer, — saw, saw, bang, bang, — look out for the drays! — bright and muddy streets, — gaudy-colored calicos, — blue and red flannels and striped ticking hanging outside the dry-goods stores, — bar-rooms, — real-estate offices, — attorneys-at-law — oceans of them. . . . the new theater, newly painted canvas, . . . stuffed seats in the dress circle, . . . new drop curtain — a medallion of Shakespeare . . . over the center, with, 'One touch of nature makes the whole world kin,' written under him, and a large, painted brick-red drapery looped up by Justice, with sword and scales, showing an arena with a large number of gladiators hacking away at one another in the distance to a delighted Roman public. . . . There were two private boxes with little white-and-gold balustrades and turkey-red curtains, over one box a portrait of Beethoven and over the other a portrait of Handel. . . . The dome was pale blue, with pink-and-white clouds, on which reposed four ungraceful ballet girls representing the seasons, and apparently dropping flowers, snow, and grapes into the pit. . . . With what delight the actors looked forward to the opening of a new theater in a new town, where dramatic entertainments were still unknown — repairing their wardrobes, studying their new parts, and speculating on the laurels that were to be won!" Chicago was in the midst of the boom which brought thousands of people to northern Illinois in the years which followed the Black Hawk War.

THEATRE.

MESSRS. MACKENZIE & JEFFERSON respectfully announce to the citizens of St. Louis that they have fitted up the SPLENDID BALL ROOM, CONCERT HALL, for Dramatic representations.

MONDAY,

Will be presented the drama in three acts, called
THE IDIOT WITNESS,
A TALE OF BLOOD.

Gilbert, the Idiot, ... Leicester
Walter Arlington, the Queens page, Mrs Ingersoll
Dome Tuggecull, - - - - " MacKenzie

To Conclude with the national drama, called
RIP VAN WINKLE,
OR; THE
Demons of the Cattskill Mountains.

Rip Van Winkle, - - - - Jefferson
Knickerbocker, - - - C S Green
Demon of the mountain - Burke
Dame Van Winkle - Mrs Jefferson.

In preparation with new Scenery, Dresses, &c.
HIGH LOW JACK & THE GAME.

Doors open at 7; performance to commence at half past 7 precisely.

Tickets to the parquette, 75 cents each; seats as back of parquette, 50 cents. Gallery, for persons of color, 50 cents.

439 Jo Jefferson, II, as Rip Van Winkle, from an announcement in the *Daily Missouri Republican*, March 23, 1840

440   Early Travel in the Northwest, from advertisements in the *Daily Missouri Republican*, March 9, 1840

441   Lincoln as a Lawyer, from the model by Herman A. MacNeil (1866–), in the possession of the artist

BARNSTORMING IN THE NORTHWEST

AFTER a short and moderately successful season at the Chicago Theater, the Jeffersons with their little company began a barnstorming tour in much the same manner that Smith and Ludlow had conducted theirs during the two preceding decades. Jefferson's descriptions have an accumulation of detail and pictorial beauty, however, that no other chronicle possesses. From Chicago across the prairies to Galena, Illinois, they traveled during the coldest days of the winter, in an open wagon, seated on skin-covered trunks off which they kept sliding at every bump in the rough road. To get from Galena to Dubuque, Iowa, they went by sleigh over the frozen Mississippi River. Just as Douglas (see p. 126) and the Drakes, and Smith and Ludlow had been in the past, so now were the Jeffersons eager to play during a session of a state legislature. To accomplish this they made their way to Springfield, Illinois. On their arrival the prospects seemed promising. Plans were being completed for the opening of the new theater, when news was received that a certain religious sect had secured an injunction against the opening. "In the midst of their troubles," wrote Jefferson in his *Autobiography*, "a young lawyer called on the managers. He had heard of the injustice, and offered, if they would place the matter in his hands, to have the license taken off, declaring that he only desired to see fair play, and he would accept no fee whether he failed or succeeded. The case was brought up before the council. The young lawyer began his harangue. He handled the subject with tact, skill, and humor, tracing the history of the drama from the time when Thespis acted in a cart to the stage of today. He illustrated his speech with a number of anecdotes. . . . His good-humor prevailed and the exorbitant tax was taken off. This young lawyer was very popular in Springfield, and was honored and beloved by all who knew him; and after the time of which I write he held rather an important position in the government of the United States. He now lies buried near Springfield, under a monument commemorating his greatness and his virtue — and his name was Abraham Lincoln." Lincoln remained throughout his life a friend of the theater, and derived a keen enjoyment from good performances behind the footlights.

A HEROINE OF THE THEATER

442 Cornelia Burke Jefferson, from an engraving in the
Harvard Theater Collection

In spite of the victory of the young advocate over the religious revivalists, the Springfield season was not as great a success as the sanguine Jefferson had hoped. The partnership with MacKenzie was dissolved, and the Jeffersons proceeded southward. From this period forward it was Mrs. Jefferson who directed the financial affairs of the wandering family. Though she was at one time, under the name of Cornelia Burke (see p. 72), a prominent New York and Philadelphia actress, she submitted without complaint to the hardships and privations of western travel and to the insecurity caused by her husband's improvidence. It was she who collected the money from the Memphis billiard-room keeper, who had failed to pay Jefferson for the decorations the latter had painted for him; it was she who insisted that they travel steerage on the Mississippi steamboat, so as to have a little capital when they arrived at Mobile. It was she who, on the death of her husband from yellow fever on November 24, 1842, opened in Mobile a boarding house for actors. There were boarders enough, but at the end of an unsuccessful season their salaries were not forth-coming, and Mrs. Jefferson was the ultimate loser. Both young Jo and his sister were given juvenile parts in the St. Emanuel Company, but their small salaries were scant contribution to the depleted family exchequer. From Mobile the Jeffersons went as part of a company to play Nashville and then tour Tennessee. But business was bad, and the company soon started on a barge for New Orleans. For sails they used great sheets of stage scenery, and to increase the amazement of the steamboat passengers who stared at them they realistically staged mock duels and murders. During the season of 1843–44 young Jefferson, aged fourteen, appeared at the New St. Charles. Unfortunately in his *Autobiography* he dismisses the season as being in no wise eventful except for the appearance of Mrs. Mowatt, Mrs. Kean, and James H. Hackett. For the summer season he went with the St. Charles company to St. Louis, where he was humiliated by forgetting the lines of the first verse of *The Star-Spangled Banner*, which he was supposed to sing. The following years found the Jeffersons in various companies and theaters — in the backwoods of Mississippi, in Galveston, Houston, and Point Isabel, Texas, and then in 1846 following the American army about to invade Mexico to Matamoros, where a small company amused the soldiers with theatricals. And finally, when the army was ordered on to Monterey, Jo and his mother started a restaurant in a Spanish saloon, by which they made enough money to get them once more back to the East.

THEATRE.

MESSRS. MACKENZIE & JEFFERSON respectfully announce to the citizens of St. Louis that they have fitted up the SPLENDID BALL ROOM in CONCERT HALL, for Dramatic representations.

WEDNESDAY.
THE DENOUNCER;
Or, seven Clerks and three Thieves.

Claude D'Arnaud,	Mr. Germon
Hans Hoogpot	" Green
Victorine,	Mrs Germon

After which A DANCE, by Mr. Burke.

To conclude with
A ROLAND FOR AN OLIVER.

Sir Mark Chase,	Mr. Sankey
Hon. Alfred Highflyer	" Leicester
Selberne,	" Sullivan
Fixture,	" Jefferson
Maria Darlington,	Mrs McKenzie
Mrs Fixture,	" Jefferson

Doors open at 7; performance to commence at half past 7 precisely.
Tickets to the parquette, 75 cents each; seats back of parquette, 50 cents. Gallery, for persons of color, 50 cents.

443 Mrs. Jefferson as Mrs. Fixture in *A Roland for an Oliver*, from an announcement in the *Daily Missouri Republican*, St. Louis, March 18, 1840

THEATRE

MESSRS. MACKENZIE & JEFFERSON respectfully announce to the citizens of St. Louis that they have fitted up the SPLENDID BALL ROOM in CONCERT HALL, for Dramatic representations

ON MONDAY, MARCH 9, will be presented,
THE LADY OF LYONS
OR LOVE AND PRIDE.

Claude Melnotte,	Mr. Leicester
Colonel Damas,	" Jefferson
Deschapelles,	" Sankey
Madame Deschapelles,	Mrs. Jefferson
Pauline Deschapelles,	" Ingersoll
Dame Melnotte,	" Mackenzie

AFTER THE PLAY.

SONG —" *The Last of Gowrie*"	Mr. Germon
COMIC SONG,	Master Jefferson
SAILOR'S HORNPIPE,	Mr. Burke

TO CONCLUDE WITH,
AN AFFAIR OF HONOR.

Major Limskey,	Mr. C.L. Green
Martha,	Mrs. Germon

Doors open at 7; performance to commence at half past 7 precisely.
Tickets to the parquette, 75 cents each; seats back of parquette, 50 cents. Gallery, for persons of color, 50 cents.

444 Mrs. Jefferson's Sons, Joseph, III and Charles T. Burke, in St. Louis, 1840, from an announcement in the *Daily Missouri Republican*, March 9, 1840

NEW THEATRE.

THE public are respectfully informed **MISS PLACIDE** is engaged for 12 nights, and will make her first appearance this evening. Also, MISS RUSSELL'S first appearance.—THIS EVENING, June 16, Shakspeare's fashionable comedy of **MUCH ADO ABOUT NOTHING.** Benedict. Mr. Caldwell, Beatrice. Miss Placide. After which the operatic farce of the SPOILED CHILD. Little Pickle Miss Russell, with the original songs and a *Sailor's Hornpipe*. ☞Second night of Mr. and Mrs Sloman's engagement on Wednesday.

445 A Sailor's Hornpipe by Miss Marie Ann Russell (Mrs. Farren), from an announcement in the *National Banner and Nashville Whig,* June 16, 1829

THE FARRENS

IN the records which Ludlow and Smith have left of their management at New Orleans and St. Louis, there is no mention of the 1843 appearance of Joseph Jefferson, nor of his mother, Cornelia Burke, whom Ludlow had known long ago in 1820, when they had been together as members of Caldwell's New Orleans company. Smith's prophetic eye, which had singled out Forrest from an inferior cast in Cincinnati, was evidently not arrested by any suggestion of genius in Jefferson's New Orleans performances. The two popular standbys of the New Orleans, St. Louis, and Mobile theaters for the ten years preceding Jefferson's unnoticed appearance were George P. Farren, and his wife, who was a daughter of Richard Russell, to whom in 1833 Caldwell had leased the Camp Street Theater and the Ohio Valley theaters. Miss Russell had made her début at the Chatham Garden Theater on July 5, 1824, as the Page in the farce of the *Purse*, and, wrote Ireland, "evinced, even at that early period of her life, considerable talent, which was cultivated with so much success, that, a few years later, she was engaged at the Park, where she made her début with much applause, on the 11th of September, 1828, as Young Norval and Little Pickle." In 1832 she went with her parents to New Orleans, where she married George P. Farren, a nephew of the famous English comedian, William Farren. Sol Smith, who had known Mrs. Farren from her childhood, and under whose management she acted for eight years, praised her as an "excellent woman and fine actress, who always did her duty and more." She received from Joe Cowell an unusually lyrical tribute. "The *amiable woman* and the *talented actress* were never more happily blended than when nature selected her as the model for both. Every one who knows her, loves her, the endearing

446 Mrs. George P. Farren as Katherine in *Henry VIII*, from an engraving in the Fridenberg Collection

freshness of childhood still remaining to adorn the well-borne duties of the wife and mother." George Farren was an excellent actor of old men, receiving especial praise from Tyrone Power. In 1845–46 the Farrens left Ludlow and Smith's management, and appeared in starring engagements at the St. Louis, New Orleans, and Mobile theaters, while Mrs. Farren also appeared with some success at the Broadway, Niblo's, and Wallack's in New York. "She...is fully capable of sustaining the leading heavy business in a first class theater," wrote Ireland in 1866, as though giving a public recommendation.

THEATRE

MANAGERS,   LUDLOW & SMITH.

☞ FIRST NIGHT OF

MRS. FARREN!

Who is engaged for

SIX NIGHTS ONLY!

WELCOME HOME OUR FAVORITE!

Mr. C. Mason

☞ The celebrated Comedian and "Droll."

Mr. WINCHELL!

Is engaged for a very few nights, and will appear in his truly singular performances

TO-MORROW EVENING.

PRICES OF ADMSSION:

Dress Circle,	75 cents.
Children, to Dress Circle,	50 "
Parquette,	50 "
Second and Third Tiers of Boxes,	25 "

PRINTED AT THE REVEILLE OFFICE.

447 Mrs. Farren at the New St. Charles, New Orleans, from a playbill in the Louisiana Historical Society, New Orleans

448 George P. Farren, from a drawing by August Toedteberg in the Harvard Theater Collection

449 Mrs. Fanny Fitzwilliam, from an engraving in the
Fridenberg Collection

THEATRE.
State-Street.

MANAGERS,.................LUDLOW & SMITH.

MRS. FITZWILLIAM'S BENEFIT,
And last of her engagement.

THIS EVENING, MARCH 3, 1841,
Will be performed the comedy of
FOREIGN AIRS AND NATIVE GRACES.
Emily Staples,.....................Mrs. Fitzwilliam
M'selle Ziphorine Eutrachet,.....Mrs. Fitzwilliam
Signorina Salfadoremi,.............Mrs. Fitzwilliam
Susan Acorn,.......................Mrs. Fitzwilliam
In which she will give a Song and Gitano a la Tag-
lioni; Recitative Italiano; a Trio-tie Solo,
and Grand Sinfonia, and an English
Medley.
After which the celebrated monologue called the
WIDOW WIGGINS—or Music Mad.
In which Mrs. Fitzwilliam sustains SIX characters,
sings several Songs, and performs on the
Guitar, Piano Forte, and Harp.
Widow Wiggins,.................Mrs. Fitzwilliam!
Miss Totterly Rosebud,........Mrs. Fitzwilliam!!
Andrew,.......................Mrs. Fitzwilliam!!!
Fanchette,....................Mrs. Fitzwilliam!!!!
Master Jacky Wiggins,.......Mrs. Fitzwilliam!!!!!
Euphrosine Juliet Hobbs,....Mrs. Fitzwilliam!!!!!!
With other entertainments.

Box Book open at the Waverly House. Performance to commence at quarter after 7.

450   Mrs. Fitzwilliam in Mobile, from an announcement in the
Mobile Daily Advertiser and Chronicle, March 3, 1841

"A DARLING OF AN ACTRESS"

BUT more popular even than Mrs. Farren was Fanny Fitzwilliam, who, after her New York and Philadelphia performances, made her first appearance at Ludlow and Smith's Poydras Street American in 1841. She had come to New Orleans, expecting an engagement with Caldwell, but, a misunderstanding having arisen, she inquired of Caldwell's rivals if they could offer any inducement to her remaining. Ludlow explained that it had been their intention to run the new theater without stars, depending on "the novelty of our perform-ances, and the attraction of a new theater and a good stock company." The managers decided, however, in view of her reputation to give her a two weeks' trial. "The lady by her inimitable acting, filled the theater almost every night to its utmost capacity," wrote Ludlow, "and her engagement was extended to two more weeks on the same terms." In a sketch called *Foreign Airs and Native Graces,* she played the rôle of a French danseuse, which enabled her to give imitations of Fanny Elssler (see No. 280), who was appearing the same week at the St. Charles. "There was a short piece," wrote Ludlow, "I remember to have seen her perform in . . . in which she enacted three or four characters in an inimitable manner; one of the characters was, if I remember right, a female street-singer, who screamed out her ballads to a hand-organ accompaniment by herself, that used to convulse the house with laughter; and in ten minutes after, as a wandering Savoyard boy, she uttered her words with so much pathos and feeling that she filled the eyes of the same people with tears. Thus would this admirable artist sway the feelings of her audience as she willed. Her representa-tions of Irish characters . . . I am of opinion, have never been equalled by any lady on this continent." At the end of the four weeks at the American, a special company was sent with Fanny Fitzwilliam to the "Swamp Theater," Mobile, which because of its poor location had lost money for the joint-managers. For the first time in its history it was filled for two weeks straight before Mrs. Fitzwilliam returned to New Orleans. Sol Smith in a letter to a New York friend was quite as enthusiastic as Ludlow. "Mrs. Fanny Fitzwilliam, the 'bright particular' luminary, is cramming the American every night, and throwing from nine hundred to a thousand people into fits (of laughter) and causing them to forget the hard times, short crops, and everything else of a disagreeable nature. Isn't she a darling of an actress?"

451   John B. Buckstone, 1802–79, as Tony Lumpkin, from an engraving in the Fridenberg Collection

AUTHOR AND ACTOR

WHEN Mrs. Fitzwilliam returned from her successful Mobile engagement, she reopened at the Poydras Street American opposite John B. Buckstone, who had just completed a starring engagement with Caldwell at the St. Charles. For ten nights Buckstone and Mrs. Fitzwilliam appeared together in pieces in which they had often played opposite each other on the London stage. "It was really a treat," wrote Ludlow, "to see these two artists perform. They had so frequently acted together, and understood each other so well, that they mingled pleasantly their comic touches of humor and facial expression, producing a combination that quite charmed their hearers, and rendered them insensible to everything but the exquisite acting before them." Buckstone was an author as well as an actor. He had made his American début at the Park in August, 1840, as Peter Pinkey in his own comedy of *Single Life*. Ludlow is authority for the statement that Buckstone wrote over one hundred plays, many of which were successful. Francis Wemyss emphasized Buckstone's genius as a dramatist rather than as an actor. "As a star, he has no pretensions to notice, and wisely joined his fortunes to Mrs. Fitzwilliam, who found in him an able assistant. . . ." Yet Sol Smith wrote of him: "His acting is a treat to see." Ludlow and Smith's first season in their new theater, in competition with the old established monopoly of Caldwell, netted them a profit of twenty thousand dollars, and certainly without Buckstone and Mrs. Fitzwilliam the profits would have been appreciably less.

452   Buckstone as Launcelot Gobbo in *The Merchant of Venice*, from an engraving in the Fridenberg Collection

AN INFANT PRODIGY

A STAR of an unusual order presented to Manager Ludlow, during the season of 1844 at Mobile, a somewhat perplexing problem. Jean Davenport, who shared with Joseph Burke the honor of being the most versatile infant prodigy since Master Betty and John Howard Payne (see No. 157), had made her first appearance at the age of eleven. In the popular rôle of Young Norval in Home's *Douglas* she had received tremendous applause. In the four years that had followed she had played with marked success a variety of rôles, including a performance of Richard III at Richmond, Virginia, in which she had worn the same hat which Edmund Kean had used in his famous characterization of the hunchback king. In spite of the reputation which preceded her to Mobile, and in spite of the generally accepted rumor that she was the original of Dickens' "infant phenomenon" in *When Crummles Played*, Ludlow found difficulty, owing to her rapidly maturing figure, in maintaining the infant prodigy illusion; while on the other hand she refused to attempt mature rôles. Her dilemma became increasingly apparent, however, and shortly afterward she retired for a number of years, returning as a charming and graceful woman. During this latter period of her career she won many triumphs not only in America but also in Holland, Germany, and England. In 1860 she married General Lander of the Union Army, who was in 1862 killed in battle. After his death she appeared as Mrs. General Lander.

453   Jean Davenport Lander, 1829–1903, as Juliet, from an engraving in the Fridenberg Collection

454 Julia Dean, 1830–68, from a photograph in
the Madigan Collection, New York

A CHILD OF THE FRONTIER

MORE truly even than Joseph Jefferson, Julia Dean, the daughter of Julia Drake (see p. 126), and the granddaughter of Samuel Drake, the patriarch of the western stage, was a product of the colorful theatrical frontier beyond the Alleghenies. And her career — her steady rise from an actress with a local reputation to an outstanding position of national prominence — was in many ways an epitome of

455 Miss Dean as Beatrice, from an engraving
by C. E. Price in the Fridenberg Collection

the increasing power of the theater in the Mississippi Valley. It was undoubtedly with a feeling of security that, shortly after the death of her mother and the remarriage of her father, she turned to Ludlow, who many years before had so eagerly accepted the offer of her grandfather to make the journey from Albany to Lexington, Kentucky. During the season of 1844–45 she played under the direction of the veteran manager. It was during this engagement that she first met Joseph Jefferson, also in the Mobile stock company. In his *Autobiography* Jefferson has recorded his memories of life behind stage in Mobile and his admiration and affection for the young actress beginning her career: "In the various dramas produced during this season Julia and I had gone hand in hand, alternately espousing the cause of tyranny and virtue for the small sum of six dollars a week. For this reward we were content to change our politics and our costume at the will of the stage-manager. As brigands, gentle shepherds, or communists we gained our daily bread together. We changed our religion without the slighest compunction; as Catholics we massacred the Huguenots, while as Pilgrims we bade sad adieu to our native land, from which we had been driven by religious persecution. So we trudged on with perhaps a lurking thought that some day we might lead to victory as we were then following to the

456   Miss Dean as Juliet, from an engraving in the
Fridenberg Collection

death." In the same mellow vein the old actor, recalling his youth, recorded how the victory came first to his friend. One of Ludlow's stars had fainted; the green room was in a "high state of excitement" until Julia Dean in a "clear and steady voice" and with winning confidence, persuaded the skeptical manager to substitute her. After the briefest of rehearsals, she appeared. She spoke in a voice — "so low, so sweet and yet so audible. It sinks deep into the hearts of all who listen. They are spellbound by her beauty, and as she gives the lines with warm and honest power a murmur of delight runs through the house, and from that moment our lovely friend is famous." In the following May Julia Dean made her New York début at the Park as Julia in *The Hunchback*. Her success was instantaneous. Her position in the East was secured; in the Middle West she was without a rival; and when after her marriage to the son of the famous southern statesman, Robert Hayne, she moved to California, she repeated her triumphs. But none of her followers, not even David Belasco, who worshipped her, has passed on the secret of her charm quite as vividly as did her first admirer, Joseph Jefferson.

457 Dan Marble, 1807–49, as Samson, from an engraving in the Harvard Theater Collection

"DELIBERATE NONSENSE"

ONE of the oldest friends of Ludlow and Smith, and the traveling actor who appeared probably most frequently in the Ohio and Mississippi Valley theatrical centers, was Dan Marble. In the portrayal of rustic Yankee characters he was second only to George H. Hill. Born in Danbury, Connecticut, in 1807, Marble worked for a time in a dry goods store in Hartford, going from there to New York, expecting to learn the silversmith's trade. Unable longer to suppress his love for the theater, he joined an amateur company, and before long was behind the scenes at the Chatham, where by paying the sum of twenty dollars he secured permission to appear in a minor rôle. On March 6, 1832, he appeared under his own name at the Richmond Hill Theater, attempting with discouraging results the tragic rôle of Damon in *Damon and Pythias*. For the next two or three years in country theaters he gained a modicum of reputation for his Yankee stories and for one or two of his Yankee characters. In 1836–37 at Buffalo he finally found the Yankee character of Sam Patch, to which he was ideally suited and in which he gained a great reputation in his tour of the South and West. In 1838 he made his début at the Park, and in September of 1844, after frequent reappearances on the Ludlow and Smith circuit, he opened at the Strand in London, where in the rôle of Deuteronomy Dutiful in *The Vermont Wool Dealer* he was overwhelmingly successful. Other well known Marble plays were: *Sam Patch in France*; the nautical drama of *Black-Eyed Susan*; *Sam Patch, The Jumper of Niagara Falls*; *The Backwoodsman*; *Luke, The Laborer*; *The Vermonter*; and *Jonathan in England*. Joe Cowell was enthusiastic in his praise of Marble's acting: "No matter if you have the toothache, the headache, or the heartache; the cool, quiet deliberate *nonsense, if you please*, . . . would make you laugh at a funeral."

"THE NATURAL HUMOR OF THE MAN"

ANOTHER actor, whose fame rests upon his interpretation of Yankee character, was Joshua S. Silsbee, who was born on December 1, 1813, in Steuben county, New York. Not until he reached the age of twenty-five did he make his début in a humble capacity at the Natchez, Mississippi, theater, at that time directed by Caldwell. From Natchez he transferred to Cincinnati, where he was employed for fops and juvenile parts. He attracted little attention until 1840, when he volunteered a Yankee story which made a decided hit. His first eastern engagement was at Boston, his second at Philadelphia. In 1843 he starred at the New Chatham in New York, and the following year on a tour of the South and West appeared for an engagement at the Mobile Theater, which Ludlow had recently bought from the retiring Caldwell. Silsbee's reputation gradually increased. His tour of the country in 1850 was everywhere successful. In England he appeared at the Adelphi, the Haymarket, and other theaters. A London critic in *Tallis's Magazine* gave what was perhaps the most revealing impression of Silsbee's technique and manner. "His style of acting differs considerably from either Hill's or Marble's, and is indeed so far peculiar that it may be said to form a new and original school. Faithfully as he performs the Yankee character, his performances are permeated with the natural humor of the man. His looks, gestures, and actions, even the arch twinkle of his eye, impress the spectator with ludicrous emo-

458 Joshua Silsbee, 1813–55, as Jonathan Ploughboy in Woodworth's *The Forest Rose*, from an engraving by J. Moore after a daguerreotype by Mayall, in the Fridenberg Collection

459 Silsbee as Curtis Chunk, from an engraving in the Fridenberg Collection

tions, and his inflexible countenance, rigidly innocent of fun while his audience are in roars of laughter, gives an additional zest to the humor of the language and the absurdity of the situation."

A YANKEE IN THE FLESH

A NATIVE character as eccentric and as colorful as any of those portrayed by Hill, Marble, and Silsbee was Andrew J. Allen, who claimed, among many other titles, that of " Father of the American Stage." Sol Smith first saw him — "through the knot-hole of a pine board under the boxes" — at Bernard's Green Street Theater at Albany in 1815. In an extravagant production called *The Battle of Lake Champlain*, Allen sang a pleasing negro song, which Smith incorrectly believed to have been the first sung on the American stage. But in general Allen played stern villains, and clowns in pantomimes. From Albany he went to New York where he acquired a moderate success and such enormous debts that he was forced to depart hurriedly for Pensacola, Florida, where he managed the theater, on which, as has been noted (see p. 137), Ludlow cast longing eyes in the summer of 1820. Allen, having evidently failed at acting and at managing, appeared next in 1822 at Cincinnati, where Smith discovered him sending up balloons, asking the public patronage on the plea that he was a native American, whereas the rival balloonist was a Frenchman.

460 Andrew J. Allen, from a lithograph by Pendletone in the Fridenberg Collection

Later Allen toured the highways and byways of Virginia sending up balloons from every village. "When Mr. Edwin Forrest began to rise in his profession," wrote Smith, "Allen determined to rise with him, and attached himself to that tragedian as a costumer, in which capacity and that of a fighting gladiator, he traversed this country and Great Britain." The costumer's conceit was a great source of merriment to the actors who often amused themselves at his expense. It is reported that Allen, with great seriousness, asked Forrest where the latter would have gotten, had it not been for his fortune in having Allen to design his costumes.

JULIET IN ST. LOUIS

"OF all the star actors and actresses I have had to deal with," wrote Sol Smith, "Mr. and Mrs. Kean [see No. 250], separately and together, were the most agreeable and friendly. It was a positive pleasure to have them with us. . . . During their engagement they were so unassuming and kind in their demeanor, that, were it not for the immense receipts they attracted, you would not have supposed to see them, that they were anything but the humblest members of the stock company." An incident at the appearance of the Keans at St. Louis in 1850 gives an interesting sidelight into life behind stage in the early western theaters. Outside of New Orleans no theaters were equipped with gas. The oil-burning lamps which lighted the stage were always in danger of flaring up suddenly and setting fire to the scenery. It was necessary, Smith

461 The Keans in St. Louis, from an engraving *Scene in Romeo and Juliet — Swabbing!* by A. R. Waud, in Smith, *Theatrical Management*, New York, 1868

revealed, to swab them frequently. Often it happened that Romeo or Lear or Lady Macbeth just previous to making a brilliantly dramatic entrance would pause and give the lamps a good swabbing. On one particular night which Smith described neither Romeo nor Juliet had paid due attention to the lamps. Charles Kean, forgetting all else in the intensity of his outburst of love for Mrs. Kean on the balcony, spoke his lines in a manner that the most exacting Shakespearean scholar might have approved. Mrs. Kean took a few more liberties with her text. For just after the opening of the scene she observed from her elevation that the lamps were flaring higher and higher. "Romeo, who had entered from the right-hand side," wrote Smith, "and had not seen the flaring lamp, went on with his speech, interrupted from time to time by the lovely Capulet. . . . Juliet (aside) 'will nobody get the swab? We shall all be burnt up!' . . . Romeo: 'See how she leans upon her hand.' . . . Juliet: 'Ah me!' (aside) 'We'd better not go on. Where is the swab?' Romeo: 'She speaks! Oh, speak again, bright angel!' Juliet (aside) 'If that swab isn't brought this instant, I'll come down. I will. Ah! there's Mr. Sol Smith with the swab at last.' Romeo: (speaks the balance of the speech unheeded by Juliet, who is watching the swabbing)."

462 Noah Miller Ludlow, Veteran of the Frontier Theater, from a lithograph in the Fridenberg Collection

AN ARISTOCRAT ON THE FRONTIER

IF the Keans were popular with the western managers, William Charles Macready (see No. 217), with his aristocratic pretensions, his intellectual snobbery, and continual fault-finding was sincerely hated by both Smith and Ludlow. In March of 1844 Macready was at Mobile, where Ludlow was in charge. "Although the play was going off, as I supposed, excellently well, yet Mr. Macready sent for me at the end of the first act, requesting I would step to his dressing room. I went there, and he commenced a

463 William Charles Macready, Aristocrat, from a photograph in the Davis Collection

tirade on the inadequacy of the company, and their neglect of the business of the play as laid down in his book. I told him that the play had been rehearsed three times, that I had attended to these rehearsals myself, and had been careful in pointing out to all the performers in it the business as set down in the marked book that had been given to me by him for that purpose. But he was not satisfied, and at the end of the second act he sent Thompson, to summon me again to his presence. Not having been educated to that kind of managerial servility which perhaps Mr. Macready had found accorded him in his own country, I declined . . . and requested Thompson to say that I had business in my office to attend to, and that if Mr. Macready had any matter of importance to communicate, and would send it in writing, I would give it all due consideration. I never heard any more complaints from Mr. Macready that night, nor any night thereafter." Immediately afterward, Macready proceeded to New Orleans where he had the same trouble with Manager Smith. "When he came to himself between the acts, he was irritable and fault-finding; never satisfied with those who acted with him, sending for this one and that one for the purpose of administering a lecture, and often, until I gave him notice I would not go, dispatching his servant to the manager, to whom he would pour out complaint after complaint, until the rising of the curtain called him to his duties upon the stage."

PLACIDE'S VARIETIES

THE closing of the second New Orleans American theater in 1843 had presumably brought to an end Caldwell's power in the theatrical world. In the following year he had sold his Mobile theater to his successful rival, Ludlow, and for a period of time his name had entirely disappeared from dramatic activities. In 1850, however, there was opened on the north side of Gravier Street near Carondelet Street a new theater called the Varieties Theater. It had been built by a group of men in New Orleans, known as the "Varieties Club." Thomas Placide (see No. 199), who had often appeared during the past few years at the St. Charles and the Mobile Theaters, was nominal head and manager. But Ludlow discovered to his surprise that his old rival, Caldwell, had been one of the chief promoters and backers of the new organization, which was now attempting to dispute the monopoly of the St. Charles. On June 25, 1852, Ludlow visited the Varieties and saw *The School for Scandal*, "which, for the excellence of cast and characters, has seldom, if ever, been equalled in the United States." This tribute is especially noteworthy as it was Placide's policy to dispense altogether with stars, and revert to the

464 The Varieties Theater, New Orleans, from a sketch in John S. Kendall, *History of New Orleans*. Copyright Chicago, 1922, Lewis Publishing Company

old stock-company idea. In 1854 the Varieties was destroyed by fire, but was replaced the following year by Dion Boucicault's (No. 544) Gaieties. Boucicault remained as manager for a year, and was succeeded by William H. Crisp, a prominent western actor; by John E. Owens (No. 495); Mrs. Chanfrau and others. During these later managements its original name of Varieties was resumed. Burning in 1870, it was replaced in 1872 by the Third Varieties Theater on Canal Street near Bourbon — called also the Grand Opera House. Here Lawrence Barrett (No. 614) was in control for a number of years, and played for the first time the classical rôles with which he later won national fame. This theater, boasting the finest staircase in America, was by far the most famous of its day in the Southwest.

465 Ben de Bar, from a portrait, artist unknown, in the Missouri Historical Society, St. Louis

A NEW MANAGER IN ST. LOUIS

THE St. Louis monopoly which Ludlow and Smith had enjoyed since 1835 was ended on January 8, 1851, when John Bates opened a new theater on the north side of Pine Street between Third and Fourth Streets. Earlier in life, having accumulated a considerable fortune from a confectionery and soda-water establishment in Cincinnati, Bates had later lost it in unwise banking investments, and then attempted to make another by theatrical management in Cincinnati and Louisville.

466 Field's Varieties Theater, St. Louis, from a photograph in the Missouri Historical Society St. Louis

In 1846 he had bought a theater in Louisville which Caldwell had abandoned in a half-completed state. But neither his Louisville nor his Cincinnati theater proved as profitable as had the confectionery business. He had arrived in St. Louis hoping at last to make up all he had lost. On his stage William J. Florence (No. 566) and the Barney Williamses (No. 571) had their first western successes — and after the retirement of Ludlow and Smith in 1853, all the leading visiting stars appeared on his boards. In 1856 the Bates Theater was sold to Ben de Bar, who renamed it the St. Louis Theater. De Bar was a London actor, who in 1837 had been brought by Caldwell to the first St. Charles, where he had thrilled the New Orleans audiences by the daring of his equestrian performances, "perilling his life every night for eighteen dollars a week." From 1850 he had been stage manager at the St. Charles under Ludlow and Smith, who, when they retired in 1853, left the entire management to him. De Bar, after 1856, ran the St. Louis Theater for a number of years, leasing it in 1874 to William Mitchell, who renamed it the *Théâtre Comique*. The building was burned in 1880. Another St. Louis theater which ultimately found its way into the hands of Ben de Bar was the St. Louis Varieties on the south side of Market Street between Fifth and Sixth. Built by a stock company of gentlemen living in St. Louis, and managed by Joseph M. Field (No. 407), this theater, handsomely decorated and furnished, and capable of holding from eleven to twelve hundred persons, was opened on May 10, 1852, with a stock company described as being the best that had ever appeared in St. Louis. But, according to the evidence of Ludlow, Field was not a shrewd manager, and his enterprise failed. It was closed, taken over by an unsuccessful German stock company, and, after two other managements had failed, was bought in 1873 by De Bar, who rechristened it De Bar's Opera House, under which name it ran until it was closed in 1881. Other St. Louis theaters of the period were the Olympic (1866–82) and the People's Theater (1852–81).

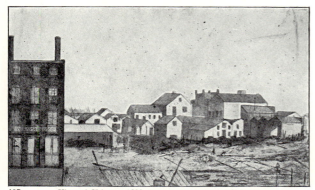

467   View of Chicago, 1839, from a sketch in the Chicago Historical Society

BEGINNINGS IN CHICAGO

THE first actors who came to Chicago in 1837 were discouraged from giving any performances by the license fee, which exceeded the limits of their small purses. Shortly afterward, however, Isherwood and MacKenzie bought a license, and opened with Kotzebue's *The Stranger* in the dining room of the Sauganash Hotel, fitted up tentatively into a crude theater. The modest bills which were printed and distributed through the town seem to have drawn a crowd, for the venture was successful — so much so that it was decided to open a regular theater on the upper floor of a wooden building and to call it The Rialto or the Chicago Theater. Space was limited but the appointments were good. In 1842 the second theater was opened in the Chapin building, where for a short time the managers succeeded. In 1844 the first museum was opened in the Commercial Building.

468   James H. McVicker, from a photograph in the Davis Collection

JAMES H. McVICKER, 1822–1896

THE first Chicago building intended exclusively for a theater was built in 1847 on Randolph Street by J. B. Rice, who was later for many years Mayor of Chicago and Congressional representative at Washington. In May of 1848 James H. McVicker, excellent for singing and dancing rôles, and, owing to the number of parts which he had mastered, dependable in almost any emergency, joined Rice's company as first low comedian. McVicker, who was destined to become the outstanding figure of theatrical life in the Middle West, had, in 1837, at the age of fifteen, emigrated from his home in New York to St. Louis, where he had been a printer on the *St. Louis Republican*. As often as his small salary allowed, he had visited Ludlow and Smith's theater and soon became stage-struck. From 1843 to 1846 under the management of Ludlow and Smith, he had been call boy at the second St. Charles, and before his departure for Chicago had been at the American Theater, also controlled since 1845 by the joint managers.

In 1850, the year of the burning of Rice's first theater, McVicker purchased from the widow of Dan Marble all of that actor's Yankee plays, and went on a long tour specializing in Yankee parts. His first experience at stage management was at the People's Theater, St. Louis, as assistant to the manager. In 1855 McVicker was favorably received in England in various Yankee characters. In 1856 he appeared at Burton's Chambers Street Theater in New York, and then proceeded for starring engagements in St. Louis.

McVICKER'S THEATERS

FROM St. Louis McVicker hurried to Chicago where he immediately began arrangements for the erection of an elegant theater on Madison Street. After an outlay of eighty-five thousand dollars McVicker opened the doors of his new theater on November 5, 1857. Its excellencies were soon acknowledged. There was every convenience for the actors and for the audience. The acoustics were splendid, the stage property extensive, stock and stars of the first order. Its supremacy as the handsomest playhouse in the West came gradually to be recognized. For some time, however, there was severe competition from Rice, who in 1850 had built a second theater — this time of brick — on the site of the original wooden structure which had burned in that year. But when Rice was elected to Congress, and was no longer able personally to supervise his theater, McVicker made rapid strides to the front. Another competitor was North's National Amphitheater, which had opened on November 10, 1855, a wooden structure, seating three thousand people, with a performing ring forty-two feet in diameter and with stabling quarters for an entire stud of horses. Charles

469   Rice's Second Theater, Chicago, from an engraving in *Chicago's First Half Century*, Chicago, 1883

R. Thorne had, on October 7, 1856, refitted the Metropolitan Hall Theater, which had opened without much success in 1854. But in spite of these numerous competitors McVicker's Theater gradually outdistanced all of them, until by the time of the great fire of 1871 it was preëminent. McVicker was the first to build after the fire, and on August 15, 1872, opened the doors of his palatial new two hundred thousand dollar building. This burned in 1892 and was replaced by the third McVicker Theater which still remains, one of the finest outside New York City.

470   McVicker's First Theater, Chicago, from a lithograph in the Chicago Historical Society

OTHER CHICAGO THEATERS

In 1863 several rooms on the north side of Randolph Street east of Clark were fitted up as a museum, in which were displayed a collection of natural history objects, a hall of paintings, and a panorama of London. In the following year Colonel Wood became proprietor of the museum, bought the adjoining building, and organized a stock company, which was prominent in Chicago theatricals until the fire. Other Chicago theaters of the decade before the fire were: the Aiken, built in 1869 and replaced by the Adelphi, which itself burned in 1874, to be followed by the second Adelphi of J. H. Haverly; Crosby's Opera House, 1865; Smith and Nixon's Hall; the Academy of Music; the Staats Theater; and Hooley's Theater, which was rebuilt after the fire and during the closing years of the century occupied a prominent place in the theatrical life of Chicago.

471 Wood's Museum, Chicago, from an engraving in J. Seymour Currey, *Chicago: Its History and its Builders*, Chicago, 1912. Courtesy of the S. J. Clarke Publishing Co., Chicago

THE MORMON THEATER

472 Hiram B. Clawson, from an engraving in Horace G. Whitney, *The Drama in Utah*, Salt Lake City, 1915. © *The Deseret News*

Not only did the Mormons lay the foundations of Nauvoo-on-the-Mississippi; they laid even more lasting foundations for cultural and social activity. Nauvoo, with its bands and choral societies, boasted many evidences of musical interest. It enjoyed such intellectual pursuits as the study of Hebrew, Latin and Greek in schools, and a widespread enthusiasm for the drama. Its high mission was clarioned by the voice of the prophet, Joseph Smith, who himself formed the city's first dramatic company. Among the first players were Brigham Young and Thomas Lyne, a well known tragedian (see No. 403). To Lyne one day "The Prophet" brought a young man clever at mimicry. Lyne who was presenting *Pizarro*, in which Brigham Young played High Priest, gave him the only thing open, the rôle of throwing down, at the appointed signal, fire from heaven. The young man, who was Hiram Clawson, eagerly accepted this opening to a long and successful career. The Mormons did not confine their activities to Nauvoo. When Brigham Young led his followers westward and settled in "The Valley" the activities of the Nauvoo musicians, students and actors were barely interrupted. In 1850, less than three years after the arrival of the first pioneers, and simultaneous with the first issue of *The Deseret News*, one of the first English plays in the Far West was produced. The play, *Robert Marave*, featuring Hiram Clawson was given in the Bowery, a crude building of boughs and lumber, which served also for a house of worship. It was to be superseded two years later by the opening of a Social Hall, considered then a splendid edifice, and that in turn by the famous Salt Lake Theater. This magnificent structure, which Brigham Young caused to be erected in 1861 as a permanent temple of the drama, cost more than one hundred thousand dollars and was more than six months under construction. It is said that public interest during this winter alternated between the events of the great Civil War, news of which was posted on a wall in front of the press, and the progress of the huge theater. For the first night Brigham Young extended invitations to church officials and the families of the workers. The house, which held from twelve hundred to fifteen hundred, could not, however, meet the demand for seats; so a second night, March 8, was set apart, the attendance this time being paid,

473 The Salt Lake City Theater, from an engraving in E. V. Fohlin, *Salt Lake City Past and Present*, Salt Lake City, 1908

474   The First Theater in Monterey, California, from an engraving in the Harvard Theater
Collection, Cambridge, Mass.

THE CALIFORNIA FRONTIER

Long before the Mormons built their theater in Salt Lake City, the disciples of an older religion had transplanted from Spain a type of drama which traced back to medieval Catholic rites. Not only in Spain, but also in France, and England and Italy, devout members of the village congregation had staged, on the occasion of church anniversary festivals, miracle plays, in which, for the edification and amusement of the congregation, the recognized personalities of Good and Evil were graphically portrayed in dramatic settings. During the intervening centuries of Spanish occupation of Southern California, the *padres* in their various missions along the King's Highway had employed the same time-honored device for inculcating in the minds of the native acolytes the salient doctrines of the Catholic religion. One of the most vivid pictures of these transplanted miracle plays describes the ceremony in the Cathedral at San Diego in 1832, attended by "stately Spanish grandees with handsome wives and lovely daughters on their arms; busy Mexican mothers with broods of swarthy-faced, black-eyed children." In 1847, the second year of the Mexican War, which brought to an end the long Spanish domination in California, a group of American soldiers, volunteers from New York state, had been commissioned to arrest General Vallejo, the commander of the Spanish post at Sonoma, California. The general proved himself an amenable prisoner, and in addition a most conscientious host. For the amusement of his captor-guests he fitted up a crude theater, in which the American soldiers gave what proved to be the first legitimate English play in California, Benjamin Webster's popular domestic drama, *The Golden Farmer*. At about the same time other American soldiers gave performances — entirely, it seems, of the minstrel variety — in San Francisco, Santa Barbara, and at the theater in Monterey, which enjoys the distinction of being the oldest California Theater. It was at the Eagle Theater, Sacramento, however, that the first English professional dramatic performance in California took place on October 18, 1849. Though built at a cost of seventy-five thousand dollars, it was forced, probably because of the heavy nightly expense of six hundred dollars, to close on the fourth of the following January. It was shortly followed by the Tehama and the Pacific theaters, which became important units of the California circuit — along with Stockton, Monterey, and Nevada — over which visiting stars regularly traveled. After

475   The First English Professional Dramatic Performance in California, from a play-bill in the Hall of California Pioneers, San Francisco

closing at Sacramento the Eagle Theater Company went to San Francisco, and on January 16 gave the first professional dramatic performance there on the second floor of Washington Hall. The first theater building in San Francisco, the National, which was opened in February by a French company, soon burned and was replaced by an Italian theater. Other early San Francisco theaters were Rowe's Olympic and the Dramatic Museum.

476   View of San Francisco, 1849, from an engraving in *The Bay of San Francisco*, Chicago, 1892

477   The Second Jenny Lind Theater, from an engraving in John P. Young, *History of San Francisco*, San Francisco, 1912, courtesy of the S. J. Clarke Publishing Co., Chicago

478   The Bella Union Theater, San Francisco, from an engraving in John P. Young, *History of San Francisco*, San Francisco, 1912, courtesy of the S. J. Clarke Publishing Co., Chicago

GROWTH IN SAN FRANCISCO

In December, 1850, Tom Maguire, who was destined to play an increasingly important part in the history of the San Francisco Theater, opened over his Parker House saloon on Kearney Street a new theater, which as a tribute to the brilliant singer from Sweden was christened the Jenny Lind. In the fire of 1851 the building was destroyed along with the other crude theaters. Maguire, realizing the ever-present danger of fire in San Francisco, began the erection of a large stone theater, capable of holding two thousand persons. The second Jenny Lind was opened October 4, 1851, and ran for over a year until it was sold to the civic authorities as a City Hall. The two most important actors to appear at the Jenny Lind were Lewis Baker of Philadelphia and his wife, formerly Alexina Fisher. After two series of performances at the Jenny Lind, and short engagements at Sacramento, followed by a tour of smaller California towns, the Bakers assumed the management of the Adelphi Theater, a French theater on Dupont Street, opened in 1851. Their first season at the Adelphi from August, 1852, to May, 1853, was the most prosperous and brilliant that California had yet enjoyed, with a profit to the management of thirty thousand dollars. Baker then took over the direction of the American Theater, which with equal success he managed until January, 1854. "It had been no trifling task," wrote Soulé, "to restore order out of the chaotic confusion of the theater in San Francisco. . . . With the advent of Mr. and Mrs. Baker, however, commenced a new era in the California drama. . . . He introduced . . . careful rehearsals and paid all needful attention to the necessary accessories of the stage. Under such auspices, the citizens were presented with entertainments of a refined character, and in a style of excellence fully equal to those of the best theaters in New York or Philadelphia." The ascendancy of the American was ended by the opening of the elegant Metropolitan Theater, built and managed by Mrs. Catherine N. St. Clair, aided by James E. Murdoch (see No. 242) and an excellent stock company. Though there were numerous smaller theaters such as the Bella Union, the Metropolitan for the next fifteen years dominated the theatrical life of San Francisco. On its boards appeared practically all the leading stars of the East, attracted to California by the huge salaries which the western managers, thanks to the high prices of admission, were able to pay. But with the opening of the California Theater, under the joint direction of John McCullough (see No. 610) and Lawrence Barrett (see No. 614) a still more brilliant era was ushered in.

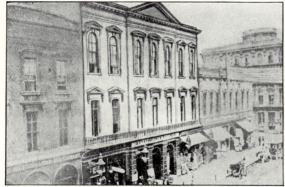

479   The Metropolitan Theater, San Francisco, from an engraving in John P. Young, *History of San Francisco*, San Francisco, 1912, courtesy of the S. J. Clarke Publishing Co., Chicago

480   The California Theater, San Francisco, from an engraving in John P. Young, *History of San Francisco*, San Francisco, 1912, courtesy of the S. J. Clarke Publishing Co., Chicago

481   Edward J. Baldwin, from a photo-
         graph in the Davis Collection

482   Baldwin's Hotel-Theater, San Francisco, from an engraving in David Belasco's
              "My Life Story" in *Hearst's Magazine*, June 1914

"PERFECT TYPES OF THE RUGGED WEST"

McCullough and Barrett produced on a sumptuous scale which set the standard for the numerous new entries into the production game. The most prominent of the new competitors were, in Belasco's words, two "perfect types of the rugged west," Thomas Maguire, an illiterate ex-cabman, who, as already noted, built the Jenny Lind Theater, and Edward J. Baldwin, a former hostler, who, having risen from the stable to a position of influence in the financial world of San Francisco, had come to be called by his admirers "Lucky." Maguire's Opera House — which later became the Bush Street Theater — was opened in 1873, followed the next year by another Maguire theater, the old Alhambra, of which David Belasco was stage manager. "Lucky" Baldwin on March 6, 1876, in conjunction with Maguire opened Baldwin's theater, a combination hotel-theater, of which James A. Herne (see No. 830), Maguire's personal representative, was for a number of years stage manager. Six years later Al Hayman bought out Baldwin's interest in the theater and organized one of the strongest stock companies in our history. The most picturesque production in San Francisco annals was *The Passion Play* at the Grand Opera House, written by Salmi Morse, and directed by Belasco — in which James O'Neill played the part of Christ. Although Maguire and Baldwin, the promoters, spent huge sums on the production, and although O'Neill gave a most impressive performance, the play in the end had to be withdrawn because of the religious bitterness aroused.

BACK COUNTRY

The theater-going of the thousands of new settlers who were yearly pouring into the country west of the Rockies was by no means confined to such established centers as the stages of Baldwin and Maguire. San Francisco was the headquarters for numerous troupes — legitimate, minstrel, and variety — which barnstormed through mud and rain over the newly built roads of the hinterland. Their experiences in Oregon and Idaho and Wyoming on the improvised stages of mining camps, where drunken gamblers threw purses and gold nuggets on to the stage, were similar to the "gagging tours" of Smith and Ludlow.

483   A Variety Show at Cheyenne, Wyoming, from an engraving in *Frank Leslie's
                 Illustrated Newspaper*, Oct. 13, 1877

484 Charlotte Crabtree, 1847–1924, from a photograph in the Davis Collection

"THE PET AND PRIDE OF CALIFORNIA"

THE trouper, *par excellence*, of this far-western circuit was Joseph H. Taylor, an adventurous minstrel player from the East, who arrived in San Francisco at the period when theaters were just gaining a firm foothold. His rambling, humorous anecdotes furnish an invaluable picture of various nomadic groups of entertainers, and of boisterous audiences with daggers and pistols. He painted on a broad canvas — from Sacramento to Puget Sound and British

485 Lotta, from a photograph in the Davis Collection

Columbia, from Olympia and Seattle and Tacoma to Hogum, Idaho, and back again with a group of minstrels who during the Civil War crossed to Honolulu and Pekin. On one of his tours Taylor crossed the path of another group of performers, which included a girl who was destined for twenty years, 1865–85, to outshine all her companions. "While travelling with Backus Minstrels in 1856 or 7," wrote Taylor in *Joe Taylor, Barnstormer*, New York, 1913, "we were in Shasta, when Lotta, who had been travelling with Mart Taylor, met us, and Mrs. Crabtree asked us if we would be pleased to have Lotta go on, and sing Topsy's song. Knowing Mrs. Crabtree very well, I asked if Lotta would black up. . . . This proved a great success for she was forced to respond to several encores, each time filling her slipper with money which was being showered on the stage. From this time Lotta sprang into prominence. She was an amiable, lovely and an ambitious child, who became the pet and pride of California." In 1858 Lotta made her legitimate début as Gertrude in *Loan of a Lover*. Most of her early California plays were written especially for her, sensational, sentimental melodramas centering around a heroine, who, though a ragged waif among drink-crazed miners, regenerates

486 Lotta, from a photograph in the Davis Collection

them — with the ever-pleasing coincidence that they find gold and become fabulously wealthy. The actress herself, as a result of her enormous popularity throughout the country, in such plays as *Zip, Musette, The Little Detective, Mam'selle Nitouche*, and *Little Nell and the Marchioness*, amassed a fortune, which, in striking contrast to many theatrical stars, she saved and by wise investment increased to over four million dollars at the time of her death in 1924. This in large part she left to the veterans of the World War.

487 Lotta as Topsy, from a photograph in the Davis Collection

CHAPTER VIII

RIVALRY IN THE EAST

THE growth of the American theater recorded in the previous chapter may be said to have culminated during the 'fifties in a rivalry more extensive and more keen than our stage had yet known. The competition was naturally most evident in New York, which by the end of the decade contained over a dozen playhouses. The famous old Park had passed forever, but with the Bowery, Burton's, Wallack's, the Old Broadway, Brougham's Lyceum, Laura Keene's, and Niblo's all eagerly competing, the New Yorker had little occasion to lament the older régime. In particular Burton, Wallack and Laura Keene each assembled a brilliant company and vied in an effort to capture the most influential following. The contest was sharply waged, but in the end it was the Wallacks who gained a long preëminence in the New York field, partly because of greater versatility and more uniform excellence in the troupe, but chiefly because an uncanny instinct for the theater seems to have been a Wallack characteristic. Philadelphia's major theatrical activities were carried on at the Walnut Street, Chestnut Street and Arch Street houses; but under the direction of William Wheatley and John Drew the Arch Street soon won the upper hand and remained in practical control of the situation for a number of years. In Boston spirited competition was responsible for the erection of the Boston Theater, in its day one of the outstanding theatrical buildings in America. The company it housed and that of the Boston Museum, where William Warren was the favorite actor, long rivaled each other in merit and provided Boston with a quality of stock acting that has not often been surpassed in the United States.

In the contest among the various theaters the stars played a considerable part, but it is interesting to find that it was largely a struggle between rival stock companies, for despite the undeniable appeal which the famous individual player had exercised for half a century, the older stock system had not yet succumbed before the inroads of the star. Perhaps the main cause for the failure of the stars to dominate the eastern stage lies in the rapid development of the theater in numerous thriving towns from one end of America to the other. These communities offered the traveling star a new field in which he might display his brilliant but limited repertory in a hundred different theaters. This contact between the noted actor and the remoter audiences was possible during this period as it had never been before because the decade of the 'fifties was an era of the development of trunk-line railroads. Already there were a number of short and disconnected routes in the United States, but in 1849 a mania for railroad building seized the country that added several thousand miles annually to the nation's lines and that soon bound distant points together by continuous trunk roads. In 1853 Chicago and the East were connected by an all-rail route, and by the end of 1854 the total trackage in the United States amounted to over twenty-one thousand miles, with some lines making tentative thrusts beyond the Mississippi. Before the beginning of the Civil War it was possible to travel by rail from New York City to Albany and Buffalo over a route that was soon to be controlled by the recently organized New York Central; or to go from New York to Pittsburgh over the Pennsylvania Railroad; or to journey between Baltimore and St. Louis, largely because of the development of the Baltimore and Ohio. The actor was not slow to take advantage of the enormous opportunity this new mode of transportation provided him, and not only individuals but whole companies went on tour with a degree of speed and comfort that would, to be sure, discourage a trouper of today, but that must have seemed like the last perfection of progress to those who may have remembered our first traveling star, T. A. Cooper, and his covered wagon. As a matter of fact the adventurous player who aspired to appear in the Far West was still forced to resort to the stagecoach or perhaps even the humble covered wagon; but when in 1869 the last spike was driven that completed the transcontinental railway, the United States became one great circuit, and it was then possible for Jo Jefferson, for instance, to make Rip Van Winkle as familiar and beloved a figure in San Francisco as he was in New York.

A particularly significant achievement of this period was the writing of *Francesca da Rimini* (1855) by George Henry Boker, a tragedy which excelled any drama that had yet been written in America. Definitely as this play surpasses its predecessors, it must not be regarded as a miraculous blossom on a dead bush. Rather, to change the figure, it is the peak of a succession of romantic tragedies that may be said to have begun with Dunlap's effective *Leicester* in 1794, and to have been developed and perfected by such successful plays as Barker's *Marmion*, Payne's *Brutus*, Smith's *Caius Marius*, and Bird's *The Gladiator*, until it reached its climax in the work of Boker. In these romantic and poetic dramas the playwrights of the time are to be seen at their best, and the product is such as to command the respect and even admiration of the present-day reader. Neither is there any occasion for surprise that the summit of this development should have fallen about the middle of the century, for during the fifth and sixth decades America was enjoying a standard of literary excellence that had not been approached before in this country and has scarcely been equaled since. Between 1840 and 1855 appeared some of the best work of Poe, nearly all that of Hawthorne, Thoreau's *Walden*, Emerson's *Essays*, much of the most distinctive writing of Longfellow, Holmes, and Lowell, the *Moby Dick* of Melville, and Whitman's *Leaves of Grass*. When we consider also the stimulus that the group of remarkable actors then on our stage must have imparted to an imaginative playwright, we realize that the time was ripe for a great drama.

As we today review the history of the 'fifties, the Civil War looms so imminent that little else seems to matter. But the contemporary theater appears to have been almost oblivious of these momentous events. To be sure the slavery question found its way to the stage in the dramatization of *Uncle Tom's Cabin* and in Boucicault's *Octoroon*, but the great issue was reflected in drama less than in any other literary form. People have always gone to the theater, not to be disturbed, but to be entertained. Perhaps there is significance in the fact that John Brown's raid at Harper's Ferry and the opening of a new theater in New York by George Fox, the popular clown, occurred only a few weeks apart.

488   William Evans Burton, 1804–60, from a photo-graph in the Davis Collection

"BROAD HUMOR"

DURING the early 'fifties Burton's Theater in Chambers Street replaced the vanished Park as New York's aristocratic theatrical center. Its proprietor, William Evans Burton, as a lad had set out to be a printer in his native London, but the stage soon proved irresistible and he played in provincial theaters until 1831, when he began a London engagement. In 1834 he was playing at the Arch Street Theater, Philadelphia, and early in 1839 he began starring at the National in New York, soon transferring to the Park. Burton's great hold on the public

489   Burton as Captain Cuttle, from a photo-graph in the Davis Collection

began in 1848 with the opening in New York of a theater bearing his name. Here his acting as Bob Acres, Tony Lumpkin, Mr. Micawber, Captain Cuttle in *Dombey and Son*, and many other comic characters gave him a position without a rival among the lovers of broad humor. In 1858 he commenced a starring tour of the country, and the name of Billy Burton became a household word in almost every quarter of the Union. Laurence Hutton has written in *Plays and Players:* "Burton was probably the funniest man that ever lived. . . . Burton in his day was the best known man in New York, if not in America." In Joseph Jefferson's *Autobiography* occur these sentences: "Burton was thoughtful and saturnine . . . one of the funniest creatures that ever lived. . . . As an actor of the old broad farce-comedy Mr. Burton certainly had no equal in his day . . . Captain Cuttle and Micawber were his greatest achievements; his face was a huge map on which was written every emotion that he felt." To quote again from the indispensable Ireland: "Mr. Burton's humor was

490   Burton, as Falstaff, opposite Mrs. Burton in *The Merry Wives of Windsor*, from a photograph in the Harvard Theater Collection

broad and deep, and sometimes approached coarseness, but at the same time always genial and hearty, and generally truthfully natural, while in homely pathos, and the earnest expression of blunt, uncultivated feeling, he has rarely been excelled. . . . His features were flexible, and without unmeaning distortion, full of rich and most varied comic expression, and with his clear, strong voice, and his plump and somewhat pussy figure, were admirably adapted to the general class of characters in which he appeared."

491   Burton as Bottom, from a gravure by Gebbie and Co., in the possession of the publishers

BURTON AS MANAGER

W. E. BURTON had extensive experience not only as an actor but also as a manager. His first theater was Cook's Olympic Circus in Philadelphia, of which he obtained control in 1840. The next year he undertook the management of the new National Theater in New York, built in 1840 on the site of the old National, which had burned the preceding year. This new theater was decorated within in the Oriental style, even to the ladies' saloon and anteroom. Two boasted features of the house were the installation of a bell in each box so that "immediate attendance, refreshments, etc." might be obtained without quitting the box, and the provision of ample space for each person in the audience. Burton's tenancy of the new National was very brief, for on May 29, less than seven weeks after the beginning of his occupancy, it, like its predecessor, was totally destroyed by fire. Thereafter he controlled for a time the Chestnut Street and the Arch Street Theaters in Philadelphia, and at the same time took over the management of the Washington Theater and the Front Street Theater, Baltimore. His most important venture, however, was the leasing of Palmo's Opera House, New York, which he opened as Burton's Theater, July 10, 1848. Thanks to his own comic talents, the excellent services of John Brougham as actor and playwright, and the original and gifted Caroline Chapman (see p. 152) the theater became immensely popular and its proprietor waxed rich. "For several years," wrote Ireland, "Burton's Theater was the resort of the most intelligent class of pleasure seekers, and there beauty, wit, and fashion loved to congregate, without the formality or etiquette of attire, once deemed necessary at the Park." But in time his clientele, fancying they detected a trace of vulgarity about Burton's, began going elsewhere. Thereupon, to meet the strong competition of Wallack, Burton in 1856 took a theater on Broadway near Bond Street, which had been known as Laura Keene's Varieties, but which he rechristened Burton's New Theater. After two years of indifferent success in his new home, the proprietor withdrew permanently from managership. The Civil War with its disruption of American life was at hand. In still another field of endeavor Burton gained prominence, that of journalism. In the 'thirties he established at Philadelphia Burton's *Gentleman's Magazine*, of which for a time the assistant editor and leading contributor was Edgar Allan Poe.

492   Interior of Burton's Theater, Chambers Street, from a print
in the New York Historical Society

493   Performance at Burton's Theater, from a playbill
in the New York Historical Society

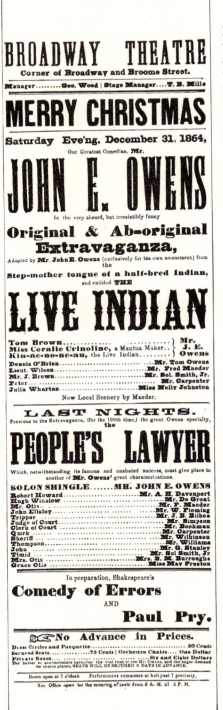

494 Owens as Kin-ne-no-ne-au, the Live Indian,
from a playbill in the Davis Collection

A BORN COMEDIAN

BURTON'S chief disciple was John Edmond Owens, a man of Welsh ancestry, who was born at Liverpool. At the age of three he was brought to America. In 1840, having resolved to go on the stage, he went to Philadelphia and became associated with Burton. In 1850 he made his New York début as Mr. Fright in *Crimson Crimes* at Brougham's Lyceum. He next went on an extensive trip to Europe, ascended Mont Blanc, returned to America, and gave entertainments describing this ascent, with panoramic illustrations. He continued his former successes, and in 1864 at the Broadway Theater began a most brilliant engagement as the Yankee, Solon Shingle, in *The People's Lawyer* and as Caleb Plummer in *The Cricket on the Hearth*. By 1864 the people of the North had recovered from the financial depression of 1861. Industry was booming, prices were soaring, and the theater again flourished. In 1865 Owens carried his Yankee rôles to the London Strand. His career as a successful actor continued until 1882, in which year he made his final stage appearance at the Harlem Theater as Solon Shingle. During much of his active life he added to his fortune by managing theaters in Baltimore, New Orleans, and Charleston. Owens belonged to that happy breed of comedians of whom Burton was perhaps the outstanding representative. William Winter wrote in *The Wallet of Time:* "Owens was born to be a comic actor. He was intrinsically funny. . . . He was thoughtful in mind and affectionate in heart, but above all he was a creature of buoyant, merry temperament. . . . 'His humorous vitality was prodigious. It sparkled in his bright brown eyes; it rippled in the music of his rich, sonorous, flexible voice; it exulted in the bounteous health of his vigorous constitution; it rejoiced in his alert demeanor, his elastic step, his beaming smile, his exuberant and incessant glee."

495 John Edmond Owens, 1823–86, from a
photograph in the Davis Collection

496 Owens as Solon Shingle, from a photograph in the Davis Collection

MOSE THE FIREBOY

I<small>F</small> Owens was a distinguished impersonator of the long familiar stage Yankee, it was Francis S. Chanfrau who popularized another native type, the tough city lad. Chanfrau, a native of New York City, after receiving a substantial education became a ship carpenter. Before long, however, he began appearing at the Bowery as a super, and there he attracted attention by his excellent impersonations of Forrest and other stars. In 1848 he leaped into fame by

497   Francis S. Chanfrau, 1824–84, from a photograph in the Davis Collection

appearing at Mitchell's Olympic as Mose the Fireboy in *A Glance at New York*, written by Mitchell's prompter, Benjamin A. Baker. This play, a lineal descendant of *Tom and Jerry*, capitalized the contemporary fire fighters, whom A. H. Quinn in *A History of the American Drama* thus describes: "The volunteer fire companies were well known institutions. They were not only fire fighters, they were also rude social and political forces, and their methods of dealing with fires were appalling, to say the least. Rivalry was keen between the companies and the first one to reach the scene had to spend time in intrenching its position for a siege before it turned its attention to the fire." Chanfrau looked and acted the part to perfection with his plug hat, red shirt, turned up trousers, "soap locks," and impudence. The play is filled with rapidly shifting scenes and unceasing action. The underworld of the city is vividly disclosed, and in making the rounds thereof Mose finds ample opportunity to satisfy his love of battle. For seventy nights he delighted the "Bowery B'hoys." During this run Chanfrau started a companion piece, *New York As It Is*, at the Chatham Theater, of which he was now the manager, acting in both plays every evening. There followed a succession of Mose plays — *Mose in California*, *Mose in a Muss*, *Mose's Visit to Philadelphia*, *Mose in China*. Other actors, including John E. Owens and Junius Brutus Booth, Jr., began appearing in similar plays. But the originator of the species continued its most popular interpreter. According to Ireland, Mose "carried him as a star triumphantly through every theatrical town in the Union." Chanfrau's ability was, however, by no means limited to this range of character. A decidedly handsome and well-bred man, he was thoroughly qualified to assume a wide variety of rôles.

498   Chanfrau's Benefit at Troy, New York, from a playbill in the Davis Collection

499   Chanfrau as Mose the Fireboy, from a hand-colored print after a miniature by A. Morand, in the Fridenberg Collection

500   The Old Broadway, from a print in the New York Historical Society

THE OLD BROADWAY

A HOUSE that endeavored to compete with Burton's during the 'fifties was the Broadway Theater. Projected by Thomas S. Hamblin (see No. 222), who was prevented from completing it by his loss of the Bowery, it was erected in 1847 on Broadway between Pearl and Anthony Streets by Colonel Alvah Mann. The theater, which was modeled after the London Haymarket, had an immense auditorium divided into a pit for men and boys only, a dress circle, a family circle, a gallery, and a "colored gallery." The Broadway was opened September 27, 1847, with *The School for Scandal*, the company including Henry Wallack and George Vandenhoff. Forrest and Macready won their greatest laurels here, and here Forrest "thundered" during the years of his waning glory. For a time, beginning in 1850, George Barrett (see No. 191) was stage manager for the company; in 1852 Celeste (No. 248) made her reappearance at this theater; and in 1857 Charles Mathews, Jr. (No. 276). But, although the Broadway stage was trodden by numerous distinguished players, and although the house was a handsome one, calculated to catch the esteem of the wealthy and intellectual, it never gained prestige during its career of a dozen years, and in 1859 it was torn down to make way for a warehouse.

"ELOQUENT IDEALISM"

A POPULAR comedian connected with the Broadway between 1848 and 1851, and serving for a time as stage manager, was William Rufus Blake. Here he created his most famous rôle, that of Jesse Rural in Boucicault's *Old Heads and Young Hearts*. In speaking of the interrelation of tears and laughter, Oliver Wendell Holmes wrote in *The Autocrat of the Breakfast Table*, "If you want to choke with stifled tears at the sight of this transition from laughter to weeping as it shows itself in older years, go and see Mr. Blake play Jesse Rural." He was also excellent in such other characters as Sir Anthony Absolute, Old Hardcastle, and Sir Peter Teazle, old men's parts in which he was declared by contemporary observers to have equaled even John Gibbs Gilbert (No. 243). These were the rôles of a later period, however, for at the beginning, when he was handsome, slim, and graceful, he delighted New York audiences with his young heroes and lovers. His début was made in 1824 at the old Chatham Garden Theater, on which occasion he played Frederick in Colman's *Poor Gentleman*, and the three characters of Percival, Pertinax and Peregrine Shingle in the protean farce, *The Three Shingles*. He became at once a success as an actor, starring in the United States and Great Britain. In 1837 he originated the idea of building the Olympic Theater and was the manager for a year. During the 'fifties he was a leading comedian in the Burton, Wallack, and Keene stock companies, one of his

501   William Rufus Blake, 1805–63, from a photograph in the Davis Collection

most successful rôles being Old Dornton in *The Road to Ruin*. W. L. Keese wrote that Blake's acting was marked by "broad heartiness, suggestive sentiment, and eloquent idealism." His wife, formerly Caroline Placide, sister of Henry and Thomas (see No. 198), was a prominent actress for many years.

MOSE THE FIREBOY

IF Owens was a distinguished impersonator of the long familiar stage Yankee, it was Francis S. Chanfrau who popularized another native type, the tough city lad. Chanfrau, a native of New York City, after receiving a substantial education became a ship carpenter. Before long, however, he began appearing at the Bowery as a super, and there he attracted attention by his excellent impersonations of Forrest and other stars. In 1848 he leaped into fame by

497 Francis S. Chanfrau, 1824–84, from a photograph in the Davis Collection

appearing at Mitchell's Olympic as Mose the Fireboy in *A Glance at New York*, written by Mitchell's prompter, Benjamin A. Baker. This play, a lineal descendant of *Tom and Jerry*, capitalized the contemporary fire fighters, whom A. H. Quinn in *A History of the American Drama* thus describes: "The volunteer fire companies were well known institutions. They were not only fire fighters, they were also rude social and political forces, and their methods of dealing with fires were appalling, to say the least. Rivalry was keen between the companies and the first one to reach the scene had to spend time in intrenching its position for a siege before it turned its attention to the fire." Chanfrau looked and acted the part to perfection with his plug hat, red shirt, turned up trousers, "soap locks," and impudence. The play is filled with rapidly shifting scenes and unceasing action. The underworld of the city is vividly disclosed, and in making the rounds thereof Mose finds ample opportunity to satisfy his love of battle. For seventy nights he delighted the "Bowery B'hoys." During this run Chanfrau started a companion piece, *New York As It Is*, at the Chatham Theater, of which he was now the manager, acting in both plays every evening. There followed a succession of Mose plays — *Mose in California, Mose in a Muss, Mose's Visit to Philadelphia, Mose in China*. Other actors, including John E. Owens and Junius Brutus Booth, Jr., began appearing in similar plays. But the originator of the species continued its most popular interpreter. According to Ireland, Mose "carried him as a star triumphantly through every theatrical town in the Union." Chanfrau's ability was, however, by no means limited to this range of character. A decidedly handsome and well-bred man, he was thoroughly qualified to assume a wide variety of rôles.

BENEFIT OF

F.S. CHANFRAU

And last Night of the Engagement
OF
Miss ALBERTINE and Mr. CHANFRAU!

CHANFRAU   as the   FRENCHMAN and the IRISHMAN
And his singularly truthful personation of
MOSE!

Miss ALBERTINE as   The DEBUTANTE
Miss ALBERTINE as   LIZE

The Beautiful Piece of the

FIRST NIGHT;

The Far-Famed Local Extravaganza of the

GLANCE at NEW YORK

And the side-splitting Farce of

PADDY MILES' BOY!

Chanfrau in all Three Pieces!
ON THE SAME EVENING.

F. S CHANFRAU AS   MONS. ACHILLE TALMA DUFARD.

A severe and well known critic in New York remarks, "That the above arduous and peculiar character is almost unapproachable, unless by actors of that high order, now so rarely to be found in the profession of the histrionic art; but CHANFRAU's representations of the eccentric warm hearted Dufard was, indeed, a finished and most brilliant performance ; he fully proved his intellectual superiority, over every contemporary, who have attempted to personate this difficult character. It was, in fact, the alchemist transmutation of the baser metal into pure Gold, which GENIUS in its adaptative faculty, can alone achieve.

"Some things have been done, others are doing."

Monday Eve., May 14th, 1855

Will be acted the highly popular and truly laughable Burletta, of a very peculiar construction, entitled the

FIRST NIGHT!

OR, THE DEBUTANTE!

Mons. Achille Talma Dufard,...an old French Actor,.F. S. Chanfrau
M'lle Rose Antoinette Dufard,...the Debutante,...Miss Albertine
Bertie Findangle,.............a Theatrical Speculator...........G. S. Lee
Timothess Flat,............Manager of the Theatre,.........W. H. Dimond
Hyacinth Parnassus,.............an Author,.............C. L. Allen
Theophilus Vamp,.............Stage Director,.............H. P. Stone
George,..................the Call Boy,.................A. W brown
Miss Arabella Fitzjames,....the leading Actress.............Miss Kate Fisher

To be followed with the ever memorable Extravaganza entitled the

GLANCE

AT

NEW·YORK

Mose,...........Mr. F. S. Chanfrau
Lize,..................Miss Albertine
GEORGE PARSELS,..VINING BOWERS
Harry Gordon,..................G. S. Lee
Jake,..................W. H. Dimond
Mike,.............G. McWilliams
Major Gates,..................C. L. Allen
Mr. Morton,..................D. Worrester
Sykesy,..................H. F. Stone
Ben,.............B. C. Thompson
Sam,.............A. B. Yeomans
News Boy,..................Browne

Walters, Loafers, Dancers, &c

Mrs. Morton,..................Mrs. Archbald
Jenny,..................Miss Kate Fisher
Mary,.............Miss McWilliams
..................Miss Schmidt

Ladies, Passengers, Dancers, &c

498 Chanfrau's Benefit at Troy, New York, from a playbill in the Davis Collection

499 Chanfrau as Mose the Fireboy, from a hand-colored print after a miniature by A. Morand, in the Fridenberg Collection

500   The Old Broadway, from a print in the New York Historical Society

THE OLD BROADWAY

A HOUSE that endeavored to compete with Burton's during the 'fifties was the Broadway Theater. Projected by Thomas S. Hamblin (see No. 222), who was prevented from completing it by his loss of the Bowery, it was erected in 1847 on Broadway between Pearl and Anthony Streets by Colonel Alvah Mann. The theater, which was modeled after the London Haymarket, had an immense auditorium divided into a pit for men and boys only, a dress circle, a family circle, a gallery, and a "colored gallery." The Broadway was opened September 27, 1847, with *The School for Scandal*, the company including Henry Wallack and George Vandenhoff. Forrest and Macready won their greatest laurels here, and here Forrest "thundered" during the years of his waning glory. For a time, beginning in 1850, George Barrett (see No. 191) was stage manager for the company; in 1852 Celeste (No. 248) made her reappearance at this theater; and in 1857 Charles Mathews, Jr. (No. 276). But, although the Broadway stage was trodden by numerous distinguished players, and although the house was a handsome one, calculated to catch the esteem of the wealthy and intellectual, it never gained prestige during its career of a dozen years, and in 1859 it was torn down to make way for a warehouse.

"ELOQUENT IDEALISM"

A POPULAR comedian connected with the Broadway between 1848 and 1851, and serving for a time as stage manager, was William Rufus Blake. Here he created his most famous rôle, that of Jesse Rural in Boucicault's *Old Heads and Young Hearts*. In speaking of the interrelation of tears and laughter, Oliver Wendell Holmes wrote in *The Autocrat of the Breakfast Table*, "If you want to choke with stifled tears at the sight of this transition from laughter to weeping as it shows itself in older years, go and see Mr. Blake play Jesse Rural." He was also excellent in such other characters as Sir Anthony Absolute, Old Hardcastle, and Sir Peter Teazle, old men's parts in which he was declared by contemporary observers to have equaled even John Gibbs Gilbert (No. 243). These were the rôles of a later period, however, for at the beginning, when he was handsome, slim, and graceful, he delighted New York audiences with his young heroes and lovers. His début was made in 1824 at the old Chatham Garden Theater, on which occasion he played Frederick in Colman's *Poor Gentleman*, and the three characters of Percival, Pertinax and Peregrine Shingle in the protean farce, *The Three Shingles*. He became at once a success as an actor, starring in the United States and Great Britain. In 1837 he originated the idea of building the Olympic Theater and was the manager for a year. During the 'fifties he was a leading comedian in the Burton, Wallack, and Keene stock companies, one of his

501   William Rufus Blake, 1805–63, from a photograph in the Davis Collection

most successful rôles being Old Dornton in *The Road to Ruin*. W. L. Keese wrote that Blake's acting was marked by "broad heartiness, suggestive sentiment, and eloquent idealism." His wife, formerly Caroline Placide, sister of Henry and Thomas (see No. 198), was a prominent actress for many years.

502 Julia Margaret Mitchell, 1832–1918, from a photograph in the Davis Collection

503 Maggie Mitchell in *The Cricket*, from a photograph in the Davis Collection

504 Maggie Mitchell as Mignon in *The French Spy*, from a photograph in the Davis Collection

PLEASING IMPROVISATIONS

MAGGIE MITCHELL, a popular comédienne and soubrette for over three decades, made her first appearance on any stage in June, 1851, when she played the child Julia in *The Soldier's Daughter* at Burton's Theater. In February, 1852, at the Bowery Theater she took the rôle of Oliver Twist in the play of that name, and in 1853 at Purdy's National Theater she was appearing in light comedies. After her first engagements in New York she made tours about the country, her repertory including *Katty O'Shiel*, *Satan in Paris* and *The French Spy*. She was even more popular in the South and West. In 1857 she was a principal attraction at Burton's, offering besides the plays just named, *The Wept of Wish-Ton-Wish*, *The Pet of the Petticoats*, and *The Four Sisters*. In 1860 *La Petite Fadette* of George Sand was translated for her as *Fanchon* and soon became a brilliant success. She, like Clara Fisher and Lotta Crabtree, was most successful in building up delightful personations, particularly of children. Her sketches were not careful studies, but pleasing improvisations. In her later career she played in *Jane Eyre*, and *Elsa* with ability, but *Fanchon* was her chef d'œuvre and endeared her to the public for many years.

"BEAUTIFUL BUT RECKLESS"

505 Lola Montez, 1818–61, from a daguerreotype in the Davis Collection

THE most notorious person ever to appear at the Broadway was Maria Dolores Eliza Rosanna Gilbert. Though she was born in Limerick of an Irish father, her mother was of Spanish descent, and for this reason she felt justified in assuming the name of Lola Montez when she went on the stage. Famous at an early age as both a beauty and a dancer, she enjoyed court life in London until expelled because of scandal. She then toured the continent, appeared as a dancer at the Théâtre St. Martin in Paris, captivated the Czar on a trip to Russia, and, as a climax to her career, became the favorite of the King of Bavaria. Banished at length, with the title of countess, she accepted an offer from America and appeared at the old Broadway, December 29, 1851, in a ballet written for her, called *Betty the Tyrolean* and later in a sketch called *Lola Montez in Bavaria*. As her dancing alone could not hold the public by its merit, she organized receptions to which anyone paying a dollar was admitted, with the privilege of shaking the hand of the celebrity. She appeared on the stage at Boston and Philadelphia, and then, after some clever advertising, proceeded to New Orleans. Her next appearance was in California, where with great éclat she made a tour of the mining camp theaters of those boisterous and colorful days following the gold rush of 'forty-nine. After an eventful engagement in Australia in 1855 and after revisiting Paris in 1856, she returned to America, this time in the more prosaic rôle of lecturer, announcing such intriguing titles as "Beautiful Women," "Wits and Women of Paris," and "The Comic Aspects of Love." At the age of forty-three she died. In her prime Lola Montez was, in the words of Ireland, "graceful but not brilliant, beautiful but reckless."

THE IMMORTAL LOVERS

506 George Henry Boker, 1823–90, from an engraving in the Fridenberg Collection

507 Lawrence Barrett as Lanciotto in Boker's *Francesca da Rimini*, in the Davis Collection

THE most important figure whose name was associated with the Broadway Theater was the distinguished American dramatist, George Henry Boker. A native of Philadelphia and a graduate of Princeton, he grew to manhood in an atmosphere of culture, and resolved on a career of letters. His first play, *Calaynos*, in which the true bent of his talent was revealed, was produced at Sadler's Wells Theater, London, in 1849, and first presented in America at the Walnut Street Theater, Philadelphia, in 1851. A tragedy based on the theme of Spanish aversion to Moorish blood, *Calaynos*, in its romantic remoteness illustrates the type of material that challenged Boker's interest throughout his career. His second play, *Anne Boleyn* (1849), never reached the stage. It was followed by a romantic comedy, *The Betrothal*, first played at the Walnut Street Theater in 1850 and presented later in the same year at the Broadway. It was given in England in 1853 but met with disapproval from the press because of its American origin — at least so its author believed. After two unimportant pieces *Leonor de Guzman* appeared, another tragedy laid in Spain. It was played at the Walnut Street in 1853 and at the Broadway the next year. Then came Boker's masterpiece, *Francesca da Rimini*, which, after long study and preparation, was written in three weeks. It had its première at the Broadway, September 26, 1855, with E. L. Davenport and Madame Ponisi in the cast. Boker's was the first play in English on the theme of Dante's immortal lovers, and it is still among the best in any language. In the delicate and just drawing of the characters and the force and beauty of its blank verse it surpasses all native plays that preceded it, and even to-day it must be regarded as one of the greatest plays ever written by an American. The drama has been subsequently revived with much success by Lawrence Barrett and Otis Skinner. In December, 1855, Boker's poorest play, *The Bankrupt*, a prose melodrama of contemporary times, was brought out at the Broadway with Julia Dean as the heroine and Charles Fisher as the villain. It ran for only three nights. The nation was drifting swiftly into war and Boker turned from the fictitious emotion of the drama to participation in the stirring events of national life. He helped form the Union Club in Philadelphia, which under his influence became the center of intense loyalty to the Union cause. In 1871 Boker was appointed minister to Turkey, and four years later was made Minister Plenipotentiary to Russia.

CASTLE GARDEN

ANOTHER theater that, like the Broadway, housed celebrities in the 'fifties does duty to-day as the New York Aquarium. This ancient edifice was originally built as a fort, called Castle Clinton, for the defense of the city in the War of 1812. In 1822, Congress having ceded the fort to the city, it was converted into a public assembly hall with the name of Castle Garden. Here Lafayette, Kossuth, and other notables were given great public receptions. It was transformed into a theater about 1845 and at the outset housed a troupe of minstrels.

They were soon succeeded by a regular company containing George Holland and others. Beginning in 1850 it was used at times as a grand opera house. An interesting occurrence here was the celebration on September 6, 1852, of the centenary of what was then thought to be the introduction of drama in America — the coming of the Hallams. The bill consisted of *The Merchant of Venice* and *Lethe*, of which the first had been given, and the second was erroneously thought to have been given, on the Hallams' opening night at Williamsburg just a hundred years before. But the most notable event that ever occurred at Castle Garden was the American début of Jenny Lind,

508   Castle Garden, from an engraving by Dougal after a drawing by Wade, in the Fridenberg Collection

509 Jenny Lind, 1820–87, from an engraving by N. A. Singer after a drawing from life, in Mener's *Monats-Heste*, New York, August 1853

510 Cartoon, satirizing the after-effects of Jenny Lind's visit, from *Yankee Notions*, 1852

"THE SWEDISH NIGHTINGALE"

IF only because her visit was the first occasion of ticket speculation, and her success the result of canny advertising, the advent of Jenny Lind was epoch making. One ticket, sold at auction for her first concert in Boston, brought two hundred and twenty-five dollars, a fact which impelled her to write in a letter to her parents, "It is amazing what heaps of money they have here." Only a few months before this, the name of Jenny Lind was unknown to America, despite the fact that she had been for some years one of the outstanding figures on the operatic and concert stage in Europe and England. But P. T. Barnum, hearing of the furore she had created in London, resolved to risk his fortune in order to bring her to America. Having deposited one hundred and eighty-seven thousand dollars in her London bank as a security to the singer, he set about advertising her so well that the curiosity of a million people was awakened. Her first recital at Castle Garden, September 11, 1850, was attended by a huge enthusiastic crowd. In a short time she was the most talked of woman in America, and her concert tour of one hundred and thirty-seven cities, including Havana, was a continuous triumph. In 1852 she and Barnum dissolved their contract, which had netted each a fortune, and for a short time she continued her concert work alone, but in the same year she married Otto Goldschmidt, a Boston pianist, and returned to England, which was her home for the rest of her life. According to an English critic quoted by Ireland, "Her voice is a pure soprano, of the fullest compass of voice belonging to this class, and of such evenness of tone, that the nicest ear can discover no difference of quality from the bottom to the summit of the scale. Her lowest notes come out as clear and ringing as the highest, and her highest are as soft and sweet as the lowest: mellow roundness distinguishes every sound she utters. Much of the effect of this unrivaled voice is derived from the physical beauty of its sound, but still more from the exquisite skill and taste with which it is managed, and the intelligence and sensibility of which it is the organ." Jenny Lind captured the American public not alone by her voice but also by the probity, the graciousness, and the generosity of her nature. The last quality was demonstrated by her distribution of more than fifty thousand dollars in charity during her visit to the United States. She toured America at a peculiarly happy time. The fierce conflict of interests which had flared up between North and South had been resolved by the Compromise of 1850. The desire to forget the controversy was widespread. In 1852 as Jenny Lind was nearing the end of her American triumph, the nation mourned the passing of those prophets of nationalism whose last great work had been the settlement of 1850, Webster and Clay.

511   First Appearance of Jenny Lind at Castle Garden, September 11, 1850, from an engraving in possession of the publishers

512 Phineas Taylor Barnum, 1810–91,
     from a photograph in the Davis Col-
     lection

513   Caricature of Barnum by Spy, in
              Vanity Fair, London, 1889

514   Barnum and Commodore Nutt, from a pho-
        tograph in the Davis Collection

THE MASTER SHOWMAN

JENNY LIND'S American manager was born in Danbury, Connecticut. Before he started his Big Business he was in turn clerk, storekeeper, lottery agent, auctioneer, newspaper editor, and boardinghouse keeper. In 1835 he purchased Joice Heth, a toothless, withered, old negro woman, and introduced her as the one-hundred-and-sixty-one-year-old nurse of General George Washington to a public that seemed to be waiting to be taken in. With the money gleaned from the pockets of the curious, Barnum purchased a boat and sailed down the Mississippi, playing theatricals and making a collection of odd and interesting objects as he went along. In 1841 he purchased Scudder's Museum at the corner of Ann Street and Broadway, New York, and gave his own name to the new Emporium. Having placed there his patiently assembled curiosities, Barnum soon popularized his museum as an institution unique in New York and in the United States, a reputation retained until, in 1868, the building was destroyed by fire. It was here in 1842 that he exhibited the dwarf Charles Stratton, or Tom Thumb, with such success that the ambitious promotor was inspired, in 1847, to present his new attraction to the audiences of Europe. While abroad he heard continuous talk of Jenny Lind, but it was not until three years had elapsed that he conceived the plan which, when executed, marked the climax of his career. The fortune he made from her concerts was lost in speculation, and, for a number of years, he retired to private life. In 1890 he again appeared before the public with a prize novelty, his big traveling menagerie and circus. His last spectacular feat was the introduction to America of another European favorite, "Jumbo, King of Elephants," an introduction effected with much the same strident publicity as when, forty years before, he had announced the arrival of the "Swedish Nightingale." Barnum's philosophy is summarized in his words, "The American people love to be humbugged," and his success proved the validity of his dictum.

515   Barnum's Roman Hippodrome, from *Frank Leslie's Illustrated Newspaper*, May 9, 1874

516 Exhibition at Barnum's Museum, from a poster in the New York Historical Society

BARNUM'S MUSEUM

BARNUM'S MUSEUM, for decades the most talked-about and popular resort in America, and the home of Nature's pet abnormalities, was in a sense the forefather of the modern circus "side-show." The woolly horse, the white negress, the automaton writer, the Japanese mermaids, the white whales, gave continual delight to the inquisitive of the 'fifties, just as the wild man of Borneo, the lion-faced boy, and the Siamese twins did in more recent years. The career of the midgets, Tom Thumb, Commodore Nutt,

517 Exhibition at Barnum's Museum, from a poster in the New York Historical Society

Minnie and Lavinia Warren, which extended over continents, began at Barnum's Museum. In conducting this institution Barnum applied his theory that the one indispensable qualification of a good showman is "a thorough knowledge of human nature, which of course included the faculty of judiciously applying *soft soap* . . . the faculty to please and flatter the public so judiciously as not to have them suspect your intention." Besides the exhibit rooms, however, there was a "Moral Lecture Room" in which moral plays and farces were presented in a manner unique to New York — as many as twelve being sometimes given in one day. Here, during the early days, appeared many actors, later prominent on the legitimate stage, such as George Chapman, Maria Barton, Barney Williams, E. A. Sothern, and the Martinetti Family. The matinee performances, popular particularly with the children of New York and of nearby communities, were well patronized until the destruction of the Museum by fire in 1868. A characteristic production was that of *Dred*, a dramatization of Mrs. Stowe's novel of that name, in which Tom Thumb played the part of Tom Tit.

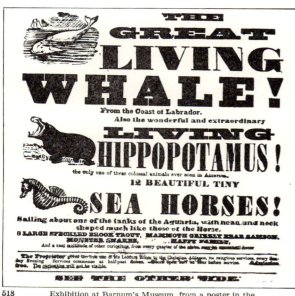

518   Exhibition at Barnum's Museum, from a poster in the
New York Historical Society

519   Exhibition at Barnum's Museum, from a poster
in the New York Historical Society

520   George C. Howard as St. Clare, from a lithograph
        in the Houdini Collection

521   Cordelia Howard as Little Eva, from a lithograph by
        C. Currier after a drawing by J. L. Magee, in the Houdini
        Collection

UNCLE TOM'S CABIN

A PRODUCT of the intense antipathy of the anti-slavery elements in the North to the Fugitive Slave Law of 1850 was *Uncle Tom's Cabin* (see Volume XI). Mrs. Stowe's novel both expressed and augmented the vivid emotions of the times. It achieved political significance. Scarcely had the book appeared and begun its extraordinary success when dramatic producers recognized that it contained the elements necessary for a gripping melodrama. In August, 1852, a stage version by C. W. Taylor was produced at Purdy's National Theater, New York, but it failed after eleven performances. A version prepared by George L. Aiken met a very different fate. First played in September, 1852, at the Museum in Troy, New York, with G. C. Howard, manager of the theater, as St. Clair, Mrs. Howard as Topsy, and their daughter Cordelia as Eva, it ran for a hundred nights before it was transferred to Albany and then to New York, where it was performed over two hundred successive times. During the latter part of this run it was given eighteen times a week, the company eating their meals in costume behind the scenes. The Howards later toured the nation as far west as St. Louis and as far south as Baltimore. Their success as well as that of the book itself aroused the bitterest resentment in the South, whose people considered the work an inexcusable misrepresentation of conditions in their section. The Howards with their play followed the book to successes in Great Britain. In contrast with its success in America, however, the vogue of *Uncle Tom's Cabin* abroad ended with the Civil War.

522   Mrs. George C. Howard, 1829–1908, as Topsy,
        from a lithograph in the Houdini Collection

523   Performance of *Uncle Tom's
        Cabin*, 1859, from a poster in the
        Harvard Theater Collection

524 Harriet Beecher Stowe, 1811–96, from a
photograph in the Davis Collection

THE LATER HISTORY OF *UNCLE TOM'S CABIN*

THAT *Uncle Tom's Cabin* contained the elements of successful melodrama and was not dependent for its effect merely upon the emotions of the times has been demonstrated by the persistence of the play after the close of the great sectional conflict. In the 'nineties it was part of the repertoire of every touring company and was referred to as the "Tom Show." In 1902 there were sixteen companies acting the melodrama in tents. There exists a cycle of stories about these mushroom shows — one, for instance, of the stage manager, who, on the illness of the lead-

525 Liza, crossing on the Ice, from a lithograph in the Houdini Collection

ing actress, took the rôle of Topsy himself, although he rejoiced in the possession of a heavy black beard. In spite of such absurd makeshifts and glaring inconsistencies of action and character, a generation of theatergoers from Boston to Red Gulch followed with unfailing interest the fortunes of Eva, Topsy, Miss Ophelia, Shelby, St. Clair, Simon Legree, and Uncle Tom. And in the year of sophistication, 1928, *Uncle Tom's Cabin* became one of the sensations of the silver screen.

THE BOSTON THEATER

ALTHOUGH before the Civil War New York was becoming more and more completely the heart and center of American theatrical activity, it would be an error to assume that its former rivals were giving up the struggle. During the 'fifties and 'sixties there were five theaters in Boston, the Adelphi, the National, the Howard Athenæum, the Boston Museum, and the Boston Theater. When this last named company was incorporated in 1852 the historic Federal Street Theater, with its venerable associations, had been destroyed by fire earlier in the same year. Thomas Barry, later a close friend of Edwin Booth, was appointed manager of the new theater, and immediately sailed for Europe for the purpose of securing adequate stage scenery and costumes. The new house was constructed in more modern fashion than either of its older rivals, being noted for beauty of line as well as for its size and appointments. Barry opened the new theater on September 11, 1854. The auditorium, which was lighted by a "great chandelier, the admiration and delight of the century," had a seating capacity of over three thousand. The paneled clock over the proscenium, the spacious lobby, the smoking room,

526 Thomas Barry, 1799–1876, from an engraving in the Fridenberg Collection

were other features that aroused the enthusiasm of the first-nighters. This enthusiasm was not universally shared, however, for on the Sunday preceding the opening a bitter sermon of denunciation was preached in Mt. Vernon church, entitled, "The Love of Pleasure, occasioned by the opening of a new theater in Boston." In spite of these criticisms, the new theater prospered, and became a part of the social and intellectual life not only of Boston but also of Harvard College and of the Massachusetts Institute of Technology, students of both institutions often appearing on its stage as supers. During the first season there were presented such favorites as *The Rivals, The Loan of a Lover*, and *A New Way to Pay Old Debts*. Julia Dean was the first star to appear, and she in turn was followed by Forrest. It was at the Boston Theater that Rachel played in 1855, and Edwin Booth in 1857. Until 1870, when its prestige began to wane, the Boston Theater had one of the finest stock companies in America.

ARCH STREET THEATER

527 John Drew, Sr., 1827–62, from a photograph by Handy in the Madigan Collection

528 Mrs. John Drew, 1820–97, from a
reproduction of a miniature in the John
Drew Collection, in *Scribner's Magazine*,
November 1899

IN the 'fifties the star system, so deplored by William Wood in his *Personal Recollections*, showed signs of breaking down. Wallack and Burton were working against it in New York, and the new managers of the Arch Street in Philadelphia were initiating a stock company there. Since its opening in 1828 this theater had had many managers, among them William Forrest, William Jones, Francis Wemyss, and W. E. Burton, and was identified, more than the other houses, with native American drama and dramatists. Stock companies had been attempted, but it was not till 1853 that a resident company was formed comparable to that of the old Chestnut Street of Warren and Wood. In that year John Drew, who, as well as his wife (Louisa Lane), had appeared on the Philadelphia stage during the 'forties, and William Wheatley, of a wide theatrical experience, leased the Arch Street Theater, and soon formed a company that attracted the finest audiences in the city. After the second season Drew left the partnership, and until 1860 Wheatley conducted the theater alone. In that year he leased the theater to Mrs. John Drew, and two years later opened Niblo's Garden with great success. Mrs. Drew developed a stock company at the Arch Street Theater that not only was famous throughout the country, but also served as a training school for some of the best actors of later years.

ANOTHER OPERA HOUSE FOR NEW YORK

FOUR times grand opera had attempted to obtain a permanent domicile in New York, and four times the effort had ended in quick failure. When in 1854, however, the Academy of Music was built at the corner of Fourteenth Street and Irving Place, the city at last obtained a house which proved to be a continuous home of at least moderately successful opera for a long term of years. The Academy, with a seating capacity of four thousand six hundred and an immense stage, was one of the largest theaters in America. At the outset the house was under the management of James H. Hackett, who opened it with Bellini's *Norma*, October 2, 1854. Ole Bull, the famous Norwegian violinist, became the lessee in February, 1855, but his management was brief and disastrous, and the stockholders soon took over the control of the house. In April they brought out Rossini's *William Tell* and in May Verdi's *Il Trovatore*, both for the first time in New York. Later managers were Max Maretzek, at one time conductor at the Academy, Maurice Strakosch, and Bernard Ullmann.

WHEATLEY AND DREW'S
ARCH ST. THEATRE
MANAGERS, - - - {WM. WHEATLEY / JOHN DREW.}
AGAIN
RESTORED!
To-Night, Tuesday, Oct. 10, 1854
SHAKSPEARE'S
PECULIAR & POPULAR
COMEDY
OF
ERRORS
80th Time by the Star Company

529 Program of the Arch Street Theater,
in *Scribner's Magazine*, November, 1899. Original in the John Drew Collection

The house was destroyed by fire, May 21, 1866, but was rebuilt and reoccupied in March of the following year. It continued as the center of grand opera in New York, during its later years under the direction of Colonel James H. Mapleson, until it was superseded in 1883 by the Metropolitan Opera House. The Metropolitan steadily grew in significance until to-day it is the most important opera house in the world.

530   The Academy of Music, New York, from an engraving in the
Fridenberg Collection

531 Giuseppe Mario, 1810–83, from a photograph in the Davis Collection

A GREAT STAGE LOVER

ONE of the most distinguished singers ever to appear at the Academy of Music was Giuseppe Mario, Count of Candia. The most famous tenor of the nineteenth century, he had had a brilliant career in Paris and London, in the latter city being regarded as the greatest stage lover ever seen. When he came to America his powers were at their height. Moreover he was known as the handsomest man on the stage. It is not surprising, therefore, that during his engagement for the season of 1854, he achieved a triumph here and brought in large finan-

532 Julia Grisi, 1811–69, from an engraving
in the Davis Collection

cial returns for himself and the management. A co-star who splendidly supported Signor Mario and gained an equal success was the soprano, Julia Grisi, a native of Milan. After singing on the Continent she gained a preëminent reputation in London in 1834. As a vocal artist she was thought to surpass all rivals by virtue of the exquisite purity of her voice and her high gift as a tragic actress. At the time of her American appearance she was somewhat past her prime as to both voice and personal appearance, but she too was received with great acclaim. Two years after their season here these brilliant vocalists became husband and wife.

"WALLACK'S"

A HOUSE that became as much of a New York institution in the field of drama as did the Academy of Music in the field of opera was Wallack's Lyceum. Built in 1850 as Brougham's Lyceum at the corner of Broadway and Broome Street, it had enjoyed scant success until taken over and opened September 8, 1852, by James W. Wallack. Its prosperity, thanks in part to the low prices of fifty and twenty-five cents, was almost instantaneous. It "soon succeeded," wrote Ireland, "not only in rivaling, but in a measure superseding Burton's Theater in public esteem. The hand of a master was visible in every production, and the taste, elegance, and propriety displayed about the whole establishment gave it a position of respectability never hitherto enjoyed in New York, except at the old Park Theater." Year after year Wallack brought out a succession of new comedies, English, French, and American that had never before been seen in this country. To interpret these plays he gathered about him a company of marked excellence, to which he continued to add new actors of distinction at frequent intervals. In consequence the Lyceum was recognized as the leading theater of the city as long as Wallack occupied

533   Wallack's Broome Street Theater, from a print in the
New York Historical Society

it, and when he moved up Broadway to Thirteenth Street in 1861, to take possession of a new theater, he transferred this excellent reputation along with his other effects. This new house, known as Wallack's Theater, was the home of a brilliant stock company until 1882.

534   Lester Wallack (left) and James W.
Wallack, Sr., from a photograph in
the Davis Collection

535 John Lester Wallack, 1820–88, from a photograph in the Davis Collection

536 Lester Wallack as Rob Roy, from a photograph in the Davis Collection

537 Lester Wallack as Leon del Mar in *The Veteran*, from a photograph in the Davis Collection

"MR. LESTER"

One of the popular figures at Wallack's Lyceum was the son of the manager. John Lester Wallack was born in New York while his parents were making their first visit to this country. Educated in England, he made his first stage appearances there, and eventually reached the Haymarket Theater, London, where among other rôles he played Mercutio to Charlotte Cushman's Romeo. On September 27, 1847, he made his American début at the old Broadway, New York, and in 1850 he was connected with Burton's Theater. For a time he appeared as "Mr. Lester," the name he had used in England, but before many years he was designated only as Lester Wallack. His rise in public favor was steady and by 1852 he was a member of his father's company, taking leading parts and also serving as stage manager. Being a Wallack, he was a handsome man — according to Ireland (1867) "for many years the handsomest man on our stage, the most graceful and gallant in his carriage and bearing . . . he is, nevertheless, rather slender in person, and his fine features are somewhat deficient in variableness of expression. With the highest capabilities otherwise for his profession, and with undoubted merit as the general juvenile hero of all modern comedies, he has had but one rival and no superior during all this time, and we know of no one who can justly be called his peer. His worst faults . . . are a tendency to turn legitimate comedy into farce, and a habit of being too familiar with his audience." Among his rôles were Orlando, Benedick, Young Marlow, Captain Absolute in *The Rivals*, Charles Surface in *The School for Scandal*, and Count de Jolimaître in *Fashion*. His activities included the writing of a number of plays, among them *The Veteran* and *Rosedale*, and the adapting of several others.

538 Lester Wallack as Eliot Grey in *Rosedale*, from a photograph in the Davis Collection

539 Lester Wallack as Leon del Mar from a photograph in the Davis Collection

540 Lester Wallack as Charles Marlow in *She Stoops to Conquer*, from a photograph in the Davis Collection

"A FUND OF QUIET HUMOR"

ONE of the most popular comédiennes at Wallack's Lyceum was Mary Gannon, whose first stage appearance had been made at the age of three. When Garrick's farce, *Lilliput*, was given at the National Theater, New York, in 1837, she played the part of Lady Flimnap, and at Philadelphia her acting in the same play earned her the name of the "Lilliputian Wonder." In 1848 she was playing adult rôles at Mitchell's Olympic, New York, and winning a delighted following. She became one of the Wallack company in 1855, and quickly took her place among the most brilliant members of the troupe. "Entirely original in her style," wrote Ireland, "with a truthfulness to nature almost unparalleled, and a fund of quiet humor apparently inexhaustible, she has in some characters never been approached in merit, is in none surpassed, and is now [1866], universally acknowledged to be the best general comic actress in the city."

541 Mary Gannon, 1829–68, from a photograph in the Davis Collection

A SENSE OF THE THEATER

CONNECTED for a short time with Wallack's as a writer of plays and general director was the brilliant and erratic Dion Boucicault. Born in Dublin of a French father and an Irish mother,

542 Dion Boucicault, 1822–90, from a sketch by Spy in *Vanity Fair*, London, 1882

he was educated to be an architect and engineer, but the success of his comedy, *London Assurance*, which was produced at Covent Garden in 1841 with Charles Mathews and Madame Vestris in the cast, convinced him that the theater was his proper field. In 1853 he came to America, where for years he carried on an active career as a playwright. His first considerable play to be written in this country was *The Poor of New York*, adapted from a French piece, *Les Pauvres de Paris*. It was brought out at Wallack's in 1857, and was later altered by its adapter into *The Poor of Liverpool* and *The Streets of London*. Among Boucicault's most successful plays was *The Octoroon* (1859), based on Mayne Reid's novel, *The Quadroon*. Though dealing, like *Uncle Tom's Cabin*, with negro slavery, *The Octoroon* is in no sense a propagandist play, but employs the theme solely for its dramatic value. So successfully did the author accomplish his purpose that the play was loudly applauded on both sides of the Mason-Dixon line. *The Octoroon* was long popular and was performed in many American cities as well as in London. Shortly after this success Boucicault began exploiting his native Ireland for dramatic purposes. *The Colleen Bawn*, again a dramatization of a novel, was first produced at Laura Keene's Theater in 1860, where it had an unusual run, and it proved even more popular in England and Ireland. Other dramas of a similar sort followed, among the most effective being *The Shaughraun*, brought out at Wallack's in 1874. The dominating character in the play is the lovable, irresponsible wanderer, Conn. Boucicault's Irish plays are important as being among the most truthful delineations of the Irish temperament ever written in

America. Another division of Boucicault's work consists of dramatizations of famous English novels, including *The Cricket on the Hearth*, *Nicholas Nickleby*, and *The Heart of Midlothian*. Always a writer of great industry, he wrote or adapted at least one hundred and twenty-four plays, many of them based on French originals. Boucicault possessed little originality in the matter of plot invention, but in theatrical effectiveness, in the devising of thrilling stage business and striking contrasts of character and motive, he was something of a genius. In a word he possessed in an unusual degree a sense of the theater.

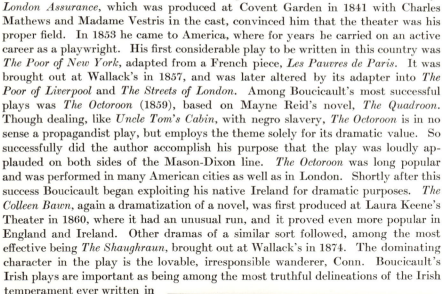

543 Scene from Boucicault's *The Colleen Bawn*, from a woodcut in the 1864 edition of the play

544   Dion Boucicault, from a photograph
         in the Davis Collection

BOUCICAULT AS ACTOR

BOUCICAULT's talents were not confined to the writing of plays. The success of his dramas was due to some extent to his skillful acting of character parts in them. Irish rôles were peculiarly congenial to him, and he made one of his most distinctive stage impressions in this country as the loyal and self-sacrificing Myles-na-Coppaleen in *The Colleen Bawn*. His impersonation of Conn in *The Shaughraun* was equally admired. His acting, however, was all of the intellect, according to William Winter,

545   Boucicault as Conn in *The Shaughraun*,
        from a photograph in the Davis Collection

who wrote in *Other Days:* "He was himself as cold as steel, but he knew the emotions by sight, and he mingled them as a chemist mingles chemicals; generally, with success." He was associated with various New York theaters, including Niblo's Garden, and for a short time in 1859 was one of the managers of the Winter Garden, formerly the Metropolitan Theater. Here he brought out several of his plays, including *The Octoroon*. But after this play had been running a week, he withdrew from the establishment because of a disagreement over his salary. In 1860 he took *The Colleen Bawn* to England and remained there for some years engaged in various theatrical ventures. He returned to America in 1872 and spent most of his remaining years here. Although he made a fortune through his plays, his manner of living was extravagant and he died in greatly reduced circumstances.

Boucicault has been credited by his biographer, Townsend Walsh, and by Dr. Arthur Hobson Quinn in *A History of the American Drama from the Beginning to the Civil War*, with responsibility for the development of the traveling company with a single play. He conceived the idea of sending a second company around the theatrical circuit while the play was enjoying a New York run. His first play to be so presented was *The Colleen Bawn* in 1860. "There were obvious difficulties," writes Dr. Quinn, "but the success of the project from a financial point of view led the managers, one by one, to adopt the new idea and the disintegration of the stock companies began."

"THE FAIRY STAR"

WHEN Dion Boucicault came to America in 1853 he was accompanied by his wife, the lovely Agnes Robertson. The beauty and simplicity of this young Scottish woman quickly won for her a devoted following in this country. William Winter in *Other Days* declared her to be "one of the most charming players, in *ingénue* parts and in light comedy, who have graced our stage." These qualities gained her the name of "the fairy star." Not only in New York but also through the South and West she was an outstanding favorite. At Boston an engagement of two weeks was extended to eight by popular demand, and four hours after Miss Robertson consented to add a ninth week every seat was sold. She played in numerous dramas by her husband, originating such rôles as Jeanie Deans in his version of *The Heart of Midlothian*, the Scotch heroine of *Jessie Brown, or The Relief of Lucknow*, Zoe in *The Octoroon*, and Smike in *Nicholas Nickleby*.

546   Agnes Robertson Boucicault, 1832–1916, from a wash-drawing
        by Henry Tanner, in the collection of Montrose J. Moses

THE SENSATION OF A SEASON

Dumas' languishing and consumptive courtesan, Camille, was first represented in this country by Jean Davenport (see No. 453), but it was Mathilda Heron who, at Wallack's Lyceum in 1857, made the part the sensation of a season. Her peculiar success arose, no doubt, from what William Winter has called her "repulsive naturalness, her wildness of emotion, force of brain, and vitality of embodiment." Before this triumph Miss Heron had been acclaimed in many other rôles. Born in Londonderry, Ireland, she grew up with a desire to act, studied with Peter Richings, and in 1851 at the Walnut Street Theater played Bianca in *Fazio*, studying Lady Macbeth, Juliet, Mariane (*The Wife*) and Pauline (*The Lady of Lyons*) at the same time. In 1852 she played Juliet to Charlotte Cushman's Romeo, with such talent that T. S. Hamblin engaged her for the Bowery, where she presented Lady Macbeth in August, 1852. The next year she went to the Arch Street Theater, and to Boston, playing with J. E. Murdoch. In 1854 she appeared in California and soon became a royal favorite in the West. After this she made a début at Drury Lane, and paid a visit to Paris. Seeing Madame Doche in *La Dame Aux Camelias* inspired her to make a translation and present it to an American audience. She was at Wallack's many years and in addition to her regular repertoire played in *Lesbia* and *Mathilde and Gamea*, two plays from her own pen. During these later years, however, *Camille* was her only real success.

547 Mathilda Heron, 1831–77, from a photograph in the Davis Collection

OUR FIRST WOMAN MANAGER

To Wallack's must be given the distinction of having introduced to America the actress who later became the first woman manager in the United States. Laura Keene, while still a child in her native city of London, received great inspiration from some performances of Rachel given in a theater so near her home that the great tragédienne's voice could be easily heard. She studied with Madame Vestris, and in 1851 appeared at the Olympic as Pauline in *The Lady of Lyons*. In September, 1852, she began an American engagement at Wallack's Lyceum, but after a short time she left, despite her success there, and opened a theater of her own in Baltimore. Soon after, she started on a tour around the world. Late in 1855 she took over the New York Metropolitan Theater, erected in 1854, which she altered throughout and opened to the public under the new name of Laura Keene's Varieties. The next year, Burton having obtained this house through a flaw in her lease, she built a new playhouse by subscription, on Broadway near Houston Street, and for eight years Laura Keene's theater was one of the popular establishments of New York.

548 Laura Keene, 1820–73, from a photograph in the Davis Collection

549 Laura Keene, from a photograph in the Davis Collection

XIV—14

OUR AMERICAN COUSIN

At Laura Keene's New Theater occurred in 1858 the first performance on any stage of Tom Taylor's *Our American Cousin*, with Miss Keene as Florence Trenchard. This once famous comedy had a continuous run of one hundred and forty nights. For years Miss Keene was closely identified with this play. It was during one of her performances of *Our American Cousin* in Washington that President Lincoln was assassinated. In 1869 Miss Keene became manager of the Chestnut Street Theater, Philadelphia, and organized a strong stock company in which she was a prominent

550   Laura Keene (left) and Mrs. Dion Boucicault in *The Heart of Midlothian*, from a photograph in the Davis Collection

551   Laura Keene as Lady Teazle, from a playbill in the Davis Collection

performer. As an actress Miss Keene possessed considerable talent, being especially distinguished by her unusual versatility. As a manager she was imperious and tempestuous and was often involved in quarrels with her company. She was a woman of courage and resolution and, considering the troubled period during which she labored, she achieved an honorable success.

552   Interior of Laura Keene's New Theater, from a print in the New York Public Library

553 Edward Askew Sothern, 1826–81, from a photograph in the Davis Collection

554 Sothern as David Garrick, from a photograph in the collection of H. A. Ogden, New York

555 Sothern as Lord Dundreary, from a photograph in the Davis Collection

"LORD DUNDREARY"

Our American Cousin brought fame to others besides the manageress. The name most intimately associated with Taylor's comedy is that of Edward Askew Sothern, whose impersonation of the rôle of Lord Dundreary was largely responsible for the long popularity of the play. Sothern, a native of Liverpool, was destined by his father for medicine, but he resolved to make a player of himself. After acting for a time in the English provinces under the name of Douglas Stuart, he came to the United States and made his American début at Boston, November 1, 1852. His performance was a failure. To gain experience in varied parts he obtained a position as comedian at Barnum's Museum, New York, where performances were given two or three times a day. The fall of 1854 saw him a member of the company at Wallack's where he supported some of the principal actresses, in particular Mathilda Heron, to whose Camille he played the lover Armand Duval. In later years he regarded his work in this part as the "worst performance ever seen." In 1858 Sothern, now a member of Laura Keene's company, was cast for the slight and seemingly barren part of the English fop, Lord Dundreary. Joseph Jefferson's *Autobiography* presents this account of the matter: "Sothern was much dejected at being compelled to play the part. He said he could do nothing with it, and certainly for the first two weeks it was a dull effort, and produced but little effect. So in despair he began to introduce extravagant business into his character, skipping about the stage, stammering and sneezing, and, in short, doing all he could to attract and distract the attention of the audience. To the surprise of everyone, himself included, these antics, intended by him to injure the character, were received by the audience with delight." By degrees he improved the part, by magnifying the British lord's vacuity, bland self-assurance and gravity, until it became the hit of the play and made him a famous and eventually wealthy comedian. In his hands the rôle became a caricature of a certain type of English "swell" not unknown at the time, a type that affected long side whiskers, sometimes called "Piccadilly weepers," and a drawling, haw-haw style of speech. *Our American Cousin* held the stage for years, largely because of Sothern's Dundreary. London also received the character with immense satisfaction, for by this time it had grown until it was the central feature of the play. Sothern appeared in numerous other rôles, including Benedick and Charles Surface, but he never duplicated the Dundreary success. Of this impersonation William Winter has written in *Other Days*: "The prodigious sapience of Lord Dundreary's disjointed colloquies with his sweetheart and with his servant rose to the height of comic humor. The manner in which the man's mind stumbled and fell over itself cannot be described. No one but Sothern could do it, or has ever done it since." That being true, Sothern must shoulder the chief responsibility for the popular conception of the English aristocrat that has ever since widely prevailed among us.

556   Joseph Jefferson, III, 1829–1905, from a
           photograph in the Davis Collection

A NEW STAR

OUR AMERICAN COUSIN gave another comedian his first great opportunity. After the Mexican episode (see p. 169) Joseph Jefferson
had journeyed to Philadelphia and obtained a small position at
the Arch Street Theater, where his half-brother, Charles Burke
(see No. 273), was second comedian under the managership of
W. E. Burton. On Burke's withdrawal from the company
Jefferson was elevated to his rôles. Shortly after leaving Burton
he was engaged as low comedian at Foster's Amphitheater in
Philadelphia, but Jefferson was not long in discovering that the
task of being the funny man in an equestrian show was a very
serious business indeed. His next undertaking was in the managerial field on the southern circuit, the troupe performing in
such towns as Macon, Savannah, Charleston, and Wilmington,
North Carolina. At
Charleston his play-
ers were joined by
the beautiful Julia
Dean, with whom he
had acted in the
utility ranks seven
years before under
the management of
Ludlow and Smith.

557   Jefferson as Caleb Plummer in Boucicault's *Dot*,
         from a photograph in the Davis Collection

But Miss Dean was now a rising star, and thanks to her great
popularity Jefferson and his partner, at the end of the week,
divided between themselves the — to them — unheard of sum
of eighteen hundred dollars. Leaving management, Jefferson
accepted an engagement as first comedian at the Chestnut
Street Theater.
After several
other ventures he
was engaged in
1857 as leading
comedian by
Laura Keene, for
her New York theater. He first appeared as Dr. Pangloss
in Colman's *Heir-at-Law*, and was described by one of the
critics as a "nervous, fidgety young man, by the name of
Jefferson." But when Miss Keene the next year cast him
for the part of the Yankee, Asa Trenchard, in *Our American
Cousin*, this young man by the name of Jefferson immediately became one of the town's favorite actors. He and
Miss Keene, however, often had serious differences of opinion in respect to the conduct of the play, on one occasion
even exchanging high words in the midst of the performance
and in full view and hearing of the audience. Consequently
at the end of the season he deemed it the part of wisdom to
withdraw from her company. After taking *Our American
Cousin* on tour for a time, he accepted an advantageous
offer from the Winter Garden, where he first appeared as
Caleb Plummer in Boucicault's *Dot*, an adaptation of *The
Cricket on the Hearth*, and later played a prominent part in
the same playwright's *Octoroon*.

558   Jefferson as Rip Van Winkle, from an engraving after the
        painting by N. R. Brewer, in *Leslie's Weekly*, May 1, 1902

"A POET AMONG ACTORS"

559   Jefferson as Young Rip, from a photograph in the Davis Collection

560   Jefferson as Old Rip, from a photograph in the Davis Collection

In 1859 Jefferson reworked three old stage versions of Irving's *Rip Van Winkle*. The new play was first presented at Washington, and its author's fame and fortune were assured. In 1861 Jefferson made a professional trip to California, and from there took ship for Australia, where he acted with much success during the four years of the Civil War in such plays as *Rip Van Winkle*, *Our American Cousin*, and *The Octoroon*. In 1865 he left for England, stopping on the way for an informal visit in South America.

In London Boucicault rewrote *Rip Van Winkle* and gave the play its permanent form — except that Jefferson always felt free to make any change he wished. Its London run, with Jefferson in the title part, lasted one hundred and seventy nights. On his return to America he devoted himself largely to the character of Rip, in which he repeatedly traversed the country from one end to the other. Second only to Jefferson's Rip in public favor was his Bob Acres. He had assumed this rôle first as a young actor, but it was not until he made his revision of Sheridan's comedy that Acres became one of his famous characters. It was, however, primarily as Rip Van Winkle that Jefferson retained his place in the hearts of countless thousands of American playgoers until his final appearance in the rôle in 1904, the year before his death.

Jefferson's admirers were by no means confined to the ranks of the casual theatergoers. The dramatic critic, William Winter, wrote in *Other Days:* "The magical charm of his acting was the deep human sympathy and the loveliness and individuality by which it was irradiated, — an exquisite blending of humor, pathos, grace and beauty, that made it an intimate and confidential impartment to each and every mind and heart in all the vast auditory that he addressed. . . . Discovery of the charm of Jefferson's acting was not difficult to those who saw him act. Designation of it was never easy. . . . Examination of the characters of Rip and Acres, — in which two parts he fully revealed himself, — with analysis of his interpretation and expression of them would arrive at the result, disclosing and defining an exceptionally rich and various nature, combined with great felicity of dramatic art. Those parts he, literally, created; for Rip, as Jefferson displayed him, never existed until he made him manifest; and the Acres that he embodied was a higher and finer type of man than the Acres drawn by Sheridan, a far more exquisite fabric of whimsical humor." Winter awarded him "the rank of a poet among actors. . . . *Rip Van Winkle* . . . as interpreted by Jefferson . . . had the irresistible charm of poetry."

561   Joseph Jefferson, from a portrait by John Singer Sargent (1856–1927), in the Grand Central Art Galleries, New York

562   Jefferson as Bob Acres, from a painting by John Singer Sargent in the Players' Club, New York

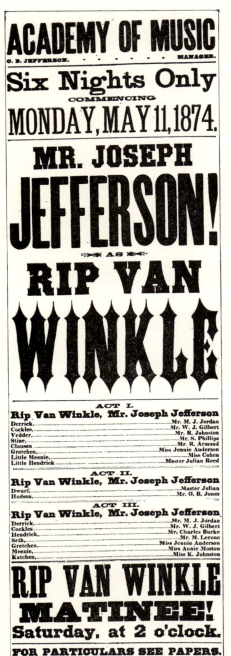

563   Jefferson as Rip, from a playbill in the
Davis Collection

ALL HIS WARD-ROBE IN A GRIP-SACK

OTHER critics have found Jefferson not devoid of faults. Henry Austin Clapp has said in *Reminiscences of a Dramatic Critic:* "Personally, I make little account of that cheerful, chirping libel upon Dickens's creation which Mr. Jefferson has labeled Caleb Plummer, and no very great account of that effervescent *petit maître*, light of step and glib of tongue, into whom he has trans-

564 Jefferson as Dr. Pangloss in Colman's *Heir-at-Law*, from a photograph in the Davis Collection

formed Sheridan's clodborn Bob Acres, though I admit the actor's delicate drollery in both impersonations. Mr. Jefferson can point, it seems to me, to but one work of supreme distinction, the sole and single product of his life, the masterpiece of our stage, — the figure of the immortal Rip." Charles Mathews accused him of carrying all his wardrobe in a gripsack, that is, of being a one-part actor, and he added: "Look at that huge pile of trunks — mine, sir, mine! Examine my list of parts! Count them — half a hundred, at the very least; you ought to be ashamed of yourself." To which Jefferson replied: "My dear Charlie, you are confounding wardrobe with talent. What is the value of a long bill of fare if the stuff is badly cooked? You change your hat, and fancy you are playing another character. Believe me, it requires more skill to act one part fifty different ways than to act fifty parts all the same way." In *Sixty Years of the Theater* by John Ranken Towse occurs the following estimate of Jefferson's ability as an actor: "Now none of the parts in which Jefferson delighted his audiences could by any stretch of the imagination be called great. None of them sounded the heights or depths of emotion, lofty flights of imagination or passion, or demanded the

565 Jefferson (right) and W. J. Florence in *The Rivals*, from a photograph in the Davis Collection

exhibition of uncommon intellectual, moral, or dramatic power. They all lay within the limits of the middle register. . . . Wherein then . . . is to be found the secret of Jefferson's popularity and fame? The answer is easy. In his consummate artistry and his personal fascination." Jefferson was by no means the greatest actor America has produced, but he was in all probability the best beloved.

THE FLORENCES

566 William James Florence, 1831–91, from a photograph in the Davis Collection

567 Florence as Hon. Bardwell Slote in *The Mighty Dollar*, from a photograph in the Davis Collection

A FAVORITE actor who supported Jefferson in some of his leading rôles was the Irish comedian, William James Florence. He was born at Albany with the family name of Conlin. Making his début on the professional stage at Richmond, Virginia, in 1849, after some vicissitudes he joined the company at Niblo's Garden, New York, in 1850, and also acted at the Broadway and Brougham's Lyceum. In 1853 he married Malvina Pray, and the pair entered upon a long period of starring, appearing often in Irish or Yankee plays of his writing. Florence also composed many songs, in the singing of which his wife delighted the public. In 1856 the Florences visited London and appeared successfully at Drury Lane, where Mrs. Florence was the first American comic actress to play on the English stage. A very profitable tour of England, Scotland, and Ireland followed. Returning to America in 1861 Florence played at Wallack's for a time, produced several burlesques there during summers, and in 1863 brought out at the Winter Garden Tom Taylor's *Ticket-of-Leave Man*, giving one of the best performances of his life in the character of Bob Brierly. The most famous of his rôles, however, was that of the Hon. Bardwell Slote in *The Mighty Dollar* by Benjamin E. Woolf. At one time he was associated with Jefferson, playing Sir Lucius O'Trigger to his Bob Acres, and Zekiel Homespun to his Dr. Pangloss. Jefferson listed Florence among the most successful comedians of his time.

568 Malvina Pray Florence, 1830–1906, from a photograph in the Davis Collection

569 Mrs. Florence as Mrs. Gilflory in *The Mighty Dollar*, from a gravure by Gebbie & Husson, in the possession of the publishers

570 Barney Williams, 1823–76, from a
photograph in the Davis Collection

MR. AND MRS. BARNEY WILLIAMS

A PAIR somewhat comparable to the Florences were Mr. and Mrs. Barney Williams. Bernard O'Flaherty, born in Cork, Ireland, had come as a boy to America and in 1840 made his first hit, under the name of Barney Williams, as Pat Rooney at the Franklin Street Theater, New York. Small, agile, quick of apprehension, a fair singer, and a good dancer, he was soon regarded as a powerful attraction. In 1850 he married Mrs. Charles Mestayer, formerly Maria Pray, sister of Mrs. Florence, and by assuming the characters of the Yankee "gal" and the Irish boy the couple introduced to the stage several new pieces which

571 Mr. and Mrs. Williams, from a
photograph in the Davis Collection

proved highly successful because of the humor and vivacity of the principals. In 1854 Mr. and Mrs. Williams made a successful tour of the Union, not stopping until they reached California, and in 1856 they entered upon a long and equally prosperous series of performances in London and the English provinces. On their return to America in 1860, they were enthusiastically welcomed when they made their reappearance at the newly named Winter Garden, formerly Burton's Metropolitan Theater. During the succeeding years they were popular favorites at Niblo's Garden, the Broadway, and the Winter Garden, and made annual starring tours, appearing with equal success in the West, South, and East. The acting of Mrs. Williams was marked by brilliance and versatility. Her husband lacked the finish of Power and Brougham, but as the conventional Irishman of low life he was unrivaled in popularity although he had many imitators. As the author of several successful plays Williams increased his already large income until he became one of the richest actors of his day.

"THE FIRST ACTRESS OF THE WORLD"

THE decade which saw the American appearance of such celebrated foreign women as Lola Montez, Jenny Lind, and Julia Grisi witnessed also the reception in this country of Elizabeth Rachel Felix, the greatest tragédienne of France. Born in Switzerland of poor Jewish peddlers and reared in poverty and ignorance, she early rose to become, in Ireland's phrase, "the first actress of the world." After many vicissitudes she made a début at the Théâtre Français in 1838, and the fame of Rachel was established. For several years her brother Raphael, stirred by the tales of Barnum's fabulous profits from Jenny Lind's tour, urged her to make a trip to the United States, promising her riches and honor. But Rachel had no desire to venture into a "wilderness," and it was not until 1855 that she reluctantly consented to undertake the venture. The company, which included her sister Sarah, made its first American appearance at the Metropolitan Theater, New York, on September 3, in Corneille's *Horace*. One of Rachel's most applauded rôles was that of Camille in this tragedy, but its true proportions could hardly be appreciated by an audience only five per cent of which understood French.

572 Elizabeth Rachel Felix, 1821–58,
as Phèdre, from a photograph in the
Davis Collection

Most of the spectators tried to follow the drama with a translation, and Leon Beauvallet, a member of the troupe, describes in his amusing history of the tour the clamor that fell upon his startled ears as one thousand leaves crackled simultaneously. Gate receipts as a whole fell far below expectations, her première bringing in less than a third as much as the Nightingale's opening night. Subsequent appearances at Boston and Philadelphia likewise proved disappointing financially, partly, it is probable, because Rachel's powers were deteriorating as a result of continued ill health. During her tour a consumptive tendency from which she suffered was aggravated by a severe cold. She made her last appearance on any stage at Charleston on December 17, and then returned to France, where she died scarcely more than two years later.

AN ARTIST IN TRAVESTY

573 George L. Fox, 1825–77, from a photograph in the Davis Collection

574 Fox, the Clown, from a photograph in the Davis Collection

575 Fox in a burlesque of *Hamlet*, from a photograph in the Davis Collection

DESPITE the steadily increasing rumblings that presaged the Civil War, the decade of the 1850's was a decade of comedians. Another of the genial brotherhood to place alongside Burton, Owens, Chanfrau, Florence, and Williams was George L. Fox. His first stage appearance was made at the age of five in Boston and his New York début occurred in 1850. As a clown and pantomimist he soon came to hold a unique place. In 1859 in partnership with the actor James W. Lingard, Fox opened the New Bowery Theater near Hester Street, and here for the edification of the East Side he presented a little of Shakespeare and a good deal of *Fast Women of a Modern Time* and other sensational pieces. In the early 1860's he was for a short time manager of the old Brougham Lyceum, which now went under the name of George L. Fox's Olympic. After serving as a volunteer in the Civil War, he took over the old Bowery and later held the post of stage manager at Mrs. John Wood's Olympic. At this house in 1868 he appeared in the once famous pantomime *Humpty Dumpty*, in which he is said to have acted twelve hundred and sixty-eight times in New York alone. His peculiar art was best seen, however, in his travesties of Hamlet and Macbeth and in similar burlesques. Edwin Booth declared his Hamlet to have such beauty of understanding in its humor that it was a very great Dane indeed. Laurence Hutton ranked his Bottom in *A Midsummer Night's Dream* among the best and thought him "one of the few really funny men of his day upon the American stage." By providing humorous diversion during the Civil War, Fox served the Union as genuinely as he did in the field.

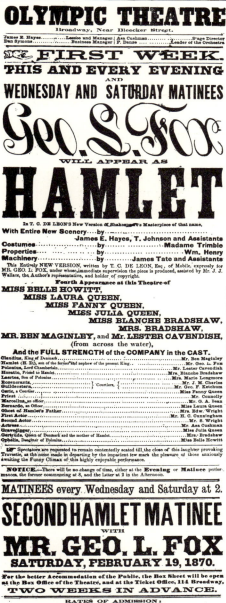

576 Fox as Hamlet, from a playbill in the Davis Collection

CHAPTER IX

EDWIN BOOTH AND CONTEMPORARIES

WE have seen that the theater was not seriously affected by the troubled events which immediately preceded the Civil War. This is, perhaps, not surprising. But surely, one would suppose, the cataclysm of the Civil War itself must have a profound influence on the stage. Yet such appears not to have been the case. At the very outset a number of theaters were closed because of the unsettled state of affairs, but by 1862 theatrical business seems to have been in a comparatively normal condition once more. In fact the history of the northern theater during the 'sixties is to a very considerable degree a record of growth and success. In this it reflects the increasing prosperity of the North; for the conflict, instead of checking, rather augmented the development of industrialism in that quarter, and war profiteering brought into being a new and large class of men of wealth, as it has been known to do in more recent times. As for the playwrights, they occasionally took their themes from the war during the years of the struggle, sometimes dramatizing important events almost as soon as they occurred, but from the standpoint of theatrical art the results were entirely negligible. Between 1861 and 1865 the plays that were performed by the most prominent and successful companies were in the main standard British pieces. Into the lives of numerous actors, to be sure, the conflict introduced certain changes. Some, abandoning for the time their stage careers, hastened to join the colors. Others employed their talents for the entertainment or inspiration of the soldiers in the field, as did many of the profession during the World War. But the majority of actors continued their accustomed work far from the danger of battle. Perhaps they were suspected of timidity or disloyalty for their failure to shoulder arms, but such an attitude would have done them injustice. As we found during the recent war, the actor performs a service of the highest value by employing his best efforts for the entertainment of the civilian population at a time when men's nerves are stretched to the breaking point and their spirits are on the edge of panic. In such a crisis an ably presented play, by bringing self-forgetfulness through laughter or through sympathy for others, does more than is commonly realized to preserve a calm and rational state of mind when that element is vitally needed.

There is one respect in which the stage, about the middle of the century, showed the shaping influence of certain Civil War conditions. Oratory in America was never so widespread or on so high a plane as during the years that preceded and included the great conflict. The appeal of the cause of abolition to the loftiest human sentiments, and the tragic consequences to the Union latent in the irreconcilable opposition of North and South, inspired eloquence such as the nation has known at no other period of its history. This was the era of Henry Clay, of Theodore Parker, of Henry Ward Beecher, of Edward

Everett, of Wendell Phillips, of Daniel Webster, of the Lincoln-Douglas debates, of the Second Inaugural and the Gettysburg Address. From almost every platform in America some passionate voice was speaking. The platform within the theater responded to this condition, and the stage rang with a noble eloquence that took something of its tone from the fervor pervading the national struggle. The great actors of the day, Edwin Forrest, Charlotte Cushman, John McCullough, Lawrence Barrett, and above all Edwin Booth, were products of a time which felt the greatness of the spoken word and was swayed by its power.

A consideration of such names as those just listed brings the conviction that the middle decades of the nineteenth century represent almost the high-water mark of American acting. Logically the period should have been peculiarly distinguished by the staging of great dramas. But this was not the case. The outstanding sensation of the 'sixties was *The Black Crook*, as gorgeous in decoration as it was barren in substance; and it was followed by others of its kind whose incredible banality caused the judicious to grieve. Possibly this situation should be laid in part at the door of the war, which left the public weary in spirit and with a preference for mere diversion when it went to the theater. The blame must certainly be shared by the poverty of the contemporary drama of England, upon which source our producers had always heavily relied. But the major responsibility must be assumed by the American managers and theater owners, who, in their desire to profit as richly as possible from the popularity of the stage, were building immense theaters in whose splendid distances the legitimate type of drama was almost lost. In enormous houses like Niblo's Garden, where *The Black Crook* was brought out, little could be successfully produced except elaborate spectacles full of color, movement, and music.

The Black Crook was the most sensational innovation of the 'sixties, but it was not the most important or far-reaching one. During that decade the so-called "combination system" was introduced, a pronounced change in theatrical procedure which has remained with us to the present day. This system abandoned the stock company tradition; abandoned also, in part, the individual star; and instead established the method of choosing the actors with special reference to the play in which they were to appear, each performer being selected because by temperament and appearance he was adapted to a particular rôle. Joseph Jefferson, who took to himself much of the credit or blame for inventing the system, thus defended it in his *Autobiography:* "The performers themselves are not better than those who acted under the old form of dramatic government, but on the principle of 'selection' a more perfect unity has been evolved. And further, the vast continent of America, with its wonderful and progressive cities thousands of miles apart, seems to have demanded the establishment of this important institution. The inhabitants of these distant places, having fine opera houses, enjoy the advantages of seeing the same plays acted by the same companies as those of the larger cities. If they can afford and appreciate it, then they deserve it, and these entertainments can only be administered by the combination system." In the development of this idea is clearly evident one of the significant effects of the expanding railway system upon the American stage. Henceforth "the road" was to exert a powerful influence on the theater.

577   Lester Wallack, from a photograph
in the Davis Collection

578   . Wallack's Thirteenth Street Theater, from a print in the New York
Historical Society

WALLACK'S IN THE SIXTIES

DURING the 1860's, as during much of the preceding decade, the most brilliant company in America was that assembled under the Wallack banner. Carrying on a distinguished family name and a time-honored form of theatrical organization — the stock company — this group made the new Wallack Theater, erected in 1861 at the corner of Broadway and Thirteenth Street, the most famous playhouse in this country. When James W. Wallack died in 1864, his son Lester (see No. 535) succeeded him in the control of the theater. He pursued his father's excellent policy of maintaining a talented stock company instead of relying for his appeal on visiting stars. It was essentially a company of comedians, among the best of them being Wallack himself, and not only were the outstanding comedies of the day produced but the older English comedy from Shakespeare to Holcroft was given renewed attention and presented with great spirit. In the field of artificial comedy — that is, in such plays as *The School for Scandal* — the company has probably never been surpassed in America. Wallack continued his lavish and varied seasons at the Thirteenth Street house until 1882, when Wallack's again moved north to the corner of Broadway and Thirtieth Street. Here Lester continued to rule and occasionally to act until his retirement in 1887, a year before his death.

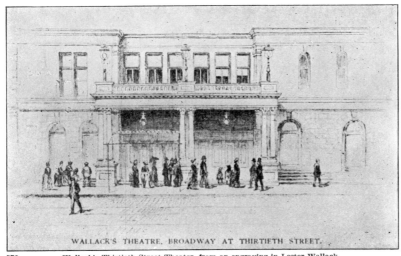

WALLACK'S THEATRE, BROADWAY AT THIRTIETH STREET.

579   Wallack's Thirtieth Street Theater, from an engraving in Lester Wallack,
Memoirs of Fifty Years, New York, 1889

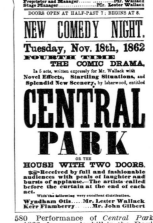

580   Performance of *Central Park*,
1862, from a playbill in the Davis
Collection

581 Elizabeth Ponisi, 1818–99, from a photograph in the Davis Collection

582 Harry J. Montague, 1843–78, from a photograph in the Davis Collection

583 Effie Germon, 1849–1914, from a photograph in the Davis Collection

584 Mrs. John Hoey, d. 1893, from a photograph in the Davis Collection

585 John Gilbert (right) with Dion Boucicault in *The Shaughraun*, from a photograph in the Davis Collection

586 Madeline Henriques, from a photograph in the Davis Collection

THE WALLACK STARS

The company that Wallack assembled in the 'sixties was of an excellence that, according to William Winter, could not have been matched in the second decade of the present century except by combining the best actors of a dozen of the best companies in America. Madeline Henriques, for several years the leading lady, had had only amateur experience before joining Wallack's in 1860, but by her exquisite refinement and the beauty with which she depicted the milder emotions, she soon rose to first line parts. Perhaps the most remarkable member of the company was John Gilbert, who was connected with the house from 1861 until 1888. He was one of the best impersonators of old men our stage has ever known. Mark Smith, who entered the company in 1862, was a much loved player, hearty in everything he did, careful and studied, yet thoroughly natural in his acting. In 1872 Mme. Elizabeth Ponisi, an English actress, joined the ranks. In the rôles of old women and aristocratic dames she occupied a distinguished place. Harry J. Montague was an attractive and clever light comedian, who first appeared at Wallack's in 1874 and shortly became the matinée idol of the house. Other noted players who were associated with Wallack's at one time or another were E. L. Davenport, George Holland, Rose Eytinge, Charles Fisher, John Brougham, Effie Germon, Rose and Charles Coghlan, Dion Boucicault, and Mrs. John Hoey.

587 Junius Brutus Booth and Edwin Booth,
     from a photograph in the Davis Collection

EDWIN BOOTH,
1833–1893

THE 'sixties and later years were also marked by the prominence of an actor who, like Wallack, bore a distinguished name and who represented the newer system of the individual star. Edwin Booth, son of the gifted and erratic Junius Brutus Booth, was born in Harford County, Maryland. After a brief education he began accompanying his father. His first stage appearance was made in 1849 at the Boston Museum as a

588 Edwin Booth, from a photograph in the
     Davis Collection

minor character in *Richard III*. During the next two years he played many small parts with his father without attracting much attention. An illness of the elder Booth in 1851 gave Edwin a sudden chance to assume the rôle of Richard III and he successfully stood the test. From 1852 to 1856 he was playing in California, Australia, and the Sandwich Islands, and developing an enviable reputation. On his return to America he toured the South and then in 1857 made his first important appearance in New York at Burton's Metropolitan Theater as Richard III. Four years later he appeared in London, but his English popularity was not great at this time. Returning to America in 1862, he soon became one of the proprietors of the Walnut Street Theater, Philadelphia. The next year he joined with two others in leasing the New York Winter Garden, where he gave a series of Shakespearean productions surpassing in magnificence anything this country had yet seen. As Hamlet he appeared for one hundred consecutive nights, establishing a Shakespearean record for America. During this period occurred a memorable performance of *Julius Caesar* with the parts of Cassius, Mark Antony and Brutus taken by the three brothers, Junius Brutus, Jr., John Wilkes, and Edwin. Five months later the mad act of John Wilkes Booth plunged the nation into mourning. Overwhelmed by the tragedy, Edwin withdrew from the stage for several months. His reappearance at the Winter Garden in January, 1866, on the insistence of the public, was hailed with the greatest enthusiasm.

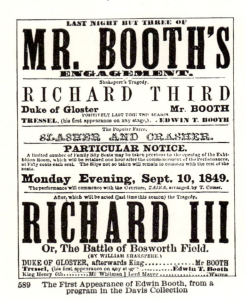

589   The First Appearance of Edwin Booth, from a
        program in the Davis Collection

590   Booth as Hamlet, from a photograph in the
       Davis Collection

591   Edwin Booth, with his wife and daughter, from a photograph
in the Madigan Collection

592   Booth as Iago, from a photograph in the
Davis Collection

BOOTH'S LATER CAREER

In 1867 the Winter Garden was destroyed by fire. Booth shortly set about building a theater of his own at the corner of Sixth Avenue and Twenty-third Street. This house, erected at a cost of a million dollars, was opened as Booth's Theater, February 3, 1869. No effort had been spared to make the house safe for the audience and comfortable for the actors. The proprietor organized an excellent stock company and devoted himself chiefly to Shakespearean productions of a splendid and expensive nature. Although he was admirably supported by the public, his management was highly uneconomical, and his enormous expenses forced him into bankruptcy in 1874, with the attendant loss of his entire fortune. During the remainder of his career Booth devoted himself to starring tours throughout the country, with three visits to London, where at the Haymarket Theater he achieved a brilliant success. In 1882 he visited Germany and was received with the highest approbation. His health declining in his last years, he took his farewell of the stage at the Brooklyn Academy of Music as Hamlet, April 4, 1891, two years before his death.

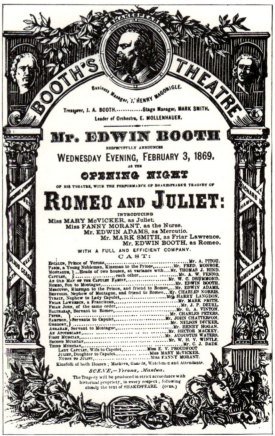

593   Booth's Theater, 23d Street and 6th Avenue, New York City,
from an engraving in the Fridenberg Collection

594   Opening Night of Booth's Theater, from a program
in the Davis Collection

595   Booth as Richelieu, from a photograph
            in the Davis Collection

BOOTH'S PLACE AS AN ACTOR

Was Edwin Booth a great actor? Certainly he had his limitations, for in comedy he was seldom happy. His physique was not sufficiently massive for the wholly successful assumption of such characters as Macbeth and Othello. By habitually surrounding himself with supporting players who lacked training or ability, he committed one of the gravest errors of the starring system. But in his proper sphere Booth was superbly endowed. His beautiful head, his rich, melodious voice, his remarkably clear enunciation, his penetrating intellect, and his perfected art splendidly fitted him to impersonate some of Shakespeare's most subtle and profound tragic figures. As Shylock, Hamlet, Iago, and Lear he reached a height of dramatic impressiveness that has probably not been seen since his day. If he was preëminently

596   Edwin Booth, from the portrait by John
Singer Sargent, in possession of the Players' Club,
New York

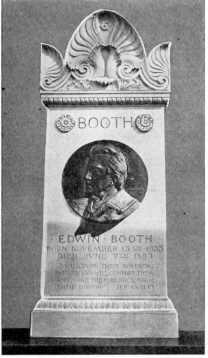

598   Tombstone of Edwin Booth, from a photograph in the Davis Collection

the interpreter of the royal Dane, a part for which his extraordinary grace, beauty, and eloquence peculiarly fitted him, perhaps the explanation is found partly in a sentence from *Sixty Years of the Theater* by John Ranken Towse: "In his life the sweet and the bitter were mingled in almost equal proportions; and there can be little doubt that his private afflictions, most courageously endured, added to his artistic temperament that touch of grave and tender melancholy so well suited to his Hamlet. . . ." In view of the fact that his name looms so large in the consciousness of later generations, perhaps it is not too much to style Edwin Booth the foremost actor America has produced.

597   Booth and Barrett in *The Merchant of Venice*,
from a playbill in the Davis Collection

599 Group of the Founders of the Players' Club, from a photograph in possession of the Players' Club, New York

600 Library at the Players' Club, from a photograph in possession of the Players' Club, New York

"THE PLAYERS"

BOOTH's influence upon his fellow actors was widespread and beneficent. It took its most tangible form in the organization of The Players in 1888, a club in whose inception he was a moving spirit.

Booth, Lawrence Barrett, Augustin Daly, and Albert M. Palmer conceived the idea of establishing a club similar to the Garrick Club in London, where the theatrical profession might mingle with writers, artists, and interested men of affairs. A luncheon to adjust preliminaries, held at Delmonico's, was attended by those named above, as well as by Mark Twain, Thomas Bailey Aldrich, Brander Matthews, John Drew, and others, and here Aldrich proposed the name of "The Players." Booth, with the approval of his associates, purchased at his own expense the house at 16 Gramercy Park, and presented it to the organization, reserving for his own use a suite of rooms on the third floor. Stanford White immediately undertook the remodeling of the house. In his address at the formal opening Booth said in part: "Although our vocations are various, I greet you all as brother Players. At this supreme moment of my life, it is my happy privilege to assume the character of host, to welcome you to the house wherein I hope that we for many years and our legitimate successors for at least a thousand generations, may assemble, for friendly intercourse and intellectual recreation." The mellow quarters on Gramercy Park continue to house The Players, which is to-day the leading theatrical club of the United States. From the point of view of the public its most valuable activity is the all-star revival of old English dramas, which for some years has been one of the most delightful events of each spring season.

601 John Sleeper Clarke, 1833–99, from a photograph in the Davis Collection

"THE EASE OF A SECOND NATURE"

A COMEDIAN associated in various ways with Booth was John Sleeper Clarke. He obtained his first taste of acting as a member of a Thespian Club in his native Baltimore, a society of which Booth was an active member. After first appearing professionally at the Howard Athenæum, Boston, in 1851, he rose rapidly and was soon serving as leading comedian at the Front Street Theater, Baltimore, and later at the Arch Street, Philadelphia. From 1861 he was a conspicuous favorite in New York. Two years later he became associated with Edwin Booth, whose sister he had married in 1859, as joint-manager of the Winter Garden. The association was of short duration, however, for Clarke was drawn away by an interest in the Walnut Street Theater, Philadelphia, and the Boston Theater. In 1867 he went to London and, achieving immediate success, made his home thereafter in England except for an American tour in 1870, during which he appeared at Booth's Theater. "At the beginning of his career," wrote William Winter, in *The Wallet of Time*, "Clarke wished to play tragedy, but he soon discovered his true bent, and throughout life he was faithful to the Comic Muse, and by her he was abundantly rewarded." His most popular rôle was that of Major Wellington De Boots in *Everybody's Friend*, a part he played over a thousand times in America. Other impersonations of his were Bob Acres, one of the Dromios, Dr. Pangloss, and Dr. Ollapod. "Life struck his mind," again according to Winter, "at the comic angle, and his constitutional methods of response to its influence were either drolly playful or downright comic. . . . He acted with the ease of a second nature, that makes the observer oblivious of the skill which alone could produce such effects."

602 The Arch Street Theater, Philadelphia, from a photo-engraving in *The Delineator*, September, 1923

AN IRISH COMEDIAN

JOHN DREW, SR., who was associated with the Philadelphia stage more intimately than Clarke, was, like him, a comedian of unusual powers. Coming to America from Ireland, he made his début at the Richmond Hill Theater, New York. Following his marriage to Louisa Lane (see No. 528) in 1850, his name became prominent in the Philadelphia theaters, and in 1853 the Arch Street Theater came under the management of Drew and William Wheatley. Three years later Drew acted a star engagement under Jefferson's management in Richmond, Virginia, and between 1858 and 1862 he toured California, Australia, and England. Among his rôles were Sir Lucius O'Trigger, one of the Dromios, and Goldfinch. But his proper line was the Irish peasant, to whose impersonation he was able to bring a blend of comedy and sentiment that few could equal. "I think it has been generally conceded," wrote Jefferson, "that since Tyrone Power [see No. 427] there has been no Irish comedian equal to John Drew. Power, as a light and brilliant actor, . . . was undoubtedly unparalleled in his line, but I doubt if he could touch the heart as deeply as did John Drew."

OUR SECOND WOMAN–MANAGER

IN 1861, during her husband's absence on his foreign tour, Mrs. John Drew took over the control of the Arch Street Theater, and provided Philadelphia with one of the outstanding chapters in its theatrical annals. Some of the most celebrated actors of the time, such as Lester Wallack, Edwin Booth, and Charlotte Cushman, appeared in her theater, and in her own stock company were developed several future stars. Her success lasted for about eight years, and during that time her establishment ranked among the most important and artistic theaters in America; but with the decay of the stock company she was compelled to adapt her organization to the newer combination system, under which her prosperity declined. She remained in charge of the Arch Street, however, until 1892. Of Mrs. Drew as a manageress it has been said: "She was always a wonderful disciplinarian; hers was said to be the last of those green-rooms that used to be considered schools of good manners. Some women descend to bullying to maintain their authority — not so Mrs. John Drew. Her armor was a certain chill austerity of manner, her weapon a sharp sarcasm, while her strength lay in her self-control, her self-respect."

603 Mrs. John Drew, from a photograph in the Davis Collection

604 Mrs. Drew, from a photograph in the Madigan Collection, New York

605 Mrs. Drew as Mrs. Malaprop, from a photograph in the Davis Collection

606   Performance at the Arch Street Theater, Philadelphia, from a sketch in *Frank Leslie's Illustrated Newspaper*, December 27, 1879

607   Interior of Niblo's Theater, New York, from a sketch in *Ballou's Pictorial*, February 24, 1855

WILLIAM WHEATLEY, 1816–1876

DREW's partner in the management of the Arch Street Theater, William Wheatley, was a native American, both of whose parents were actors. He began his stage career as a juvenile actor at the Park Theater, New

608   William Wheatley, from an engraving in the Fridenberg Collection, New York

York, and while still a boy scored heavily in the play of *Tom Thumb*, which was arranged especially for him. He gradually rose to more mature responsibilities at the Park, and in romantic comedy parts gained an excellent reputation, especially in rôles of a showy and pictorial nature, such as Captain Absolute. In such characters as Romeo and Hamlet he satisfied the eye by his handsome face and fine person, but his interpretation left something to be desired in the matter of depth and intensity. In 1853 Wheatley became associated with Drew in the management of the Arch Street Theater, where he also appeared often on the stage. After Drew left, Wheatley conducted the theater alone for a time, and then in partnership with John Sleeper Clarke until his own withdrawal in 1861. A year later he leased Niblo's Garden, New York, and brought that house into great favor by producing the most elaborately romantic and spectacular dramas the city had ever seen. Before his retirement in 1868 his theater had been visited by many of the leading stars of his time, including Forrest, Hackett, Mathilda Heron, and Booth. Wheatley exerted a very considerable influence upon the art of the stage, chiefly in the direction of theatrical display.

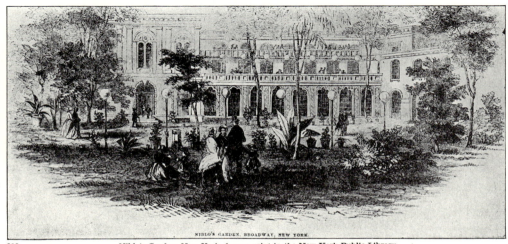

NIBLO'S GARDEN, BROADWAY, NEW YORK.

609   Niblo's Garden, New York, from a print in the New York Public Library

610 John McCullough, 1832–85, as Virginius, from
a photograph in the Davis Collection

"GENERAL JOHN"

DURING their co-management of the Arch Street Theater, Drew and Wheatley introduced to the professional stage an actor who later became one of the most celebrated players of his time. John McCullough, born of a humble family in Ireland, was so uneducated when he emigrated to America at the age of fifteen that he could not even write. His first contact with acted drama was sufficient to convince him that his vocation was the stage.

611   McCullough as Othello, from a photograph in the Davis Collection

After his first professional appearance, in 1857 at the Arch Street Theater, he gradually rose by dint of hard work until, in 1861, Edwin Forrest engaged him to play opposite him in such parts as Laertes, Macduff, Iago, and Edgar. In this capacity McCullough traveled through the country for several seasons and in 1866 he accompanied Forrest to California. Here he made so favorable an impression that influential citizens induced him to remain as manager of the California Theater in San Francisco in partnership with Lawrence Barrett. McCullough continued his managership for eight seasons, and then, returning to the East, made his first starring appearance in New York as Spartacus in Bird's *The Gladiator*, one of the favorite vehicles of Forrest. Numerous American tours followed, which greatly increased his popularity and profits. The summer of 1881 was spent at Drury Lane Theater, London, where he was somewhat coolly received. His final years were occupied with further touring in America until his health and mind broke in 1884. A year later he died insane. McCullough was essentially an actor of heroic parts. He was imperfectly fitted for Hamlet, but as Othello, Brutus, Coriolanus, and above all Virginius in Sheridan Knowles' play of that name, he came near to greatness. For such parts his noble presence, classic features, and ringing voice excellently equipped him. "A dis-

612 McCullough as Spartacus, from a photograph
in the Davis Collection

ciple of Forrest," wrote John Ranken Towse in *Sixty Years of the Theater*, "he emulated the methods of his exemplar with considerable success, and in stormy bursts of passion he exhibited vast power. Moreover, he could assume a lofty dignity, in which Forrest was lacking, and had a notable mastery of virile pathos. He excelled in broad strokes, in the vivid contrasts between raging passion, portentous calm, and the inner convulsions caused by repressed emotions. But he was not an intellectual, imaginative, or analytical performer." At the same time his acting was always profoundly sincere.

613   McCullough as Coriolanus, from a photograph in the Madigan Collection, New York

614 Lawrence Barrett as Cassius, from
a photograph in the collection of H. A.
Ogden, New York

615 Barrett as Hamlet, from a photograph in the Davis Collection

LAWRENCE BARRETT, 1838–1891

For the first four years of his California managership, McCullough had as partner a greater actor than himself. Like McCullough, Lawrence Barrett, though born in this country, was the son of Irish parents and was reared in ignorance and penury. He early gained a humble position in a theater in Detroit, whither his parents had gone from his native town of Paterson, New Jersey. After being entrusted with a few minor rôles he obtained an engagement at Pittsburgh where for two years he played with a stock company and then in 1856 essayed New York. Here he soon obtained a place at Burton's Theater and was allowed to act with Edwin Booth and Charlotte Cushman. Two years later he joined the Boston Museum stock company. When the Civil War broke out Barrett entered the army and served for a time with distinction as captain in the 28th Massachusetts infantry regiment. In 1863–64 he was a member of Booth's company at the Winter Garden. From 1867 to 1870 he was associated with McCullough in the California project. Thereafter he acted mainly in the East except for a few professional visits to London. In 1882 he revived Boker's *Francesca da Rimini* (see No. 507) and made the part of the deformed Lanciotto one of his most brilliant characters. Five years later he assumed the management of Booth and later toured the country as a joint star with him in a repertory that included the great Shakespearean tragedies. This highly successful tour was terminated by Barrett's sudden death. Barrett was especially impressive as Lanciotto, Cassius in *Julius Caesar*, Richelieu in Bulwer-Lytton's drama, and Gringoire in *The King's Pleasure* adapted from the French by Alfred Thompson. Those who knew Barrett have left record of his austere and intellectual cast of mind, his tragic face, his beautiful voice, his remarkable elocution, his range, and his lofty ideals. "In losing Lawrence Barrett," wrote Winter, in *The Wallet of Time*, "the American Stage lost the one American actor who served it with an apostle's zeal because he loved it with an apostle's love."

MURDOCH IN THE CIVIL WAR

The Civil War inevitably brought profound changes into the lives of actors as of other citizens. Barrett is illustrative of the player who temporarily abandoned his profession for the soldier's vocation. Some found other modes of service, among them James E. Murdoch (see No. 242). While he was appearing at Pittsburgh in the spring of 1861, Murdoch learned that a favorite son had enlisted. Abruptly closing his engagement, he went to Washington, and there he associated with many prominent people in the work of arousing the patriotic spirit of the nation. Feeling that he could best serve through his art, he began giving patriotic readings and by his recitation of Drake's *The American Flag* he aroused his Washington audience to an uproar of enthusiasm. "From that time onward," it is said, "he gave himself up as absolutely to the country as any soldier in the field." He appeared in all the principal cities of the North, in soldiers' hospitals, in the camps of the army, sometimes even within sound of the enemy's guns, reciting such poems as Read's *The Wagoner of the Alleghanies*, Janvier's *The Sleeping Sentinel*, Bryant's *The Battle-field*, and Whittier's *Barbara Frietchie*. On one occasion, at a hospital camp near Indianapolis, after reading Taylor's *Scott and the Veteran*, Murdoch was almost overwhelmed by a crowd of excited veterans who rushed up to him to express their appreciation of the poet's heroic sentiments so indelibly impressed upon them by the reader's ringing eloquence.

616 James E. Murdoch, from an engraving in the Fridenberg Collection, New York

617 Avonia Jones, 1839–67, from a photograph in the Davis Collection

AN AUDIENCE OF SECESSIONISTS

YOUNG Augustin Daly had dreams of managerial greatness, and, like a wise man, he seized the first opportunity for experience that offered. Accordingly in 1864 he undertook to manage a southern tour of a minor star, Avonia Jones. His experiences were interesting and often amusing. The following is from Joseph Francis Daly in his *Life of Augustin Daly*, published by The Macmillan Co.: "Memphis, November 13, 1864. On Friday night I had my first taste of 'war.' You must know that everybody belongs to the militia here. No resident is exempt. They drill every week and all the stores are closed that day to let everyone turn out — white and black. When danger to the town is apprehended and these soldiers are needed the signal given for assembling is four reports of cannon and the ringing of all the bells. Then all have to seize their muskets and trot to rendezvous. Well, Friday evening about 9½ o'clock, and while the performance was going on to the biggest and most fashionable audience in the theater since it was built, the four cannon were heard and the bells commenced to ring. Lord! you never saw such a lot of scared people in your life as the men were. They started for the door pell-mell. . . . I told them there was nothing the matter, that those shots were only fired in honor of another victory of Sheridan in the Shenandoah. But it was no good. I only had my lie for my pains. 'Dat's all berry well, bress yer soul, Massa,' said one old codfish, 'but what for dem dere bells ringin'?' and off he went followed by the entire gallery. In three minutes we had only an audience of secessionists remaining."

ON THE WAY TO RICHMOND

PERCY MACKAYE in recounting the early Civil War days of his father, Steele MacKaye, quotes a vivid description from a contemporary newspaper of performances by a Thespian society of New York Union Volunteers, in Baltimore, Maryland, temporarily halted on their way to the Virginia front. "To break the monotony of camp life the soldiers formed 'The Seventh Regiment Amusement Association.' A stage was built within the hollow square, formed by the wings of the barracks. There on acting nights the trees of the parade ground blazed with Chinese lanterns. The scene presented the guise of a fashionable ball, for the audience of soldiers in dress uniform were all volunteers from among the first New York families, and the fair guests in crinoline . . . were drawn from the best society of Baltimore . . . for the evening of August 2, 1862, festal preparations ushered a scene from Othello in which J. Steele MacKaye played Othello and John H. Bird, Iago. . . . the evening ended with dancing and refreshments, while Grafulla's band played under the moonlit leaves, and the marching tread of passing regiments, going to the front, accompanied the dancers' feet. Growing ambitious the Association on August 8 rendered the *Merchant of Venice*, in which J. Steele MacKaye acted Antonio." *The Merchant of Venice* was followed by *Julius Caesar*, and on August 15 by *Hamlet* — a production, "remembered by Baltimore society as the most brilliant dramatic offering ever given in their midst."

7th REGIMENT
Amusement Association!

FORT FEDERAL HILL,
Baltimore, Aug. 15th, 1862.

THE REGIMENTAL BAND

OVERTURE—Fra Diavolo	AUBER
ALLG WELL	
POLKA REDOWA	GRAFULLA
WALTZ	STRAUSS

After the overture will be performed the Fourth and Fifth actions of the Tragedy of

HAMLET!

HAMLET	J. K. MAKATH
GHOST	P. D. GULAGER
HORATIO	B. A. SPRING
MARCELLUS	D. C. KISORLAND

Musical Interlude

Air, PER SEMPER—Aria Puritani	BELLINA
	A. K. VALENTINE
COMIC SONG	E. F. ROBERTS

618 Military Thespians at Baltimore, from a playbill in the possession of Percy MacKaye, Windsor, Vermont

---

The Performances will terminate, by a series of Tableaux, Illustrative of our

Victories at Fort Donelson!

In order to give Tone and effect to our series of

Living National Pictures,
☞ FIFTY U. S. SOLDIERS

Will appear in Military Groups.

Box Book now Open.   **Tickets for Sale everywhere.**

619 Representation of a Civil War Battle, from a playbill in the New York Historical Society

"LIVING NATIONAL PICTURES"

ANOTHER reflection of the Civil War is the notice of a performance at the Old Bowery Theater, New York — temporarily under the management of S. P. Stickney's National Circus — on March 5, 1862, which concluded with tableaux, depicting the Union victory at Fort Donelson under General Grant. Shortly after this, in May, the Bowery was taken over and occupied by Union troops.

THE ACTRESS LOOKS AT STATESMEN

620 Rose Eytinge, 1835–1911, from a photograph in the Davis Collection

OTHER war-time contacts were experienced by the actor, as *The Memories of Rose Eytinge* makes clear. That beautiful and uncontrollable actress, who performed with some of the leading players of her day, was a member of Wallack's company during the war, and spent a considerable time in Washington when the troupe was playing that city during the early period of the conflict. The company was lodged in a private house on Seventh Street, and thither the personalities of Lester Wallack and E. L. Davenport drew a group of prominent officials. In Miss Eytinge's words, "To those men who were making our history at that time in Washington, whose lives were so full of the hurry, the worry, and the fury of the fight, the talk of these two bright men offered such a sense of respite and refreshment that often, when the performance was over, we were joined at supper . . . by some of these more-or-less 'grave and reverend signiors,'" not to mention many of the leading newspaper men of the time. The company, playing in an insignificant little white-washed house called the Washington Theater, proved so welcome a diversion that it was able to play for many weeks to the best people in the city. Men and women of fashion, foreign ambassadors, and "boys in blue" were always much in evidence. President Lincoln attended several of the performances, and on one occasion invited Wallack and Davenport to the White House. They went, taking Miss Eytinge with them. "When, in my turn," she wrote, "I was presented to the President, he took my hand, and, holding it while he looked down upon me from his great height, said: 'So this is the little lady that all us folks in Washington like so much?'" On another occasion she met Secretary Seward, of whom she wrote, "It is impossible to think of two more contrasting personalities than those of Lincoln and Seward: the one so simple, warm-hearted, and free-spoken; the other so stately, cold, and dignified. When Mr. Seward spoke a few complimentary commonplaces to anyone, the person addressed felt as if he or she were participating in history."

THE ASSASSINATION OF LINCOLN

As all the world knows, the most tragic event of the Civil War period occurred in a theater. On the night of April 14, 1865, five days after the surrender of General Lee, Abraham Lincoln, worn by the long labors of his office, was attending a performance of *Our American Cousin*, given by Laura Keene's company at Ford's Theater, Washington. In the midst of the performance John Wilkes Booth, an actor (see p. 216), who had entered into a conspiracy with other Southern sympathizers to assassinate the principal officers of the nation,

621 John Wilkes Booth, 1839–65, from a photograph in the Davis Collection

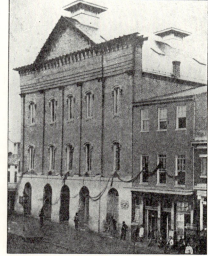

622 Ford's Theater, Washington, draped in mourning after the assassination of Lincoln, from a photograph in the Davis Collection

stealthily entered the President's box and from the rear fired a bullet into his brain. Then flourishing a huge knife, with which he wounded Colonel Rathbone, who tried to hold him, Booth leaped to the stage. In the fall his leg was broken, but, according to the legend, with the theatrical cry of "Sic Semper Tyrannis" he rushed through the stage door and escaped on a horse that had been made ready. Lincoln was carried to a house across the street, where he died at seven o'clock the following morning. As quickly as possible after the fatal act, a patrol was formed, which set out in pursuit of the assassin. Twelve days later he was shot down in a barn.

KATE BATEMAN, 1842–1917

623   Kate Bateman as Leah, from a photograph in the Davis Collection

THE repertory that Miss Avonia Jones used on her southern tour contained several plays adapted from foreign drama by her manager, Augustin Daly. But his first effort at adaptation had brought him into contact with a greater celebrity than Miss Avonia Jones, to wit, Kate Bateman. In their first youth Kate and her younger sister Ellen, daughters of theatrical parents, were the famous "Bateman children," widely known as the precocious impersonators of Richard III and other adult characters — a form of entertainment that once found high favor on our stage. At the age of twenty Kate played in New York as Juliet and Lady Macbeth, and then her father, Hezekiah Linthicum Bateman, looking about for a vehicle especially suited to her, hit upon Mosenthal's *Deborah*, which was then electrifying Vienna. Daly, at Bateman's insistence, had the play translated, and then adapted it into *Leah the Forsaken*. Bateman, staking all he had on the play, engaged an expensive company and brought it out in Boston, December 8, 1862. It was an immediate success and six weeks later was brought to Niblo's Garden, New York, where its prosperity continued. Thereafter Miss Bateman took the play to London where her tenderness, pathos, and dignity as the hapless Jewish maiden gained her an enthusiastic following. After her marriage to George Crowe in 1866 she confined her acting largely to the English stage, where, under her father's management, she appeared for a time with Henry Irving.

MRS. JOHN WOOD, 1831–1915

OWING to the success of *Leah the Forsaken* Daly was now in some demand as a writer of plays for the exploitation of special talents. One of those who thus engaged his services was Mrs. John Wood, manager of a New York theater. She had come from England to the Boston Theater in 1854; two years later she made her New York début with John Wood at Niblo's Garden, and before the year was out was acting at Wallack's. Her forte was burlesque, and in this field she became a general favorite, appearing in such burlesque pieces as *Hiawatha* and *Shylock*, in the latter of which she played Portia to her husband's title-rôle. Mr. and Mrs. Wood also appeared together in several musical burlettas. From 1863 to 1866 she was manager of the house that had been opened in 1856 as Laura Keene's Varieties, now called Mrs. John Wood's Olympic. In the first year of her managership she prevailed on Daly to provide her with a comedy; accordingly, with the aid of a friend, Frank Wood, he adapted Sardou's *Le Papillon* under the title of *Taming a Butterfly*. In 1869 she undertook the direction of St. James' Theater, London, but was back in the United States in 1872 and was

624   Mrs. John Wood, from a photograph in the Davis Collection

for a time a member of Daly's company (see Chapter X). In her later years Mrs. Wood returned to the London stage and was identified with a number of modern successes. Mrs. G. H. Gilbert in her *Reminiscences* wrote of her: "I think she is the most absolutely funny woman I have ever seen, both on and off the stage. The fun simply bubbled up in her. Then she could sing and dance a bit, and in the burlesques and farces she did, such as *The Sleeping Beauty* and *The Fair One with the Golden Locks*, she was inimitable." Ireland referred to her as "the charming Mrs. John Wood . . . generally acknowledged the best burlesque actress of the day."

625   Mrs. Wood, as Lady Gay Spanker in Boucicault's *London Assurance*, from a photograph in the Davis Collection

DALY AS A PLAYWRIGHT

626 Augustin Daly, 1838–99, from a photograph in the Davis Collection

627 Daly's Dramatization of *Griffith Gaunt*, from a playbill in the New York Historical Society

AMONG those who besought Daly to provide a play was Laura Keene, who wrote him saying she had an excellent idea and asking him to work it into a good acting part for her. Nothing came of this project, but, shortly after, Daly established connections with an able actress who starred in his next two plays. In November, 1866, he brought out, under his own management, his *Griffith Gaunt*, a dramatization of Charles Reade's novel. The rôle of the heroine, Kate Peyton, was entrusted to Rose Eytinge, a principal actress at Wallack's, who was released from her contract for this particular purpose. The effective acting of Miss Eytinge, especially in the murder trial scene, helped make the play a considerable success, and the next year when Daly produced his original play, *Under the Gaslight*, she again carried the lead. This melodrama contained, perhaps for the first time, the famous device of the hero bound to the railroad tracks by the villain, but released by the heroine just before the train reaches him. Such devices, added to a realistic setting, gave the play a long lease of life. Indeed it has been one of the most popular melodramas ever written in English, and naturally its author became something of a celebrity. In subsequent plays, such as *A Flash of Lightning* and *The Red Scarf*, he employed similarly thrilling tricks, in the latter, for instance, the device of the sawmill, in which the hero is rescued from the moving log just before it reaches the saw. These plays made a strong appeal by their realistic stage devices, and by the unblushing extravagance of their situations they cause Daly to rank as one of the leaders of the "ten-twenty-thirty" school of melodrama. He was, however, to do more substantial work in such pieces as *Horizon* (1871), a drama of the West, and *Divorce* (1871), a study of jealousy. On the whole, perhaps Daly's chief claim to importance as a dramatist lies in the fact that the fidelity of his settings and characters places him among the first of our modern stage realists.

628   Scene from Daly's *Under the Gaslight*, from a woodcut in the Davis Collection

629   John T. Raymond, 1836–87, as Colonel Mulberry Sellers, from a photograph in the Davis Collection

"THERE'S MILLIONS IN IT"

As a boy John T. Raymond ran away from home to go on the stage. He made his first bow at Rochester before he was seventeen; from there he moved to the Philadelphia theater, and later played on the southern circuit for several seasons. On Jefferson's departure from Laura Keene's Theater in 1861, Raymond was engaged to succeed him in such rôles as Asa Trenchard in *Our American Cousin* and other comedy parts. Six years later he acted Trenchard in London to the Dundreary of Sothern and then toured Britain and appeared in Paris with him.

630   Raymond and Mark Twain, from a photograph in the Davis Collection

In 1874 in New York he achieved the real success of his career as the cheerful speculator, Colonel Mulberry Sellers, in *The Gilded Age*, a dramatization, largely by Mark Twain, of his own novel; and in this character, with his famous tag phrase — "There's *millions* in it!" — Raymond gained much popularity throughout the United States and Canada. In 1879 he added to his artistic laurels by creating the part of Ichabod Crane in a dramatization of Irving's *Wolfert's Roost, or The Legend of Sleepy Hollow*. It was, according to William Winter, "one of the most quaint, humorous, and touching performances that have graced the comedy stage in our time." Raymond is said to have lacked the refinement and versatility of such an actor as Sothern, but his humor was marked by an abundance of animal spirits, a rich extravagance, and a solemn composure of countenance that made him a public favorite. The popularity of figures like Colonel Mulberry Sellers and Ichabod Crane indicates a continued interest in the dramatic presentation of distinctively American types of character, types hitherto illustrated by the Yankee, Rip Van Winkle, and Mose the Fireboy.

DAVY CROCKETT

ANOTHER actor of this period who gained his fame largely by his impersonation of a native American type was Frank Mayo, who began his career in 1856 at the American Theater, San Francisco. By 1865 he was leading man at the Boston Theater. But it was not until he assumed the title-rôle in Frank H. Murdoch's *Davy Crockett* in 1872 that Mayo became a celebrity. This thoroughgoing melodrama of the frontier, based on the historical figure of the Tennessee hunter who "found out what was right and went ahead," tells a thrilling tale of an unlettered backswoodsman with an arm of steel and a heart of gold, a maiden of superior station but an understanding soul —

"WOLVES! What can save us?"   "The strong arm of a Backwoodsman."

631   Scene from *Davy Crockett*, from a poster in the New York Public Library

and wolves. The play, produced by Mayo, was at first coldly received, but before long, by virtue of the actor's quiet, restrained manner, which gave reality to the extravagant romance, it caught on, and held the stage successfully for many years.

632   Frank Mayo as Davy Crockett, from a photograph in the Davis Collection

ADAH ISAACS MENKEN, 1835–1868

THE career of Adah Isaacs Menken provided her with more thrills than the heroine of *Davy Crockett* ever dreamed of. Her mother appears to have been a Creole and her birthplace New Orleans. At the age of thirteen she began her career as a ballet dancer at the Opera House in New Orleans, afterward filling a brief engagement in Havana. In 1852 she joined a traveling hippodrome and rapidly became an expert equestrienne, but, finding the hardship too great, a year later accepted the position of *première danseuse* at the Opera House in Mexico City. Captured by Indians in Texas, she escaped and returned to her native city where she practiced the art of poetry. In 1856 she married John Isaacs Menken, a Galveston Jew. Soon bored with her husband, she made her début as an actress in 1858 at New Orleans, and then played for five weeks on the southern circuit with great applause. In 1861 she appeared at the Green Street Theater, Albany, as the hero in *Mazeppa*, a popular and sensational play based on Byron's poem. Conscious of her fine figure, she created a great stir by allowing herself, clad in tights, to be bound to the horse for the scene of Maz-

633 Miss Menken in *Mazeppa*, from a poster in the Davis Collection

eppa's wild ride, whereas hitherto a dummy had always been used for the purpose. This feat made her an international character. To New York, Pittsburgh, St. Louis, California, London, Paris, and Vienna she carried the wonders of *Mazeppa*. She essayed other rôles, including Richmond in *Richard III* and yearned to attempt Rosalind, Julia, Beatrice, and Macbeth. Among her friends, she counted Mark Twain, Swinburne, Dickens, and the elder Dumas. Her career has become almost a legend.

634 Adah Isaacs Menken, from a photograph in the Davis Collection

A SMASH

ADAH ISAACS MENKEN's daring display of her charms in *Mazeppa* was a prophecy. *The Black Crook* was its fulfilment. This extravaganza would never have been the spectacular thing it became but for the burning of the Academy of Music just as Jarrett and Palmer, producers, were on the point of introducing a large group of imported ballet dancers in the opera, *La Biche au Bois*. William Wheatley, manager of Niblo's Garden, conceived the idea of incorporating the idle ballet troupe in a play by George Barras, called *The Black Crook*, which he had contracted to produce. In order to do this Wheatley found it necessary to make so many changes that practically nothing was left of Barras' manuscript but the title. After an elaborate advertising campaign, this spectacle opened September 12, 1866, and, in spite of the dreary twaddle of which the play consisted, at once became the great sensation of the day. It was the *corps de ballet* that captured the town.

A hundred beautiful girl dancers clad, according to Olive Logan, "in close-fitting flesh-colored silk 'tights,' and as little else as the law will permit," were such an alluring sight as American eyes had never seen. Small wonder that *The Black Crook* "intoxicated playgoers," in the words of Joseph Francis Daly, "and brought train-loads of people from every point of the compass to see Bonfanti, Sangalli, and Rigl and a hundred pretty coryphées." Small wonder that it ran for sixteen consecutive months and brought in more than one million, one hundred thousand dollars. Small wonder that John Ranken Towse "marveled at the scenic glories and the unutterable stupidity of *The Black Crook*."

635 The chorus of *The Black Crook*, from a photograph in the Davis Collection

636　Lydia Thompson, 1836–1908,
in *Robinson Crusoe*, from a photograph in the Davis Collection

SINCEREST FLATTERY

NOR is it any occasion for surprise that imitations followed. *The Black Crook* was succeeded by *The White Fawn*. Then in 1868 came the "British Blondes" presenting a burlesque show called *Ixion*, which likewise capitalized the female form, and once more the ghosts of the Puritan fathers squeaked and gibbered. At the head of this company was Lydia Thompson, a dancer and pantomimist from the London Haymarket and Drury Lane. As an actress she was sufficiently gifted to have inspired the younger Dumas to write a play especially for her. Her efforts in *Ixion* were ably seconded by those of Pauline Markham, who played Venus in the show, and by Eliza Weathersby, a particularly popular dancer and singer. These young ladies were apparently competent performers, but they shrewdly relied on the shapeliness of their persons for no inconsiderable part of their box-office appeal.

637　　　　Pauline Markham, from a photograph in the
Davis Collection

638　　　　The Lydia Thompson Girls, from a photograph
in the Davis Collection

OLIVE LOGAN OBJECTS

INEVITABLY such displays aroused a storm of protest in certain quarters. Preachers fulminated and editors denounced. The New York *Tribune* summed it all up as "a revel of Cyprians, on the money of prosperous counter-jumpers." But the most ardent crusader against the new iniquity was Olive Logan, an actress of some ability, a novelist, a playwright, and one of the first American champions of woman's rights. In various articles and in her book, *Before the Footlights and Behind the Scenes*, she dealt unsparingly with what she was pleased to call the "Nude Woman Question," and from them the following excerpts are taken: "Considering it a burning disgrace to the theatrical profession that there should be in its ranks a class of so-called actresses, whose claim on public patronage lay in their boldness of personal display, I have persistently made war upon them for several years past." "When *The Black Crook* first presented its nude woman to the gaze of a crowded auditory, she was met with a gasp of astonishment at the effrontery, which dared so much. Men actually grew pale at the boldness of the thing; a deathlike silence fell over the house, broken only by the clapping of a band of claqueurs around the outer aisles; but it passed; and, in view of the fact that these women were French ballet-dancers after all, they were tolerated." "An army of burlesque women took ship for America, and presently the New York stage presented one disgraceful spectacle of padded legs jigging and wriggling in the insensate follies and indecencies of the hour." ". . . they do not either act, dance, sing, or mime; but they habit themselves in a way which is attractive to an indelicate taste, and their inefficiency in other regards is overlooked." Miss Logan congratulated herself that her doughty blows and those of her fellow crusaders had driven the enemy from the field. It is to be doubted. For a time fourteen out of sixteen theaters in New York were given over to such burlesques and spectacles, and the burlesque show has been with us ever since. Legs had come, and they had come to stay.

639　Olive Logan, 1839–1909, from a photograph in the Davis Collection

640 Adelaide Ristori, from a photograph
in the Davis Collection

641 Ristori as Marie Antoinette, from a photograph in the Davis Collection

642 Adelaide Ristori, from a photograph
in the Davis Collection

ADELAIDE RISTORI, 1822–1906

In the year in which the "painted Jezebels" from Europe were setting America agog with *The Black Crook*, a European woman of quite different type also made a pronounced impression on the New York public. Adelaide Ristori, daughter of Italian strollers, early gained a dominant position in Italy. When she made a professional visit to Paris in 1855, her reception was enthusiastic, and violent partisanship sprang up between her supporters and those of Rachel. After appearing in various European countries Ristori came to America in 1866. In spite of the fact that her plays were acted in Italian, she was immensely admired in such rôles as Legouvé's Medea, Schiller's Mary Stuart, Giacometti's Queen Elizabeth, and Lady Macbeth. Subsequently she revisited this country three times. Her farewell visit in 1884–85 was almost a failure because her support was execrable and because she attempted to act in English, a language she did not understand. At its best her acting was marked by subtlety, finish, spontaneity, and fire. Her Queen Elizabeth was generally acknowledged to be her masterpiece, and here, wrote John Ranken Towse, "the haughty carriage, imperious address, fierce temper, blunt humor, masculine sagacity, petty vanity, and feminine jealousy, were all indicated with surpassing skill and blended into a consistent whole with finished artistry." Ristori deserves to rank among the great actresses of the century.

643 Fanny Janauschek as Meg Merrilies,
from a photograph in the Davis Collection

FANNY JANAUSCHEK, 1830–1904

The year after Ristori's American appearance there arrived an actress of comparable genius, the Bohemian, Fanny Janauschek. Her stage début had been made at Frankfort in 1848, and by the time of her arrival here she was ranked among the greatest European tragédiennes. At the outset of her career in the United States, which began at the New York Academy of Music in 1867, she acted in German, and when, in the following year, she played Lady Macbeth to Edwin Booth's Macbeth at the Boston Theater, she used her native language while Booth used his. But she rapidly mastered English and as soon as possible substituted it for German. Among her most impressive characters were Lady Macbeth, Medea, Mary Stuart, and, above all, Brunhilde. Into these powerful rôles she injected an immense passion, and also an element of tenderness that kept them human. "Her face was strong and expressive," wrote Towse, "her voice deep, full, and vibrant, her port majestic, and her vigor great. Of the technique of her art she was a perfect mistress, and her versatility was remarkable in all characters compounded of strong intellectual or emotional elements. . . . It was in great dramas that she shone, and when they disappeared from the stage her occupation . . . was gone." It was her tragedy that when, in her later years, the taste for heroic characters had passed, she was compelled to perform in crude melodrama as a means of livelihood. But, wrote Towse, "she was a grand artist to the last."

644   Clara Louise Kellogg, 1842–1916, from a photograph in the Davis Collection

AN AMERICAN *DIVA*

THE Academy of Music, which was the scene of Janauschek's American début, had for some years witnessed the triumphs of a native American star in an art closely allied to the drama. Clara Louise Kellogg, born in Sumterville, South Carolina, and educated for the musical profession in New York, could well boast, when she made her début in *Rigoletto* at the Academy of Music, February 27, 1861, that she was an American product. Her subsequent achievements quickly disproved the conventional belief that America could not produce great singers, for her beautiful soprano voice and her artistic gifts soon gained her

645   Miss Kellogg, from a photograph in the possession of the publishers

an enthusiastic public. Her fame crossed the ocean and in 1867 and 1868 she appeared in London as prima donna in French and Italian opera, her initial rôle being Marguerite in *Faust*. From this time she was recognized as one of the leading singers of her day both in London, where she appeared at intervals, and in America. In 1874 she organized her own opera company, which toured the country with great success and in the direction of which she displayed unusual ability. In 1887 she married her manager Carl Strakosch, nephew of Maurice Strakosch (see p. 198), and retired from public life.

"A COMPLETE TRIUMPH"

ADELINA PATTI, although born in Madrid, might almost be claimed as another product of America. Her parents, the father an Italian, the mother a Spaniard, and both singers, came to the United States when Adelina was a small child. At the age of seven she made her first public appearance in the concert halls of New York and astonished the town by her remarkable voice and execution. Trained by Maurice Strakosch, who had married her sister, Amelia, Patti made her operatic début in *Lucia di Lammermoor* at the Academy of Music, November 24, 1859, before she had reached her seventeenth year. Ireland said that "her triumph was complete." Other rôles followed rapidly, and her fame rose with each new performance. On May 14,

646   Adelina Patti, 1843–1919, from a photograph in the Davis Collection

1861, she appeared at Covent Garden, London, in Bellini's *La Sonnambula*, and from this time on she held the supreme place among living vocalists. She sang in all the principal musical centers of Europe and America, and her repertory included all the important rôles in Italian opera. Although Patti sang in opera until the end of the 'eighties and much longer in occasional recitals, her voice retained an amazing freshness, largely because of her admirable method of tone production. Next to Jenny Lind she must be regarded as the greatest soprano of the nineteenth century. To the older generation of opera-goers there is still magic in the name of Patti.

647   Patti, from a photograph in the Davis Collection

"A GREAT ACTOR IN A SMALL FIELD"

NOT all the distinguished artists of foreign extraction who visited America during this period were women. Charles Fechter, son of French parents, though his mother was of Italian, and his father of German lineage, was a great favorite in Paris and London before he came to the United States in 1870. At the time of his arrival he had a fluent command of English, though he spoke with a foreign intonation. Not long after his début at Niblo's Garden, New York, he undertook the management of the Globe Theater, Boston, but he soon quarreled with his associates, and the project came to an end. A few years later he undertook management in New York, but again he failed. Fechter had, according to Dickens, who was an ardent admirer, "a perfect genius for quarreling," which probably should be laid to his vanity, and which unfitted him for the work of manager. As an actor he was much more successful. While inadequate in Shakespearean parts, he was often extremely powerful in romantic and melodramatic characters, such as Ruy Blas, Monte Cristo, and Claude Melnotte in *The Lady of Lyons*. In rôles of this nature he often displayed a reckless frenzy that

648 Charles Fechter, 1824–79, from a photograph in the Davis Collection

was highly thrilling. William Winter rightly said: "It was seen that he was a great actor in a small field, that he elevated little subjects, and that the illumination of his subject was secondary to the display of himself. . . . Fechter chiefly announced and interpreted his picturesque, spasmodic self." Joseph Francis Daly confirmed this estimate when he wrote in his *Life of Augustin Daly:* "The impression he left upon me was that of a consummate actor consciously displaying his art." His powers declined early and he found it expedient to retire in 1878.

"UNEQUALED SINCE GARRICK"

A MUCH greater actor than Fechter and without Fechter's limitations was that amazing genius, Tommaso Salvini. Salvini first visited the United States in 1873 after already achieving extraordinary success in his native Italy, as well as in France, Spain, and elsewhere. He made a total of five visits to America, the last being in 1886, and he left an indelible impression on all who saw him. "When he was first seen here," wrote Henry Austin Clapp in *Reminiscences of a Dramatic Critic*, "the beauty and strength of his classic face, the grand proportions of his figure, and the vibrant, sympathetic sweetness of his voice — a voice as glorious as ever proceeded from a man — combined to overpower the observer and listener." His emotional range was remarkable; he could completely embody the cyclonic fury of Othello's murderous passion and the heartbreaking pathos of Corrado's renunciation in Giacommetti's *La Morte Civile*, while in Italy his high comedy was as much admired as his tragedy. Some critics found fault with his Shakespearean interpretation, which,

in such parts as Hamlet and even Othello, inclined toward an excess of violence. But in continental tragedies such as *La Morte Civile*, Alfieri's *Saul*, Saumet's *The Gladiator*, and Munsch-Bellinghausen's *Ingomar* he was colossal and his audience was swept as by an irresistible tempest. This result is the more remarkable in that Salvini always acted in Italian, sometimes with Italian support, sometimes with English. In 1886 he played Othello with Booth as Iago, each speaking his native tongue.

"Tommaso Salvini," wrote the critic John Ranken Towse, "was not only incomparably the greatest actor and artist whom I have ever seen, but one who has never had an equal, probably, since the days of Garrick."

649 Tommaso Salvini, 1829–1916, from a photograph in the Davis Collection

650 Salvini as Othello, from an engraving by Gebbie and Husson, 1890, in the Davis Collection

CHAPTER X

THE AUTOCRAT OF THE STAGE

"WHEN the accursed star system, and the general disorganization of the stage accompanied the other disorganizations of the war, Wallack's *alone* held fast to the good, and even now, at Wallack's alone can one see the whole of a fine play finely played. Good actors gravitate to it, attracted as it were by an innate feeling that there is the management where study and refinement will be turned to account, and there assemble audiences capable of appreciating the artistic results of both." These sentiments, written on December 30, 1870, by a conservative New York dramatic critic, are typical of the prevailing attitude of the average New York theatergoer in the second year of Grant's first administration. The name of Wallack carried with it a prestige and historical association covering a half-century of the stage's development. During the decades when the theatrical center of New York was in the vicinity of Park Row, near the square where the City Hall stands, the Wallacks and their wives had risen to positions of eminence. When, by the middle of the century, the fashionable residential section of New York had moved northward to Union Square, the Wallacks leased the nearest available theater on Broome Street; and when Burton and Laura Keene intervened with new theaters on Bond and Houston Streets, the Wallacks, going still further north, opened on Thirteenth within a stone's throw of Union Square, on a site accessible to the many new exclusive clubs, restaurants and hotels going up in the neighborhood. During the decade of the Civil War the older downtown theaters had one by one closed. Their best actors had drifted northward to Wallack's to take their parts in the suave, gracefully directed British comedies and romances which well-bred New York considered the acme of histrionic art, and, like many of the "deeper truths" of society and religion, not open to question or criticism.

At a short distance from Wallack's were to be found also the offices of various penny newspapers, which increased with great rapidity during the 'fifties and 'sixties to meet the demands of the masses of workers brought into existence by the new industrial era in which the noise of machines was to be heard on every hand. New York had almost ceased to be a city in the old sense, and became overnight a monstrous population center, sprawling aimlessly and chaotically beyond the confines of the ante-bellum city. In the factories babbled many strange tongues. Opportunity in America drew to the shores of the nation vast hordes from Europe. The American people faced problems in the assimilation of this rapidly growing foreign population which was revolutionizing the methods of life in American cities. Abject poverty was to be found in slums filled with vice and misery. In other parts of the urban centers was the garish and the new. To such wide and varied classes the newspapers of the 'sixties were forced to direct their appeal. The early nineteenth-century newspapers, such as *The Evening Post,* and the *Commercial Advertiser*, had been designed for a comparatively small circle. In those days the dramatic criticism of Washington Irving and William Coleman had been followed by only a few thoughtful subscribers. But by 1860 the number of dramatic critics had trebled and the readers of dramatic criticism were yearly increasing in number. It was during this period that William Winter and Nym Crinkle were serving their apprenticeship in preparation for their great critical work of the ensuing years. But far more important than these was another young dramatic critic, Augustin Daly, who was destined to rise far above the fields of criticism into a career of thirty years of independent producing, and to a position of influence and importance in the theatrical world beyond that even of Lester Wallack.

Fascinated from his earliest boyhood by the staging of shows and spectacles, and determined to overcome all handicaps that stood between him and his ambition to become the greatest producer in New York, Daly entered with great enthusiasm into his work as dramatic critic. "I had the good fortune when a boy," he once said, "to see Burton's and Wallack's theaters in their prime, and from those stages drank in my first draught of Shakespearean nectar, and understood then, and from them, what a dramatic company truly meant, and what a real manager must be."

In the struggle to achieve his ambitions Daly was without fear. Having decided on the next step to be taken, he was without misgivings as to his ability to execute it. His relentless self-confidence, his unswerving energy in working out his plans, and his complete absorption in one ambition, give to his career a broader significance than mere theatrical success. He was akin to many of the younger industrial leaders who in the period after the Civil War were stimulated by the electrifying forces of a new era; who had visions of new developments; and who to attain their one ambition freely sacrificed all lesser desires. To these new "Captains of Industry" the conception of a leisurely well-balanced life, such as had become familiar in cultured Atlantic centers in the period before the War, was insufficient. For Augustin Daly, who felt these great changes that were taking place in the nation, the assured position and the complacent smugness and condescension of the Wallack type of mind held no terrors.

Four years after Lee surrendered at Appomattox, Daly opened a New York theater eleven blocks further north than Wallack's, a little distance from Madison Square. The prospects of success on this theatrical frontier seemed negligible. In one play after another the young manager presented to his audiences unfamiliar faces, and the New York critics facetiously recommended that he go and study the art of Wallack. But in spite of criticism he persevered. In 1873 his first theater burned, and his fortunes were low in a panic year. But he had even at that early date the satisfaction of realizing that there was an increasingly large public which could be satisfied only by the new type of realistic staging and scenic effect which he had so laboriously worked out with his subordinates. Albert Palmer at the Union Square Theater was a disciple, if not a plagiarist. A new taste was fast being formed which would replace the old, and Daly realized that the years ahead were to be his period of attainment. No longer would conservative New York critics dare suggest that "at Wallack's alone can one see the whole of a fine play finely played."

651   Daly reading a play to his company, from a photograph in the Davis Collection

AUGUSTIN DALY

THE opportunity for which Augustin Daly had diligently planned during the preceding decade of his dramatic apprenticeship materialized in 1869. For in the spring of that year John Brougham admitted failure at last in his final attempt at theatrical management. In consequence, the Fifth Avenue Theater on 24th Street, built by James Fisk, Jr., was open to a new applicant. Displaying a temerity that stunned the skeptical capitalist, Daly announced his intention of leasing the theater; and thanks to the aid of his father-in-law the veteran producer John Duff, the ambitious youth presented to Fisk a check furnishing the requisite security. With the unsparing energy that characterized his thirty years of management, Daly began the redecoration and reupholstering of the former Brougham Theater. In a study of the personality and career of Daly there is a recurring suggestion of an earlier American manager, William Dunlap of the First Park. Like his predecessor, Daly was forced for many years to summon his entire energy and resourcefulness to stave off failure, which again and again seemed inevitable. Each of the two men was endowed with unswerving integrity and pride, and each was forced to pay the penalty of mistakes of judgment in casting and in the selection of plays; and the powers of each expanded by this process of trial and error. Both Dunlap and Daly were authors of original plays, which proved popular enough with their respective audiences; but each was forced to resort again and again to adaptations from contemporary German dramatists — Dunlap from Kotzebue, Daly chiefly from Rosen and the Von Schönthan brothers. The obvious difference is, of course, that Dunlap, after a few years of heroic struggle, failed and retired to a subordinate position, while Daly, in spite of fires and broken contracts and popular indifference, became before many years the most powerful producer in New York. The explanation of this difference lies, perhaps, in Daly's absolute

652   Augustin Daly, from a photograph in the Davis Collection

autocracy. He delegated no authority; he supervised personally every phase of the activities of his theaters; his life, his sole interest was concentrated in the one enterprise. He demanded from his subordinates a simi-

653   Interior of Daly's Theater, from an engraving in the Davis Collection

lar loyalty and energy. Perfection of production was his standard; the number of rehearsals of no moment. Confident of the ultimate success of such honest methods, he experimented as his judgment dictated, and if he himself was satisfied with the outcome, the severest critic did not affect him; and when at last his position was assured, he was equally unaffected by the eulogies and flatteries of his many admirers. Daly's unswerving loyalty to his high artistic standards is particularly notable because he worked in a period marked in some other phases of art by confusion of taste and decline of standards.

"ADAPTABLE AND CREATIVE"

THE most complete biography of Augustin Daly is by his brother, Joseph Daly, whose interest in the growth and development of the Daly theaters never slackened. According to this biographer Daly's "purpose was to break away from tradition; to free actors from the trammels of 'lines' into which they had settled as in a groove. It was with a great wrench that the old favourites were pried out of the rut, but the result was soon a mobile force, adaptable and creative. He astonished his players by throwing them into parts for which they thought they had no fit-ness. . . . From the beginning he got the reputation of an unyielding disciplinarian, but if he was rigid with others, he also sacrificed himself. It was soon seen that no one else could do so much with men and

654   Scene from Augustin Daly's production of *The Merchant of Venice*, from a photograph in the Ada Rehan Collection, New York Public Library

women of the stage as he." William Winter in *The Wallet of Time* has left the following appraisal of Daly's work: "He gathered the ablest men and women in the dramatic pro-fession; he presented the best plays that were available; he made the theater important, and he kept it worthy of the most refined taste and the best intellect of his time. His fertility of resource seemed inexhaustible. He was quick to decide, and the energy with which he moved, in the execution of his plans, was the more splendid because it was neither deranged by tumult nor marred by ostentation." In the tribute of John Ranken Towse, whose British background sometimes blinded him to the mer-its of American producers and American actors,

655   Scene from Augustin Daly's production of *The Merchant of Venice*, from a photograph in the Ada Rehan Collection, New York Public Library

there are a number of qualifying criticisms. "His actual achievement has been vastly overrated. There is very little solid foundation for the common belief that his contributions to the revival, or survival, of the literary and poetic drama were of any great or lasting value. It is true that he was a man of artistic tastes, and impulses, and a most liberal, en-terprising and courageous manager, who could be daunted by no disaster, but was always ready with a fresh ex-periment. It is true that he had for many years the best light-comedy company in the country and that he was the author of many delightful en-tertainments, prepared and served in irreproachable fashion. But these in the main were of an entirely ephem-eral and unimportant kind. . . . Some of the pieces that he produced were unmitigated trash, flagrant melodramatic absurdities, with no other possible object than to catch the mob."

656   Scene from Augustin Daly's production of *Midsummer Night's Dream*, from a photograph in the Ada Rehan Collection, New York Public Library

"THE GOVERNOR"

THE most intimate glimpses which have been preserved of Daly and of life inside the Daly theaters are contained in Dora Knowlton's *Diary of a Daly Debutante*, Duffield and Company, New York, 1910. "He has a very agreeable smile," wrote Miss Knowlton, a minor member of Daly's company, describing "The Governor," "and is a distinguished-looking man. He is tall and slender, with a pale complexion and the most remarkable blue eyes; they are of so dark a shade and have such long, thick, curving black lashes they remind me of the blue fringed gentian. . . . Mr. Daly sat on an old wooden chair on the stage with his back to the footlights . . . the actors moved slowly about the stage with manuscript copies of their rôles in their hands and read their lines aloud. Mr. Daly would often bounce up to rush to some actor, bristling and turning him about, waving his long arms, and going through the funniest motions showing him how to do things; then he would return to the kitchen chair, push that hat a little farther to the back of his head, and watch the action until he felt called upon to bounce up again. I wonder whether he ever takes his hat off; I haven't seen him do it yet. Still more do I wonder where he ever bought such a queer hat."

657 Augustin Daly, from a photograph in the Davis Collection

AGNES ETHEL

ON the opening night of Robertson's *Play* the first Daly audience saw in the leading female rôle of Rosie Farquehere an unfamiliar face of alluring beauty, with "candid eyes, flowing auburn hair, . . . and regular features always lit up by an expression of childish appeal. These and a low voice of penetrating quality dwelt in the public memory from the moment she appeared on the Fifth Avenue stage." Agnes Ethel, completely inexperienced except for a few rôles at the Union League Club on Twenty-sixth Street, had been a pupil of Mathilda Heron (see No. 547), and Daly had seen in her the possibilities of an appealing actress. Her success during the next two seasons amply justified his judgment. On the evening of February 12, 1870, Daly presented to the Fifth Avenue audience his adaptation of the popular Parisian melodrama, *Frou-Frou* by Meilhac and Halévy, and, carrying out one of his strongest principles, that of developing and training untried talents, he gave the leading rôle to the novice, Agnes Ethel. It was the first great success of the new company. "The naïveté of the beginner gave reality to the thoughtlessness of the character," wrote Joseph Daly. "Dramatic force was wanting, but there was the effect of a searching cry from a weak and despairing heart. . . . The play was an unquestioned success. It became the town talk, and everybody crowded to the Fifth Avenue Theater. Daly had justified prediction. James Fisk, Jr., looked as if he felt that his sagacity in leasing the theater to the untried manager had been vindicated." Unfortunately the various other rôles which followed, such as Viola in *Twelfth Night*, Hero in *Much Ado about Nothing*, and Julia in *The Hunchback*, were not equally sensational, and, in the fall of 1872, jealous of the popularity of the rôles of certain other Daly actresses, Agnes Ethel accepted the offer of A. M. Palmer, and transferred her services to the Union Square Theater, where she had a brilliant run in a new Sardou play, *Agnes*, rewritten especially for her. At the end of a year, however, having decided to marry, she retired from the stage.

658 Agnes Ethel, 1852–1903, from a photograph in the Davis Collection

659 Agnes Ethel, from a photograph in the Davis Collection

FANNY DAVENPORT

660 Fanny Davenport, 1850–98, as Rosalind, from a photograph in the Davis Collection

661 Fanny Davenport as Fedora, from a photograph in the Davis Collection

IN the month following the début of Agnes Ethel, Daly, continuing his experiments, introduced in a star rôle another actress, almost as young as Miss Ethel, and almost equally inexperienced. Fanny Davenport, a daughter of Edgar Loomis Davenport, had been brought to America in 1854 at the age of four, and for the next eight years had been subjected to an erratic education in Boston, interrupted by numerous stage appearances in juvenile parts. In 1862, after having appeared at Niblo's Garden in New York, she had been engaged by Mrs. John Drew, under whom she served at the Arch Street until she attracted the eye of Daly, ever on the search for promising material. When Daly announced her as the Lady Gay Spanker of *London Assurance*, a sarcastic critic dubbed the manager's confidence, "New York Assurance." But Daly's faith in her youthful beauty and spirit and presence, and in her unshakable self-confidence, was not impaired; and he had the satisfaction of seeing her soon acknowledged as the best Lady Gay of her times. Her very exuberance and brusqueness saved her from the super-sophistication with which the rôle had often been burdened. As Effie Remington in *Saratoga*, Lu in *Divorce*, and Lady Teazle in *The School for Scandal* she was pleasing; but it was not until 1874 in *Charity* that the audience began to appreciate the brilliance of Daly's choice. According to Joseph Daly "the appearance of Miss Fanny Davenport, hitherto the representative of fashion, beauty, and comedy, in the rags of Ruth Tredgett, with matted, straggling hair, and furtive, hunted eyes, acted upon the audience like an electric shock. As if recognizing immediately her true dramatic instincts and feeling the promise of power to come, they broke into the wildest welcome; and then watched through the play the truth with which she struck every note of the character." In December of the following year Miss Davenport became a universally recognized star as Mable Renfrew in Daly's original play of *Pique*, which opened at the Fifth Avenue Theater on December 14, 1875, with such success that it enjoyed a run of two hundred and thirty-eight performances in New York and a long tour of the country. "The estimate of her work by the press was so unanimously flattering and sincere," wrote Joseph Daly,

662 Fanny Davenport as Cleopatra, from a photograph in the Davis Collection

"that the young girl enjoyed her triumph to the full." She remained with Daly until 1877, playing a wide range of parts, varying in scope from the dignity of Shakespeare to the artificialities of old comedies and the furies of the contemporary melodrama. In 1877–78 she starred at the Union Square in a dramatization of *The Vicar of Wakefield*. This was followed by an extensive tour, supported by John Drew. Her most famous rôles after leaving Daly were in the Sardou plays, *Tosca*, *Cleopatra*, *Fedora*, and *Gismonda*, in which, at the head of her own company, she toured the country.

663 Fanny Davenport as Blind Posthumia, from a photograph in the Davis Collection

664 Clara Morris, from a photograph in the collection of H. A. Ogden, New York

CLARA MORRIS, 1846–1925

THE greatest, perhaps, of all of Daly's discoveries was Clara Morris, who, unheralded and with only an unimpressive apprenticeship in Cleveland, Cincinnati, and other mid-western towns behind her, had come with her mother to convince metropolitan managers of her genius. With the exception of Daly, there had been no response. Even he had been evasive, promising in a general way to bear her in mind for a comedy part. But when to the general surprise Agnes Ethel refused the part of Anne Sylvester in *Man and Wife*, the young manager "recalled the mobile countenance and impressive voice of Miss Morris, and intrusted that leading rôle to her. The result was that the first night of the new play presented to a deeply interested audience another of Mr. Daly's discoveries." But it was not until Daly's production of *Article 47* in April, 1872, that the true greatness of Clara Morris was revealed. "In this play Miss Morris reached the height of her achievement," wrote Joseph Daly. "The scene in which, baffled of her vengeance, which had become a monomania, her overwrought emotion unseats her reason, and she passes through the stages of fear, cunning, and loss of control to raving madness was electrifying, and when the curtain fell, she was the mistress of the American stage. This triumph had not been effected without extreme preparation. Long rehearsals with her ambitious and painstaking manager had shaped every movement and guided every inflection." And yet, as happened in many cases, after the careful drudgery and training from Daly, the full benefit was reaped elsewhere. For in the fall of 1873, while in Cincinnati with a company in *Divorce*, Miss Morris became piqued at the applause which the comedy parts received, and in her irritation broke her contract with Daly to join Palmer at the Union Square. There she made her début in Feuillet's *The Sphinx*, and later gave a brilliant interpretation of Camille, which Towse considered the equal of Bernhardt's or Modjeska's, "in realistic pathos, though not in art." For a while she left the Union Square to star as Lady Macbeth, a performance in which she rose on occasion to some of her greatest heights, but which as a whole was unsound. She afterward returned to the Union Square. There her most striking new rôle was Miss Moulton in a dramatization of *East Lynne*. Towse praised her as "one of the very few American actresses to whom the gift of genius may be properly ascribed. . . . If judged by her artistic equipment only, she could not establish a claim to any very high place in the ranks of her contemporaries. She was far behind many of them in artistic cunning, but she distanced all of them in flashes of convincing realism and in poignancy of natural emotion. . . . Miss Morris's genius, while unmistakable, was of a very special and restricted order. It was not manifested in romance, in high comedy, or in the heroic emotions, whether good or evil, but shone out resplendently in the intensification of the commoner passions of ordinary human nature, and particularly in the depiction of pathetic suffering, whether mute or tearfully eloquent." Her last performance was in 1904 in a revival of *The Two Orphans*.

665 Clara Morris as Cora in *Article 47*, from a photograph in the Davis Collection

666 Clara Morris as Marguerite Gauthier in *Camille*, from a photograph in the Davis Collection

667 Clara Morris as Evadne in the play of that name, from a photograph in the Davis Collection

668   Bronson Howard, from a photograph in
the collection of Montrose J. Moses

BRONSON HOWARD,
1842–1908

ONE of Clara Morris's most pleasing comedy rôles was that of Effie Remington in a play by a hitherto unknown dramatist from Detroit. Bronson Howard, the author, submitted his work to Daly with no further recommendation than that it had been produced at Macaulay's Theater in Louisville. It was at a time when American dramatists were ignored by the producers of the East, who concentrated on adap-

669   Scene from Bronson Howard's *Saratoga*, from
a photograph in the Davis Collection

tations of the leading contemporary plays of Europe or on revivals of the old classics. Plays with American types such as Metamora, Solon Shingle, and Davy Crockett were fast losing their popularity by the time that Daly opened his new theater. But in the manuscript submitted to him by Howard the young producer saw possibilities of a clever, satirical study of the foibles and affectations of a section of contemporary American society, gathered at the fashionable resort of Saratoga. He made several constructive suggestions which the delighted young author eagerly incorporated. The long run of *Saratoga* justified the producer's faith, and at the same time was a powerful incentive to the American drama, which during the following decades found an increasingly large number of exponents. Howard's play was adapted for the English stage, and afterward achieved the distinction of being the first American drama to be translated into German. But with all the significance to which *Saratoga* is justly entitled, it has, by the fact of its priority in time, tended to obscure the greater contribution of its author, who, according to Dr. Arthur Hobson Quinn in *A History of the American Drama from the Civil War to the Present Day*, is of importance primarily in that he "illustrates in the broadening of his own grasp of dramatic material and the refinement of his own skill, the development of American playwriting during the period of his creative achievement from 1870 to 1906." Daly's other Howard productions were less successful than *Saratoga*. *Diamonds*, which opened the season of 1872, had a short run, and *Moorcroft*, produced in 1874, lasted only two weeks; while *Wives*, a prose adaptation and combination of two of Molière's plays, was never popular. The four other plays on which Howard's fame most securely rests are: *The Banker's Daughter*, produced by A. M. Palmer at the Union Square in 1878; *Young Mrs. Winthrop*, which, according to Dr. Quinn, "placed on the stage for the first time in America a

670   Scene from Bronson Howard's *The Banker's Daughter*, from an engraving in *Frank Leslie's Illustrated Newspaper*, Jan. 4, 1879

group of characters, whose actions are determined by the power of social laws and the interruption of social distractions, without making the prevailing note one of satire"; *The Henrietta*, produced at the Union Square in 1887, a brilliant study of a Wall Street capitalist and his two sons; and finally *Shenandoah*, produced by Charles Frohman in 1889, which, with the possible exception of William Gillette's *Secret Service*, is the finest study in drama of the Civil War background. His other plays include *One of our Girls*, produced at the Lyceum in 1885, *Only a Tramp*, produced in 1881 at Hull, England, *Hurricanes*, a three-act farce comedy, produced at Chicago in 1878, and *Peter Stuyvesant*, written in collaboration with Brander Matthews, and presenting an interesting picture of life in colonial New York.

671   George Clarke, from a photo-
      graph in the Davis Collection

GEORGE CLARKE, 1844–1906

ANOTHER of Daly's hitherto unknown beginners was George Clarke, whom Joseph Daly described as "a handsome youth, beginning to win favor." In the manager's adaptation of *Pickwick Papers* Clarke played the rôle of Bob Sawyer, in which he was "fearfully made up to double the 'scorbutic youth' of Bob's little party." He was especially well received in Daly's numerous Shakespearean revivals: a swaggering and cringing Malvolio in *Twelfth Night;* a romantic Orlando in *As You Like It;* an impressive Leonato in *Much Ado About Nothing;* a gay, clever Biron in *Love's Labour's Lost.* As Charles Surface in *The School for Scandal,* he was especially pleasing in its first presentation. But when, on the unexpected failure of Bronson Howard's *Moorcroft,* Sheridan's classic had to be suddenly revived, there was trouble. For in *Moorcroft* (1874) Clarke's part had called for a moustache, which he had grown for the occasion, and which he had every intention of keeping. Unfortunately it was one of Daly's ironclad rules that there should be neither beards nor moustaches in Sheridan revivals. So that when Charles Surface appeared with an all too apparent moustache, he was severely reprimanded by the manager. Resentful of this unappreciativeness, Clarke immediately left the theater refusing to finish even the one performance, and, in an ill-judged interview with newspaper reporters, severely critized Daly and predicted his early downfall. He was soon penitent and wrote Daly a note of apology, but it was not until 1880 that he appeared again on Daly's boards. Towse described Clarke as a "versatile and well-trained actor, expert in all the tricks of his trade, intelligent, but without a particle of inspiration."

"AN ARTISTIC AND FRIENDLY COMPANIONSHIP"

ONE of Daly's greatest finds was James Lewis, "a very young man who had made in a small way some acceptable appearances in brief seasons of burlesque and extravaganza." Under the painstaking tutelage of his new manager he developed into one of the most versatile comedians of the time, ranging with equal facility through rôles of low and high comedy, juveniles, and testy old men. With Lewis more completely than with any other of his actors Daly upset the long established actor tradition of concentrating on one line of business. Towse characterized Lewis as a "quaint, dry, chipper, and magnetic little comedian who contributed very largely to the merriment of his generation. . . . In almost any circumstances he was amusing, and even when most grotesque his impersonations had a finish and consistency which gave them artistic value." With the exception of one season Lewis remained with Daly until his death in 1896. "His loss to the theater was well nigh irreparable," wrote Joseph Daly, "but it was as nothing compared to the void made in an artistic and friendly companionship of twenty-five years. He was of the same age as his manager. In their long association there were moments of irritation on both sides, but the deep-seated mutual respect they felt made such differences trivial. Lewis regarded Daly as the creator of his career. Of all the thousands who witnessed Lewis's impersonations none enjoyed them more than his manager. After some particularly good bit, Lewis and my brother, meeting for an instant behind the scene, would exchange a glance from kindling eyes. No words were needed to tell the artist that he had fulfilled the ideal of the author and director."

672   James Lewis, 1840–96, in *7–20–8,* from a
      photograph in the Davis Collection

673   Lewis as Mr. Clarkson in *The American,* from
      a photograph in the Davis Collection

A MASTER OF MAKEUP

"OFTEN, on the first night of a play or at dress rehearsal," continued Joseph Daly, "Lewis would surprise and delight the manager by the novelty and felicity of his make up, of which art he was a born master. Without being grotesque or extravagant, his very clothes talked. He once appeared in a hat that was a whole comic almanac . . . no matter what his part might be, the voice suited it perfectly." Although Lewis detested old comedy, he was good as Touchstone and Sir Toby Belch, and as Puff in Sheridan's *Critic*, while his rôle of Grumio in *The Taming of the Shrew* was one of his greatest. Winter wrote of him, "Lewis did much more than 'make the people laugh.' He touched their hearts, he entered into their lives, and he gained their friendship. He was an uncommon man, and he was a comedian of a high order. A more conscientious, thorough, scrupulously fastidious actor has not been known in our time. He acted many parts and he acted every part well . . . he ever strove to merge himself in the character he represented, and to this design he was strenuously devoted."

674 James Lewis and Mrs. Gilbert in *A Night Off*, from a photograph in the Davis Collection

"GRANDMA" GILBERT

IN addition to such beginners as Ethel, Davenport, Morris, Clarke, and Lewis, Daly also enlisted the services of various actors and actresses whose reputations were already established. Mrs. G. H. Gilbert, whose name is linked so closely to that of Lewis and who was later known as "the grand old woman of the stage," had made her American début as a dancer at Chicago in 1851. Not until six years later in Cleveland had she attempted the legitimate drama. After seven years' stock experience on the western circuit in old women's parts she had made her New York début at Mrs. John Wood's Olympic as the Baroness in *Fifine*. She first attracted the attention of Daly in 1867 at the Broadway Theater, New York, where she made a great hit as the Marquise de St. Maur in *Caste*. Her aristocratic features and majestic carriage fitted her admirably for the rôles of venerable dowagers. Mrs. Gilbert was with Daly longer than any other of his troupe. During the thirty years from 1869 to 1899, she was away only once. As with Lewis, so with Mrs. Gilbert, Daly insisted that she must not confine herself to the dowager type, and, as the years passed, her acting became increasingly versatile and her interpretation of varying types more profound. Mrs. Gilbert and Lewis were the first two of the group always referred to as Daly's "Big Four," whose names are synonymous with the glories of the Daly régime. John Drew and Ada Rehan had not yet appeared. Her relations with the manager and with the other members of the company were always most cordial, and to her intimates she always signed herself "Grandma." "Her sympathy with the young," wrote William Winter, "was deep and quick: she was always ready and glad to speak the word of genial encouragement to inexperience. . . . It was a technical education to watch and study

675 Mrs. Gilbert and May Irwin in *A Night Off*, from a photograph in the Davis Collection

her employment, in speech, movement, and gesture, of pause, rapidity, or deliberation. She never obtruded herself. Each of her performances possessed the invaluable attribute of seeming inevitability. . . . To age she would not surrender, and she was indescribably amusing, and often a little pathetic, in her politely brusque resentment of any intimation that she . . . required attention or assistance. . . . As example of artistic coöperation, the ability and willingness to 'play together,' for the right effect, without regard to self, I have seen nothing finer than Joseph Jefferson and W. J. Florence in *The Rivals*, and Mrs. Gilbert and James Lewis, in the Daly comedies."

676 Mrs. Gilbert, 1822–1904, from a photograph in the Davis Collection

677   William Davidge, from a photograph
         in the Davis Collection

WILLIAM PLEATER DAVIDGE, 1814–1888

ANOTHER veteran comedian who appeared in a great variety of rôles during the first eight years of Daly's management was William Davidge, who, on August 19, 1850, had made his American début as Sir Peter Teazle in *The School for Scandal* at the Broadway Theater, New York, where he remained for the next five years in "leading comedy" and "old men" rôles. In 1867 with Mrs. Gilbert he had appeared in the production of Robertson's *Caste*. Under Daly he was most famous for his parts in Shakespearean comedy. He was a perfect Sir Toby Belch in manners and looks, displaying a "rich liquorish humor" and giving a performance which Towse considered the best, with one possible exception, ever given on the American stage. He was, continued Towse, "a racy and eccentric personality, . . . a low comedian of wide range and infinite experience, brimful of a robust humor which could be dry, saturnine, unctuous, or Bacchic at will. Moreover, he had a considerable command of choler and pathos, but neither in visage nor figure was he adapted to the principal characters in high comedy. . . . In his degree he was a rare and invaluable performer." His Touchstone in *As You Like It*, his Dogberry in *Much Ado*, and his Holofernes in *Love's Labour's Lost* were especially pleasing. Davidge remained with Daly until 1877, playing a wide range of parts. Two years later he was the first American Dick Deadeye in Gilbert and Sullivan's *H. M. S. Pinafore*, and from 1885 until his death he was at the Madison Square Theater under Palmer.

FOR OLD COMEDY

THE addition of Charles Fisher, another veteran, to the Daly company in 1872 enabled the ambitious manager to extend the range of his old comedy revivals. Fisher's first appearance in America had been in 1852 at Burton's Chambers Street Theater, as Ferment in *The School of Reform*, and for a number of years prior to joining Daly he had been connected with Wallack's, where his reputation as a finished actor had steadily increased. Fisher was most at home in the old comedies, and his performances created a standard which stimulated the efforts of his new and less expert associates. His Sir Peter Teazle had "old comedy style and finish"; his Mercutio was "gay and buoyant in spirit, and brilliant in technique"; his Malvolio, "a finely finished bit of eccentric comedy," lacked only "a touch of quixotic pride and gravity to perfect it." Towse, the source of the above appreciations, thus summarized the work of Fisher: "At the head of Daly's histrionic forces in 1874 stood Charles Fisher, an actor of trained skill and vast experience. Long past his early prime, he was still in full possession of his physical and artistic resources. He was tall, handsome, dignified, with

678   Charles Fisher, 1816–91, as Sir Peter Teazle
         in *The School for Scandal*, from a photograph
         in the Davis Collection

the precise, bold, free execution and courtly grace of the old school of comedy. He was capable of sparkling and spontaneous gayety . . . of sly humor, vigor, robust passion, and many forms of pathos, but not of tragic emotion." Joseph Daly wrote of Fisher's Falstaff: "Fisher's fat knight was all nature. There never seemed to be anything theatrical about his bulk nor anything assumed in voice or gait. The rolling eye and smacking lip had no suggestion of the theater, and seemed to have no taint of grossness." Until his death in 1891, Fisher remained a loyal member of the Daly company.

679   Charles Fisher as Falstaff in Shakespeare's
         King Henry IV, from a photograph in the
         Davis Collection

THE "TYPICAL AMERICAN" OF 1872

"YOUNG and phenomenally successful theatrical managers," wrote Joseph Daly, "are never satisfied with one theater." In the same year that Charles Fisher joined the cast of the now prosperous Fifth Avenue Theater Daly verified the aphorism of his brother by securing the lease of the Grand Opera House, which had been built by Samuel Pike in 1868 to compete with the Academy of Music. Daly's first great spectacle in his new theater was *Le Roi Carotte*, with music by Offenbach and book by Victorien Sardou, the prolific French dramatist on whom Daly and Palmer and Wallack drew so consistently during the next twenty-five years. Though much less elaborate, the most sensational production of the first season at Daly's new opera house was Sardou's *Uncle Sam*, a biting satire on American life by the distin-

680   Grand Opera House, New York, from a print in the New York Historical Society

guished French dramatist, who was then visiting America. In spite of having been officially suppressed in France as conducive to bad feeling, it was enjoyed during many performances in New York. American real estate speculation, the slowness and inefficiency of American legal procedure, the puerile rivalries of our political parties, the replacement of home life by hotel life, the coquetry and inconsiderateness of the American girl, were all attacked shrewdly and without condescension. The element of hyperbole is of course ever present, as in the description of the typical American, who "sold brooms at the age of twelve, was porkpacker at seventeen, manufacturer of shoe-polish at twenty, made a fortune in cocoa, lost in tobacco, rose again with indigo, fell with salt pork, rebounded with cotton and settled definitely upon guano. He rises at six, rushes to his office in an omnibus, is greedy, extravagant, cunning, and credulous; without scruples, yet a good fellow; will throw you overboard for a hundred dollars, and spend two hundred to fish you out. . . ." After many years of friendly relationships Daly and Sardou quarreled bitterly, the former accusing the French dramatist of having given to Wallack a play which he had contracted to give to Daly. Sardou was incensed at the accusation, and their dealings ended.

"EXQUISITE FOOLING"

THE next most thrilling hit of Daly's Grand Opera enterprise was a burlesque performance of the last act of *Richard III* with George L. Fox (see No. 573) as the King and Frederick Vokes as the Earl of Richmond. "The bare announcement of this desecration of the classic drama," wrote Joseph Daly, "was sufficient to attract a vast audience, which awaited with emotion the respective appearances of Fox and Vokes and their desperate combat on Bosworth Field. When it is understood that all the characters delivered the immortal lines . . . with the utmost gravity; that the falling of Fox's steel visor, whenever he attempted to speak, cut off most of his lines until he reversed the helmet . . . that in the combat, his Humpty Dumpty shuffle was opposed to the incredible agility of Vokes, whose Richmond escaped death by feats of legs as well as of arms, the whole stupendous joke may be faintly realized. Until we have another Fox and another Vokes we cannot expect to see such exquisite fooling." Frederick Vokes was but one of the large Vokes family,

681   The Vokes Sisters, from a photograph in the Davis Collection

consisting of himself, Rosina, Fawden, Victoria, and Jessie, who were famed the world over for their entertainments. They sang, danced, gave pantomimes and burlesques. In 1872, four years after they had made their début in London in the pantomime of *Humpty Dumpty*, they came to America in their best and most successful offering, *The Belles of the Kitchen*, an entertainment made up very largely of incidents which they themselves had written. They appeared first at the Union Square Theater, at that time a variety house, where the Ravels, de Angelis, Harrigan and Hart (see No. 828) had achieved some of their greatest triumphs. In August of 1875, while the Daly company was on its annual western trip, the Vokes troupe appeared at the Fifth Avenue Theater in the well-known *Belles of the Kitchen*, followed by *A Bunch of Berries*. They were popular for many years. "Rosina Vokes," wrote Towse, "was one of the cleverest and most piquant actresses who ever adorned the stage. She had the most infectious laugh ever heard in a theater, and a merry devil lodged in her eye."

682 Augustin Daly as "An Atlas of Theaters," from a caricature in the New York *Daily Graphic*, Nov. 11, 1873

"AN ATLAS OF THEATERS"

IN spite of such occasional hits as *Uncle Sam* and burlesques on *Richard III*, the Grand Opera enterprise proved more and more a losing business, and the year 1873 one of the blackest in Daly's career. On the first day of that year the Fifth Avenue Theater, which he had leased from Fisk and remodeled with such pains, was destroyed by fire, along with carefully accumulated wardrobes, furniture, and manuscripts. Undismayed, Daly called immediately on A. T. Stewart, owner of the New York Theater, secured a lease for two years, and within three weeks had converted the dilapidated interior into a resemblance of the burned Fifth Avenue. In the summer of 1873 plans were begun for a more permanently suitable theater on Twenty-eighth Street, while the temporary structure of Stewart, renamed Daly's Broadway Theater, was to pay expenses by a combination of star and stock arrangement. Thus with two theaters, the Grand Opera and the Broadway, open and a third under construction, and with three companies to maintain, the adventurous young manager watched with disconsolate eyes the ravages of the Panic of 1873 on all business, and its reflection in the increasingly thin lines of theater patrons. It was not until the following year that Daly was able, even at a great loss, to dispose of the two white elephants and concentrate on his New Fifth Avenue Theater.

WELCOME!

Welcome, thrice welcome to our virgin dome,
The Muses' shrine, the Drama's new-found home!
Here shall the statesman rest his weary brain,
The worn out Artist find his wits again,
Here Trade forget his ledgers and his cares,
And sweet communion mingle Bulls and Bears.

. . . .

Here shall the timid pedants of the schools,
The gilded boors, the labor-scorning fools,
The grass-green rustic and the smoke-dried cit,
Feel each in turn this tingling lash of wit
And as it tingles on some part
Find balsam in his neighbor's smart.

THUS ran the concluding periods of the long address written by Oliver Wendell Holmes for the opening of Augustin Daly's second Fifth Avenue Theater on December 3, 1873. "At a certain point," wrote a contemporary critic, "the curtain parted, disclosing the entire company ranged upon the stage, and Mr. Daly came forward and bowed in acknowledgment of the vociferous calls and the hearty public plaudits. . . . The assembled company, a noble and interesting group, received emphatic recognition and welcome. There were twenty-eight persons on the stage." From Joseph Daly we get an inside view of the manager, worn by the strain of the preceding year, and by the efforts to hold his own against the depression of the panic. "His physical labors for forty-eight hours in preparing for the opening were so exhausting that he fell asleep for a moment behind the scenes during a part of the performance."

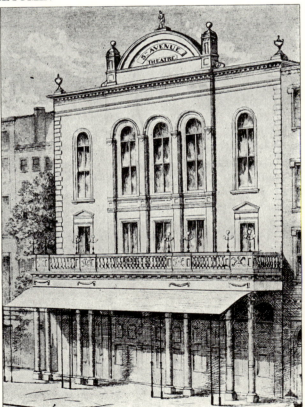

683 Exterior of Daly's New Fifth Avenue Theater, from an engraving
in the New York *Daily Graphic*, Nov. 20, 1873

684   Ada Dyas, 1843–1908, from a photograph
in the Davis Collection

685 Miss Dyas and Harry Montague, from
a photograph in the Davis Collection

AN ARISTOCRAT IN A DEMOCRACY

DALY watched the English theatrical market for possible additions to his cast, which in the matter of actresses was somewhat weakened by the successive desertions of Agnes Ethel, Fanny Morant, and Clara Morris. He counted greatly on the arrival of Ada Dyas, an English actress, who had been considered so excellent in her own country that plans had been formulated to send her as a star with her own company to America. Endowed with youth and beauty, she had been educated in the most refined English circles — in distinct contrast to the discouraging struggles which Clara Morris had been forced to make in the Middle West. This difference of background was most interestingly revealed in Miss Dyas' début on January 3, 1874, in the rôle of Anne Sylvester in *Man and Wife*. The character, "portrayed by Miss Morris as a passionate, emotional creature, was now represented as a woman of not less intense feeling, whose wrongs burned through a surface of womanly dignity and calm." Miss Dyas' popularity with the audience steadily increased in *Foline*, in *The Fast Family*, and in *Divorce*. But it was impossible for her to dismiss from her mind the idea of starring. Unfortunately it was the foundation of Daly's structure that there should be no stars. He reasoned with Miss Dyas, who, continuing to object to his democratic leveling, broke definitely with her new manager, and in the fall of 1874 joined Wallack's.

686   John Drew, II, from a photograph
in the Davis Collection

687   Drew as Robin Hood, from a photograph
in the Davis Collection

JOHN DREW, II,
1853–1927

IN spite of the absence of Ada Dyas, Daly determined to concentrate during the season of 1874–75 on revivals of old comedies. The precipitate desertion of George Clarke, the handsome and romantic lover, left, however, a perplexing vacancy. A happy solution was found in the person of young John Drew, Jr., eldest son of Louisa Lane (see No. 528) of the Philadelphia Arch Street Stock Company. With her Daly had always preserved most cordial relations, and her note, introducing her son, the New York manager considered ample recommendation. Drew had already made his Philadelphia début under his mother's supervision, evincing an unusual coolness and nonchalance on the "fateful" night. This initial self-assurance seldom deserted John Drew during the half-century of his prominence on the American stage. His début at the second Fifth Avenue on February 17, 1875, as Bob Ruggles in *The Big Bonanza* was, according to Joseph Daly, filled with intelligence but lacked the finish and polish of his later performances. It was still a period of apprenticeship — comprising, during the next four years, supporting rôles to Edwin Booth, barnstorming tours into Texas, and seasons with Fanny Davenport.

688   John Drew as Petruchio, from a photograph in the Davis Collection

DISTINGUÉ

IT was not until Daly in 1879 moved into his final theater that Drew took his place as one of the most distinctive actors on the American stage. "John Drew," wrote Booth Tarkington in his preface to Drew's memoirs, "would play Simon Legree into a misunderstood gentleman, I believe." No other native actor has portrayed so convincingly the distingué, amusingly cynical man of the world, whether as diplomat or banker or lawyer or soldier or dilettante. His name is inseparably connected with that of Ada Rehan, opposite whom he played in countless rôles in Daly's comedies adapted from the German. In 1892 he joined Charles Frohman (see No. 840). Some of his finest effects were secured in revivals of old comedies, as Charles Surface in *The School for Scandal*, Orlando in *As You Like It*, Petruchio in *The Taming of the Shrew*, and the King of Navarre in *Love's Labour's Lost*.

ADELAIDE NEILSON, 1846–1880

Two years after joining Daly's forces, Drew, in *Twelfth Night* and *Cymbeline*, played opposite one of the finest interpreters of Shakespeare that the American public had seen for many years. Her "range of characters," wrote Joseph Daly, describing these performances of Adelaide Neilson at his brother's theater in 1877, "was limited for a star . . . but there were actually no bounds to her control of her audiences, who hung upon her words and followed her motions with rapture . . . everything she did appeared to be unconscious . . . her voice did not penetrate — it enveloped." Since her New York début at Edwin Booth's Theater in 1872, she had, by her beauty and by her alluring romantic background, seized the imagination of the American public. Though born amid the miseries of an English factory town she had come under the spell of Shakespeare, and had gradually worked her way upward through the provinces to a brilliant performance of Juliet at Drury Lane in 1870 at the age of twenty-four. In the pages of William Winter this feeling for Neilson as the avatar of a romantic ideal was strongly expressed. During her various American tours, in addition to Viola and Imogen she played Rosalind, Beatrice, Juliet, Isabel in *Measure for Measure*, Amy Robsart, Pauline in *The Lady of Lyons*, Julia in *The Hunchback*, and Lady Teazle. Towse was less enthusiastic than Winter: she was "ravishingly pretty and had a measure of dramatic genius, but not of the high, inventive, intellectual type." Her untimely death in 1880, while still in the height of her powers, increased the romantic attachment of the American public to her name. "I never saw such wonderful eyes," wrote David Belasco, who danced with her in the minuet in *Romeo and Juliet* at San Francisco in 1874, "or heard a voice so silver-toned, so full of pathos, so rich and thrilling."

689   Adelaide Neilson as Imogen in *Cymbeline*, from a photograph in the Davis Collection

690   Adelaide Neilson as Pauline in *The Lady of Lyons*, from a photograph in the Davis Collection

691   Adelaide Neilson as Juliet in *Romeo and Juliet*, from a photograph in the H. A. Ogden Collection

692 Maurice Barrymore, 1847–1905, from a photograph in the Davis Collection

THE BARRYMORES, SENIOR

IN the same year, following John Drew's début at the Fifth Avenue, his sister Georgiana, or, as she was more commonly called, Georgie, became a member of the Daly company. Her first rôle was the sympathetic one of Mary Standish, substituting for the popular Jeffreys Lewis, who was touring in *Pique*. When Amy Fawsitt, English actress, whom Daly had engaged to play Lady Teazle suffered a physical collapse and returned to England, Georgie Drew was selected to replace her. After a season with

693 Maurice Barrymore in *Alabama*, from a photograph in the Harvard Theater Collection, Cambridge, Mass.

Daly she supported successively Edwin Booth, Lawrence Barrett, John McCullough, and Helena Modjeska. In 1890 she played opposite William H. Crane in *The Senator*. After her death in California in 1893 she was survived by three children Lionel, Ethel, and John Barrymore, and by their father Maurice, with whom in 1876 she had played at Daly's and whom soon afterward she had married. Maurice Barrymore, born in India and christened Herbert Blythe, had enjoyed the highest English education, with a view to his becoming a barrister. The appeal of the stage having proved too strong, he had made his début at Windsor as Cool in *London Assurance*, and after an apprenticeship in London and the provinces he had in 1875 come to America on a tour with the English star Charles Vandenhoff. On January 23, 1875, he made his American début at the Boston Theater as Ray Trafford in Daly's popular melodrama, *Under the Gaslight;* and after a revival of the *Shaughraun* in Boston, had joined the Daly company on its annual summer tour. His first metropolitan appearance was at the Fifth Avenue on August 23, 1875, where, wrote Joseph Daly, he was "liked fairly." In the later rôle of the "honest, obtuse, 'pig-headed,' and faithful" Talbot Champney in *Our Boys* he was "cordially accepted." After two seasons with Daly he toured for a number of years — with his new brother-in-law, John Drew, to Texas, where one of the troupe was murdered in a restaurant brawl and he himself wounded; supporting Jo Jefferson in *Rip;* and opposite Fanny Davenport in Shakespearean rôles. From 1879 to 1881 he was leading man at Wallack's. In 1881 in London, he presented *Honor* — his own adaptation from the French. For the five years preceding his wife's death, Barrymore was at the Madison Square under Palmer, appearing in *Alabama*, *Lady Windermere's Fan*, and *Colonel Carter of Cartersville*. His last years, until his death in 1905, were filled with great physical and mental suffering. Modjeska's description of the young Barrymore is

694 Mrs. Barrymore, with her children, Ethel, Lionel, and John, from a photograph in the Davis Collection

at the present day doubly interesting: "Maurice Barrymore was one of those handsome men who also have the rare gift of winning all hearts. He was much admired by women, but was too intellectual to be a mere matinee idol. . . . Sentimental girls used to send him flowers, to his great amusement." Barrymore was an intimate friend of Augustus Thomas (see No. 834) who records many amusing incidents of their association.

695 Georgie Barrymore, 1856–93, from a photograph in the Davis Collection

696 Helena Modjeska, from a photograph
in the Davis Collection

HELENA MODJESKA, 1844–1909

IN 1882 Maurice Barrymore had signed a four-year touring contract with an actress who for a number of years was one of the most striking figures on the American stage. Helena Modjeska, born in Cracow in 1840, a Polish actress of experience and distinction, had been forced by political expediency to flee with her husband. At a safe distance, in the fastnesses of the California valley, they had settled and turned to the raising of chickens. But the lure of the theater could not be evaded, and in 1877, having learned a little English, Mme. Modjeska went to San Francisco, where in August at the California Theater she appeared in one of her famous roles, Adrienne Lecouvreur. After an overwhelming triumph in the West, she appeared

697 Modjeska as Juliet, from a photograph in the Davis Collection

later in the same year at Daly's, and was equally acclaimed by the Metropolitan critics. The beauty of her Camille, her Mary Stuart, her Juliet, her Viola, her Beatrice, and her Rosalind became generally accepted throughout the country. In 1883 her production of Ibsen's *The Doll's House* was less popular and had to be withdrawn. Its indirect result was Maurice Barrymore's *Nadjeska*, a play of Polish life inspired by her performances of Ibsen, though not following at all closely Ibsen's outline. Barrymore's play proved such a strain on the actress that after three weeks of performances she was forced to rest, and Barrymore, irritated at her refusal to present it each night, withdrew the play; and with his wife and Beerbohm Tree produced it with a modicum of success in London. In 1886 Modjeska returned to America from one of her numerous visits to Europe, and played in support of Edwin Booth. Her repertoire steadily increased, including, toward the end, over one hundred rôles. Returning often to Poland, she came again and again to America on "farewell" tours. Towse in his study of Modjeska's performance of Paul M. Potter's adaptation of *Les Chouans* has furnished one of his most illuminating pieces of criticism: "She proved herself as capable of melodramatic emotional expression as Bernhardt herself. In scenes of love, grief, terror, indignation, and rage she exhibited every phase

698 Modjeska as Rosalind, from a photograph in the Madigan Collection, New York

of passionate tenderness, abject misery, hauteur, and stormy passion, revealing a physical vigor surprising in a woman of her slender form." He emphasized the "ease with which she could turn from the extravagance of melodrama to the naturalism of serious domestic comedy. She was equally effective as the loving wife and the outraged woman, being especially impressive in her moments of righteous anger and contemptuous scorn. . . . It was in comedy, social or romantic, in melodrama, and in poetic romance, that her versatility, imagination, emotional eloquence, and almost inexhaustible artistry were manifested most triumphantly. For many years she was the brightest feminine ornament of the American stage."

699 Modjeska as Viola in *Twelfth Night*, from a photograph in the Madigan Collection, New York

700 Emily Rigl, from a photograph
in the Davis Collection

701 Mrs. Scott-Siddons, 1843-96, from a photograph in the Davis Collection

702 Linda Dietz (left) and Sarah Jewett, from
a photograph in the Davis Collection

703 Carlotta Leclercq, from a photograph
in the Davis Collection

704 Daniel H. Harkins, 1835-1902, from a photograph in the Davis Collection

705 Jeffreys Lewis, from a photograph in
the Davis Collection

706 Louis James, 1842-1910, from a photograph in the Davis Collection

XIV—17

DALY'S ACTORS

"WE rehearse almost all day long," wrote
the Daly debutante in her Diary. "I
wonder whether all managers have such
tremendous rehearsals as Mr. Daly has.
He is a wonderful teacher of acting; I
believe he could teach a broom-stick to act;
. . . he seems to know instinctively just
how everything should go . . . suddenly
he will stop someone in the midst of a
speech — and request that person to repeat
the lines or perform that bit of business
in a different manner. . . . When things
go well he tiptoes about softly as if he went
on velvet paws; but if there is any trouble
he tears about like a madman."

707 Edith Kingdon, 1841-1921, from
a photograph in the Davis Collection

708 John Parselle, 1820–85, in the Union Square success, *A Celebrated Case*, from a photograph in the Davis Collection

709 Sara Jewett, 1847–99, as Adrienne in *A Celebrated Case*, from a photograph in the Davis Collection

710 Agnes Booth and E. M. Holland (right), in the Madison Square success, *Jim the Penman*, from a photograph in the Davis Collection

INCREASING COMPETITION

By the time that Maurice Barrymore made his début at the New Fifth Avenue Theater, the competition against which Daly had been struggling since 1869 had become appreciably more severe. He had always recognized and made due allowance for the power of Wallack's organization. The increasingly powerful company at the Union Square Theater was more startling. Since the desertion of Agnes Ethel, Daly had watched a number of the actors and actresses whom he had carefully trained transfer the benefits of their experience to the rival company; but each such crisis had evoked new resourcefulness on his part, and the efficiency of his administration was on the whole enhanced. When Sheridan Shook, a capitalist with no pretensions to dramatic taste, had built his small theater on the south side of Union Square between Broadway and Fourth Avenue, and his first manager had failed to produce from his raucous variety entertainment the returns which the investor expected, Shook turned to a young lawyer who happened to be in his internal revenue office, and suggested that he try his hand at the enterprise. Albert Marshall Palmer, who was thus presented with an unpromising opportunity for which his legal training had in no way fitted him, was endowed with a native ingenuity and sensitiveness of appreciation that enabled him to overcome his original handicap, and take ultimately his place beside Wallack and Daly as an intelligent constructive promoter of the drama. For eleven years, 1872–83, he controlled the destinies of the Union Square Theater, adding each year to the strength of his cast and his repertory. Leaving in 1883 with the intention of retiring, he returned after a year abroad to the Madison Square Theater where he gathered a company of strong players whom he presented in many important successes. In 1891 he surrendered the Madison Square Theater and moved to the old Wallack's Theater at Broadway and Thirtieth. Here he enjoyed less success, and, with his powers fast failing, decided in 1896 to withdraw entirely from management.

711 Scene from *Jim the Penman*, from a photograph in the Davis Collection

712 Exterior of the Union Square Theater, from *The Theatre Magazine*, Mar. 1903

713 Albert Marshall Palmer, 1838–1905, from a photograph in the Davis Collection

714 Henry E. Abbey, 1846–96, from a photograph in the Davis Collection

NEW YORK MANAGERS

An appreciation of Palmer as a producer invites a comparison of his methods and of his personality with those of other New York managers, a comparison that suggests certain obvious differences. Wallack was an actor, with a long inheritance of the green-room tradition and spirit; was dramatist on occasion; and always understood the particular problems of adaptations. Daly was, par excellence, the draughtsman, the technician, the adapter, the promoter, who since childhood had been interested in the framework of plays, in the subtle laws governing the mind of an audience, and in the economics of a box office. With no personal desire to act, he slaved with his troupe in endless rehearsals, striving to submerge the identity of the actor in the dramatic figure that would hold the eye and heart of the spectator. He had the zeal of the crusader, the monomania of the idealist. There were other New York managers who, though overshadowed by Daly and Wallack, were active and prosperous at the time that Albert M. Palmer was building up the Union Square Company. Henry C. Jarrett and Henry Palmer, who had promoted the famous Black Crook Review (see No. 635) were associated from 1868 to 1874 as co-managers of Niblo's Garden, and from August 10, 1874, to September 12, 1877, as co-managers of Booth's Theater. In the fall of 1876 Henry E. Abbey, backed by Lotta Crabtree (see No. 484), gained possession of the New Park Theater between 21st and 22nd on Broadway, which he managed until it was destroyed by fire in 1882. Albert M. Palmer was neither actor, nor dramatic adapter, nor capitalist, nor stage general. He was, as Towse epitomized him, "a man of considerable cultivation, suave, shrewd, worldly, somewhat hesitant and timid in judgment, but with first-rate executive ability, and a remarkable faculty of finding means to serve his ends." Realizing his own limitations and those of his company, Palmer made few pretensions to literary production. He selected his actors with unusual discrimination, but in the preparation of plays the responsibility was entrusted to the brilliant adapter and house dramatist, A. R. Cazauran, a Bohemian. Steele MacKaye is authority for the statement about Palmer that "three of his biggest managerial successes, *The Two Orphans*, *Jim the Penman*, and *Alabama* are said to have been urged upon him against his own will and judgment." Palmer himself developed few great actors, but he was blessed again and again by the addition of a new member who had been thoroughly drilled by Daly, the autocrat.

715 Henry C. Jarrett, 1827–1903, from a photograph in the Davis Collection

716 Henry Palmer, d. 1879 from a photograph in the Davis Collection

717 Kitty Blanchard (left) and Kate Claxton in *The Two Orphans*, from a photograph in the Davis Collection

718 Fanny Morant as Countess Diane De Lanieres in *The Two Orphans*, from a photograph in the Davis Collection

719 Kate Claxton, 1849–1924, as Louise in *The Two Orphans*, from a photograph in the collection of H. A. Ogden, New York

THE TWO ORPHANS

THOUGH much less of an autocrat than Daly, Palmer, thanks to his "first-rate executive ability" and the "suave, shrewd, worldly" use of his stage managers and house dramatist, had succeeded by the summer of 1875, the period of Barrymore's first tour with Daly, in establishing the Union Square Stock Company as a powerful rival to the two older houses. *The Two Orphans* written by d'Ennery and Carmon, and adapted especially for the Union Square Theater, ran for one hundred and eighty consecutive nights from December 21, 1874, to June 15, 1875. Fanny Morant and Kate Claxton, both of whom had formerly been with Daly, played two of the leading rôles. This play proved an unfailing favorite. Kate Claxton bought the rights from Palmer and traveled for twenty years in her rôle of the blind sister. It was *The Two Orphans* which was being given at the Brooklyn Theater when the scenery caught fire, and, before many had managed to escape, the entire building was burned. Miss Claxton was saved, escaping through the parquette. Her gratitude did not take the form displayed by her grandfather, likewise an actor and likewise a near victim of another famous fire — that of the Richmond theater in 1811 (see No. 155) — who, having been thus shown the judgment of the Almighty, immediately repented of his sinful Thespian ways and became a preacher.

720 F. F. Mackay, 1836–1923, as Pierre Frochard in *The Two Orphans*, from a photograph in the Davis Collection

721 James O'Neill, 1847–1920, in *The Two Orphans*, from a photograph in the Davis Collection

STEELE MACKAYE, 1844–1894

DURING the summer after the first run of *The Two Orphans* Palmer was busily engaged at his home in Stamford, Connecticut, supervising the work of a young American dramatist, whose new play he hoped to produce during the coming season. Steele MacKaye, Palmer's new neighbor, had since 1870 suffered discouraging years of ups and downs, of sudden changes from "cheese cloth to ermine" and back again to cheese cloth. In 1870 he had become a warm friend and enthusiastic admirer of Delsarte, supreme master of the aesthetic philosophy of facial and vocal expression, whom numerous French stars acclaimed as the source of their art. Returning to America, MacKaye had preached the philosophy and given practical demonstrations of the methods of his new teacher. After a financially unsuccessful season (1872–73) as actor and manager of the old St. James Theater on Twenty-eighth Street and Broadway, where he had attempted to prove that Delsarte's methods were feasible behind the footlights, MacKaye had returned to Paris to study under Regnier, of the Conservatoire, who, since the death of Delsarte, was the outstanding maestro of Paris. MacKaye had given *Hamlet* in French, had

722 Steele MacKaye, from a photograph in the collection of Montrose J. Moses, New York

made his London début in the same rôle at the Crystal Palace in 1873, had toured the English provinces, and had collaborated on plays with Charles Reade, Tom Taylor, and other prominent English dramatists. During the interval between his return to America in 1874 and the summer at Stamford with Palmer, he had toured the country lecturing for Redpath, bringing to American audiences the gospel of Delsarte, and describing the school for dramatic expression which he had begun in New York. Only two of MacKaye's plays had been produced: *Monaldi*, in which he had made his début, and *Marriage*, an adaptation of Feuillet's *Julie*, produced at the St. James in 1872. But when Palmer asked him to undertake the adaptation of *Rose Michel*, a French success by Ernest Blum, MacKaye, with that independence which characterized all

723 MacKaye as Col. Servasse in his own play, *A Fool's Errand*, from a photograph, courtesy of Percy MacKaye, Windsor, Vt.

his relationships, accepted only on condition that he have an absolutely free hand, and that he be allowed "to take only the central idea of the play and work out his own characters and plot." MacKaye worked eagerly on the play, indifferent to the numerous annoyances of getting settled in a new home. Palmer would drop in, seat himself on the still unpacked boxes, and listen to the lines which MacKaye had finished during the day. *Rose Michel* was one of MacKaye's most popular dramas. It was eclipsed later by *Hazel Kirke*, which he produced in 1879 at the Madison Square, and which, on the basis of its performances in New York and on the road, held the record for the longest run of any play in America until *Lightnin'*. *The Twins* for Palmer, *Won at Last* for Wallack, and *Through the Dark* for Daly, were less popular. *Anarchy* (also called *Paul Kauvar* and *The Vagabond*), an embodiment of MacKaye's passionate interest in the French Revolution, is generally considered his most powerful play. For the first time on the American stage, there was a disciplined and carefully trained mob, which gave to the revolutionary scenes a thrilling realism. The effect on the audience was electrifying.

724 James H. Stoddart as Pierre Michel in *Rose Michel*, from a photograph in the Davis Collection

725 J. H. Stoddart in *Miss Moulton*, from a photograph in the Madigan Collection

JAMES H. STODDART, 1827–1907

"To me," wrote James H. Stoddart in the section of his *Recollections of a Player* dealing with *Rose Michel*, "it read like an ordinary melodrama, but it was set with such care and acted in such a refined manner that it was raised to a high grade of performance. The scenic effects produced on that small stage were indeed extraordinary." Stoddart, who had joined Palmer's company the preceding year, and who in *Rose Michel* played the rôle of the old miser, Pierre Michel, is an interesting example of the stock actor, whose career, in its details, gives life and coherence to the succession of theaters and managers. Having come to New York in 1852, with only a few years of experience in the English provinces, he had been elated at being accepted on his first application by Wallack, who had only recently organized his first stock company. He was satisfied, of course, with minor parts such as Gol-o-gog in Brougham's *Po-Ca-Hon-Tas*, and delighted at his reputation of having the best wigs in the cast. In 1855 he joined a company of E. A. Sothern to tour Canada. In 1856 he went with Sothern and J. T. Raymond for a season at Halifax, Nova Scotia, and later in the year joined Laura Keene's Varieties, with which he remained until 1858, when he joined his wife, also a stock actress, at the Mobile Theater, then under the direction of Duffield. From Mobile he went for a summer season to Montreal, and then to the theaters of John Ford at Baltimore, Washington, and Alexandria, Virginia. For two years he was with Boucicault, concentrating on "old men" at the Winter Garden; then again for a short period with Laura Keene; and later with Mrs. John Wood, whose management of the Olympic Stoddart very highly praised. In 1867 he rejoined his old manager, Lester Wallack, and for six years he was given the leading eccentric comedy rôles, in which he gained an increasingly wide reputation. In 1873 he was tempted to try starring, but after a completely unsuccessful venture, he was glad to accept Palmer's offer to become a member of the Union Square Company. Stoddart, according to Towse, was "an eccentric comedian of rare ability, who shone in fierce passion as well as in broad humor and simple pathos."

THE SUCCESS OF THE PLAY

"When *Rose Michel* was produced [November 23, 1875] at the Union Square Theater," wrote Stuart Robson, "Mr. Stoddart achieved the success of the play, aided in no very small degree by your humble servant."

726 Stuart Robson (left), 1835–1903, and William H. Crane as the two Dromios in *A Comedy of Errors*, from a photograph in the Davis Collection

727 Stuart Robson (right) and William H. Crane in *Our Bachelors*, from a photograph in the Davis Collection

Stuart Robson, who took the part of Moulinet, was the established comedian of Palmer's forces, and Stoddart had been forced to change his own line from eccentric comedy to character work. Robson's appreciation of his own contribution to the success of *Rose Michel* was substantiated by Towse, who was convinced that Robson was "not much of an actor, but had a quaint and comic personality that brought him great popularity." Robson, like Fanny Davenport and the young Drews, had served his apprenticeship at the Arch Street under Mrs. John Drew, and was associated for a number of years with William H. Crane. (See No. 881.)

CHARLES R. THORNE, JR., 1840–1883

At least an equal sharer in the success of the play was Charles R. Thorne, Jr., who won his audience during the preceding season by his dashing, romantic Maurice de Vaudray in *The Two Orphans*. And now for one hundred and twenty consecutive nights he gave a similarly spirited presentation of the Count de Vernay, the appealing hero-lover, opposite the Rose Michel of Rose Eytinge (see No. 620). According to Towse, Thorne was, in spite of a certain stiffness, "an intelligent and forceful actor, whose stalwart form lent verisimilitude to all virile parts." Other famous rôles of Thorne's were the husband in Bronson Howard's *A Banker's Daughter*, and the title-rôle in Sardou's *Daniel Rochat*. Thorne's father, born in New York in 1814, had made his début at the second Park in 1830, and had been for a time manager of the Federal Street, Boston, and of the New Chatham, New York.

728 Charles R. Thorne, Jr., as Maurice de Vaudray in *The Two Orphans*, from a photograph in the Davis Collection

CHARLES COGHLAN, 1842–1899

Daly watched with some apprehension the growing popularity and extended runs of his new rival at the Union Square. Joseph Daly recorded his brother's next move to offset the unexpected success: "To strengthen the company where it had sometimes been found weak, that is, with regard to a masculine actor who possessed the authority of Wallack, the charm of Montague [see No. 582] . . . or the force of Thorne, Daly brought over one of the latest favorites of London, Charles Coghlan. He was the superior of all those named, in youthful appearance, manners, and taste, and was presented on September 12, 1876, as Alfred Evelyn in Bulwer's *Money*." His success was immediate and overwhelming: as a charmingly romantic Orlando opposite Fanny Davenport's Rosalind; as Charles Surface — a performance which was described by Joseph Daly as "a miracle of elegance, dress, and distinction"; and as the Duc de Septmonts, in *The American*, Daly's adaptation of Dumas' *L'Etrangère* — in which, according to Towse, Coghlan gave "a microscopic study of cold, smooth, steely villainy." "Charles Coghlan," epitomized Towse, "was one of the best all-round actors of his generation. He was infinitely superior to any of the leading men of his era or of the stars of today. . . . In poetic romance, melodrama, and artificial and social comedy he was without a rival, but in tragedy his best faculties seemed to suffer paralysis." Winter was equally enthusiastic: "He had a figure of rare symmetry, a handsome face, — remarkable not only for regularity of features but for variety, dignity, authority, and sweetness of expression, — a voice of wide compass and sympathetic quality, and a natural demeanor of intrinsic superiority." The prospects for Coghlan's second season seemed brighter than any that Daly had known for some time — and then, recorded Joseph Daly, quite too laconically, "dissatisfaction manifested itself in the company. Coghlan was not pleased with the numerous changes of bill, or with his new parts. Lewis also

729 Charles Coghlan, from a photograph in the Davis Collection

began to complain. Both gentlemen . . . appear to have been invited to a chat with Mr. Palmer of the Union Square. Coghlan was the only one that Palmer succeeded in getting; but he was a severe loss to Daly." His most famous rôle at Palmer's was Jean Renaud opposite the Madeline of Agnes Booth in *A Celebrated Case*, which ran one hundred and eleven nights. During the next two decades Coghlan was an outstanding favorite with the American public, wherever he appeared. He was the author of several plays, *The Brothers*, *A Quiet Rubber*, and *Lady Barter*.

730 Coghlan as Orlando in *As You Like It*, from a photograph in the H. A. Ogden Collection, New York

731   Rose Coghlan as Rosalind, from a photograph in the Davis Collection

732   Rose Coghlan as Lady Teazle, from a
photograph in the Davis Collection

ROSE COGHLAN, 1850–

THOUGH the phenomenal brilliance of Charles Coghlan was never attained by his sister, Rose, her stage career in America covered a longer period,

733   Rose Coghlan in *Forget-Me-Not*, from a photograph in the Davis Collection

and identified her even more closely with the American tradition. Her first New York appearance had been at Wallack's on September 2, 1872, as Jupiter in *Ixion*. For the next six years she appeared, at intervals of varying length, on the board of Wallack's Thirteenth Street Theater. On March 23, 1878, the critic of *The Spirit of the Times* in his review of her Magdalen Atherleigh in *False Shame* gave an indication of Miss Coghlan's increasing popularity, "She does not strike you blind by the instant refulgence of her genius. . . . But she wins you surely if you go more than once to Wallack's. I like her sturdy, direct, Anglo-Saxon style." But it was not until her brilliant performance of the rôle of Countess Zicka in Sardou's *Diplomacy* that the excellence of her acting was generally applauded. "Miss Coghlan is conspicuous," wrote the critic in *The Spirit of the Times* of April 13, 1878, "among those whose personations are town talk. This clever lady has

734   Rose Coghlan as Lady Gay Spanker
in *London Assurance*, from a photograph in the Davis Collection

made an immeasurable advance by her latest assumption, and altogether the fair creatrice of the Countess Zicka bids fair to rival her talented brother in the estimation of theater-goers." During the years that followed, Miss Coghlan's popularity increased steadily. Her Rosalind was declared the best to be seen on the American stage; her Lady Teazle was unrivaled; her starring rôles — under the direction of Augustus Pitou — which included Lady Gay Spanker in *London Assurance*, Mrs. Arbuthrust in *A Woman of No Importance*, and Peg Woffington, were invariably successful. Her voice, which was able to express all the emotions and give the righ tone to light comedy or heavy drama, became celebrated.

735   Rose Coghlan as Lady Teazle, from a photograph in the H. A. Ogden Collection

736 Francis Bret Harte, 1839–1902, from an engraving in the New York *Daily Graphic*, October 9, 1873

AH SIN

WHILE still unaware of the impending loss of Charles Coghlan, Daly on July 31, 1877, offered to his public the work of two of the most famous American men of letters of the time, *Ah Sin* by Bret Harte and Mark Twain. It was the strongly nourished ambition of both of them to turn their remarkable gifts of vivid fiction and character portrayal to the demands of the stage. Daly had earlier tried to supervise a working agreement between Harte and Boucicault, but the professional dramatist had soon refused to continue the collaboration. Harte had completed the work alone and in 1876 given it

737 Samuel Langhorne Clemens, (Mark Twain) 1835–1910, from an engraving in the New York *Daily Graphic*, October 9, 1873

to the Union Square public as *The Two Men of Sandy Bar*, but it had not proved popular. The author then undertook with Mark Twain *Ah Sin*, a play of the western life which they knew so well. "There was a distinguished gathering on the first night," wrote Joseph Daly, ". . . A speech being of course demanded, Twain . . . responded with his usual gravity. Some of the papers next day thought the speaker better than the play. Here it is: 'This is a very remarkable play. . . . The construction of this play and the development of the story are the result of great research, and erudition, and genius, and invention — and plagiarism. . . . When our play was finished, we found it was so long, and so broad, and so deep — in places — that it would have taken a week to play it. I thought that was all right; we could put "To be continued" on the curtain, and run it straight along. But the manager said no; it would get us into trouble with the general public, and into trouble with the general government, because the Constitution forbids the infliction of cruel or unusual punishment; so he cut out, and cut out, and the more he cut the better the play got. . . . I believe it would have been one of the very best plays in the world if his strength had held out so that he could cut out the whole of it.' "

ON THE ROAD

ON September 12, 1877, Daly, discouraged by the continued financial difficulties which had beset him during the past year, called together the members of his company to inform them of his decision to close the New York theater and to take whatever volunteers offered themselves on a tour of the southern and southwestern circuit. To the disappointment of the manager, only a few of his stars accepted, and with an inferior company he left in early October for a tour that eventually included Paterson, Wilmington, Baltimore, Richmond, Raleigh, Charleston, Savannah, New Orleans, Mobile, and Nashville. A letter from Savannah, February 12, 1878, gives an invaluable picture of the type of house in which the touring company performed. "The theater is the oddest old building you ever saw. . . . The proscenium is very old & odd too and has an opening each

738 The Savannah Theater, from an engraving in *The Autobiography of Joseph Jefferson*, New York, 1889. © The Century Co.

side for the stars to answer calls without disturbing the curtain. I believe 'tis the oldest theater in America now, since the Holliday Street house in Baltimore was burned. And its very dinginess is suggestive. Kean & Booth & Macready & Fanny Kemble & Charles Kemble and Ellen Tree and the elder Mathews and all the lights of Art so long sunken in their sockets flashed forth from these creaky boards their brightest fires — & warmed two generations past into enthusiasm." After his return to New York, Daly began negotiating for a new theater, but seeing little possibility of concluding at the moment the desired arrangement, sailed for an eight months' visit to England.

739   Ada Rehan, 1860–1916, as Lady Teazle in *The School For Scandal*, from a photograph in the H. A. Ogden Collection, New York

ADA REHAN

WHEN Daly returned from Europe in the spring of 1879 he brought with him a dramatization of Emile Zola's *L'Assommoir* — lurid and morbid in spirit, but possessed of certain scenes which had thrilled London audiences. Daly's production in the inaccessible Olympic Theater added nothing to his laurels, either artistically or financially, except the person of a new actress, who was destined during the twenty remaining years of the manager's life to help tremendously in so establishing the reputation of the Daly theater that it was without a close rival. The se-

740   Ada Rehan, left (with Virginia Dreher), as Mistress Page in *The Merry Wives of Windsor*, from an engraving in possession of the publishers

lection of the cast for the Zola play had been entrusted to the stage manager of the Arch Street Theater, who recommended to Daly's close attention a young pupil of Mrs. Drew's who was appearing at the time in New York opposite Fanny Davenport. Daly saw Ada Rehan, was greatly impressed by the spontaneity and brilliance of her person and voice, chose her for a minor rôle in *L'Assommoir*, soon promoted her, and was pleased to accept her as a permanent member of the Fifth Avenue Company, which he was re-forming. On the opening night of Daly's final New York Theater, September 19, 1879, the audience gazed with amazement at the unbelievable transformation that Daly had within a few months effected in the old Broadway Museum on the corner of 30th Street — gazed with delight at the beautiful freshness of Ada Rehan who made her first Daly appearance in a comedietta, *Love's Young Dream*. The last of the famous "Big Four" had arrived. But during that first season of 1879–80 only one of the other three was present, John Drew. Mrs. John Gilbert and "Jimmy" Lewis did not return until the following year. Rehan's first great success was as the Countess in *Odette*, Sardou's latest Parisian sensation. Here, as in the scores of clever comedy adaptations from the French and German, Rehan played opposite Drew, a pair widely regarded as more complementary and mutually stimulating than any in our stage history. Whether in revivals of old comedies, as Hypolita in *She Would and She Would Not*, Peggy Thrift in Daly's expurgated *Country Wife*, Sylvia in *The Recruiting Officer*, Katherine in *The Taming of the Shrew*, Rosalind or Viola or Portia, or as Mistress Page in *The Merry Wives;* or in modern comedy adaptations as Phronie in *Dollars and Sense*, Annie Austin in *Love on Crutches*, or Niske in *A Night Off*, she was equally sparkling and brilliant. During her twenty years with Daly she played over two hundred parts, and her popularity with all generations was unfailing. "I have written wonderful books," protested Mark Twain in a letter to Daly, "which have revolutionized politics and religion in the world; you may think that is why my children hold my person to be sacred; but it isn't so; it is because I know Miss Rehan and Mr. Drew personally."

741   Ada Rehan, center (with Henrietta Crosman), as Rosalind in *As You Like It*, from a photograph in the Davis Collection

742 Ada Rehan as Katherine in *The Taming of the Shrew*, from a photograph in the Davis Collection

"LIKE THE DAUGHTER OF FINGAL"

FROM the plethora of adulation that has been heaped upon this most popular American comédienne, it is difficult to select tributes, representative of the audience, and yet mellowed with a certain salt of critical judgment. William Winter devoted to her an entire volume of biographical study and appreciation, and yet even he admitted his failure to visualize for posterity the artist who appeared on the boards of Daly's theater. "Cibber

743 Ada Rehan and John Drew in *Dollars and Sense*, from a photograph in the Madigan Collection

could have caught and reflected the elusive charm of Ada Rehan. No touch less adroit and felicitous than his can accomplish more than the suggestion of her peculiar allurement, her originality, and her enchanting, because sympathetic and piquant, mental and physical characteristics." "Art can accomplish much," he wrote elsewhere, evading the critic's task of esthetic evaluation, "but it can not supply the inherent captivation that constitutes the puissance of Rosalind. Miss Rehan possesses this quality, and the method of her art is the fluent method of natural grace." Ellen Terry, after her first visit to a Rehan performance, wrote to Daly, "You've got a girl in your company who is the most lovely, humourous darling I have ever seen on the stage." "It was Ada Rehan!" . . . continued Terry in her *Memoirs*. . . . "The audacious, superb, quaint, Irish creature! Never have I seen such splendid high comedy! Then the charm of her voice . . . her smiles and dimples, and provocative, inviting coquetterie! I can only exclaim, not explain!" Arthur Lynch in *Human Documents* gave an extraordinary picture of her, "She is all alive; she whirls round and comes into the action with a bold ringing stroke that has been adjudged to perfection. She can stride — not like a man, for she is always a fine woman — but like the daughter of Fingal, the sister of Ossian. She can bang a door

744 Ada Rehan and John Drew in the *Railroad of Love*, from a photograph in the Davis Collection

like a chord of martial music. . . . We find flesh and blood throughout and everywhere the fire of the soul that animates it." And even Towse, usually so judicial in his critical estimates, did not qualify his generalization. "From the first Miss Rehan was in her element in every variety of piquant, tender, mischievous, high-spirited, alluring, whimsical and provocative girlhood. Her humor was infectious, her charm potent, her pertness delicious, her petulance pretty, and her flashes of ire or scorn brilliant."

745 Ada Rehan, from the painting by John Singer Sargent (1856–1927), in the Grand Central Galleries, New York

746 Laying of Cornerstone of Daly's London Theater, from a photograph in the Ada Rehan Collection, New York Public Library

EUROPEAN TOUR

ON May 10, 1898, Daly received a letter from the Mayor of Stratford-on-Avon, announcing that the Executive Committee of the Shakespeare Memorial Theater had "honored themselves and the institution by making Miss Rehan a Life Governor," and wishing her manager to convey to her the sentiments of the distinguished fellow-townsmen of Shakespeare: "We find she is now as thoroughly identified with our good old Town and all its prized associations as if she lived amongst us, as I know she does in spirit." As Daly relayed to Miss Rehan this sincere testimonial of the Stratford authorities there must have come to each of them many memories of their numerous tours of England and of the continent: of the opening London season of 1884, and the chill welcome extended to the hardy American company that ventured as pioneers in the exclusive British market; of the many seasons that followed, culminating in a success trumpeted by recanting critics; of the struggles to continue the London Daly Theater, opened in 1893 and forfeited finally in 1897; of the performances in Hamburg and Berlin before uncomprehending audiences — the first performances in English in three hundred years; of the two Paris appearances and the surprisingly naïve hostility of the French critics; of days at the home of Tennyson, who wrote for Miss Rehan the lyrical rôle of Maid Marian in *The Foresters*, which Daly produced in New York; of letters from Oscar Wilde begging Rehan to play the rôle of Mrs. Erlynne in *Lady Windermere's Fan*, "more fitted to her than to any other English actress"; of Rehan's own cottage on the rocky coast of Wales, where the Dalys, exhausted by the strain of London productions, retired for recuperation; of the long walking trips in France and Italy of Augustin Daly and his wife and Ada Rehan. But chiefly, in thinking of the letter, they must have remembered the two performances of the Daly company at Stratford: the first in 1888 with Rehan as Katherine, in the first known performance of *The Taming of the Shrew* in the birthplace of the author; the second in 1897, an open-air performance of *As You Like It* with Rehan in one of her greatest rôles as Rosalind; memories of the reception by the town officials, and of their quiet entertainment; memories of the afternoon in the punts on the Avon; of the thundershower which interrupted the bucolic charm of the evening's performance; of the resumption of the performance indoors before a crowded audience. And there were in their minds probably plans of new tours and new successes. In the following fall, of the year before his death, Daly sent to the Stratford authorities a bronze bust of Ada Rehan to be placed permanently in the Memorial Library — a becomingly modest symbol and announcement of the American theater's coming of age; a humble tribute to the shrine of the canon saint, who, since the days of the infancy of the American theater under the first American stock manager, William Dunlap, had been revered as the source of English drama in its old home and in its new.

747 Daly's Company in the Banquet Scene from *The Taming of the Shrew*, from a photograph in the Davis Collection

748 Daly's Company in *A Night Off*, from a photograph in the Davis Collection

CHAPTER XI

THE STAR MAKERS

ON February 4, 1880, the Madison Square Theater, a marvel of beauty in the eyes of contemporaries, was opened in New York City. It was equipped with new and fascinating mechanical devices — evidences of the fact that the age of applied invention was beginning to have its effect on the theater. In other respects Americans were swift to utilize the devices produced by an industrial era in their adjustment to the conditions of the new cities. The decade of the 'eighties saw the beginnings of trolley cars and telephones. Men were experimenting with new forms of locomotion, particularly the bicycle of the old high-wheel type. In industry, the dominant phase of the development between 1880 and 1910 was the swift rise of the corporation — the trust, as it was commonly called in those days. Industrial magnates were dreaming dreams, which to an earlier generation would have seemed incredibly vast, and were making them come true. The American people were exploiting one of the richest natural environments in the world, and were deriving therefrom tremendous wealth. The genius of the people expressed itself in material things — in railways, in factories, in deep mines, and, after the beginning of the new century, in the automobile and in the aeroplane. Side by side with the industrial development following the Civil War had gone the emergence of the modern American newspapers, magazines, and universities. The culture of the American people was being both broadened and deepened. It was to such a public that the American theater of this period directed its appeal; and the man who idealized this public and who accepted its judgment as final was Charles Frohman, the most typical theatrical figure of his day.

An analysis of Frohman's career reveals a number of seeming contradictions. If a single characteristic of his régime be chosen which would differentiate it most clearly from the preceding period, and ally it most closely to the activities of his great rival, David Belasco, it would be undoubtedly the tremendous number of "stars" whom Frohman introduced each year to the public. On one occasion, returning from his yearly trip to London, he showed to his friends a crude sketch which he had made of "C. F." in a top hat, gazing up at the moon and saying to her, "I will make a star of you yet." Again and again he expressed his deep faith in the star system. "Over here we regard the workman first and the work second. Our imaginations are fired not nearly so much by great deeds as by great doers. There are stars in every walk of American life. It has always been so with democracies. Caesar, Cicero, and the rest were public stars when Rome was at her best, just as in our day Taft, Roosevelt, and some others are of a much finer brilliance than any public service they actually render." "A star has a unique value in a play," he once wrote in a letter to Billie Burke. "It concentrates interest. In some respects a play is like a dinner. To be a success, no matter how splendidly served, the menu should always have one unique and striking dish that, despite its elaborate gastronomic surroundings, must long be remembered." Acting on these fundamental beliefs, Frohman elevated to the ranks of stardom actors with only a few years of experience. There had been stars in the American theater since the days of Thomas Cooper at the First Park down through the era of Edwin Booth and Lawrence Barrett, but in each case there had been years of patient ground work. In the opinion of both Frohman and Belasco the long laborious ascent was superfluous, and with their numerous productions each year it was essential to draft all available talent, and cast around it the greatest glamour possible. Yet Frohman often disclaimed ever having made a star. "I don't believe any manager living ever made a star," he once wrote. "An actor or an actress is made by the audience. The manager does not watch the actress' methods, but he watches the methods of the audience. When the electric actor is on the stage, he then sees his chance and takes it." Frohman conceived of himself as a cabinet minister directly responsible to his constituents — the audience. He never doubted the justice of their verdict, however great the financial loss to him as producer. There is throughout Frohman's entire career a spirit of calm, mellow acquiescence in the judgments of the American public, to which in sentiment and taste he felt himself peculiarly akin.

Along with the conception of Frohman as the star maker has grown in the public mind the figure of Frohman, the financial wizard, who had his thumbs in countless theatrical pies, from all of which he succeeded in extracting juicy plums; the wizard of commerce comparable to Harriman; the relentless monopolist who exerted every energy to crush his chief rival, Belasco. Across his memory fall the shadows of Al Hayman and the other members of the Theatrical Syndicate, which was responsible, in the eyes of many, for the commercialization and subsequent demoralization of the American theater. In New York and London alone Frohman's theaters were worth over five million dollars. He paid thirty-five millions in salaries each year to upward of ten thousand employees; his yearly bill for advertising was over half a million; over three-quarters of a million was necessary to transport his troupes in their annual tours of America and Europe — with an extra half a million for baggage. A twenty-thousand dollar Pullman was built for him, and the railroads accorded his coach the same precedence of schedule that they did to the President's Special. He controlled the bookings in the large, barn-like theaters which were growing up like mushrooms over the country to house the increasing number of road companies emanating from New York over the complex network of railroads which had by now been completed. He excluded from his New York stages those plays which he felt would not be popular on the road. He worked incessantly, reading plays and rehearsing, but to him the theater was a hobby, and his fund of humor softened the strain. His broadsides against rival managers in the provinces read like the edicts of Napoleon: "I have found no difficulty in placing my plays along the Thames, the Seine, the Rhine and the Hudson, so I hardly expect to find much difficulty in placing them alongside the Erie and the Missouri." Yet Sir James Barrie wrote of him, "I have never known anyone more modest and no one quite so shy. . . . For money he did not care at all. It was to him but pieces of paper with which he could make practical the enterprises that teemed in his brain." He shunned publicity and abhorred photographers; and he gave to dramatists a greater share of profits than they had ever before received. His contributions to the higher art of the theater were negligible, and after his death in 1915 his organization lost its preëminence, but during his lifetime he was the personification of the American theater.

749 Exterior of the Madison Square
Theater, from a print in the possession
of Percy MacKaye, Windsor, Vt.

"THE MOST EXQUISITE THEATER IN THE WORLD"

"TONIGHT," wrote the dramatic critic of the *Spirit of the Times* on February 4, 1880, "Mr. J. Steele MacKaye [see No. 722] will open the most exquisite theater in the world, and all New York will assemble to do honour to the realization of his artistic visions. On Monday morning, before noon, every seat was sold. Mr. Augustin Daly and Miss Rose Coghlan will have boxes. The play is now called *Hazel Kirke* after the heroine. Mr. MacKaye

750 Interior of the Madison Square Theater,
from a photograph, courtesy of Marshall Mallory,
New York

will play the drama through with only two minute waits between the acts, and will then exhibit the double stage . . . so that the audience can appreciate the value of his invention. Mr. Hughson Hawley, the scenic artist, . . . will be a celebrity after tonight. . . . Not to have seen the Madison Square Theater is to be behind the age in theatrical intelligence and artistic knowledge."

"TO THE ADVANTAGE OF MANKIND"

"NEW and splendidly handsome, his house will receive all merited attention, respect, and public good-will," wrote William Winter on the following day in *The Tribune*, "but the influences which proceed from its stage are its soul. . . . These, from the guarantee of the opening performance, will be such as the best friends of the drama could desire — a theater administered in a pure and high spirit, to the advantage of mankind in beauty, . . . liberal and fine intelligence, and thus in happiness." "The characters are sharply individualized," commented Nym Crinkle, another critic. "In the Dunstan of Mr. Couldock, all the mellow power of this superb old artist is brought to bear upon this part." The management and booking of the road companies of *Hazel Kirke* were in the hands of Gustave and Charles Frohman, brothers of MacKaye's business manager, Daniel Frohman. From this apprenticeship Charles Frohman learned the technique of booking and distribution which was later to make him one of the theatrical autocrats of America. The numerous companies

751 The original *Hazel Kirke* Company, from a
group picture in the Davis Collection

of *Hazel Kirke* gave openings to many actors, who soon rose to stardom. In the beginning the dynamic personality of Mac-Kaye was everywhere felt.

752 Steele MacKaye as Dunstan Kirke
(with Mrs. Thomas Whiffen), from a
photograph, courtesy of Percy MacKaye,
Windsor, Vt.

753 Charles W. Couldock, 1815–98, from a photograph in the Davis Collection

754 Cartoon attacking the Mallory Brothers, in the collection of Percy MacKaye, Windsor, Vt.

"STRANGE DISILLUSIONS"

PERCY MACKAYE, who has written a most brilliant apologia for his father, gives the following picture of the Madison Square manager during the early months of *Hazel Kirke*. "As he stood then, Director of his Theater's Art, acclaimed by his peers, in the well-earned 'ermine' of his royal endeavors for his calling; glad in the fellowship of his loyal co-workers; keen for the trail to higher peaks of his pilgrimage; yet humble before that vision of his far goal — 'the perfected art of his country,' — Steele MacKaye, doer of dreams, characteristically foresaw the bright ascents, but imagined far less vividly the obscure, **retarding** obstacles, along that ruin-heaped path which would

755 Rev. George Scoville Mallory, from a photograph, courtesy of Trinity College, Hartford, Conn.

lead him toilsomely on, to strange disillusions." It is difficult to discover from existing records all of the facts and ramifications of the quarrel between MacKaye and the owners of the Madison Square, the Mallory brothers, two churchmen, who in 1879 had drawn up a contract which MacKaye signed. As the huge profits from *Hazel Kirke* began to pour in, and MacKaye received nothing but his paltry salary, he read, presumably for the first time, the contract which he had signed the year before, and felt that he had been the victim of flagrant injustice. He was unwisely persuaded to take the matter to court, and, failing there to secure redress, he resigned from the Madison Square organization and resumed his independent activities. "Contract or no contract, however," wrote William Winter, "MacKaye and the Mallorys could not have remained long in association on amiable terms, because they were as antagonistic as fire and water." Popular sympathy was almost unanimously on MacKaye's side when it became generally known that he had not secured a cent of royalty from *Hazel Kirke*, and that shortly after his withdrawal the Mallorys removed his name as author.

756   Steele MacKaye as Paul Kauvar in his own play, *Anarchy*, from a sketch, courtesy of Percy MacKaye, Windsor, Vt.

757 Mary Anderson, 1859–, as Perdita in *The Winter's Tale*, from a photograph in the Davis Collection

MACKAYE, WILDE, AND ANDERSON

"Do NOT despair," wrote a brilliant English dramatist to MacKaye in 1882, "you and I together should conquer the world, why not? Let us do it." In the year following MacKaye's resignation from the Madison Square, he was thrown into intimate contact with Oscar Wilde, who at the time was on a lecture tour of America. MacKaye confided to his new friend his dream of an ideal theater, to be fitted with most modern improvements, and to be conducted according to the

758 Mary Anderson as Ophelia, from a photograph in the Davis Collection

highest standards of aesthetics and art. In the same building was to be a hotel, the profits of which would take care of any deficits in the theatrical end. MacKaye was already in conference with prominent financiers. Wilde was enthusiastic at the prospects. He would write the plays; MacKaye produce them. The first was to be Wilde's *The Duchess of Padua*, the scenario of which Mary Anderson had already seen and approved. In 1875 when she made her début in her home town of Louisville, Kentucky, and for thirteen years thereafter, Miss Anderson held the public's attention here and in England as a star. She was one of the few who shone at the top without previous stage training. Encouraged by Edwin Booth, she studied for a time with George Vandenhoff and she went forth with Charlotte Cushman's blessing. "My child," Miss Cushman said, "you have all the attributes that go with a fine actress." Her connections with the best in drama and literature give

759 Mary Anderson as Hermione in *The Winter's Tale*, from a photograph in the Davis Collection

her personal *Memories* a delightful flavor. Her beauty and her power of declamation marked her work. Unfortunately for Wilde and MacKaye her rôles never included the Duchess of Padua, nor did she ever appear at the Hotel-Theater. MacKaye had his customary misfortunes with the prospective financiers; Wilde's completed version of the Duchess was not satisfactory to Miss Anderson, and MacKaye returned to his barnstorming tours over the country which he had begun shortly after his resignation from the Madison Square Theater.

760 Mary Anderson as Parthenia, from a photograph in the Davis Collection

761 The Lyceum Theater, New York, from a photograph,
     courtesy of Daniel Frohman, New York

THE LYCEUM THEATER

THOUGH the visionary temple for which MacKaye and Wilde were so eager never materialized, to MacKaye goes the credit for the beautiful Lyceum Theater, which stood for so many years on the west side of Fourth Avenue between Twenty-third and Twenty-fourth Streets, adjoining the Academy of Design. Intended primarily for the use of the Lyceum School of Acting, of which MacKaye, Gustave Frohman, and Franklin Sargent were associate managers, it soon became more famous for the excellence of its professional plays. *The Morning Journal* of April 7, 1885, carried the following headline "Wilde Outdone by MacKaye: The Gorgeous Lyceum Theater Opens." "It belongs to no school," the article continued, "unless the ultra-aesthetic — the school of Wilde outdone by MacKaye. . . . Everything was a departure from the hackneyed forms of theatrical decoration. The electric light from the clustered globes pendant from the ceiling is soft and pleasantly diffused. Similar lights smoulder under green sconces along the face of the gallery, like fire in monster emeralds.

. . . But these things are not obtrusive. A master hand has blent them into a general effect, avoiding all aggressive detail. . . . Under the theater four steam engines are constantly running. Two furnish the electricity with which the house is lighted throughout; one works the ventilating apparatus, which supplies the auditorium with medicated air, charged with ozone; the fourth raises and lowers an elevator car in which the musicians are placed. . . . There are four wide aisles on the first floor, besides the extra aisles which the patent chairs make when folded. The chairs are arranged in groups of three and four, so that nobody will be incommoded by people pushing past, and so that one may take a row of seats, as one would take a private box. . . . The Lyceum Theater is in every respect a unique creation, unlike any other place of amusement. The ideas of Steele MacKaye have been called impracticable; but we have seen them carried out, not only practically but profitably in the miraculous Madison Square and they appear to be equally practical in his new theater. Here he has organized the American Theater Building Company, which owns the theater; he has personally supervised every detail of its erection and decoration; invented its novelties, written the play, and carefully rehearsed all the actors and supernumeraries." Great interest was displayed by the critics in the opening of MacKaye's new theatrical venture. In the course of his litigation with the Mallorys he had won an increasing amount of popular sympathy. Dispossessed of his first creation, the Madison Square, he was now returning, after the intervening years of hardship, as the most potential rival to the Mallorys and to Palmer. The preliminary skirmishes were very encouraging to MacKaye. From the Madison Square he drew the most able men, Gustave and Daniel Frohman, and Richard Mansfield. But, again, as at the Madison Square, MacKaye soon reached an insurmountable impasse with the Lyceum proprietors, who were dissatisfied at the early closure of *Dakolar* on June 6, 1885. On the same day the Lyceum School of Acting was

dissolved, and Franklin Sargent instituted an independent New York School of Acting in the direction of which he was soon joined by David Belasco. The final issue between MacKaye and the proprietors came over the attempt of the latter to introduce a burlesque show by E. E. Rice. MacKaye realized that his ideal of a stock company, though temporarily successful, would never be realized, and feeling, therefore, that his services were no longer needed, he resigned on November 7, 1885.

762   The Interior of the Lyceum Theater, from an engraving in Percy MacKaye,
       Epoch, New York, 1927. © Boni and Liveright

THE WORLD FINDER

THE most ambitious of Steele MacKaye's enterprises, and the one in which he hoped to correlate a lifetime's experience as actor, dramatist, producer and experimenter in stage mechanics, was his projected Specta-

763 Model showing Columbus' Ships in the harbor of San Salvador, from an engraving in Percy MacKaye, *Epoch*, New York, 1927. © Boni and Liveright

torium at the Chicago World's Fair in 1893, in which was to be presented a pantomimic pageant chronicling on an unprecedented scale the outstanding episodes in the life of Columbus, the World Finder. For many years MacKaye had planned a dramatic biography of the restless, indomitable explorer whose courageous idealism he felt peculiarly akin to his own. The ambitious American producer, in spite of the discouraging experiences of the past, still clung to his guiding ideal of an art theater dedicated "to the advantage of mankind." This ideal was most clearly stated in MacKaye's own words, which are included in a later "Introduction" to *The World Finder*. "When the amusement of the multitude can be made the means whereby lives benumbed by overwork, . . . may be brought to the clear consciousness of the real worth of life which is created by the contemplation of the heroism history reveals, then indeed the temple of entertainment performs its worthiest function and attains its highest rank." For two and a half years MacKaye worked with frenzied eagerness to convince skeptical Chicago capitalists of the practicability of his scheme for an auditorium which would seat ten thousand spectators, and for additional space for twenty-five telescoped stages to be moved on miniature railroads. Small models of the Spectatorium and of the six scenes were completed by him and submitted for the approval of the backers of the Columbian Celebration Company, which had been organized to finance the Spectatorium. After numerous delays, the enterprise entered its final stages. Laborers were at work. Actors were being chosen for the leading pantomime rôles; scenic artists were in Spain making researches. The organizing and

764 Two drawings by Robert Edmund Jones, showing proposed interior and stage of MacKaye's Spectatorium, from engravings in Percy MacKaye, *Epoch*, New York, 1927. © Boni and Liveright

training of the huge musical department was well under way. The celebrated Bohemian composer, Anton Dvorák, was at work on the choral and orchestral scores; Anton Seidl was conductor of the orchestra; Victor Herbert was composing the incidental pantomime music; Percy MacKaye, under the direction of his father, was writing the choral odes; and Steele MacKaye was heralded as a great pioneer. The collapse was swift. The panic of 1893 paralyzed the finances of the country. Subscribers defaulted. Promoters withdrew. MacKaye fought desperately. In June, 1893, a receivership was demanded and granted. Workmen deserted the incompleted building. In July it was sold at a price of two thousand two hundred and fifty dollars for old junk. On July 18, the Chicago Building Commission ordered it removed.

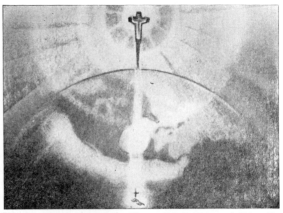

765 Imaginative Drawing by Norman-Bel Geddes, symbolizing the Vision of Columbus, from an engraving in Percy MacKaye, *Epoch*, New York, 1927. © Boni and Liveright

766   Robert Mantell (*ca.* 1885), from a photo-
         graph in the Davis Collection

767   Mantell as Monbars in *The Secret Warrant*, from
         a photograph in the Davis Collection

ROBERT MANTELL, 1854–1928

THE first performance at the Lyceum was on April 6, 1885, with Robert Bruce Mantell as Dakolar in a play of that name by Steele MacKaye, based in part on a French dramatization of George Ohnet's novel, *Le Maître de Forges*. Mantell, born in Scotland and educated in Ireland, had made his American début in 1878 at the Leyland Opera House, Albany, as Tybalt in Madame Modjeska's production of *Romeo and Juliet*. He had been for several seasons with Modjeska, and later with Fanny Davenport, opposite whom in 1884 he had played in *Fedora* at Stetson's Fifth Avenue. His first starring engagement was in *Tangled Lives* at the same theater during the season following his Lyceum début. For many years he starred in the western theaters. When he returned to New York, it was felt by many that the early promise which he had given had not been realized. "Beyond question," wrote Towse, "he had in him the makings of a really great actor, and it is a pity that circumstances, in the formative period of his career, kept him for so many years from the metropolitan stage. In that long exile he acquired great experience and an imposing repertory, but grew little in artistic stature. His execution gained in precision and authority, but became mannered. His acting lost the old glow of inspiration. He learned to rely more and more upon exaggerated points — always sure of a round of applause from the gallery — and he strained his voice until it lost much of its flexibility and mellowness."

Mantell was the last of the old-school Shakespearean actors. His Lear and Macbeth and Othello reveal strength beyond the range of most of his contemporaries. His vigorous, dramatic Richard III was always popular. He was at his best, perhaps, as Romeo, a character especially suited to him, since "it is in romantic action and the portrayal of the simple, direct emotions that his faculties have been displayed to best advantages." Among his most popular non-Shakespearean plays were *The Corsican Brothers*, *The Marble Heart*, *Louis XI*, and *Richelieu*.

768   Mantell as Richard III, from a photo-
         graph in the Davis Collection

769   Mantell in *The Corsican Brothers*, from a
         photograph in the Davis Collection

770 Richard Mansfield as Beau Brummel, from a photograph in the Davis Collection

771 Mansfield as Shylock, from a photograph after a painting by Edward Cameron, in the collection of Montrose J. Moses, New York

772 Mansfield as Richard III, from a photograph in the H. A. Ogden Collection, New York

RICHARD MANSFIELD, 1857–1907

THE second production at the Lyceum, September 15, 1885, was another adaptation from the French by Steele MacKaye; this time from Sardou's *Andrea*, renamed *In Spite of All*. The leading figure, Kraft, was played by Richard Mansfield, who two years earlier had leaped into prominence at the Madison Square by his graphic delineation of Baron Chevrial in *A Parisian Romance*. The dominant personality of Richard Mansfield found outlet in a series of character portraits, definite, picturesque, romantic, and melodramatic. He was eccentric; his rôles were eccentric — polished, suave, brittle as his manner of reading. He followed his will in all things, but never touched a rôle that he did not etch deeply in memory. He took the player's art seriously, and was inclined to be intolerant of those who did not, whether audience or actor. His memorable characterizations were Baron Chevrial in *A Parisian Romance*, the dual rôles in *Dr. Jekyll and Mr. Hyde*, Cyrano in *Cyrano de Bergerac*, Brummell in Clyde Fitch's *Beau Brummell*, the title-rôle in Ibsen's *Peer Gynt*, Reverend Dimmesdale in *The Scarlet Letter*, and Bluntschli in Shaw's *Arms and the Man*. As Henry V, Shylock,

773 Mansfield as Henry V, from a photograph in the Davis Collection

and Richard III he maintained the best traditions of the theater. "His manner, on the stage and off," wrote Towse, "was apt to be stiff, precise, and angular, but, nevertheless, there was about his presence a certain forcefulness — a suggestion of latent power that concentrated attention and excited interest. His voice was deep, resonant, and musical — few actors have been gifted with a finer organ — but he never learned to take full advantage of it, adopting a falling inflection ending upon the same note at every period, which soon wearied the ear, and was especially fatal in the delivery of blank verse."

774 Mansfield as Baron Chevrial in *A Parisian Romance*, from a photograph in the Davis Collection

775 Daniel Frohman, 1853–, from a photograph,
     courtesy of Daniel Frohman, New York

DANIEL FROHMAN'S LYCEUM COMPANY

Two months after Mansfield's Lyceum début, Helen Dauvray acquired the lease of the Lyceum Theater, from which MacKaye had now withdrawn. For one season she undertook the direction of the theater, acting at the same time the leading female rôles. Her first presentation was Bronson Howard's *One of Our Girls*, written expressly for her, in which she took the part of Kate Shipley opposite the Captain John Gregory of E. H. Sothern. In Howard's *Met by Chance*

776 Members of the Lyceum Stock Company,
     detail from a group picture, courtesy of Daniel
     Frohman, New York

she was Stella van Dyke, and Sothern was Harrington Lee. Later rôles included Peg Woffington in *Masks and Faces*, Walda Lamar in the play of the same name, and Constance in *The Love Chase*, in all of which Sothern was her leading man. "Helen Dauvray," writes Percy MacKaye, "brought to our native stage the fresh simplicity and rather mannish directness of her unspoiled personality." The difficulties of management, however, required a firmer hand, and on May 24, 1886, following the resignation of Miss Dauvray, Daniel Frohman assumed direction, and announced himself as manager, presenting Frank Mayo (see No. 632) in *Nordeck*. Frohman's first popular hit was *The Highest Bidder*, in which Sothern, as the auctioneer, made a startling success. Frohman gradually built up the personnel of his company until its excellence was generally recognized. Many of the actors and actresses who later became famous as Charles Frohman stars learned the fundamentals of their profession on the stage of Daniel Frohman's Lyceum. The elder Frohman also introduced to this country the works of the leading British dramatists, Arthur Wing Pinero, Haddon Chambers, Henry Arthur Jones, and others. "During the fifteen years of its existence," writes Hornblow, "the Lyceum was successful in catering to an intelligent and refined clientele. The theater never attained the brilliancy of Wallack's. It was not in any sense a rival of Daly's. The tone of the house and the quality of

many of the plays was distinctly *bourgeois*. But if Daniel Frohman, in his effort to please popular taste, never attempted productions in the big manner of his famous predecessors, what he did do was well done. The plays given were well staged and excellently acted." The last performance at the old Lyceum occurred March 22, 1902, and in the following year Frohman moved into the New Lyceum on Forty-fifth Street near Broadway. From 1899 to 1903 he was also manager and lessee of Daly's Theater. Since his brother's death in 1915 he has been joint-manager of Chas. Frohman Inc.

777   Bill-board Poster, advertising a Lyceum Performance of Pinero's *The Amazons*, from
      a print in the New York Historical Society

778 Edward Hugh Sothern as Hamlet, from a
photograph in the Davis Collection

779 Sothern as Shylock, from a photograph
in the Davis Collection

780 Sothern as Romeo, from a photograph
in the collection of Montrose J. Moses,
New York

E. H. SOTHERN, 1859–

FROM the time of his phenomenal success as Jack Hammerton in *The Highest Bidder*, May 3, 1887, to his final Lyceum appearance as Godfrey Remden in *A Colonial Girl*, October 31, 1898, Edward Hugh Sothern, son of Edward Askew Sothern (see No. 553), was the main support of Daniel Frohman. There are three periods in the career of Mr. Sothern: the first his broad comedy in *Chumley* (1888); then his romantic comedy in *The Prisoner of Zenda* (1891), *An Enemy to the King* (1896), and *The King's Musketeers* (1899); finally, his Shakespearean ventures, which began in 1899 with a performance of *Hamlet*. Had he contented himself with such plays as *The Highest Bidder* (1887) or *Letterblair* (1891), had he continued to be ambitious along the line of the Villon play, *If I Were King* (1901), he could have made a fortune. As it is, for years he has presented his Shakespearean repertory, in conjunction with Miss Julia Marlowe (see No. 880), to the country at large, meeting with failure at times, as in his venture with *A Winter's Tale*, but always drawing when they gave *The Merchant of Venice*, *Romeo and Juliet*, *Twelfth Night*, *Macbeth*, *The Taming of the Shrew*, or *Much Ado About Nothing*. Once his Hamlet was compared with that of Forbes-Robertson; now it has to submit to comparison with the newer methods of Walter Hampden and John Barrymore, even as Miss Marlowe's Juliet has to stand beside that of Jane Cowl. Sothern's approach toward his art is serious. He has written a partial autobiography in *The Melancholy Tale of Me*, and is the author of various plays and poems. In 1907 Sothern and Marlowe played in London with pronounced success. His Malvolio, wrote Arthur Symons, "is an elaborate travesty, done in a disguise like the solemn dandy's head of Disraeli. He acts with his eyelids, which move while all the rest of his face is motionless; with his pursed, reticent mouth, with his prim and pompous gestures; with that self-consciousness which brings all Malvolio's troubles upon him. It is a fantastic, tragically comic thing, done with rare calculation, and it has its formal, almost cruel share in the immense gaiety of the piece."

781 Sothern (center) in Jerome's *The Maister of Woodbarrow*, from a photograph,
courtesy of Daniel Frohman

782 Georgia Cayvan as Minnie Gilfillian in *Sweet Lavender* (with Herbert Kelcey), from a photograph in the Davis Collection

GEORGIA CAYVAN, 1858–1906

GEORGIA CAYVAN, Sothern's leading lady in the Lyceum stock company from 1887 to 1894, began her theatrical career as an elocutionist and reader in Boston. Her professional début was made in November 1880 at the Madison Square as Dolly Dutton in *Hazel Kirke*, after which she appeared as Daisy Brown in Gillette's *The Professor*, Ilica in Boyesen's *Alpine Roses*, and May Blossom in the play of that name by Belasco and DeMille. She first attracted widespread attention by her performance of Jocasta in George Riddle's production of *Œdipus Tyrannus*. After a period of starring at the California Theater, San Francisco, she was engaged by Frohman. Her first appearance, November 1, 1887, at the Lyceum was as Helen Truman in Belasco and DeMille's *The Wife*. Her most famous rôles were Minnie in Pinero's *Sweet Lavender*, Ann Cruger in Belasco and DeMille's *Charity Ball*, Lady Harding in Haddon Chambers' *The Idler*, Lady Alice in Boucicault's *Old Heads and Young Hearts*, Camilla Brent in Pinero's *Lady Bountiful*, Beatrice in Clyde Fitch's *The American Duchess*, and Lady Noeline Beltenbet in Pinero's *The Amazons*. In 1894 a nervous breakdown necessitated her withdrawal from the Lyceum. After a year's rest in Europe she organized her own company to tour America, but another collapse ended definitely her theatrical work.

MINNIE MADDERN, 1865–

IN the second Lyceum production, *In Spite of All* (1885), the part of Alice Glendenning was taken by a young actress, who, though only twenty, had behind her already many years of stage experience. Since her first appearance at the age of three in Little Rock, Arkansas, Minnie Maddern had steadily risen: in 1870 at Wallack's with J. K. Emmett; at Niblo's Garden, 1871; at the old Theater Comique, 1872; and at Booth's, 1874, with John McCullough. Her first adult rôle — at the age of thirteen — that of Widow Melnotte in *The Lady of Lyons*, had been followed by engagements with E. L. Davenport (see No. 299) and Mrs. Scott-Siddons (No. 701). At the end of the Lyceum engagement of *In Spite of All*, Miss Maddern toured the country in that and in *Caprice*, in which she had previously appeared at Henry Abbey's New Park Theater.

783 Minnie Maddern, aged 8, from a photograph in the Davis Collection

784 Juvenile Performance of Minnie Maddern (with Jo. Emmet), from a photograph in the Davis Collection

785 Minnie Maddern, from a photograph in the Davis Collection

786 Mrs. Minnie Maddern Fiske, from a photograph in the collection of Montrose J. Moses, New York

MRS. FISKE

IN 1889, following her marriage to Harrison Grey Fiske, a New York journalist and dramatist, Minnie Maddern retired for four years. She returned under her new name to play the lead in *Hester Crewe*, a play by her husband. Mrs. Fiske's most signal contribution to the development of drama in America has been her devotion to Ibsen, and her practical, constructive sponsoring of his plays at a time when many of her admirers inveighed pompously and piously against the corrupting Norwegian pessimist. Her first Ibsen rôle was Nora Helmer in *A Doll's House*

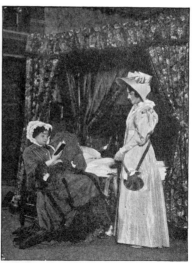

787 Mrs. Fiske (right) as Becky Sharp, from a photograph in the possession of the publishers. © Byron

in 1894, followed later by Hedda Tesman in *Hedda Gabler*, Rebecca West in *Rosmersholm*, and Laura Hessel in *The Pillars of Society*. Her interest also embraced the experiments of some of the younger American dramatists: Cynthia Carslake in Langdon Mitchell's *New York Idea*; Nell Sanders in Edward Sheldon's *Salvation Nell*, and Mary Page in his *The High Road*; and Dolce in John Luther Long's play of that name. Other famous rôles, many of them at the Knickerbocker, of which her husband became manager and lessee in 1901, include Gilberte in *Frou Frou*, Tess, Magda Giulia in *Little Italy*, Becky Sharpe, Mary in *Mary of Magdala*, Leah Kleschna in the play of that name; Juliet Miller in *Erstwhile Susan*; Nelly Daventry in *Miss Nelly of N'Orleans*, Mrs. Malaprop, and Mrs. Page in George Tyler's revival of *The Merry Wives of Windsor*.

MRS. THOMAS WHIFFEN, 1845–

ON November 1, 1887, while Minnie Maddern was still touring with *In Spite of All* and *Caprice*, Daniel Frohman produced *The Wife*, a play by the new house dramatists of the Lyceum, David Belasco and Henry DeMille. The rôle of Mrs. Amory was taken by Mrs. Thomas Whiffen, an English actress who in

788 Mrs. Thomas Whiffen, from a photograph in the Davis Collection

1868 had come to America with her husband as a member of the Galten Opera Company, which had opened at Wood's Museum, New York, and had then toured the country. After a performance of Buttercup in *Pinafore* Mrs. Whiffen had secured her first legitimate engagement at the Madison Square, where she had played in one of the *Hazel Kirke* companies, in *Esmeralda*, *The Rajah*, *May Blossom*, and *The Private Secretary*. Under Frohman's management from 1887 to 1900, she appeared in a great number of plays, including *Bladion*, *The Wife*, *Sweet Lavender*, *The Charity Ball*, *The Amazons*, *The Benefit of the Doubt*, *An Ideal Husband*, *The Princess and the Butterfly*, and *Trelawney of the Wells*. Her last appearance at the Lyceum was as Mrs. Hartley in Jerome K. Jerome's *John Ingerfield* on March 29, 1900, after which she became a member of the Empire Stock Company of Charles Frohman. After various new rôles at the Empire, she joined forces for a season with Mary Mannering, with whom she had often played at the Lyceum. In 1905 Mrs. Whiffen opened with Margaret Anglin in *Zira*, and supported her in the significant production of William Vaughn Moody's *The Great Divide* at the Hudson, 1905–07. Her later plays include *The Brass Bottle* (1910), *Electricity* (1910), *Cousin Kate* (1912), *The Indiscretion of Youth* (1912), *Just Suppose* (1920), and *Trelawney of the Wells* (1927).

789   William J. LeMoyne, from a photograph
in the Harvard Theater Collection

790   LeMoyne as Dick in *Sweet Lavender*, from a
photograph in the Davis Collection

VETERANS

In the original cast of *The Wife*, along with Mrs. Whiffen, appeared the names of four actors, who during the years to come were to form the backbone of the Frohman supporting cast. Herbert Kelcey (1856–1917), who played the part of John Rutherford, was an English actor with experience at Drury Lane and the Royalty in London, who had come to America in 1882, when he had made his début at Wallack's. Subsequently Kelcey like many others of the Lyceum had been for a number of seasons at the Madison Square before transferring to the more progressive theater. Nelson Wheatcroft, an excellent "heavy" actor, who took the part of Matthew Culver, was until his death in 1897 one of the most dependable of Frohman's assets. W. J. LeMoyne, whose first professional appearance dates back as far as 1852, was the finest stock actor in America of old men's rôles. William Winter wrote of LeMoyne: "His impersonations of eccentric, humorous, peppery old gentlemen were among the finest and most amusing that our stage has known." Charles Walcot, who had long been a favorite at Wallack's, was an eccentric comedian of the first order. The reputation of these four men has been obscured by the more spectacular rise of the younger Lyceum stars, such as E. H. Sothern, Virginia Harned, James K. Hackett, Henry Miller, and William Faversham, but as the preservers of the spirit of the older stock companies they were invaluable.

791   LeMoyne and Henry Miller in *Sweet Lavender*, from a photograph, courtesy of Daniel Frohman, New York

792   Herbert Kelcey (right) and Nelson Wheatcroft in *The Charity Ball*, from a photograph in the Davis Collection

793   Mr. and Mrs. Charles Walcot in *Sweet Lavender*, from a photograph in the Davis Collection

VIRGINIA HARNED, 1872–

VIRGINIA HARNED, the first wife of Edward H. Sothern, was for a number of years the leading actress of the Lyceum Stock Company. When on August 26, 1890, she made her Lyceum début opposite Sothern as Clara Dexter in *The Maister of Woodbarrow*, her stage experience consisted of a tour with George Clarke (see No. 671) in *The Corsican Brothers* and *False Shame*, a performance as Florence Featherley in *A Long Lane* at the Fourteenth Street Theater, 1890, and two appearances in the same year at Palmer's in *The Editor* and *Lora*. During her first Lyceum engagement she played Drusilla Ives in *The Dancing Girl* and Fanny Hadden in *Captain Letterblair*. After an absence at Palmer's in 1894 and at the Garden Theater — where in 1895 she gained an overwhelming success as Trilby — Miss Harned returned to the Lyceum on September 1, 1896, as Julie de Varian in *An Enemy to the King*. During the final years of the Lyceum she was a universal favorite. In independent productions she played opposite her husband in *The King's Musketeers*, *Hamlet*, and *Alice of Old Vincennes*.

794 Virginia Harned as Trilby, from an engraving in *The Gallery of Players*

795 James K. Hackett, from a photograph in the Davis Collection

JAMES K. HACKETT, 1869–

JAMES K. HACKETT, the son of James H. Hackett, the celebrated American comedian (see No. 207), made his first Lyceum appearance on March 31, 1892, as the Duke of Bayswater in *The Duchess of Bayswater & Company*. His most important period at Frohman's Theater did not begin, however, until 1895, when he appeared as Morris Lecaile in *The Home Secretary*. For the next four years he was the leading romantic actor of the company, enjoying great popularity, especially in *The Prisoner of Zenda* and *Rupert of Hentzau*.

796 Hackett as Rupert of Hentzau, from a photograph in the Madigan Collection, New York

797 William Faversham, from a photograph in the Davis Collection

WILLIAM FAVERSHAM, 1863–

WILLIAM FAVERSHAM, another Lyceum favorite, after a short apprenticeship in England, made his New York début in 1887 at the Union Square Theater. On May 3, 1887, he made his first appearance at the Lyceum as Parkyn in *The Highest Bidder*, followed in 1888 by Robert Gray in *The Wife*. Subsequently to his Lyceum connection, he played at the Madison Square with Mrs. Fiske, was a member of the Empire Stock Company from 1893 to 1901, and since then has been starred in many rôles.

798 William Faversham and Hilda Spong in *Miss Elizabeth's Prisoner*, from a photograph in the Davis Collection

GENERAL ASSISTANT

799   David Belasco, 1853–, from a photograph in the Davis Collection

800   Belasco as Uncle Tom, from a photograph in the Davis Collection

IN the spring of 1887 the manager of the Lyceum, intent on building up a strong stock company, retained the services of David Belasco as stage manager, adviser and general assistant. It was a rôle which Belasco's years of apprenticeship qualified him to fill. When in 1882 at the age of twenty-nine he had left California, Belasco already had behind him a practical experience in the problems of theatrical production which few of his contemporaries could equal. During his years in San Francisco he had been thrown into contact with the outstanding theatrical figures of the West, and with the visiting celebrities from the East; he had acted one hundred and seventy parts, ranging from super to lead; he had altered, adapted, rewritten or written more than one hundred plays, and had directed over three hundred. Through Gustave Frohman, with whom he had produced a revival of the *Octoroon* at Baldwin's Academy, he had met Charles Frohman, and together they had journeyed East, where the third Frohman brother, Daniel, was business manager of the newly opened Madison Square Theater. The contract which Belasco was forced to sign with the Mallorys (see No. 755) for a slight sum bound over his entire services, executive and creative, to the exacting churchmen. Though dissatisfied, Belasco remained until the arrival of the new manager, A. M. Palmer, whom he refused to have present at rehearsals. Thereupon he went to the Lyceum as assistant stage manager and general helper to Steele MacKaye. But when Belasco frankly expressed his disapproval of MacKaye's *Dakolar*, the sensitive author became estranged. In the interval between his break with MacKaye and his contract with Daniel Frohman, Belasco adapted for Lester Wallack a play *Valérie*, which proved moderately successful. But it was during the second Lyceum connection that his important work as a dramatist began. In collaboration with Henry C. DeMille, a playwright of no great experience, he wrote, between 1887 and 1890, four popular plays of which *The Charity Ball* was probably the most substantial. These pieces are marked by strong and even violent conflicts of emotion that produce a telling effect on the stage, however unconvincing they might seem in the reading. What part each of the collaborators had in the finished product it would be hazardous to say. In all probability Belasco, with his stage experience and his keen sense of the theater, was the more ready at inventing effective situations, but DeMille had the larger share in the verbal expression of the plays. When Belasco severed his connection with the Lyceum in 1890, he had earned the reputation of being a successful dramatist.

801   Scene from Belasco and DeMille's *The Wife*, at the Lyceum Theater, from a photograph, courtesy of Daniel Frohman, New York

802   Henry C. DeMille, 1850–93, from a photograph in the Davis Collection

803 Photograph, *ca.* 1884, of Charles Frohman, 1854–1915, in the Davis Collection

"C. F."

WITH his production of Bronson Howard's *Shenandoah* on September 9, 1889, at the Star, Charles Frohman's long years of apprenticeship and unrequited struggle came to an end. The Frohman name thereafter becomes more and more distinguished. The Charles Frohman era stretches from 1889, the year of the opening of *Shenandoah*, until 1915, when he met his death in the *Lusitania* tragedy. It was a period entirely dominated by his personality — a lovable one that captivated the mind of J. M. Barrie, and gained the love

804 Last Photograph of Charles Frohman, taken on the *Lusitania*, 1915, courtesy of Daniel Frohman, New York

and trust of all who worked with him. He was the product of a commercial system; the methods of his production, the quality of his taste in choice of plays, his advice to authors who wrote under his order — all these were governed by the necessity of satisfying the box office, which was to be sole arbiter of the kind of drama acceptable. The idea governing a production was that it could be built up by many people doing their special work, which was finally brought together and focused at dress rehearsal. The "star" system in the Frohman era was the one calculable thing to which a manager might pin his faith. Frohman created a galaxy of bright luminaries; he blazoned the night skies with their names in incandescent lights; he press-agented them into existence. An actor's worth was measured by his drawing power; a play's eligibility depended on the earmarks of success it might contain, as proved in other plays that had succeeded. The new dramatist found it difficult to gain hearing, since the commercial system relied for its plays on a very few men — in the great majority of cases European masters, whose reputations were already well established, and occasionally a few Americans such as Clyde Fitch and Augustus Thomas. Frohman felt that these men knew, by experience, what was most likely to attract the crowd. In other words seeing was believing;

805 Charles Frohman (right-center), Co-Proprietor of the Callender Minstrels, 1883, from a group-photograph in the Davis Collection

there was little artistic faith. "An extraordinary man, Charles Frohman," wrote Cosmo Hamilton in *Unwritten History*, "a kind, simple, loyal, courageous, resilient, hard working, honorable man, to work for whom it was a privilege and a pleasure. For one whose business it was to control theaters, collect plays and create stars on both sides of the Atlantic, who was the Czar, the high Panjandrum, whose room was the Mecca of the dramatists, who loved Barrie as a brother, Sutro as a cousin, Pinero, Marshall, Guitry, Rostand, Haddon Chambers, Somerset Maugham, Granville Barker, Augustus Thomas, and an army of others, equally gifted, as his friends, but was scared to death by Bernard Shaw, Frohman knew more about the theater but less about plays than any man I know." J. M. Barrie, in *Introduction to Charles Frohman: Manager and Man*, paid him the following tribute: "Lamb was fond of the theater, and I think, of all those connected with it that I have known, Mr. Frohman is the one with whom he would most have liked to spend the evening. Not because of Mr. Frohman's ability, though he had the biggest brain I have met with on the stage, but because of his humor and charity and gentle chivalry and his most romantic mind." John D. Williams writing of "C. F." in the *Century* for December, 1915, called him "a quaintly romantic personality, possessed of almost hypnotic power in influencing and often in entirely reshaping the lives of countless others."

806 Henry Miller, from a photograph, courtesy
of Henry Miller, New York

807 Henry Miller (right) with William Faversham in Henry A. Jones' *The Masqueraders*,
1894, from a photograph in the Davis Collection

HENRY MILLER, 1860-1925

WHEN the time came to begin casting for the new play from which he hoped much, Charles Frohman remembered a young actor, whose work in San Francisco he had admired, many years before, and to whom he had promised, "When I get a theater in New York and have a big Broadway production, you will be my leading man." It was this memory which caused Frohman to search out Henry Miller at the Lyceum, and offer him the position of leading man in the forthcoming production of *Shenandoah*. Miller at the time was playing Rodolph de Chaméry in *The Marquis* for Daniel Frohman, under whose direction he had been since April 1887, in such dramas as *This Picture and That, Ernestine, Sweet Lavender*. Previous to the Lyceum engagement Miller had, since his Toronto début, been in turn at Booth's Theater in Shakespearean rôles opposite Adelaide Neilson (1880), at the Grand Opera House (1880), at Daly's (1882), at the Madison Square (1882–85), and at the Star (1886). From the successful first night of *Shenandoah*, September 9, 1889, until January 11, 1897, Miller played as a member of Charles Frohman's company, and after the opening of the Empire was leading man of the Empire Stock Company. On January 11, 1897, he was first presented as a Frohman "star," in *Heartease*. After various other star rôles under Frohman he joined Margaret Anglin in 1903,

808 Henry Miller (left) as Colonel West in Bronson
Howard's *Shenandoah*, from a photograph in the
Davis Collection

playing Dick Dudgeon in *The Devil's Disciple*, and Armand Duval in *Camille*. In 1906 the Princess Theater came under his management, and it was there that he and Miss Anglin presented Moody's *The Great Divide*. Two years later, in Moody's second great play, *The Faith Healer*, he played Ulrich Michaelis opposite Margaret Anglin. Subsequent rôles include Richard Craig in *The Havoc* (1911), Neil Summer in *The Rainbow* (1912), and Jervis Pendleton in *Daddy Long Legs*. In 1918 he opened his own theater — the Henry Miller — with *The Fountain of Youth*.

809 Henry Miller as Stephen Ghent in William V.
Moody's *The Great Divide*, from a photograph,
courtesy of Henry Miller, New York

810 Wilton Lackaye as Svengali in Potter's dramatization of *Trilby*, from a photograph in the Davis Collection

WILTON LACKAYE, 1862–

IN contrast to Henry Miller, Wilton Lackaye, who was chosen by Frohman to take the part of General Haverill in *Shenandoah*, did not form an enduring association with his new director, but pursued the independent, migratory path which has characterized his entire career. Born in Loudoun county, Virginia, Lackaye, one of the few southern actors of his time, made his first appearance (1883) in support of Lawrence Barrett in Boker's *Francesca da Rimini*. In 1885 he appeared in MacKaye's *Dakolar*, in 1892 in Howard's *Aristocracy;* and later on various occa-

811 Wilton Lackaye as Gen. Haverill in Bronson Howard's *Shenandoah*, from a photograph in the Davis Collection

sions played opposite Fanny Davenport. Shortly after his Frohman engagement Lackaye, in 1891, toured England with George Alexander in *The Idler*. His season of 1894 at Palmer's, during which he played Van Buren Crandall in Augustus Thomas' significant play *New Blood*, was followed by his creation at the Garden Theater of the rôle of Svengali in Paul Potter's dramatization of Du Maurier's *Trilby* — a rôle which he played for two years. In the following year he toured with Nance O'Neil in *East Lynne*. Later appearances include Shemmel in *The Children of the Ghetto* (1899), Petronius in *Quo Vadis* (1900), Richard Sterling in Clyde Fitch's *Climbers* (1903), Jean Valjean and M. Madeline in his own dramatization of *Les Miserables*, Fagin in *Oliver Twist*, James Ralston in *Jim the Penman*, the Doctor in *Damaged Goods* (1913) and Prince Alexis in *The Awakening* (1918).

VIOLA ALLEN, 1869–

To another southerner Charles Frohman entrusted the leading feminine rôle of Gertrude Ellingham in *Shenandoah*. Viola Allen, born in Huntsville, Alabama, in 1869, made her first appearance on the New York stage on July 4, 1882, when she succeeded Annie Russell at the Madison Square (see No. 871) in the title-rôle of Frances Hodgson Burnett's popular *Esmeralda*. Two years later she was appearing with John McCullough in *Virginius, The Gladiator, Othello,* and *Richard III*. On the opening night of the Lyceum, April 7, 1885, she appeared as Madeleine in *Dakolar*, and in the following year played leading rôles opposite Tommaso Salvini (see No. 649). For a short time after the conclusion of *Shenandoah* she appeared as Lydia Languish in *The Rivals* supporting Joseph Jefferson and William J. Florence, and for a while was at Palmer's in Bronson

812 Viola Allen, from a photograph in the Davis Collection

Howard's *Aristocracy*. It was not until 1893 that she became more permanently attached to Frohman as a member of the Empire Stock Company, where she had leading parts in such plays as *The Younger Son* by Belasco, *John-A-Dreams, The Importance of Being Earnest, Bohemia,* and C. Haddon Chambers' *Under the Red Robe* and *The Conquerors*. Her first starring engagement was as Gloria Quayle in *The Christian* (1899), followed later by *In the Palace of the King, The Hunchback, Twelfth Night, A Winter's Tale, The Toast of the Town, As You Like It,* and *Cymbeline*.

813 Viola Allen as Gertrude Ellingham (with Henry Miller) in Bronson Howard's *Shenandoah,* from a photograph in the Davis Collection

814   Charles Frohman, from a photograph, White
Studios, courtesy of Charles Frohman, Inc.,
New York

A PICTURESQUE FRIENDSHIP

"*SHENANDOAH* led to a picturesque friendship in Charles Frohman's life," wrote Isaac Marcosson, Frohman's biographer. "On the opening night a grizzled, military looking man sat in the audience. He watched the play with intense interest and applauded vigorously. On the way out he met a friend in the lobby. He stopped him and said 'This is the most interesting war-play I have ever seen.' The friend knew Charles Frohman, who

815   General William T. Sherman, from an engraving
in the possession of the publishers

was standing with smiling face watching the crowd go out. He called the manager over and said 'Mr. Frohman, I want you to meet a man who really knows something about the Civil War. This is General William T. Sherman.' Sherman and Frohman became great friends, and throughout the engagement of *Shenandoah* the old soldier was a frequent visitor at the theater. He then lived at the Fifth Avenue Hotel and he often brought over his war-time comrades." On the two hundred and fiftieth performance, April 19, 1890, General Sherman publicly praised the production for its historical and technical accuracy.

ODETTE TYLER OF SAVANNAH, 1869–

IT is an interesting coincidence that, on the night when Sherman made his curtain speech to the Frohman audience, the lead in *Shenandoah* was taken by a girl who, only five years after the general's devastating "March to the Sea," had been born in Savannah, Georgia. The daughter of General William W. Kirkland, Miss Kirkland, known professionally as Odette Tyler, had made her New York début at the Star Theater in 1884, and had subsequently appeared in *Caprice* at the Bijou Opera House and in *Featherbrain* at the Madison Square. Shortly after the removal of *Shenandoah* from the Star to Proctor's Twenty-Third Street Theater, the young southern actress had been selected by Frohman to take the place of Viola Allen, who had been bound by contract to Jefferson and Florence. Miss Tyler became one of the leading members of Froh-

man's stock company at Proctor's, appearing as Kate Delafield in *Men and Women,* and as Polly Fletcher in *The Lost Paradise;* and on the formation of the Empire Stock Company in 1893 was Lucy Hawksworth in Belasco's *The Girl I Left Behind Me,* and Margaret in his *The Younger Son.* Her association with Frohman ended in 1894. Later rôles included two other southern heroines, Caroline Milford in Gillette's *Secret Service* and Maryland Calvert in Belasco's *Heart of Maryland.*

816   Odette Tyler (left) as Kate Delafield in Charles Frohman's production of Belasco and DeMille's
Men and Women, from a photograph in the Davis Collection

817 Maude Adams in *The Lost Paradise*, from a photograph in the Davis Collection

818 Maude Adams, from a photograph in the collection of Montrose J. Moses, New York

819 Maude Adams as Joan of Arc, at the Harvard Stadium, from a reproduction of a poster, in the *Theatre Magazine*, June 1906

MAUDE ADAMS, 1872–

MAUDE ADAMS, who made her first appearance under Frohman's management in William Gillette's *All the Comforts of Home*, September 9, 1890, will be best remembered for her charming delineation of Peter Pan in James M. Barrie's masterpiece. Other outstanding successes include *The Little Minister*, *Quality Street*, *What Every Woman Knows*, and *A Kiss for Cinderella* — all from the pen of the author of *Peter Pan*. As early as 1892 she was John Drew's leading lady in *The Masked Ball* and other plays, and continued in that capacity in *Butterflies* (1894), *Christopher, Jr.* (1895), and *Rosemary* (1896). Then, still under the Frohman régime, she came into her stardom. At different times she has made such ambitious efforts as *Romeo and Juliet*, *Twelfth Night*, *L'Aiglon*, *Chantecler*, and Schiller's *Joan of Arc*. Although quiet and retiring, and avoiding publicity wherever it was possible, she became, nevertheless, a national figure. Within recent years, Miss Adams' interest has been centered on experimenting with stage lights, and for that purpose she entered the laboratories of the General Electric Company for a time.

820 Maude Adams as Peter Pan, from a photograph in the Davis Collection

821 Maude Adams as Peter Pan, from a photograph in the H. A. Ogden Collection

822 William Gillette, from a photograph in
the collection of Montrose J. Moses, New
York

823 Gillette as Johnson in his
own play, *Too Much Johnson*,
from a photograph in the collection of Montrose J. Moses,
New York

824 Gillette as Sherlock Holmes, from a photograph in the collection of Montrose J.
Moses, New York

WILLIAM GILLETTE, 1855–

THE author of Miss Adams' opening play under the Frohman management was William Gillette.   At about the age of twenty he began acting professionally, and during these early years he occupied his spare time with study at the College of the City of New York and later at Harvard and Boston University.   The first play from his pen, *The Professor* (1881), is typical of his later work in that it is built about one character of a distinctive and appealing sort.   *Esmeralda* (1881), written in collaboration with Mrs. Frances Hodgson Burnett, ran for a year, but Gillette's fame as a playwright depends on three subsequent plays.   *Held by the Enemy* (1886) is a drama of the Civil War in which the most memorable figure is a heroic spy.   The spy had already been treated sympathetically in American literature, especially in Dunlap's drama, *André*, and Cooper's novel, *The Spy*, both concerned with the Revolution.   Plays dealing with the Civil War had begun to appear in considerable numbers, just as plays of the World War have appeared in recent years, but *Held by the Enemy* was the first one of any importance.   With its rapid and skillfully managed action and its emotional tensity, this melodrama possessed qualities that assured it of success.   Gillette's best known play,

Secret Service (1895), is a melodrama of uncommonly expert construction, in which he achieved his greatest triumph as an actor in the rôle of Captain Thorne, a spy who devotedly serves the cause of the Union.   Gillette has also gained wide fame as the impersonator of the imperturbable Sherlock Holmes.   Using Conan Doyle's detective stories as a basis Gillette constructed his *Sherlock Holmes* (1899), for which he invented his own episode and created most of the characters. Despite its stage appeal this piece lacks the reality of the Civil War dramas. Gillette has written in all twenty full length plays, including his adaptations from foreign pieces.   In these his high skill as a dramatic technician is prevailingly present, and his major characters are marked by a cool restraint, a polish, and a charm that have been so delightfully evident in his own acting.

825   Scene from William Gillette's *Secret Service*, from a photograph.
© White Studio, New York

CHARLES HOYT,
1860–1900

826 Charles Hale Hoyt, from a photograph in the collection of Montrose J. Moses, New York

827 Charles Hoyt (right) with Julian Mitchell, from a photograph in the Davis Collection

MISS ADAMS' last appearance before her Frohman engagement had been with Charles Hale Hoyt in *A Midnight Bell*. Hoyt was essentially a writer of broad and obvious farces, the quality of whose humor is suggested by the names of some of the characters, such as Christian Berriel the undertaker, Vilas Canby the plumber, and Kneeland Pray the hypocrite. Nevertheless he had a keen perception of what would go well on the stage, and in the hands of a vivacious cast his plays are actable in the extreme. Hoyt's first real success was *A Bunch of Keys* (1882), a name which still stirs pleasant memories in the minds of many playgoers. *A Texas Steer* (1890) is full of amusing situations and represents his farcical talents almost at their best. *A Trip to Chinatown* (1891) was given six hundred and fifty consecutive times, the longest run, so Dr. Quinn writes, of any play given in the United States up to that time. Comedies of a somewhat more serious intent are *A Midnight Bell* (1889) and *A Temperance Town* (1893), the latter a satire on prohibition hypocrites. Hoyt's plays are justified by the fact that they provided clean laughter for countless playgoers. But to his gift of pure farce was added a keen if superficial perception of varied American types, which he converted into vivid acting parts.

THE CREATOR OF THE MULLIGAN GUARD

EDWARD HARRIGAN (1845–1911), another writer of farces, like Hoyt made capital of certain humorous phases of American life. Beginning his connection with the stage as an actor, he soon became associated with Tony Hart, and shortly the pair were famous as a team of Irish comedians. Harrigan's plays had their inception as vaudeville sketches, consisting of songs and dialogues, which he wrote for himself and Hart. Out of these grew his full-length plays centering about the New York Irish, of which the most important are

828 Harrigan and Hart as Negro Minstrels, from a photograph in the Davis Collection

829 Harrigan and Hart in a *Mulligan Guard* play, from a photograph in the Davis Collection

the series dramatizing the adventures of Dan Mulligan and the Mulligan Guard. This cycle was first definitely launched with *The Mulligan Guard Ball* (1879), and the theme was developed in no less than eight subsequent plays. In these the hostility between the Irish and the German immigrant is humorously treated. Extravagant as these plays are, they are based on observation and they present a not untrue picture of certain conditions in New York life of about 1880.

830   James A. Herne, from a photograph in the
Davis Collection

JAMES A. HERNE,
1839–1901

831   Herne as Nathaniel Berry in his own *Shore Acres*, from *The Gallery of Players*, No. 2

DURING the last two decades of the nineteenth century there was a definite trend in American literature toward realism under the leadership of William Dean Howells, Hamlin Garland, and Mary E. Wilkins. In the drama of the same period this movement was championed by James A. Herne. In comparison with the writings of our sophisticated and cynical contemporaries, Herne's realism is of a mild sort; in fact the plots of the great majority of his plays are more or less romantic and sentimental. The realism lies in the presentation of character. His men and women are recognizable American people, who think and talk in a familiar way. His realism also lies in the fact that the emotions and situations he dramatizes are of the simpler and less violent kind that are akin to those of the average man. Herne, who began his connection with the stage as an actor, wrote some early plays in collaboration with David Belasco. Outstanding among these was *Hearts of Oak* (1879), which was based on an earlier English play and in which Mr. and Mrs. Herne appeared for many years. Among his first independent pieces was *The Minute Men of 1774–75* (1886). It contains two characters, a charming, simple girl and a lifelike farmer, who give promise of better things to come. *Drifting Apart* (1888) is a drama of domestic life, marked by fidelity to the simple people involved in its plot. In *Margaret Fleming* (1890) we find a faithful study of the cultivated American gentlewoman, which has been compared with some of the work of Howells and Henry James. Herne's greatest success was *Shore Acres* (1892), a drama of New England rustic life, which in its general type harks back to Woodworth's *Forest Rose* and other rural plays. But *Shore Acres* shows by contrast how far Herne had gone in the direction of realism, for here we have veracious farm people, an accurate setting, and simple action. Herne wrote one of our able Civil War plays in *The Reverend Griffith Davenport* (1899), which tells the story of a Virginia circuit-rider, who, hating slavery, espouses the Northern cause and is captured by his own son. Herne's final play, *Sag Harbor* (1899), is a revision of *Hearts of Oak*, and is of interest chiefly as showing how far its author had advanced in the intervening years in the direction of naturalness and truth. Not a little of Herne's success as a playwright was due to his gifted wife, Katherine Corcoran, who by her advice and her acting in leading rôles gave invaluable aid.

832   Scene from Herne's *Sag Harbor*, from a photograph in the collection of Montrose J. Moses, New York

833   Advertisement of Herne's *Shore Acres*, from a lithograph by Hugo Ziegfeld, in the collection of Montrose J. Moses, New York

834 Augustus Thomas, from a photograph, courtesy of Augustus Thomas, New York

835 Scene from Thomas' *Alabama*, from a photograph in the Davis Collection

AUGUSTUS THOMAS, 1857–

PERHAPS none of our dramatists has ever been more representatively American than Augustus Thomas. The son of a father who served during the Mexican War, and who, during a part of the Civil War, conducted the St. Charles Theater in New Orleans for the entertainment of the Federal troops, Thomas was reared in an environment colored by some of the most stirring events of our history. The play which first gave him a wide reputation, *Alabama* (1891), presents the post-war conflict between the Southerner who has retained all his sectional prejudices and the one who thinks in national terms. No less an authority than Colonel Henry Watterson of Louisville declared that *Alabama* did a great amount to reconcile the North and the South. *In Mizzoura* (1893), though lacking any special historical element, is a play built about an American locality and containing characters studied from American life. It was long a favorite stock piece. *The Capitol* (1895), a comparative failure, is a powerful study of Washington politics. This was followed by *Arizona* (1899), which stresses western characters and ideals, and by the unsuccessful *Colorado* (1901). Perhaps the most skillful and, in some ways, most effective of Thomas' distinctly American plays is *The Copperhead* (1918), in which the heroic spy once more appears. At Lincoln's behest Milt Shanks, an Illinois farmer, at the cost of life-long ostracism, allies himself with the "Copperheads" (a Northern organization of Southern sympathizers), in order to report on their activities. Coming as it did during the most crucial period of the World War, this drama of patriotic self-sacrifice, as acted by Lionel Barrymore, was genuinely moving. As Dr. Quinn has well written, Milt Shanks is a "type of the undistinguished American, the average man, who in times of national peril shows the potential devotion to his country which has led him to give his best without display." Another division of Thomas' work consists of what might be called plays of ideas. *The Witching Hour* (1907) is based on the themes of hypnotism and telepathy, and involves the question of the moral responsibility of those who exercise occult power over others. The success of *The Witching Hour* was so great that Thomas undertook to exploit the same general theme of mental suggestion in *The Harvest Moon* (1909). But this play did not achieve the popularity of its predecessor. Probably his most thoughtful play is *As a Man Thinks* (1911), which is in effect a discussion of the double standard of morals for men and women. In this drama Thomas' major fault, a too great fondness for didacticism, is apparent. Nevertheless he must be credited with having injected into our drama a number of well constructed and well thought out situations arising from a conflict of ideas.

836 Heavy Box Office Receipts of Thomas' *In Mizzoura*, at the Broad Street Theater, Philadelphia, from a facsimile in the Davis Collection

837 Clyde Fitch in his study at Greenwich, Conn.,
from a photograph in the collection of Montrose J.
Moses, New York

CLYDE FITCH,
1865–1909

AMONG the most prolific and most gifted American dramatists Clyde Fitch takes a prominent place. He wrote thirty-three original plays besides making numerous adaptations of foreign pieces. His work is of rather widely varying types, but for our purpose his historical plays and his social dramas are of chief importance. His studies in American history were a product of the contemporary movement in American literature toward the exploitation of our past, which is best seen in the

838 Caricature of Clyde Fitch by Max Beerbohm,
in the collection of Montrose J. Moses, New York,
courtesy of the artist

novels of Mary Johnston, Paul Leicester Ford, and Winston Churchill. Fitch's first venture into this field was *Nathan Hale* (1898), in which he contrives to weave a love theme into the story of Hale's last days. In his *Barbara Frietchie* (1899) Fitch took the liberty of converting his heroine into a young girl, out of whose love for a Union officer grows the tragedy of the play. *Major André* (1903) like *Nathan Hale* and many of our other war plays has a spy as its hero — in this case a spy who, though an enemy of America, has strongly appealed to numerous American playwrights from William Dunlap to those of our own time. Though Fitch's drama is the most expert of all the André plays, it met with much the same lack of success as its predecessors. The appeal of the André theme to American audiences seemingly is not irresistible.

In Fitch's social dramas the influence of Ibsen is discoverable in the moral earnestness with which he attacks certain problems that grow out of social relationships. His first significant effort in this direction was *The Climbers* (1901), a picture of the heartless social ambition displayed by certain types of New Yorker. *The Girl with the Green Eyes* (1902) which, despite a forced happy ending, is one of his most powerful plays, is a study of an inherited tendency toward jealousy that, without cause, comes perilously near wrecking an otherwise ideal marriage. It is especially in *The Truth* (1907) that a certain kinship with Ibsen is apparent. By an almost incurable habit of lying the heroine brings several characters to the verge of tragedy; yet the author treats her sympathetically because this weakness was bred into her by her father. Because of the strength of its theme, the vividness of its characters, and the skill of its construction, *The Truth* seems of all Fitch's plays the one most likely to endure. His last drama, *The City* (1909), deals tellingly with another social idea, the power of the city in bringing out the strongest qualities of the individual, whether good or bad. It also reiterates one of Ibsen's favorite themes, the visiting of the sins of the fathers upon the children. When one considers the best work of Clyde Fitch it is not difficult to rate him as the equal of any playwright America had produced up to his time.

839 Clyde Fitch after the dress rehearsal of his own play,
Barbara Frietchie, from a photograph in the collection of
Montrose J. Moses, New York

840   John Drew, from a portrait by Joseph de Camp, in the
Players' Club, New York

841   John Drew in his home at Easthampton, L. I., from a
photograph, 1902, in the collection of Montrose J. Moses,
New York. © Byron

" THE FIRST GENTLEMAN OF THE STAGE "

In an early play by Clyde Fitch Charles Frohman introduced to his public the first of the long line of "stars" who in the next two decades were to make him internationally famous. Frohman's analysis of the American theatrical market in 1890 convinced him that he was witnessing the end of an era. The older stars of the post-bellum period were rapidly dying. In another decade they would be gone. It was essential, therefore, that newer, younger ones be rapidly created, without the hallowed procedure of a long apprenticeship and slow, laborious rise. At Daly's Theater John Drew (see No. 686), in spite of his unfailing successes opposite Ada Rehan, was dissatisfied. Sensing, like Frohman, the probability of great changes, he realized that Daly's contribution, however great, was of the past, and that more adaptable managers would now dominate. Henry Miller brought Frohman and Drew together, and, after preliminary feelers, Frohman offered a three-year contract, which Drew, to the amazement and chagrin of Daly, promptly signed. On October 3, 1892, as Paul Blondel in Fitch's *Masked Ball*, Drew appeared on the stage of the old Wallack's opposite Maude Adams, who for many years was his leading lady until she herself was made a star. From 1892 until 1915, the fall opening of John Drew was the outstanding event of the Frohman season. During that time he played over

842   John Drew opposite Maude Adams in *Christopher,
Jr.*, from a photograph in the Davis Collection

thirty rôles, which included John Armsley in *That Imprudent Young Couple*, Mr. Kilray in *The Squire of Dames*, Comte de Condale in *A Marriage of Convenience*, Richard Carvel, James Delancey in *Delancey*, Hilary Jesson in *His House in Order*, Benedick in *Much Ado About Nothing*, Major Arthur Pendennis in *Pendennis*, and the Marquis of Quex in *The Gay Lord Quex*. His death occurred in 1927.

843   John Drew (center) as Frederick Ossian in *Butter-flies*, at the Empire Theater, from a photograph in the Davis Collection

844   Interior of the Empire Theater, New York, from a photograph, courtesy of Charles Frohman, Inc., New York

845   The Empire Stock Company, from a group-photograph in
the Davis Collection

THE EMPIRE THEATER

ELATED by the success of his first "starring" venture, Frohman decided that it was now time to realize his life-long dream of a New York theater of his own.   William Harris, a theatrical promotor and speculator and always one of Frohman's closest friends, was persuaded to assume half the responsibility of the enterprise. Harris was making all preparations to open negotiations with Palmer, who had placed the Union Square Theater on the market.   Al Hayman (see No. 920) dissuaded them, pointing out that theatrical activity was fast moving uptown and would soon center around certain lots on Broadway and Fortieth Street

which he owned and was willing to sell on reasonable terms. Hayman's offer was accepted,
and work on the new theater began. "He was
like a child during the building of the theater,"
wrote Marcosson of Frohman. "Every minute that he could spare from his desk he would
walk up the street and watch the demolition
of the old houses that went to make way for
this structure."   The completed building became a nucleus around which grew up an
entirely new theatrical district.   Frohman
established his offices on the third floor and
practically the entire remainder of the available space was occupied by his booking office.
"The Empire Stock Company became an ac-
credited institution. A new play by it was a
distinct event, its annual tour to the larger
cities an occasion that was eagerly awaited.
To have a play produced by it was the goal of
the ambitious playwright, both here and
abroad."

846   Vestibule of the Empire Theater, New York, from a photograph,
courtesy of Charles Frohman, Inc.

THE RISE OF BELASCO

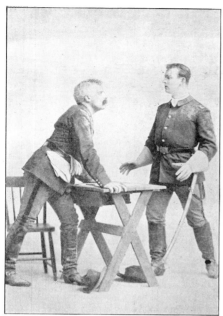

847 Scene from Belasco and Fyles, *The Girl I Left Behind Me*, from a photograph in the Davis Collection

848 Belasco, the Collaborator, from a photograph in the Davis Collection

THE play with which the Empire opened was *The Girl I Left Behind Me*, written by Belasco in collaboration with Franklin Fyles. It was another substantial success for Belasco. The scene is an army post in the Sioux country, and throughout the play runs the theme of Indian rebellion, out of which grow some of its most striking situations.

The Indian uprising was a timely theme, for Sitting Bull, the famous Sioux leader, had been killed in 1890, and the massacre of Indians at Wounded Knee was in all minds. *The Girl I Left Behind Me*, according to Dr. Quinn, is "one of the most vivid plays of Indian and army life which our drama contains." Again in 1895 Belasco scored heavily with *The Heart of Maryland*, in which Mrs. Leslie Carter played the leading rôle. This Civil War melodrama proved to be enormously popular — indeed it is probably still being acted in the provinces. It was not until his association with John Luther Long, however, that Belasco began producing work of real distinction. *Madame Butterfly*, based on Long's story of that name, had its première at the Herald Square Theater in 1900. Telling a wholly romantic story of the kind Belasco loved, it possessed the qualities that are certain to captivate an audience, as Puccini's operatic version of the play still proves. In their second joint effort, *The Darling of the Gods* (1902), Belasco and Long wrote another Japanese romance. This drama of heroism, patriotism, and love ran for two years, and was performed in several foreign countries. The final product of Belasco's and Long's literary partnership was *Adrea* (1904), in which Mrs. Carter found her most famous rôle. This romantic tragedy, laid in the Roman Empire of the fifth century after Christ, presents in the heroine Adrea a figure of great power, and is declared by Dr. Quinn to be "the finest of the plays written by Belasco and Long." The figures in Cut No. 849, from left to right, are Gatti-Casazza, Belasco, Toscanini, and Puccini, the composer.

849 Belasco (second from left), with group prominent in operatizing *Madame Butterfly*, from a photograph in the Davis Collection

850 Scene from *The Girl I Left Behind Me*, from a photograph in the Davis Collection

851   Mrs. Leslie Carter, from a photograph
in the Davis Collection

MRS. LESLIE CARTER, 1862–

THOUGH *The Girl I Left Behind Me* enjoyed an overwhelming success, its author was not satisfied. Since his arrival in New York in 1882, Belasco had been devoting his energy and his maturing craftsmanship to the service of others. In succession he had toiled without recognition at the Madison Square, the Lyceum, and now at the Empire. His unshaken ambition to produce and direct his own plays could be satisfied only by a definite cleavage with the established organizations. The penalty of his independence was years of discouraging struggle to launch his first "star." In 1890 a prominent young Chicago society woman, Mrs. Leslie Carter, who had received much unenviable publicity when she and her husband were divorced, had made a dramatic appeal to Belasco, and had eventually convinced him of her sincere desire for a professional stage career and of a latent genius for emotional rôles. With indomitable courage and patience the new teacher imparted to her the technique of a most exacting art, handicapped always by the prejudice of cautious theater owners afraid of incurring popular disapproval by sponsoring the much criticized Mrs. Carter. Success finally came in 1895 in *The Heart of Maryland*, with the rôle of Maryland Calvert designed in detail by Belasco to suit the peculiar qualities of his pupil. This was followed in 1899 by *Zaza*. William Winter, who greatly opposed the projection of immoral women on the stage, conceded that Mrs. Carter's performance was "much admired and extravagantly commented on. . . . The method of the execution was direct, broad, swift, — and coarse. The best technical merit of it was

852   Mrs. Leslie Carter (center) in a scene from *Du Barry*, from a
photograph. © Byron, New York

clarity of utterance. . . . It was the utter, reckless abandon, the uncontrolled physical and vocal vehemence, the virago-like intensity of her abuse of her lover, which, communicating themselves to the nerves of her auditors and overwhelming them by violence, gained the actress her success in the part." Her rendition of Du Barry in 1901 aroused Winter to exaggerated sarcasm. "In serious business the method of Mrs. Carter as Du Barry was to work herself into a state of violent excitement, to weep, vociferate, shriek out, become hoarse with passion, and finally to flop and beat the floor." But the final triumph, which even Winter praised, was as Adrea in the beautiful play of that name by Belasco and John Luther Long in 1905. "Mrs. Carter," Winter wrote, "had long been known for her exceptional facility of feminine blandishment, her command of the enticing wiles of coquetry and the soft allurement of sensuous grace — known, likewise, and rightly admired for the clarity and purity of her English speech, always delightful to hear: but observers studious to see and willing to be convinced had not supposed her to be an actor of tragedy. It took a long time for Belasco to bring her to a really just victory but she gained it in *Adrea*." In the summer of 1906 Mrs. Carter broke her connections with Belasco, and under her own management toured in *Du Barry* and *Zaza*. In the following year she revived *Tosca*.

853   Mrs. Carter (center) in a scene from *Du Barry*, from a photograph.
© Byron, New York

OLGA ISABEL NETHERSOLE, 1870–

AN English actress, who aroused almost as much moral opposition as Mrs. Leslie Carter did, became in the third year of the Empire Theater Charles Frohman's first foreign star. Olga Nethersole's first American engagement, after seven years' experience gained in London, the provinces, and Australia, was at Palmer's Theater on the fifteenth of October, 1894, in A. W. Gatti's *The Transgressor*, where by the intensity and realism of her acting she disturbed many of the more puritanically inclined observers. On December 2 of the following year Charles Frohman presented her as Denise in the play of that name, followed in turn by Gilberte in *Frou Frou* on December 5, by Marguerite Gauthier in *Camille* on December 9, and by Carmen on Christmas Eve. Miss Nethersole made many subsequent tours of America, all under the management of "C. F." In 1896 she added the new rôle of Emma in *The Wife of Scarli*, and in 1899 that of Paula in Pinero's *The Second Mrs. Tanqueray*. In 1900 she horrified the more conservative New York theatergoers by her interpretation of Emmy Legrant in Clyde Fitch's *Sapho*, resulting in the fulminations of such

856 Olga Isabel Nethersole, from a photograph in the Davis Collection

critics as William Winter, and culminating in the unsuccessful attempt of the righteous to have the theater legally closed. In 1904 Miss Nethersole toured as Sudermann's unconventional heroine in *Magda;* and in 1910 at Winthrop Ames' New Theater interpreted Maeterlinck's *Mary Magdalene.* Concluding her tour of America in 1911, she returned to England where she remained.

THE KENDALS

ANOTHER English actress who aroused violent discussion in the United States by her interpretation of Paula Tanquerary was Madge Robertson Kendal, who made her American début on October 7, 1889, in *A Scrap of Paper*, and subsequently toured with great success during five seasons. She was the youngest sister of the well-known British dramatist, Tom Robertson, whose plays such as *Caste, Play,* and *Our Boys* had been produced many times during the 'seventies and 'eighties by New York managers. One of Miss Robertson's earliest rôles in England had been that of Georgina in a London production of *Our American Cousin* with Edward Askew Sothern in 1867. She was later engaged as juvenile woman at the Haymarket Theater in London, where she played opposite William Hunter Kendal, whom she soon married. "For many years," wrote Daniel Frohman, the promoter of the Kendals in America, in *Memories of a Manager*, "Mr. and Mrs. Kendal reigned in London as the chief and most interesting couple in the British metropolis. While they were in partnership with John Hare, the St. James Theater, their dramatic home, became the resort of the modern drama." *The Scrap of Paper*, with which the Kendals opened in New York, proved very popular, running to capacity houses for four weeks. "Mrs. Kendal," wrote Frohman, "won her audience in a moment after her

857 William Hunter Kendal, 1843–, from a photograph in the Davis Collection

first entrance on the first night of her American engagement. Her exuberant spirits, her beauty and captivating comedy qualities, the subtlety of her humour, her splendid poise and handsome appearance justified, to her new audiences, the splendid reputation that had preceded her. . . . The applause was tumultuous. . . . American audiences, too, are remarkably hospitable in their first greeting to foreign artists and when these make good they become lasting favourites."

858 Madge Robertson Kendal, 1844–1917, from a photograph in the Davis Collection

857   Henry Irving as Thomas Becket, from a
photograph in the Davis Collection

858   Irving as Shylock, from a photograph in
the Davis Collection

859   Irving (right) and Edwin Booth, from a
caricature in the Davis Collection

SIR HENRY IRVING, 1838–1905

ALTHOUGH not universally acclaimed as a great actor, Sir Henry Irving was deemed by His Majesty's Government worthy of a knighthood and of a burial in Westminster Abbey. In the opinion of many he was an intellectual rather than an emotional actor. "He could charm by his delicacy," wrote Towse, with his customary aloofness, "dazzle by his brilliance, thrill by his intensity, but he could not overwhelm." His professional début was made on September 8, 1856, in the rôle of Gaston, Duke of Orleans, in *Richelieu*. It was not until ten years later, however, when at the Saint James in London he appeared as Doricourt, that he succeeded in winning the favor of the critics. By the time of his first tour of America in 1883 he was firmly established as an outstanding theatrical manager and Shakespearean actor and scholar. The brilliance of the productions at Irving's Lyceum had ushered in a new period of the English theater. His leading rôles during his eight tours of America were Mathias in *The Bells*, Charles XI, Hamlet, Shylock, and Thomas Becket.

ELLEN TERRY, 1848–1928

IRVING was accompanied on his tours of America by an English actress whom he had first met in 1867, and whom eleven years later he had elevated to stardom under his management at the Lyceum. Ellen Terry, by virtue of her beauty and charm and by the intensity of her acting during the long period of her ascendancy

860   Ellen Terry, from a photograph in
the Davis Collection

on the London stage, came gradually to be recognized as the best beloved actress of England. Excelling alike in comedy and tragedy, she appealed to every taste. She was an entrancing Beatrice, a majestic, awe-inspiring Lady Macbeth. Her interpretations of the heroines of Shakespeare revealed unsuspected possibilities of treatment. Her influence in continuing and bringing new life to the Shakespearean tradition in America was profound. In addition to her tours with Irving, Terry gave to American audiences readings from Shakespeare and modern comedies.

861   Ellen Terry as Lady Macbeth, from a photograph in the Davis Collection

862 Forbes-Robertson and Mrs. Patrick Campbell in *Romeo and Juliet*, from a photograph in the Davis Collection

ROBERTSON AND CAMPBELL

THE names of Sir Johnston Forbes-Robertson and Mrs. Patrick Campbell are joined together in the minds of the English public almost as closely as are those of Henry Irving and Ellen Terry. Their association began in 1895 at the

863 Mrs. Patrick Campbell as Paula Tanqueray, from a photograph in the Davis Collection

Lyceum Theater, London, of which, at the time, Forbes-Robertson was manager. At the Lyceum they played opposite each other in many rôles, the most famous being Romeo and Juliet, and Hamlet and Ophelia. Forbes-Robertson had made his American début ten years earlier touring opposite Mary Anderson as Pygmalion, Romeo, Ingomar, Orlando, and Claude Melnotte. Subsequent American tours were numerous: in 1891, 1903–04, 1906, 1909, and 1913–16. Mrs. Campbell, who made her American début in Sudermann's *Magda*, January 13, 1902, also made many tours of America: in 1904, 1907–08, 1910, and 1914–16. Her Paula Tanqueray was especially popular.

LILLIE LANGTRY, 1852–1929

EMILY CHARLOTTE LEBRETON, born on the island of Jersey and married to Edward Langtry of London, was for many years a celebrity on the English stage, referred to affectionately as Lillie Langtry, the "Jersey Lily." The year following her London début she came to America, and on November 6, 1882, appeared at Wallack's as Hester Grazebrook in *The Unequal Match*. At the Fifth Avenue Theater on November 25 she made a great success as Juliana in *The Honeymoon*. Her popularity was still further enhanced by her interpretations at the same theater of Galatea, April 23, 1883, Pauline in *The Lady of Lyons*, October 18, 1886, and Lady Clancarty, April 25, 1887. On January 15, 1900, at the Garden Theater, New York, she gave a disappointing performance of Mrs. Trevelyan in *The Degenerates*.

864 Lillie Langtry, from a photograph in the Davis Collection

BENOÎT COQUELIN, 1840–1909

THE influx of European stars during the closing decades of the nineteenth century was not confined to English celebrities. After twenty-three years of success at the Comédie Française, Jean Benoît Coquelin in 1888 formed a dramatic company in association with Jane Hading, a well-known French actress. On October 8th of that year, they opened at Palmer's Theater, New York, in Molières *Les Précieuses Ridicules*. Coquelin's interpretation of Mascarille was, according to William Winter, "welcomed with enthusiasm . . . in that character . . . he evinced the complete mastery of technical method, the consummate knowledge of the machinery of his profession, for which at all times he was distinguished." In the spring of 1889, after a tour of America, Coquelin was again in France. He returned to America with Jane Hading in January 1894, for a short tour. His final visit to America was in 1900 with Sarah Bernhardt, when he introduced to the American public Rostand's great character of Cyrano de Bergerac. Opposite Bernhardt he also played Flambeau in *L'Aiglon*, Scarpia in *La Tosca*, and the first grave digger in Bernhardt's attempt at *Hamlet*.

865 Benoit Coquelin as Mascarille in *Les Précieuses Ridicules*, from a photograph in the Davis Collection

866   Sarah Bernhardt, the Sculptress, from a
        photograph in the Davis Collection

867   Sarah Bernhardt, from a photograph in the
        collection of Montrose J. Moses, New York

868   Sarah Bernhardt as Cleopatra, from a
        photograph in the Davis Collection

SARAH BERNHARDT, 1844–1923

SARAH BERNHARDT, who in 1900 played a retiring Roxane to Coquelin's Cyrano, was a product of the Comédie Française and was its crowning glory. She came to America for nine tours — the last time fresh from the battlefields of France, where her patriotism had fired the poilus of 1917, even as it had those of 1870–71. During her first tour, in 1880, she appeared in a favorite rôle, Adrienne Lecouvreur. She also played in *Frou-Frou, Ernani, Phèdre,* and *La Dame aux Camélias.* On subsequent visits she made significant additions to her repertory: in 1886–87 *Le Maître de Forges* and *Théodore;* in 1891 *La Tosca* and *Cleopâtre, Jeanne D'Arc, La Dame de Challant,* and *Leah;* in 1896 *Izeyl, Magda,* and *Gismonda.* In 1905 she encountered difficulties with the American Theatrical Syndicate (see No. 920), and was on numerous occasions forced to play in a tent.

ELEANORA DUSE, 1859–1924

ELEANORA DUSE, the most brilliant figure on the Italian stage since Adelaide Ristori (see No. 640), refused to resort to the superficial technique and artifice of the stage, and it seems that her connection with it was due only to the coincidence of her having been born of poor strolling players, who impressed her into service long before the element of choice was present. Thus almost accidentally a world audience came to know and worship this brooding idealistic woman, who, in the words of Arthur Symons, was "a chalice for the wine of

869   Eleanora Duse as Camille, from a photograph
        in the Davis Collection

imagination." She first came to America in 1893, playing in *Camille,* and again in 1903, when she brought the repertory that D'Annunzio had created for her, *Francesca da Rimini, La Città Morta,* and *Gioconda.* After an absence of almost twenty years from the stage she returned again to America in 1923, and shortly afterward, broken in health and fortune, died in Pittsburgh. "Duse," wrote George Bernard Shaw in *Dramatic Opinions and Essays,* "produces the illusion of being infinite in variety of beautiful pose and motion. Every idea, every shade of thought and mood, expresses itself delicately but vividly to the eye."

870   Eleanora Duse, from a photograph
        in the Davis Collection

871 Annie Russell, from a photograph in
the Davis Collection

872 Annie Russell in *Esmeralda* at the Madison Square Theater, from a photograph in the Davis Collection

873 Annie Russell, from a photograph in
the Davis Collection

ANNIE RUSSELL, 1864–

IN the year following Olga Nethersole's first Frohman appearance, a veteran American actress with years of stock experience was promoted to the ranks of stardom. After three years of touring South America and the West Indies as Josephine in a juvenile opera company's rendition of *H. M. S. Pinafore*, Annie Russell entered the legitimate drama as Hazel Kirke in a Madison Square road company. In October of the same year she enjoyed her first big hit as Esmeralda in the play of that name, on the regular stage of the Madison Square in New York. Later rôles at the Madison Square included Lady Vavir in *Broken Hearts*, Maggie MacDoulane in *Engaged*, Elaine in a dramatization of Tennyson's poem, and Mabel Seabrook in *Captain Swift*. For several years thereafter, owing to a serious illness, she withdrew from the stage, reappearing again at Palmer's in 1894 as Margery Sylvester in *The New Woman*, followed by Mrs. Thornton in *Keeping Up*. On September 16, 1896, she eclipsed all her former popularity by her Frohman rôle of Sue in the play of that name by Bret Harte and T. E. Pemberton, and in 1898 introduced the character to the British public. Other Russell starring plays under Frohman management were *Catherine* (1898), *Miss Hobbs* (1899), *A Royal Family* (1900), *The Girl and the Judge* (1901), *Mice and Men* (1903), *Brother Jacques* (1904), and *Jinny the Carrier*. In 1910 at Ames' New Theater she appeared as Georgiana Byrd in Edward Sheldon's *The Nigger*, as Liz Piecemeal in *Liz, the Mother*, and as Viola in *Twelfth Night*. In 1912 at the 39th Street Theater, Miss Russell organized an Old English Comedy Company which presented *She Stoops to Conquer*, *Much Ado About Nothing*, and *The Rivals*. Her last appearance was as Madame La Grange in *The Thirteenth Chair*.

874 Annie Russell, from a photograph in
the Davis Collection

875   Annie Russell, from a photograph in the Davis Collection

876   Julia Marlowe as Mary Tudor in *When Knighthood was in Flower*, from a photograph in the collection of Montrose J. Moses, New York

877   Julia Marlowe as Viola in *Twelfth Night*, from a photograph in the Davis Collection

878   Julia Marlowe in Clyde Fitch's *Barbara Frietchie*, from a photograph in the Davis Collection

JULIA MARLOWE, 1870–

JULIA MARLOWE, who in 1898 made her Frohman début in the title-rôle of Countess Valenska, has been identified primarily with Shakespearean plays. Her repertory has embraced *Romeo and Juliet*, *Twelfth Night*, *The Merchant of Venice*, *Cymbeline*, *Macbeth*, *The Taming of the Shrew*, and *As You Like It*. In addition, she has been seen in *The Hunchback*, *The Lady of Lyons*, *The Love Chase*, *Pygmalion and Galatea*, *She Stoops to Conquer*, *Ingomar*, and *The Rivals* (all-star cast with Joseph Jefferson and Mrs. John Drew, 1897). She had a triumph in Clyde Fitch's *Barbara Frietchie*, October 23, 1899, and during the vogue of the dramatized novel, she lent color to such pieces as Charles Major's *When Knighthood was in Flower*, January 14, 1901. After she became co-star with E. H. Sothern (1904), whom she later married, she added to her list of dramas *Much Ado About Nothing*, *Hamlet*, *Jeanne D'Arc* by Percy MacKaye, and *The Sunken Bell* by Hauptmann. Both Mr. and Mrs. Sothern have been unswerving in their devotion to the classic drama. In quality of voice and gesture Miss Marlowe maintains the best standards. Of her Juliet, Arthur Symons wrote, "No one else has rendered, with so deep a truth, with so beautiful a fidelity, all that is passionate and desperate and an ecstatic agony in this tragic love which glorifies and destroys Juliet. . . . Miss Marlowe is not only lovely and pathetic as Juliet; she is Juliet. . . . In Juliet Miss Marlowe is ripe humanity, in Ophelia that same humanity broken down from within. As Viola in *Twelfth Night* she is the woman let loose, to be bewitching in spite of herself. . . . In Miss Marlowe there is something young, warm, and engaging, a way of giving herself wholly to the pleasure of pleasing, to which the footlights are

879   Julia Marlowe as Ophelia, from a photograph in the collection of Montrose J. Moses, New York

scarcely a barrier." A. B. Walkeley, distinguished London critic, has left the following picture of her: "In the purely sensuous element in Shakespeare, in the poet's picture of frankly joyous and full-blooded womanhood, the actress is in her element, mistress of her part, revelling in it and swaying the audience by an irresistible charm. . . . High arched brows over wide-open eloquent eyes; a most expressive mouth, now roguish with mischief, now trembling with passion; a voice with a strange croon in it, with sudden breaks and sobs — these, of course, are purely physical qualifications. . . . But behind these things in Miss Marlowe there is evidently an alert intelligence, a rare sense of humor and a nervous energy which make . . . a combination really fine."

880   Julia Marlowe as Beatrice (with E. H. Sothern) in *Much Ado About Nothing*, from a photograph in the collection of Montrose J. Moses, New York

WILLIAM H. CRANE, 1845–

IN the season following Julia Marlowe's success as Barbara Frietchie, Frohman launched as a star one of the most brilliant of the older American comedians, William H. Crane, who had begun his career as a negro minstrel. In 1877 he became associated with Stuart Robson (see No. 726). They were the two Dromios in *A Comedy of Errors* and Sir Andrew and Sir Toby in *Twelfth Night*, before they dissolved partnership in 1888. Crane was then starred as General Hannibal Rivers in *The Senator*, and in *The American Minister*. In later years he appeared in Jefferson's all-star cast of *The Rivals*, and in a special production of *She Stoops to Conquer*. For many seasons he was counted one of Frohman's most valuable stars. He created the chief rôles in *Peter Stuyvesant, David Harum, Business is Business, His Wife's Father, The Governor of Kentucky,* and *His Honor, the Mayor*.

881 William H. Crane as Gen. Hannibal Rivers in *The Senator,* from a photograph in the Davis Collection

NAT GOODWIN, 1857–1919

NATHANIEL CARL GOODWIN, almost as well-known for his acting as for the number of his wives, made his first New York appearance in 1875 at Tony Pastor's Variety Hall, which for many years was the most famous institution of its kind in the city. After a period of burlesque and mimicry of favorite stars, he settled down to legitimate comedy, and an occasional tragedy. His London début was in 1889 as Silas Woolcott in *A Gold Mine*. His most famous later rôles were Jack Medford in *The Candidate*, Chauncey Short in *A Gilded Fool*, Jim Radburn in Augustus Thomas' popular success *In Mizzoura*, Beresford Cruger in *An American Citizen*, and the title-rôle in *Nathan Hale*.

882 Nat Goodwin, from a photograph in the Davis Collection

FRANCIS WILSON, 1854–

FOLLOWING his début at the Chestnut Street Theater, Philadelphia, in 1878, Francis Wilson was for many years a star in musical comedy, touring with Annie Pixley, making numerous appearances at the Casino Theater, the center of musical comedy in New York, and finally in 1889 organizing his own company at the Broadway Theater. One of his best known rôles was Cyrano de Bergerac in a musical version of Rostand's masterpiece. Abandoning musical comedy in 1902, he appeared with great success as William Jenks in *Cousin Billy*, 1905, Sir Guy de Vere in *When Knights were Bold*, 1907, Thomas Beach in his own play, *The Bachelor's Baby*, 1909, and Stephen Atwill in *The Spiritualist*, also written by him.

KYRLE BELLEW, 1855–1911

HAROLD KYRLE BELLEW, a British actor, who made his American début at Wallack's Theater, New York, in 1885, and who afterward attained a popularity in this country almost as great as did Crane, Goodwin, and Wilson, made his first

883 Francis Wilson, from a photograph in the Davis Collection

stage appearance at Solferino, New South Wales, in 1874. After two years in America, 1885–87, in which he played a variety of rôles, he toured for many years, going as far as India and Australia. Returning again to America in 1901, he achieved great success as Romeo and Hamlet, as Raffles in a play of that name, as Richard Voysin in *The Thief*, Jacques in *The Sacrament of Judas*, Lord Delcode in *A Marriage of Reason*, and Edward Thursfield in *The Builder of Bridges*.

884 Kyrle Bellew as Hamlet, from a photograph in the Davis Collection

885 Ethel Barrymore, from a photograph in the collection
of Montrose J. Moses, New York

886 Ethel Barrymore and Bruce McRae, in Galsworthy's *The
Silver Box*, from a photograph in the Davis Collection

ETHEL BARRYMORE, 1879–

ETHEL BARRYMORE, who became a Frohman star in 1901, is a member of a noted American actor-family which covers over a century of American theatrical history (see No. 694). She became a Frohman star after she had worked her way without influence to the top. She served her novitiate in minor parts played in her uncle John Drew's company, and came for a while under the watchful eye of Henry Irving in London. Finally, in Clyde Fitch's *Captain Jinks of the Horse Marines*, February 4, 1901, she entered her own orbit. Since then she has gained wide popularity in *A Country Mouse*, *Cousin Kate*, Ibsen's *A Doll's House*, Barrie's *Alice-Sit-by-the-Fire* and *A Twelve Pound Look*, and Pinero's *Mid-Channel*. Personality is a large part of her effectiveness. Perhaps her most brilliant accomplishment was in the Players' Club revival of *The School for Scandal*, where in the spring of 1923 she played Lady Teazle to John Drew's Sir Peter. In the popular imagination Ethel Barrymore at the present time (1929) still reigns, in spite of the rise of numerous younger actresses, as the mistress of the legitimate stage. In her honor the Schuberts have named their beautiful new theater the Ethel Barrymore, and it is an impersonation of Miss Barrymore that affords some of the most diverting moments of *The Royal Family*, the Jed Harris success written by Edna Ferber and George Kaufman.

887 Ethel Barrymore, from a photograph
in the Davis Collection

888 Ethel Barrymore in *Captain Jinks*, from
a photograph in the Davis Collection

889 Ethel Barrymore Colt and her children,
from a photograph in the Davis Collection

890 Margaret Anglin, from a photograph in the collection of Montrose J. Moses, New York

891 Margaret Anglin as Medea, from a photograph in the collection of Montrose J. Moses, New York

892 Margaret Anglin as Ruth Jordan in Moody's *The Great Divide*, from a photograph. © Strauss-Peyton, Kansas City

MARGARET ANGLIN, 1876–

MARGARET ANGLIN, who rose to Frohman stardom in the title-rôle of Camille, is fundamentally an emotional actress. She was seen at her best in Jones' *Mrs. Dane's Defense* while she was leading lady at the Empire Theater under Charles Frohman. Her humor is sparkling, as best witnessed in the Oscar Wilde comedies. Her first marked success was won when she played with Richard Mansfield in *Cyrano de Bergerac*. Her ambition has taken her into the classic drama, and she has met success in *The Taming of the Shrew, Twelfth Night, Antigone, Iphigenia, Electra*, and *Medea*. She is the type of actress who would prosper in a theater of her own. But, in accord with theater conditions of the past, she has been forced to be on the road. She was responsible for the acceptance and playing of Moody's *The Great Divide* (1906). She has produced Greek drama at the Greek Theater, University of California, Berkeley (1910 *seq.*), and subsequently in New York. "I often wonder," wrote Miss Anglin in 1915, "whether the modern audience feels as deeply as the actor the tremendous difference between the ancient and modern stage. To me there is the difference between vastness and precision, and there is a sweep of the hills encircling the Greek amphitheater. I feel the physical difference as I leave the stage door of our modern playhouse, and go to any one of the stadia built at our universities; I feel it overwhelmingly as I stand amidst the classic beauty of the Hearst theater at Berkeley, California. There is a spiritual exaltation, not alone in the Greek drama itself, but in the architectural beauty of the Greek theater."

893 Margaret Anglin (standing, center) as Dora in Sardou's *Diplomacy*, from an engraving in the *Theatre Magazine*, June 1901

894 Two views of Margaret Anglin as Ruth Jordan in *The Great Divide*, from engravings in the *Theatre Magazine*, November 1906

895 William Vaughn Moody, from a photograph. © Brown Bros., New York

896   Scene from Moody's *The Great Divide*, from a photograph. © White Studio, New York

WILLIAM VAUGHN MOODY, 1869–1910

THE author of *The Great Divide* was a playwright whose untimely death deprived America of a dramatist of large powers and larger promise. William Vaughn Moody was a poet and thinker as well as writer of plays, as his earlier triology of verse dramas, *The Masque of Judgment* (1900), *The Fire Bringer* (1904), and the uncompleted *Death of Eve* had made evident. These three plays are based on one of Moody's cardinal principles: the duty of man to rebel against all that thwarts the development of his own highest nature. In *The Great Divide* (1906) the same theme recurs in the conflicts between the free impulses of the western hero and the prejudices and traditions of his New England wife. *The Great Divide* is characterized by an unusual breadth and significance, since it presents with reality the conflict between the ideals of our eastern and our western states. In his only other drama, *The Faith Healer* (1909), Moody depicts the struggle between love and a mission, and reaches the highest level of his philosophy.

EDWARD SHELDON, 1886–

LIKE Moody, Edward Sheldon has presented in his plays certain facts and conflicts in American life that had seldom been dramatically treated before. In his first success, *Salvation Nell* (1908), he painted a vividly realistic picture of slum life, and showed the heroine's struggle against her sordid environment. *The Nigger* (1909) deals with the tragedy implicit in the discovery by a southern patrician of the existence of a negro ancestor. Sheldon next wrote *The Boss* (1911), a study of the crude and ruthless political dictator, whose type is a well-known phenomenon in our public life. *The Princess Zim-Zim* (1911) is interesting to-day mainly because its romance is enacted against the background of a Coney Island side show in which the heroine officiates as snake-charmer. *The High Road* (1912), again involving a study of politics, is centered about a heroine who begins as an ignorant farm drudge and ends as the wife of the Governor. From the romantic element in *The High Road* it was not a long step to Sheldon's outstanding success *Romance* (1913), which had a long run in New York and was given over eleven hundred times in London.

897   Scene from Sheldon's *Salvation Nell*, with Mrs. Fiske, from a photograph. © Bryon, New York

LANGDON MITCHELL, 1862–

ONLY one important play has come from the pen of Langdon Mitchell but it is of a type that has been rare in American drama, the comedy of manners. *The New York Idea* (1906) is, to some extent, a satire on easy marriage and easy divorce. One of the characters puts it thus: "Marry for whim! That's the New York idea of marriage. . . . Marry for whim and leave the rest to the divorce court!" It must not be assumed, however, that the play is a solemn tract against the divorce evil; it is primarily a brilliant and witty comedy based on the contrast between the almost impossibly complacent and self-sufficient repre- sentatives of the self-appointed aristocracy and the unconventional, vivid, spontaneous members of the sporting circle. The clear social picture, the sharply etched characters, and the sparkling dialogue all go to make a play that can bear comparison with the best of the mod- ern social comedies. *The New York Idea* had a long run when it was first brought out with Mrs. Fiske in the leading rôle, and it was success- fully revived in 1915. It has also been given in Germany under Max Reinhardt's direction, and has been translated into several European languages.

898 Langdon Mitchell, from a photograph, cour- tesy of Langdon Mitchell, Philadelphia

JESSE LYNCH WILLIAMS, 1871–

899 Jesse Lynch Williams, from a photograph, courtesy of Henry Mead Williams, New York

THE subject of marriage and divorce has been of even greater interest to Jesse Lynch Williams than to Langdon Mitchell. In his delightful and thought-provoking comedy, *Why Marry?* he asks some frank questions about matrimony and he reaches the conclusion that it is very far from an ideal institution. Seeing so much of hypocrisy and baseness in marriage, the hero and heroine, because their love for each other is deep and honest, resolve to deprive themselves of the benefit of clergy, but they are cleverly trapped by the Judge, spokes- man of the author, into taking their legal vows without realizing what they are doing. Its sanely modern views on a difficult sub- ject and its ingenious and vigorous plot made *Why Marry?* one of the most enjoyable plays of the New York season of 1917–18. *Why Not?* (1922), which also treats the subject of divorce, was less suc- cessful on the stage because it lacks the sharpness of characteriza- tion and the clarity of point of *Why Marry?* It is, in Williams' own phrase, a "comedy of Human Nature *versus* Human Institutions," and while it offers no solution it causes one to consider that, since human nature cannot be changed, perhaps it would be well to change some human institutions.

OWEN DAVIS, 1874–

IT would be difficult to imagine a type of drama more removed from that of Mitchell and Williams than the early work of Owen Davis. Davis, though a Harvard graduate with certain ambitions toward serious poetic work, became gradually intrigued by the type of melodrama which was flourishing in New York under Al Woods' patronage. The titles of the plays which Davis wrote for Woods are sufficiently indicative of the ma- terial contained in them. *Convict 999, The Millionaire and the Circus Rider, Jack Sheppard the Bandit King, Chinatown Charlie,* and *Creole Slave's Revenge,* are typical of this enormous output. According to Davis' own estimate he reached an annual audience of over seven million people. This outburst of crude melodrama was bound to be followed by a correc- tive reaction, and Davis, sensing the coming change, altered his methods to meet it. In *Detour* (1921), and the Pulitzer Prize Winner, *Ice Bound* (1923), Davis has written two plays of high artistic value.

900 Owen Davis, from a photograph, cour- tesy of Owen Davis, New York

901   Otis Skinner, from the portrait by George Luks in the Kraushaar Galleries, New York

902   Skinner as Antonio in *Mister Antonio*, from a photograph in the collection of Montrose J. Moses

903   Skinner in Edwin Booth's Room at the Players' Club, from a photograph in the collection of Montrose J. Moses, New York

OTIS SKINNER, 1858–

OTIS SKINNER, who became a Frohman star in 1906, was born in Massachusetts of several generations of clergymen. In 1879 he was in the support of Edwin Booth. In 1880–81 he was at the Boston Theater. Then followed three years in the company of Lawrence Barrett, and in 1884 he began a five year's association with Augustin Daly. After this he became the leading man with Margaret Mather, and then joined Modjeska. In 1903 he was co-star with Ada Rehan in classic repertory. Then he became a Frohman asset. He was starred in such pieces as *His Grace de Grammont*, *The Duel*, and *Kismet*. He has a style of acting easily suited to rôles of a braggadocio nature. Recently he has published his reminiscences, in the course of which he writes, "I am glad that I was able to be in at the death before the old system quite passed away (*circa* 1878–79); glad that my novitiate was one of hard knocks that compelled me to swallow my technique in great gulps; glad of the vast experience that gave me every sort of character . . . and glad that my dramatic kindergarten was placed among men and women filled with the knowledge of their trade and with honor for their calling. . . ."

904   Skinner (second from left) as a member of Daly's Stock Company, from a photograph in the Davis Collection

905   Skinner as Count Paolo in Boker's *Francesca da Rimini*, from a photograph in the Davis Collection

906   Skinner as Lanciotto in *Francesca da Rimini*, from a photograph in the Davis Collection

907 Edna May, 1878–, from a photograph in the Davis Collection

908 Marie Doro, 1882–, from a photograph in the Davis Collection

909 Maxine Elliott, 1871–, from a photograph in the Davis Collection

FROHMAN'S WOMEN STARS

"The last decade of Charles Frohman's life," wrote his biographer Isaac F. Marcosson, "was one of continuous star-making linked with far-flung enterprise. He now had a chain of theaters that reached from Boston by way of Chicago to Seattle; his productions at home kept on apace; his prestige abroad widened. It was during the closing years of Frohman's life that his genius for singling out gifted young women for eminence found its largest expression. Typical of them was Marie Doro, a Dresden-doll type of girl who made her first stage appearance, as did Billie Burke and Elsie Ferguson, in musical comedy. . . . With her, as with the other young women, he delighted to nurse talent. He conducted their rehearsals with a view of developing all their resources, and to show every facet of their temperament. . . . Indeed, as Barrie so well put it, he regarded his women stars as his children. If they were playing in New York they were expected to call on him and talk personalities three or four times a week. On the road they sent him daily telegrams; these were placed on his desk every morning and were dealt with in person before any other business of the day. . . . When his women stars played in New York he always tried to visit them at night before the curtain went up. He always said of this that it was like seeing his birds tucked safely in their nests. Then he would go back to his office or his rooms and read manuscripts until late."

910 Billie Burke, 1885–, with Daniel Frohman, David Belasco, and Gilbert Miller, from a photograph, courtesy of Daniel Frohman, New York

911 Elsie Ferguson, 1883–, from a photograph in the collection of Montrose J. Moses, New York

912   Blanche Bates, from a photograph in the
            Davis Collection

913   Blanche Bates, from a photograph in the
            Davis Collection

BLANCHE BATES,
1873–

In 1913 Frohman presented as the leading lady in his *The Witness for the Defense* an actress who had risen to fame under Frohman's chief managerial rival, David Belasco. Miss Bates' first Belasco rôle was Cora in *Naughty Anthony* in January 1900, followed by Cho-Cho-San in *Madame Butterfly* and Cigarette in *Under Two Flags*, in both of which she scored great successes. In Belasco's own theater, which he secured from Oscar Hammerstein in 1902, Miss Bates was the original Yo-San in the beautiful Japanese play by John Luther Long and Belasco called *The Darling of the Gods*, a rôle which she played for two years. "Blanche Bates gained the greatest success of her professional career by her impersonation of Yo-San," wrote Winter. "She was an entirely lovely image of ardent, innocent, ingenuous, noble womanhood — such an image as irresistibly allowed by piquant simplicity, thrilled the imagination by an impartment of passionate vitality and by its exemplification of eternal constancy in love, — the immortal fidelity of the spirit — captured the heart. Her facility of action and fluency of expression were continuously spontaneous and she was delightful both to see and to hear. . . . Her appearance was beautiful, her action graceful, alert, vigorous, and free from all restraint of self-consciousness. . . . The clear, keen, healthful north wind was suggested by it, the reckless dash of mid-ocean wave, the happy sea-bird's flight." In 1905 at the Belasco she appeared as The Girl in *The Girl of the Golden West*, in which she toured for several years, reappearing later in New York as Anna in *The Fighting Hope* (1908), opposite Frank Worthing. More recent rôles include Countess Zicka in *Diplomacy* (1914), the title-rôle in *Medea* (1919), and Nancy Fair in *The Famous Mrs. Fair* (1919).

914   Blanche Bates and George Arliss in Belasco and
            Long's *The Darling of the Gods*, from a photograph.
            © Byron, New York

915   Blanche Bates as Cigarette in *Under Two Flags*,
            from a photograph in the Davis Collection

916 David Warfield as Simon Levi in *The Auctioneer*, from a photograph in the Davis Collection

917 Warfield as Herr Anton Von Barwig in *The Music Master*, from a photograph in the Davis Collection

918 Warfield in *The Return of Peter Grimm*, from a photograph, courtesy of David Belasco, New York

DAVID WARFIELD, 1866–

AT the conclusion of Blanche Bates' run of *Under Two Flags*, in June, 1901, Belasco concentrated on his new scheme of bringing forth as a legitimate star a burlesque actor with Weber and Fields, who had attracted his attention many years earlier in San Francisco. On September 23, 1901, David Warfield, under Belasco's management, appeared at the Bijou Theater as Simon Levi in *The Auctioneer*. His success in the rôle of the East Side Jew — a type which he had perfected during his music-hall and burlesque apprenticeship — was instantaneous. After one hundred and five consecutive performances in New York *The Auctioneer* ran over a period of two years on the road, netting approximately two hundred thousand dollars. *The Music Master*, September 12, 1904, was an even greater success, and for years was a favorite on the road. Later Warfield plays include *The Grand Army Man*, 1907, *The Return of Peter Grimm*, 1911, *Van der Decken*, 1915, and *The Merchant of Venice*, 1922. "Of all the many players, male and female," wrote William Winter in *The Life of David Belasco*, "whom Belasco has guided and helped to develop none, in my judgment, owes more to his fostering care and assistance than Warfield does: it is extremely probable that, without Belasco's aid, he would have remained to the end of his career a denizen of the music-halls, instead of becoming, as he has become, one of the most loved and admired actors of our stage."

919   Warfield (right-center) as Shylock in *The Merchant of Venice*, from a photograph.   © White Studio, New York

920 Al Hayman, 1866–1921, from a photograph, courtesy of Charles Frohman, Inc., New York

921   Marc Klaw, from a photograph, courtesy
of Marc Klaw, New York

THE THEATRICAL TRUST

THE attempts of Belasco to secure booking on the road for Warfield in *The Auctioneer* brought him for the first time into active conflict with a group of magnates who during the preceding years had been secretly gaining control of the theaters of the country, and since the season of 1895–96 openly grouping them together into a powerful theatrical trust. These men were Sam Nixon and Fred Zimmerman of Philadelphia, Al Hayman, Charles Frohman, Marc Klaw, and Abraham Erlanger of New York. They coralled the theaters of the country; they turned the owners of the out-of-town theaters into janitors of their buildings, subject, for the year's attractions, to the dictates of the trust. Though in some ways the business of the theater became stabilized and the salary of the actor more certain, there immediately became evident the dangerous concentration of power in the hands of a small group, with the attendant temptation to direct all art traffic to their own advantage and sell it on their own terms. The country was in the hands of Broadway commercial interests. Actors might protest, as they did, but with small effect. The independent attitude of James A. Herne, Francis Wilson, James O'Neill, Mrs. Fiske, and Richard Mansfield was one of protest against monopoly of this sort. "The Syndicate," as it was called, discounted all opposition theaters and closed its doors to all actors who refused its terms. It fought Harrison Gray Fiske, who refused to be a docile follower; it forced Mrs. Fiske to seek halls to play in; it required Madame Bernhardt to resort to a circus tent.

922   Fred Zimmerman, from a photograph.
© Brown Bros., New York

923   Abraham Erlanger, from a photograph,
© White Studio, New York

924   Sam Nixon, from a photograph. © New
York *Evening Post*

925 David Belasco, from a photograph in the collection of Montrose J. Moses, New York

926 Belasco at work in his Studio in the Belasco Theater, New York, from a photograph in the Davis Collection

FIGHTING THE TRUST

For almost ten years Belasco, at the price of great inconvenience and hardship, maintained his fight against the theatrical trust. He was outspoken in his contempt of it. There was open hostility. At a revival of *Zaza* on November 16, 1904, at the Belasco Theater, a representative of Charles Frohman interrupted the performance by serving a summons on Mrs. Leslie Carter. For many years Frohman and Belasco did not speak. In the same year, when Belasco desired to present *The Darling of the Gods* at the St. Louis World's Fair, every syndicate theater was closed to him, and he was forced to resort to an out-of-the-way building. In spite of persecution, Belasco increased each year in power, both as producer and dramatist. His two plays, dealing with romantic California themes, *The Girl of the Golden West* (1905), and *The Rose of the Rancho* (1906), were powerful by virtue of their dramatic intensity of action and appeal. The realism of his scenery and the subtlety of his lighting became each year more perfect. In 1907 he leased a second theater, the Stuyvesant — shortly afterward renamed the Belasco — where every modern improvement was installed. Two years later, so firmly established was Belasco's position, and so greatly were his plays in demand on the road that the theatrical trust was forced to make overtures of peace — which were eventually accepted.

927 Belasco's Settings for *The Merchant of Venice*, from a photograph, © White Studio, New York

928 Belasco's Settings for *The Merchant of Venice*, from a photograph, © White Studio, New York

930   Frances Starr, from a photograph in the
Davis Collection

931   Frances Starr, from a photograph in the
Davis Collection

FRANCES STARR, 1880–

FRANCES STARR, the outstanding actress of many of Belasco's best known later successes, began her stage career as a member of the stock company at Albany, New York, as Lucy Dorrison in Tom Robertson's *Home*. After six years more of stock experience gained in New York City, San Francisco, and Boston, she was in 1906 playing in an old fashioned race-track melodrama called *Gallops*. Belasco, who had been advised to keep his eyes on the young actress, was immediately captivated by the brilliance of her acting in the scene where the heroine waits anxiously on the pavilion porch as the news of the crucial race is relayed to her. "As the race was described," wrote Belasco in his memoirs, "Miss Starr's facial expression was so remarkable that she held the audience for several minutes. The various expressions of hope, despair, and joy came and went according to the movements of the horse. The tumult of applause was a tribute . . . to the perfection of Miss Starr's acting. And as an exhibition of pantomime I have seen nothing to surpass it." That same night Belasco offered her a contract. Her first rôle under the new management was the leading woman, Helen, opposite David Warfield in *The Music Master*. Her first independent starring rôle was as Juanita in Belasco's romantic drama of old California, *The Rose of the Rancho*, a rôle in which, according to William Winter, "she gained and merited general admiration." Her versatility is indicated by the wide range of parts which she capably filled — from the prostitute in Eugene Walter's disturbing and bitterly attacked play, *The Easiest Way*, to the almost unbelievably innocent nun in *Marie-Odile*. "The most completely finished and artistic performance of her career," according to Winter, was her Gabrielle Jannelot in Henry Bernstein's *The Secret*. Another popular rôle was Becky in Edward Locke's *The Case of Becky*.

932   Frances Starr as Becky, from a photograph
in the Davis Collection

933   Frances Starr, right, with David Belasco, at the Belasco Theater, after a rehearsal of *The Rose of the Rancho*, from a photograph.   © Byron, New York

935   Ditrichstein, center, in a scene from *The Great Lover*, from a photograph.
                        © White Studio, New York

LEO DITRICHSTEIN, 1865–1928

THE Belasco season of 1909–10 opened at the Stuyvesant Theater on Forty-fourth Street with a play by an Austrian dramatist, who during the past twenty years had been in America, and had gained increasing recognition both as actor and adapter. Leo Ditrichstein, who for Belasco adapted *Is Matrimony A Failure?* from a German original, had made his New York début at the Amberg Theater in 1890. Five years later he had enjoyed his first great success as Zou Zou in Du Maurier's *Trilby*. In July, 1910, Ditrichstein appeared at the Stuyvesant, by that time renamed the Belasco, as Gabor Arany in his own adaptation *The Concert*. Subsequent appearances under Belasco's direction include Jacques DuPont in *The Temperamental Journey*, 1913, and Sascha Taticheff in *The Phantom Rival*, 1914. His most famous rôles were Jean Porel in *The Great Lover*, 1915, and Armand in *The Purple Mask*, 1920.

GEORGE ARLISS, 1868–

ANOTHER actor-author of foreign extraction, who has become one of the most important figures on the American stage, was for a time a Belasco star. George Arliss began his stage career in England, coming to America for the first time in 1901 as a member of Mrs. Pat Campbell's company. At the end of the tour he signed a contract with Belasco to appear as Sakkuri in *The Darling of the Gods* (see No. 914). "He had an exceptional success," wrote William Winter, "even for an actor who always acts well." Later under the management of Harrison Grey Fiske, Arliss appeared opposite Mrs. Fiske in *Becky Sharpe*, *Leah Kleschna*, and *The New York Idea*. His most famous later characters were Disraeli, Alexander Hamilton, Nicolo Paganini, the Rajah in *The Green Goddess*, and Shylock in Shakespeare's *Merchant of Venice*.

CHAPTER XII

OUR CONTEMPORARY THEATER

THE second decade of the twentieth century may one day be looked upon as a turning point of considerable importance in the development of the civilization of the American people. By this time the first phase of industrialism, as it had manifested itself in the last third of the nineteenth century, had passed. During that period men had been absorbed in exploring the vast natural resources of the nation, and in taking the first steps toward their exploitation. It had been a period of swift material development, of the building of factories, and of the creation of great combinations of men and capital. By the second decade of the twentieth century the foundations of the new industrial America had been largely completed. Great wealth had been accumulated. American capital began seeking opportunities for profitable investment outside the national boundaries. Suddenly in the four years of the World War the relative positions of the United States and Europe were reversed. America became a creditor instead of a debtor nation and the money center of the world. America profited greatly in a material sense as a result of the tragedy which left Europe with devastated areas, with staggering debts, and with a deranged economic system. After the Armistice both Europeans and Americans began to realize as never before that a new and much more significant United States was taking its place in the society of nations.

The years following the World War have demonstrated completely that the American people have entered upon what may properly be called a period of maturity in the development of their civilization. Among other things they have become conscious of themselves and of their peculiar characteristics. A literature of iconoclasm pointing out the deficiencies in American character sprang up before the completion of the demobilization of the World War armies. Communities all over the United States became conscious of their sectional peculiarities, and began to emphasize in local ceremonies and celebrations their peculiar heritage. America was settling down, the restless movement of its people was declining in relative importance. Quite naturally Americans turned again to the drama, the development of which had been interrupted by the conflict, as one of the most effective modes of expressing the ideals and emotions of the new day.

When men sought to use the drama on a scale which had not heretofore been attempted in America, they discovered that the commercial control of the theater was an obstacle to its popular usefulness. They discovered also that the sudden rise in cost of living, which had characterized the second decade of the twentieth century, had made it commercially unprofitable to send plays on "the road" to the extent to which it had been done in pre-World War days. With the rapid growth of the quieter, more intimate type of drama, the cavernous "road" theaters which grew up in the 'eighties and 'nineties were found increasingly unsatisfactory, and for the most part were converted to other uses. As a step toward remedying this situation, and to provide a stage for the new type of drama, theatrical enthusiasts in smaller towns throughout the country organized local amateur organizations, and set about the production of plays in centers generally called

Little Theaters. As more and more such organizations spread throughout the country, their activities came to be called the Little Theater Movement. This successful attempt of the individual community to provide its own amusements constituted the first important effort of the American people to use the theater, in a wide sense, as a mode of self-expression. Thanks to the high level of intelligence and taste of the promoters, many plays are presented each year in the Little Theaters of the country which under the commercial régime would never have been seen. The surprising success of this movement is in large part attributable to the growing wealth of the American people, and to their desire to encourage worthwhile artistic and intellectual endeavors. Colleges and universities had been growing steadily before the World War, but the years which followed that conflict saw an educational expansion of vast proportions. In spite of the high cost of living, life was becoming more and more comfortable as the per capita wealth increased. Average Americans had sufficient money to assist in defraying the cost of the Little Theater Movement. They had the leisure to participate in its activities, and they had the desire, quite unprecedented in the national history, to share in its cultural advantages.

On the other hand, the fate of that institution which Arthur Hopkins referred to as "the facetiously called commercial theater" shows signs of being in the midst of one of its periodic depressions. For the last decade prominent critics have been deploring the low estate of the Broadway theater, drawing until recently equally barbed rejoinders from its defenders. But after 1925 there was a discernible decline, culminating in the generally lamented season of 1928–29, which in the eyes of numerous critics represented the lowest level yet reached in the twentieth century. On every side the unanswered question was broadcast, "What is the matter with the theater?" Whereas formerly the low quality of acting and drama was held responsible, the attack was gradually shifted to the management and the entire commercial structure of present-day theatrical organization. The crushing difficulties of modern theatrical management were widely discussed. Broadway managers declared themselves to be seriously handicapped in their efforts to produce better plays, by the alleged high-handed methods of labor unions, which had resulted in raising to an impossible figure the salaries of stage mechanics, carpenters, electricians, truckmen, and other back-stage laborers. So desperate seemed the situation that one prominent producer announced the transfer of his center of activities to the cheaper labor market of London. To meet the unusual crisis producers and managers were called to a conference to discuss methods of more intelligent coöperation between the various branches of the theatrical profession. When set against the background of the history of the American theater this clamor in the market place becomes less disturbing. As Charles Frohman enjoyed observing, pessimists have been bemoaning the decadent state of the theater and the drama since the days of Shakespeare. It is undeniable that too many theaters have been concentrated into a small area of New York City; that the popularity of the movie and the movietone is (in 1929) at a high point; and that the 1928–29 season suffered from an unhappy selection of plays. But the general standard of acting, the skillful directing and staging, and the sincere efforts of a number of able native dramatists, suggest that the American theater will in time emerge from its depression, and continue that healthy development which we have traced through two centuries.

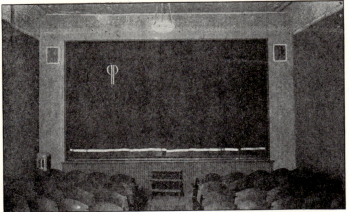

938   Interior of the Prairie Playhouse, Galesburg, Ill., from a photograph,
                courtesy of J. Allen Crafton, Lawrence, Kansas

"HOUSES OF VISION"

ALTHOUGH there had been occasional sporadic attempts, as far back as 1891, to organize independent theaters in America for the production of plays of unusual merit, the Little Theater Movement proper had no continuity in this country until the second decade of the twentieth century. In Europe, on the other hand, there has been uninterrupted activity since 1887, when André Antoine established in Paris the Théâtre Libre, dedicated to experimentation in the art of the theater. Two years later a similar organization was started in Germany by Theodore Wolff and Maximilian Hardin, formulating for the first time a policy, which since then has served as the guiding principal of the Little Theater Movement: "It is the plan of these assembled to found a stage, independent of any existing theaters, yet not in rivalry with them, which shall be free from . . . financial pre-occupations. There shall be given . . . performances of modern plays of outstanding interest, which, because of their nature, might find difficulty in being presented elsewhere." The Moscow Art Theater in 1890 and Max Reinhardt's Kammerspielhaus in 1905 are the most famous examples of the countless art-theaters that sprang up following Antoine's. In these various new playhouses the idea of intimacy between players and audiences was the primary consideration, with a corresponding minimizing of pecuniary profit as a motive for production. To their directors, men of the type of Reinhardt and Stanislavsky, the theater was a "house of vision," not a machine of amusement. The same ideals have characterized the Little Theater in the

939   Workshop of the Little Country Theater, Fargo, N. D., from
          a photograph, courtesy of the Fargo Little Country Theater

United States, and, though no groups have been formed comparable to the three famous European organizations, they have spread spontaneously and become a popular, nation-wide institution in a way undreamed of in other countries. In 1911 there were four American organizations which had taken up the gauge against commercialism: "Plays and Players" in Philadelphia; the Toy Theater in Boston; the Little Theater in New

940   Yale University Theater, New Haven, Conn., from a photograph,
                courtesy of the University Theater

York; and the Little Theater of Maurice Brown in Chicago. Six years later there were fifty such organizations, housed in remodeled stables, chapels, art museums, masonic temples, private houses, stores, and even saloons. Though united by a common ideal, their particular policies have varied markedly. Some have specialized in American plays only, while others have confined themselves to the European classics. Some have produced only one-act plays, and others have alternated the one-act form with full-length plays. The Little Theaters have greatly encouraged the American dramatist and their experiments in scenic effects have stimulated the native scenic artist.

GROWING DISCONTENT

THE number of Little Theaters increases yearly. They are born overnight; they die every hour; they serve their particular purposes, and then develop into something else. But they are all a part of our present national art restlessness — symptoms of that dissatisfaction which the American people have been showing for more than a decade because the commercial theater, since the breakdown of the first-class road company, has failed to give them what they want. From New York to San Francisco, the map is dotted with Little Theater groups. Not alone in the large cities, but in the villages of the western plains, the movement has taken root. Prairie houses seem as fond of Chekov, the Russian play-

941 Interior of the Carnegie Institute of Technology Little Theater, Pittsburgh, from a photograph. © Wm. W. Beaudry, Pittsburgh

wright, and of Shaw, the British satirist, as they are of the memory of Buffalo Bill. At random, take any theatrical journal and note what is going on in the amateur field. A hotel is advertising that it has established a Little Theater for the entertainment of its guests. St. Louis, Cleveland, and Chicago are showing pride in

942 Community Hall, promoted by the Little Theater, Fargo, N. D., from a photograph, courtesy of the Fargo Little Theater

their Civic Theaters. In the Wisconsin town of Ripon, they discover that they can have a Little Theater so contrived as to cost them sixty dollars, and they emulate Professor Baker at Yale by establishing "English *Cog* Dramaturgy." Columbia, Missouri, experiments with a Children's Theater. California teachers, met in convention, insist on a play produced in the latest style as part of their entertainment program. The Society of Arts and Crafts in Detroit, the Pasadena Community Play House, the Cleveland Play House, and the Dallas, Texas, Little Theater are winning the confidence of their clientele to such an extent as to finance substantial buildings and complete equipment. The Little Theater of Philadelphia, owned by the seven hundred and ninety-seven members of "Plays and Players," is a four-story edifice worth one hundred and fifty thousand dollars, and enjoys the assured support of the social and financial interests of the city. In Mobile, New Orleans, and Dallas the mayors issue official proclamations welcoming Little Theater Week. In one city booths are built in the

financial district for a Community Theater "Drive." In another city subscription lists have to be closed with a pledged membership of three thousand with new members clamoring at the door, and with the treasury having fifty thousand dollars to its credit. In Chicago a Memorial Theater is dedicated to the memory of a Little Theater dramatist — Kenneth Sawyer Goodman; in New Haven a new Gothic theater, equipped as a workshop, houses the manifold activities of Professor George P. Baker and the Department of Drama at Yale University.

943 Entrance to Playhouse, Society of Arts and Crafts, Detroit, Mich., from a photograph, courtesy of the Society of Arts and Crafts

UNIVERSITY PRODUCTIONS

944   George Pierce Baker, 1866–, from a photograph in the collection of Montrose J. Moses, New York

945   Brander Matthews, 1852–1929, from a photograph. © Brown Bros., New York

IN 1913 Professor George Pierce Baker began his famous 47 Workshop at Harvard, where he taught successfully the fundamentals of playwriting, and sent to Broadway many of his promising students. He was the pioneer college enthusiast, and if the university to-day is showing vital concern for playwriting, workshops, university production, it is to Professor Baker — now at Yale — that most of the credit is due. Meanwhile Professor Brander Matthews has written his popular books on dramatic theory; and his historical essays on the drama have been instrumental in the establishment of a Dramatic Museum at Columbia University and in the reissue of important essays on the theater in his Dramatic Museum Series of brochures. The universities have elsewhere contributed workers in similar fields: Professor Hatcher Hughes, professor of playwriting at Columbia, and author of the Pulitzer Prize Play *Hell-Bent for Heaven*; Professor Donald Clive Stuart, through whose initiative Princeton plans for the future a theater of her own; and Professor Samuel Eliot of Smith. Colleges yearly become more and more concerned about the theater. The Yale Dramatic Association and the Harvard Delta Upsilon in their classic productions are representative of the complete departure that has been made, in many directions, from the customary musical comedies. The Zelosophic Society of the University of Pennsylvania, where Langdon Mitchell is conducting three courses in playwriting, has for a number of years successfully produced American plays of a historical interest. Professor Frederick Koch of the University of North Carolina has brought the playwriting department to a high point of practical efficiency, and has presented his own students in amateur productions throughout the South and East. These folk plays dealing with the everyday life of the North Carolina type have become models for numerous other university groups engaged in working out a local drama. At the Carnegie Institute of Technology in Pittsburgh, the College Theater, conducted by Thomas Wood Stevens and B. Iden Payne, has for thirteen years been presenting plays of high quality, though often exotic in theme. Each year there is a meeting of university men interested in theatrical production.

946   Frederick Henry Koch, 1877–, from a photograph, courtesy of F. H. Koch, Chapel Hill, North Carolina

947   Production of John Masefield's *Esther* at the Carnegie Institute of Technology Theater, from a photograph, courtesy of the Department of Drama, Carnegie Institute, Pittsburgh

948 Percy MacKaye, 1875–, from a photograph, courtesy of Percy MacKaye, Windsor, Vt.

949 Scene from the Pilgrim Pageant, directed by George P. Baker, from a photograph, courtesy of George P. Baker, New Haven, Conn.

"AN ELEMENTAL INSTINCT FOR ART"

"CRUDE though it often be, then, pageantry satisfies an elemental instinct for art, a popular demand for poetry. This instinct and this demand, like other human instincts and demands are capable of being educated, refined, developed into a mighty agency of civilization. . . . By so doing, the development of the art of public masques, dedicated to civic education, would do more than any other agency to provide popular symbolic form and tradition for the stuff of a noble national drama." Percy MacKaye, the author of this idealistic credo, has contributed more than any other individual, since the death of his father, Steele MacKaye, to the advancement of a civic theater, dedicated "to the advantage of mankind." Believing that the highest mission of the theater is to provide "expressional opportunity for the largest number of individual participants," he has given the best of his energy to such large scale out-door masques as *The Canterbury Pilgrims*, with fifteen thousand participants,

950 Scene from Pageant of Joan of Arc, given by Entertainment Section of the Y. M. C. A. at Domremy, France, from a photograph in the United States Signal Corps, Washington, D. C.

and *Caliban* with over twenty-five thousand. His St. Louis Masque of 1914, tracing the history of the city, is the finest example of his combination of social and artistic forces. Under the influence of MacKaye the number of pageants and out-door performances in America has increased appreciably.

951 Out-door Performance of *Twelfth Night* by the Coburn Players, on the White House Grounds, from a photograph, courtesy of the Coburn Players, New York

952   Scene from a production of Maeterlinck's *The Blue Bird* at the New Theater, from a photograph, courtesy of Winthrop Ames, New York

THE NEW THEATER AND THE LITTLE THEATER

THOUGH the idea of an American theater unhampered by commercialism and devoted to art crystallized in 1911, a distinct movement in that direction had been made in November 1909 under the direction of Winthrop Ames by the endowment and establishment of a New Theater, dedicated to repertory. Praised as "the most beautiful theater in the western hemisphere," this house, the present Century Theater, had an enormous stage suited to great spectacles, which unfortunately were not forthcoming. Some of the repertory plays, however, such as *Don*, *Sister Beatrice*, *The Blue Bird*, *The Piper*, and *The Arrowmaker* contributed ideas for new scenic and stage effects, which were of permanent value to the American theater. But the enterprise failed in its second season, because the productions were too intimate for the great auditorium, and also because they lacked democracy of appeal. With his Little Theater in 1911 Mr. Ames achieved more lasting commercial success as well as true artistic production.

953   Scene from a production of Pinero's *The Thunderbolt* at the Little Theater, from a photograph, courtesy of Winthrop Ames, New York

It was a Little Theater only in an architectural sense, for the identifying characteristics of a Little Theater, resident company, experimentation, repertory, and subscription system, were all lacking in the new Ames enterprise.

THE NEIGHBORHOOD PLAYHOUSE

THE Neighborhood Playhouse was the most noteworthy representative of the institution which grew up in answer to a social demand. It sprang from the dramatic work conducted by Miss Alice and Miss Irene Lewisohn in a New York settlement house. In 1915, in order to provide larger accommodations, they founded the Neighborhood Playhouse in Grand Street. Their purpose was twofold: to set before tenement audiences plays which they could not otherwise see, and to give the younger people of the neighborhood an opportunity to act in plays and festivals. The festivals, a unique feature of the playhouse, have included *The Kairn of Koridwen*, *Petroushka*, *Jeptha's Daughter*, and *The Grand Street Follies of 1924*. The fame of the Playhouse spread rapidly through the country, and the force of its influence may be judged by the results of a single play performed there. Lord Dunsany's *A Night at an Inn* (1917) was produced by the players before the author was well known to America, and so favorably was it received that this as well as the other plays of Dunsany were everywhere in demand by the Little Theater groups of America.

954   The Neighborhood Playhouse, New York, from a photograph, courtesy of the Neighborhood Playhouse

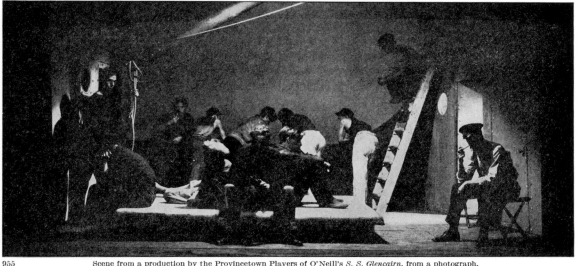

955   Scene from a production by the Provincetown Players of O'Neill's *S. S. Glencairn*, from a photograph,
courtesy of the Provincetown Players, New York

THE PROVINCETOWN PLAYERS

FOUNDED in a fish house on a wharf at Provincetown, Massachusetts, in 1915, the first company of Provincetown Players made some of the most significant experiments of the modern theater. The Wharf Theater, with
an excellent modern stage lighting system, came to be used as a laboratory
for experimentation. After successful try-outs there, plays were produced
at the Provincetown Players Theater on MacDougal Street, New York City,
which was maintained by associate membership with the help of the Stage
Society of New York. Tickets were not sold at the door, but a membership
fee of four dollars entitled the purchaser to ten performances. The special
purpose of the Provincetown Players was to produce plays by living American authors, and their theater, called The Playwrights' Theater, was essentially a place for trying out plays and a feeder for other theaters up town.
Because the program was varied every three weeks, and because the players
were unable to devote all their time to the demands of the theater, the performances were extremely uneven, as was the quality of the plays presented.
Yet it was by the first Provincetown Players that the plays of Eugene O'Neill
— especially such early plays as *Bound East for Cardiff*, *The Long Voyage
Home*, *Before Breakfast*, and *Emperor Jones* — were first produced, and in
such a way as to win general recognition. Susan Glaspell and David Pinski
were other notable dramatists introduced by the Players. *Suppressed
Desires* by Susan Glaspell and George Cram Cook was a noted comedy success

956   Scene from a production by the
Provincetown Players of O'Neill's *All
God's Chill'un Got Wings*, from a photo-
graph, courtesy of the Provincetown
Players, New York

of the company. A large percentage of plays tried out on MacDougal Street have been performed in other
Little Theaters, or have appeared in magazine or book form. In 1924 the first company was dissolved because

957   Scene from a production by the Provincetown Players of Paul Green's *In
Abraham's Bosom*, from a photograph, courtesy of the Provincetown Players

of the growing feeling that there was not
enough satisfactory material available to
enable them to maintain the high standard of
American plays which they had set themselves.
A second company was thereupon formed by
Eugene O'Neill, Robert Edmond Jones, and
Kenneth MacGowan. Among the most notable
productions of the second Provincetown group
are a revival of Mrs. Mowatt's *Fashion*,
O'Neill's *All God's Chill'un Got Wings* and
Desire under the Elms, Stark Young's *The Saint*,
and Paul Green's *In Abraham's Bosom*.

958   Eugene O'Neill, from a photograph.
              © Nikolas Muray, New York

EUGENE O'NEILL, 1888–

THE most hopeful situation in the present-day American theater is the existence of a group of sincere, intelligent, and able playwrights, who are writing more good drama than has been written in any corresponding period in our past. By common consent Eugene O'Neill stands supreme among the current group of playwrights. His career as a dramatist began in 1913 with the writing of one-act plays, and for a few years his efforts were largely confined to this form. The best of his one-acters are *Bound East for Cardiff*, *The Long Voyage Home*, *In the Zone*, and *Ile*, all of them presented by the Provincetown Players, and all dealing with the sea, which O'Neill had known as a common sailor. These early plays showed a tense power and a sense for dramatic material that augured well for the future. The promise was more than fulfilled in his first full-length play to reach the stage, *Beyond the Horizon* (1920). In this tragedy of a dreamer of far places who is confined to the narrow limits of a New England farm, the author revealed a vein of poetry and mysticism that had hardly more than been hinted at in his previous work. In his next successful play, *The Emperor Jones* (1920), O'Neill first showed himself to be a daring experimenter. Essentially a one-character drama, *Jones* is presented in eight episodes, most of which depict merely states of mind. The result is a play of strange and thrilling power. With the *Hairy Ape* (1922) O'Neill carried his experimentation into the field of symbolism. Brute force in human form, with its aspiration and its tragedy, is represented in a series of startling scenes that produce a grippingly dramatic effect. *All God's Chill'un Got Wings* (1923) is probably the most powerful treatment in our literature of the tragedy implicit in the efforts of the negro to compete on terms of equality with the white race. *Desire Under the Elms* (1924), which, like *Anna Christie* (1921), won the Pulitzer Prize, is a somber study of the dark passions of human nature. *The Great God Brown* (1926) is again definitely experimental, the mask being used — to the confusion of the audience — to indicate different phases of the same character. *Marco*

959   Charles Gilpin in O'Neill's *The Emperor Jones*, from a photograph in the collection of Montrose J. Moses, New York

Millions (1927), superbly produced by the Theatre Guild, is a satire on Babbitry stated in terms which, though symbolic, are readily comprehensible. In *Lazarus Laughed* (1927), perhaps the most poetic of his plays, O'Neill again deals in symbols, this time to voice the daring and beautiful theme that Love and Joy can conquer Death. O'Neill's most interesting innovation is found in his latest play, *Strange Interlude* (1928). This nine-act drama, in which the characters think aloud as much as they converse, produces, by its length and its analysis of the mind, an effect more nearly akin to that of the novel than has ever been produced in drama before. Combining as he does the poet, the mystic, the psychologist, and the experimenter, O'Neill is undoubtedly the most significant figure in the American theater to-day.

960   Scene from O'Neill's *Marco Millions*, from a photograph, courtesy
                of the Theatre Guild, New York

THE THEATRE GUILD

THE most successful Little Theater group from the point of view of development of prestige and power was organized in 1915 by some habitués of the Washington Square Bookshop. It was composed of actors, authors, and artists "interested in stimulating and developing new and artistic methods of acting, producing and writing for the American Stage." Having small capital, they rented the Bandbox Theater, seating two hundred and ninety-nine persons, manufactured their own scenery and costumes, and produced for their first performances the four one-act plays, *Interior, Licensed, Eugenically Speaking*, and *Another Interior*. Such was the ability of their scenic artists, R. E. Jones and Lee Simonson, that with scant

961   The Bandbox Theater, New York, from a photograph, courtesy of the Theatre Guild, New York

material they achieved the subtle atmosphere of Maeterlinck in this last play. Tickets were fifty cents at first and the theater was popular from the start. Although the players were still classed as amateurs, the

962   Scene from the Theatre Guild's Production of *John Ferguson*, from a photograph, courtesy of the Theatre Guild, New York

company during the second season moved to the Comedy Theater in the Broadway district with a seating capacity of seven hundred, and a scale of prices from fifty cents to two dollars. Most successful in 1917–18 was *The Bushido*, with the longest run of any one-act play in New York. After another successful season at the Comedy, the Washington Square Players moved in the spring of 1919 into the old Garrick Theater on Thirty-Fifth Street, where more adequate space and better accommodations allowed them to produce full-length plays. Under the new name of the Theatre Guild, they presented on April 14, 1919, Jacinto Benavente's *The Bonds of Interest*, followed the next month by St. John Ervine's *John Ferguson*. During the succeeding seasons at the Garrick and at the beautiful new Guild Theater on Fifty-first Street, the board of directors have insisted on carrying out the original program of the Washington Square Players "to produce new works by American authors, and important plays by foreign dramatists that would not otherwise be given a hearing, always maintaining our custom of free experiment, without which we believe progress in the theater to be impossible." Under the

leadership of a most capable governing board of six directors, the Theatre Guild, by efficiently organizing into a subscription membership the superior types of discriminating playgoers, has succeeded in maintaining the highest standard of plays, at the same time enjoying a considerable amount of commercial returns. Thanks to the Theatre Guild, the New York public has been able to see excellent productions not only of the best European plays by Shaw, Molnar, Milne, and Andreyev, but such significant American plays as Behrman's *The Second Man, Porgy* by Dorothy and DuBose Heyward, and O'Neill's *Strange Interlude*. One of the most encouraging signs of the present-day theater is the alliance of O'Neill, America's greatest living dramatist, and the Theatre Guild, our finest producing organization.

963   Scene from the Theatre Guild's Production of *The Masses*, from a photograph. © Bruguiere, New York

964 Helen Westley, from a photograph, courtesy of the Theatre Guild, New York

965 Dudley Digges, from a photograph, courtesy of the Theatre Guild, New York

966 Lynne Fontanne, from a photograph, courtesy of the Theatre Guild, New York

THE THEATRE GUILD ACTING COMPANY

"THE most important news of the year of grace 1926," wrote William Lyon Phelps in the *Theatre Guild Quarterly* for April, 1926, "is the announcement that our beloved New York Theatre Guild, which has blithely undertaken so many high-hearted adventures, will make the bold and risky experiment of repertory. All honour to its directors! . . . All over the United States lovers of what is best in the theatre are looking at the New York Theatre Guild; if the Guild succeeds in establishing repertory, it will be perhaps not altogether a vain hope that small villages like Cleveland, Buffalo, and St. Louis may some day have a theatre, where the inhabitants may actually be permitted to see good new plays." The repertory system as worked out by the Theatre Guild differs in many respects from the common practice of Europe, and from such a repertory schedule as that of the Civic Repertory Theater in our own country (see page 323). Instead of changing plays every night the Theatre Guild, at the inception of its new policy, alternated from week to week. By 1926 the effective personnel of the Guild Acting Company had grown sufficiently large so that two companies could be performing at the same time. By such an arrangement, *Ned McCobb's Daughter* (see No. 975) and *The Silver Cord* were presented by the Guild on alternate weeks at the John Golden Theater, while *Pygmalion* and *The Brothers Karamazov* alternated at the Guild Theater. Although visiting players are sometimes invited to participate, the casting is done almost entirely from the ranks of the Guild Acting School, which was begun in the summer of 1925 by Winifred Lenihan (see No. 973). In the fall of 1928 the Guild extended still further its activities, by sending out road companies to present either current Guild successes such as *Porgy* or revivals of old successes such as *John Ferguson*. The subscription system, as perfected in New York, has been extended to other towns, and the number of subscribers has grown.

967 Clare Eames, from a photograph, courtesy of the Theatre Guild, New York

968 Tom Powers, from a photograph, courtesy of the Theatre Guild, New York

969 Margalo Gillmore, from a photograph, courtesy of the Theatre Guild, New York

MARGARET WYCHERLEY, 1881–

MARGARET WYCHERLEY made her first appearance on the stage with Madame Janauschek in 1888, followed by associations of varying lengths with Richard Mansfield, Edith Wynne Matthison, Ben Greet, and Arnold Daly. In 1910 at Winthrop Ames' New Theater she played Light in Maeterlinck's *The Blue Bird;* in 1913 she was the Woman in *Damaged Goods;* in 1916 Rosalie La Grange in *The Thirteenth Chair,* a play by her husband Bayard Veiller. Her subsequent rôles include Clare in *The Verge* (1921), the Voice of the Serpent, the Parlor Maid, the Oracle, and the She Ancient in Shaw's *Back to Methuselah* (1922), Mrs. Gaylord in *Taboo* (1922), the Mother in Pirandello's *Six Characters in Search of an Author* (1922), and Daisy Devore in *The Adding Machine* (1923).

970   Margaret Wycherley, from a photograph, courtesy of the Theatre Guild, New York

EVA LE GALLIENNE, 1899–

EVA LE GALLIENNE, daughter of the well-known poet, Richard Le Gallienne, after completing her education in London and Paris and after a short engagement in English theaters, came to America in the autumn of 1915. Her original rôle of Rose in *Mrs. Boltay's Daughters* was followed by Jennie in *Bunny,* Patricia Mallory in *Mr. Lazarus,* Ottiline Mallinson in *Lord and Lady Algy,* Delia in *Belinda,* and Elsie Dover in *Not So Long Ago.* Her first great success was as Julie in Molnar's *Liliom.* After a long run with *Liliom* she took the part of Simonetta in *Sandro Botticelli* (1923), followed with Julia in *The Rivals,* and Alexandra in *The Swan.* In 1924 she appeared in Hauptmann's *Hannele,* in *La Vierge Folle,* and in *The Master Builder.* In 1925 she appeared in Paris, rendering in excellent French Mercedes di Acosta's *Jeanne D'Arc,* and on her return to America appeared in Schnitzler's *The Call of Life.* In the autumn of 1926 she opened on 14th Street the Civic Repertory Theater, which, under her management, has presented during the past three seasons plays by Ibsen, Chekov, and other standard European dramatists. In the attempt to encourage American drama, *The First Stone,* a play by Walter Ferris, of Cheshire, Connecticut, was in 1928 included in the stock company's repertory.

971   Eva Le Gallienne in *The Three Sisters,* from a photograph, courtesy of the Civic Repertory Theater, New York

RICHARD BENNETT, 1873–

RICHARD BENNETT, who in 1920 played the leading rôle of Robert Mayo in Eugene O'Neill's *Beyond the Horizon,* made his first stage appearance in 1891 at the Standard Theater, Chicago. After serving a long apprenticeship in New York at the Knickerbocker and at Hoyt's, at The Academy of Music and the Lyceum, he made his London début in 1906 as Jefferson Ryder in *The Lion and the Mouse.* Returning to America in 1908 he played, among other rôles, the Reverend Lindon in *The Hypocrites,* William Lake in *The Deep Purple* (1911), George Du Pont in *Damaged Goods* (1913), Colonel Barnard in *Rio Grande* (1916), Peter Marchmont in *The Unknown Purple,* Andrew Lane in Gilbert Emery's excellent play *The Hero* (1921), He in Andreyev's *He Who Gets Slapped* (1922), Tony in Sidney Howard's Pulitzer Prize play, *They Knew What They Wanted* (1924), and the title-rôle in the dramatization of Jim Tully's *Jarnegan* (1928).

972   Richard Bennett, from a photograph, courtesy of the Theatre Guild, New York

973   Winifred Lenihan in a scene from Shaw's *Saint Joan*, from a photograph. © Francis Bruguiere, New York

WINIFRED LENIHAN, 1898–

WINIFRED LENIHAN, who in 1923 so brilliantly introduced to the American public Shaw's masterpiece, *Saint Joan*, had made her début only five years before, following the completion of her studies at the American Academy of Dramatic Arts. Her début rôle of Bellini in *The Betrothal* was followed by Anne Woodstock in *For the Defense*, Betty Lyons in *The Survival of the Fittest* (1921), Anne in Milne's *The Dover Road* (1922), Anne Hathaway in Clemence Dane's *Will Shakespeare*, and Juliet in *The Failures*. Subsequently to *Saint Joan* she has appeared in *Nerves* by John Farrar and Stephen V. Benet, in Philip Barry's "glorious failure," *White Wings*, and in Shaw's *Major Barbara*.

HELEN HAYES, 1895–

HELEN HAYES made her début at the Herald Square Theater in 1909 as Lille Mime in *Old Dutch*, followed the next year by Psyche Finnigan in *The Summer Widowers*, and in 1911 by Fannie Hicks in *The Never Homes*. In 1917–18 she toured as Pollyanna Whittier in *Pollyanna*, and returned in September as Margaret Schofield in Tarkington's *Penrod*. Her New York plays, in which she has won increasing recognition for her winsome, whimsical pathos and humor, include Margaret in *Dear Brutus*, Cora Wheeler in *Clarence*, Bab in a play of that name, Seeby Olds in *The Wren* (1921), Mary Anne in *Golden Days*, Elsie Beebe in *To the Ladies* (1922–24), Mary Sundale in *We Moderns*, Dinah Parther in *Quarantine*, Maggie Wylie in *What Every Woman Knows*. Her first attempt at tragedy was as Norma in Jed Harris' production of George Abbot's and Anne Preston Bridgers' *Coquette*, in which she displayed unexpected depths of emotional intensity.

974   Helen Hayes, from a photograph, courtesy of Jed Harris, New York

ALFRED LUNT, 1893–

ALFRED LUNT, the outstanding actor of the Theatre Guild, made his first big hit opposite Helen Hayes in *Clarence*. The year following his début at the Castle Square Theater Stock Company in Boston (1913), he had toured with Margaret Anglin, appearing with her in her Greek plays at the Berkeley, California, Stadium, and later toured with Lillie Langtry and Laura Hope Crewes. His New York rôles include: Claude Estabrook in *Romance and Isabella* (1917), George Tewkesbury Reynolds in *The Country Cousin* (1918), Ames in *The Intimate Strangers* (1921), Charles II in *Sweet Nell of Old Drury* (1923), David Peel in *Robert E. Lee* (1924), Mr. Prior in *Outward Bound* (1924), the Actor in *The Guardsman* (1925), Dmitri in *The Brothers Karamazov* (1927), the Bootlegger in *Ned McCobb's Daughter* (1927), and Marco in *Marco Millions* (1928).

975   Alfred Lunt, from a photograph, courtesy of the Theatre Guild, New York

976   Basil Sydney (center) in a scene from a modern dress production of *Hamlet*, from a photograph. © White Studios, New York

BASIL SYDNEY

BASIL SYDNEY, after an apprenticeship in England with Lawrence Irving, was engaged by Granville Barker, 1914, for a tour of the United States in Shaw's *Fanny's First Play*. His permanent residence in the United States did not begin, however, until 1910, when he accompanied his wife, Doris Keane, the star of Edward Sheldon's *Romance*. In this play he appeared at the Playhouse in the rôles of the Bishop and Thomas Armstrong. In 1922 he achieved his first independent success as Harry Domain in *R. U. R.* His Mercutio to Ethel Barrymore's Juliet and his Sandro Botticelli at the Provincetown Theater established his reputation as a serious actor of unusual possibilities. Later rôles include Dick Dudgeon in Shaw's *The Devil's Disciple*, young Marlowe in Goldsmith's *She Stoops to Conquer*, Raskolnikoff in a dramatization of Dostoievsky's *Crime and Punishment* (1926), Hamlet in modern dress (1925), Petruchio in a version of *The Taming of the Shrew*, also given with modern settings and costumes, and Pietekin in Bruno Frank's *The Twelve Thousand* (1928). In these last three plays, he appeared opposite Mary Ellis.

JOHN BARRYMORE, 1882–

JOHN BARRYMORE, who, before his desertion to the motion pictures, gave the greatest promise of any of the younger actors, made his first New York appearance in 1903, and in 1905 made his London début. The following year he toured Australia in the company of William Collier. At Winthrop Ames' Little Theater in 1912 he achieved great success as Anatole in Schnitzler's *The Affairs of Anatole*. His rôles of the next few years included George Macfarland in *Believe Me, Xantippe* (1913), Julian Rolfe in *The Yellow Ticket* (1914),

William Folder in Galsworthy's *Justice* (1916), Peter Ibbetson (1917), and Protosov in Tolstoi's *Redemption* (1918). His most popular rôle was as Gianni Malespini in Sem Benelli's *The Jest*, in which he played opposite his brother Lionel. In the spring of 1920 Barrymore made his first Shakespearean venture as the Duke of Gloster in *Richard III*, which was followed two years later by a brilliant run of *Hamlet*, first in New York and later in London. In both places it was hailed as one of the high-water marks of the modern theater.

977   John Barrymore as Hamlet, from a photograph in the collection of Montrose J. Moses, New York

978   John Barrymore as the Duke of Gloster in *Richard III*, from a photograph in the collection of Montrose J. Moses, New York

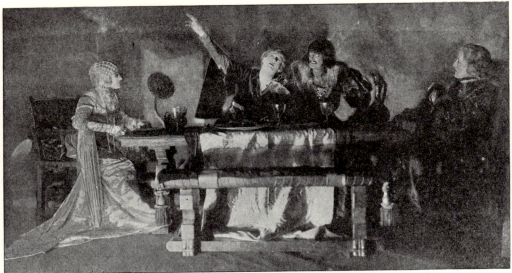

979   Scene from Sem Benelli's *The Jest*, Lionel Barrymore, right center, John Barrymore, left center,
                    from a photograph in the Davis Collection

LIONEL BARRYMORE, 1878–

LIONEL BARRYMORE, the older brother of John, appeared for the first time on the stage in 1893 in the company of his grandmother, Mrs. John Drew (see No. 603), under whom he played in *The Rivals* and in *The Road to Ruin*. In 1897 he toured in the company of Nance O'Neil and in 1900 with James A. Herne (see No. 830) in *Sag Harbor*. He then played two seasons with his uncle John Drew (see No. 840) in *The Second in Command*, *The Mummy*, and *The Humming Bird*. In 1917 he played Colonel Ibbetson in *Peter Ibbetson*, and in the following year scored a great success as Milt Shanks in Augustus Thomas' *Copperhead*. In 1919 he appeared as Neri in *The Jest*, in 1920 as Mouzon in *The Letter of the Law*, in 1921 as Macbeth in Arthur Hopkins' production and as Achille Carleton in *The Claw*, and in 1923 as Tito Beppi and Flik in *Laugh, Clown, Laugh*.

WALTER HAMPDEN, 1879–

WALTER HAMPDEN, the most active exponent of the Shakespearean tradition on our stage at the present time, though born in Brooklyn, New York, served the greater part of his theatrical apprenticeship in England. From 1901 to 1904 he was with F. R. Gerigan's stock company at Brighton, playing about seventy parts of wide range, a list which he extended still further at the Adelphi in London, and at Glasgow. In 1907 he was engaged by Henry Miller to appear opposite Alla Nazimova at the Bijou Theater in New York, in an Ibsen repertory. He later played opposite Viola Allen, and in 1908 achieved independent success as Manson in Charles Rann Kennedy's *The Servant in the House*. In 1913 he joined the company of the Fine Arts Theater, Chicago, where he remained for a short engagement. In 1916 he established permanent headquarters in New York. His subsequent rôles include Caliban in *The Tempest*, Elihu in *The Book of Job*, Mark Antony in *Julius Cæsar*, Macbeth, Romeo, Hamlet, Shylock, and Cyrano de Bergerac, Dr. Stockmann in *An Enemy of the People*, Caponsacchi in a dramatization of Browning's *The Ring and The Book*, and King Henry in *Henry V*.

980   Walter Hampden as Othello, from a photograph. © Strauss-
                    Peyton, Kansas City

JANE COWL, 1887–

JANE COWL, who has enriched the Shakespearean tradition by her beautiful performance of Juliet (1923), made her professional début in 1903 on the stage of the Belasco Theater in *Sweet Kitty Bellairs*. Under Belasco's management she subsequently appeared in support of David Warfield in *The Music Master* and *A Grand Army Man*, and of Frances Starr in *The Rose of the Rancho* and *The Easiest Way*. In 1912 she appeared as Mary Turner in *Within the Law*, followed by Jeannine in *Lilac Time* (1917), The Duchess of Towers in *Peter Ibbetson* (1918), Mary Lawrence in *The Crowded Hour* (1919), Kathleen Dungannon and Moonyeen Clare in *Smiling Through* (1920). After a long run of Juliet she appeared as Melisande in Maeterlinck's *Pelleas and Melisande*, and shortly afterward as Cleopatra in Shakespeare's play. Her most recent success was as Amytis in Robert E. Sherwood's farce, *The Road to Rome* (1926–27). In the spring of 1928 Miss Cowl staged *Diversion*, an excellent play by John van Druten, produced by her husband, Adolph Klauber.

981   Jane Cowl as Cleopatra, from a photograph, courtesy of Jane Cowl

MARJORIE RAMBEAU, 1889–

MARJORIE RAMBEAU, after ten years stock experience in California, Oregon, and Washington, made her first New York appearance in 1913 as Nelly in *Kick In*, opposite Willard Mack. Her most famous later rôles were Nan Carey and Ruth Brockton in *Cheating Cheaters* (1916), Gina Ashling in *Eyes of Youth* (1917), Madame Reine in *The Fortune-Teller* (1919), Margaret Emerson in *The Unknown Woman* (1919), Mrs. Lafe Regan in *The Sign on the Door* (1920–21), Edith Fields in *Daddy's Gone-a-Hunting* (1921), Jenny in *The Goldfish* (1922), and Dora Kent in *The Road Together* (1924).

982   Marjorie Rambeau, from a photograph in the Davis Collection

LAURETTE TAYLOR, 1887–

LAURETTE TAYLOR, whose first substantial success was in 1910 as Rose Lane in *Alias Jimmie Valentine*, began her career seven years before in stock at the Boston Athenæum and served a long apprenticeship as stock star in Seattle, Washington, and other western centers. Her second success was as Luana in *The Bird of Paradise* (1912), followed the next autumn by *Peg o' My Heart*, which ran over six hundred nights in New York and five hundred in London, and was revived in 1921. Her other rôles include 'Aunted Annie in *Out There* (1917), L'Enigme in *One Night in Rome* (1917), Marian Hale in *The National Anthem* (1922), Sarah Kantor in *Humoresque* (1923), and Nell Gwynne in a revival of *Sweet Nell of Old Drury* (1923).

983   Laurette Taylor as Peg o' My Heart, from a photograph in the Davis Collection

984   Pauline Lord, from a photograph in the
Davis Collection

PAULINE LORD, 1890–

PAULINE LORD, whose brilliant interpretation of Eugene O'Neill's *Anna Christie* (1921) constitutes one of the high-water marks of the post-war stage, made her first professional appearance in 1903 with the Belasco Stock Company in San Francisco. Two years later she was engaged by Nat Goodwin, with whom she toured and filled New York engagements. Her first metropolitan success was in 1912 as Ruth Lenox in *The Talker*. Her later successes include 'Aunted Annie in *Out There* (1917), Sadie in *The Deluge*, Nancy Bowers in *April* (1918), Nasbia in Hopkins' beautiful production of Gorki's *Night Lodging* (1919), Dagmar Krimback in *Samson and Delilah*, and, after the long New York and London runs of *Anna Christie*, Amy in Howard's *They Knew What They Wanted* (1924). Her play, *Salvation*, (1928), likewise by Howard (and MacArthur) was less successful. The difficulty of securing an adequate play has handicapped her appreciably for a number of years.

LENORE ULRIC, 1894–

LENORE ULRIC, after several years of stock experience in the Middle West and upper New York state, made her first metropolitan success as Wetona in Belasco's production of *The Heart of Wetona*. The next year she won still greater popularity as Rose Bocion in *Tiger Rose*, and in 1919 as Lien Wha in *The Sun Daughter*. Since then she has starred as Kiki, Lulu Belle, and Mima.

985   Lenore Ulric as Kiki, from a photograph in the
Davis Collection

986   Katharine Cornell, from a photograph, courtesy of Gilbert Miller,
New York

KATHARINE CORNELL

KATHARINE CORNELL, who in 1916 made her début with the Washington Square Players at the Comedy Theater in *The Bushido*, first aroused the enthusiasm of the New York critics by her brilliant performance of the disquieting Mary Fitton in Clemence Dane's *Will Shakespeare*. Later emotional rôles include Laura Pennington in Pinero's *The Enchanted Cottage* (1923), Henriette in *Casanova* (1923), Lalage Sturdes in *The Outsider* (1924), Suzanne Chaumont in *Tiger Cats*, Candida in Shaw's play of that name, and Iris Marchbanks in Michael Arlen's *The Green Hat* (1926). Her performance (1929) in a dramatization of Edith Wharton's *The Age of Innocence*, in which Miss Cornell with her beauty and with her gorgeous costumes created an illusion of charming romance, was highly praised.

ALINE MacMAHON

ALINE MacMAHON, by her portrayal of such widely varying characters as the patient American wife in the 1926 revival of O'Neill's *Beyond the Horizon*, the Mexican peasant in Jed Harris' production of *Spread Eagle*, and Bella, the French prostitute, in Ernest Boyd's adaption of *Maya*, gives promise of developing rapidly into a tragédienne of unusual sincerity and depth. Her voice is remarkable for its richness and its variety.

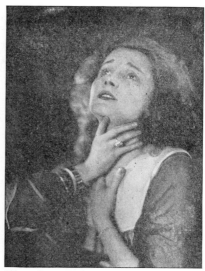

937 Aline MacMahon, from a photograph, courtesy of Jed Harris

988 Jeanne Eagels, from a photograph in the Davis Collection

JEANNE EAGELS, 1894–

JEANNE EAGELS' overwhelming success as the tragic Sadie Thompson in *Rain* (1922–24) came only after eleven years of preparation in rôles both comic and tragic, during which she had toured with George Arliss and Julian Eltinge. Her latest performance, *Her Cardboard Lover* (1927), reveals Miss Eagels as an excellent comédienne, fully capable of the subtleties of French farce.

INA CLAIRE, 1892–

INA CLAIRE, whose interpretations of Polly Shannon in *Polly With a Past* (1917), Jerry Lamar in *The Gold Diggers* (1919–21), Monna in *Bluebeard's Eighth Wife* (1921), and the American social climber in Somerset Maugham's *Our Betters* (1928), place her near the top of the list of American comédiennes, began on the vaudeville stage in 1907, and four years later made her New York début as Molly Pebbleford in *Jumping Jupiter*. She was for a time one of the leads in Ziegfield's Follies.

PEGGY WOOD, 1894–

PEGGY WOOD, another leading comédienne, made her début in New York in 1910. Her first rôle was as Vera Steinway in *The Three Romeos* (1911), followed by Fanchette in *Mlle. Modiste* (1913). Later rôles include Julie in *Buddies* (1919), Antoinette Allen in *The Clinging Vine* (1922), and Portia in *The Merchant of Venice* (1928), opposite George Arliss.

989 Ina Claire, from a photograph. © Underwood & Underwood

990 Peggy Wood, from a photograph in the Davis Collection

991   David Belasco, from a photograph in the collection of
                    Montrose J. Moses, New York

DAVID BELASCO

SINCE the death of Charles Frohman in 1915 David Belasco (see Chapter XI) has reigned with undisputed title as the dean of American producers, the patriarch of the American stage. In his youth a daring experimenter in new methods of production, he stands to-day a venerable conservative, a living symbol of an older period of the American theater, which has become almost completely obscured in the mass of new tendencies and new experiments. His energy has, however, been little impaired by his advancing age. His activities since the war include a number of notable productions: *Tiger Rose; Tiger! Tiger!; The Gold Diggers; Deburau; The Wandering Jew; Shore Leave; The Merchant of Venice; Mary, Mary, Quite Contrary; Lulu Belle;* and *The Bachelor Father*. His latest offering, *Mima*, an adaption of Ferenc Molnar's *The Red Mill* is the most elaborate production that Belasco has ever made, and embodies the results of his years of exhaustive experimentation in the possibilities of lighting and stage effects. In 1924 the French Government decorated Belasco in the presence of the director of the Odéon Theater, Paris.

WINTHROP AMES

WINTHROP AMES, whose connection with the direction of the New and Little Theaters is elsewhere treated (see Nos. 952–53), took over in 1904 the management of the Castle Square Opera House in Boston. Four years later he was called to New York to take charge of the New Theater. At the present time he is owner of the Little and the Booth Theaters, at which he has made many notable productions, including *Prunella*, Galsworthy's *The Pigeon*, *Pierrot the Prodigal*, *Children of Earth*, *Truth*, *Hush*, *The Green Goddess*, various Gilbert and Sullivan revivals, Philip Barry's *White Wings*, and Galsworthy's *Escape*.

JED HARRIS

THE most widely acclaimed and phenomenally successful of the younger producers is Jed Harris, who, after only a few years apprenticeship as theatrical agent in New York and on the road, began production with *Weak Sisters*, which was followed by *Love 'Em and Leave 'Em*. In his next presentation, *Broadway* (1926), written by Philip Dunning and George Abbott, Harris achieved one of the most distinctive commercial successes of the post-war theater. *Spread Eagle* (1927), though more pretentious artistically, had a comparatively short run. In 1928 he had two eminently successful productions: *Coquette*, a tragedy of life in the South, written by George Abbott and Ann Preston Bridgers; and *The Royal Family*, a satiric comedy woven by Edna Ferber and George Kaufman around the domestic life of the Barrymores. *The Front Page* by Ben Hecht and Charles MacArthur was the outstanding theatrical success of the 1928–29 season.

992   Winthrop Ames, from a photograph in the collection of Montrose J. Moses, New York

993 Jed Harris, from a photograph, courtesy of Jed Harris, New York

ARTHUR HOPKINS, 1878–

SINCE his successful arrival on Broadway with *The Poor Little Rich Girl* in 1912, Arthur Hopkins has held a high place among the more serious New York producers. Since that date he has to his credit more sincere artistic productions than has any competitor. These include among others *A Successful Calamity, Redemption, The Jest, Night Lodging, Richard III, Macbeth, The Wild Duck, Hedda Gabler, A Doll's House, We are Seven, Daddy's Gone-a-Hunting, Anna Christie, The Hairy Ape, Rose Bernd, Hamlet, Romeo and Juliet, What Price Glory?* and *The Second Mrs. Tanqueray.* It is felt by many that his earnest desires for the betterment of the commercial theater have been hampered at times by his theory of *laissez-faire,* according to which his rôle is merely to bring together the artists in the various phases of theatrical production, tell them his general purpose, and hold them responsible for the execution of the details. However, his enormous service to the contemporary theater has been generally recognized, especially by George J. Nathan, the most exacting contemporary critic.

994   Arthur Hopkins, from a photograph, courtesy of Arthur Hopkins, New York

ALBERT HERMAN WOODS

A. H. WOODS, one of the best known Broadway managers of the present day, began producing in 1902. During these early years he confined himself to sensational presentations, which, from the price of admission, were known as 10–20–30 melodramas. The titles of a few are indication enough of the general character: *Queen of the White Slaves, Tracked around the World,* and *Fast Life in New York.* In recent years he has taken his place beside the more conservative producers with *Friendly Enemies, Eyes of Youth, Fair and Warmer, Potash and Perlmutter, Cheating Cheaters, The Thirteenth Chair, Within the Law,* and *Up in Mabel's Room.*

995   Albert Herman Woods, from a photograph, courtesy of A. H. Woods, New York

MORRIS GEST, 1881–

MORRIS GEST, whose chief contribution to the American theater lies in his importation of significant European productions, began his career in Boston in 1893. Since 1905 he has been associated with F. Ray Comstock in the production of over fifty plays, which include such outstanding successes as *The Wanderer* (1917), *Chu Chin Chow* (1918), *Aphrodite* (1919) and *Mecca* (1920). In 1922 he introduced to America Balieff's *Chauve Souris,* and in the following year brought over the Moscow Art Theater, which under the leadership of Stanislavsky gave two seasons of Russian masterpieces. In 1924 he imported Max Reinhardt to stage *The Miracle.*

996   Morris Gest, from a photograph. © Wide World Photos

GILBERT HERON MILLER, 1884–

GILBERT HERON MILLER, the son of the famous actor Henry Miller (see No. 806) and Bijou Heron, daughter of Mathilda Heron (see No. 547), has since 1921 been manager of Charles Frohman, Inc., and responsible for all Frohman productions. His first independent production was *Daddy Long-Legs* in London in 1916, followed by *The Willow Tree* (1917), *Nothing But the Truth* (1918), *Monsieur Beaucaire* (1919) and *Daniel* (1921). From 1921 to 1928 Mr. Miller's headquarters were in the Empire Theater on Broadway, and under his auspices a number of successes, financial and artistic, were produced, including *Polly With a Past* (1921), *The Bat* (1922), *The Green Goddess* (1923–24), *The Patriot* (1928), and Molnars' *Olympia* (1928). In December of 1928 Mr. Miller announced that, owing to the enormous expense of producing in New York, he intended to transfer his center of operations again to London, and bring to this country only those plays which by actual test had proved themselves successes.

997   Gilbert Heron Miller, from a photograph, courtesy of Gilbert Miller, New York

JOHN GOLDEN, 1874–

JOHN GOLDEN, the producer of Frank Bacon's *Lightnin'*, which until *Abie's Irish Rose* held the record for the longest run of any play in America, was formerly an actor, journalist, and song-writer. He is the author, either alone or in collaboration, of *The Candy Shop, Hip, Hip Hooray, The River of Souls, The Big Show, Flying Colors,* and *Eva the Fifth.* Other Golden productions, a number of which have been great successes, include *Forward March, Thank You, The Wheel, The First Year, Dear Me, Thunder, Three Wise Fools, Seventh Heaven, Nite Hostess,* and *Four Walls,* an excellent play by Dana Burnet and George Abbott, in which Muni Wisenfrend in his first Broadway appearance gave a brilliant performance.

998   John Golden, from a photograph in the Davis Collection

GEORGE CROUSE TYLER, 1867–

GEORGE CROUSE TYLER, who is best known in the theatrical world to-day for his elaborate all-star revivals of Shakespeare and of former successes in this country, began his career as a reporter and editor on various Ohio newspapers. In 1894 he entered the theatrical business as manager for James O'Neill. Three years later he organized the firm of Liebler and Co., which over a period of eighteen years was one of the most powerful forces in the theater, managing such stars as Charles Coghlan, Viola Allen, who in *The Christian* played to almost two million dollars in three years, Duse, William Faversham, William H. Crane and Ada Rehan. Tyler's most notable all-star revivals were Pinero's *Trelawney of the Wells,* Sardou's *Diplomacy,* Goldsmith's *She Stoops to Conquer,* and *The Merry Wives of Windsor* and *Macbeth.*

999   George Crouse Tyler, from a photograph in the Davis Collection

1000   Sam Harris, from a photograph
in the Davis Collection

SAM HARRIS, 1872–

SAM HARRIS, lessee and manager of the Sam Harris and the Music Box Theaters, and the Bronx Opera House in New York, and of the Sam Harris Theater and the Grand Opera House in Chicago, was for a time in the producing firm of Sullivan, Harris & Woods, and then for sixteen years (1904–20) was associated with George M. Cohan in the production of numerous Broadway successes. Since 1920 he has been an independent producer, with a succession of notable hits.

1001   George Michael Cohan, from a photograph
in the Davis Collection

GEORGE MICHAEL COHAN, 1878–

GEORGE M. COHAN, who to-day is known throughout the country as a writer of songs, as an actor and dancer, as the author of many popular successes, and as an enterprising Broadway producer, began his stage career at the age of eleven in *Daniel Boone*. His name is most closely associated with the plays produced in conjunction with Sam Harris, many of which he himself wrote and in many of which he played the leading rôle—plays such as *George Washington, Jr.*, *Get Rich Quick Wallingford* and *Broadway Jones*.

EDGAR SELWYN, 1875–

EDGAR SELWYN, president of Selwyn and Company, prominent Broadway producers, has had a long career as actor, author, and producer. His first appearance on the stage was in 1896 at the Garrick Theater in William Gillette's *Secret Service*. Subsequent rôles include Tony Mastaro in Augustus Thomas' *Arizona*, and Foreman in Gillette's *Sherlock Holmes*. He is the author of many plays such as *The Arab*, *Rolling Stones*, *Nearly Married*, *Judy*, and *Possession*.

1002   Edgar Selwyn, from a photograph, courtesy
of Edgar Selwyn, New York

WILLIAM A. BRADY, 1863–

WILLIAM A. BRADY, the husband of Grace George and the father of Alice Brady, has been for many years one of the most influential producers and managers on Broadway. In 1896 he became manager of the Manhattan Theater, where he produced *Mlle Fifi*, *Women and Wine* and *Way Down East*. Later Brady successes include all-star revivals of *Uncle Tom's Cabin*, *The Two Orphans*, *Trilby* and *The Lights of London*.

1003   William A. Brady, from a photograph.
© Underwood & Underwood

1004   Sam Shubert, from a photograph.
© Matzene, Chicago

THE SHUBERTS

AT the present time the Shuberts, Jacob J. and Lee, are the most powerful agency controlling theater sites and buildings in New York City and throughout the country. They first came into prominence around 1900 in their fight against the Theatrical Trust. At that time an older brother Sam was alive, and it was he who had taken the initiative and persuaded his two younger brothers to transfer their theatrical activities from Syracuse to the wider market in

1005   Lee Shubert, from a photograph.
© Strauss-Peyton Studio

New York City. In 1900 the three Shuberts subleased the Herald Square Theater, and, as leaders of the Independent Movement, gradually gained control of a chain of good theaters from coast to coast. To day the Shubert-owned theaters dwarf those of the nearest competitor. Though the Shuberts have managed a number of stars and produced much legitimate drama, they are best known, from the producing angle, for their brilliantly staged operettas and musical comedies.

FLORENZ ZIEGFELD, 1869–

THE greatest rival of the Shuberts in the musical comedy field is Florenz Ziegfeld, who, since his first humble start in 1907, has presented each year a revue called The Ziegfeld Follies, which, with increasing splendor and variety, has accomplished its aim of "glorifying the American girl." With each new Ziegfeld show there is a fresh outburst of praise from the critics. His name has become synonymous with elaborate production. Within the last few years he has advanced to more dramatically pretentious efforts. From Edna Ferber's *Show Boat* he contrived a strikingly pictorial drama of the lives of the actors along the Mississippi. His production of operetta made from Dumas' *Three Musketeers* was even more dramatic and colorful.

1006   Florenz Ziegfeld, from a photograph
in the Davis Collection

1007   Scene from a Ziegfeld Revue, from a photograph.   © White Studio

RACHEL CROTHERS, 1878–

WHILE women dramatists have been known in America since the days of Mercy Warren (see No. 43), it is only in recent years that they have become an impressive force in the theater. Conspicuous among the playwrights of the present are Zoe Akins, Edna Ferber, Susan Glaspell, Clare Kummer, Anne Nichols, Lula Vollmer and Maurine Watkins. But the most prolific and perhaps most competent woman now writing for the stage is Rachel Crothers. After three years of valuable experience as an actress, Miss Crothers turned to the writing of plays. Her more important dramas, such as *He and She* (1911), have dealt with certain problems of modern life, especially as they affect women. *A Man's World* (1909) and *Ourselves* (1913) criticize the double standard of morality. In *Nice People* (1920) the lax conduct of the younger generation is realistically depicted and their need of reformation is shown. *Expressing Willie* (1924) provides a vivacious satire on the prevailing fad of self-expression.

1008   Rachel Crothers, from a photograph.
© Underwood & Underwood

1009   Sidney Howard, from a photograph, courtesy of
the Theatre Guild, New York

SIDNEY COE HOWARD, 1891–

BUT an even more encouraging sign than this new prominence of the woman dramatist is the rise of a group of younger men who are turning with earnest sincerity to a study of various phases of American character, and then incorporating their observations into well made plays. One of the most able of these is Sidney Howard, who, after beginning with romantic dramas, turned to the realistic treatment of American life. *They Knew What They Wanted* (1924), a love triangle involving an Italian grape-grower in California, received the Pulitzer Prize. *Ned Cobb's Daughter* (1926), which has as heroine a shrewd, courageous New England woman, is definitely superior to the earlier play. It in turn was surpassed by *The Silver Cord* (1926), a tense drama of a mother who will brook no rival in the affections of her sons.

GEORGE KELLY, 1887–

GEORGE KELLY has likewise made capital of certain phases of the American scene. The first play to win him a public was *The Torch-Bearers* (1922), a satire on some of the absurd persons who have associated themselves with the Little Theater movement. Next came his delightful comedy, *The Show-Off* (1924). Kelly offered a more serious play, which, incidentally, won the Pulitzer Prize, in *Craig's Wife* (1925), essentially a tragedy of the woman who puts the perfect orderliness of her house before all other considerations. *Daisy Mayme* (1926), though inferior to its predecessor, is marked by some acute character observation, in which Kelly excels. His latest play, *Behold, the Bridegroom* (1927), in which Judith Anderson was starred, is an emotional, somewhat sentimental, study of a restless, disillusioned society girl, who, under the stimulus of an unrequited love for a self-made man, realizes the hollowness of her own life and yet is unfitted to go on to anything better.

1010   George Kelly, from a photograph.
© Wide World Photos

1011   Paul Green, from a photograph.
              © Wide World Photos

PAUL GREEN, 1894–

WITH the growth of artistic consciousness in America has come an increased interest in provincial life as material for drama. The North Carolina playwrights have taken the lead in this search, and preëminent among the North Carolinians is Paul Green. His first play of importance, *The Last of the Lowries* (1920), is an effective one-acter built about a historical gang of outlaws that flourished shortly after the Civil War. Before long Green turned to the negro, and in 1926 published *Lonesome Road*, a volume of one-act plays in which negro life is handled with understanding and sympathy. Green came into prominence when his full-length drama, *In Abraham's Bosom*, was produced at the Provincetown Theater in 1926 and won the Pulitzer Prize. This tale of a man of mixed blood, who dedicates his life to the betterment of himself and his race but is rejected by both whites and blacks, presents a tragedy that has often been enacted in reality. In *The Field God* (1927) Green turned again to the southern whites.

GILBERT EMERY, 1875–

GILBERT EMERY, whose three outstanding plays reflect a phase of American life different from Paul Green's, yet as sincerely honest, is a man of the theater, and knows from his experience as an actor the possibilities and limitations of spoken dialogue. Emery's first success was produced in 1921, only a few years after his return from the war. *The Hero*, a study of a returned soldier, who is a moral coward but a physical hero, as he proves in the end, is striking by reason of its effective dialogue, its preciseness of character, and its well-contrived situation. *Tarnish*, one of the successes of the season of 1923–24, centers about a sensitive New York girl who finds her whole environment, including her parents and her lover, "tarnished." Of Emery's later plays, *Episode* (1925), though a failure on the stage, is the most important. It is a social comedy of the modern school.

1012   Gilbert Emery, from a photograph, courtesy
              of Arthur Hopkins, New York

1013   Philip Barry, from a photograph, courtesy
              of Arthur Hopkins, New York

PHILIP BARRY, 1896–

AMONG the outstanding writers of social comedy at present is Philip Barry who first won public attention with *You and I*, a skillful play of family life, written in Professor George P. Baker's workshop at Harvard, and awarded the Harvard Prize in 1923. *White Wings* (1926) is a satiric comedy based on the social distinctions which exist in America. One of the conspicuous plays of 1927–28 was Barry's *Paris Bound*, which is a well-sustained attempt to analyze marriage into those elements which are permanent and those which belong only to an unpleasant passing phase. The author succeeds surprisingly well in maintaining the crisp, brittle atmosphere of sophistication, in spite of situations essentially sentimental in character. In *Holiday* (1928–29) he succeeds equally well. With such gifted people writing plays about life in the United States, there is little occasion for any friend of the stage to lament the decay of American drama.

CHAPTER XIII

THE NEW STAGECRAFT

IF we place the name of Gordon Craig by that of David Belasco, we have the contrast of two entirely different systems of play mounting. As early as 1898 Craig was the prophet of a new order, earnestly preaching against the method of staging which, in an effort to produce a living reality by minute reproduction of actual life, produced unreality. He, together with Adolphe Appia, a German interested primarily in the stage use of light, may be considered the father of the revolutionary movement in scenic art during the last quarter-century. Being unwilling to compromise with existing conditions, however, he has had less influence in remodeling the existing theater than some of his followers, such as Max Reinhardt. Craig's banner was inscribed "Unity," a unity to be achieved by creating in scenery an expression of the deepest meaning of the play. All artificiality, triviality, and falseness should be eliminated, and the action of the play should develop in a setting that sustains and reinforces it, but of which the eye itself is hardly conscious. Concretely, he attacked the painted backdrop or box set, and the clutter of meaningless furniture, and developed as a contrast to the former a "plastic stage" with all columns, lintels, panelings, and stairs projected, thus doing away with false shadows. The second evil of the painted drop, false perspective, was vigorously denounced, and the efficiency of modulated lights on a white plaster wall, or monotone curtains and screens, was demonstrated. These "cushions of light" give a sense of distance and infinity that the most perfect pictorial curtain could not achieve. After Craig and Appia, formulating the revolt against realism, have come hundreds of theorists and experimenters, such as Granville Barker, Max Reinhardt, Meyerhold, Jacques Copeau and Joseph Urban. The work of such men has established three simple principles of staging: simplification, suggestion and synthesis.

The rapid flowering of the Little Theaters brought out a score of young artists keenly awake to the new developments in play producing and eager to try them — Robert Edmond Jones, Norman-Bel Geddes, Cleon Throckmorton, Rollo Peters, Sam Hume, Lee Simonson, and Raymond Johnson. With the Little Theater as their nursery, they were to try out the rich possibilities of color, line, and mass in building a more expressive stage — the effects of simple suggestive touches such as a single, soaring Gothic pillar for a church, or a flat wall and noble doorway for a palace, or a cramped room and straight stairway for a cellar; the effect of simple decorative screens and backdrops; the use of a primary or skeleton frame with slight additions or changes throughout a whole play; the value of plastic sculptural forms to denote abstract feelings. Yet in their various experiments there is this common plan: "For a positive purpose the new stage craft sets itself to visualize the atmosphere of a play. Its artists aim to make in the settings called for by the text an emotional envelope appropriate to the dramatic mood of the author, a visualization in color, line and light of the dominant emotions to be pictured by the actors."

1014   Setting by Joseph Urban for the Courtyard Scene of *Tristan and Isolde*, from a photograph, courtesy of the artist

JOSEPH URBAN, 1872–

A VIENNESE architect and scene painter, Joseph Urban came in 1913 to the Boston Opera House, where his sets for *Hansel and Gretel, Pelleas and Melisande,* and *Tristan and Isolde* had already created a sensation. He was later engaged at the Metropolitan Opera House, and in 1916 became the designer for Ziegfeld's productions. He has a more distinctive and fixed style than any other designer, but his highest achievement is in the pictorial background which was raised to new heights by his rich imagination. His influence in America as an apostle of the new stage decoration, with its fresh coloring, love of light, and freedom from excessive detail, was tremendous. Though not a great experimenter, he was the first in America to use the temporary "portals," inside the proscenium, and in 1916 he introduced "pointillisme," the system of painting spots of different color on a drop and then revealing them in turn by a play of different colored lights. This ensures freshness of color, atmosphere, liveliness, and vibration of light. In addition to designing the scenery for numerous musical comedy spectacles and operas, he is a practicing architect in New York City and Palm Beach.

1015   Setting by Joseph Urban for the Tavern Scene of *Carmen*, from a photograph, courtesy of the artist

ROBERT EDMOND JONES, 1887–

A GRADUATE of Harvard in 1910, Jones, after studying with Reinhardt, began designing for the stage in New York in 1911. His work with the Washington Square Players, begun in 1915, brought him to fame. Later he staged productions for Arthur Hopkins, the triumph of his art, perhaps, being *Richard III* in 1919–20. His most notable designs, besides this, were created

1016   Setting by Robert Edmond Jones for the Throne Scene in *Richard III*, from a photograph in the collection of Montrose J. Moses, New York

for *The Man who Married a Dumb Wife, The Jest, Macbeth,* and *Redemption.* He and Norman-Bel Geddes stand as leaders of the revolutionary stage in the United States, and at the present time enjoy the greatest international reputation of any of the American school of scenic artists. In *The Devil's Garden,* an unsuccessful Hopkins production, the three outstanding tendencies of the new staging are illustrated (see p. 337). In *Richard III,* "the most interesting experiment in structural form in America," the deepest mood of the play is captured and held in the grim, ponderous walls of the Tower, which are visible in some form, at least in Jones' design, throughout the play. This use of a principal frame through several acts is a step in the direction of a per-

1017   Setting by Robert Edmond Jones for *Hamlet*, from a photograph in the collection of Montrose J. Moses, New York

manent setting, or architectural stage, which the most forward-looking artists have been trying to develop. In *The Seven Princesses* (1919), a skeleton of a Gothic apse is set up very effectively, being formal in the same way as the Tower in *Richard III*, but at the same time abstract in treatment, designed for a space

stage, and a forerunner of Constructivism. In *Macbeth* (1921) Jones turned to Impressionism to project the mysterious forces from which the action springs. In the palace scenes there are two sets of arches disturbingly aslant. Above the witches three great eyes are represented, and in the throne scene brooding and malignant shapes are present. Of late Jones has devoted a large part of his time to architecture, and his stage settings, as in *Machinal, Holiday,* and *Serena Blandish,* are of a more conventional order.

1018   Setting by Robert Edmond Jones for Arthur Hopkins' production of *Macbeth*, from a photograph in the collection of Montrose J. Moses, New York

1019   Setting by Norman-Bel Geddes for a Scene from the *Boudour Ballet*, from a photograph
in the collection of Montrose J. Moses, New York

NORMAN–BEL GEDDES

"More than through any other channel, the artist in the theater has direct intercourse with his audience. We have less conception of the possibilities in drama than geographers had of the world in the fourteenth century. . . . Up to this time no effort has been made to develop a technique that builds permanently." Thus Norman-Bel Geddes wrote in 1919. He is perhaps the most distinctly American of all our stage designers, having developed his technique in the United States. Born in Detroit, he first became interested in stage problems when he attempted to produce an Indian drama which he had written. After studying painting for several years he began his experimentation in the Los Angeles Little Theater, and later staged various productions for the Chicago and Metropolitan Opera Houses. The most stupendous of his sets was for Max Reinhardt's production of the gigantic spectacle, *The Miracle*, at the Century Theater, New York, in 1925. His drawings for a stage presentation of Dante's *The Divine Comedy* are the farthest removed from customary stage practice and show a more sweeping vision than any that have come out of America, and point to him as a prophet of the type of Craig. Geddes is the best representative of abstraction in stage setting. He uses no painted drops or realistic furniture, but depends on sculptural forms placed on a vast stage, surrounded with curtains, and played upon by fluctuating lights to produce the moods of the drama. It is his policy to recreate his own style and develop new and distinctive technique for each production. It would, according to Sheldon Cheney, be "a blind spectator who fails to single out Norman-Bel Geddes as the possessor of the most vivid imagination in the American professional theater."

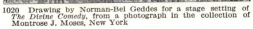

1020   Drawing by Norman-Bel Geddes for a stage setting of
The Divine Comedy, from a photograph in the collection of
Montrose J. Moses, New York

1021   Setting by Norman-Bel Geddes for *King Lear*, from a photograph
in the collection of Montrose J. Moses, New York

1022   Setting by Lee Simonson for *Tidings*, from a photograph, courtesy of the artist

1023   Setting by Lee Simonson for *Peer Gynt*, from a photograph, courtesy of the artist

LEE SIMONSON, 1888–

ONE of the original group who formed the Washington Square Players in 1915, Simonson had gained a wide experience from study and travel. He had studied in Paris with Julien and afterward had made several exhibitions of paintings. His career since 1916 has been identified first with the Players and then with the Theatre Guild, and he has given notable examples of his ability to adapt new principles to different necessities. He has not striven for the deeper spiritual interpretation, the ideal of Jones and Geddes, nor does he show the intense poetical imagination of Urban. In *Pierre Pathelin* (1916), he made one of the first uses in this country of permanent portals and an inner proscenium. In the production of Masefield's Japanese play *The Faithful* (1919), the action is developed in front of delicately painted screens placed before neutral hangings. His most significant work, perhaps, was his creation of the illusion of distance — as in a scene in *The Power of Darkness*, where a shadowed doorway is used effectively, or in the graveyard scene of *The Treasure*, or most notably in *Liliom*, where an arch in a railroad embankment gives a distant view of factory chimneys. Again in the limited use that has been made in America of projected scenery, Simonson has been one of the most successful. In *The Failures* and *The Goat Song* he put an isolated bit of reality in the center of the stage, surrounded by a space, small room, or scrap of a scene, set as if floating in toned light. In this way, the locale is fully pictured and yet achieves theatrical detachment.

1024   Setting by Lee Simonson for *Back to Methuselah*, from a photograph, courtesy of the artist

1025   Setting by Lee Simonson for *Liliom*, from a photograph, courtesy of the artist

1026   Setting by Sam Hume for *The Romance of the Rose*, courtesy of the Arts and Crafts Theater, Detroit

SAM HUME AND ROLLO PETERS

A HARVARD graduate and a pupil of Gordon Craig, Sam Hume, after giving an exhibition of stagecraft in New York in 1914, spent the years 1916–18 as stage designer at the Arts and Crafts Theater in Detroit. His most significant work in the Detroit theater was the application of Craig's patented system of panels by the rearrangement of which an entire drama or several dramas could be staged. Hume devised a mechanism of pylons and draperies, together with steps and arches, which could be used as a permanent setting for the acts of a play, or a series of plays. Thus in one season nineteen plays were presented with twenty scenes, eleven of which were constructed from this permanent setting. The scope of the mechanism allowed such widely differentiated scenes as the interior of a medieval castle in *The Intruder*, the gates of Thalanne in *The Tents of the Arabs*, the interior of a palace in *Helena's Husband*, and the wall of heaven in *The Glittering Gates*. Hume's later activities have been as lecturer and professor of dramatic literature and art, and as director of the Greek Theater of the University of California. Rollo Peters like Robert Edmond Jones and Lee Simonson came from the Washington Square Players. One of his most successful productions was the *Bonds of Interest* for the Theatre Guild in 1919. His style is simple and delicate. Later he aided Jane Cowl in her productions of *Romeo and Juliet*, *Pelleas and Melisande*, and *Anthony and Cleopatra*. He is also an actor.

1027   Setting by Rollo Peters for Jane Cowl's production of *Romeo and Juliet*, from a photograph, courtesy of the artist

NOTES ON THE PICTURES

1. The Visscher Map of 1616 shows the Globe, the Hope, and the Swan Theaters.

3. The Fridenberg Collection, New York, is an excellent source for American theatrical engravings and prints.

13. The Harvard Theater Collection in the Widener Library at Cambridge is one of the most valuable sources for pictorial material covering all periods of the American theater. It is especially useful for its early programs and for its engravings of early actors and theaters.

37. The Madigan Collection, New York, contains many engravings and photographs of theatrical interest.

40, 42. Two of the earliest examples of the work of American engravers.

46. The presence of the woman in the next to the last row of the pit is due to a mistake on the part of the engraver. At this early date women sat only in the boxes to the side.

64. The late Harry Houdini, in addition to his activities as magician and spiritualist, maintained an interest in the theater, and assembled an excellent collection of theatrical illustrations. Since his death in 1926, his collection has been sold.

65. The Dunlap Society in New York City was for many years most active in promoting research in the history of the American theater.

72. Dunlap's interest in painting is attested by his excellent *History of the Arts of Design in the United States* (see Vol. XII). For a criticism of his work as a painter, see Volume XII, pp. 21, 30.

84. For work of John Neagle, see Vol. XII, p. 28.

108. The New York Historical Society has a very full collection of engravings and playbills covering the activities of the theater in New York.

120. Professor George C. D. Odell of Columbia University, during the course of his exhaustive researches on the New York stage, has collected many rare theatrical engravings. See also Nos. 148, 175.

128. By far the largest collection of American theatrical photographs is owned by Albert Davis of Brooklyn. For almost half a century Mr. Davis has been gradually increasing the number of his photographs and playbills. If properly indexed and lodged the Davis Collection will constitute an invaluable pictorial source for future students of the American theater.

135. For work of Thomas Sully, see Vol. XII, p. 27.

142. The Players' Club on Gramercy Park, New York City, possesses many fine paintings of American actors. For the work of Gilbert Stuart, see Vol. XII, pp. 18–20.

169. For work of J. W. Jarvis, see Vol. XII, p. 22.

170. For the work of A. B. Durand as engraver, see Vol. XII, pp. 233–35.

210. For work of Henry Inman, see Vol. XII, p. 17.

239, 240. For work of John Sartain, see Vol. XII, p. 239.

243. For work of John W. Alexander, see Vol. XII, p. 140.

278. By a well-known English caricaturist, whose real name was Leslie Ward.

302. Henry A. Ogden, well-known military artist, has always been interested in the theater. He has collected many fine photographs of leading actors and actresses.

311. The date 1796 on the notice is evidently a mistake, and may denote that there had been a performance in Washington the preceding year.

315. The accuracy of this painting is not guaranteed by St. Louis historians.

341. The spelling, "Douglass," in the advertisement is an error.

364. For the work of Felix O. C. Darley, see Vol. XII.

394. Occasionally the dates given by Ludlow in his autobiography do not coincide with the dates of local newspaper notices. Owing to irregularity of newspaper files, it is impossible to check accurately, and the dates given by Ludlow in his text have been followed consistently. See p. 396. The same is true occasionally of Sol Smith's autobiography. See p. 399.

400, 415, 461. By a well-known American illustrator.

561, 562. For the work of John Singer Sargent, see Vol. XII, pp. 138–142.

654. The Ada Rehan Collection in the Reserve Room of the New York Public Library is a valuable source for pictorial and program material on the theatrical activities of Augustin Daly.

764. For the work of Robert Edmond Jones, see p. 339.

765. For the work of Norman-Bel Geddes, see p. 340.

838. By a distinguished British author and cartoonist.

840. For the work of Joseph DeCamp, see Vol. XII, p. 144.

901. For the work of George Luks, see Vol. XII, p. 150.

INDEX

Titles of books under author and plays as titles are in italics; titles of illustrations under producer are in quotation marks.